ALSO BY KAREN SWENSON:
Barbra: The Second Decade

AND WRITTEN WITH JAMES SPADA:
Judy and Liza

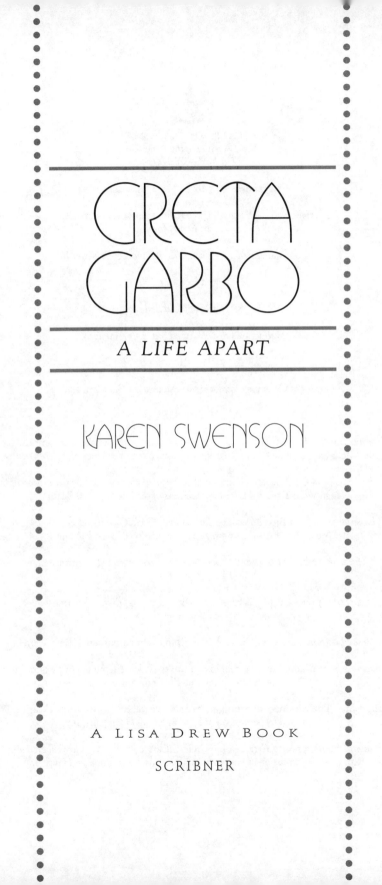

GRETA GARBO

A LIFE APART

KAREN SWENSON

A LISA DREW BOOK

SCRIBNER

A LISA DREW BOOK/SCRIBNER
1230 Avenue of the Americas
New York, NY 10020

Designed by Colin Joh

Set in Goudy Old Style

Manufactured in the United States of America

1   3   5   7   9   10   8   6   4   2

Library of Congress Cataloging-in-Publication Data is available.

ISBN 0-684-80725-4

For Justin, Heather, Tyler, Erienne, and Caitlyn—
the sons and daughters of an immigrant nation

ACKNOWLEDGMENTS

The search for the truth is an ongoing process. More so than with any other contemporary figure, the telling of Greta Garbo's life story is largely dependent on what she would have considered the indiscretion of her friends and coworkers. Many sought to explain or defend a person they felt had been unfairly maligned, some had more self-serving motives—all would provide insight, if not into the Garbo psyche then into the world she inhabited. Reconstruction is the ultimate challenge: a biographer must always consider an individual's reasons for recording their experience, weigh this against other written accounts or interviews, and, finally, balance each with historical fact. (Even surviving personal correspondence may have been selectively maintained and therefore is subject to this rule.) What remains is a mosaic of words in which the reader must fill in some of the tiles in order to view the final image.

"One almost feels grateful to Garbo for keeping herself so resolutely to herself, for leaving us a little mystery," an admiring Joan Crawford once told a reporter. Indeed, Garbo refused to destroy the illusion by peeling away the mask—for anyone. She may have reinvented herself as Harriet Brown, but the concept of divinity still followed her. It has been more than fifty years since her last movie offering, and time has made clear that much of the mystery surrounding Greta Lovisa Gustafsson—a legacy that began in Sweden, was defined in Hollywood, and then was polished through decades of her wandering from continent to continent—will remain intact despite the sincere efforts of biographers to penetrate it.

And yet who can resist the temptation to try? Even as we acknowledge the right to privacy, our natural instinct—human curiosity—bids us to explore Garbo's life story. A highly original and independent spirit, she was, significantly, a woman shaped by her times every bit as much as those times were shaped by her.

For their help in illuminating this subject, the author wishes to thank: Lew Ayres, Letitia Baldrige, Claude Botteron, Sven Broman, Jose Chavez, the late, great J. J. Cohn, Raymond Daum, Bill Edmundson, Betty Estevez, Luis Estevez, Douglas Fairbanks, Jr., Leatrice Gilbert Fountain, Dr. Arnold Fox, Åke Sven Fredriksson and family, Samuel Adams Green, Dori Guler-Bischsel, Lars Gumpel, Monica Halford, Scott Harrison, Patrice Hellberg,

Jean Howard, Jörg Jannings, Herbert Kenwith, Dr. Kenny Kingston, Sally Kirkland, Jack Larson, former ambassador Leif Leifland, Joseph Lombardo, Mary Anita Loos, Carlos Martinez, the late Patsy Ruth Miller (another unfortunate loss), Barbara Kent Monroe, Stella Montoya, Laila Nylund, Anita Page, James Pendleton, Mimi Pollak, Marcella Rabwin, E. Max Sarnoff, Ruth Scheuber, L. Jeffrey Selznick, Lillian Burns Sidney, Marian Silver, Betty Spiegel, Robert Sterling, Elizabeth Taylor, Emily Torchia, Nancy Tuckerman, Nicholas Meredith Turner, Leonard Valdes, former ambassador Wilhelm Wachtmeister, Professor Gösta Werner, James Wharton, Noel Woods, and Fred Zinnemann.

My sincerest appreciation to the entire Reisfield family. While this book was never authorized by the Garbo estate, it was done with their knowledge and limited cooperation. As the final mauscript took shape, Gray Reisfield, her husband, Dr. Donald Reisfield, and three of their children, Scott, Derek, and Gray, helped to correct a handful of errors and/or clarify the family's viewpoints on certain topics. It would have been so easy to say "no," and yet when they were most needed they were prompt in their responses and generous with their time. It is important to note, however, that this book in no way represents the opinions or conclusions of either the Reisfields or the Garbo estate (which reserves the right to publish its own book in the future).

Conducting the research on A Life Apart was an international undertaking—and always a challenge for a Swedish-American with only a rudimentary knowledge of other languages. I am therefore eternally indebted to the following people and institutions for their generous assistance. In Stockholm, my tireless researcher, assistant, translator, and supporter, Marie Peterson; George and Anki Wood, who took me in after a short chat on the shuttle between Heathrow and Gatwick—and made much of the rest possible; Margareta Nordström, Barbro Everfjärd, Elisabet Helge, and Rolf Lindfors of Svenska Filminstitutet; Ann-Christine Jernberg and Ulla Orre of Kungliga Dramatiska Teatern; Ingrid Lutekört, who shared some of her research on Dramaten with me; Nordisk Film's Bengt Forslund; Ulf Forsman from Katarina archivet in Södermalm; Jens Wallén and Bo Elthammar of Stadtsarkivet; Gun Edholm, who did genealogical research in Vadstena; the staff at Högsby Församling archivet, and at Visby Landsarkivet; Lillemor Hedström of Frustuna archivet; Birgitta Björkrot of Brännkyrka; Birgitta Hjalmarsson from Sofia kyrka; Brita Petersson of Stockholms Stadsmuseum; and research assistant Sanna Wennberg. Local history was compiled from research materials provided by many of the above institutions, as well as The American Swedish Institute in Minneapolis, Svenska Institute/Sverigehuset in Stockholm, and the excellent exhibition *Den Svenska Historien* at Statens Historiska Museum and Nordiska Museet.

Berlin came alive thanks to Hans Helmut Prinzler, Wolfgang Jacobsen, Wolfgang Theis, and Peter Latta from Stiftung Deutsche Kinemathek. Paris was made easy by an industrious student from NYU in France, the late Kimberly Pasquale. I found Kimberly through her supervisor, Maud Walther—whom I located based on a suggestion from Claudine Freulon of Bibliothèque du Cinéma André Malraux. A grateful nod is also owed the library and photo staffs of La Cinémathèque Française (now the Bibliothèque du Film). Klosters became a place I wanted to return to thanks to the attentive staff of the Chesa Grischuna, particularly Marianne Hunziker and Thomas Tunkel.

In England, I would like to acknowledge Gillian Hartnoll and John Riley from the venerable British Film Institute; the resourceful and accommodating Tony Fletcher from The Cinema Museum; research assistant Janne Olsen; Dr. Peter Beale; author Hugo Vickers, who makes all things about Cecil Beaton possible; Peter Cowie for his background on Scandinavian cinema; Alexander Walker, who got to the Metro legal files before all of us; and the film historian's film historian, Kevin Brownlow.

The primary research in New York was conducted at the Library for the Performing Arts at Lincoln Center; Ronald J. Grele and his staff helped me scan the vast array of oral histories that are part of Columbia University's American Biography Project; Charles Silver and Mary Corliss opened up the film and still archives at the Museum of Modern Art; Maxime La Fantasie provided invaluable last-minute aid in perusing Erich Maria Remarque's papers in New York University's Fales Library; and Gregory J. Plunges of the National Archives, Northeast Region, helped with locating passenger lists on ships arriving in New York Harbor. Thanks also for the generous assistance of David Columbia, Michael Gross, Cari Beauchamp, Charles Hamilton, Joan Kramer, Mark Vieira, Allison Waldman, and my selfless New York aide-de camp on a host of projects, Michel Parenteau (whose enthusiastic and unqualified support will be dearly missed).

I remember the Margaret Herrick Library when it was located in a small, overcrowded room of a modest two-story theater building on Melrose Avenue in Los Angeles. Its file cabinets were overflowing, and stacks of unsorted clippings and photographs were placed wherever there was room. Over the years, the library has moved twice and increased its staff as well as its expertise in the preservation of fragile motion picture history resources. With all due respect to the British Film Institute, La Cinémathèque Française, Stiftung Deutsche Kinemathek, Svenska Filminstitutet, and even the Library of Congress, the Academy Motion Picture Research and

Study Center has become the premiere facility for motion picture study (and an immensely pleasurable one in its new location). I owe its entire staff a debt of gratitude, but most especially Sam Gill, Stacey Behlmer, Carol Cullen, Dan Woodruff, Bill Holden, Bob Cushman, and Faye Thompson.

A deep bow as well to Ned Comstock, the able and ready curator of Special Collections at the USC Film and Television Library; Paul Christopher and Dacy Taube of the USC University Archives; Brigitta Kueppers, who manages the Special Collections at the UCLA Theater Arts Library; Daniel Einstein, the UCLA Film and Television Archive's busy curator; Charles Hopkins at UCLA's Archive Research and Study Center; the incredible Charles Sachs and his edifying Scriptorium; the staff at the American Film Institute's Louis B. Mayer Library; Diane S. Nixon and Bill Doty from the National Archives, Pacific Southwest Region; Diana R. Brown of Turner Entertainment, who gave me the opportunity to study at length the continuity script for the missing film *The Divine Woman*; Sara S. Hodson, curator of Literary Manuscripts at the Huntington Library in Pasadena; Kevin Carter of *Entertainment Tonight*; fellow biographers Rudy Behlmer, Charles Higham, and James Curtis (who introduced me to the world of David Lewis); Professor Terry Castle of Stanford University, whose opening essay in her book *The Apparational Lesbian* challenged and motivated me; Jim Kepner of the International Gay and Lesbian Archives in Los Angeles; Joseph Spano, the Sheraton-Miramar Hotel's own historian; John Farquar; researchers Rebecca Lindau and Eve Sullivan; Palm Springs historian Fred Rice; and finally, John Whitaker for his superb Silver Lake legwork.

In Washington, D.C., I would like to begin by thanking George Coupé, Sr., who generously made his collection available to me—thus providing extraordinary new information on Greta's relationship with Mauritz Stiller, among many other surprises. At the Library of Congress, I relied on Patrick Sheehan, Patrick Loughney, Madeline Matz, and Rosemary Hanes of the Motion Picture Division, and Sam Brylawski in Recorded Sound, as well as the library staff in the Manuscript Division. Government files were made available courtesy of J. Kevin O'Brien at the U.S. Department of Justice, Freedom of Information Privacy Acts Section; Milton O. Gustafson of the National Archives, Civil Reference Branch; John P. Butler of the Archives' Textural Reference Division; Rosemary Melendy and Karen A. H. French from the U.S. Department of State, Office of FOI and PA Classification Review; Barry J. Kefauver, U.S. Department of State, Passport Services; Francisco J. Carmona, U.S. Department of State, Office of Program Support, Passport Services; John H. Wright at the Central Intelligence

Agency's Freedom of Information Privacy Acts Section; Magda S. Ortiz of the U.S. Immigration and Naturalization Service, Freedom of Information Privacy Acts Section; and Vincent Sanudo from the Department of Health & Human Services, Social Security Administration.

Thanks to the foresight of a number of motion picture producers, artists, and technicians, as well as the enterprising staffs of a number of top American universities, I was able to avail myself of a wealth of information—the key was looking under every single rock and file folder. For their help in this regard, I am grateful to (in no particular order): Dr. Charles Bell, archivist and cinema historian at the Harry Ransom Humanities Research Center of the University of Texas at Austin; Karen Mix in the Special Collections department of Mugar Memorial Library at Boston University; David Powers of the John F. Kennedy Library; Dr. Ronald L. Davis and Kay Bost at SMU's DeGolyer Institute for American Studies in Dallas; William B. Eigelsbach and Curtis Lyons from the University of Tennessee's Hoskins Library in Knoxville; Harold L. Miller, Bill Budreau, Maxine Fleckner Ducey, and Crystal Hyde from the Center for Film & Television Research at the State Historical Society in Madison, Wisconsin; David Lagerman from the *Milwaukee Journal-Sentinel;* George Cukor's definitive biographer, Patrick McGilligan; Elizabeth Fuller and Doug Parsons of the Rosenbach Museum and Library in Philadelphia; Orlando A. Romero at the Museum of New Mexico's History Library; Phyllis M. Cohen from the Museum of Fine Arts in Santa Fe; Dr. Rolf Carlson, my consultant for the ongoing psychological profile; Milton Green, who helped with the Florida contingent; Ed Stratmann at the George Eastman House in Rochester, New York; and Walter Wanger biographer Matthew Bernstein.

I am further indebted to a handful of dedicated women who transcribed and translated reams of material brought home from various research trips. They include Lori Ann Ingalsbe, Laura Levitt, Simone Rodman, Gina Nugent, Christina Coleridge, and Valerie Von Weich. Thanks also to Sandra Chapa at the OfficeMax in San Antonio, who rescued me one day when I was en route, out of paper and out of time.

That this book even survived when delays and the competition loomed before us was due, in large part, to my editor, the ever-patient, always observant, never anything less than supportive Lisa Drew, and to her assistant, Marysue Rucci; my gratitude for their eternal diligence. To my agent, Loretta Barrett, her assistant Gary Morris, and Laura Van Wormer, a writer's ultimate cheerleader, thanks for hanging in there.

Last but certainly not least, no major undertaking like this is possible without the support of friends and family. This book was conceived and created thanks to the largesse of both. A friend named Jimmy Bangley took me to a Los Angeles County Museum screening of *The Torrent* a few short months after Garbo's passing, and an idea was born. I shared this idea with another writer, Steve Sanders, and wound up with an introduction to his editor. Jim Spada recommended an agent (as a matter of fact, he was responsible for my first book contract—so much for writers worrying about the competition). While I was preparing my proposal for the book, my father and brother traveled to Wisconsin to research one of the first important collections. Marty Erlichman and Barbra Streisand kept me solvent during the crucial early period; Christine Chapman, Michael Hawks, Victoria English, and my stalwart landlord, Virgil Rome, helped me through leaner times. Vernon Patterson, Linda Frank, and Christopher Nickens read and critiqued nearly everything I wrote.

For their encouragement and moral support, I would also like to salute Guy Vespoint, Rain Burns, Greg Rice, Lisa Madden, Deb Whitney, Mark Epstein, Shaun Miller, Manfred Thönicke, and Karina Michael. A special nod to the host of pet sitters who looked after my "family" when I was away for weeks at a time.

Thank you all for believing in me.

Most of all, thank God for my family. Mom, Dad, Barb, Arne, Diane, Tim, Len: You have, of course, noticed that I put the kids up front—but this one is for you, too. *Tack så mycket med kärlek.*

—*Karen Swenson*
Los Angeles
October 1996

What a waste of the best years of my life—always alone—it was so stupid not being able to partake more. Now I'm just a gypsy, living a life apart . . .

—Greta Garbo to Cecil Beaton, March 1948

Coming Home

She went home to Sweden in triumph in 1928, and again in 1932, 1935, 1937 . . . and to still-greater glory in 1946. But there was no final homecoming for Greta Lovisa Gustafsson in 1990. No memorial service at Stockholm's Storkyrkan, the historic Old Town cathedral where St. George and the Dragon watch over the proceedings. No floral tributes laid in the Royal Dramatic Theatre lobby, where the names of Strindberg and O'Neill and Bergman are spoken reverentially. The public paid its respect in the media, and Greta Gustafsson—known to intimates as "G.G.," "Miss G," or sometimes "Harriet Brown," but better known to the rest of the world as Greta Garbo—passed on as she lived: in dignified silence. She kept her good-byes to herself.

Years later, friends would note with sadness that she had yet to find a proper resting place. Their unhappiness begs an old question: Will Garbo ever be allowed to find peace? As of this writing, private investigations by her family have not yielded a burial plot that meets their special security requirements. Ironically, the indecision perpetuates the cycle for a restless spirit who spent decades wandering around the world—rarely at home in the place of her birth, and yet never truly at home anywhere else.

She appeared "at home" in front of a movie camera. For the sixteen years she lived and worked in Hollywood, Greta Garbo's craft consumed her. And though she was uninterested in the life of a movie star while she was one, she reinvented the role to suit her once she had retreated from motion pictures. "You're so beautiful," one admirer exclaimed. "Why have you hidden yourself away?" Garbo smiled mischievously. "Because," she replied before disappearing, "I want to keep the myth alive."

Because of the extraordinary measures she took to ensure that the truth would always remain elusive, any biography of Greta Garbo by nature struggles to walk the line between fiction and fact. Between Garbo and Gustafsson. Between Hollywood . . . and New York . . . and Paris . . . and Klosters . . . and Stockholm. Inevitably, the story returns to Sweden as the pages of a life are filled with images of Tistad, Hårby, Råsunda, Dramaten, Drottninggatan, Södermalm, Blekingegatan, and Småland.

Don't be intimidated by the vocabulary. Study it; absorb it. These are exotic words for the uninitiated, but home for a laborer's daughter looking to make something better of her life.

PART ONE

*To know Greta—one must know the North. . . .
She will always be Nordic with all its sober and
introvert characteristics. To know her one must
know—really know—wind, rain and dark
brooding skies.*

—Mercedes de Acosta, 1960

CHAPTER 1

A Scandinavian Profile

magine a photograph taken just before dusk. A tall, dark figure stands in the foreground in deep silhouette against the rolling hills of a Swedish countryside. The background is in focus, but it is the mysterious shadow which draws one's attention. The rest has been forgotten.

Of course there were happy times: The fresh, clean look of Södermalm when the first snow of the season alighted its streets. Snow angels and skating in the park. The rich aroma of pine logs being put on the fire in the winter. Christmas carols, Santa Lucia. The brilliant color of the flowers and the sky when spring burst forth. Basking in the sun during joyous midsummer festivities. Greta Gustafsson could obscure her nationality by changing her surname to Garbo, but Sweden was always there.

"Let's not talk of me!" she pleaded with a journalist during one of her last official interviews. "It is New Year's Eve. In Sweden that means so much, so very much. There we go to church and eat and drink and see everybody we know. I have been so blue all day. At home, in Stockholm, they are skiing and skating and throwing snowballs at one another. The cheeks are red—oh, please, let's not talk of me."

The nation most of the English-speaking world knows as Sweden is called Sverige ('svæ-rē-yə) by its people: "land of the Sveas," the early inhabitants of central and southern Sweden. Built on ancient bedrock, it is the fourth-largest country in Europe, encompassing about the same square area as Germany, France, or California (which it resembles in form as well as size). It is a country of immense contrasts—of great beauty and profound desolation. Far from the frigid stereotype, southern Sweden is blessed with a moderate climate, thanks to warm Gulf Stream currents and the region's protection from the cold North Atlantic by the mountains of Norway. However, Sweden's vast northern expanse is a sparsely populated, inhospitable land of lakes, forests, and remote mountain terrain pounded by seemingly endless winters.

It is Sweden's geographic isolation that provides the key to the history of her people. The first inhabitants of Scandinavia migrated north after the ice cap melted. Sweden's earliest settlers chose to live and work near the water, gravitating toward the more fertile, temperate regions of the south. As time passed, farming became the way of life. Farms in the southern provinces of Skåne, Blekinge, and Småland supported most of Sweden's population from the Middle Ages up until the beginning of the nineteenth century.

For centuries, the ancestors of Greta Gustafsson lived uneventfully on this land, farming and tending cattle, never venturing far from the family homestead. There was no gentry or nobility in their distant past, no peerage—they were simple people who lived out their days battling nature and carved out their nights in meager one-story wooden houses with thatched roofs. Some actually owned the property they worked, others were merely tenants; one was a blacksmith, one served in the army of Gustav II Adolf (Gustavus Adolphus) during the Thirty Years War, one worked briefly as a bailiff on the ancient island of Gotland; a few may have served as deacons in the church.

Each and every one of them, from the time of Gustav Vasa on through to the present day, was a Lutheran. In Sweden, by proclamation, a child is considered Lutheran unless his or her parents request a waiver. This is what it means to be a Swede. Generations and generations of *bönden*—peasants, farmers—and modern generations which, even when removed from that humble existence, still feel the land is an intrinsic part of them.

The nineteenth century was a dismal period throughout Scandinavia. Unable to keep up with the rapid pace of the Industrial Revolution, Sweden and its neighbors were thrown into economic turmoil. Swedish agriculture declined while the various social classes struggled to maintain power and influence.

Greta's great-grandparents were from the first new generation to be caught in this conflict. A succession of bad crops, especially in the southern agricultural region of Småland, increased the misery of the Swedes and strengthened the resolve of many of them to emigrate. In the spirit of his Viking forefathers, Karl Johan Nilsson escaped to America in 1864—only to return in defeat a few years later. In 1882, his son Johan August attempted a similar venture, with the same disappointing results.

Life was hard on each succeeding generation as they tried to hold on to land they felt was cursed . . . and finally, inevitably, just to hold on to a job. This was particularly true for the family of Karl Alfred Gustafsson. He was the second of seven children and the eldest son of Johan Agathon Gustafsson and Lovisa Andersdotter. Born Karl Alfrid Johansson on May 11, 1871, in Frinnaryd, he later assumed his father's surname, reflecting the new trend in Sweden.[1] Three younger brothers and a sister died before

---

[1]He adopted the more common spelling of his middle name, Alfred, around the same time.

they turned five, two within a day of each other. Karl Alfred never knew his paternal grandfather, Gustaf Adolf Gustafsson, who died of "inflammation of the chest" at the age of forty-four. His maternal grandfather, Anders Persson, also passed away before Karl Alfred was born; he succumbed to tuberculosis and left his widow, Lovisa Jaensdotter, a pauper.

The land of Säby and Frinnaryd had not been kind to the Gustafssons. The competition for jobs as indentured servants on local farms was great, even among kin. In 1881 Lovisa Andersdotter, Karl Alfred's mother, died from complications following a difficult childbirth; she was thirty-five years old. As Sweden's population grew and farms continued to fail, life became increasingly difficult for working-class families. Karl quit school early in order to find work. Finally, in the spring of 1887, Johan Agathon moved his family, including his second wife, Johanna Karlsdotter, and their two infant children, to Gotland Island, the former domain of Goths and Vikings ninety kilometers off the mainland in the Baltic Sea.

Surviving on an assortment of jobs in local industry, the Gustafssons remained on the island until May 1891. By that time, Karl Alfred had ideas of his own and, like many young men, he looked to Stockholm for answers. Compared to the hardship of country life, this handsome, civilized "Venice of the North" was paradise: fourteen islands held together by a series of bridges and locks which separate the fresh water of Lake Mälaren from the salty Baltic Sea; east of the city lies an archipelago of 24,000 islands, skerries, and islets, and beyond them—the sea. Factories dotted the southern islands, and new homes and businesses were being built to the north and west.

Unskilled labor was in demand in the capital city, although the supply was plentiful and wages were low. At the 1897 Jubileum Exposition in Djurgården, the king's deer park, the main pavilion boasted advances in science and industry, including a French invention called *le cinématographe*. Across the river, however, farmers still traveled in horse-drawn wagons or on small boats to deliver their produce to Stockholm's open-air markets. Working women toiled in private gardens, at waterfront stalls, in local bakeries, or at the candle factory. Men found employment loading and unloading ships, in the steel mills, cleaning streets, shoveling coal, or cutting lumber.

It is not clear when Greta's parents first met. It is possible they were introduced during one of Karl Alfred's excursions to the mainland; Anna Lovisa's home in Högsby is not far from the area where one of the Gotland ferries is based. Another theory suggests that he was a farmhand and she was a kitchen maid on the same estate in southern Sweden. More likely, they met socially or at work in Stockholm.

Karl Alfred, or Kalle as he was known to friends, was tall, slim, and possessed of an aristocratic face framed by short blond hair and deep-set, somber eyes that belied his cheerful manner and good sense of humor. He would have been considered a good match for a twenty-five-year-old farmer's daughter from Småland. When she wasn't hiding behind her long blond lashes, Anna Lovisa's blue eyes pierced sensitively into the object of her attention, never threateningly but projecting instead benevolent understanding. The third of eight children, she was born on September 10, 1872, in Högsby, and was the eldest daughter of Johan August Karlsson and Emma Kristina Adamsdotter.

Anna Lovisa belonged to the first generation of Swedish women to acquire independent legal status; they were no longer considered wards of their husbands, fathers, or male guardians. Shy, tolerant, hardworking, Anna was a careful person with a typically Scandinavian attitude about minding one's business. Not surprisingly, Karl Alfred took notice of this gentle young woman with an attractive figure and light chestnut hair. In 1897 they met, matched, and were working together in the city; by year's end, Anna Lovisa was pregnant with their first child.

At the turn of the century in Stockholm, it was neither unusual nor socially unacceptable for a poor, unmarried couple to be living together. In April of 1898, Karl and Anna dutifully reported to the parish church that they had moved to Gotlandsgatan 4 in Södermalm; he listed his occupation as gardener's apprentice. On April 24, Pastor Klefbeck made his first of three betrothal announcements to the Katarina congregation. The couple was married on the eighth of May. Ten weeks later on July 26, 1898, their son, Sven Alfred, was born at Södra Maternity Hospital.

Södermalm, Stockholm's southside district, is a large rocky island with magnificent cliffs that tower dramatically over Lake Mälaren, the many isles of the city, and the bustling harbor activity below at Skeppsbron. In the early 1900s, the smell of coal, tar, and whale oil still lingered in the air. Progress approached the working-class community in a leisurely fashion. Few streets in 1900 were paved; the best were cobblestone, most were narrow dirt and gravel roads winding around the island. Primitive one- and two-story dwellings—the majority of them painted dark red—lined the back roads. In the winter, milk was delivered throughout the neighborhood by sleigh, while Stockholm's first steam-powered streetcar transported residents from their homes in the suburban Södermalm to unfashionable jobs in the fashionable inner city.

To accommodate the influx of laborers, larger apartment buildings were built near the main thoroughfares. After the birth of their second child,

Alva Maria, on September 20, 1903, the Gustafssons moved into one such building at Blekingegatan 32. The modest fourth-floor tenement was small but comfortable by city standards, and Anna Lovisa kept it clean and well-ordered. Their new home featured a kitchen with a wood-burning stove and running water, a living room with two windows facing the street—and down the stone stairs, through the hallway and past the back courtyard, a "modern" outhouse.

"Where we lived, all the houses and apartments looked alike, their ugliness matched by everything surrounding us," Greta recalled. "Even the grass gave up trying." Churches loomed at both extremes of Blekingegatan: on the east atop a hill stood Sofia *kyrka* with its dominant cathedral spires, to the west the more modest Alllhegona *kyrkan*.[2] The grounds of Alllhegona served as the local playground.

By all accounts, the Gustafsson family fit well into their new neighborhood. Sven had inherited his father's lean good looks and temperament. He was also, secretly, his mother's favorite. As Alva got older, she looked more and more like her mother—but she was, perhaps not so secretly, her father's little girl and shared his same sense of fun. The drudgery of his work in various odd jobs from the sanitation department to the slaughterhouse did not cross the threshold into Karl Alfred's home—except when it came to his health, which was inconsistent at best. He always had a friendly greeting for his children. As far as their day-to-day existence was concerned, Anna Lovisa was the resourceful mate, always willing to haggle with shopowners or barter with neighbors regarding whatever her family needed, whether it be food for the dinner table or flowers and curtains for their living quarters.

In September of 1905, while Stockholm anxiously awaited news of the treaty dissolving the union between Sweden and Norway, Karl and Anna Gustafsson were anticipating the birth of their third child. Anna had become pregnant the previous Christmas. The family's joy was nearly obscured by financial worries. Knowing of their circumstances, Karl Alfred's employer had reportedly offered to adopt the baby, but Anna Lovisa was resolute. "If God gives you a child," she told her husband, "he also gives you bread."

Hospital records reveal that labor began at 3:00 on the afternoon of September 18. The mother was admitted to Södra Maternity Hospital at 5:20 P.M. A doctor's examination revealed that the baby was in place, its head facing downward and slightly to the right; the heartbeat was strong.

---

[2]The sound of the Swedish language is much more pleasing to the ear than the word on the printed page would suggest. As in church, the beginning is soft: *kyr-ka*='sheer-ka.

At 7:30 that same Monday evening, Greta Lovisa Gustafsson was born. Delivery nurses Hanna Karlson and Ida Sten carefully measured the baby girl: she was 52 centimeters long and weighed 3.5 kilograms (the equivalent of approximately 20.47 inches and 7.7 pounds, respectively).

Greta Lovisa was christened the following day by Pastor Hildebrand of Katarina *kyrka*. Since both mother and child were pronounced healthy and strong, they were released by the hospital a week later. Seven-year-old Sven Gustafsson moved his bed into the kitchen of apartment 14C and, for the time being, both the baby and her two-year-old sister slept in the larger living room quarters with their parents. Despite the crowded situation, the Gustafssons bore their circumstances with reasonable humor. "My mother was almost always in a good mood," Greta said. "I cannot remember [her] ever saying a cross word to me." The child bonded quickly to both parents, but most particularly to her mother—"the center of my life"—who was always at home cooking, sewing, watching over the family while her father worked odd evening hours and came home in the morning with strange smells on his clothes (and sometimes his breath).

"Born into a home of non-intellectual parents . . . Garbo's childhood fluctuated on a plane between two points: pleasure and pain," psychologist Eric Drimmer explained.[3] "Work, illness, and poverty come under the heading of pain. Food, home, and comfort come under the heading of pleasure." Karl Alfred was dreadfully aware that his lack of education trapped his young family in Södermalm. Contrary to his motto that "Things will be better tomorrow," there was very little likelihood they ever would be. During the summer of 1909, a national labor strike crippled the country; after six weeks of struggle, most workers would return to their jobs with conditions unchanged. For little Greta, nicknamed "Kata" because of her inability as a toddler to pronounce her own name, the tension at home was sometimes palpable. It was as if "there [was] danger in the air."

In the winter, claustrophobia set in as the windows of the apartment were sealed to keep out the cold, and the children huddled around the same stove that heated their water and cooked their food. "It was eternally gray—those long winter's nights," Greta said. "My father would be sitting in a corner, scribbling figures on a newspaper. On the other side of the room my mother was repairing old clothes, sighing. We children would be talking in very low voices or just sitting silently."

That is, perhaps, the most descriptive statement Greta Garbo ever made about her childhood. Were her parents, whom she described as loving to laugh and sing, reduced to fighting about money? Did Karl Alfred

---

[3]Drimmer would treat Garbo when she worked at MGM.

drink excessively? Was there physical as well as emotional abuse? She never said. But the sensitive, youngest child seemed to take everything to heart, later referring to those years as "brutal."

As further evidence of her hypersensitivity regarding strained relationships between people—even strangers—Garbo would admit, "If I see an accident or hear two people quarreling, I am just sick all over." She did not like any kind of trouble. A Metro publicist vividly recalled the comments of a journalist after interviewing Greta. "That girl has been hurt—deeply, terrifically hurt. I wonder what it is?"

Childhood fantasies took on a new importance. Greta and her friends often played among the clotheslines and lilac bushes that defined the back court; occasionally, she and neighbor Elisabet Malcolm climbed on top of the latrine to sunbathe on its gently sloping roof. There her imagination took flight. "We are on a sandy white beach," she would explain in hushed tones. "Can't you see the waves breaking the shore? How clear the sky is, Elisabet! And do you hear how sweetly that orchestra at the Casino is playing? Look at that girl in the funny green bathing suit!" Elisabet thought her friend was "a show in herself," with a vivid imagination that easily transformed the tin roof of an outhouse into an elegant, glistening beach.

During the winter, Alllhegona Hill was dotted with toboggans and sleds as well as snow fights, and the square echoed with delighted screams as sporting children navigated the hill on their descent back on to Blekinge-gatan. To Greta, said Elisabet Malcolm, the barren, twisted trees might be an enchanted forest guarding an evil king's castle; her blue sled (a hand-me-down from her brother) the means for a romantic knight to free a lady in distress. When she didn't have a sled she coasted on tattered coattails, much to the dismay of her mother.

Despite the fact that she was a natural leader in games, Greta usually preferred to play alone. "I never enjoyed playing with others," she said, "even with my sister and brother, but preferred to sit alone with my dolls and picture books . . ." Actually, she preferred a friend's set of tin soldiers over dolls. "Greta was different from any other kid I ever knew," her uncle, David Gustafsson, said. "I used to think it strange that so pretty a child should wish always to hide herself away. She would crawl under a table and sit there for a long time. 'What are you thinking of, darling?' I would say to her, and she would look at me with her big shining eyes and say, 'I am thinking about what I am going to do when I grow up.' . . . 'And what will that be?' I asked her. Quick as a flash, her head would go back and she would cry, 'Why, first of all, I shall be a great diva and then a princess.' "

Not everything was so serious. Greta told Mercedes de Acosta about an encounter with one of her uncles at home one Sunday afternoon. Greta, who was then about six years old, interrupted her games to inquire, "Does Uncle care a lot about Jesus?" Her uncle, with his mind intent on his news-paper, answered absentmindedly, "Yes, yes. Uncle cares a lot about Jesus." Greta went off and played for a while, and then returned. "Are you *sure* Uncle cares a lot about Jesus?" "Yes, yes, indeed. Uncle cares a lot about Jesus." She disappeared again—but not for long. "Are you *absolutely* sure that Uncle cares a lot about Jesus?" she asked for a third time. Finally, the poor harassed uncle jumped to his feet, flung down the paper, and shouted at the top of his lungs, "Uncle doesn't give a damn about Jesus!" Whenever she wasn't interested in something, Greta would proclaim, "Uncle doesn't give a damn about Jesus."

As she got older, there were times, Greta admitted, when she could be a holy terror. "I was awful as a child! We used to do all the tricks of ringing doorbells and running away, and next door to us was an embittered old spinster and she made the mistake of going for us. Then we let her have it! We were a gang . . . and I was the ringleader. I wasn't at all like a girl. I used to play leapfrog, and have a bag of marbles of my own—a tomboy."

There were glimpses of Garbo very early on. Greta's friend, publisher Lars Saxon, ghosted a personal memoir for her in *Lektyr,* a Swedish men's magazine, in which she explained that when she was very small and could barely talk, "I had a certain mania to paint—not on paper, as most children do, but on my own face. With the aid of some watercolors my father had given me I painted my lips and face, believing that this is what real actresses do. No one in my family could escape my paintbrush." A child might not have recognized it, but it *was* what "real actresses" do when they are young.

"Greta was stagestruck long before she saw a stage or knew about the existence of any actresses," her brother, Sven, stated. "We all had to dress up in old costumes and do as we were told. Usually she liked to play the part of the boy. Sometimes she would say terrible things. She would point to me and say, 'You be the father,' and then to my sister, 'You be the mother.' Then I would ask her what part she was playing, and she would say, 'I am your child who is drowned.' " When she was young, he noted, you couldn't help but believe in her.

Small wonder that such an imaginative child would eventually find school confining. On August 22, 1912—while most of Stockholm was recovering from hosting the Olympic Games—Greta Gustafsson enrolled at Katarina Södra Folkskola, the local elementary school located a few blocks away on Sofiagatan. Instead of reveling in this new world, she seemed to withdraw even further. Katarina Folkskola was typical of most

Swedish schools of the period, adhering to the Lutheran principle that "Where sin is punished, God is honored and praised." Sometimes Greta surprised herself by confronting her teachers. For the most part, however, she "lived in a constant state of fear, disliking every moment of it . . ."

Her least favorite subjects were geography and mathematics. "I could never understand how anyone could be interested in faraway places or in trying to solve such ridiculous problems," she later said. She did not share the same disdain for history, reading her textbooks as if they were novels and often daydreaming about fantastic adventures in class. The fantasies dissolved when Greta was confronted by Mrs. Ronnell, one of her teachers. Asked to repeat a historical elaboration, the red-faced student could not separate fact from fabrication. "[And] my embarrassment was taken as proof of my ignorance," she lamented, earning her low marks in her favorite class.

Fellow student Ebba Antonsson had a different recollection. "I didn't find school as easy as Greta," she said. "She never seemed to do any homework but knew all the answers anyway." Judith Ronnell felt that "she was a strangely appealing girl. She was very careful and attentive at her lessons, but her mind was always on the stage. I remember that when any of the students were scolded, she waited for them in the corridor after class and flung her arms around them. She hated what she thought was injustice."

The outbreak of the First World War in 1914 brought a number of changes to Södermalm. Sweden immediately declared its neutrality in the European conflict, insisting upon their right to ship non-contraband essentials (much of which originated in the United States) to Germany and Prussia. England, however, suspected the Swedes of secretly backing the enemy and gradually gained support to enforce an Allied blockade of the area, severely reducing trade—most particularly the importation of food into Sweden. As the rationing of items like sugar, butter, coffee, and grain became necessary, soup kitchens sponsored by the Salvation Army increased in popularity in disadvantaged neighborhoods.

Greta found the Salvation Army storefronts a safe haven; it was here that her unexpressed theatrical ambitions found an outlet when she participated in neighborhood shows. In addition to singing in the choir at Sofia *kyrka*, Greta earned "an occasional krona here and there singing with a very good friend named Sigurd Hudin," Sven Broman reported. "She had a lovely contralto voice." Treasurer John Philipsson organized some of the programs and was struck by young Greta Gustafsson's enthusiasm for them; she was a standout. Impressed by her tenacity, wooed by the first sparks of her emerging charisma, an official at the local branch offered her a chance to make extra money by hawking *Stridsropet* (Battle Cry), the Salvation Army newspaper. "It worked to some extent in the building we lived in, but I was never any great shakes as a newspaper seller," Greta insisted. An upstairs neighbor, Mrs. Karin Gustafsson, disagreed. She thought that "[Greta] was a real cadger in those days. On paydays when the men came home from work she would stand in the street smiling at them with an outstretched hand . . ."

The yin-and-yang of life in Stockholm often meant that a child like Greta was cheerful and bright one moment—and the next, painfully certain there was nothing left for her. Then spring would come again, followed by the summer when the sun smiled on the Northern Hemisphere and Sweden basked in its brilliance. Nowhere is the sun more celebrated than in Scandinavia, where the mood of the people is dramatically elevated by nature's rebirth; their faces follow the light.

Those summers during the First World War were no exception. Somehow, despite the wretched poverty that threatened them at every turn, Karl Alfred managed to follow the Södermalm tradition of renting small plots of land just outside the city. Each plot contained a modest gardening hut that could provide shelter for the family during the summer, and enough land to grow a tasty crop of fruit and vegetables. On the Gustafsson allotment in Enskede, Alva and Greta felt revitalized and took to their gardening chores with new fervor, planting carrots, beets, and potatoes in addition to two raspberry bushes and some red currants. When the soil was generous, the girls took pleasure in selling their surplus.

Greta was very fond of her older sister, whom she referred to as "Lillan," little one. The two spent many happy summer days soaking up the sun in Enskede and sometimes at a little hotel run by their paternal grandparents ninety kilometers further south in Sparreholm. "She wanted to be a tightrope walker," Johanna Gustafsson, the second wife of Karl Alfred's father, recalled of one visit. "I will never forget it. . . . [She] tied ropes between the trees and had everybody on the place worried stiff." These carefree summer days impressed Sven as one of the few times he could remember his sister as being truly content.

Just at a time when the girls were developing their first crushes, the boys of Katarina Folkskola were preparing for military service. The last two years at school for Greta were also marked by illness. Reportedly suffering from a "sinus problem," and wary of more serious complications, she was allowed five "vacation" days in 1917. The following school term she was absent for another eight days due to illness, and was truant—"absent without permission"—once.[4] Accounts of her absence vary: one suggests she ran away with two other girls and was caught across town by an elderly shopkeeper; another insists she was discovered by a conductor on the train to Skåne; a third account simply states that she was lost in the hypnotic fantasies of youth. Whatever occurred, her teacher Linnea Rosenqvist put a black mark on her report card, and Greta learned that the punishment for getting caught was severe (though she was spared the rod, thanks to her sister's intervention).

The youngest Gustafsson was already living in two separate worlds, juxtaposing the grim reality of home life with the dream world of theater. And there can be little doubt which one was more important to her—or where she felt more understood. By the time she was twelve, Greta had reached her full height of five feet seven inches, a point most evident in school photos where she has hidden herself, straight hair and straight-faced, in the back of the classroom with Elisabet Malcolm and Sonja Eriksson. The physical difference only emphasized her alienation; emotionally she was already distanced from most girls her age. "I think I used to sleep much less than other children," she confided to a friend. "I was out running far too late in the evenings." The reason for her evening escapades: across the island at Mosebacke Torg (Square) Greta had discovered the excitement of watching the actors come and go from the theater.

Like most children, Greta often spent her pennies (öre) at the nickelodeon, thrilling to the celluloid antics of Charlie Chaplin, Mary Pickford, Mabel Normand, and Douglas Fairbanks, or Swedish films like Victor Sjöström's *Terje vigen* (*A Man There Was*) and *Herr Arnes pengar* (*Sir Arne's Treasure*) by Mauritz Stiller. She first began sneaking away from home to frequent the popular Södra Teatern and the Mosebacke cabaret theater at the tender age of seven years. She went alone. Because she rarely had the money to see the shows (she wouldn't manage that until she was twelve), she would wait for hours in the cold, dimly lit alley to get a glimpse of the actors backstage.

"I used to go there at 7:00 in the evening . . . and wait until 8:30. Watch them come in; listen to them getting ready." Greta crept closer to observe favorites such as Josef Fischer and Sigurd Wallén. "Listen to their voices doing their parts in the productions! Smell the greasepaint! There is no smell in the world like the smell of the backstage of a theater. No smell will

[4]There are at least three different stories of Greta skipping school, but only one recorded absence.

mean as much to me—ever. . . . Night after night, I sat there dreaming. Dreaming when I would be inside—getting ready."

Always the center of artistic activity, Mosebacke, meaning "Moses Hill," was regarded as Stockholm's Montmartre. Adjacent to the theaters was (and is) an outdoor café, the same café celebrated in the opening of Strindberg's novel *The Red Room*. From here, Greta could take in the impressive panorama below, admiring the ships as they sailed across the Strömmen and perhaps peering with some interest at the elegant Grand Hôtel across the waterway. Greta rarely ventured into that other land— the posh neighborhoods on the north side of Stockholm—but she could envision the day when she would be accepted there.

During the winter, the sun would set by 4:30. When Greta didn't show up after dinner, her father or brother usually went out into the black of night to retrieve her. Though they tried to reason with her regarding her increasingly obsessive behavior, "even as a child she had her own unflaggable opinions," her uncle David noted. David Gustafsson began chauffeuring her in his taxi so that he could keep an eye on her. Sometimes on the way home she would regale family members with stories about what she had seen at Mosebacke Square; more often than not she was quiet and introspective all of the way back to Blekingegatan.

Down the street from the Gustafsson apartment was a *tobak*, the local newsstand and tobacco shop run by a widow named Agnes Lind. Among her wares, Mrs. Lind sold postcards of theatrical celebrities and occasionally gave Greta one in exchange for an errand or chore. She recalled that the teenager's favorites were Naima Wifstrand, a popular star of light opera, and a dashing young Danish performer named Carl Brisson: her first matinee idol. In 1918, the former boxer headlined the Mosebacke with his revue, "Brisson's Blue Blondes." He later remembered one bitter-cold evening when a girl slipped out of the shadows and touched his hand. "For a girl to speak to me at the stage door was at the time most unusual . . . I stammered politely, and she held out something toward me with a smile. I took it. It was a bunch of violets. Violets in Stockholm in January! . . . I think I was more nervous than she was. I stood hatless and silent, and she made little rings with her shoe in the snow."

Brisson signed an autograph and gave his new admirer a card that admitted her to any performance at the theater. One evening, he took advantage of Greta's enthusiasm by throwing the spotlight on her and encouraging her to sing the next chorus of his song. "She hesitated and blushed, but she answered my smile and rose to her feet as the orchestra swung into the chorus." From then on, whenever she was in the audience and Carl Brisson asked for a volunteer, Greta cheerfully called out, "I'll sing!"

Such illicit adventures were an effective way of "hiding in plain sight": a child who already felt different now used her imagination and creativity as a means of distancing herself from the pain and adversity of her adolescence. Henceforth, Greta rarely associated with children from her own neighborhood. Curiously, her withdrawal had the equal and opposite effect of determining the rules under which she would accept people into her life. "Elisabet, we are going to be actresses," she announced one day. The occasion her friend Elisabet Malcolm later described resembled a scene from *Little Women*, with Greta as Jo playing the lead roles and orchestrating the production. "You must come in like this and pretend you are very much surprised to see me and look like this," she instructed her cast. Elisabet tried to follow her directions, but Greta was not satisfied. "This will never do," she proclaimed. "You see, Elisabet, you've got to act. Now take that chair and sit down. You can be the audience and I'll show you how one really *acts*." And Greta re-created an entire variety skit.

"After that day Greta and I played theater whenever we had a chance," Elisabet recalled. "When we weren't actually imitating actors and actresses we would dress up as boys, making good use of her brother, Sven's, belongings. Once we even went to the shoemaker's down the street rigged up this way. I felt a little embarrassed at showing myself in public in boy's clothes, but not Greta! 'I'm Gustafsson's youngest boy, you know,' she said to the shoemaker, 'and this is a pal of mine.' She then proceeded to whistle and act the part of a boy as best she could until the shoemaker and his assistants roared with laughter."

When she was thirteen, Greta created her own theatrical company, which she called The Attic Theater. "By this time she had given up any hope of making an actress of me," Elisabet said. "Some of her other playmates were more promising, and they became the members of her 'company.' We all brought old furniture from our homes to serve as props, and for costumes we used anything we could lay our hands on." Their first show was a musical revue in which Greta portrayed everything from the Goddess of Peace to a three-year-old in red rompers.

Although she concentrated her best efforts on stage work, one winter day Greta and a friend hiked all of the way to Lidingö (one of Stockholm's outer islands) in search of the Svenska Bio movie studio. The pair held out hopes of being "discovered," but their ringleader neglected to get proper directions; they reached the end of the streetcar line without having enough money to cross the toll bridge to the island. "We'll have to walk across the ice," Greta said, leading the way down a steep embankment and across the frozen, treacherous waterway. They wandered haphazardly around Lidingö looking for the large glass barn where most of the major

Swedish films made between 1912 and 1920 were produced. They never found it. After several chilling hours, they returned home, tired, dejected—and in the dark.

On June 14, 1919, Greta graduated from public school. Typically, a girl from Södermalm did not pursue her education any further, and the Gustafsson children were no exception. Alva studied shorthand while working in an insurance office. Sven struggled with a number of low-paying jobs after military service. He earned a few kronor a week at the local *konditori* (bakery) where he met a young dairy maid named Elsa Hägerman and soon began a family. When she became ill following her pregnancy, they moved back home with his parents. There were now seven people living in three rooms at the Gustafssons'.

The mood at home became further strained when Karl Alfred began missing work. Life in Södermalm—living in drafty buildings and working menial jobs—was all about survival; even the toughest had to confront life-threatening illnesses such as anemia and tuberculosis. Karl's latest job had been in street maintenance where he had to lift heavy outhouse barrels as well as sweep the sidewalks and streets. During the winter of 1919, a devastating strain of the Spanish flu that had spread throughout Europe at the end of the war finally overtook Stockholm, filling the already crowded hospital wards with thousands of new patients. Hoping to avoid the epidemic, Anna Gustafsson carefully monitored her family's health.

But Karl Alfred's problems extended beyond the flu season, and family finances soon became an issue. Sven and Alva already had jobs; Anna Lovisa found day work at a jam factory and took in extra money as a seamstress; Greta contributed by working in a local barber shop as a *tvålflicka*, lathering men's faces before they were shaved. Her principal assignment, however, was to look after her father at home. She became in effect the caregiver in the family.

According to church records, Greta was confirmed by Pastor Runo Ahlfeldt of Katarina *kyrka* on Sunday, April 18, 1920. Interestingly, photographs of her in her white confirmation dress are dated almost two months later. The pictures reveal a slightly overweight teenage girl with uncharacteristic (for her) kewpie doll curls. Not surprisingly, in the group photo she is somberly standing at the center in the back. The confirmation was her coming of age; according to classmate Eva Blomkvist, Greta wept silently all throughout her first communion. It was one of the few times she permitted her friends to see her tears.

Approximately once a week, Greta accompanied her father to a public clinic. Late one day in May, she came home and found her father in agony;

he was burning with fever and complained of nausea. She later described to playwright S. N. Behrman the long, poignant ordeal as she took her father to Maria Sjukhus, a charity hospital nearby. By this time, Karl Alfred was so ill he could barely stand up; both father and daughter were helpless to do anything except wait in line. Their humiliation was compounded when they finally reached the reception window. "The man told Karl Gustafsson to take off his hat and asked a hundred questions, all seeming to indicate . . . that the hospital was principally interested in their ability to pay for treatment," Behrman related. His body was racked with pain, a lingering pain that grew until Greta believed her father was dying right in front of her. A few days later, on the first of June, he did.[5]

"God, what a feeling," she shared with *Photoplay* reporter Ruth Biery in Hollywood. "Someone you love is there, then he is not there. Gone where you can't see him, can't talk with him. . . . The same flesh, the same blood—yet he is gone, never to return." For months to come, the sobbing and moaning at the Gustafsson home resounded in the halls of their apartment building. For Greta, the very public grieving of her brother and sister robbed them of their privacy and dignity; it was too much for her to bear. "I often had to ask them to be quiet," she told her friend, Lars Saxon. "To my mind a great tragedy should be borne silently. It seemed disgraceful to me to show it in front of all the neighbors by constant crying. My own sorrow was as deep as theirs, and for more than a year I cried myself to sleep every night. For a time after his death I was fighting an absurd urge to get up in the night and run to his grave to see that he had not been buried alive."

Karl Alfred Gustafsson was laid to rest in a simple plot at Södra Skogskyrkogården, the "cemetery in the woods" across the river from Södermalm. It was, fittingly enough, the final trolley stop on the north-south line traversing Stockholm.

---

[5]The official cause of death, according to records at the Katarina archive, was "nefrit chronicus," a chronic inflammation of the kidneys.

CHAPTER 2

Dramatiska Teatern

"Lots of things can happen to a child of fourteen who is very advanced," Greta would say many years later. Understandably, her father's death changed many things for fourteen-year-old Greta Gustafsson. The summer of 1920 was the first in some time that she was not able to enjoy the garden in Enskede or chase *idol* fantasies at Mosebacke. Anna Gustafsson wanted her daughter to stay at home, "but we badly needed every penny," Greta said, so she looked for new work.

Her casual employment as a *tvålflicka* became a full-time job when she accepted an apprenticeship with a second barber, Einer Widebäcke, and then a third, Arthur Ekengren. Ekengren's shop on Götgatan was the largest and busiest in the neighborhood; there young Miss Gustafsson could make tips nearly equal to her salary of seven kronor a week. She proudly turned over her earnings to her mother—but kept the tips to herself, often spending them on chocolate treats. A comparison of photographs taken between winter 1919 and fall 1920 reveals a startling change: the Greta Gustafsson of late 1920 is nearly unrecognizable behind chubby cheeks, a sagging chin, bloated eyelids, and shorter, permed hair. Suppressing her unhappiness, it was another way of hiding in plain sight.

Her confusion and insecurity is evident in a letter she wrote to a friend on the seventh of July, just one month after her father's death. First she chided Eva Blomkvist for contriving to meet another actor, a popular variety performer named Valdemar Dalqvist. Then she accused her of trying to take over on a personal front. "One other thing I have to say," Greta wrote, "if you and I are to remain friends, you must keep away from my girlfriends as I did from yours. I'm sure you wouldn't like it if you met me with your most intimate friends and I completely ignored you. I didn't mind your going out with Alva, but then I realized that you intended to do the same with all my acquaintances. Eva, I am arrogant and impatient by nature, and I don't like girls doing what you have done. If you hadn't written, I should never have made the first move toward reconciliation. . . . Frankly, I think you are making yourself ridiculous."

Jealous, possessive, controlling, distrustful, dramatic, opinionated, hypercritical and self-analytical. Such a letter was undoubtedly written by a woman of fourteen going on thirty-five and illustrates something of the contrasting reports that exist of Greta Gustafsson during this transition period. Did she have close friends or not? Boyfriends? Girlfriends? Was she impatient and ambitious or reticent and withdrawn? She was, it seems, all things: part man, woman, *and* child, as actress Eleanor Boardman aptly described her in Hollywood. And already exuding that magnetic quality that encouraged people like Eva to play by her rules if they wanted to remain in Greta's circle; otherwise she withheld herself from them.

Still, according to Sally Ekengren, Greta was an immediate favorite on Götgatan and attracted a number of regular customers. "The shop was always full in the evenings," Ekengren noted. "Some clients would phone and make special appointments and then, if Greta was not there, find some excuse for postponing them." Whether decorating her cubicle with theatrical postcards or joking with the customers, she "filled the place with her laughter and vitality."

A good soap girl did more than simply put lather on the faces of students, sailors, and businessmen. She gently rubbed the soap into the skin, massaging each man's face and preparing him for the barber. It could be a enjoyable, even sensual experience for the patron and certainly put a teenage girl in the position of dealing with unwelcome advances along with the camaraderie. According to fellow assistant Märta Thörnland, Greta "always kept her dignity and never allowed men to get fresh with her."

At the advice of friends, she looked uptown for a better job. It didn't take her long to get up the courage to fill out an application at Paul U. Bergström's department store. Greta temporarily assumed the more genteel spelling of "Gustavsson" and stated her age as fifteen—a very well-mannered fifteen. After a second interview, she was given a job running errands and unpacking hats in the millinery department at a starting salary of 125 kronor per month. "Can you imagine me as a shop girl?" Greta wrote Eva Blomkvist. "But don't worry, I haven't given up my ideas about the theater. . . . I'm just as faithful to them as before." On Monday, July 26, she reported to the millinery department for work.

For some time, as the dynamics of her family shifted, Greta had been treated by friends and family alike as the eldest sibling; her carriage and deportment, her manner, her speech, even her attire demonstrated a maturity beyond her years. "I feel as though I have been alive for an eternity," she mused, though she was aware that she was something of a curiosity to fellow workers. "They all look at me with such interest there because I'm only fifteen," the fourteen-year-old shop girl wrote in another letter to Eva. "If you were to come, I'll bet they'll all ask you if it's true."

After her training, Greta was transferred to women's clothing; she was the youngest of ten salesgirls working in the department under the supervision of Magda Hellberg. Miss Hellberg remembered employee #195 as "very ambitious, quiet, and [she] always took great care about her appearance. Even at her young age one could sense her self-restraint." Carl Brisson unexpectedly ran into Greta Gustafsson behind the hat counter at Bergström's. "She had matured, half grown up," he remarked. "Her clothes were smarter, and she had acquired the self-possession of the typical shop girl."

It was only natural that Greta's conservative nature and keen observance of people had helped her to understand the importance of a refined presentation and good manners. Back at home, dressmaker Hanna Rumberg agreed that Alva Gustafsson's kid sister had impeccable taste; she wasn't as sure about her manners. "Alva would come weeks ahead, and talk and plan. But Greta would rush in wildly at the very last minute and demand that I make her a dress to wear that very evening! . . . Once I basted a dress on to her to wear to a party. How cross I was, too. How could a dressmaker do her best work so? I told this to Greta, and I scolded her very well for it. . . . She looked at me with a strange grave look that she had. Then she put her hand upon my lips to quiet me. 'Don't scold,' she said."

Her self-possession was further apparent in a gradual weight loss, and in the way she conducted herself around friends. Oden Lindstrom, a friend of Alva's who also worked at Bergström's, noted that both girls were known to be sympathetic, likable young women—not particularly intelligent, he said, but "one never feared of having a boring time in their company." According to Ms. Kaj Gynt, Greta had always been popular with the boys from Södermalm, although she rarely seemed to pay them much attention.

Eva Blomkvist believed her friend aspired to something more romantically impossible. Every evening after work, Greta would walk down Drottninggatan, the Queen's Street, across the river and past the royal family's winter palace on Gamla Stan on her way home. "One of the princes might catch sight of me," she told Eva hopefully. That attention would come in time.

Meanwhile, she had a new opportunity. Bergström's department store, more popularly known throughout Sweden as PUB, was a pioneer in the area of mail-order catalog sales. One day, store manager Ernst Lundgren asked Magda Hellberg to suggest someone to model hats for the upcoming spring 1921 catalog. She replied without hesitating. "Miss Gustafsson should be perfect for that. She always looks clean and well-groomed and has such a good face." Greta accepted the assignment with rare excitement. "Aunt Hellberg can arrange anything for me," she reportedly told coworkers and friends. "Oh, how happy I am!" Magda Hellberg believed her response was "probably the longest sentence I ever heard her say at one time."

Pages 108 and 109 of the spring catalog show Greta Gustafsson imper-sonating several different characters in an assortment of hats and poses—most of them solemn; only in one photograph does she reveal a slight smile while hiding her eyes under the broad brim of her chapeau. Her success prompted another catalog offer, as well as the opportunity to earn extra money as a fashion model at exclusive PUB shows.

Although her coworkers felt that Greta was content with her position, they didn't know that she was willing to risk everything in her continued pursuit of theater or motion picture work. Like her childhood friends in Södermalm, they recalled that she talked constantly about movies and theater, and were surprised when she did not participate in PUB's theater group. They assumed that she did not have the stamina to follow through with her dream. Doubtless, Greta Gustafsson, age fifteen, considered ama-teur productions a waste of time. She aspired to be a professional, and she needed that time to determine how to propel herself toward her goal.

The six-story brick-and-iron building that houses PUB is located in Norr-malm on the corner of two main boulevards: Kungsgatan, the King's Street, and Drottninggatan. Adjacent to the store is Hötorget, a public square where merchants still sell their wares in an open-air market; across the square stands the Konserthuset, home to Stockholm's Philharmonic Orchestra; further on down Kungsgatan is Oscars Teatern. The neighbor-hood is, in fact, rich with theaters and museums. As one of the top depart-ment stores in Sweden, PUB attracted a variety of upscale clientele including actors, directors, producers, writers, and other artisans.

Shortly after her first modeling triumph, Greta met Captain Ragnar (Lasse) Ring, a former cavalry officer-turned-writer and actor who was now directing short films and commercials (then exhibited in local movie houses as "advertising films"). Everyone at PUB knew about the fortieth anniversary film that was being produced and directed by Ring for Bergström's. Professional actors and actresses would be cast in the leading roles, but there was a possibility that a few of the store's six hundred employees might be assigned "bit" parts in the production. Lasse Ring, "a large, smiling man," according to Greta, with a round childish face and booming voice, appeared in her department, made some notes, and was just about to leave when the advertising manager stopped him. "There is a girl here who has done very well modeling hats for us," he said, directing Ring's attention to the stylish young woman standing behind the counter. "Perhaps we could use her." There was a pause. "I felt my heart palpitat-ing," Greta recalled. "Captain Ring looked at me. 'I'm sorry,' he said, 'but our star Olga Andersson will do very well for the hats.' " Nevertheless, he offered to pay the salesgirl 10 kronor a day for a supporting role. Rehearsals began soon after.

Evidence suggests that this film has been improperly identified in the past as *Från topp till tå* (*From Head to Toe*) or *How Not to Dress*. The latter title refers to one of the segments of the story in which Greta and other models are comically depicted wearing an assortment of outrageous out-fits. Magda Hellberg was told the film was going to be the story of a family whose home had been destroyed by fire and how they are helped by the staff of Bergström's. Greta was assigned the role of the eldest daughter who comes to PUB with her family to replace their lost wardrobe; they are redressed "from head to toe" (one of the store's mottos). The short film is officially registered with the local censorship board as *Herr och fru Stockholm* and at Svenska Filminstitutet as *Herrskapet Stockholm ute på inkop* (*Mr. and Mrs. Stockholm Go Shopping*).

Actor Ragnar Widestedt mistook Greta's selection of and willingness to model outlandish costumes. "When she put on her black-and-white checkered costume I thought that the effect was exaggerated and absurd. She looked grotesque . . . I leaned toward Ring and suggested that we shouldn't use her. 'She's impossible,' I said." Widestedt claimed that Lasse Ring shared his opinion "but [he] was a decent fellow, he didn't want to disappoint Greta or break his promise. 'We can always leave some film on the cutting room floor,' he answered. But then something remarkable happened. When she started acting we noticed that she had studied the situation so very carefully and played her role with such intuitive feeling that the result was far too good to throw away."

For Ring the pivotal moment came when producer Hasse Tullberg arrived on the set one day. When the lights were turned on Greta, Tullberg grabbed hold of the door post. "She is so beautiful that it really pains my heart just to see her," the producer told Ring. The director was taken by surprise. Although he had been charmed by Miss Gustafsson, he was "really ashamed that another, an outsider, had opened my eyes."

The twenty-three-minute advertisement was first screened in Stockholm theaters on December 12, 1920. Later that same month, Greta received permission to take an unpaid week off from work; she and Alva had been promised work as extras in a motion picture entitled *En lyckoriddare* (*A Fortune Hunter*, also known as *The Gay Cavalier*). The historical drama was to be produced and directed by John W. Brunius for Skandias Filmbyrå and would feature Gösta Ekman, one of Sweden's finest actors, as the dashing rogue who steals the heart of the ethereal Mary Johnson. Greta and Alva were cast as maid-servants in a bawdy tavern scene. According to Eugene Nifford, who claimed to be one of the cavaliers, a dance sequence was shot in the basement of the Palladium Theatre in downtown Stockholm.[1] He chose Greta Gustafsson as his partner "because I was attracted by her soft, rounded curves. . . . As we danced I became fascinated with the thick, long curling lashes fringing the most unusual eyes I have ever seen. Smoldering gray-blue eyes that glowed like moonlight on a blue lake when she looked up at me and said, 'It must be wonderful to be a star.' "

The stars were still in her eyes when she returned to work. In addition to Lasse Ring, Greta had attracted another older admirer during the making of *Herr och fru Stockholm*. Max Gumpel, a bachelor in his early thirties, lived nearby and came to the set to watch his seven-year-old nephew, Erick Fröander, perform. A leading citizen in the community, Gumpel was the owner and manager of one of Sweden's most successful construction firms. By his own account, he was immediately taken with the actress playing Erick's older sister; she, in turn, was taken with his affable style and manner. He invited Miss Gustafsson to dine with him and, in time, she accepted.

Gumpel's glamorous apartment at Drottninggatan 73 was Greta's initiation into the lifestyle she had always dreamed about. "I remember we ate crown artichokes, which at that time were fairly rare," Max wrote in a privately published memoir entitled *Tales and Reality (Sagor och verklighet)*. "I have to admit that I was very fond of the girl, so much so that I made her a present of a tiny gold ring with a small diamond in it." The ring was comparatively modest, but the diamond was real; it was a true gesture of friendship.

Anna Gustafsson seemed pleased to see both her daughters becoming acquainted with such fine gentlemen—especially with circumstances still lean at home—but she understood why her youngest sometimes worried about being out of her depth. When Max Gumpel showed up at the apartment on Blekingegatan with an expensive gift, Greta was horrified; none of her new friends from the north side of town had ever seen where she lived.

Eventually, says Sven Broman, the romantic relationship matured into a sexual one. Laila Nylund, Max's youngest daughter, isn't so sure. "My father was not the kind of man to brag about that kind of thing," she explains. "He never said anything to us other than he thought she was charming and they had a deep friendship. If she had ever needed any help,

---

[1]Since Greta and Alva were employed as extras, their participation in this film cannot be verified and is dependent on Nifford's story and a reference Greta made to it in *Lektyr*. Nifford's name doesn't appear in the brief cast lists currently available on the motion picture. However, if his memory is correct, the sequence he refers to was most probably filmed at Skansen, an open-air museum and year-round cultural fair on the island of Djurgården.

he would have been there for her. Maybe they did have a sexual relation-ship, but I think that is highly speculative." Max and Greta continued to date on a casual basis for the next year. Inevitably, they drifted apart, but Gumpel remembered their separation as an amicable one. They parted "like the good friends we had always been." She would not be easy to forget.

Lasse Ring did not forget Greta Gustafsson either, selecting her to essay another comedic role in a promotional piece he directed for the Con-sumer's Cooperative Association of Stockholm.[2] Her part was filmed on Sundays, Greta's day off from PUB. The twenty-seven-minute short, a ver-itable time-capsule vision of Stockholm in the early 1920s, depicts leisure activity in and around the capital city during the summer. In an intriguing bit of foreshadowing, during the first sequence Greta and a group of friends have tea on the rooftop terrace of the Strand Hôtel, across the street from the Royal Dramatic Theatre. Greta finishes her coffee and pastry while the camera pans to reveal the popular actor Lars Hanson at an adjoining table. Within two years she would be working with Hanson in one of the most important films of both their careers.

By August of 1921, Greta had been employed at PUB for over a year. Things were going well for her; she liked her work, she'd been an extra in her first motion picture, and her Stockholm promotional film was set to be shown at the Tokyo World's Fair. She was on the verge of getting what she wanted—yet confessed that she had become "pretty indifferent to every-thing."

She found the energy to renew her effort in the fall. Greta was offered a part in a feature-length motion picture: "a Nordic love story" to be directed by Lasse Ring and filmed on location two hours outside of Stock-holm. This time, however, the personnel department refused to arrange additional time off from work. According to Ring, when he tried to inter-vene with Greta's boss he was reprimanded for giving the girl "crazy ideas about the movies." Greta reluctantly declined the role.

It wasn't long before she captured another filmmaker's attention. Pro-ducer/director Erik A. Petschler first observed Greta in front of a shoe store in Norrmalm. He was transfixed. "I was fascinated by her profile, and as I came closer, I saw her eyes and lips, which appealed to me greatly," he stated. "As soon as she saw me looking at her she gave me the kind of glance which expressed more clearly than words: 'Go away and leave me alone!' "

[2]Konsumtionsföreningen Stockholm med omnejd. Once again, information—albeit incomplete—indicates that this is the advertising film formerly known as *Our Daily Bread*.

"He stared at me so intently that I became embarrassed and quickly disappeared into the crowd," Greta admitted to Lars Saxon. Two days later, he saw her behind a counter at PUB—but decided not to bother her, reasoning that the young saleswoman would prefer the security of a weekly paycheck to anything he could offer. Fortunately for Greta, one of his party stayed behind. "She was Tyra Ryman, one of Mr. Petschler's favorite actresses . . ." They began to talk: ". . . and she told me who he was and about the film he was planning. I asked her if there was any chance I might be able to get a part. She laughed at this and said she was sure I was just what the producer wanted!"

Ryman gave her the director's telephone number, and Greta did "one of the boldest things I have ever done"—she called Petschler from a public telephone at work (the Gustafssons still didn't have a phone). The following afternoon, she went to see the director during her lunch hour. After a brief interview in which Greta recited a poem in lieu of a dramatic scene, Petschler offered her a part in his upcoming film. Although her role would take two weeks to shoot, Greta accepted it at once, thinking she could rearrange her vacation schedule. Her request was again declined by the personnel department. Even Petschler's direct plea to Mr. Bergström failed to get her a release. "Miss Gustafsson, in spite of her youth, is one of the best saleswomen in my entire company," Bergström responded. He wanted her behind the counter where she belonged.

Greta discussed her dilemma with her mother. Much to her daughter's amazement, Anna Gustafsson supported her decision to leave PUB. Miss Gustafsson tendered her resignation, and on July 22, 1922—almost two years to the day from her fateful move uptown—she completed her final day of work at PUB. Personnel records state her reason for leaving: "to work in film." She was sixteen years old. She would never hold another job outside the world of entertainment.

Luffar-Petter (*Peter the Tramp*) was a low-budget comedy patterned after the popular Mack Sennett Keystone comedies. The production company's moderate budget of 15,000 kronor restricted them to locations in the Stockholm vicinity; the scenario was developed accordingly. It would tell the story of Max August Pettersson (nicknamed Peter the Tramp), a fireman named Erik Silverhjälm—both roles portrayed by Petschler—and the three daughters (Tyra Ryman, Greta Gustafsson, and Irène Zetterberg) of the town's mayoress (Gucken Cederborg). Greta won the role of the "second daughter," the tallest of the three girls and often their ringleader.

"Greta Gustafsson, the future film star, did not actually outshine the others, though there were occasions when she aroused a certain interest in me," Petschler remarked. "I can still see Greta sitting nonchalantly on the grass, hands thrust into her blue trousers, chin cocked up and her little head to one side, watching the [actors] with a calm, sleepy, yet interested expression, her eyes half shut."

One scene with another actor went through multiple takes before the director turned to Greta in frustration. "Miss Gustafsson, how would you do this scene?" he asked. She turned toward Petschler, looking at him "uncomprehending and startled, as if she hadn't grasped what I said. I repeated it. With a slight, embarrassed smile she got up slowly and walked . . . somewhat awkwardly to do what for her must have been a difficult task." What started out as a sarcastic comment from Petschler turned into genuine surprise when the director discovered she was able to capture the nuance of what he was talking about. He was touched; she was a comic delight.

Each day was a new adventure. Described as "shy and uneasy" when filming began, Greta gradually relaxed into her job and began to contribute to the filmmaking fun. As she became more confident, Petschler shifted the focus in her direction. The director recalled one incident in which "a sudden rain squall burst over us and . . . Greta and Tyra in their bathing suits improvised a wild Indian dance in the pouring rain. It was a sight for the gods."

The motion picture, a five-reeler, was set to open at the end of the year. In the meantime, Greta contemplated her next job. If she was lucky, she might get a new film assignment before the summer was over or pursue a legitimate production for the coming fall season. She asked her costars on *Luffar-Petter* for suggestions, then began her first (and only) rounds of producers and directors in the Stockholm area; according to Petschler, she even tried to see Mauritz Stiller, the celebrated director of such Svensk Filmindustri classics as *Erotikon* and *Thomas Graals bästa film*. Stiller had worked with both Gucken Cederborg and, more recently, Tyra Ryman—a fact which Greta, no doubt, hoped to parlay into an introduction. But the director was absorbed with completing his latest epic, *Gunnar Hedes saga*, and had no time.

Greta subsequently consulted with a number of her acting acquaintances—each of whom would take credit for her next step. Erik Petschler ran into her while she was making her casting rounds and suggested discussing her situation over coffee. Greta was afraid that she might have to accept a regular job; her family could not afford for her to be unemployed for long. Since she had quit her job at PUB in order to act in his film, Petschler felt somewhat responsible. Her problem, he thought, was that she needed to develop her craft. One of the finest acting schools in the world was located in Stockholm: Kungliga Dramatiska Teaterns Elevskola, the Royal Dramatic Theatre Academy. Auditions for the coming year would take place at the end of the summer. The director encouraged her to try for a scholarship, and promised to arrange a meeting with Frans Enwall, who had been the head of the school from 1904 to 1921 and now tutored students privately.

That is one story. However, according to Greta, she studied with Frans Enwall for six months—which means that she was introduced to him prior to her work on *Luffar-Petter* and *before* she left PUB. True to the Garbo spirit, her story is indefinite, yet precise. "I met an actor," she told Ruth Biery for *Photoplay*. "And I told him, just like millions tell actors, that I wanted to go on the stage. Asked him, just like all the others, how I could do it. He called upon another actor, better known, and sent me to him. It was Frans Enwall . . ."

During their first meeting, Enwall listened very carefully to his prospective student, noting Greta's dedication, determination, and the mysterious force driving her that told her she had "no choice" but to follow this path. He agreed to coach her for the audition. But, he warned her, only six students would be selected from dozens of applicants; two of the six were eligible to receive nominal financial support along with their scholarships. Enwall would help Greta get an invitation and recommend her for a placement. The rest was up to her.

She returned a few days later with the scene she had prepared, but the elderly teacher was too ill to work. To console her, he introduced her to his daughter, Signe, who also coached actors. Greta began her soliloquy and then stopped abruptly. "I'm sorry," she said, somewhat annoyed with herself. "That wasn't very good. May I begin again?" She started over and this time the speech flowed naturally. "She was so anxious to succeed that she was completely receptive to assistance," Signe Enwall reported. "The fact that her knowledge of the drama was not wide did not matter. What really counts in an actress is an ability to feel and understand [everyday life]. In that sense, Greta Gustafsson was extremely well-equipped."

Following her release from *Luffar-Petter*, Greta and her coach had less than a month to polish three scenes—highlights from dramatic works they had discussed at length and agreed upon for the audition. The material they selected was challenging and varied in scope, designed to demonstrate the prospective student's potential: a monologue from *Dunungen* (*The Fledgling*) by Selma Lagerlöf, the wench Catherine's speech from act 1 of *Madame Sans-Gêne*, and a whisper of Ellida in Ibsen's *The Lady from the Sea*.

A notice in *Svenska Dagbladet*, one of Stockholm's daily papers, announced that the day was at hand. Greta gathered the necessary papers from her parish, school, doctor, and a number of personal references for presentation to the Academy. According to Sven Broman, she even collected a letter from Arthur Ekengren stating that she had been a reliable assistant at his barber shop. On the day of her audition—"a beautiful day in August," she recalled—Miss Gustafsson gave the papers to the selection committee and made a declaration about her financial situation.

Greta played with the diamond ring Max Gumpel had given her while strangers observed her with curious conceit. Some of the students made it through their entire program; the less fortunate ones were dismissed after two or three halting lines. Greta heard her name called and walked out in front of the blue and gold curtain of the main theater. Assembled in the dark auditorium were the twenty jurists of the examining body: teachers and actors from Dramatiska Teatern as well as respected critics and journalists. "I remember it was right after noon . . . and I was frightened," she said. "My knees shook. I trembled all over. . . . All I could see was the black pit—that black open space. All I could hear was whispering."

She chose the piece by Selma Lagerlöf. *"There's no blood in my veins; there is only tears!"* she began, reciting the speech perfectly. According to the rules, the jury then selected the next audition piece from the two additional scenes that had been prepared by the student. In Greta's case, they decided on Sardou's *Madame Sans-Gêne.* Miss Gustafsson had barely completed her presentation when she was told that she didn't need to go any further, she would hear back from the committee in approximately three days. Sensitive about her age and the lack of proper schooling, Greta thought she was being dismissed. "Then I just ran off. I forgot to say goodbye." She immediately regretted her behavior. "I thought they would think I had not been polite," she said. She was so nervous and confused she almost fainted backstage.

A telephone call to a neighbor's phone brought her the news she so desperately wanted to hear: she had been accepted *and* would receive a small monthly stipend of approximately 50 kronor. "Oh God, I was happy! I almost died," she told an American journalist. She was on her way to becoming a *real* actress.

Skådespelerska.[3] Even without translation the word seems to carry with it the tradition of Shakespeare and all the great artists who glorified the theater. In Sweden, acting is an honorable profession and theater is an important part of many Swedes' lives. Actors are not diminished by their work,

[3]Skådespelerska: actress. Pronounced shō-des-pā-lær-ska.

people are enriched by it. A seventeen-year-old girl from the working class could not have aspired to anything finer.

Greta was asked, along with five other new students, to return to the Academy at 9:00 A.M. on September 18, 1922, for registration. It was an important day for her. As she walked across Nybroplan, the plaza where Birger Jarlsgatan, Nybrogatan, and Strandvägen all meet, Greta could marvel at the stately white marble and gold exterior of Kungliga Dramatiska Teatern (or Dramaten, as it is affectionately known in Stockholm). The blue and yellow flag of Sweden waved above the awning, beckoning her in. Up the stairs and past the friezes by Carl Milles, inside the marble foyer where she stood under the magnificent ceiling mural depicting *The Birth of Drama*. She was directed to the Academy classrooms on the third floor in the back.

A small woman with large eyes and short black hair sat in the room across from Greta. The classroom was silent. A teacher asked everyone to introduce themselves and state their age. When Greta's turn came, fellow student Mimi Pollak recalled that "Greta was so excited that instead of giving her age, she blurted out, 'It's my birthday!' Everyone, including the teacher, laughed and the ice was broken."

The theater school was a two-year program with an additional year offered to gifted students.[4] During that time they were taught acting fundamentals; performance and interpretation; voice, dance, and movement; theater history; mime; play reading and analysis; set design; and fencing. Their teachers would include the great Nils Personne, who had helped establish the Academy years earlier. Class hours were 9:00 to 5:00. After school, students also participated in Dramatic Theatre productions in small roles or as supernumeraries. During the theatrical season (typically, late September through mid-May), they often were at the theater from 9:00 A.M. until midnight. They were not allowed to take any outside work (even between terms) without permission.

After their orientation, the new students were introduced to the class of 1921, as well as former students now under contract to the theater, and were encouraged to get to know one another. Mimi Pollak invited Greta to her apartment off Birger Jarlsgatan. She had been abroad and had many stories to share with a new friend. Her father, proprietor of a business in Karlstad, was from Vienna and was of Jewish descent; her mother, a classical pianist, was from Yugoslavia. Despite her social station and background, Mimi was not arrogant about the advantages she had in life. Greta relaxed in her company.

---

[4]Prospective students also signed a contract obligating them to two years in the theatrical company following graduation.

Mimi's first impressions of Greta were of a young woman who was "a little round and wore her hair in a little knot at the nape of her neck. She wore very simple clothes . . . and she *loved* the theater." They drank coffee and smoked cigarettes "until suddenly Greta started coughing terribly. When she recovered she said it had been the first cigarette she ever had." Mimi, who was two years older than Greta, had been introduced to smoking on the Continent and thought it very smart and sophisticated. From then on, the two girls would often spend their coffee breaks having a private smoke in the backstage alley. Greta smoked first for friendship, second for the illusion of sophistication, and third because she could not quit once she started. It would be a lifelong addiction.

The two became the closest of friends, later admitting into their circle Vera Schmiterlöw and, occasionally, Mona Mårtenson, both of whom were a year ahead of them at the Academy. Vera Schmiterlöw lived in the same humble circumstances as Greta and also shared with her an early start in films. Mona Mårtenson had already distinguished herself in student productions at Dramaten and was considered someone to watch. Mimi Pollak was regarded as the most cultured and the most intelligent. Greta was the quiet one—the only one of the group who hadn't been to high school; she listened, and absorbed.

The acting technique as taught at Dramatiska Teatern stressed simplicity in motion, feeling, intellect, experience, and physical characterization—the mechanics of which were drilled into each student until they became part of his or her subconscious. "The school was wonderful," Greta enthused. "We had the very best teachers. We were given plays to study. Two pupils and a teacher would study together."

One of Greta's student notebooks—its frail, dog-earred pages now yellowing with age—is safely tucked away in the archival files of the Svenska Filminstitutet. The first part of the Dramaten notebook is interesting for its classroom observations—many of which would stand in good stead with the future screen actress. "Mime," it was recorded, "is the art of expressively reflecting various states of mind, thoughts and desires through facial expressions and gestures." The entry warns the student against stiff, angular movements; one must move beautifully, fluidly, without affectation or restraint. Other parts of the notebook document the class's instructions on how to use their bodies, what different gestures or physical characteristics communicate to the audience, and stress the subtle importance of the eyes and mouth in facial expression. A final entry underscores Greta's directions for a scene to be performed in class.

Greta acquired a reputation at the dramatic school for her uniquely offbeat way of thinking. Fellow students got to know her more quickly than they anticipated; what appeared at first to be arrogance was actually nothing more than timid reserve. They came to view her as simple, but never ordinary; thoughtful; sometimes fearful, but more often fear*less*, curious about life and always ready to laugh. While some teachers thought her most striking attribute to be her indolence, friends admired the loyal comrade who never had anything bad to say about anyone.

Another student who gained a reputation as an original thinker was Alf Sjöberg, soon to become the preeminent figure in Swedish theater and cinema. "He came in like a stormy wind with his socialism, his vision, his new ideas, his rebellion against the old," Mimi Pollak wrote. At lunch, Greta and Mimi would share a dish for a krona (then about twenty cents) at Söderberg's cafe. Alf Sjöberg often joined them. "We had decided to revolutionize the art of stage acting," Mimi recalled. "There was a lot [of talk] about the relationship between life and the theater, between reality and illusion. . . . Like all other students we understood everything better than all the other great theater workers. We criticized violently."

To read Sjöberg's account of his student years is to understand what Mimi was talking about. "Meeting the fellow students had given me the warm feeling you get when you belong to a group," he stated. "We struggled from morning to evening. Early rehearsals, late rehearsals . . . but we were young and continued our discussions, quarrels and wild parties throughout the nights." He quickly became friends with Greta Gustafsson, recognizing in her a comrade: like him, one of the working class. "She had found a friend in the short, happy, gleaming Mimi Pollak, who with her mannerisms from southern Europe, also was an outsider in the group of blond, Swedish upper-class children. They complemented each other in a fantastic way," he noted. "Greta's queenlike person, with her arm around Mimi's small graceful person. I attacked them, of course, with my ideas: revolt . . . renewal . . . rebuild this old temple! I see Greta sitting on the long, worn bench in the students' dressing room, so close and yet so distant. On the floor Mimi and I . . . arguing, smoking, fighting . . . That small one, she was so strong . . . Finally, we lay on the floor, laughing—but Greta sat there, alone, locked inside her androgynous silence. *Tintomara*—I thought, there she is sitting, only partly present . . . above all the fighting, who was she really?"

Greta Gustafsson's first public performance was on November 4, 1922. Her first play was a comedy, *La belle aventure* (*The Adventure*) by Gaston-Armand de Caillavet and Robert de Flers. The playbill lists Greta Gustafson (one *s*) in the role of Madam de Ligneray, and also credits her classmates "Mimmie" Pollak, Lena Cederström, and "Monica" Mårtenson; they were guests at a wedding that never takes place. Greta's single line of dialogue: "Excuse me, Count, for being late."

The Academy brought in a photographer to produce group photos of both student classes at Dramatiska Teatern. On the left, with one exception (Barbro Djurberg, who was engaged to classmate Arnold Sjöstrand), stood the graduating class of 1921; on the right, with one exception (the always exceptional Alf Sjöberg), stood the class of 1922. Six men and six women—all dressed in their Sunday best. Greta stayed with basic black: black dress, black tights, and new black shoes. She brushed her hair off her face, avoiding the bobs and curls of the 1920s that were the latest fad. To further distinguish herself from the rest of the group, she did something very canny: she avoided looking at the camera. While everyone else looks like they are posing for a family photo, a nearly expressionless Greta Gustafsson, with her eyes downcast, adds the element of mystery and allure.

On December 26, the belated premiere of *Luffar-Petter* was staged at the Odéon Teatern in Stockholm. Reviews of the film were mixed. The general consensus was that everyone overacted, but the girls looked wonderful in their bathing suits. Critics who singled out Greta Gustafsson did not think she could compete with American actresses "where comic situations and technical finesse are concerned," though one suggested she had freshness and charm. "Since Miss Gustafsson has thus far only had the dubious distinction of playing a 'Bathing Beauty' for Mr. Erik A. Petschler . . . we have no impression whatsoever regarding her ability," *Swing* magazine advocated. "In any case, it is a pleasure to be able to record a new name in Swedish films and we hope to have occasion to mention it again."

Greta quietly attended the film's premiere with schoolmates Mimi Pollak and Alf Sjöberg. "The film surpassed every expectation," Sjöberg reported. "I have never seen anything so ghastly. We pulled her out of the auditorium before the lights went on. As we walked up and down the streets, we demanded that she'd take a vow never to get involved in movies again. She obviously did not have even the most basic talent for it." Greta's place was in the theater, they thought.

Classes continued at Dramatiska Teatern after the Christmas holidays. "We worked hard and with great enthusiasm, but sometimes we also cried with fatigue," Mimi Pollak said. For many students, a training in theater would help them reach beyond their usual inhibitions. At seventeen, even when others had caught up to her in height, Greta felt big for her age—and awkward in class. She avoided morning exercises and was tentative in dance class. But many of her classmates thought she moved with an innate grace and possessed an elegant, noble air that she assumed to stunning effect. She made them forget she was the girl from Blekingegatan.

"The beauty that she was, Greta was constantly invited out by young men for dinner," Vera Schmiterlöw said. "On the few occasions when she accepted, she would make it clear before that she had to be home early." A Dramaten production of Holger Drachmann's *Det var en gång* (*Once Upon a Time*) brought a new admirer. Johannes Poulsen had been borrowed from the Royal Theatre of Denmark. Before the actor returned to Copenhagen, he asked Miss Gustafsson to dine with him. He arranged for a private dining room at the Strand, where they shared a romantic *tête-à-tête*. But after coffee and liqueur, just as Poulsen moved in for more intimacy, Greta got up, thanked him for the lovely dinner, and left. "There would be no playing about," Vera added. "Greta would never let herself go down in a horizontal position!"

Sometimes Vera, Mimi, and Greta went out on dates together. Mimi recalled the time Vera arranged for them to meet their escorts outside the Stockholm Stadion. It was a bitter-cold evening and the girls were early— but they quickly forgot their frozen feet when three well-dressed young gentlemen arrived in separate horse-drawn sleighs. Greta rode with Gösta Kyhlberg, whom she discovered had recently separated from his wife and was terribly unhappy. According to Mimi, he fell in love with Greta instantly.

When they reached Foresta, a fashionable restaurant on the outskirts of town, the girls were escorted to a private candlelit room; in front of a romantic log fire now stood their three smiling dates in smoking jackets. "We had landed in the midst of the operetta's magical world and we strained to look as though we were those smiling operetta stars we had seen on the posters.... The maître'd came in with goose on a silver platter, which he carried high over his head. Wine, the jingle of glasses, *skål!*" For dessert they were served juicy pears from France; as Mimi bit into her pear she thought she saw Greta slip hers into her handbag. "Don't leave me alone with Gösta in the taxi cab," Greta begged her as they gathered their hats and coats at the end of an unforgettable evening. "It wasn't the last time I got to play the third wheel during the journey to the corner of Blekingegatan and Ringvägen," Mimi said.

The next morning, Mimi rushed to get to class on time, arriving just as Nils Personne was taking attendance. But there was no sign of Greta. Her absence was noted in the teacher's book. "At that moment the door burst open and a cheerful Greta walked up to him, saying, 'Look what I have brought you, Mr. Personne.' " She curtsied as she handed him the large, juicy pear. The teacher looked at the offering appreciatively, wrapped it in his red handkerchief, and promptly erased her absence from his record. "Wasn't that clever of me?" she whispered to Mimi.

Greta, whom many classmates called "Gurra" (a derivation of Gustaf), was notoriously late during her tenure at the theater academy. "The other pupils were charming, lovely girls who were always on time," she said. "Then in would come [Gurra], late as usual. I'd come in the door and say, 'There's a rumor about that this school is still here. But I'm so tired; Gurra's so tired.' And nobody would say a word to me! . . . If I had been scolded, I'd have been there." She did not, as she feared, upset the school with her behavior. By now, they were used to her idiosyncrasies, and they accepted them because they believed in her talent. Greta always arrived in time for the morning coffee break, and off they would go to discuss the previous night's revelry.

Interviewed many years later, Academy director Gustaf Molander admitted having very little recollection of Greta Gustafsson, "for she never put in an appearance until my own lesson was over and it was time to go and have coffee. She was gifted, of course; though it seemed as though she did not dare show it, as though she did not have the courage to be truly herself. But at times it would flash out, especially if something fired her imagination."

Occasionally, Mimi Pollak saw a unique boldness emerge in her friend. Greta and Mimi participated in a celebration honoring Halvdan Christensen's final performance at the theater. After an elegant supper in the mirrored ballroom at the Grand Hôtel, there were speeches toasting the Norwegian actor, then an improvised entertainment in which the guest of honor took part. Greta leaned over to Mimi and announced that she would like to sing something. Mimi gave her an approving nod. The usually reticent acting student got up in front of an incredulous gathering and sang a song from the revue *Fru från Hagalund* (*The Girl from Hagalund*). After that performance, Mimi said, no one at the Academy pretended to know what Greta Gustafsson would do next.

"You understand that in the theater you have to be a bit forward. Though that's scarcely very womanly," Greta would tell Eva Blomkvist. "But then perhaps I'm not all that womanly." Her speech teacher Karl Nygren would have liked to have seen her show even more initiative. "I remember that now and again she seemed very depressed and troubled. She often blushed, especially when we were discussing things that she was not acquainted with," he said. "I think that this was probably due to the fact that her schooling had been meager, and she was acutely conscious of that. I was often sorry for her in the classroom.

"But when I would meet her by chance in the halls or in the theater she was not at all bashful. Once, during class, I remember I was trying to explain the way to make certain tones—I wanted to show how to speak with a kind of nasal twang. In trying to get this across I imitated the popular cabaret stars Hansi and Jean Moreau. Always after that, whenever I met Greta outside the classroom she would greet me in those nasal tones, saying, 'Good morning, Director Nygren. Is this the right way to say it?' She had a very pleasing personality, very attractive."

"Shortage of money was Greta's chief worry at that time," Vera Schmiterlöw recalled, adding that "[she] had no need to feel embarrassed in front of me, because I was just as hard up as she was." During the summer she might be allowed to make extra money modeling, but during the school year, apart from the monthly stipend she was given as a scholarship student, all she received was a three-kronor-per-night honorarium for Dramatiska Teatern productions.[5] Her sister, Alva, whom Vera believed "worshipped Greta," helped her with money whenever she could, "as did her uncle David"; on occasion, the manager at the Strand Hôtel also arranged for free meals, but it was a constant struggle.

Vera, Greta, and Mona Mårtenson appeared together in the German comedy *Sköldpaddskammen* (*The Tortoise-Shell Comb*) by Richard Kessler, which opened on April 28, 1923, and ran for forty-three performances before successfully moving over to Mindre Teatern. Greta Gustafson (still one *s*) essayed the role of Fräu von Brandt. This time, she promised Mimi, she wouldn't overdo the makeup—no black circles around the eyes. Greta had learned another secret: by arriving late backstage, she had the dressing room—which she normally would have to share with the other Dramaten students—to herself.

That weekend, the students celebrated the advent of spring, with lively festivities throughout the city streets. Bonfires dotted the parks along the Strandvägen, the elegant boulevard running along the water between the Nobel Park and Dramatiska Teatern . . . bands played nearby in the royal promenade, Kungsträgården . . . singing resounded down the narrow streets of the old city of Gamla Stan, and across the Slussen bridge toward Södermalm. *Walpurgisnacht* 1923 was no different from any other spring celebration, but for once Greta Gustafsson had cause to celebrate. She had

---

[5]Archivists at Kungliga Dramatiska Teatern were not able to confirm either the scholarship or the honorarium. Complete records for the school, which has since become an independent entity, no longer exist. Information regarding these financial arrangements comes from fellow students.

been with the Academy for less than a year, but she had made an indelible impression on most everyone. She was among her peers—and she was happy. "Happy is too big a word to use very often," she cautioned. "It means so much to our country—the word happy—that we hardly speak of it."

Shortly after she returned from Easter vacation, she received a message from Gustaf Molander to prepare herself for a new audition: director Mauritz Stiller wanted to see her.

CHAPTER 3

Flesh and the "Devil"

For all the actors and directors who mingled in the familial world of enter-
tainment in Stockholm and later took credit for bringing Greta Garbo and
Mauritz Stiller together—actor Carl Brisson in 1919, the "phantom"
Eugene Nifford in 1921, director Erik Petschler in 1922—it took a man
with solid ties to Svensk Filmindustri to finally deliver. He was the author
of Stiller's *Thomas Graal* films as well as the acclaimed *Song of the Scarlet
Flower (Sangen om den eldröda bromman)* and cowriter of *Erotikon*. He was
Gustaf Molander, the head of Dramatiska Teaterns Elevskola.

Interestingly, Molander had selected Greta Gustafsson and Mona
Mårtenson for Mauritz Stiller to consider for his new motion picture—but
not the equally attractive (and experienced) Vera Schmiterlöw whom
Molander had already featured prominently in his own films.[1] Considering
the fact that Molander had not been overly impressed with Miss Gustafsson during her first year at the Academy, it is possible that the suggestion
was made to *him* to send her over—that someone on the outside had been
interested in her progress. In 1946, director Victor Sjöström said as much
to journalist Charles Turner. Veteran actress Karin Swanström heard that
Stiller had attended the graduation performance for the class of 1921 at
Dramatiska Teatern. Although Greta's part in the gala was minor, Stiller
approached Molander after the show and told him that he must speak with
her. Greta pretended not to think about how much an introduction to
Mauritz Stiller meant. "I never get thrilled about anything until it happens," she would say. "It hurts too much to be disappointed."

Despite her alleged indifference, as soon as classes were over Greta
found her way to the director's apartment at Odengatan 90, halfway
between Dramaten and the film studios in Råsunda. It appeared that he
was not at home; Miss Gustafsson was asked by Stiller's close friend and
assistant, Axel Nilson, to wait. An hour or so later, he made his entrance
with a Russian wolfhound at his side; Greta was properly intimidated.
"Without so much as a greeting, he stared at me for a long time—a very
long time."

The director was in his element. He made no attempt to get to know his

---

[1] Schmiterlöw and Mimi Pollak were assigned to another film that summer.

guest; he was most concerned about her appearance: her face, her long eyelashes, the line of her body, her weight. He broke a long silence by making small talk about the weather and other trivialities as he continued scrutinizing her. He had a disconcerting way of staring as if he were looking right through her or, what was worse, not even looking. Greta would later discover that, whatever her perception was at the time, "[Stiller] was really looking at me every moment." She respectfully noted that a few years later he could describe in detail exactly what she was wearing that fateful afternoon—right down to her low-heeled black shoes (so she wouldn't appear too tall) and black stockings (which made her legs seem slimmer).

"Well, can't you take off your coat and hat?" he commanded, as if he had asked his guest to relax and sit down many times before. "Then he just looked at me some more and said, 'What's your telephone number?' " That was the death knell at any audition or interview. "I knew it was all over. 'He isn't interested,' I thought. 'When they're not interested they always ask your telephone number.' " Greta gave Stiller the phone number of a friend, thanked him for seeing her, and left. She did not expect to hear from the director again.

He was born Movscha Stiller on July 17, 1883, in the Jewish-Slavic quarter of Helsinki, then the capital of the Russian grand duchy of Finland. It wasn't an easy life. When Movscha was four years old, his mother committed suicide. One month later, his father passed away after a long illness. One of Movscha's older brothers and his sister were sent to live with relatives in Russia; two more brothers were shuttled off to Poland; Movscha, then known by his Hebrew name of Mosche—or Moje for short—and his younger brother, Abraham, stayed in Helsinki and were raised by family friends. Moje grew up in the home of Peretz Katzmann, a cap maker.

In a 1971 interview, Abraham Stiller described his brother as a popular figure at school. "The boys liked him because he was rebellious and he had the courage to lead the way to some bold venture. The girls admired his nice appearance—he was very good-looking as a child—and they turned to him diligently as an advisor in matters of taste." When he was thirteen years old, Moje left school. By then, three of his brothers and his sister had emigrated to the United States (most to California). At age sixteen, he drifted into acting, taking on the stage name of Mauritz Stiller. Between 1899 and 1903 he worked in two different Swedish-language theaters in Helsinki and Turku, gradually working his way up to leading roles. In the autumn of 1904, while many Finns were rising against the oppressive regime of Tsar Nicholas II, the twenty-one-year-old Stiller stole across the Swedish border with a false passport in order to avoid conscription in the

Russian army.[2] In 1905, when Greta was born, Mauritz Stiller was touring Sweden in an acting troupe. In 1911, he became the manager of the Lilla Teatern in Stockholm, and began directing as well as acting in their productions. He gained a reputation for being highly theatrical; he was—according to friends and foes alike—passionate, articulate, obsessive, and full of ideas. His strength lay in his extraordinary eye and an unequivocal belief in himself. He was perfect for the movies.

Understandably, after decades of Hollywood dominating the business, most people today believe that the film industry actually began in the United States when, in fact, up until the First World War, it was in Europe that the most spectacular advances were being made. In Sweden, under the leadership of Charles Magnusson, Svenska Biografteatern rose to prominence alongside its counterparts in France, Italy, and Germany. Magnusson moved Svenska Bio to Stockholm in 1912, built a new studio on the island of Lidingö, and invited two new directors to join his company. Their acceptance would permanently alter the face of Swedish cinema. By 1916 Victor Sjöström and Mauritz Stiller had firmly established themselves as Sweden's greatest filmmakers, positions which remained unchallenged until the rise of Ingmar Bergman thirty years later.

Sjöström gravitated toward more somber material, making lyrical films about man's battle with God and nature that were inherently Scandinavian in their themes and execution. Stiller struggled to find a singular style, vacillating between the sophisticated comedy of *Erotikon* to the psychological drama of *Vingarna* (*Wings*) or the epic *Herr Arnes pengar* (*Sir Arne's Treasure*), his first adaptation of a Selma Lagerlöf story. He loved music and often worked on the rhythm of his films the way a good musician labors over a melody, freely adapting stories to suit his dramatic sense—thus incurring the wrath of many writers, including Miss Lagerlöf, Sweden's revered Nobel Prize–winning author. But he knew how to use his charm to ingratiate himself to people he had offended; he usually won them back.

At six feet tall, Mauritz Stiller towered over most people—though his physical size was just one way he was able to dominate a situation. In a country where people preferred not to call attention to themselves, Stiller presented an impressive figure about town in his bright yellow Kiesel sports car, accompanied by a beautiful woman or his dogs. Although his hair had

---

[2]Abraham Stiller's memory was that his brother "was picked up by the gendarmes and brought to Novgorod, where our father was born." While he was under arrest, Moje's friends in Helsinki rushed to his support, forging a passport under the name of Oskar Rosqvist. But he never used the certificate, his brother stated, "because he simply ran away."

turned prematurely gray, there were striking black highlights in his thick eyebrows, closely cropped sideburns, and mustache. His eyes were brilliant blue. He wore fine clothes, most of which were specially tailored for him in London. In Stockholm, he had a regular table reserved for him at Bern's Salon; on the Continent, he was known by the maîtres d'hôtel of Europe's premier restaurants. He alternated between different apartments in town and also owned a home in the exclusive Lidingö neighborhood of Bosön. He lived extravagantly and often beyond his means despite a generous salary from Svenska Bio.

He was a restless spirit, characterized by friends as "one who was always departing." The litany of adjectives used to describe him illustrates an undeniable complexity: mercurial, seductive, ambitious, intelligent, nervous, vain, uncompromising, overpowering. Enthusiastic and inspirational one moment, impatient or despondent the next, Stiller was known on his film sets for his "brilliance and fire"—treating some of his actors like mannequins, others as favored children. His laughter, they said, was "like hearing thunder from a distance." There were so many different kinds of men gathered within him, said Victor Sjöström. "He never shirked or hesitated to call a spade a spade, to tell people straight from the hip what he thought. . . . He could say things that hurt—could hurt badly—which were, at the same time, strikingly funny. Although not so funny for the poor victim. But he was quick to make amends . . ."

He was, most probably, homosexual. Nils Asther met Stiller in 1916 in a Stockholm restaurant. The director approached Asther, whom at the age of nineteen was almost too beautiful to be real, and inquired if he was interested in acting in motion pictures. Asther was cast in a small role in *Vingarna* and quickly became Stiller's "darling favorite," the actor wrote in his autobiography. "One evening he came up to me and I was initiated into the art of loving someone of your own sex." Other reported favorites included actor Einar Hansson, the star of *Gunnar Hedes saga,* and studio technician Nils Elffors.

The suicide of Danish set designer Axel Esbensen on New Year's Day, 1923—reportedly after a "terrible quarrel" with Stiller—was one scandal the director managed to avoid. A police investigation revealed that Esbensen had been under surveillance by the local vice squad. Since the two had been rumored companions beginning with their association on *Herr Arnes pengar* in 1919, Stiller had cause for concern. There was, however, very little gossip about his sexuality—in fact, few acquaintances dared even to speculate about it. He seemed to them to be a very lonely soul with few intimate friends.

*   *   *

"There is something quite extraordinary about that girl. I must discover what it is," Mauritz Stiller declared after Greta left. A few days later, the director asked her to come out to the studios in Råsunda at 10:00 A.M. for a screen test.[3] "I was pleased, but not even yet very excited," Greta stated rather matter-of-factly.

She met Mona Mårtenson on the streetcar and they walked together through the gates of Filmstaden, the film city set in a wooded area just off Råsunda's main boulevard. Making a test for her first major film under the keen eye of Sweden's top director (Sjöström had left for the United States months earlier) was a curious experience for Greta. Again, Stiller made both actresses wait as a way of testing their resolve, and perhaps their courage, as well as disarming them in front of the camera; he wanted to see what made them tick. Confidentially, cameraman Julius Jaenzon, an artist of some reputation himself, told the girls not to let Stiller's flamboyant manner frighten them. "His bark is worse than his bite," he assured them.

Finally, the director ordered the test to begin. "I was all shaky," Greta admitted. "I come off the street . . . and they make me up and then they take me [inside] and tell me to lie in a bed and be sick. Very sick. I didn't know what it was all about. It seemed to me like a big joke, to come off the street and be right away sick. And I was ashamed [to] try and put myself over . . ." Stiller waited for her to find her rhythm, and when she didn't, yelled at her in frustration: "My God, don't you know what it is to be sick?" Then, Greta stated, "I became a very sick lady."

Before she left, Jaenzon told Greta privately that he didn't think she had done very well. Once again, she went home in defeat; it had been another bewildering encounter with the great director. Back at Råsunda, however, Mauritz Stiller had determined that he had indeed found the actress to play Elisabeth Dohna in *Gösta Berlings saga*.[4] He argued with screenwriter Ragnar Hyltén-Cavallius and other Filmindustri executives—all of whom wondered whether Greta would be able to deliver a solid screen performance. "She has no technique," Stiller explained, "so she can't show what she is feeling, but she will be all right. I'll see to that."

Ultimately, they deferred to the director because it was a supporting role and Greta Gustafsson at least looked the part; Stiller would take care of the nuances. Inexperienced players certainly worked well under his tutelage. The director outlined his theory of screen acting for a German news-

---

[3]In 1918, an investment of several million kronor by Swedish industrialist Ivar Kreuger had given Charles Magnusson the opportunity to restructure Svenska Bio as Svenska Filmindustri and move into a new studio complex in the northern suburb of Råsunda.

[4]Gösta is pronounced with a soft G—'yoes-ta.

paper the following year: "I venture the paradox that films, as well as stage productions, should really be played by amateurs, if they only could! When an actor is 'great,' he works unceasingly to simplify his craft . . . to get back to the natural simplicity that was his when he knew nothing about the technique of acting."

One condition he made clear to Greta during subsequent conversations: if she wanted to participate in *Gösta Berlings saga* she would have to lose weight. She agreed wholeheartedly. Gustaf Molander granted Greta and Mona Mårtenson (cast in the smaller role of Ebba Dohna, Gösta Berling's first love) a leave of absence from the Academy for whatever production time overlapped with their fall or winter classes. On July 23, 1923, seventeen year-old Greta Gustafson [*sic*] signed a standard player's contract with Svensk Filmindustri offering her 3,000 kronor for her services. They would pay all necessary travel expenses; she would be expected to adhere to their rules and regulations concerning conduct, and agreed to furnish her own clothes, formal if need be, for promotional appearances.

With the part actually in hand, Greta allowed herself the privilege of being excited, then diligently set about the task of slimming down before production began. "She wanted to become figure-perfect in Stiller's eyes as quickly as possible," Vera Schmiterlöw said. Mimi Pollak, who was performing in Helsingborg that summer, received a letter from Vera acknowledging that the pair were taking Turkish baths at Sturebadet hoping to lose weight. "I'm not getting anywhere," Vera reported, "I've actually put on four kilos. But Greta just gets thinner and thinner. You can't see her breasts anymore. They're just two buttons."

She did not have very much time to reach her goal of losing ten kilos (approximately twenty pounds). Production on *Gösta Berlings saga* finally began in mid-August. The delays with the film had as much to do with securing Selma Lagerlöf's approval on the screenplay by Stiller and Ragnar Hyltén-Cavallius as from the complications of casting. During their previous associations (*Herr Arnes pengar* and *Gunnar Hedes saga*), Lagerlöf had complained that the director had eliminated important scenes and changed locales—while adding his own flourishes to the story—for no apparent reason. After a series of talks between Stiller and Lagerlöf, the writer agreed to Svensk Filmindustri's production of *Gösta Berling*—but not before a thorough examination of the screenplay and a written promise from the director that he would remain faithful to the approved adaptation.

Swedes hold *Gösta Berlings saga* in the highest regard; Selma Lagerlöf had been the first writer to break the spell of stern realism cast over Scandinavian literature in the nineteenth century and make her stories a vehicle for a return to romanticism. *Gösta Berling,* her first and possibly finest work, was a heroic tale that proceeded through folklore, feuds, and fires— gathering up in its rich and sprawling narrative a tale of Värmland, the untamed land on the western perimeter of Sweden, at the end of the Napoleonic era. Finding the right actor to play the troubled hero of Lager- löf's novel would be something of a national obsession and could only be equated with the search for Scarlett O'Hara fifteen years later in America.

Among female moviegoers, the consensus favorite for Gösta Berling— defrocked minister, poet, and scoundrel—was the always-popular Lars Hanson. But Stiller, who had directed Hanson in four films, didn't think he fulfilled the physical requirements of the role. He considered a number of other actors, including Gösta Ekman, before settling on Carl Brisson— Greta's childhood idol. But Brisson was unable to secure a release from his current theatrical contract. "I think everyone in Sweden heaved a sigh of relief when, after all, Lars Hanson was chosen," Victor Sjöström conceded.

Neither Greta nor Mona was prepared for the work before them. Their previous films had been unpretentious undertakings, shot in a matter of weeks, sometimes days. Principal photography on *Gösta Berlings saga* was scheduled for August through October of 1923, with a break in mid-Octo- ber and November while the company awaited the season's first snowfall; the winter shoot would continue through the beginning of February. Forty- eight sets would be constructed, including interiors and exteriors for Ekeby Manor, the scene of a spectacular fire at the film's climax (another hint of *Gone With The Wind* to come). With a budget rumored to be the largest in Svensk Filmindustri's brief history, the arguments concerning the picture's cost and execution also were plentiful. Gone were the idyllic days of Stiller's and Sjöström's apprenticeships, when the front office scarcely knew more than the title of the films they were shooting.

When did Mauritz Stiller first realize what he had in Greta Gustafsson? Historians differ on this point. Stiller certainly knew early on that the actress was someone he could manage or control, as he typically preferred to dominate all novice performers in his productions. Doubtless, he also believed in her potential—but was his belief in her more substantial than his hopes for Jenny Hasselqvist (who had been featured in two of his most recent films) or Mona Mårtenson? "Frankly, we were inclined in those days to think Greta's good luck [was] her greatest asset," Karin Swanström, the actress who played Jenny Hasselqvist's mother, said. "None of us could understand why Stiller was so interested in this little nobody, because he had never paid any particular attention to anyone before. To us she appeared to be just an awkward, mediocre novice."

The "little nobody" admitted being so scared during the first few days of production that she was sick in earnest. Once again, Stiller at first left her to her own devices. It was a silent war of nerves: Would she be the one to ask for help? "Finally, everyone went out and left me. The electricians, the prop boys—even Mr. Stiller. He told me to practice alone." But Greta was beginning to understand him. "I knew he was in some corner watching," she said. "I looked all around and could not see him, but I *knew* he was there. So I would not practice. I would not rehearse all by myself—I would not look so stupid." The director soon took over.

For some time Mauritz Stiller had dreamed of molding an actress into his feminine ideal; someone who combined the exotic sensuality, grace, and warmth of Tora Teje, whom he had directed in *Erotikon*, with the soulful mysticism of Mary Johnson, his leading lady on his previous forays into Lagerlöf territory. Greta Gustafsson had a few advantages over the other contenders. She had extraordinary eyes—a prerequisite for any aspiring movie star and something that would separate her from the vast majority of her peers. Equally important, although her personal charisma was already in evidence, she came to him as a *tabula rasa*, a blank slate.

Stiller's careful observance of the ingenue during rehearsal revealed that she was extremely malleable. Direct eye contact was the key to impressing his will upon her. "I have to break her down . . ." he told an associate, "but when she is broken down, what a performance she gives—such calm, such concentration, such effortless knowledge. And besides all this, her face . . . when she is acting becomes a face to make the gods happy." His attitude toward Greta intensified as the days went by; later scenes were even shot differently, with more of an emphasis on close-ups. As filming continued, Stiller would note with pride that the young actress was solely his creation.

Correspondence from this period shows that Greta clearly missed the company of her Dramaten comrades. "Our desire to make her one of our little family here was never fully realized," Karin Swanström explained, "because of Stiller's jealous care of Greta. He scarcely permitted anyone else even to speak to her, and would hardly leave her out of his sight for a moment." The pair inevitably earned a nickname: "Beauty" and "the Beast." "Perhaps they were more like Svengali and Trilby, with that hypnotic power he seemed to have over her to make her do extraordinary things. But we had little idea then that he was making over her very soul. I can still see them—forever walking up and down, up and down, in the shade of that grove [outside Filmstaden] . . . Stiller was always teaching and preaching, Greta solemnly listening and learning. I never saw anyone more earnest and eager to learn."

According to another observer, however, the film was a tortuous experi-ence for Greta—she was nervous, restless, and "she cried a great deal." Stiller was, in his own words, merciless with her, pushing her farther and farther along. He fussed over her costumes; he needled her about what she ate until she was inclined not to eat at all; he studied her makeup, her walk, her gestures. One day, she actually broke down in front of the com-pany and cursed him. It was a scene made all the more memorable because the usually mild-mannered actress wasn't known to lose her temper. "It was a love-hate affair," Greta stated, "at times he loved me as much as I hated him."

He pushed her hard because he believed the results would be worth it. "As we cut the film, Stiller was pleased that even if his protégé was not a full artist, she at least never seemed artificial," Ragnar Hyltén-Cavallius noted, "what she could express was real. 'She seems touching, one feels sorry for her,' he exclaimed triumphantly." Exhausted by the ordeal, Greta was often seen lying down during breaks on a nearby sofa or bench. In an interview conducted during production, she confessed that the work had been terrifically difficult. "It has been a Gethsemane," she declared. But she was grateful to her director for being exceedingly patient with her. "Stiller is the most generous person in the world," she said. "You never get angry or sad no matter how much he bawls you out. He creates people and shapes them according to his will." According to Vera Schmiterlöw, after reading her interview with a *Filmjournalen* reporter, Stiller forbade his pro-tégé to give any more interviews during production—or indeed any at all exclusive of his attendance.

The ties that bound them strengthened. The director began driving his actress home in his sports car, then escorting her to social events. He helped her select her personal wardrobe. They attended the theater and went out to Stockholm's fashionable restaurants together. He introduced her to the elite circle of artists he mingled with, including Naima Wifs-trand, another childhood favorite. Reactions were mixed. A society matron hosted a party during which, she said, Greta added nothing to the conversation. "She just sat in a corner and seemed to be lost." Drama critic Hjalmar Lenning told Stiller he thought Miss Gustafsson was "dull, unin-teresting, and very taciturn." But Stiller's good friend, art director Vilhelm Bryde, believed the eighteen-year-old actress was just being circumspect about the way she interacted with people she considered better-educated or more sophisticated than herself. She willingly subjugated her own sense of humor and irony, even her own charm, in order to conform with her trusted friend and director's concept of how she should behave. "I always had a complex because I had so little schooling," she told Sven Broman, "but Moje used to dismiss it by saying that you could acquire knowledge in many ways. The most important things were experience and openness."

In October, during the film's hiatus, Greta had an opportunity to go back to Dramatiska Teatern and play Fisher in J. M. Barrie's *The Admirable Crichton*. Back in the main theater, she and Mimi watched Sweden's celebrated dramatic actress, Tora Teje, work on the role of Anna in Eugene O'Neill's *Anna Christie*. "We loved Tora Teje," Mimi Pollak said. "We idolized her when she came in as Anna Christie . . . and began in her dark, sensual voice: 'Give me a whiskey.' Who could imagine that [six] years later Greta would say the same line in her first talkie?"

Sometime during the break, Mauritz Stiller asked Greta to think about changing her name. It was not the first time she had considered it—in fact, many women during this period were adopting more distinctive surnames. After centuries of Adamsdotters and Karlssons, Sweden's youth looked for a new identity. Gustafsson was such a common name in Sweden, it filled countless pages in countless community directories; like many Swedes, the first thing Greta did was eliminate the superfluous *s* in her last name.[5] Magda Hellberg, Greta's supervisor at PUB, recollected that the young hopeful did not think that Greta Gustafsson was refined enough for the stage: "She wanted a shorter name which could be pronounced easily in any language."

Stiller had also pondered an appropriate name for her. Scenarist Arthur Nordén related that the director wanted a name that was "modern and elegant and international." He suggested the name Gábor, which apparently delighted Stiller, who tried out different alliterations of the name. However, according to Mimi Pollak, the director never mentioned the name to Greta before she went down to the Ministry of Justice to meet with Mimi's friend, Oscar Adelsson, to discuss the change. After looking through a stack of books and tossing around ideas with Mimi and friends, the name "Garbo" was conceived as she and Mimi walked across Norrbro Bridge on the way to the government building. It was a combination of two different surnames. "Greta thought it was wonderful. 'Now I don't have to change the initials on my towels,' she said."

On November 9, Anna Gustafson [*sic*] signed a petition asking the ministry to allow her daughter to legally change her name to Greta Garbo.[6]

---

[5]In all church, school, and medical records prior to 1922, she is Greta Gustafsson. According to *Svensk Filmografi*, her billing in *Luffar-Petter* is also as Greta Gustafsson. Once she joined the theater school, however, she simplified the name to the more contemporary Gustafson.

[6]Like her children, Anna Lovisa would follow Greta's lead and use the more contemporary spelling of her last name. "As far as I know, it has always been spelled G-u-s-t-a-f-

Interestingly, Mona Mårtenson—and not Mimi Pollak—witnessed Greta's signing as well as her mother's. The petition was formally approved by the Ministry of Justice on the twenty-first of December. By that time, Greta Garbo was back at work on *Gösta Berlings saga.*

The snow arrived in mid-December, prompting the cast and crew to pack up for the location shoot in Örebro. There Greta and Mona reportedly shared a hotel room, which gave them an opportunity to compare notes on their parts and the big scenes yet to come.[7] For the fire at Ekeby, Stiller ordered celluloid strips to be attached to the walls of the building and doused with kerosene. Special gas conduits were built behind the windows of the façade. Stiller seemed to enjoy the fire immensely, "roaring like a lion" through his megaphone, climbing up ladders to observe the action closer and suggest new angles for the camera. Lars Hanson (doubled by pyrotechnist Nils Elffors) anxiously scurried across a burning rooftop and down staircases engulfed in flames, urged along by his fearless director. "Don't be cautious!" Stiller shouted. "Keep going! If the flames come closer, that's all right—it won't look like a real fire unless you show some courage!" For some reason, the actor later recalled, Stiller decided to move the camera to cover the hero's escape even more dramatically. The fire was getting closer—and Hanson had yet to save poor Jenny Hasselqvist. "I'm burning!" Hanson cried out. "I'm very sorry," the director replied. "You'll just have to burn a little longer."

Gösta Berling was a defining experience for Greta. She would return to Dramatiska Teaterns Elevskola for the conclusion of her second term—but Mauritz Stiller had already "spoiled" it for her; she was no longer a novice. Stiller had established himself with Greta as the first protector/mentor to follow in the footsteps of her late father. "I have taught her everything," he bragged to a friend. "She takes instruction carefully and is like wax in my hands."

With typically articulate ambiguity, Stiller's Galatea later conveyed some of her feelings about this period to archivist and film historian Raymond Daum. "Someone has to come along and open your horizons," she would say. "If you're born in poverty and have nothing . . . then you're a confined little thing. You'll never get outside your narrow little margins—unless by some mir-

---

s-o-n," says Gray Reisfield. "No one in the family (that I know of) ever spelled it any other way." From now on they will *all* be Gustafsons.

[7]Years later, rumors would emerge that Greta had developed a crush on Mårtenson during filming. There is scant evidence to support this—although, curiously, Mona did conform to what might be called her physical "type" (short, brunette, dark soulful eyes, bright personality).

acle somebody gets hold of you [and] shows you another way. . . . An older someone who has lived life and seen things and made his way . . ."

It did not go unnoticed that Stiller, who was twenty-two years her senior, had a proprietary interest in the newly christened Greta Garbo. Their relationship would become the talk of the community as the director prepared his film for its March 1924 premiere. There were rumors of a romantic relationship. Vera Schmiterlöw found that scenario extremely unlikely. "She adored Stiller, but as far as I know there was never anything between them," she observed. "Everyone knew that [he] had a different kind of interest. He saw Greta as some beautiful raw material for him to shape into form." Film professor Gösta Werner characterized Stiller's feelings toward his protégé as "probably ambivalent to a great extent. But even if he found her sexually attractive—which is not improbable—it is far more likely that his feelings of power over her took precedence." Garbo was "a close, blindly attached, and affectionate person, hypnotically captured within his magic circle."

The final version of *Gösta Berlings saga* was nearly four hours (fourteen reels) long; Part I debuted on March 10, 1924, at the Röda Kvarn Theatre in Stockholm, Part II opened one week later. Stiller escorted his star to both premieres. Critical reaction in Sweden would be polite but restrained; the majority of reviews labeled the film "a beautifully staged failure." While the director was complimented on his handling of the love scenes, critics still complained about the liberties he had taken in distilling Lagerlöf's epic down to a more manageable length; Selma Lagerlöf was also displeased. Stiller's discovery earned scattered praise in the Swedish press. One critic saw Garbo as "a promise for the future," another as "a semi-plump and unseasoned bun." Bengt-Idestam Almquist, known to readers of *Stockholms-Tidningen* as critic Robin Hood, thought it was "too early to say much about Greta Garbo. She has several opportunities which she does not utilize. Spiritually, she is too small for her part. But she is wonderfully beautiful in her Empire gowns and, in spite of her still-life acting, she is one of the bright spots in the movie."

Admirers would later scrutinize *Gösta Berlings saga* for some evidence of the Garbo mystique, often concluding that there was no correlation between the neophyte Greta Garbo and the one manufactured by Hollywood. They disregarded any idea that Mauritz Stiller detected something in the early scenes of *this* particular film, something that told him she had potential as the new kind of screen actress he clearly envisioned. Her first scenes in the carriage en route to her husband's estate and in the garden with her new tutor, Gösta Berling, are light and personable, but it is not until the dinner at Ekeby that the emotion lying beneath the surface is glimpsed.

Garbo's scenes on the grand staircase are most evocative of her future persona. Svensk Filmindustri's premier cinematographer, Julius Jaenzon, took great care in lighting and framing Garbo's face. What inevitably comes through is the intensity of mood and expression in her eyes. Though she had yet to acquire grace of movement, her pleadings with Gösta Berling to stand up to those who would judge him, her lonely vigil as she walks down the stairs holding an old lamp, her moments as she contemplates love and her marriage, and her reassurance to Berling that she has always believed in him show the skill and expertise of Stiller and Jaenzon in presenting their actress to the world. It is not a picture-stealing performance—she is a bit too green to effectively eclipse the professional performances of Lars Hanson and Gerda Lundqvist—but it is a breakthrough one.

Ironically, a film that was profoundly Swedish in content and craftsmanship was better received outside of Sweden. It was a hit in Copenhagen and Helsinki, and would be distributed in various lengths to twenty-eight countries worldwide. On March 20, at the suggestion of actress Mary Johnson, a German producer named David Schratter wrote Stiller inquiring if he would be interested in making some films for Trianon Film A.-G., reputed to be Germany's largest production company. Stiller was already considering his next subject: a story of Russian refugees trapped in Turkey. In April, he traveled to Berlin to meet with Schratter.

Greta was invited to spend her Easter break at Mimi's family home in Karlstad. Unbeknownst to them, a fellow student[8] had committed them for a performance at a local boys school. When Mimi and Greta found out that notices had already been sent out, they decided to go through with it. Once at the hall, Greta had second thoughts. "We had to give her a push onto the stage," Mimi said. "She was completely stiff and white as a ghost, insisting she had forgotten everything she was supposed to read." She gathered her courage and went on anyway. The threesome collected 260 kronor for the evening's work.

Studies continued back in Stockholm. Greta and Mimi Pollak played farmgirls in La Malquerida (Mother's Rival) by Jacinto Benavente. They also had supporting roles in a special matinee performance of Madame Sans-Gêne; Greta essayed Madam de Vintermille. The illustrious cast included her teachers, Nils Personne and Gustaf Molander; Ellen Cederström, the actress who played her mother-in-law in Gösta Berlings saga, and

[8]Sten Lindgren, class of 1923.

Mona Mårtenson. She received her best billing to date as Mathilde in *Min vän Teddy* (*My Friend Teddy*), a comedy by André Revoire and Lucien Besnard. Before the season was over, Greta was asked to sign on for a third term as a premier student.

That spring she found out about Mimi's engagement to actor Nils Lundell. Greta wrote her friend after hearing the news, assuring Mimi that her love and respect translated into love and respect for Mimi's betrothed as well. Miss Garbo had also met someone new: a young newspaper man named Lars Saxon. She and Saxon, the son of writer and publisher J. L. Saxon, would become close friends. For his part, Saxon was quite taken with the young actress. Greta saw him only as a friend, and charitably set him up with her sister, Alva.

On May 22, after David Schratter was introduced to Mauritz Stiller's protégé, the director and the producer signed a rough draft of an agreement concerning their first production together. Germany remained an incredibly important market for Swedish films; Stiller's success there would bode well for Svensk Filmindustri's continued survival. In the deal memo, handwritten on Grand Hôtel stationery, Stiller promised to deliver two films to Trianon—each against a guarantee of 75,000 kronor. There was an option for two additional films at 100,000 kronor each. Stiller retained all Scandinavian rights (including Finland).

The director sent his star a note instructing her not to make any plans for the summer. He retired to his home on Lidingö to work on the screenplay for *Odalisken från Smolna* (*The Odalisque from Smolensk*), his next project. Greta got her driver's license, did some print ads with Vera Schmiterlöw, and settled into the camaraderie of her theatrical friends. Later in the summer, she continued her diet and exercise regimen in the seclusion of a country cabin outside of Stockholm; there she took long walks and hot baths, and ate simple food prepared for her by an old couple named Andersson. "It is so wonderful alone in our country in the summer," she enthused. "In the midsummer you can read all night long, in the open. The little noises of the country, the wonderful air . . . Ah, it gets to you."

A new arrangement between Trianon and Svensk Filmindustri allowed *Gösta Berlings saga* to be substituted as the first film under Mauritz Stiller's contract. Fritz Mischke, head of Trianon's distribution department, reiterated Schratter's invitation to Herren Stiller and Hanson, as well as to Damen Garbo, Lundeqvist, and Hasselqvist, to come to Berlin for the August premiere of their film; Trianon offered to pay all expenses for the trip. Mischke stressed in particular the importance of Selma Lagerlöf (who was held in high regard in Germany) attending the opening. Stiller confirmed only Fräulein Garbo.

In a supplemental deal, Schratter agreed to advance his Swedish partner 5,000 kronor to buy his new star a more appropriate wardrobe for her promotional trip—an undocumented agreement that would come back to haunt Garbo.

CHAPTER 4

Wilkommen

Moje should have seen the trouble signs earlier. In 1923, Germany faced a crippling inflation that grew to such a frenzy that in November of that year the exchange rate had fallen to an incredible 1.3 trillion reichsmarks to one U.S. dollar. German cinema, however, had managed to thrive during this period and had not only kept up the level of attendance around the country (although box-office receipts were virtually worthless as soon as they were earned), but also increased its distribution income from abroad. Ironically, as soon as the mark stabilized in 1924 with the introduction of a new currency, joint-stock production companies (denoted with the initials A.-G.) began failing, one after another.

Trianon Film A.-G. had been in existence for a brief ten months when producer David Schratter first approached Mauritz Stiller. At that time, Moje was cognizant enough of Germany's economic situation to demand payment in Swedish kronor. Their original agreement proposed a July or August 1924 start date. At the beginning of July, he sent a cable to Schratter informing him that they had a script ready. Schratter's response was mystifying. "This telegram has been the first sign of life in six weeks . . . and made me wonder if you would keep our contract," he suggested. In fact, Stiller had readied the screenplay in scarcely more than a month and it was Schratter who stalled. He suggested that the director either come right away or delay his proposed visit for another two or three weeks, giving Trianon time to make "new financial arrangements" while they prepared for the premiere of *Gösta Berlings saga* in Berlin. A red flag should have gone up then, but Moje was oblivious to any impending complications.

Greta's instructions were clear. "Get packed in the blink of an eye . . . You're traveling with me on Saturday to Berlin and must before that take care of your passport," Stiller wrote her on August 13. "I have worked myself into a frenzy getting the manuscript ready, and am still working on the last act. . . . Call me as soon as you get here! Hope you are now rested from all the parties of late . . . Your friend is longing for you. Moje." Finally, on the sixteenth, the director left for Berlin accompanied by Greta Garbo and Gerda Lundeqvist, the venerable actress who had effectively dominated much of *Gösta Berling*'s story. Mindful of what she had heard about

Germany's devastated economy, Anna Gustafson put together a parcel of food and tucked it away in Greta's suitcase. The journey took the better part of two days.

Berlin. Greta had never ventured beyond Sweden's tranquil borders, yet there was something familiar about the German capital to "an old soul"— even an eighteen-year-old one. "I will never forget when I came to [Berlin]. The smell of the city," she reminisced. "You can feel it in your breast, when it is coming. . . . I could *feel* the smell long before we were really inside the city—it was as though I had smelled it before . . . been there before . . ."

Germany's creative community embraced its Scandinavian visitors warmly, flooding the Hotel Adlon with floral greetings. Officials from Trianon took them on a tour of the city, exhibiting with great pride their modest studio facilities. Photographs and interviews with the stars—most prominently, Greta Garbo—appeared in local newspapers and magazines (although not always quick enough for Stiller, who often made many of the introductions himself). It was, of course, no small matter that Moje felt totally at ease in this bustling cosmopolitan environment. It was also reassuring that Greta could make herself understood in a foreign country; with her keen ear picking out the Germanic similarities to her own language, it did not take her long to assimilate key words and phrases.

The August 20 premiere of *Gösta Berlings saga* at the Mozartsaal Theatre was carried off with great pomp and circumstance. A warm summer evening did not deter the audience from enjoying the film and delivering a thunderous ovation at the movie's end. Mauritz Stiller gave an appreciative speech from his box and, according to reports, pulled Greta into the spotlight with him to acknowledge the applause. The German press hailed the picture as "a masterwork of beauty and characterization"; Garbo's notices were equally encouraging.

Gösta Berling was exactly the kind of romantic European epic that Berliners loved, and they showed their appreciation at the theater and within the community itself. "The German people are wonderful," Greta would say. "They do not touch you, yet they have their arms around you— always."

Once back in Stockholm, Mauritz Stiller reviewed a number of different career alternatives for himself, as well as for his protégé. In September he received a letter from his brother William in Los Angeles thanking him for a letter that had been hand-delivered by actor Einar Hansson. It was the first direct correspondence between the brothers in thirty years. With his friend and colleague Victor Sjöström now making films in Hollywood, Stiller appeared to be exploring that option for himself—but on September

20 he signed a new contract with Svensk Filmindustri assigning Scandinavian distribution of his Trianon films to SF. At the same time, he was corresponding with Trianon regarding a new start date on *Odalisken från Smolna.*

Until now, the cordial tone of the correspondence from Trianon had successfully masked their financial difficulties—but Stiller may have begun to get suspicious. At Schratter's request, he agreed to go back to Berlin to meet with the producers. But Stiller had unfinished business in Stockholm: his protégé was not yet free of her contractual obligation to Dramaten. Following an admonishment from Schratter, Moje made a number of telephone calls from the home of a friend, resulting in Garbo's release from Dramatiska Teatern. Her student contract would be nullified upon repayment of 800 of the 1,200-kronor advance she had accepted from Dramaten that year.[1] "It's a huge responsibility," he told Alma Söderhjelm, an associate from Finland. "Let's hope it works out for the lass."

"The lass," in the meantime, was allowed to continue with her daily routine in Stockholm, returning to Dramatiska Teatern for several productions as a premier student. Beginning September 25, she played "a guest" in the Russian drama *Höstens violiner* (*The Violins of Autumn*) by I. Surgutsjev. In October and November, she portrayed the prostitute in Pär Lagerkvist's *Den osynlige* (*The Invisible*). Lagerkvist, a local playwright who would soon make a national name for himself, became so nervous and distraught during the performance that he left the theater before the second act was over. As soon as the curtain went down, Greta took it upon herself to phone him at home and let him know that everything had gone well. That empathy would soon be missed at the Academy.

New people entered her life. Mimi Pollak recalled Greta inquiring about Moje's new assistant, Carlo Keil-Möller. Another undated letter to Mimi relates the "jolly time" she had on a dinner date with a young suitor named Hans Spiro. Nils Asther was also introduced to Greta around this time. They met at Dramatiska Teatern. "I didn't notice anything special about her except that she had a wonderful voice, dark, almost plaintive. She lowered her eyes and when she finally raised them I was thunderstruck. I stared, bewitched and bewildered," Asther recorded. The fascination turned into an obsession and, a few days later, he got up the courage to propose to her. "Without mercy, she turned me down. She said she definitely would not marry me or anyone else for that matter. She had decided to dedicate herself to her art, to film and the theater."

---

[1] By mutual agreement (dated April 8, 1925), the monies she returned were applied toward the school's scholarship fund.

Nils Asther was not the first person of means she had turned down—
and he would not be the last—but the actor didn't give up. "Several times
I walked outside her house at Blekingegatan 32 . . . but the curtains were
drawn. Maybe the family had gone away. Perhaps I wouldn't see her again.
I felt so hopeless . . ." Asther heard that Greta's father was buried at Södra
cemetery and that she often visited his grave. He walked around the
immense shaded grove of the cemetery hoping to run into her, but she was
nowhere to be found. "I thought I was going crazy," he admitted.

On the thirteenth of November, Greta performed in her final production at Kungliga Dramatiska Teatern, a French farce entitled *Knock or le
Triomphe de la Médecine*, by Jules Romains. She provided the offstage voice
of Mariette, the doctor's receptionist. Over the years, many other performances have been added to her credits: Hermione in *A Winter's Tale*, a
small role in an Arthur Schnitzler comedy entitled *A Farewell Supper*; perhaps these, like her performances as Amman in Tolstoy's *Resurrection* and
Katri in the Finnish play *Daniel Hjort*, were actually student projects.[2]
What is known is that a short time later, Greta was again bidding farewell
to her family and on her way back to Berlin with a new contract in hand.

Mauritz Stiller had planned on scouting locations in Constantinople much
earlier.[3] Advertisements placed by Trianon in the industry trade paper
Film-Kurier proudly announce the return of "the celebrated master
Swedish director" to Berlin in the September 29 issue; and on October 3,
that he is en route to Constantinople to explore the location of his upcoming epic motion picture. According to Swedish film historian Gösta
Werner, however, after arriving in Berlin late in September of 1924, Stiller
became ill, and not until the first week in October did he feel well enough
to supervise tests at Trianon's studios in Berlin. Unhappy with the results,
he told David Schratter he could not accept their cameraman. He wired
Stockholm to secure the release of cinematographer Julius Jaenzon.

On the nineteenth of October, Moje sat down at his desk at the Hotel
Esplanade and wrote a somber letter back home. "Dear little Greta!" it
began. "I am longing for you and yet I don't let you hear a word from me—
can you understand that? . . . But these days I blame it all on my illness . . .
I am far from back to normal health. I am wandering around aimlessly. My
mood changes around how my stomach is. In the meantime I'm trying to

---

[2]The first known mention of *A Winter's Tale* and *A Farewell Supper* would be in a bio of
Garbo generated by the MGM publicity department. The Dramaten's book of playbills from
the 1920s does not list Greta Gustafson-Garbo for either drama.

[3]It wasn't until 1930 that the Turkish capital changed its name back to Istanbul.

go to Constantinople in a few days. . . . I am tormented over the loss of my former energy. What if it never returns!?" He went on to discuss finances. "Tomorrow morning you will receive 5,000 kronor from Trianon.[4] It is my mistake. Schratter hints that I never said a word about money. It could have possibly happened that I have been so absentminded that I forgot to tell them. I have been so tempted for a long time to send for you, it would help to relieve my misery . . . it is a terrible sorrow to be all alone. Nobody to stroke my stomach. . . . Oh, dear Greta, how wonderful it is going to be to have you here on foreign soil! If I could just be really well so the play could go with life and gusto. . . . Send a note to me. Above all, don't forget me. Kiss me. . . . Moje."

Stiller continued on to Constantinople, where on November 8 he received a communication from Alexander Aronson, the head of Metro-Goldwyn's newly established Paris office. Aronson was in Rome with Louis B. Mayer to check on the progress of *Ben-Hur.* "HAVE HAD EXCELLENT REPORTS OF YOUR WORK," he wired Stiller. "PERSONALLY FEEL CAN INTEREST OUR COMPANY IN YOU . . . HAVING [Mayer] LOOK AT SOME OF YOUR PICTURES . . ." Aronson asked if it was possible for the threesome to meet in Rome. But Stiller received the wire just as he was getting ready to return to Berlin. On November 13, Aronson sent another telegram to the Hotel Esplanade. "FEEL I HAVE INTERESTED MR. MAYER IN YOUR ABILITY," he declared, again expressing the hope that they could all meet in Rome. Stiller's response to either wire is not recorded—but the fact is that he stayed in Berlin; Louis B. Mayer made the journey to the German capital. "A man capable of such films belongs in Hollywood," he reportedly told associates.

By the time Mayer arrived in Berlin ten days later, he had done his research on Mauritz Stiller. He knew that Trianon, which had expected to recoup its investment in *Gösta Berlings saga* in four weeks, had earned it in one, and that the film had grossed 750,000 reichsmarks in Germany alone. More important still, Svensk Filmindustri was considering a deal to align their productions with UFA in Germany or Pathé in France to increase the consortium's international market and challenge Hollywood. Mauritz Stiller and Victor Sjöström had been major forces in the success of the Swedish film industry, and now with Stiller involved in a recovering German cinema he appeared to be an additional threat. Hollywood's unspoken "divide and conquer" strategy had succeeded in increasing the quality of their productions while weakening their foreign competitors, with the integral defections of Sjöström, Ernst Lubitsch, Max Linder, and Pola Negri, among others, to the United States. Hollywood provided for its dis-

---

[4]The money Schratter had promised in July.

tribution abroad by investing in European film companies and purchasing their options; Louis B. Mayer's second objective in Berlin was to discuss just such an arrangement with Universum-Film A.-G. (UFA).

A few discreet inquiries would have revealed that Stiller was dissatisfied with the lack of opportunities in Sweden; the word was he was unhappy, underappreciated, and undercompensated. Victor Sjöström, a man whose opinion L. B. Mayer respected, had praised Stiller in no uncertain terms and urged the studio chief to sign him. The only possible obstacle was the question regarding the director's young protégé: Would MGM be expected to take her, too?

They always seemed to be at opposite ends: Greta Garbo, who came by train from the north and reached Berlin around the same time as Mayer and his family, who arrived from the south. On the twenty-sixth of November, Stiller was introduced to Mayer in the studio mogul's suite at the Hotel Adlon. They discussed films and filmmaking, occasionally together in Yiddish, more often through an interpreter who spoke in German to Stiller and English to Mayer. The director had also done his research (he had a copy of Sjöström's contract with Metro-Goldwyn) and was adamant about the terms under which he might agree to come to Hollywood.

Much has been written about the likelihood of someone of Mauritz Stiller's stature demanding that Metro take an unknown actress if they wanted him, whether anyone would be willing to bank a Hollywood career on a nineteen-year-old girl with scant film or theater experience. As fantastic as the "legend" appears, there is little doubt that it is true—first and foremost because Moje believed Greta Garbo was an integral part of his future. An inspired, creative director could make films anywhere; this was his chance to develop the glittering screen presence he had always imagined. He did it for himself as much as for her. That isn't to say that Stiller didn't genuinely believe in Greta's talent—but he believed even more in his own ability to nurture her to greatness.

Stiller sensed L. B. Mayer's hesitation in considering Garbo. He arranged for a private showing of Gösta Berlings saga at UFA's screening room nearby at Potsdamerplatz. According to Irene Mayer Selznick, Louis B.'s younger daughter, her father was sold on Greta Garbo by the end of the first reel. "It was her eyes," she wrote in her autobiography. There was a softness and a womanliness about her that L. B. found quite appealing. "Dad said, 'I'll take Stiller, all right. As for the girl, I want her even more than Stiller. I can make a star out of her.' " Greta immediately established herself in Louis B. Mayer's mind as something more than Stiller's "excess baggage."

Three and one-half hours later, the group adjourned to the Adlon to continue the negotiation. Stiller and Mayer walked ahead. When Mrs. Mayer and her two daughters stepped into the elevator, "a nice-looking but slightly heavy-set woman who looked faintly familiar also entered. She wore a large-brimmed black taffeta hat and a fairly long, dark, full skirt. No one could possibly have guessed that she was a girl between Edith and me in age."[5] Selznick's first impression of Moje Stiller was equally distinct: "Stiller frightened the life out of me. He was an awesome physical sight.... [Though] his personality was at odds with his appearance, as he was a quiet and very gentle man. He and the girl were an odd combination indeed."

Garbo was not the usual diminutive actress Louis B. Mayer encountered when looking for new beauties, yet she was poised, polite, and perfectly amenable to suggestions. Whether or not Mayer actually told Basil Wrangell, a business acquaintance who served as the interpreter, "Tell her that in America men don't like fat women," is questionable. Greta had already lost a considerable amount of weight since filming *Gösta Berling*. Pictures of her taken in Stockholm, Berlin, and Constantinople attest to the success of her diet. In fact, what Greta recalled of that November meeting in Mayer's hotel suite (and their subsequent dinner together) was that the studio chief scarcely looked at her. "I guess he looked at me out of the corner of his eye, but I did not see him," she said. "All of the business was done with Mr. Stiller."

Following their meeting, Mayer dictated a detailed memo to Stiller. Typed on Loew-Metro-Goldwyn/Berlin stationery and dated November 27, 1924, the letter confirmed their oral agreement, which Mayer considered a bond. He proposed securing "Maurice" Stiller's exclusive services for one year, with a second- and third-year option at the studio's discretion. Mayer pledged "the same kind of advertising and publicity" for Stiller as for Victor Seastrom (Sjöström's newly anglicized name). Metro-Goldwyn would pay his first-class fare to Los Angeles; Stiller was to set sail no later than May 1, 1925. A standard conduct and morals clause demanded that he abide "by all reasonable rules and regulations of the Studio.... It is also understood and agreed that you will conduct yourself in America in a manner that your name and standing shall not become in ill repute with the public of America." Neither the memo nor its accompanying correspondence contains any mention of Greta Garbo. Stiller did not countersign the letter and waited two months before committing either himself or Garbo to another contract.

*   *   *

[5]Edith Mayer was two years older than her sister, Irene.

According to Greta's datebook, which has recently been discovered, on November 30 she and Moje left Berlin on the Balt/Orient Express. They arrived in Constantinople on the third of December with cinematographer Jaenzon, screenwriter Hyltén-Cavallius, and art director Stefan Lhotha. Representatives of the Swedish and German embassies escorted them to the Péra Palas Hotel, surely the most exotic and glamorous destination of Greta's travels to date. Actors Einar Hansson and Conrad Veidt were scheduled to follow.

For Mauritz Stiller and his associates, the days in Constantinople were filled with preparations and urgent, chaotic work. The director had argued that it would be cheaper to shoot his film in Turkey. But there hadn't been much time to make the proper arrangements during his previous trip to the gilded city, and it soon became apparent that production in Turkey would be complicated by the unstable political situation (many foreigners were suspected of being spies) and little certainty the company would be issued the proper work permits.

One hindrance may have been the scenario itself. *Odalisken från Smolna* told the story of an aristocratic Russian girl, Maria Ivanovna, who flees from the political confusion of her homeland and stows away on a ship, hoping to find her lover in Constantinople. But the ship's crew sells her into slavery as an odalisque (concubine) in the harem of a Turkish prince. Stiller's adaptation of the original story by Vladimir Semitjov concerned itself with the moral conflict of the heroine's fate in Constantinople and her terrifying, dramatic escape from her captors. Since it also involved the dilemma of whether murder (of Ivanovna's Turkish captor) is ever justified, little about the script was designed to ingratiate the filmmakers to their hosts.

Stiller hired actor Mouschin Bey as an interpreter and all-around assistant, then busied himself with ironing out his problems with Turkish officials, retrieving his equipment (which had been detained at the border), checking out additional locations, and casting locals in secondary roles. While the production company awaited further word from Berlin, Greta joined Jaenzon and Stiller for location tests.

Within two weeks of their arrival, the company's finances were in a precarious state. Thus far, it appears that Stiller had been using the money advanced to him by Svensk Filmindustri. Only a modest amount of money had been collected from Trianon itself. Actor Conrad Veidt had mysteriously failed to appear on location. Suddenly, the Berlin office became deaf to telegrams from Constantinople. Stiller saw no alternative but to go back to Berlin to find out what had gone wrong. He arrived in Berlin on Christmas Eve.

Trianon Film A.-G. was on the verge of bankruptcy. The company had reportedly taken government funds intended for the construction of movie theaters and spent them on film production, although few films had been released to date. The director of Trianon's investment bank was arrested for improperly speculating with bank money. David Schratter and his wife left the country and were later found in London. There would be no *Odalisken från Smolna*.

Greta actually appeared to enjoy her Byzantine misadventures—and her first Christmas away from home. Moje had seen to it that she would be taken care of while he was gone. She was invited to the Swedish consulate several times and went to parties there twice. On New Year's Eve, she attended one such gathering in an Oriental gown of red and gold silk Stiller had purchased for her; it created quite a sensation when she joined in the native Swedish folk dances. She brightened her daily routine with the company of interpreter Mouschin Bey, who showed her around his city along with fellow travelers Ragnar Hyltén-Cavallius and Einar Hansson. Although they were rumored to be "romantically involved" in Stockholm, in Constantinople Garbo and Hansson generally preferred keeping their own company.

She was not lonely. She was constantly entertained by the anonymous throngs that filled the streets and bazaars of Turkey's great metropolis. There was so much to divert the eye and fill the senses on long solitary walks throughout the old, narrow street of the inner city, an intoxicating blend of aromas, sights, and sounds ripened by time and a generous sun. Greta recalled following one old Turk around for hours. "I do not know how many hours I followed him," she told Ruth Biery. "He did not go any-where, did not have to go anywhere but wander"—neither did she. Locals viewed the actress from the north with great curiosity. Ragnar Hyltén-Cavallius watched the Turkish and Armenian shopkeepers and traders "from old, wilted men to our fifteen-year-old guide . . . devour this beauti-ful stranger with their eyes . . ." Hyltén-Cavallius began to believe that Stiller had been right about her.

"One day in the lobby of the Pera Palace [sic] Hotel I saw one of the most hauntingly beautiful women I had ever beheld," Mercedes de Acosta wrote in an oft-quoted passage of her autobiography, *Here Lies the Heart*. The woman she imagined to be a refugee Russian princess turned out to be, said she, a Swedish actress. Unfortunately, Mercedes' own passport records contradict this rather romantic story of mystical coincidences. She did visit Constantinople—with her husband, Abram Poole, in August of 1922; Greta Garbo appeared as that magnificent apparition in December of 1924 through January 1925—and never the twain did meet (for at least another seven years).[6]

On January 20, 1925, Greta received a cable from her director. "HERE IT IS IMPOSSIBLE," he declared. "PACK MY THINGS IN TRUNK AND BUREAU. MONEY COMING TODAY TO SWEDISH CONSULATE CONSTANTINOPLE. FIVE HUNDRED DOLLARS . . ." She was to take care of her visa and wire Stiller of her departure. Incredibly, according to Greta's datebook, she was able to get everything done and leave that very day. "It was a shock not making that picture," she would say. "But none of it was my fault. Although I was restless, why should I have worried? There were other companies and I was young . . ."

Einar Hansson was instructed to leave with Greta. He told friends that she seemed unconcerned about the turn of events. "Everything will take care of itself," she assured him. "Moje will see to it." She never lost faith and continued to put a positive spin on things in letters back home. "In two days I shall be back in Berlin and we'll see what happens then," she wrote her mother. "But it will be all right.—It's been a good beginning, in spite of everything."

Word spread quickly around the German film community that Trianon had collapsed, leaving Mauritz Stiller and his company in Constantinople with their leased lights and equipment. Marc Sorkin was employed as an assistant to filmmaker Georg Wilhelm (G. W.) Pabst and had helped the director acquire backing from French investors for his company, Sofar-Film. According to Sorkin, when Pabst heard the news, against the wishes of his partners, he went to the Trianon offices to inquire about Garbo's status. "We know your people are in Constantinople," he told them. "We want to use Garbo. Give us your contract with her." Despite seemingly insurmountable problems, Schratter and his brothers were surprisingly uninterested in selling any of their contracts. "Nobody can make a picture with her," they stated, assuring Pabst that it was "only a rumor that you have heard. We will make a big picture in Constantinople."

In the meantime, Stiller had arrived in Berlin—and was livid. He could not go forward with his film, but neither was he completely free to make

[6]According to passport records on file at the Rosenbach Museum in Philadelphia, Mercedes received permission to travel to Constantinople (via Hungary, Yugoslavia, and Bulgaria) from the American Consulate in Vienna on August 8, 1922; she continued on to Budapest but didn't get reciprocal permission from the Swedish Embassy (acting on behalf of the Bulgarians) to travel through Bulgaria on the way to Constantinople until August 21, 1922.

new plans. Nor could he pay back the money he owed in Sweden.[7] A rumor reached Stockholm that the Americans might furnish completion funds for the Constantinople film; however, Stiller was advised by lawyers in Berlin that Trianon might attempt to collect on any film he did not direct for them in Germany. With the status of his contract unsettled and uncertain, and a number of unpaid bills lingering before him, he did the next best thing: disregarding Trianon's prior claim, he sold the services of Garbo and Hansson to G. W. Pabst.

The director drove a hard bargain, and then changed tactics. When he perused a draft of the screenplay by Willy Haas, he realized how demanding Greta's role would be and offered to release Pabst from their agreement. "You can have her, if you dare take the risk," he reportedly told the director. "But I must warn you that you are tackling a stiff proposition. Beautiful pictures can be made of Greta Garbo, if you know how to make pictures, but she cannot act." Pabst's belief in Garbo did not waiver. The filmmakers came to terms, and Sofar-Filmproduktions advanced Stiller 6,000 kronor on Greta's contract, half of which he then wired to Constantinople to bring her back.

Greta arrived in Berlin on Friday, January 23. The following week she met with Pabst and his producers to discuss her participation in *Die freudlose Gasse*. The director and his producers did not discuss the financial aspects with Greta—Stiller had negotiated those details before she arrived. She would learn the terms in a letter of confirmation dated the twenty-eight of January. She agreed to make herself ready for the film, which was to be shot between February 12 and March 26, 1925. "For this you will receive a payment of 15,000 Swedish kronor; 6,000 of which has been paid to you on account," the letter stated. If retakes were needed, her compensation would be 500 kronor per day. Sofar-Film would supply her wardrobe.

Two days later, yet another contract was drafted on Miss Garbo's behalf. For the past few weeks, Stiller had attempted to secure more favorable terms with Metro. Despite receiving word from N. A. Reichlin, general manager of Loew-Metro-Goldwyn/Berlin that Metro could not participate in his deal with Svensk Filmindustri, on the third of February he went ahead and sent Greta in to sign her letter of intention. "Gentlemen," it began, "In consideration of your providing me with first-class steamer and railroad passage from Berlin to Culver City U.S.A., I agree to enter into a

[7]In addition to the personal monies Stiller owed, Svensk Filmindustri helped to bail out the remainder of his cast and crew. Much of their equipment and materials was left behind in Constantinople as collateral on bills from Turkish creditors.

written contract with you for my services as a motion picture actor . . ." The contract would begin on the day she reported to work at the studio; Metro-Goldwyn was granted the right of four annual options, extending the agreement to five years. Greta was guaranteed forty weeks' work each year, commencing at the rate of $400 a week and escalating to $1,250 in her final year.[8] The contract, witnessed by N. A. Reichlin, further stated that Metro would furnish "gratis" the clothes for her films. She was to leave no later than April 15, 1925. A formal contract would be signed in Culver City, California.

Between Garbo's commitments in Berlin and Hollywood, there would be precious little time to visit family in Sweden (Greta was not to see them for another two months). Still she did not question the logic. "I was a little too young to determine those things," she would say. "Whatever Mr. Stiller said I knew was always the best thing to do. I would say, 'Is it good?' and if he said, 'It is good,' I would do it."

Because she had signed the Pabst/Sofar-Film agreement first, Metro-Goldwyn made allowances for her to honor that commitment. On February 16, she reported for a preliminary film test; sets had been constructed on a stage in the Zeppelin industrial area of Staaken, a suburb of Berlin. Moje made a private arrangement with Pabst for Garbo to be photographed on Kodak-Pathé film, then considered the finest film stock available (most European productions used the less sensitive Agfa film). Due in part to the especially strong lights they had used, the test with cameraman Guido Seeber[9] revealed a nervous twitch. The more film they shot, the more it became obvious to Greta that something was wrong. Some 290 of the first 300 feet shot were allegedly deemed unusable until Seeber employed an old cinematic trick: by shooting at a faster film speed, the blinking would barely be perceptible when the footage was projected at the normal speed.

Die freudlose Gasse began principal photography the following day. The first scenes to be shot were the crowd scenes outside the butcher shop, a microcosm of the greed and suffering in the Viennese streets.[10] Greta was so sure she was going to be awful without Mauritz Stiller to guide her that

[8]Early evidence of the studio's belief in Garbo's potential. The standard rate for contract players was $75 per week. Joan Crawford started at Metro in 1925 at such a rate, and in 1943 June Allyson was given a contract for much the same terms.

[9]Stiller had been unable to secure the job for Julius Jaenzon—though Pabst would later employ a second cinematographer, Curt Oertel, to shoot Garbo's close-ups.

[10]This is the scene popularly believed to feature Marlene Dietrich as one of the extras in line with Garbo and Asta Nielsen. The actress mistakenly identified as Dietrich is actually Hertha von Walther; Dietrich was at home nursing her three-month-old daughter, Maria.

she wrote Mimi Pollak about it. Finally, Moje agreed to coach her on the side. She spent twelve- to fourteen-hour days with G. W. Pabst, then returned to the hotel to work with Stiller on the next day's scene. Garbo's technical skill grew tremendously under the gentle, perceptive prodding of Pabst, enriched by the detailed intensity of Stiller's suggestions. There was always a noticeable improvement between the rehearsals and the final take. If Pabst knew anything of his silent collaboration with Stiller he never let on, but it was a strain on Garbo. Eventually, Moje declined to continue his behind-the-scenes role, feeling that Greta was strong enough to continue without him, and he returned to Stockholm to conclude unfinished business.

Regarding the status of her relationship with Stiller, Greta confessed to Mimi that it was too complicated to delve into. Although they had apparently settled into a comfortable, seemingly paternal relationship, Moje's emotional demands weighed heavily on her. She was convinced that the problem was entirely her own. She simply could not, would not, adjust to a lifestyle dependent on someone else, she wrote Mimi in March of 1925, and feared that her "awful temper" might ruin everything for them. Yet if Greta had begun to resent, in some small way, the director's subtle (and not so subtle) manipulation of her, she also found that without Stiller around to guide her she felt directionless. She could not wait to return to Sweden.

He couldn't wait to leave. "Dearest Greta," Mauritz Stiller wrote from the Grand Hôtel on the twentieth of March, "It was wonderful to come back to Sweden again—and just as sad and small, when one has been here for a few days. No, I think we have to find our way over the Atlantic. It is probably for the best. Have you gotten better? Do you take care of yourself? I am longing for you so. Can't you write a few lines to me?" No longer lured by the false optimism of their German venture, he expressed the wish that she would be free by the twenty-sixth of March "so you can leave the dreadful Berlin. I am working here with the lawyers and Svensk Filmindustri and [the business] is full of unpleasantness. Have you heard anything about Trianon?[11] . . . Did you know your sister has done some screen tests for Ellis and they were delighted with her! . . . Dear Greta, I barely dare under the now existing circumstances to long for you, but I do anyway. . . . Moje."

Paternal, fraternal, or romantic, Greta's relationship with her friend and mentor had clearly become more intimate over the past few months. Julius Jaenzon noted how relaxed they were with each other, recalling the time

---

[11]Attorneys in Berlin were negotiating on Garbo's behalf to collect monies still owed her.

he walked into the room while Greta was sitting on Moje's knee. She took a cigarette from his mouth and scolded him playfully. "Haven't I told you that you are not to smoke?" Acquaintances in Berlin were convinced the couple would eventually marry. "How is that darling girl Greta Garbo getting on—are you married already?" one later wrote Moje. "I took an awful fancy to her, so lady-like and sweet and not like the usual actresses." There is some indication that Stiller and Garbo may have talked about marriage by this time—and that the director not only remained steadfast in his belief that neither was *ever* to marry, but impressed those views upon his young star.

Stiller's disappearance from his protégé's side left Greta alone to face the challenge of Berlin. That was the contradiction of Moje Stiller: while he purportedly wanted Garbo dependent on him, more often than not he left her on her own. But she was nineteen years old and in one of the most exciting cities in the world, a city that pulsated with the heartbeat of the liberating 1920s . . . an uninhibited city that, on the surface at least, did not seem to concern itself with social stereotypes.

A late-blooming metropolis, Berlin became a center for avant-garde ideas, Expressionist art, Bauhaus architecture, and the new psychology. The intelligentsia—the artists and the upstarts—met in the city's intriguing cubbyholes: the cafés and restaurants that lined its boulevards and back streets. The most famous of these, the Romanische Café, was "a great barn of a place" on the westside's Auguste-Viktoria Platz. Political cabarets and variety shows were also popular, each house striving to outdo the others with the most daring, controversial revue. Nollendorfplatz was the scene of Christopher Isherwood's Berlin stories. Jägerstrasse, a few blocks from the main boulevard Unter den Linden in central Berlin, was famous for its colorful bars that ranged from sophisticated dance clubs to cellar casinos. Among the best known "dives" were the infamous White Mouse Cabaret (a favored haunt of *Die freudlose Gasse*'s Valeska Gert) and the equally notorious, ambisexual Eldorado Club, where female impersonators and transvestites performed without fear of persecution.

Historians record that Berlin during the Weimar era knew no closing hours, no censors, no stultifying morality laws—though the hysterical craze for amusement had begun to seem more and more like "a dance on a volcano" with a volatile and ever-present political threat that loomed ominously in the background. Still, there were many who felt that "To conquer Berlin was to conquer the world."

Although *Die freudlose Gasse* was set in Vienna, much of the neurosis and uncertainty of life in Berlin during the 1920s was incorporated into the film. It was to be Pabst's contribution to the "street" films of the day. Greta's scenario revolved around the unseemly exploitation of her character's virtue by sinister elements. The devoted daughter of a good-natured but pathetically unlucky and unsuccessful civil servant, she faces her greatest moral dilemma when she is forced to work in a speakeasy and is unfairly tainted with its sleaze.

Garbo's Grete Rumfort still relied on men to rescue her—there would be no liberation. Not yet. Much as her own alienation worked to center Elisabeth Dohna in *Gösta Berlings saga,* so did her anxiety focus the virginal Grete Rumfort. She delivered an even, professional performance lacking in affectation—it was a much more confident, concentrated effort and a giant leap forward from her previous screen appearances. "She moves through the film with trembling radiance," biographer Robert Payne would write, "her beauty taking fire from her nervousness and excitability . . ." Pabst's camera captured "the perfect sweep of [Garbo's] face with its gentle expression of timid sadness," film historian Lotte Eisner stated.

By the first week in April, two months later than she had promised her family, Greta was allowed to return to Stockholm.[12] The world premiere of *Die freudlose Gasse* was staged simultaneously in Berlin and Paris on May 18. Stiller was more concerned with their future plans. He was still in conflict over whether to commit to Berlin or Hollywood. On the twentieth of April, at the apparent urging of G. W. Pabst, a two- to five-year contract with UFA—which improved upon Garbo's Metro-Goldwyn offer by fifty dollars a week—was drawn up and sent to Fräulein "Greta Gabor" care of Mauritz Stiller.

It was never signed. The director had been holding out against Metro hoping to change their position regarding Svensk Filmindustri's involvement in the foreign distribution of his films. Stiller wired Louis B. Mayer from Svensk Filmindustri: "MY ABSOLUTE OPINION WAS THAT METROGOLDWYN AND FILMINDUSTRI WERE ON BEST TERMS AND THAT ALL PICTURES DIRECTED BY ME USA WERE TO BE EXPLOITED BY FILMINDUSTRI." Because the Constantinople venture had put him into further debt with SF, this detail was of major significance to Stiller; a distribution arrangement would allow him to go to Hollywood free and clear of entanglements. But their answer had been no—Stiller must leave his obligations behind in Sweden. "I WAS VERY SURPRISED," he cabled Mayer. "FROM THIS I UNDERSTAND THAT I NEED NOT COME USA AND I HOPE YOU WILL CONFIRM TO ME PERSONALLY THAT THIS IS ACCORDING YOUR OWN VIEWS."

---

[12]Though Pabst reportedly fell in love with Garbo during the making of the film, she was hardly aware of it. On her final evening in Berlin, she rode the roller coaster at Luna Park.

Mayer didn't agree. On May 27 he returned the volley via a telegram sent to Stiller's home on Lidingö: "WE HAVE CONTRACT WITH YOU AND EXPECT YOU LIVE UP TO IT . . . IF YOU HAVE OBLIGATIONS WITH FILMINDUSTRI YOU MUST ADJUST THEM; YOU WERE NOT AFRAID COME AMERICA WHEN YOU TALKED WITH ME; AND SEASTROM DOING VERY WELL IN AMERICAN STOP ALL THESE MATTERS ARE YOUR PERSONAL AFFAIRS WE CANNOT CHANGE FROM ORIGINAL PROPOSITION ADVISE ME WHEN YOU SAIL."

All of this left Greta in a fearful quandary about what she was supposed to be doing next. Had Stiller changed his mind? Were they going to Holly-wood or not? How could she break through if her mentor suddenly lacked enthusiasm for a move he himself had orchestrated? Lars Saxon was one of those who tried to talk Greta into remaining in Sweden. But she saw her future linked with Mauritz Stiller's. One day, she showed up at Alma Söderhjelm's on the verge of tears. Had Moje said anything about going to America? she asked. Söderhjelm told her "in no uncertain terms" that Stiller had repeatedly stated that he planned to go on his own and stay there only until he could extricate himself from Metro. "Garbo was very upset. She asked me to put in a good word for her so that she could still go to America . . ." She had given up much to get this far; she did not want to be left behind.

Sometime during this period, Elisabet Malcolm saw her childhood friend for the first time in years. "She was the same Greta as of old, yet not quite the same," she said. "Her clothes made a big difference, of course, for now she was smart-looking and better dressed than I had ever seen her before. But she seemed tired. The friendly smile with which she greeted me, however, was unchanged. . . . [After church] Greta's restlessness seemed gone. She willingly came to my house for tea and stayed the whole evening cracking nuts and eating raisins and talking. Once, when I asked her some question about her career, she said in a strained voice, 'Don't let us talk about that tonight, Elisabet. I'll talk to you about anything else you like, but not about my work.' "

Stiller, according to friends, was a nervous wreck as well. When he had exhausted whatever objections remained concerning the Metro-Goldwyn deal, the director finally booked passage to New York—for two. On June 20, Greta filed a letter of intent at the American Embassy in Stockholm, stating that she was going to the United States for three months "to study different moving picture [*sic*] and other theatres in New York perhaps also in California." Three days later, she checked into the Strand Hôtel and bid *adjö*[13] to friends

---

[13]A-*dyə*': Goodbye

and family. "It was strange; a very strange feeling. I was looking forward to something I had never seen," she said. "I did not know how it would turn out."

On the twenty-fifth of June, she boarded the train to Göteborg. Her mother Anna, brother Sven, and sister Alva, all accompanied her to the Central Station. Though her mother didn't say very much, she reassured her daughter with a bittersweet smile that she knew Greta would be happiest pursuing her dream, wherever it took her. Greta maintained a brave front. All she could remember saying was, "I'll be back in one year. It is only twelve months." And then she was gone. The following day Stiller and Garbo were bound for the United States on the Swedish-American liner *Drottningholm.*

Mimi Pollak, Greta's "darling Mimosa," received a letter from her friend dated two weeks earlier. Unhappy about the separation, Greta expressed some pleasure in the fact that Mimi had found someone to love—and someone to love her. Yet she was afraid that she might soon be forgotten by her Dramaten companion, the only person she trusted enough to confide in. Greta wrote that she hoped they would always remain friends. Certainly, she had shared a part of herself with Mimi that she rarely revealed to others, yet each had allowed their respective lives and careers to pull them in different directions. In the future, they would be separated by more than just an ocean.

"People here do not know what it means to my people when somebody goes to America. There is always so much crying—a feeling that they will never come back to their own country and their own people," Greta said wistfully. "They feel they are going away forever." Both Mauritz Stiller and Greta Garbo left the happiest parts of their lives behind in Sweden—something neither one would ever recapture, no matter how hard they tried.

CHAPTER 5

Strange New Land

"I thought there would be almost carpets of flowers on the streets of New York City," Greta mused about her arrival in the New World. The ten days spent crossing the Atlantic Ocean provided her with ample time to focus on what lay before her. She walked the main deck, occasionally participating in recreational activities, more often content with simply observing the ocean. And, as many Swedes do, she fell in love with the sea. "I would love to do that trip over and over. You feel *free* on the ocean," she said. "There you are—and you cannot walk away. Unless you want to walk on the water."

The *Drottningholm* approached New York late in the evening of July 5, 1925, according to Greta's datebook. "When we saw the lights, lots of people screamed. . . . You felt [the excitement] with them," she recalled. It was a touching moment for Greta, who immediately began to think about a similar homecoming in Sweden. The ship officially docked at the Swedish-American berth on West Fifty-seventh Street on Monday morning. According to passport records, Greta Garbo, visa number 396, was one of the first passengers through customs. She was followed by her director. Both stated their purpose as business and apparently struggled with the correct name of their prospective employer (listed as "Loen-Mabro-Goldwyn Film Corp."). Greta declared she was bringing in approximately $1,000 in cash; Stiller declared $20,000—a generous amount for a projected three-month stay.[1] Answering questions about their respective physical conditions, sex, and politics, both stated that they were healthy and neither advocated polygamy nor anarchy.

As they disembarked from the ship that hot, muggy July afternoon, Stiller and Garbo were provided with an illustration of the esteem in which they were held by Loew's/Metro-Goldwyn. Unlike the warm, nearly extravagant receptions attended by prominent dignitaries that had been arranged for them abroad, there was to be no such ceremony in New York City. No one seemed to have much interest in the new arrivals. "Do what you can for them, but don't spend any money," Hubert Voight, the junior publicist assigned to meet them, was told. Undeterred, Voight notified all

[1]It is possible that they had incorrectly stated their funds in dollars instead of kronor.

of the daily papers of Stiller's and Garbo's arrival. With earthquakes in Santa Barbara, the Scopes controversy brewing in Tennessee, Prohibition raids on speakeasy establishments, and an "epidemic" of people falling out of windows (including an Austrian baroness), his pitch fell on deaf ears.

Instead Voight brought a photographer to the Swedish-American docks hoping to place the photos later. "I looked up at the top deck . . . and saw the loveliest young girl dressed in a suit of huge black-and-white checks," he said. "I was thrilled. Beside her stood someone massive and portentous in a heavy cap and heavy coat." Voight turned to photographer Jimmy Sileo and told him, "I don't give a damn whether that girl is Greta Garbo or not. I am going to find out who she is." When he reached them, the publicist conversed principally with Mauritz Stiller (through interpreter Kaj Gynt), while Greta watched "tearful with emotion."

After a few photographs were taken on board ship, MGM's newest imports were shuttled off to the Hotel Commodore, a Continental-style establishment adjacent to Grand Central Station on Forty-second Street at Lexington Avenue. "I remember on the way there, [Greta] wanted to see the Woolworth Building . . ." Voight continued. "She had heard of it and was so impressed when she saw it. I painted a swell picture of New York for her. She had tears in her eyes over the big buildings, but Stiller was placid and hunched down in his seat, in the corner."

They settled into their rooms at the Commodore, and Greta headed straight for the bath. The temperature hovered in the mid-eighties all day and well into the evening. With the possible exception of their time in Constantinople, it is fair to say that neither Stiller nor Garbo had experienced such heat or humidity before; Greta could neither cool down nor catch her breath. She would remember spending more time taking cold baths than seeing the sights during her first days in New York.

Greta borrowed a Swedish-English dictionary from a friendly waiter at the Commodore, but until she had a grasp of the language even something as simple as using the telephone would be a terrifying prospect for her. Hubert Voight, accompanied by Kaj Gynt, became her principal guide to the mysteries and pleasures of New York City. Her first request: she wanted to go to Coney Island and find "the most exciting and horrible roller coaster." "She stayed on the darn thing for almost an hour," Voight exclaimed, vividly recalling her gleeful, childlike cries of delight.

Garbo got a cold that night and was in bed for several days. Voight had arranged for her to do an interview with *Motion Picture* magazine the next morning. When W. Adolphe Roberts arrived at the Commodore, Voight took him upstairs to Greta's room. "We knocked on the door, but she did not answer. We pounded. Still no answer," the publicist said, "my heart was in my mouth. I was crazy about her and I thought of all sorts of things she might have done on account of some mood or other." Although Voight had only known Garbo a short time, he was already acquainted with her changing moods. When he opened the door, he saw Greta sitting calmly in bed— reading. "Hoo-bert . . . Go avay and stay avay!" she demanded. (Voight remembered her responding in English, though there is no evidence that she knew more than a few words at this time.)

The publicist got her to agree to do the interview from bed while he and Roberts remained in the other room and Kaj Gynt nervously guarded the doorway. "Miss Garbo says she adores America, but is it always as hot as this in summer?" Ms. Gynt told them. "She looks forward to her work in America—if she survives the heat—marvelous skyscrapers here—the world's best movies—but heat, *heat, HEAT!*" It was the first time Voight experienced what he would call her *"I tank I go home now"* attitude. "She simply crawled into her shell. She had moods occasionally that were frightful. They made her miserable, and me miserable, and everyone else . . . but she made up for them by the highs she hit later . . . She would be so rollicking and so much more fun that [it] got so that I didn't mind them at all."

Back at the Metro-Goldwyn office, Voight's coworkers were convinced he was unduly infatuated with their latest foreign acquisition. "Everyone treated it as a big joke," he said. Many thought Voight's girl an awkward, unlikely prospect for movie stardom. He introduced Greta to his new boss, Howard Dietz, who was singularly unimpressed. "He just thought I had fallen for this gal—hook, line, and sinker," Voight said. "I phoned [Loew's vice president and general manager] Nicholas Schenck and asked him if he wouldn't like to meet Garbo . . . but Mr. Schenck said, 'No-thank-you-he-was-much-too-busy.' Besides, he added, he had seen Miss Garbo in the lobby of the hotel and that was sufficient."

Mauritz Stiller continued to march to a different drummer as he ironed out the details of Greta's contract with Metro junior vice-president Major Edward Bowes.[2] Contrary to the basic terms they had agreed upon in Berlin, the director now argued that Metro-Goldwyn should match the proposed offer from UFA, and he enlisted the support of a New York attorney to help negotiate a shorter term (from five years to three) as well as an increased payment. In addition, there was a disagreement regarding who was to pay the couple's living expenses while they languished in New York. (Thus far, according to one source at MGM, they had insisted on

[2]Although Stiller wasn't scheduled to sign *his* contract until he reached Culver City, MGM changed its plans and presented the contract for signature on July 9, 1925.

paying their own way rather than accept an advance from the company.)

One of the advantages of being assigned to a junior publicist is that they are rarely blasé about their work and often are willing to put in the extra effort. During the day, Hubert Voight concerned himself with promoting "a new star out of the eastern skies," but at night he took Garbo to movies at the cavernous Capitol Theatre and, when she expressed an interest, the Ziegfeld Follies and other Broadway shows. He seemed to spend most of his spare time (and spare change) on her. Occasionally, Moje would join them. "He had a great soul," Voight said. "And if a young girl like Garbo loved him, it is understandable. As I look back on it and think of her expressions and her mannerisms when near him, I recall her as being decidedly filial and most reverential."

One evening, Moje and Greta were set to have dinner with a new friend, photographer Arnold Genthe. When Dr. Genthe arrived at the Commodore, a distressed Stiller was already in the lobby. "Miss Garbo has a terrible headache and won't be able to come tonight," he explained. Genthe phoned her room to express his regrets. "Is Moje really upset?" she inquired mischievously. Genthe told her he was. "At that she laughed—really laughed, like a child pleased at having achieved her purpose. 'Oh, but how *splendid!*' she spoke between laughs. 'Did he really believe I wouldn't go? . . . Of course I'm coming! All I wanted was that he should believe I wouldn't.'" Once again, she had applied the lessons of withholding herself—albeit temporarily—in order to make a point.

Struck by Garbo's youth and charm during their first meeting, Genthe immediately acceded to Stiller's request that he take their pictures. But Greta wasn't prepared. "Look at the dress I have on, and my hair—oh no, not now!" she pleaded. Genthe wasn't interested in pictures of her clothes or hair—he wanted a portrait of her *soul*. "You are here and I am here—and my camera is ready," he stated. She finally consented.

Arnold Genthe's series of photographs would be the first serious study of Garbo as an Artist. Each pose reveals a new facet of her persona: sensual, dramatic, vulnerable, intensely female, always distinctive. Genthe's Greta Garbo emerges as a woman for whom easy labels such as "The Norma Shearer of the Sweden" would not be necessary. His pictures expose an actress.

The photographer's recollection of Garbo that summer was that she seemed extremely concerned about her status at Metro. Two weeks after their initial encounter, she came to his studio to say good-bye. "They don't like me here, and so I think I shall have to go home. I'm just a 'type,' they say." If Greta really believed Metro-Goldwyn would not honor their contract with her, it was most likely because of Mauritz Stiller—hedging on her contract was another means of trying to get him in line. As their money dwindled, a resolution to their situation became imperative. Stiller called upon his American lawyer, Joseph S. Buhler, to help settle their differences.[3]

A number of factors began to weigh in Greta's favor. First, at Genthe's suggestion she had sent copies of his photographs to Metro; Victor Sjöström delivered a second set to Louis B. Mayer in Hollywood. It is said that Mayer didn't recognize the subject as the actress he had signed in Berlin. Then too by August the studio would have been aware of *Die freudlose Gasse*'s extraordinary success in Paris (it would play at Les Ursulines Theater for nearly two years) and the positive reaction to Garbo's performance.

At last, on August 26, she went with Kaj Gynt to the Loew's/Metro-Goldwyn offices atop the State Theater at Broadway and Fifty-fifth to sign her contract. As orchestrated by her director/manager, the actress's new contract was for a shorter term but no additional money. "Are you satisfied with your contract?" an executive asked through Kaj Gynt, fully expecting a perfunctory but positive response. Greta looked at the various framed photographs of Metro-Goldwyn contract players on the office wall. "Is not enough," she declared. According to Ms. Gynt, Greta incorrectly believed that all Hollywood studios provided its stars with cars, an arrangement not included in her contract. It was explained that this wasn't true. Thus ended her first contractual dispute with MGM.

She concluded her remaining days in New York writing letters, continuing her private study of English, and shopping for new clothes and things to send home. Although she had been much more active in New York than she let on, there was a dramatic difference between the excitement of Constantinople and Berlin, and the alienation she felt in New York City. The language barrier was one problem, Stiller's growing melancholia was another—both aggravated by Metro-Goldwyn's failure to make its artists feel welcome in this strange new land. In a letter back home, Greta would describe this as the most miserable period of her career to date. "I feel suicidal," she stated. "I will either drown myself in the bath or jump out of the window, but I lack the courage . . . Everything is a mess."

On the thirtieth of August, Greta and Moje, along with interpreter Olaf Rolf, boarded the *20th Century Limited* for Chicago. As Greta's trunks were being carried out of her room, she wrote a letter to Lars Saxon. She had been away a brief two months and already longed most poignantly for the company of friends. The correspondence begged Saxon not to forget her,

[3]Buhler also made personal loans to both Stiller and Garbo during this time.

and to write her care of Metro-Goldwyn Studios. Garbo was now on her way to *"soliga land"*: sunny California.

"I know you went over there [to America], not knowing how things would turn out and even sort of afraid," a friend would commiserate with Mauritz Stiller. If Moje was anxious, he did not let anyone but his closest friends know it. Cognizant that they were expected in Los Angeles by September 12, the director booked a leisurely, scenic route north and west. From Chicago, they traveled across Wisconsin and Minnesota and up into Canada. They spent an extra day in Banff and at Lake Louise; Greta liked this vacation area enough to collect extra postcards to send back home. After crossing the Canadian Rockies, they spent the night in Vancouver and a day in Victoria, their final stop in British Columbia.

By the eighth of September they were back in the United States and on their way to San Francisco, where Moje was reunited with two of his brothers. One took Stiller by surprise, approaching him on the train as it pulled into the station. "Greta whispered to me to be careful—he was surely a pickpocket who wanted to get my wallet," Moje revealed in a letter to Axel Nilson. They would spend their final night of freedom dining with his relatives. The next day, they proceeded on the *Padre* through earthquake-rattled Santa Barbara (a tremor had struck the region days earlier) to their final destination.

Greta Garbo's contract with Metro-Goldwyn went into effect when the duo arrived in downtown Los Angeles on the morning of September 10, 1925. This time, MGM had organized an appropriate reception. When Stiller and Garbo alighted from the train, Moje's brother William rushed forward to embrace him. The Scandinavian welcoming committee included Jean Hersholt, Warner Oland, Anna Q. Nilsson, Erik Stocklassa, Karl Dane, and Gertrude Olmstead. Six-year-old thespian Muriel Frances Dana, representing Little Miss California, and seven-year-old Evelyn Erikssen, representing Little Miss Sweden, were also part of the ceremonies, bringing bouquets of flowers along with the speeches and hugs.

The newly renamed Metro-Goldwyn-Mayer was represented by Pete Smith, head of the publicity department in Hollywood. Greta had been practicing her English as she made her way west. She told Los Angeles journalists she was happy to be there and diplomatically complimented the American people on their high spirits.[4] At one point, she noticed the plainly wrapped presents several members of the contingent had brought

[4] There is no mention in these newspaper accounts of Greta's desire to find a home "with a nice family." This remark was reported in subsequent fan magazine stories.

with them. After the Scandinavians adjourned to a suite at the Biltmore Hotel, the packages were opened: they were bottles of Prohibition booze.

"I spent my first night in the Hotel Biltmore, looking out of the window, frightened and alone," Greta acknowledged to a friend years later. The next day, Pete Smith escorted his guests to their new homes in Santa Monica, a popular oceanside community that has attracted many foreign artists. Greta was deposited in a residential apartment at the Miramar Hotel and Apartments on Wilshire Boulevard at Ocean Avenue; Moje in a nearby Pacific Palisades bungalow. Soon after, Garbo and Stiller were brought to Louis B. Mayer's office and introduced to Irving Thalberg and his associates; later they were given a tour of the lot.

While en route to California, the Metro-Goldwyn legal staff discovered that "the most beautiful woman in Sweden" was technically a minor—no one had checked her birthdate before. Legal minds anticipated further "quibbling," but there was none. The studio sent a copy of her new contract to Stockholm to be ratified by her mother; Garbo re-signed the contract on her twentieth birthday.

Moje's laugh preceded his entrance into Victor Sjöström's home. "Only one person could laugh that way," Sjöström recollected. "I yanked open the door [and] there stood Moje." In the background stood a quiet young woman he didn't know. Stiller introduced his young protégé and while the two directors brought each other up to date on the last two and a half years, Greta played with Sjöström's adolescent daughters, Gunn (Guje) and Karin (Caje). Moje nodded in her direction. "You'll see. She will be something," he said. "You don't say," Sjöström replied.

As time passed without word of a project, there were reports that Stiller had become particularly restless. Driven in part by concerns about his own health, the director worried that he had made a horrible mistake and told friends that he still hoped to find a way out. Greta was deeply affected by Moje's negative moods. "They were a melancholy pair," a Swedish acquaintance shared. Friends recalled a recurring image of Greta and Moje sitting on a terrace and staring out at the ocean, always tragically detached from everyone else. With Stiller often wrapped in an old blanket, many referred to the couple as "Grandma" and "Grandpa."

Garbo's days weren't always idle. There were a number of tasks designed to keep the actress busy while her director searched for the perfect script.[5] New photos were taken, and Greta filled out a basic ques-

---

[5] Moje had *Odalisken från Smolna* translated into English, "but the powers that be at MGM didn't like it, so the proposal had to be dropped," Victor Sjöström reported.

tionnaire giving the publicity department the unembellished details of her biography: father, mother, education, stage experience, hobbies, et cetera. (Given the inaccurate stories that subsequently emanated from this very department, one might wonder if they ever referred to it.)

In keeping with the Hollywood standard of homogenous beauty, Greta allowed her permed hair to be modified to a softer, more attractive style before appearing in her first screen test. She also had a small blemish removed from her hairline. In a final concession to imagemakers regarding her looks (and smile), it has been said that Garbo submitted to the costly and time-consuming process of having her teeth capped. MGM employed the best dental technicians in the business and their skills were highly prized by their celebrity patients. However, an examination of photographs taken between 1922 and 1927 reveals that, at best, Greta required minor corrective work to fix the alignment between her front teeth. Indeed, according to studio dentist Scott Christianson, Garbo had the only perfect teeth of all their stars.

Metro employees prided themselves on the "family atmosphere" of their lot—compared with the intimate surroundings of Svensk Filmindustri, however, the Culver City studio was disturbingly monolithic. "The studios are hideous and everything is confused and overcrowded," Greta would complain in a letter home, "just like my head sometimes." Unbeknownst to her, Mauritz Stiller's maneuverings on their mutual behalf had not endeared him to MGM executives. No doubt they suspected they had imported another Erich von Stroheim to the studio.[6] The girl they could take care of, but the harder Stiller worked to re-create an environment similar to what he was accustomed to in Europe, the more Metro-Gold-wyn-Mayer would fight his efforts. The studio hierarchy appeared determined to "break" him in order to fit him into their accepted work mode; he was equally determined never to bend.

The first year in California would be difficult and unyielding for everyone. Language remained a problem. With the possible exception of the personal assistant Moje had hired in New York, there was no interpreter assigned to help the pair; they relied on friends. Victor Sjöström drove them around town, to acquaint them with major landmarks and thorough-fares. Los Angeles revealed itself to be a web of communities connected by telephone lines and asphalt, a city that virtually closed down at night. Surprisingly, the twenties did not roar here. In fact, at that time, Stockholm

---

[6]Production chief Irving Thalberg's personal experience with von Stroheim's excesses on *Foolish Wives* at Universal and *Greed* at MGM had distressed him so much that he apparently disappeared during the studio's battles with the director over *The Merry Widow*.

surpassed Los Angeles in size as well as in the cultural activity of its population.

Long periods alone in a lazy, sprawling city with no center, where the glaring monotony of the sun seemed as relentless as the sparsely landscaped environment, had already taken its toll on Greta. "It could be so beautiful here if the Americans themselves had not made it so ugly with their big buildings, the millions of cars, and noise," she confided to a friend. Sweden was getting farther and farther away. Separated from her homeland by a two-and-a-half-week journey, she longed for mild temperatures, cool breezes, fall colors, rain. "The first year or so in Hollywood wasn't a happy time for Greta. She was very lonely and wanted me to come over," Mimi Pollak said. "But I was supposed to get married just then and couldn't travel, and then nothing came of it."

With directors Sjöström, Stiller, Benjamin Christensen, and writer/director Svend Gade independently established at the studio, in addition to actors Lars Hanson, Karl Dane, Jean Hersholt, Warner Oland, Gertrude Olmstead, Garbo, and soon Einar Hansson, MGM was quickly becoming the principal employer of Scandinavian talent in Hollywood. Yet Greta still had trouble making the adjustment. Scarcely five weeks after she arrived in Los Angeles, she wrote Lars Saxon that he was quite right in his assumption that she didn't feel at home. "I'm dreaming of the theaters which must be opening now. Oh you lovely little Sweden, I promise that when I return to you my sad face will smile as never before. . . . I haven't started work yet. It seems to me it will take time, and I am sad to say that I am not sorry."

During the first two weeks of October, Greta fought off a cold as well as her indifference. Apart from the occasional company of friends, the actress's solitary pleasure in Los Angeles seemed to be her placement in the Miramar, with its panoramic view of Santa Monica Bay and a variety of outdoor activities from sailing to horseback riding. What Greta enjoyed most was walking. The uncluttered beaches and palisades nearby were an invitation for exploration. She learned every path, every side street in Santa Monica.

As soon as she was able to determine her expenses, Greta began sending money home to her mother and paid back a $500 debt to attorney Joseph Buhler. Finally, there was news of a project: for Garbo, *not* Stiller. She was cast as "La Brunna," the unconventional diva in Vicente Blasco-Ibáñez's *Entre naranjos*, which Metro had re-titled *The Torrent*. Budgeted at $250,000, it was to be a prestigious motion picture production under William Randolph Hearst's Cosmopolitan banner. Although Moje and Greta had counted on working together, another director (Monta Bell) was given the assignment.

It was, of course, at Mauritz Stiller's insistence that Garbo had been given a chance at Metro. After her first screen test, executives again appeared to lose interest. Due to Moje's perseverance, however, Greta was given a second test—which Stiller personally directed—the inevitable result being that Irving Thalberg sat up and took notice, gradually coaxing the studio machinery into motion.

Dorothy Farnum's synopsis of The Torrent suggested that the purpose of the story was "to tell the story of a Woman of Destiny, a creature born to shine as a star to be the light of all men—but out of the reach of any one." Several Metro players had been suggested for the male lead, but as late as October there were no female candidates. Monta Bell was in a screening room viewing newsreel footage of torrential floods when he saw the Stiller-directed Garbo test and immediately offered her the role of Leonora Moreno, the beautiful young Spanish peasant who becomes "La Brunna." Despite his disappointment at not being the one to direct his protégé's American debut, Stiller urged her to accept the part. Greta was summoned to Louis B. Mayer's office, where the mogul tried to get her to sign a longer contract. But she remained resolute—albeit in broken English. "Meester Mayer," she said, "I haf not done yet one picture. Let us vait until I haf been in one pictures [sic]."

To prepare herself mentally and physically for her work, Greta retreated to the Mission Inn in Riverside, in the midst of southern California's citrus belt and vineyards. Just like the wild holly, olive, and palm trees, the oranges and grapes were imported, but they seemed to thrive in an arid region formerly inhabited by eucalyptus, sagebrush, and cactus. Greta Garbo also would thrive, but never be truly sustained, in Hollywood.

In early November, a struggling young actor named Sven-Hugo Borg received a special-delivery letter from the Swedish consulate requesting his services as an interpreter. "The salary was small, but it seemed like an opportunity to bring myself to the notice of studio officials, so I accepted," Borg remarked. At 10:00 A.M. on November 14, Garbo reported to the studios at Metro-Goldwyn-Mayer to commence makeup and wardrobe tests. Following these, for the first and only time, she allowed a stylist to dye her hair black, a color more befitting a Spanish diva.

"Carpenters, electricians, painters, etc., were still working on the set when I arrived," Borg remembered. "All was confusion. . . . With features frozen with fear, [Greta] stood clinging to Stiller's arm like a frightened child. As I came up, she was saying to Stiller, in Swedish: 'Oh, Mauritz, it is so terrible and confusing! What am I to do? What do all these people talk about?' I was introduced to both Stiller and Garbo and, with a smile, he said to her: 'Here is a man who has nothing to do except tell you what they talk about . . .' "

Production on *The Torrent* began two weeks later. "Greta starts working with a well-known director and I think the part she got is an excellent one," Moje surmised in a letter to Axel Nilson back at Råsunda. "Provided she has the energy she will earn millions here." According to Borg, however, it was readily apparent that the switch in their fortunes had caused some friction between the two. He witnessed a typical scene in which Stiller railed at Garbo in Swedish while he was supervising a publicity photo session. "Can't we have some sex? Your legs, they are like pipe stems!" he admonished her. Turning to Borg and an assistant, he stated, "The girl is hopeless! She moves about like a cart horse . . ." Greta's tears changed the tone of his tirade. He turned to comfort her. "Aw, but, G-r-e-t-a, don't you know that it's all for your own good?"

She would approach the making of her first Hollywood film with all the excitement of a condemned person walking to the electric chair, said Borg. "Without the guiding hand of Stiller, she was lost." Moje's influence had not yet given her the self-confidence to stand alone. "As the day of 'shooting' approached, I was afraid she would collapse. Of course, she was constantly with Stiller, spending every possible moment with him—but knowing that when the camera's eye was turned upon her and the picture that would decide her fate began, he would not be there, terrified her. 'Borg, Borg, do something!' she would plead, wringing her hands. 'Make them let me have Mauritz! Why won't they let me have Mauritz?' "

The Torrent was another in a long line of motion pictures seeking to capitalize on the Latin-lover craze ushered in by Rudolph Valentino. For the role of Don Rafael Brull, production chief Irving Thalberg settled on Ricardo Cortez, a player on loan-out from Paramount Pictures. Ironically, Cortez was the least "Latin" of all the prospects; he was actually Jacob Kranz from Hester Street in New York. But with films like *The Spaniard, The Swan,* and *Eagle of the Sea,* Cortez was obviously being groomed as a romantic rival.

On Friday, November 27, the first day of principal photography, Greta was a bundle of nerves, too agitated to even drive the short distance between Santa Monica and Culver City, Sven-Hugo Borg reported. It was obvious from the beginning that she didn't have much rapport with her leading man, who rarely spoke to her unless the moment required it. She moved silently in the background and gave little indication that she was conscious of his snub—"except those long, sideward glances I caught [her at] when he was unusually discourteous," Borg said. Not only had Garbo seemingly replaced Cortez's girlfriend, Alma Rubens, in the role, but she received an excessive amount of individual attention; she had her own personal assistant (Borg), and executives from the front office (like studio manager Eddie Mannix) were sneaking on to the set to watch the unknown ingenue—not him.

Relations between the actors deteriorated to the point that after filming a flood scene, Cortez took the blankets Borg was holding for Garbo as she came out of a studio-manufactured rainstorm. The astonished assistant began to protest, but Greta stopped him. "Let him have them," she said, "you mustn't let yourself be bothered about a pumpkin like that." She would not respond in kind when it came to temperament.

There was a discernible change in the attitudes of workers as they witnessed Garbo's transformation. In a now-famous episode, cameraman William Daniels noted that the first time he heard her speaking a complete sentence in English, she had confused the words "important" and "imported": he thought she was asserting her *importance,* but she meant imported like Norwegian sardines. Members of the normally boisterous film crew began to watch what they said when they realized their foreign star was learning English.

Just as Greta Gustafsson's face had habitually followed the sun in Sweden, Greta Garbo turned into the intense light of the MGM dream factory and became someone else. Although in many of her early productions she acted in Swedish (title cards would take care of the language difference), what Garbo radiated was universal. "I've been down watching that new girl work," a Metro writer told journalist Helen Louise Walker. "I don't know what it is that she has but I do know that everyone on the lot who can get away for a few moments from whatever he is supposed to be doing goes to watch her. There is a stillness about her, a power . . ."

But inside she was still a frightened young woman, running home to share her problems with the man she trusted. The quick pace of American productions was dizzying to the newcomer. Production on *The Torrent* was scheduled over a four-week period on a typical Monday through Saturday shooting schedule. If Garbo had a 9:00 A.M. call, she was expected to be on the set in full makeup and costume at precisely 9:00 A.M., ready to do the scene. (According to Greta, because of the European film community's reliance on theatrical artists, schedules there were more lax.)

Sven-Hugo Borg vividly recalled one incident: "One evening late, Mr. Bell was trying to catch a fast-fading sunset before it died. The scene called for a bomb to be exploded and the first 'take' was a failure, but a piece of the flying bomb had stuck on Garbo's lip. Noticing that she had left the set, Mr. Bell told me, 'Get that woman back here, Borg. If we don't shoot in five minutes we'll have to wait for another sunset.' I found Garbo offstage,

Greta's father, Karl Alfred Gustafsson, as a young man. (Courtesy Åke Fredriksson)

Greta's mother, Anna Lovisa Gustafsson, sitting beside her husband's grave. (Courtesy Åke Fredriksson)

Straight hair, straight-faced and the tallest one in her class, Greta Gustafsson (in back) poses with her class at Katarina folkskola. Teacher Märtha Eiverstam stands to her right. (Courtesy Kungl. Dramatiska Teatern)

A striking change: two portraits separated by one year and one tragedy. (left) Greta, winter 1919, scarcely six months before her father died; and (right) sometime around her fifteenth birthday. (Courtesy Åke Fredriksson)

One cannot imitate a Keystone comedy without the prerequisite scene of Sennett-styled bathing beauties. Greta on location with actresses Tyra Ryman and Iréne Zetterberg, director Erik Petschler, and cameraman Oscar Norberg for *Luffar-Petter,* 1922. (Courtesy Svenska Filminstitutet)

(Left) Greta's first step toward a new career was modeling hats at PUB. (Courtesy Kungl. Dramatiska Teatern)

At Dramaten, Greta formed friendships that lasted a lifetime: (left) with Mimi Pollak and Vera Schmiterlöw (Courtesy Svenska Filminstitutet); (above) with Mona Mårtenson. (Courtesy Bibliothèque du Film)

A glimpse of the Garbo to come in *Gösta Berlings saga*, directed by Mauritz Stiller.

With Karin Swanström, the actress who characterized Greta's relationship with Moje as "Beauty and the Beast." (Courtesy Academy of Motion Picture Arts and Sciences)

With Mona Mårtenson, playing her sister-in-law Ebba Dohna. "What are these young and charming girls but clay in the hands of the master-modeler?" scenarist Ragnar Hylten-Cavallius asked. (Courtesy Academy of Motion Picture Arts and Sciences)

Exploring Constantinople with Einar Hansson (left) and scenarist Ragnar Hyltén-Cavallius (center). (Courtesy Svenska Filminstitutet)

(Below) A rare costume test for *Odalisken från Smolna*: Greta poses in one of the shawls Moje bought her.

(Above) *Die freudlose Gasse* was voted one of the ten most important films of the silent era in a survey by the Deutsche Kinemathek. (Courtesy Academy of Motion Picture Arts and Sciences)

A rare candid photo of Greta with her friends from Dramaten taken before she left Sweden for America. Front row (left to right): Karl-Magnus Thulstrup, Mimi Pollak, Greta (with her arms around) Håkan Westergren. Back Row: Lena Cederström, Mona Mårtenson, Vera Schmiterlöw (in shadow) and Alf Sjöberg. (Courtesy Svenska Filminstitutet)

The Garbo that arrived in New York during the summer of 1925 was "slender, smart [and] beautifully groomed," said Irene Selznick. Nonetheless there was scant attention paid to either Garbo or her mentor Mauritz Stiller while on the east coast. (Courtesy Academy of Motion Picture Arts and Sciences)

In Los Angeles a few months later, Greta (wearing the same checkered suit) was greeted by Little Miss Sweden and Little Miss California.

A gathering of "the Scandinavian contingent" on the MGM lot: (left to right) Stiller, Garbo, Otto Mattiesen, (unidentified), Gertrude Olmstead, Karl Dane, Victor Sjöström, Sven-Hugo Borg, and Lars Hanson. (Courtesy Academy of Motion Picture Arts and Sciences)

USC track coach Dean Cromwell critiques Greta's form as a potential long-distance runner in one of the sports-oriented pictures shot by photographer Don Gillum.

Mixing the masculine with the feminine in another early publicity portrait for Metro. (Courtesy Academy of Motion Picture Arts and Sciences)

Affecting a casual pose in Palisades Park.

Photographer Ruth Harriet Louise highlights a softer, earthier quality in a portrait session for *The Torrent*. (Courtesy Åke Fredriksson)

Garbo rode a trick horse in the elaborate charity circus opening for the Stiller-directed version of *The Temptress*. (Courtesy Academy of Motion Picture Arts and Sciences)

Alva Gustafson sent her sister this snapshot, taken shortly after Greta left Stockholm for the United States. Alva died unexpectedly one year later.

Though tragedy had surrounded her during the making of *The Temptress*, Greta was grateful to director Fred Niblo, Stiller's replacement, for being sensitive to her situation. Here they prepare to retake the final scene with costar Antonio Moreno. (Courtesy Wisconsin Center for Film and Television Research)

Greta's first day on *Flesh and the Devil* with John Gilbert. (Courtesy Academy of Motion Picture Arts and Sciences)

Prelude to love: Garbo and Gilbert find a chiaroscuro hideaway. (Courtesy Academy of Motion Picture Arts and Sciences)

Greta didn't "disappear" the day of
the Vidor-Boardman wedding—
September 8, 1926—she went to
work. (Courtesy Wisconsin Center
for Film and Theater Research)

Solemnly dressed for the communion scene, Greta poses the following day (September 9) on the set with studio chief Louis B. Mayer,
costar Lars Hanson, and her interpreter/assistant Sven-Hugo Borg.
(Courtesy Wisconsin Center for Film and Theater Research)

A few days later, there is no sign of trouble between Greta and Jack.
(Courtesy Wisconsin Center for Film and Theater Research)

A rare appearance: Garbo and Gilbert arrive at the Los Angeles premiere of *Flesh and the Devil*. Also pictured: MGM publicist Howard Strickling (far left), studio executive Paul Bern, and Mr. and Mrs. Emil Jannings.

With Karin Molander (left) and Edith Sjöström (right) in Santa Monica circa 1927. (Courtesy Svenska Filminstitutet)

New contract, new car: Greta shows off her "little Lincoln" in a snapshot she sent home to her family. (Courtesy Åke Fredriksson)

With director Edmund Goulding and Jack Gilbert on the set of *Love*. (Courtesy Academy of Motion Picture Arts and Sciences)

Metro's Swedish stars—Lars Hanson, Garbo, and director Victor Sjöström—collaborate on *The Divine Woman*. (Courtesy Wisconsin Center for Film and Theater Research)

An important aspect of *A Woman of Affairs* was the sensitive relationship conveyed between Garbo and Dorothy Sebastian (who played the woman John Gilbert eventually marries), which is established well before they even meet.

(Below) A scene from the lost film, *A Man's Man*. Jack Gilbert is interviewed by Fred Niblo while a pair of fans (Josephine Dunn and Mae Busch) confront Garbo. (Courtesy Wisconsin Center for Film and Theater Research)

(Above) Greta, in costume for *Wild Orchids*, looks over a sketch with designer Gilbert Adrian née Adrian Adolph Greenberg and finally, simply, Adrian.

Mimi Pollak and Greta's brother Sven meet her boat when Greta returns to Sweden in 1928. (Courtesy Library for the Performing Arts at Lincoln Center)

Anna Gustafson, Greta, and Mimi's husband, Nils Lundell, on board the train between Göteborg and Stockholm. (Courtesy Svenska Filminstitutet)

Obviously happy to be home, and once again within the gates of Råsunda on a visit to the film city, January 1929.

With John Mack Brown in *The Single Standard*.

(Left and above, right) Two portraits from *The Kiss*. (Courtesy Åke Fredriksson)

picking the burned fragment from her lip, and delivered Mr. Bell's message. 'Tell him not to get excited, Borg,' she said, 'there are plenty of other sunsets coming.' " She might have been frightened, but she would not be pushed.

In another letter to Mimi Pollak, Greta solemnly described her daily routine: up at 6:00 in the morning, at work by 9:00 A.M., back to her hotel residence by 6:00 or 7:00 in the evening—and straight to bed. She wrote of being unable to sleep and of feeling emotionally exhausted and alone. She rarely went out, she stated. She had no energy left to meet and converse with other film people, and no desire to make small talk. The only thing that gave her pleasure amidst the "soul destroying" monotony of American industry was to go to the bank and send money home to her family, she explained to Mimi. Echoing her letter to Eva Blomkvist years before, Greta was obviously aware of the curious way people at the studio viewed her, and though their intent might have been hospitable, she thought it odd. Perhaps, she admitted, they found her a bit odd as well.

In addition to her homesickness, Garbo's loneliness in this early stage of her Hollywood career—while she was still in the company of friends—was most profound. She recalled a previous letter to Mimi in which she wrote that she was going to get married. But she had been confused and unable to truly articulate her feelings, she confessed. Now she believed she would never marry. She proclaimed a decided lack of interest in either men or women—for her, there was only "old Moje." At this rate, she imagined, she would wind up a spinster. She sent similar correspondence to other friends back home, even going so far as to decorate one letter with a picture of a woman crying. Looming over her veil of tears is one word: *hemlängtan.* Homesick.

Greta withdrew completely into her work and associated only with a small circle of friends from home. It was considered extraordinary behavior for someone who had yet to make her mark in town. In Sweden, her friends had always accepted her solitary stance—not so in Hollywood. While coworkers often found her to be quite friendly, there were others on the lot who dutifully followed the expected routine—with smiles on their faces— and thought her peculiar for not doing the same.

The Torrent introduced Garbo to cinematographer William Daniels. Daniels had been assigned to Tony Gaudio as his first assistant until Gaudio injured himself during the first week of tests. The new cameraman empathized with his young actress, who seemed to him out of her element—always isolated from the others by the need for an interpreter. Daniels took great care with her and the effort showed. "We lit very much to find [an actor's] best features and accent those features strongly. Especially eyes. And Garbo had magnificent eyes," he said. "[She also] had natural long eyelashes, and in certain moods I could throw the light from quite high, and show the shadows of the eyelashes come down on the cheeks: it became a sort of trademark with her."

The first publicity photos of Garbo as "La Brunna" were rushed to national papers before principal photography was even completed. Production wrapped just before Christmas; the shoot had taken only twenty-three days. There was great excitement in executive offices over the rushes—especially after Louis B. Mayer's validation. "She's got it," he reportedly told associates as he rocked back and forth in his chair, "that is, if the public likes her."

A rough cut was assembled and previewed at a local Loew's theater in early January. In attendance along with the MGM executives was a large segment of the Scandinavian community, including Garbo, Stiller, Victor Sjöström and his wife, Edith, Lars Hanson, and Karin Molander. After the screening, the mood among the Scandinavians was somber. "We all thought the picture was a flop and that Garbo was terrible," Lars Hanson stated. Stiller was very upset. He was convinced that such a failure would reflect poorly on Garbo's future in films—and that, after two and a half years of careful grooming, Metro had effectively ruined her.

Greta Garbo's friends, it has been noted, might have been astute critics but they were a poor support group and even poorer prophets. They were not in a position to predict how an audience of strangers would respond to her unique seduction of the movie camera. "Greta Garbo, who showed in her personification of Leonora, surprising qualities of realistic acting, is superb in the varied ironical expression in which she showed her contempt for this would-be lover," an MGM employee noted of the preview cards. While Don Rafael (Cortez's character) was termed weak, spineless, a simpleton, and a boob, viewers felt that "with the true feeling of the artist Miss Garbo reacted naturally to the character of Rafael as delineated in the story. She instinctively feels that a fellow like that is not worthy of her love . . ."

What Greta's friends and associates thought clumsy and unsophisticated, audiences would find captivating: her peculiar animal grace, the idyllic love scenes in which Garbo took the dominant masculine position, tenderly cradling her lover in her arms. She would dare to take a love scene farther—without risking censure—than any actress to date. Exciting stuff for normally puritanical Americans.

The movie, now entitled *Ibáñez's Torrent* (to distinguish it from a similarly named motion picture), opened simultaneously in New York and Los

Angeles on February 21, 1926. Greta attended the L.A. premiere at the Loew's State Theatre downtown and was introduced to the audience by actor Conrad Nagel. *Variety*, the industry's respected trade paper, called Garbo "the find of the year. This girl has everything, with looks, acting ability, and personality." Most of the nation's periodicals would agree. "Young, slim, with strange haunting eyes . . . she proves that the murmurs of praise which heralded her appearance were too feeble by far," Eileen Creelman of the *New York American* recorded. "Greta Garbo is sure to prove as much, if not more, of a sensation than did Pola Negri in her first appearance." Other reviews would compare her favorably to Norma Shearer, the Talmadge sisters, and Barbara LaMarr.[7]

Greta's second Christmas away from home was far from the rewarding adventure that had consumed her the previous year. She was bored, unhappy, and trapped in a contract, the nuances of which she still did not understand; she only knew she could not go home. And, surprisingly enough, she was cold. She had been unprepared for the sudden plunge in temperature when the marine layer settled in Santa Monica at night. Greta mentioned this in a November 1925 letter home and a few weeks later received a Christmas package containing a pair of mittens her sister, Alva, had knitted for her, as well as gingerbread from her mother.

"It almost makes me ill when I think that I can't come home and spend Christmas with you, have a spruce, *lutfisk*,[8] and nuts. Can't go out and feel that wonderful Christmas atmosphere," she wrote in another touching letter home, "no popping in and out of the shops in Drottninggatan and Regeringsgatan laden with parcels. I suppose I'm stupid and ungrateful, when you consider that perhaps there are millions whose dearest wish is to be in my shoes. But there it is. Moje is not well . . ."

It would be another Christmas without snow.

---

[7]LaMarr's recent death after years of battling sickness and addiction inspired Adela Rogers St. Johns to call her "the woman who was too beautiful."

[8]A holiday delicacy: boiled ling fish soaked in lye tubs and specially prepared with cream, butter, or mustard sauces.

PART TWO

Anyone who has a continuous smile on his face
conceals a toughness that is almost frightening.
—Greta Garbo to Raymond Daum

CHAPTER SIX

Trial by Fire: Becoming Garbo

báñez's Torrent was a hit. "Greta Garbo—Perfection!" the ads proclaimed. "Discovered by Metro-Goldwyn-Mayer in stark Sweden—She is setting the heart of America aflame!" The picture's success was attributed almost entirely to interest in its rising new star. "The picture is not unusual, but this girl is," *Variety* declared in its weekly roundup of box-office grosses, terming the movie's first week at the five-thousand-seat Capitol Theatre in New York City "sensational."

The MGM publicity department was unprepared for the requests for photographs and information that inundated their offices. Garbo made a valiant effort to cooperate with publicity requests. She posed for photos in Palisades Park across from her hotel, on the beach, swimming in the ocean, playing the ukulele, driving her car . . . even with monkeys and lions. Pete Smith and his department tried to make her Everywoman: sexy, shy, provocative, mysterious, elegant, reserved, an outdoors girl. She was not unreasonable in assuming they knew what they were doing. They didn't.

The director of sports publicity at the University of Southern California, C. E. "Teet" Carle, recalled getting a call from MGM during the spring of 1926. Sports photographer Don Gillum had been hired to capture a list of contract players with his new stop-action lens. Someone suggested having Garbo pose with the USC track-and-field team. According to publicist Howard Strickling (who was in Europe with director Rex Ingram at the time), Garbo resisted the idea initially, but when she saw that $25 had been deducted from her salary for refusing, she asked where she could find a track suit.

Teet Carle and coach Jannes Anderson, a fellow Swede, noted that the young actress seemed to be getting more frightened as the session progressed. "Don had been trained by news photographers who abound in 'guttiness.' Shyness isn't sacred to them," Carle said. The publicity director leaned over and whispered to Anderson that the poor girl looked unhappy. "She's appalled," the coach replied. "She thought she was going to be an actress over here, not a performer." The next week, Gillum took her to Gay's Lion Farm. Posing with the lion cub was easy enough, but the young adult male terrified her. She was coaxed into one picture seated in a chair beside his seemingly untethered perch, the lion eyeing her as she nervously moved to the farthest edge of the chair.

Though she hardly needed the initiation, she was learning important new lessons about the way Hollywood worked. "[Garbo] lost all faith and confidence, and properly so, in the judgment and taste of the Publicity Department," producer David O. Selznick stated. Two years after the studio's incorporation, most departments were still defining their roles in a fast-moving business where the rules were being made up as they went along.

Metro Pictures Corporation was founded in 1915 by a group of exhibitors looking to secure a steady flow of product for their movie houses. Included among the investment partners was a merchant of many trades, Louis B. Mayer. Born Lazar Meir thirty years earlier in the Russian Ukraine, Mayer had made his way with his family to the United States via Canada. As a young man, he helped to expand his father's business from scrap metal to dry goods; as a married man with two small daughters, he entered motion picture exhibition in time to participate in its finest hour. The same year as his Metro deal, the enterprising distributor made a half million dollars bringing *The Birth of a Nation* to the Northeast.

Like many immigrants of the period, he made ambitious plans for the future. "Louis B. Mayer was a marvelous organizer—with hypnotic qualities," observed producer David Lewis. "He was a great promoter; he had vision and foresight and, above all, dynamism. He was one of the three men I ever knew in the industry who would have been important in anything he had done." A powerful, physical man, Mayer was tough and infuriating, ingratiating and sentimental; a man of the Old World who honored the memory of his mother, but was occasionally known to hit subordinates when he lost his temper.

In 1920 Loew's, Inc., which operated a first-class circuit of vaudeville houses, music halls, and moving-picture palaces, made a substantial investment into Metro and took over the company. One of the principal suppliers of product to the newly restructured Metro was Louis B. Mayer's company. His photoplays were produced on moderate budgets and featured up-and-coming players like Barbara LaMarr, Norma Shearer, Renée Adorée, Hedda Hopper, Claire Windsor, Lewis Stone, and Wallace Beery. In 1923 Mayer invited twenty-three-year-old Irving Thalberg, a charismatic, frail, but incredibly savvy young executive who was supervising production at Carl Laemmle's Universal Pictures, to join his staff. Thalberg's innate sense of story and film neatly complemented Mayer's business acumen. They were both great showmen, men of vision. Together, they would form an unbeatable production team.

In the spring of 1924, Marcus Loew, assisted by attorney J. Robert Rubin and general manager Nicholas Schenck, masterminded a three-way merger between Metro, Goldwyn, and Mayer. Metro Pictures purchased Goldwyn Studios, which in turn bought out Louis B. Mayer Productions. The conglomerate was now a fully integrated unit with more than one hundred Loew theaters, Metro's producers and distribution expertise, and the Goldwyn studios in Culver City.[1] Mayer was placed at the head of Metro-Goldwyn as first vice-president and general manager; Thalberg would assume the role of second vice-president in charge of production. Marcus Loew would remain chairman of the parent company, Loew's, Inc. Nicholas Schenck, his trusted advisor, would handle the day-to-day business as vice president; his role in production was yet to be determined.

Howard Dietz, who moved over from the Goldwyn publicity department, devised a logo featuring the lion mascot of his alma mater, Columbia University, framed by an anglicized (and technically improper) Latin motto, *Ars Gratia Artis:* "Art for Art's Sake." Studio publicist Pete Smith contributed the slogan: "More Stars Than There Are in Heaven." From its inception, however, Metro-Goldwyn was a producer's studio. "My unchanging policy will be great star, great director, great play, great cast," Louis B. Mayer wrote director Lois Weber. "Spare nothing, neither expense, time, nor effort. Results only are what I am after." Privately, he was credited with the opinion that practically any director could make a good film, given the right elements and the even-handed supervision of a good producer.

Mayer and Thalberg soon devised a system of producing profitable family-oriented films for the domestic market, historical dramas and romantic classics for the prestigious foreign market. The formula was simple enough: character-driven stories enhanced the interest in their stars, and stars were the studio's most valuable asset. The company's first release schedule included two Buster Keaton features (*Sherlock, Jr.* and *The Navigator*); a Lon Chaney vehicle (*He Who Gets Slapped,* directed by Victor Sjöström and featuring Norma Shearer and John Gilbert); Erich von Stroheim's *Greed;* Blanche Sweet in *Tess of the D'Urbervilles;* and *Little Robinson Crusoe,* featuring Jackie Coogan.

By the fall of 1925, when Mauritz Stiller and Greta Garbo arrived in Hollywood, Louis B. Mayer had successfully elevated his name to complete the triumvirate of Metro-Goldwyn-Mayer. The enormous success of *The*

---

[1]The Goldwyn lot was a premier motion picture production facility consisting of six glass-roofed production stages, a three-story office building, and a dressing room complex, connected by three miles of paved road throughout the forty-acre lot.

Big Parade and *Ben-Hur* had established the company as an industry giant within the first eighteen months of operation. Mayer and Thalberg made their presence strongly felt, convincing workers that what they were doing was terribly important. But they made it clear they wanted disciplined craftsmen, not temperamental talent. Each night at midnight, they literally pulled the plug on von Stroheim's arc lights for *The Merry Widow;* and, after Mayer's European sojourn, brought *Ben-Hur* back to Culver City for completion. The message was that they were in charge and you worked either for them or against them; your opinion was good, but theirs was usually better. Ultimately, nonconformist artists were not only unappreciated at MGM, they would be suppressed—and even destroyed.

They should have had much in common—but Stiller seemed to lock horns with Louis B. Mayer almost immediately. Born two years apart (records indicate that Stiller was Mayer's senior), both were Russian Jews who had made their own way in the world. Yet, while Mayer struggled on unfamiliar immigrant streets, Stiller was embraced by the warm theatrical tradition of Sweden. Both men operated on gut instinct; Stiller was probably better at articulating himself, Mayer was a street scrapper.

In truth, it turned out, they were worlds apart. Mayer had acquired the countenance—and girth—of a studio mogul, and Mauritz Stiller was now on his turf. Somehow, somewhere, there was always someone around to supervise every step the director made. There were story consultants, accountants, assistant directors, and production managers to handle the details he had formerly considered his domain. "In my country the director is everything," Garbo explained in a 1926 *New York Times* interview. "He has no assistants." In Europe, from the germination of an idea to the final product, it was the director's choice of subject, treatment, and execution. These tasks were no longer Stiller's concern; keeping a production on budget would be.

"It is about time for me to stand up if I am not to forget my career completely," Moje wrote to Axel Nilson in Sweden. "Ideally, I would like to have my millions and be on my way, but I will probably have to wait at least three years . . ." The problem, the director offered, was that the Americans were "colossally kind . . . But there is nothing of European culture here. All of America seems to be some sort of society which now and then breaks the rules." Breaking the rules was inherent in Stiller's character, because he would never acknowledge their existence to begin with.

During his first few months on the Metro lot, Stiller appeared to develop a cordial relationship with production chief Irving Thalberg. Courageous and sympathetic, a man of extraordinary complexities, Irving

Grant Thalberg could also be frightening, remote, dark, mysterious—and tremendously creative. As a child, he had survived an attack of rheumatic fever, but it seriously weakened his heart and he was not expected to live past the age of thirty. He was a dynamic presence despite his often sickly appearance, writer Anita Loos recorded: "He was remarkably aware of everything that went on everywhere. Not only in the studio, but in the world outside . . ." The fact that he did not view his problems with self-pity was bolstered, she said, "by his sense of humor and a feeling that work is better than love, zest for achievement can replace sex . . . [and] Men who run after women are only wasting time. It would be much better to run after success . . ."

And run after success he did. Each time a relapse forced him to rest, the man Louis B. Mayer called "the greatest mind in motion picture producing today" used the opportunity to catch up on his reading. His desk was constantly piled with books and scripts. Not surprisingly, one of his primary responsibilities at MGM would be overseeing the story department.

On December 1, 1925, MGM announced Mauritz Stiller's first assignment. Stiller followed his star in aligning his first American film with William Randolph Hearst's Cosmopolitan production unit. Like *The Torrent*, the scenario was based on a story by Vicente Blasco-Ibáñez; Irving Thalberg cast Garbo in the lead role: *The Temptress*.

Scenarist Dorothy Farnum would describe Elena, la Marquise de Torre Bianca, as "a conspicuous enchantress whose lure is not alone one of beauty but also of charm and temperament." Her sense of comradeship with her victims was "what makes her a 'dangerous woman,' " Farnum noted; "her innocence is disarming." Elena was depicted as a reflection of the era in which she lived, and of every man she has attracted. Through her husband, the marquis, one views her self-indulgence and weakness; through the banker Fontenoy, her arrogance and vanity; through the Argentine bandit, Manos Duras, her capriciousness and malicious mischief; and finally through her lover, the architect Robledo, her inner strength and the power of her romantic idealism. Once again, Stiller was drawn to a complex character and story that resounded with moral ambiguity.

As Metro-Goldwyn prepared for the release of *The Torrent*, the studio demonstrated its confidence in Greta Garbo by announcing that her costar in her second major MGM production would be Antonio Moreno, a contract player who had recently been featured in Rex Ingram's *Mare Nostrum* (based on yet another Ibáñez story). With previews indicating that they had an explosive new star on the horizon, both Mayer and Thalberg lobbied heavily with Garbo to sign a new contract. "Had a conversation with the boss yesterday," Greta wrote Lars Saxon. "He was annoyed with me because he thinks I get needlessly anxious about everything. I couldn't talk to him about it.—It was like hitting your head against a brick wall." Louis B. Mayer called her into his office several times trying to convince her to sign for an additional two years. The studio boss was a formidable man who was not above using a little melodrama to make his point—but he was unsuccessful in breaking through Garbo's diffidence. "I could never understand what he meant by [his argument]," she said. "We never said anything about money. He just said he couldn't afford to advertise my pictures and put money into me if I would not sign."

Mayer worried about another studio reaping the benefits of his investment. What he didn't understand was that his only obstacle was Greta's heartfelt desire to return to Sweden. "If you call my sister don't forget to tell her that I'll becoming home quite soon," she promised Saxon in February of 1926. "Tell her also that she can be happy to be living in Sweden and shouldn't think that everywhere else is paradise."

On the twenty-third of February, Greta was arrested in Santa Monica for driving thirty-five miles per hour in a twenty-mile-per-hour zone. "As soon as she learned [to drive] she became a regular speed demon," Sven-Hugo Borg claimed. "We would get in the car at the studio and it would be sixty miles an hour until we reached the hotel." She could have received a three-day sentence for the offense, but when Garbo appeared in court two days later, accompanied by studio personnel, she simply paid a $10 fine.

She usually spent her days off walking, swimming, going to movie theaters, or reading. Greta and Moje often walked the white sand beaches of Santa Monica together, wrestling private demons. Both wrote to family and friends regularly seeking new books and plays; they read voraciously. Occasionally, Greta relaxed at the homes of friends by working in their gardens. She especially enjoyed the company of children, said Erik Stocklassa. Whenever she was invited to a new home, she would inquire, "Have they any children?" If the answer was yes, he said, she often devoted her time to talking and playing with them.

Victor Sjöström's preteen daughters, Guje and Caje, were particular favorites. She also developed a close friendship with Sjöström's wife, Edith. According to MGM production manager Joseph ("J.J.") Cohn, rumors about Greta Garbo and Edith Sjöström briefly circulated around the studio, but it was just idle gossip. "They seemed to be good friends," Cohn says, "but I don't think there was anything more to it than that."

As the factor of her celebrity multiplied, it would become increasingly important for outsiders to penetrate the elite inner circle protecting

Garbo. But who was there to break through a reserved young actress's isolation except the special few who could speak her own language? In Hollywood, she continued to depend on many of the same people who had
supported her back home. It was with them that she shared her concerns
when she began to receive reports from home that her sister, Alva, was ill.
Greta worried constantly about Alva, Irma Stocklassa remembered.
"[She] was tortured by the letters from Sweden telling her [Alva] was getting more and more sick . . ." Doctors in Stockholm didn't seem to know
what was wrong. Greta hopefully planned to bring her sister over to the
United States as soon as she was well enough to travel.

Erik and Irma Stocklassa lived with their children in a house near the
Hollywood Bowl. "Every Sunday we were invited to dinner with Mauritz
Stiller," Ingrid Kjellberg, one of the Stocklassa children, recalled. "Stiller's
housekeeper had the day off then and my mother used to help with the
dinner." But Garbo never showed up before everyone had finished dining,
because she couldn't bear to look on while they were eating. Instead, she
would walk outside, back and forth, up and down the beach until supper
was over. Then, in accordance with Moje's orders, she would be given a
plate of spinach with a slice of lemon. Stiller seemed especially concerned
that Greta maintain her figure, Mrs. Stocklassa said, and took great care
with her diet. "I honestly felt sorry for her on a lot of occasions, since she
enjoyed life and had a hearty appetite." When no one was around, Irma
Stocklassa would make a couple of sandwiches for Greta to take home.

Horseback riding became a part of Garbo's research for her new film as
well as a favored recreation. In *The Temptress*, she would be required to ride
a show horse sidesaddle; she also needed to learn how to fall off the horse
without hurting herself. She practiced on an old but reliable horse at the
Santa Monica Stables. To keep herself fit, Greta also went on daily swims
in the Pacific. She frequented the more secluded areas of the beach during
off-hours—although there were times when the wish for privacy placed
her at great peril. She described such an incident to Sven Broman. "I
nearly drowned during those first years in Hollywood," she said. "Once I
had been swimming far out to sea, when I was sent spinning by a huge
breaker . . . I hurt myself and got water in my lungs and almost lost consciousness. . . . It was a miracle that I managed to swim ashore." She was
more careful in the future, but still did not invite company.

On days when Stiller and Garbo both reported to work in Culver City, they
were regular visitors to Victor Sjöström's set. Sjöström was directing Lillian
Gish and Lars Hanson in *The Scarlet Letter*. Lillian Gish, then considered
the screen's finest actress, arrived at MGM around the same time as Garbo.

An established star who took pride in the quality of her productions, Gish had been hired by Nicholas Schenck to add prestige to the studio's youthful lineup. She quickly earned the admiration of the young contract player watching her from the sidelines. Stiller would leave Greta on the set in the morning, go about his business on the lot, take her to lunch, and then return her to the stage after the break. Gish didn't mind. "We liked an audience," she said. "They were interested and quiet."

Miss Gish had a strong recollection of having encouraged her cinematographer, a Dutch artist named Hendrik Sartov, to film a screen test with Garbo.[2] Quite obviously, by the time they met on the set of *The Scarlet Letter*, Greta had already completed her first film at MGM—unless, of course, they had met months earlier during the making of *La Bohème*. The director of that silent-screen classic was King Vidor; Gish's costar was a rising young romantic idol named John Gilbert. A chance meeting, perhaps. A brief glimpse. Gilbert in costume as the tragically fated lover; Garbo with her hair dyed black to portray the enchantress in *Ibáñez's Torrent*. There were possibilities . . .

Early in March, Greta wrote Mimi Pollak that she had received a marriage proposal from Lars Saxon. Her response is not recorded, but it doesn't seem to have been definitive: Saxon was planning to visit her by the end of the year. As they had before, Greta and Moje conducted their lives separately and together in Hollywood; seemingly, their affection for each other had not waned. In fact, seeing the couple's devotion to one another, Irma Stocklassa asked Stiller why he didn't go ahead and marry the girl. Moje was firm in his response. "No. That wouldn't be right," he said. "I'm too old. She shouldn't get married at all. It would be an obstacle to her career. She is going to be the greatest star of them all."

Mauritz Stiller's troubles with Metro-Goldwyn-Mayer had been temporarily forgotten; all of his energy was focused on the project before him. Though the director's need for self-determination ran contrary to the way that Hollywood worked, thus far he had gotten on well with production VP Irving Thalberg. Both men loved film more than anything else in their lives, and both continually sacrificed their health in pursuit of cinematic excellence.

Stiller made elaborate plans for the production of *The Temptress*, confidently boasting that he would show Metro what Greta Garbo could do. "We understood each other so well, I was sure I would be more relaxed and a better actress with him," Garbo told Lars Saxon. On the first day of pho-

[2]Later confirmed in a conversation Sartov had with film historian Kevin Brownlow.

tography—March 24, 1926—the director walked on to the production stage and was surprised to find fifty people awaiting his instructions. He had no idea what most of them did. Neither familiar with the English language nor American film production, for the first time in his life Mauritz Stiller was not the master of all he surveyed. The director had a much more difficult time learning English than did Greta (who had a good ear and a curious mind and was a quick study); even Victor Sjöström had the advantage of having spent time in the United States as a boy.

Stiller was a proud man who didn't like having to rely on an interpreter in front of the crew. He insisted on giving commands himself, speaking a combination of broken English, Swedish, and German. According to notes in the MGM files, he had a tendency to give the wrong directions: "Stop" instead of Start or Action; "Go" for Stop or Cut. Sometimes his instructions were comical as well as confusing. He told a crowd of extras to "explode" when he wanted them to applaud. When he was displeased with something he would say, in his deep voice, "Ah, that is very, very bad. I think I will go now," and he would leave the set.

All of this confusion could have been dealt with if Stiller had taken to heart the lessons presented to him. His colleagues Victor Sjöström and Benjamin Christensen had won the studio's respect and approval because they consistently delivered productions on time and on budget. Studio production manager J.J. Cohn had painstakingly broken down the *Temptress* shooting script page by page, calculating down to the quarter-hour exactly how much time would be required for each scene. The director was not accustomed to making films on this basis. "They brought me here to direct because they liked my methods. They say [the films] are something completely special," he complained to Lars Hanson. "Now they don't want me to use my method. Instead they try to teach me how I *really* should be directing films."

Ironically, the principle of isolation worked well for Metro-Goldwyn-Mayer in terms of Garbo because—through Sven-Hugo Borg—they could, in effect, control her. She was unmolded clay, and theirs to shape according to their own specifications. If she chose to continue acting in Swedish, it was no problem. Stiller's isolation, however, worked against him. His inability to learn any substantive English just made him seem temperamental, if not inept. Unable to communicate and unwilling to delegate, Stiller found that he worked poorly within the studio system.

As the production proceeded, Stiller despaired that the powers-that-be at Metro had become suspicious of his "eccentricity." The studio's lack of confidence when the director was having problems with Antonio Moreno did not bode well for the film. Moreno had accommodated Stiller's request to shave his mustache, but he apparently balked when the director asked him to wear larger boots in order to make Garbo's feet appear more petite. Aware of Stiller's close personal relationship with his leading lady, Moreno believed that he was unfairly shifting the focus of the motion picture to her.

Lars Hanson watched his compatriot flounder and make all the wrong moves; there was nothing anyone could do to help. Stiller was obviously struggling to work the way he had in Sweden. "He had his own particular way of making a picture," Hanson said. "He shot scenes as he wished, not necessarily in sequence and not necessarily the ones he intended to use. He liked to shoot everything, and then make the film what he wanted it to be by cutting. He could never stick to a schedule. He would plan to shoot a scene calling for a mob of extras and then leave them standing around idle all day while he worked on something very trivial. Mayer and Thalberg were very upset. They went to see the rushes, and they couldn't recognize what he was doing. . . . I remember Thalberg saying to me, 'Is the man mad? Has he ever been behind a camera before?' " His assistant director defended him, but his loyalty was not persuasive.

Thalberg tried to talk to Stiller and encourage him to work within their structure; the director did not appreciate the interference. He made the mistake of thinking it was his film—but it was their money, and *their* film.

Further proof of Greta Garbo's lightning ascent at MGM arrived on April 19, 1926, when Louella Parsons broke the story that for her next picture the Swedish star would be teamed with the season's hottest actor, John Gilbert. "These two Metro-Goldwyn-Mayer favorites should cause a stampede in the movie theaters," the Hearst columnist predicted. A few days later, Greta received perhaps the worst news of her life: on the twenty-first of April, her sister, Alva, had succumbed to lymphatic cancer; she was twenty-two years old. She had been taken to Sofiahemmet, a nursing home in Södermalm, where she slipped away quickly, silently, and without another word to her adoring sister. "That is the hardest," Greta said. "To be so far away when something happens. Your own flesh and blood—I couldn't understand. She had always been so healthy. She was so beautiful. Then she got sick—just a little sick . . ."

News of Alva's decline reached Garbo just as production commenced on *The Temptress*. The film's most ambitious scenes—an extravagant Parisian carnival and a dangerous, complex sequence depicting the failure of Robledo's dam—had been scheduled first. According to Sven-Hugo Borg, Stiller intercepted the telegram informing Greta of her sister's death and held it for twenty-four hours before having it delivered to her on the set. "Why he chose that moment," Borg said, "only he knew." Greta, as the temptress Elena, was performing provocatively on her horse for the amusement of her society friends. "It was a gay scene," the interpreter/assistant recalled. "Colorful costumes, magnificent settings. . . . Trained trapeze artistes performed on whirling wheels of fire . . ." Garbo rode around the ring on a magnificent white horse.

Suddenly, Borg witnessed a messenger urgently pushing his way through the crowd of extras. He handed a telegram to Stiller. The director raised his arm dramatically, stopped the action, and motioned for Greta to come over. He handed her the cable without a word, "and with a little cry she sank into a chair, his arm supporting her. . . . The set was hushed in sympathy as the word spread. For a few moments Garbo sat silent, holding her head in her hands, and then she rose to her feet. 'Come, Mauritz, let us go on,' she said, and with a smile she took her place on the set."

She did not return to work on Saturday. Her absence gave Irving Thalberg an opportunity to assess the production's progress to date. The average Metro-Goldwyn-Mayer film had a shooting schedule of approximately five weeks. Four weeks into production, Mauritz Stiller's *The Temptress* was estimated to be one-third completed and already significantly over-budget. By the time Garbo returned to the set, Mayer and Thalberg were looking for a replacement for her director. They intended to cut their losses with Stiller before the production became another von Stroheim-like exercise in excess. Mayer was concerned that Garbo would walk with Stiller. "In that case," Irving Thalberg stated, "I intend to let her."

One week later, as production wrapped for the day, Stiller was summoned to Thalberg's office. Greta, sensing trouble, did not go home immediately; she decided to remain at the studio. Thalberg's offices were located on the second floor of the MGM administration building, with one of its large picture windows facing an alley running alongside the old wardrobe building. As he passed through the alley between buildings, Albert Lewin looked up into his boss's office. He could see that Thalberg and Stiller were having a lively conversation. What intrigued Lewin even more was the sight of Garbo pacing the street across from him. "She would look up into the office where Irving and Stiller were talking, watch the characters inside for a moment, and then walk away again. I watched her for quite a time as she continued that pacing up and down, up and down. She was obviously very agitated. . . . She knew that a great decision was being made that night, and she was waiting for the word."

Stiller agreed to step down; Fred Niblo, the director credited with rescuing *Ben-Hur*, was brought in as his replacement. A cover story announced that Stiller had been replaced due to illness. Garbo was devastated. "When this thing happened to Moje, I thought the sun would never rise again.—Can you understand, Nisse, why Moje should always have such difficulties?" she wrote Axel Nilson. "Always so much to fight against! . . . You should have seen Moje, as sweet and submissive as he could be. He got so tired and depressed that he said he could not continue."

Her director had been expendable; she was now alone on the film. Although his departure would have given Garbo another excuse to return to Sweden—with or without *The Temptress* being finished—everyone around her, including her beleaguered director, argued against it. "If I were to go now . . . I would have ruined everything for myself here," she explained to Lars Saxon. "I suppose they know best.—They say that I can't think about leaving until I've done three films. But I'll go the first chance I get . . ."

The executive staff at Metro-Goldwyn-Mayer spent an anxious weekend waiting to see if Garbo would report back to work on May 3 or simply disappear. Concerned production personnel arrived on the lot early that Monday morning. Garbo appeared on time, met privately with Niblo, "and phlegmatically accepted the change," a studio associate noted. Her submission marked the end of her professional life with Mauritz Stiller. "How I was broken to pieces, nobody knows," Garbo stated later. MGM was now her official protector.

Contrary to previous reports, *nothing* of Stiller's elegant footage would be retained for the final product.[3] Antonio Moreno was told he could grow his mustache; Garbo got a new wardrobe that altered the concept of her character, making Elena less polished and sophisticated. Not only was the script rewritten to reflect the changes, but supporting roles were also recast. The alterations were substantial and clearly announced to the company that *The Temptress* was now Fred Niblo's story.

When production began again later in the month, Fred Niblo made every effort to make sure Greta was happy. "Given all that's happened," she commented, "I found it all a bit enervating." Like Moje, she had learned to distrust the smiles. "I've never seen anybody look unhappy here," she wrote Vera Schmiterlöw. "They smile and smile all day long and I sometimes get angry. I would like to say—'Shut up.' But the only thing to do is smile again and pretend that's what you've been doing all of your life . . ."

Greta complained to Mimi Pollak that American directors rarely communicated their ideas. They gave her external directions on where to sit or

---

[3]In addition to production photographs that testify to this—contrasting Stiller's striking design with Niblo's common-clay approach—further evidence is contained in the similarly plotted opening to *Mysterious Lady*, Niblo's 1928 collaboration with Garbo.

stand or walk—and then left her to imagine the rest. But Fred Niblo did not think she needed much direction. "I never saw anyone so sensitive to emotional impulses as Garbo," he told the British journal *Film Weekly*.

Even after Mauritz Stiller had been "set adrift," it was obvious to Mayer and Thalberg that he remained a major influence in Greta Garbo's life. She was naïve, impressionable, lost in a foreign land—and fully dependent upon him. His opinions were her opinions. With everything indicating that Garbo would be an important property for MGM, Louis B. Mayer felt it was time that she came to *him* with her problems. The studio boss saw himself as both father confessor and spiritual advisor to his players, and did not respond well when they sought advice elsewhere. He never acknowledged that the fundamental dynamics of employer-employee relationships dictated that he was part of their problem.

The Metro legal department, which was responsible for keeping on top of employee work permits, debated the necessity of applying for an extension to Stiller's visa. If his contract was terminated, they were under no obligation to continue dealing with immigration authorities; he would have to go home. A compromise was reached when the studio received an offer from Paramount for Stiller's services. One month after his dismissal at Metro, Stiller reported to Paramount/Famous Players-Lasky studios to direct Pola Negri in *Hotel Imperial*.

Moje was extremely excited about the new assignment; Lars Hanson described him as "bursting with energy." He was so anxious to succeed that he worked "until he was green in the face." It followed that Greta was also in a better mood. On the twenty-third of July, the Crown Prince and Princess of Sweden visited MGM. After witnessing a demonstration of American moviemaking, they were escorted to the great hall of Glencoe Castle (a set for Gish's *Annie Laurie*), where an elaborate luncheon had been prepared. A place was reserved on Gustav Adolf's left for the company's young Swedish star. "Oh, oh, oh. I arrived fifteen minutes late for lunch— a scandal!" Greta wrote home. "Wasn't my fault that I worked." Without thinking, she offered the prince a cigarette. He graciously declined; Greta gushed like a schoolgirl. "He was very friendly and I pored out all sorts of foolish things," she confessed. She had finally met her prince.

Several weeks behind schedule, retakes for *The Temptress* were finally completed the first week in August. A new project already awaited her. But when Irving Thalberg showed Garbo the script, she rebelled. The character he seemed so sure no one else could play was essentially another vamp; she didn't like the story and she resented being rushed into another film. L. B. Mayer attempted to use Sven-Hugo Borg as a mediator (and later as a spy) in order to convince Greta that the studio was acting in her best interests.

She should stop acting like an obstinate child and go back to work, he was told. His speech would have little effect. "Borg, you are terrible," Garbo responded. "Who are you to know best what to do?" But she agreed to meet with Mayer.

Louis B. Mayer sat behind his mahogany desk, a large piece of antique furniture mounted imperiously on a carpeted platform nearly a foot above the rest of the paneled office. Behind him stood an American flag and a marble statue of the MGM lion. Next to the neatly arranged paperwork on the desk were a series of telephones, a prayer book, pictures of his family, and a tintype of his mother. Greta looked up from her chair. Although many saw Mayer as an intimidating figure, he was never able to manipulate Greta Garbo. She shared her feelings with "The Chief" (as he liked to be called). "Mister Mayer, I am dead tired," she explained. "I am sick. I cannot do another picture right away." Greta felt she had been given no time to mourn her sister's death. She was so nervous and anxious, she said, she was afraid she couldn't hold it together much longer.

She was most unhappy with the new role—she did not want to play another bad woman. "I cannot see any sense in getting dressed up and doing nothing but tempting men in pictures," she said later. Mayer was paternal but firm: Greta must return to the studio right away for costume fittings or be considered in breach of contract. Clearly heartbroken, Garbo returned to her Miramar apartment to contemplate the options available to her. She did not understand why L.B. didn't make more of an attempt to make her happy. "What I wouldn't have given to have been born an American girl," she told Ruth Biery. "To have understood the American language and the American business. What could I do?" She got a lawyer. When Milton Cohen saw the state she was in, he sent her back to her apartment to rest.

On August 4, Garbo received a sternly worded directive from Mayer. The memo, typed on the Chief's famous attention-grabbing pink paper, stated that she was to report to Irving Thalberg's office at 4:30 that afternoon; if she did not receive the message in time she should report to work promptly at 10:00 the next morning. Failure to comply would result in her immediate suspension. According to her own account, Greta managed two "luxurious" days off before negative stories began appearing in the papers. "They say, 'Greta Garbo go home'—'She is temperamental—she cannot be handled,' " she recalled with dismay. Stymied by the newspaper coverage and the studio's attitude, she went back to work against Cohen's advice. It was the last time she would allow the court of public opinion to determine what she should do. "I don't understand why God suddenly hurt me so deeply," Greta wrote. "It is as if somebody cut away a piece from my inside . . . Still, I hope that there will be some happiness for me in the future."

On the seventeenth of August, she reluctantly reported for work on *Flesh and the Devil*.

CHAPTER SEVEN

Conquest

Fantasy. He had dark curly hair and dark brooding eyes—eyes that glistened mischievously when he was happy and mirrored the heartache of the world when he was sad. He was tall, attractive, and extremely photogenic; full of the fiery magnificence of a stallion tempered by the ingenuousness of a child. His winning smile warmed the hearts of women he never met. He represented American manhood in all of its glory—an exciting combination of masculine bravado and romantic simplicity. He lived his happiest moments on the screen. He was John Gilbert.

Fact. John Gilbert's silence onscreen spoke eloquently of an era that seemed to be slipping away as the world rushed through the first quarter of the twentieth century. Audiences loved Jack, as he preferred to be called, because he was charming, vital, and without the artifice of many of his contemporaries. He embodied the Count of Monte Cristo avenging his honor; the amiable southern gambler in *Cameo Kirby*; Elinor Glyn's fantasy male in *His Hour*; the dashing Prince Danilo to Mae Murray's Merry Widow; and the naïve American soldier who falls in love with a French girl in *The Big Parade*. Over a ten-year period, moviegoers had watched him mature from a bit player to the most likely contender for Valentino's crown and become MGM's top male star.

Small wonder that fireworks were expected—indeed, hoped for—when the Great Lover was teamed with the skyrocketing Swedish siren. Fueled in part by modern reinterpretation of the Garbo saga, biographers today must attempt to "explain" the significance of John Gilbert's relationship with Greta Garbo. Writers have denied, fantasized, interpreted, and compromised. How much of a seemingly idealized encounter between the ardent Gilbert and the passive Garbo could possibly be true? More than some would like to admit; less than others would like to believe. The truth, while hardly elusive, can never be definitive. It simply is.

They met, officially, on a hot production stage one summer day in 1926. He was twenty-seven years old; she was twenty (soon to be twenty-one). Previous to their formal introduction by director Clarence Brown, Gilbert and Garbo had a less than nodding acquaintance on the MGM lot. Greta recalled seeing Jack a number of times as both were hurrying to their respective movie sets. On one occasion, writer Frances Marion reported, a gregarious Gilbert hailed his fellow worker with a cheery "Hello, Greta!" Unaccustomed to a stranger speaking to her in such familiar terms, she stopped and corrected him. "It's *Miss* Garbo," she announced. Gilbert enjoyed telling the story to friends. "Imagine upstaging *me!*" he laughed.

But he had been warned. *Flesh and the Devil*, based on Hermann Suder-mann's *The Undying Past*, went before movie cameras on August 9. The first sequences were photographed on location at Lake Arrowhead while Metro-Goldwyn-Mayer and a distrustful Garbo worked out their differences. When the production unit returned to Los Angeles, Brown was notified that they had a leading lady. Contrary to his normally chivalrous behavior, Gilbert let the director bring Greta to him; this time, the meeting was on her terms. "Some instant spark, some flash seemed to pass between them the instant they looked into each other's eyes," Sven-Hugo Borg wrote. "If there was ever a case of love at first sight, that was it. I knew then that Stiller's influence was put aside forever. I felt sorry for him . . ."

It was, perhaps, a bit premature to assume that anyone could come between Greta and Moje. The inevitable result of her budding relationship with Jack Gilbert was that she would not require Borg as an interpreter much longer. Jack's unexpected first gift to her was a newfound sense of freedom. With Gilbert as an ally, Garbo would begin to unlock the mysteries of Americans and their attitude toward moviemaking. "Every morning at 9:00 he would slip to work opposite me," she said. "He was so nice, that I felt better; felt a little closer to this strange America."

Jack Gilbert was a generous listener who empathized immediately with what Greta told him of her troubles at the studio. "I don't think that we realize what America means to foreigners," he stated. "When these people come to America, their parents and friends mourn them as lost. America swallows them up. . . . submerges them as failures. . . . or overwhelms them with success. [Greta] is now the talk of Hollywood, one of the biggest discoveries of the screen. But she isn't superficial enough to accept it quickly." Jack's encouragement and support was a revelation to Garbo. He made her feel that his smile was sincere, his concern genuine.

Like so many of the people Greta would be attracted to, Jack Gilbert knew about hardship. He was born John Cecil Pringle on July 10, 1899, in the Mormon community of Logan, Utah.[1] His father ran a second-rate theatrical troupe, his mother was the leading actress. Jack's childhood was filled with loneliness, abuse, and sometimes danger. His mother, Ida Adair,

---

[1] Although his death certificate states the year as 1897, a date Gilbert himself used, his daughter Leatrice Fountain believes this to be incorrect.

was usually more concerned with her own happiness than with the comfort and safety of her son. "She did not love me," Jack said. "Sometimes I think she hated me."

Gilbert's parents divorced when he was a toddler; Jack remained with his mother, who continued the cycle of neglect by sending him home with theatrical admirers or back to her father's farm in Utah. Seldom in one city long enough to make friends or participate in normal activities like attending school, Jack had no stabilizing force in his life. Instead, there were cheap boardinghouses, filthy dressing rooms, unpaid bills—and his mother's infidelities. "God pity the theatrical child," Jack once declared. "He's a pariah among other children with homes and backyards. He doesn't know the meaning of the word home."

Ida Adair succumbed to tuberculosis in 1913. Her second husband, comedian Walter Gilbert, gave Jack ten dollars, his mother's makeup case, and a train ticket to San Francisco. Eager to succeed on his own, the fourteen-year-old tried his hand at various menial jobs, but what interested him most was acting. By 1915, he was working as the stage manager of a small stock company in Spokane, Washington. When that venture collapsed, he enlisted his stepfather's support and got a letter of introduction to Thomas Ince, then one of the industry's top motion picture producers.

Jack started in movies as a *bushwa,* one of the extras who supplied the atmosphere and populated the background of most films. From the more experienced "bushwa" and "hams" Jack learned the difference between stage and film makeup; how to ride a horse bareback; how to fire a rusty musket; how to play dead when your feet are on fire. From the directors, writers, and film cutters, he learned how to put together a film. He soon graduated to bit parts in William S. Hart westerns, Ince's epics, and an assortment of drawing-room comedies and dramas. At age nineteen, Jack accepted a job in the story department of a new film company, Paralta Pictures. His tenure was brief—the company failed a short time later.

By 1921, Jack had found limited success as an actor, writer, and director—but nothing like the lavish attention now showered by Cecil B. DeMille on his wife, actress Leatrice Joy. DeMille was grooming Leatrice for stardom and would not tolerate interference from her husband. Time after time, the ingenue was asked by both men to chose between her marriage and career, between DeMille's prestige and Jack's adoration. She loved Jack, but found it hard to resist the temptations DeMille dangled before her. Gilbert was bitter and unhappy. The couple loved, quarreled, and hated in equal measure, said reporter Dorothy Herzog, with the precarious status of their relationship serving as a barometer of Jack's current disposition. In retaliation, the actor admitted drinking heavily and carousing unrepentantly. He was convinced "that all opportunities for a brilliant or even mildly successful career were gone." His reckless behavior was early evidence of a self-destructive side that would resurface later.

Forced to endure long separations from his wife, who was working in New York, Gilbert rented a house with writers Carey Wilson and Paul Bern. Jack enjoyed the friendship of a diverse group of artists, but the boy who had taught himself how to read was always magically drawn to the craftsmen of words. He would include many of the town's most talented writers—Benjamin Glazer, Herman Mankiewicz, Donald Ogden Stewart, Anita Loos, Dorothy Parker, Ben Hecht, Adela Rogers St. Johns—in his intimate coterie of friends.

Paul Bern observed his friend perpetually on the verge of major stardom and urged him to meet with Irving Thalberg. Gilbert and Thalberg hit it off. After hearing about the imminent formation of Metro-Goldwyn, Jack signed a five-year contract with the studio. A few days later, Thalberg took him to meet Elinor Glyn, and Gilbert's career was thrown into high gear. By the time *His Hour* and *The Merry Widow* were released later in the year, John Gilbert's popularity was fully evident. "Acting, that very thing which I had been fighting and ridiculing for seven years, had brought me success, riches, and renown," the actor wrote in 1928. "I was a great motion picture star."

But Jack was uncomfortable with his new designation as a great lover. Being typed, he told the *Los Angeles Times,* "is the most damaging reputation a picture actor can enjoy—or rather endure." Gilbert's romantic screen image created more problems for him than it solved. It was one of the reasons director King Vidor resisted casting him in *The Big Parade.* Jack surprised him by really getting down in the trenches. "He was an amazing actor," Vidor remembered. "His tragedy, as I saw it, was that he didn't have enough inner peace to satisfy or to tide him over between pictures. This may be true of many actors and actresses, but in his case it was outstanding." Gilbert's touching portrayal of an American soldier during the First World War had an enormous impact on audiences; *The Big Parade* became the top-grossing film of the silent era and firmly established John Gilbert as a major star.

Jack's greatest triumph coincided with his most personal defeat. In May of 1925, an interlocutory decree was granted to the Gilberts; their divorce would become final a year later. Lawyers had advised Leatrice to file for divorce before their daughter was born. Several times over the next two years the couple contemplated a reconciliation—but always returned to separate careers on separate coasts.

* * *

Pola Negri invited her director and producer to dinner. According to the actress, before the appointed time, Mauritz Stiller called to ask if he could bring a friend. Negri was more than a little bit curious about his companion. A recent item published in *Variety* suggested that Rudolph Valentino had tired of his "Polita" and was now secretly spending time with Greta Garbo. "I do not recall what sort of seductive creature I was expecting," Negri wrote in her memoirs, "but it was certainly not the tall shy girl of extraordinary beauty who arrived—a girl so seemingly dominated that she was constantly looking to her mentor for permission before uttering a syllable."

Soon her eyes would look to someone new. Despite her lack of enthusiasm for *Flesh and the Devil,* Greta could take comfort in the fact that both of her leading men were knowledgeable about their craft and willing to share their expertise. John Gilbert and Lars Hanson were survivors of the modern star-maker machinery, and both would be critical to her successful transformation in the film.

One short week after their introduction, Gilbert and Garbo were already into their second love scene. In his excitement, director Clarence Brown reported to Irving Thalberg that they had a real-life romance on their hands. "It was the damnedest thing you ever saw," Brown said. "It was the sort of thing Elinor Glyn used to write about. When they got into that first love scene . . . well, nobody else was even there. Those two were alone in a world of their own. It seemed like an intrusion to yell 'cut!' " No time was wasted leaking the news to the press. While it could be argued that studio publicity would have fabricated such a story with or without an actual romance, most people on the lot had no doubt that was exactly what was happening on the set of *Flesh and the Devil.* "They were in love throughout the entire picture," says costar Barbara Kent. "It was common knowledge."[2]

Greta's Swedish friends noticed a change as well. One Sunday, while Irma Stocklassa was preparing brunch for her guests, Greta whispered to her that she had just met Gilbert. "They had been rehearsing together at the studio," Mrs. Stocklassa said. " 'Well, what do you think of him?' I asked. 'Ah!' was her only reply. But there was so much feeling in that one little word that I realized it was love at first sight."

Much of the Garbo-Gilbert affair appears to have moved very quickly, following almost exactly the course of the daily production schedule. They

---

[2]Kent had the thankless task of playing the necessary but always conveniently forgotten ingenue in the film, the kid sister of Ulrich (Lars Hanson) who secretly pines for Leo (John Gilbert).

meet, become lovers, separate, meet again, quarrel, agree to be friends, resume their affair . . . which is fated to end unhappily. Jack made no secret of his infatuation with Greta. "There is something eternal about her," he stated. "Not only did she baffle me, but she has baffled everyone at the studio. [She is] dangerous, too. When she comes into a room, every man stops to look at her. And every woman, which is more remarkable. She is capable of doing a lot of damage—unconsciously, of course. Upsetting thrones, breaking up friendships, wrecking homes—that sort of thing."

On August 23, 1926, Rudolph Valentino died. His passing stunned the Hollywood community and had a direct effect on the films both Greta and Moje were working on. News of Valentino's failing health had put pressure on Stiller to finish *Hotel Imperial* early so that Pola Negri could rush to New York to be with her lover—but the Italian star died before the picture was completed. John Gilbert lived on the hill opposite Valentino's Beverly Hills estate; they had a friendly rivalry. After memorial services in New York, Valentino's body was put on a special train to Los Angeles so that Hollywood could pay its respects before he was laid to rest. Gilbert was asked to be an usher at the funeral service.

Each day, as the train crept closer to Los Angeles, the mood in Hollywood sank lower. In response to the desperate, depressed mood of their friends, King Vidor and his girlfriend, actress Eleanor Boardman, decided to get married the day after Valentino's funeral. The wedding was planned with less than twenty-four hours' notice. Marion Davies opened up her Beverly Hills mansion to the bridal party, decorating it with roses, dahlias, and lilies of the valley. Davies would be the maid of honor; Irving Thalberg best man. Most of the guests came directly from work. Louis B. Mayer brought his wife and his daughters, Irene and Edith; Thalberg brought along his sister, Sylvia; also in attendance were Samuel Goldwyn, Elinor Glyn, William Haines, Lita Grey Chaplin, William Randolph Hearst, columnists Harry Crocker and Louella Parsons—and Jack Gilbert.

Gilbert arrived just before 6:30, having rushed from the studio; he was still in costume and made a quick change at the house. At the time, none of the subsequent press coverage mentioned there being anything unusual about Jack's behavior. Wedding photographs, however, appear to reveal a guest who is not in the spirit of the happy occasion. According to Eleanor Boardman, the event was supposed to have been a surprise double wedding: Vidor and Boardman, Gilbert and Garbo. In deference to their friend, they delayed the actual ceremony with another round of photographs—and champagne—until the minister pleaded that he had another appointment. Obviously, Garbo was not coming.

Jack became very agitated. In fact, said Boardman, "he was getting rather violent." The actor retreated to one of the guest bathrooms, where he encountered Louis B. Mayer. Though Mayer had raised no objection to the affair thus far, he took exception to the possibility that Gilbert might become part of his ongoing problem with Garbo. In a careless, halfhearted attempt at commiserating, he slapped Gilbert on the back. "What's the matter with you, Jack?" he said. "Why do you have to marry her? Sleep with her and forget about it." Gilbert became incensed and grabbed L.B. with both hands, throwing him backward into the bathroom. Mayer hit his head on the tile and his glasses went flying across the room—Jack had drawn blood. "You're finished, Gilbert!" the studio chief snarled as Eddie Mannix and another guest restrained them from going further. Given their adversarial relationship, Mayer's reaction could not have been anything less than revenge; he would not forget who his enemies were.

When tempers had cooled, the wedding took place; then Jack Gilbert returned to his Tower Road mansion to confront the mysteriously absent Garbo—reportedly last seen pulling out of Gilbert's driveway in her Ford coupé early that morning. That is Eleanor Boardman's story. Curiously, it is an account which did not surface until documentary producers Kevin Brownlow and David Gill began work on a series about Hollywood during the silent era for Thames Television. By that time, there was no one available to confirm her account. Neither King Vidor, John Gilbert, nor, of course, Greta Garbo ever spoke of it for public record.[3] Nor did Marion Davies, Louella Parsons, or Jack's most ardent supporter (and creator of much of the romantic fiction concerning his life), Adela Rogers St. Johns, ever write of it. Many of the guests at the Vidor-Boardman wedding later wrote books about their Hollywood years—how could they neglect such an important story?

. . . *if* it happened.

Nearly fifty years later, the first published reference to the altercation between Mayer and Gilbert was included in Samuel Marx's 1975 biography of Mayer and Thalberg—although Marx's account was not from personal knowledge (he wasn't employed by MGM until May 1930) and his source remains unknown. Eleanor Boardman's account was the first to

---

[3]Vidor's autobiography, *A Tree Is a Tree,* is also devoid of this story. One event he does recall with clarity is an intimate, dramatic scene played out by Gilbert when Beatrice Lillie crashed her car on Tower Road. According to newspaper reports, it occurred on the evening of August 24, 1926; Lillie was returning from Gilbert's house where friends had gathered to throw a wake for Valentino. If Vidor's romantic retelling is to be believed, Jack was not exclusively "that way" about Garbo at this date.

reveal full details of the double wedding scenario as well as the fight. She told nearly identical versions of her story to Leatrice Fountain in 1973 and David Gill and Kevin Brownlow in 1977.

However . . .

No records exist to indicate that a license was obtained for anyone other than King Vidor and Eleanor Boardman on that September day.[4] Most important, until *they* were told the story years later, none of the other guests ever indicated that they had any knowledge of a violent argument or brawl that had occurred between Louis B. Mayer and Jack Gilbert. "I asked Irene Selznick, who was at the wedding," Leatrice Fountain confirms, "and she was unaware of the incident." Marion Davies was identified as the only outsider who knew of the "secret" wedding plans.

There is no reason to suspect anything other than faulty memories, and perhaps a juggled chronology of events. What is known of this day—September 8, 1926—is that Greta and Jack both went to work. Photographs documenting the production of *Flesh and the Devil* reveal they were filming their final, most vividly dramatic love scene. Gilbert and Garbo had known each other for three weeks—not months and most definitely not years. There had been no time for comradely double dates with Vidor and Boardman (that would come later). Although it's not unheard of for enthusiastic couples to wed having been acquainted for less time, it is unlikely that someone as reserved as Greta Garbo would have entertained such a notion. Her relationship with Stiller was as yet unresolved, and Moje had made his feelings about marriage clear: if Greta was serious about her career, she must dedicate herself and determine *never* to marry.

"Jack was on the border of hysteria even in some of his quieter moments. So violent was his love for Garbo that he attempted to defy a studio ban on their marriage," Harry Crocker echoed in a private, unpublished memoir.[5] Though he makes the traditional mistake of sequencing the event well after the release of *Flesh and the Devil,* Crocker's account is the first from Gilbert's point of view. "The sight of his friends' happiness threw Jack Gilbert into a fine frenzy of despair," he wrote. "It is no exaggeration to say that he actually soaked the lapels of his male friends with bit-

---

[4] A search of marriage records in Los Angeles, Riverside, and Orange countries has revealed that nothing survives under Garbo's and Gilbert's various names—and that without an actual ceremony and a completed form with the proper signatures, such a record would not have been kept.

[5] Crocker was a member of the Crocker banking family of California. He worked with Charles Chaplin for many years, had his own newspaper column, and was a close personal friend of both William Randolph Hearst and Marion Davies.

ter tears while sobbing invectives at hard-hearted studio officials who came between him and his Scandinavian love."

Harry Crocker believed that Jack had convinced himself—and perhaps Greta—of the urgency of their marital union. Clarence Brown recalled that "he was always proposing in front of people, trying to coerce her into accepting. But she always kept him at arm's length." Confronted with Gilbert's passion and commitment to the romantic ideal, Greta might have been temporarily carried away. She erred in not contradicting him.

Interestingly, when Irving Thalberg ordered retakes, one of the scenes they reshot was the love scene of September 8.

On the day following the wedding, Clarence Brown and company staged the scene of Garbo, Gilbert, and Hanson taking communion. It was in this sequence—even more than in the sensational and highly erotic love scenes—that Greta Garbo proved her unique potential to Metro-Goldwyn-Mayer. In the scenario, Leo von Harden has returned from foreign service to discover that Felicitas von Rhaden, the woman he had risked his life and career for, did not wait for him as she had promised. She chose instead the financial security of marriage to his best friend, Ulrich von Eltz.

Felicitas manipulates Leo into reconciling with her husband. Much to the disapproval of their minister, they attend a church service together. As he receives holy communion, Leo compares the pious, angelic Hertha (Barbara Kent) to Felicitas. When the communal wine cup reaches Felicitas, she provocatively turns the chalice around so that she might drink from the very spot where her lover's lips have touched. In that one moment, she was able "to convert a holy rite into a sensual act and *at the same time* deflect the censor's possible objections by rendering the 'sin' almost impalpable," commented Alexander Walker.

As the epoch of flappers and vamps reached its zenith in the United States, the film industry continued to battle morality laws with regional committees across the country. For his part, the director broke precedents by filming reclining love scenes—a cinematic first—as well as allowing Garbo's unrestrained open-mouth kisses. "The results seared the screen and gave movie censors something to think about," Brown boasted unabashedly. An actress who could effectively portray carnal desire, yet place it on a spiritual level that defied most censorship, would have inestimable value to her studio. Garbo would soon add elements of fate and suffering that distanced her even further from censors' objections.

Greta turned twenty-one years old on the eighteenth of September; MGM rewarded her with an "adult" raise to $600 a week, per the terms of her contract. Three days later, they rewarded themselves by leaking a story to *Variety* "now being accepted by Hollywood" that Gilbert and Garbo were engaged. Neither star deigned to comment publicly on the affair. But Louella Parsons did. "If the stills from *Flesh and the Devil* are any indication of how Jack and Greta look together, we shall have the line forming on the right at all the film houses," she wrote.

Principal photography was completed on September 28, three days after Stiller wrapped *Hotel Imperial* at Paramount. Greta and Moje were now able to spend more time together—most times happily; sometimes unhappily, because they were to find themselves once again at odds. Greta was placed in the midst of what was to become an exhausting emotional tug-of-war between Stiller, Gilbert, and Metro-Goldwyn-Mayer, with herself as the prize. "Garbo tried in many ways, at first, to keep her romance with Gilbert hidden from Stiller," Sven-Hugo Borg divulged. But Moje seemed more amused than hurt or jealous as he watched his young protégé "testing her wings on the currents of life. . . . It was easy to see that he penetrated the subterfuges with which Garbo sought to hide her romance from his eyes."

The couple went public the following evening when they attended the Hollywood premiere of Vidor's *Bardelys the Magnificent,* a romantic swashbuckler starring Gilbert and Boardman. Clinging to Gilbert's arm, Garbo smiled broadly for the cameras and posed with studio boss Irving Thalberg and his date, Norma Shearer, as well as the newlyweds Vidor and Boardman before going inside the Carthay Circle Theatre.

After a happy ending was filmed for the picture's general release, *The Temptress* made its long-awaited debut at the Capitol Theatre in New York on October 10. As with *The Torrent,* Greta had gone to a preview of the film with Moje and other members of the Scandinavian colony. And, as with *The Torrent,* Stiller made his displeasure known immediately after the screening. He cornered Thalberg, who had been observing the audience reaction in the theater lobby. "*Es ist ein Skandal!*" he admonished the executive, continuing his tirade in German while Thalberg nodded benignly, "*Ja . . . ja . . . ja.*" Rejoining their friends, Moje told them incredulously, "When I was at Metro, that fellow pretended not to know any German. Now I find he speaks it fluently!"

The Sjöströms left the preview without saying a word to Stiller or Garbo. Writer/director Svend Gade was also trying to make a discreet exit when Moje came walking toward him. "That was rotten—dreadful," Stiller said. He suggested that they all go to Gade's house for drinks. "How the devil could you spend six months acting that without feeling how dreadful you were?" the director berated Greta in front of Gade. She again wrote dark letters home apologizing in advance for her "frightful" performance. "I was beneath contempt," she confessed to Lars Saxon, "and I've only got myself to blame.—I was depressed, tired, I couldn't sleep, and everything went wrong . . ."

The Temptress was not the film Moje had wanted to make, it was the film Fred Niblo made—and with Garbo top-billed, its impact would be keenly felt. She was beginning to project the very qualities Stiller had foreseen in her, yet many of her Scandinavian friends refused to concede this. They saw her smoldering sexuality as tasteless and banal; they were embarrassed for her. They need not have worried: critics and audiences were enthralled.

"Slim as the proverbial reed, and appealing as any siren that ever wrecked a nation, Miss Garbo is born for the seductive charms of the languid-eyed Elena," the *Los Angeles Examiner* pronounced. *Film Daily* thought that Garbo tempered her work "with intelligent restraint," while Robert E. Sherwood admitted that Garbo knocked him for a loop. "She may not be the best actress on screen—I am powerless to formulate an opinion on her dramatic technique—but there is no room for argument as to the efficacy of her allure," he wrote in *Life*.

It was appropriate that Garbo made her way into films at the end of the silent era. Her subdued acting foreshadowed a less melodramatic, more natural style on screen. With her appeal to both sexes and her contemporary looks, she was to become the model that young women the world over wanted to emulate; the girl most men wanted to possess and captivate.

The Temptress broke box-office records for its first and second week at the Capitol. "The consensus of opinion is that Greta Garbo is in a great measure responsible," *Variety* proclaimed. The film continued to set the pace nationwide throughout the fall and winter of 1926.[6] Everyone had been so sure that it would take years before Greta was well-known in the United States. Within a year of her arrival in Hollywood, however, she had exploded on the scene with a lustrous force likened only to Valentino. She *had* arrived.

Her victory would have a bittersweet taste. She had succeeded in the very production that had almost destroyed Moje's reputation. His corresponding success with *Hotel Imperial* would be critical to maintaining a balance in their complicated relationship. When Stiller went to New York to meet with Emil Jannings and discuss a new film with Adolph Zukor and

---

[6]According to an MGM accounting, the final cost was $669,216—including Mauritz Stiller's entire salary while in the United States plus a 25 percent surcharge. Despite an exceptional box-office return of $965,000, MGM took a $43,000 "loss" on the picture (which they blamed on Stiller's overages).

Jesse Lasky, Greta took advantage of her time off to relax—often at Jack Gilbert's house.

Jack opened up the magical world of life as a Hollywood luminary to Greta. He enjoyed being a movie star and shared his revelry by introducing Garbo to his friends and peers. People like Charles Chaplin, Richard Barthelmess, Colleen Moore, Bebe Daniels, and his writing pals Carey Wilson, Barney Glazer, Donald Ogden Stewart, and Adela Rogers St. Johns. These were nice people; high-strung, often brilliant companions whose repartee at Sunday brunch was as clever as any dialogue they wrote. Jack was the kind of person who never wanted to be alone for more than five minutes, St. Johns said. "He loved people. He loved games, indoors and out, loved to sit up all night with the gang and talk."

Much to her amazement, Greta was immediately accepted by this group and they made every effort to include her in social activities. Of particular importance was Jack's friendship with Irving Thalberg; the casual setting would give her an opportunity to see the studio VP in a new light. For a time, Gilbert succeeded in drawing his "svenska flicka" (Swedish girl, as he was fond of calling her) into the social life of Hollywood. Only a few months earlier, she had talked about being lonely and afraid. Finally, someone showed her the secrets to the community she resided in: where the fun spots were, how to escape the heat, what to do on a Saturday night. They were invited to Pickfair, the palatial estate of Mary Pickford and Douglas Fairbanks, where an invitation alone meant acceptance into Hollywood's higher spheres.

Most of all, Greta seemed to enjoy the Sundays at Jack's hillside home, a Spanish-style house at the top of Tower Road in Benedict Canyon. Here was sunshine, music, and laughter. Jack and his friends introduced Greta to American popular music; her first discs served as a private classroom for studying English. At 1400 Tower Grove Drive (his official address) there were lively brunches around the pool, afternoon drinks on the veranda with its impressive view of the city, and tennis matches with Charlie Chaplin, Buster Keaton, or even Bill Tilden as her doubles partner.

Carey Wilson first met Greta while she was standing on her head. After a ferocious game of tennis, several laps in the pool, and a brisk hike, he said, "she still contained so much physical exuberance that standing on her head, on a sofa pillow, seemed to be the simple and desirable thing to do." Wilson fancied himself a tennis player. "In fact, I thought I was pretty good," he said. "But with the 'Fleek,' it was something else again. The 'Fleek' played the most unorthodox tennis you can possibly imagine. Grasping the racket well up toward the throat, she would smack the ball so heartily that there wasn't much to be done about it in the event it happened to land in the court." For sixteen days, they played tennis and Wilson beat her soundly. "On the seventeenth she caught up to me." Having accomplished her objective, that was the last day they played singles.

Many acquaintances felt that Greta was a different person during this period. She was the person they wanted her to be: charming, polite, sociable, and easier to know. But many also wondered about the curious effect the solitary Swede had on Jack. He was so taken with her, his eyes never seemed to leave her. Anita Page recalled a party at Marion Davies' beach house during which Greta said nothing and Jack just sat on the floor watching her adoringly. Full of energy and ready to have some fun on their only day off, Gilbert's friends would show up at his house and "Garbo would be there, white and speechless," Adela Rogers St. Johns recalled. "She'd play two sets of tennis, which she played very well, or swim in the pool, and then disappear. . . . They never stayed long [at parties]. Then nobody would see Jack for weeks, until he'd appear unexpectedly, defiant, excited, quite mad with joy about being with his friends again."

That fall, Greta and Jack were invited to William Randolph Hearst's ranch at San Simeon. According to Eleanor Boardman, Greta was somewhat intimidated by all the stories of the newspaper magnate's hilltop "castle" by the sea. After much discussion, they went anyway. The founder of the Hearst publishing empire seemed to enjoy watching his mistress's Hollywood friends luxuriate in his generosity. "Yet," Frances Marion mused, "who could possibly fathom his labyrinthine mind as he watched Constance Bennett, Myrna Loy, Jack Gilbert, and Norman Kerry playing cards on tables inlaid with gold and lapis lazuli from the Doges' Palace in Venice; Rod La Rocque, Constance Talmadge, and Gilbert Roland swimming in a pool of Carrara marble; while Richard Arlen, Viola Dana, and Marion's most loyal friends, Eileen Percy and Seena Owen, danced the Charleston on Aubusson rugs, their heels digging deeply into beautiful and ancient patterns?"

The only record of Jack's and Greta's visit to La Cuesta Encantada (The Enchanted Hill) is a photograph taken outside the front door of the main building that weekend. It shows them in the company of Buster Keaton, Natalie Talmadge, Hal Roach, Irving Thalberg, Norma Shearer, Richard Barthelmess, Constance Talmadge, Alice Terry, King Vidor, Eleanor Boardman, Paul Bern, Aileen Pringle, Beatrice Lillie, Edmund Goulding, Nicholas Schenck, J. Robert Rubin, Harry Rapf, and Eddie Mannix. Jack is lying on the ground, looking up at the camera; Greta watches him from above and does not bother to smile for the photographer. Once again, her concentration is elsewhere, and her eyes avert closer inspection by the camera's eye.

Louis B. Mayer couldn't possibly compete with Hearst's extravagant hospitality, but his home was part of the filmland circuit of Sunday brunches and buffets. The gatherings began small and expanded until they became *de rigueur* for invited studio personnel—and even more fashionable to show up uninvited if one was important enough to bypass such formalities. "The most unexpected appearance was that of Garbo, heretofore not seen dressed up or at parties," Irene Selznick reminisced. "She came in a feminine, chic, black velvet suit, on the arm of Jack Gilbert, in itself an unlikely event in our house. It was at the height of their romance and the gay mood of their evening brought them over."

More often than not, the conventions of dress were not of concern to her. Herman Mankiewicz recalled a formal social gathering in which Gilbert and Garbo suddenly appeared at the top of the ballroom stairs. "There was a sudden silence, all eyes upon this mysterious recluse," Mankiewicz's biographer, Richard Meryman, recorded. "In a delicate gesture of independence, she removed her shoes and descended the steps in stockinged feet."

Being on parade—a showpiece for someone else's amusement or pleasure—was not something Greta would have relished, especially as her relations with Metro-Goldwyn-Mayer again disintegrated. While in New York, Mauritz Stiller had consulted with attorney Joseph Buhler concerning Greta's situation. Mayer and Thalberg were adamant that she must sign a five-year contract, but there still was no offer of additional money. Garbo could not see the logic in this and held fast to their signed agreement. "Tell Miss Garbo that I am watching the progress of her great success most attentively, and that she should be most careful about signing any contract until she has given it careful consideration," Buhler stressed in a letter to Stiller. "I am confident that . . . she can command a very much larger salary by being patient for the present."

"GRETA GARBO OFF LOT; 48 HOURS TO RETURN," the headline in *Variety* read. The paper dutifully reported that on Monday, November 4, Greta had walked off Metro's Culver City lot. Undoubtedly as a tactic to coerce her into signing a new deal, Irving Thalberg offered her a number of inferior properties. *Diamond Handcuffs*, according to *Variety*, was a Mae Murray cast-off.[7] Explaining her side of the story to the press, Greta later said that she was offered a similarly titled picture, *Women Love Diamonds*.[8] Both scenarios indicated a decided lack of foresight by decision-makers regarding

[7]The project ended up with Eleanor Boardman in 1928.
[8]Produced later in the year with Pauline Starke.

their new Swedish star—provided the studio wasn't deliberately trying to force her into an act of insubordination. On the fifth of November, MGM issued an ultimatum: If Garbo didn't report within forty-eight hours, she would be considered in breach of contract and suspended from the payroll. "Your resulting idleness would be due purely to your attitude and to your wilful [sic] disobedience of instructions," the studio charged.

On a personal front, marriage was becoming a bona-fide issue between Greta and Jack. Although she maintained her apartment at the Miramar, the inside word was that she was now spending most of her time at Jack's. Gilbert had even converted a small guest bedroom into a changing room for her. The actor made no secret that he was very much in love with this "marvelous . . . alluring . . . capricious . . . fascinating woman. . . . One day she is childlike, naïve, ingenuous, a girl of ten," he told one reporter. "The next she is a mysterious woman a thousand years old, knowing everything . . . " Sven-Hugo Borg was told that Gilbert had begged her to marry him.

What Jack offered was something much different from the artistic will and obsession with an ideal that had determined her relationship with Moje. While Pola Negri believed that Stiller was "heartbroken" when Garbo seemed to transfer her affections to Gilbert, Greta wasn't prepared to make a complete, unequivocal commitment to Jack. One week later, another headline decorated the pages of *Variety:* "GILBERT-GARBO ROMANCE OFF." Evidence of the break, according to the trade newspaper, was the fact that "Miss Garbo was seen in public with her former admirer and fiancée, Maurice [sic] Stiller, director." Other newspaper accounts reported that Gilbert was last seen getting on a train for New York; the actor was scheduled to attend an anniversary celebration for *The Big Parade.*

In an oft-quoted letter to Lars Saxon, Greta allegedly denied the rumors regarding her romance with "a certain actor." In the full context of the letter, however, the only thing she actually denied was that she and Gilbert would ever get married. She explained herself a little more fully to Mimi Pollak. While their relationship had been exploited in newspaper columns, she could not do what "they"—either the press or the studio—expected her to do, she stated. It did not suit her to be married. Once again, Greta took most of the blame for not being able to take that final step. She admitted being too nervous and too uneven in temperament. She was afraid that whoever did marry her would soon find out how scatterbrained she really was. Jack Gilbert was very sweet, she acknowledged—and very angry that she wouldn't marry him. She felt guilty about being unable to keep her promise to him. Jack had everything: a swimming pool, servants, a lovely house—and still she went home to her apartment at the Miramar. Why?

Feeling a bit conciliatory, Greta asked Mimi to help her buy some gifts and Christmas decorations for Gilbert's house.

Director Rowland V. Lee could attest to Greta's growing feelings for Jack. They met Garbo at the home of producer Erich Pommer. "We had a long conversation which Garbo opened by asking me if I knew John Gilbert," he recorded in a written history he prepared for the American Film Institute. "I told her I had practically brought him up. From then on she did all of the talking and it was all about how simply marvelous, wonderful and charming Jack was. She made no bones about being fascinated by him. . . . She did not have a large English vocabulary but she certainly knew all the complimentary phrases and adjectives."

When Jack returned to Los Angeles in December, he would find Greta waiting for him, ready to continue as if nothing had ever happened. Moje made every effort to dissuade her from giving in to a moment of whimsy. "Love has no place in her life at this time," he told Sven-Hugo Borg. Would Stiller ever concede that love was necessary and relevant in his former protégé's life?

Frances Marion, at that time arguably the industry's most successful screenwriter, provided the most vivid imagery of Garbo's conflict. "Away from the studio atmosphere Greta seemed neither mysterious nor aloof," she declared. "With simple tastes, instinctive discrimination between what was real and what was false, she hated the hypocrisy that was evident all around her." When Greta visited her home, Marion noted her great love of nature. It was not unusual to find her observing the horses in the riding ring, the birds in the aviary, climbing the steep paths around Marion's palatial hilltop estate to gather pods of wild rose for *Nypon soppa*,[9] or out on the front lawn, gazing intently at the vista. "I remember watching her in the garden one afternoon. Greta walked alone as usual. Our white peacocks waved their fans to attract her attention. She did not see them; her gaze was fixed on the opposite hill as ribbons of laughter from John Gilbert's house floated across Benedict Canyon."

[9](Nue'-pon so'-pa)- A sweet soup popular in Sweden.

CHAPTER EIGHT

MGM *vs. Garbo: Contracts, Love, and Marriage*

"I think I go home," John Gilbert said, was Greta Garbo's final word on everything. After such a declaration, she would do exactly that: leave. "Once she had been missing for days and I went to see her," he continued. "Her maid told me that she had gone to the beach. I jumped in my car and motored for miles . . ." Jack found her, at last, way beyond Santa Monica. Satisfied that she was alone, he began to approach her as she came out of the surf. She didn't see him right away and he changed his mind—but his curiosity was piqued. He wanted to see what she did when left to herself. "She stood on the beach . . . and just looked out at the ocean. And she remained so, without moving, for fifteen minutes."

Gilbert left quietly. He realized that this was when Greta was happiest: a private, serene, unbothered moment—stolen away from friends, just watching the sun sink into the ocean as the waves lapped upon the shore. "There isn't another girl in Hollywood—or in this country—capable of such complete repose," he observed.

Executives at Metro-Goldwyn-Mayer often expressed their dismay that foreign artists seemed to view them as shrewd, crafty businessmen who were more concerned with commerce than art. They complained that they were unfairly regarded with suspicion. Not without reason. Motion picture companies were especially guilty of stereotyping actors, writers, even directors. Within a few short years, they would turn casting into a science of personality and chemistry. "Miss Garbo is a type," an unnamed executive told *Photoplay* in 1927. "She cannot play guileless, sweet heroines any more than Gloria Swanson can play them. If we let her have her way, she would be ruined quickly." Conversely, during the term of her first contract at Metro, production executives would have willingly ruined Greta Garbo's Hollywood career rather than let her pursue work anywhere else. They claimed her as their investment; MGM alone would either reap the rewards of her success—or send her home.

None of Garbo's work abroad had been as restrictive as the series of manipulative vampires she had been assigned at Metro-Goldwyn-Mayer. She thought them idiotic, and the director attached to the new project even worse. "Four or five bad pictures and there would be no more of me for the American people," she opined. Greta went back to her hotel for a second time knowing that a suspension was imminent. Walking away, she wrote Lars Saxon, "is something nobody does here. . . . They think I am mad!"

Thalberg's final conversation with her had lasted nearly three hours, after which everyone patted themselves on the back for convincing the actress with their superior logic. The self-congratulations were premature. The next morning, Garbo received a call from the wardrobe department instructing her to come down and look at some costume sketches. She never showed up.

Jack Gilbert sympathized with Greta's effort to make herself understood at the studio. He did not think her temperamental. She did not yell and scream, she did not make scenes, she did not embarrass people; she simply withdrew. Jack also knew that the studio's need for control was greater than its desire to understand its artists, and that they were fully capable of utilizing their resources to make Garbo seem unreasonable. "Greta has no idea of the conventional courtesies of the studio," he stated. He personally witnessed her meeting with the director of a project she had refused. "She met him, in the lobby of her hotel, quite casually. But he immediately cornered her and argued, interminably, like a self-winding phonograph . . . After all his talk, she turned to him coldly and said, 'But I do not wish to work for you.' Naturally, he was horribly insulted. After he walked off, I told her that she really ought not to speak so bluntly. 'But,' she insisted, 'I do *not* wish to work for him.' "

With the announcement of Garbo's suspension, Metro took its commonsense argument to the press. The studio was currently—and very publicly—embroiled in disputes with actress Mae Murray (unkindly depicted as aging and impossible) and director Monta Bell (who was accused of having a "conspiracy complex"). Another promising young actress, Sally O'Neil, would soon find herself attacked in newspaper columns. Less well known at the time was the private falling out between Lillian Gish and MGM.

A perennial favorite with the public in general and critics in particular, Gish had been signed, not by Louis B. Mayer or Irving Thalberg, but by Nicholas Schenck in New York. With a few years' hindsight, the star would recognize that she had been unknowingly caught in the beginnings of a bicoastal feud between the theater owners who supplied the money (represented by Schenck) and the motion picture producers who supplied the product (represented by Mayer). She was Wall Street's attempt to fix something that wasn't broken, and Culver City resented it because they had to pay the bill. An exemplary, enormously appealing artist, Lillian Gish was a costly property to maintain nonetheless. She had the right to approve the scenario and director as well as her costars and that meant top talent, which translated into expensive productions. When Irving Thalberg, whom Gish respected, surprised her by suggesting they tarnish her sterling reputation to generate more excitement at the box office, Gish knew the end was near.[1]

"They all point to the harm they could do me by putting me out in bad pictures, which, of course, is only too true," Gish wrote her attorney. "They also tell me that it would do them no harm, as they are so organized that they would go on just the same, but that I would suffer irreparable loss." The only prestige Mayer and Thalberg were interested in was earned by selling tickets.

Film historians would speculate about another reason behind Lillian Gish's dissociation from Metro-Goldwyn-Mayer: Greta Garbo. "From the moment *The Torrent* went into production, no contemporary actress was ever again to be quite happy in herself," actress Louise Brooks wrote in a controversial essay on Gish and Garbo subtitled "The Executive War on Stars." Brooks imagined the entire studio to be watching the daily rushes "with amazement as Garbo created out of the stalest, thinnest material the complex enchanting shadow of a soul upon the screen."

Certainly, the studio was capable of positioning one player against another—though MGM was clearly in doubt regarding its future relationship with Garbo; she was hardly a reliable threat to Gish. Lillian Gish could go anywhere and make movies; she might even chose to return to the theater. But, in 1926, MGM held all the options on Greta Garbo's career in the United States. Interestingly, both contract disputes occurred around the same time.

If she had been cognizant of their mutual struggle, Greta would have felt a heartbreaking sense of irony. Lillian Gish was one of the few players on the Metro lot to express her condolences to Greta when her sister died. Because she had a close relationship with her own sister, Dorothy, she personally identified with Garbo's tragedy. "I couldn't speak to her and tell her I was sorry. So I sent her some flowers, with a note," Gish recalled. Greta tentatively approached her at the end of the day, struggling to express herself in English. Gish, sensing Greta's awkwardness, tenderly put her arms around her and they both burst into tears. That day, she became something of a heroine to Garbo, who already admired her dedication to quality, her dignity, and her sense of self. She would not forget her kindness.

---

[1] In a similar vein, the front office would later suggest changing the name of Gish's drama about feuding Scottish clans, *Annie Laurie*, to *Ladies from Hell*.

* * *

Garbo was unable to articulate her basic quarrel with MGM—she would find even the word "quarrel" inadequate, saying it was a "noisy word." But she was very much aware of how many studio employees viewed her: poor . . . dumb . . . backward . . . an ignorant, thick-headed Swede. While she privately endured the insults and slurs, Greta told friends she hoped that she would be rewarded for all the years she had "sacrificed for money. My God, imagine to go back home when the time here is over—and in addition somewhat wealthy. How good it would be," she wrote during the previous August. "But no increase of salary yet.—Those greedy people!" She chastised herself for allowing considerations about money to guide her, cynically alluding to the popular Swedish expression: "When you bring the devil aboard, you must row him ashore."

Jack Gilbert encouraged Greta to make a stand at Metro. It was not his first defiance of studio politics, but the repercussions would be significant. "That son of a bitch is inciting that damned Swede and it's going to cost us a fortune," Mayer raved to associates. Given Garbo's emerging box-office potential, Jack agreed that the studio wasn't paying her enough; he was also among those friends advising her to find stories she could suggest as alternatives to what MGM offered her. But the front office saw Gilbert's steadying influence during this conflict as a betrayal—not the least of which because the player they were negotiating with so fiercely obviously knew *exactly* what a major star made at MGM (not some inflated figure planted in the press).

Garbo's terms for nullifying her original contract and signing a new five-year deal were simple: she wanted to have a say in the parts she played, and a salary commensurate with her ascent from featured player to star; she asked for an immediate raise to $3,000 a week. Louis B. Mayer, Irving Thalberg, and the MGM lion took a hard line with their Swedish import. Hopeful that she would not be willing to risk everything so early in her career, they resorted to public—and private—intimidation. They couldn't conceive of anyone willing to sacrifice everything so soon after having earned it.

The presumed temperament and conceit of foreigners, who were accused of invading the entertainment industry and then shamefully holding it for ransom, was a marketable concept to certain members of the press. Feeding on the isolationist mentality of many Americans, producers in Hollywood—after luring the best and the brightest of the European firmament with gluttonous sums of money—switched gears and charged the "unruly" foreigners with avarice. At the same time, a series of battles over wages and contracts, including several heated confrontations with Actors Equity (and any organization purporting to represent actors), helped the

MGM publicity department refine their media skills as the first group of studio contracts came up for renewal.

Louella Parsons, whose daily exposure in Hearst newspapers across the country guaranteed a captive readership, was one of the studio's most important allies. "The way Greta Garbo's mind works is a mystery no one can fathom," she wrote in a December 1926 column. Parsons characterized the actress as ungrateful, willful, temperamental, childish, and greedy—even so, MGM felt obliged to put Hollywood on notice. "Mr. Mayer has the whip hand in the shape of a two-year contract," she announced. "Other producers, cognizant of these facts, will not be apt to so much as look in Miss Garbo's direction . . ."

The following week, Parsons listed Louis B. Mayer's Christmas wish for "a stout rope to tie Greta Garbo to the Metro-Goldwyn-Mayer studios." Likewise, James R. Quirk of *Photoplay* criticized "the luscious Swede [who] has had more good breaks in one year than any one of our talented American girls ever had." The derisiveness and condescension in the press was unmistakable. "When you learn to speak English," Quirk snipped, "inquire how many beautiful and clever girls have been absolutely ruined by playing good women without ever a chance to show how bad they could be."

Using the most common of negotiating strategies, the studio put on a public show to gain sympathy and punish the alleged offender. The whole, unfortunate misunderstanding, Metro pleaded in the press, boiled down to that demon temptation: money. "GRETA GARBO SAYS $5,000 OR NO WORK," *Variety* declared on December 15. Greta found herself caricatured in newspapers as a greedy Swede holding fistfuls of American dollars. She was hurt but unmoved by such tactics and chose not to respond publicly. Such apparent indifference marked the beginning of a maverick reputation. People thought her brave, Greta shared with Mimi Pollak, but little did they know that she simply could not articulate what she wanted because she wasn't sure herself. One thing she did know: she had no intention of continuing to play the "vampire" on screen.

Although Garbo's visa had been extended through July of 1927, there were disturbing and not very subtle threats of deportation reported in the press. In the past, MGM had ruthlessly—albeit anonymously—used the INS to plant negative stories about Mauritz Stiller, ensuring that he would have problems with future visa extensions. Evidence of outside interference can be seen in the studio's legal files.[2] Scandalous insinuations—

---

[2]Metro executives were aware of the rumors about Stiller from the beginning. A lawsuit from Carlo Keil-Möller had threated to expose their private relationship, and there had been gossip about Stiller's boys in Berlin and Los Angeles as well.

whether true or untrue—were very effective in controlling aliens who wanted to remain in the United States. Greta Garbo could easily have been painted with the same brush, if the studio required it.

From friends and acquaintances, she now heard that MGM was contemplating bringing in a replacement. Mona Mårtenson was one of several actresses who received inquiries from the studio regarding their availability. "People say that they are going to send me back home. I don't know what will happen," Greta wrote Lars Saxon. "Haven't shown up at Metro for over a month. Oh, oh. . . . I feel so unhappy and treated in such a step-motherly way.—Can you understand it?"

Ultimately, Metro-Goldwyn-Mayer was unsuccessful in maneuvering Garbo into either compliance or submission. She simply did not possess that lusty ambition so often used against actors. Threats of putting her in bad pictures for the duration of her three-year contract didn't work, because a traditional desire for the spotlight did not dominate Greta's feelings about her work. While they did all the fuming, Mayer and Thalberg learned that Greta Garbo's indifference was no ruse. "Hers was to be the triumph of the apathetic will," Alexander Walker wrote in his study of Garbo's career. Even more frightening, this was one actress who would have preferred being sent home.

Desperate to reach some kind of accord before *Flesh and the Devil* was released, Louis B. Mayer gave away his hand by turning to Sven-Hugo Borg for help. "Tell her that, to me, she has acted as a simple and ordinary dishwasher would do," he was instructed. But Borg relayed the message somewhat differently from what he'd been told. "That girl thinks I am a hard, unreasonable man and that I am paying her a salary far below what she is worth," he reported the mogul saying. "She forgets that it was I who took all the risk. She has acted like a fool and ought to be spanked . . ." Mayer wished to be fair, Borg added, "and if you have any sense you will listen."

Greta's reply effectively put her assistant on notice that she had not asked for career guidance. Borg reported back to Mayer that he'd made little headway. In an unusual move—beyond the scope of his duties as an interpreter or assistant—he took it upon himself to voice his concerns to Garbo's lawyer in New York. "The difficulties between Miss Garbo and the studio are, in my opinion, the fault of Miss Garbo," he informed Joseph Buhler. However well-intentioned his actions, it was clear where his sympathies lay. Buhler recommended that Greta show his letter to Stiller and discuss firing the subordinate. But Sven-Hugo Borg was a salaried MGM employee assigned to Garbo; they might not chose to deal with him, but they could not get rid of him.

For an intervention to work, Mayer would have to move in closer. L.B.

spoke at length with Victor Sjöström, who agreed to discuss the matter with Moje. Stiller responded on the eighteenth of December. "My dear Sir," he wrote his former boss, "After my conversation with Mr. Seastrom [sic] yesterday I wish to explain my position in regard to Miss Garbo, and especially do I hope that this letter will be the means of avoiding eventual misunderstandings between Metro-Goldwyn-Mayer and Miss Garbo." Referring to their previous negotiations, Stiller reiterated that "Miss Garbo had a much better contract with UFA than the one she now has with your company, and it was I who persuaded her to accept the lower salary at Metro-Goldwyn-Mayer, because I was directly responsible for her coming to this country, and was absolutely convinced that she would make a wonderful success in America. . . .

"The reason that Miss Garbo has been so unhappy here, notwithstanding her success, is simply a matter of the vamp roles she has been forced to play and which, she keenly feels, are outside her sphere. . . . Believe me or not, Mr. Mayer, I have been the only one who consoled her and I explained to her that the first roles she portrayed for your company whether they were vamp roles or others more suited to her, made absolutely no difference whatsoever. I also told her that I had expressed my opinion in this case to Mr. Thalberg and he personally assured me there would be a change and Miss Garbo need have no fear that she had to play vamp roles exclusively in the future."

Stiller reminded L.B. that Greta had always been against signing a long-term contract. When MGM pressed its case in Hollywood, the director stated that he had "advised Miss Garbo not to be contrary but seriously consider a contract for a longer period of years." As far as the salary demands were concerned, he could only stress his belief that "she is one of the best attractions a film company can possess and, I myself, would not hesitate a moment to pay her the amount her representative has asked for, especially when there is an option every year and the firm can terminate her contract practically any time." In the interest of moving everything forward, Stiller suggested, and Greta agreed to, a lesser salary of $2,500 per week for the first year, $3,000 for the second, and $1,000 increases each year thereafter. Under the new proposal, she would not be making the widely reported $5,000 a week until the fourth year.

A truce was called. On December 21, the studio issued a statement that Garbo had "given in" and, for the time being at least, they were going to take her back under the terms of her original contract.

"Greta Garbo is a very great actress," Clarence Brown enthusiastically told a Los Angeles Times reporter. "She has all any actress has in the way of talent and looks, and then something. She doesn't have to register sex appeal. It just photographs." Brown's collaboration with cinematographer William Daniels added a striking number of dramatic effects to the irrepressible chemistry of Gilbert and Garbo in *Flesh and the Devil.* The intimate shots of Gilbert and Garbo dancing . . . the chiaroscuro of the seduction in the arboretum . . . the duel in silhouette . . . the daring, almost sacrilegious scene in the church as Garbo toasts her lover with communion wine . . . the final love scene in front of a winter fire of fading embers. All contributed to the visual excitement of the photoplay for audiences.

"Here is a picture that is the 'pay-off' when it comes to filming love scenes," *Variety* concluded. "There are three in this picture that will make anyone fidget in their seats and their hair to rise on end—an' that ain't all. It's a picture with a great kick, a great cast and great direction. . . . This film is a battle between John Gilbert, starred, and Greta Garbo, featured, for honors and if they don't star this girl after this picture Metro-Goldwyn doesn't know what it's missing."

There has been little argument that in films such as *Ibáñez's Torrent* and *The Temptress,* Greta Garbo's true love affair was with the motion picture camera. Although Antonio Moreno was, possibly, the most virile figure of her costars to date, Greta had little chemistry with him. In John Gilbert she would meet her match: a dynamic, appealing presence who projected similar, unspoken feelings on film regarding the sanctity of love and "that strange, all-consuming, mysterious, unfathomed passion" that cannot be denied. Gilbert's sexual electricity was based on masculine drive; Garbo's empowering eroticism reflected the duality of a profane masculine side and a spiritual feminine one. The combination would mesmerize audiences.

Garbo's third American picture in less than a year was again booked into Loew's spectacular Manhattan movie palace. On January 9, 1927, *Flesh and the Devil* opened at the Capitol Theatre in New York City. The crowds milling about outside the theater at Broadway and Fifty-first left no doubt that, even with a capacity of five thousand seats per show, the Capitol was doing turn-away business. The leading contributor to this frenzy, reported industry trades, was Greta Garbo. No such expectations had greeted Gilbert's *Bardelys the Magnificent,* the *Los Angeles Times* reminded readers, yet *The Temptress* (playing in a much larger theater) drew crowds for each performance.

During its record-breaking month-long engagement at the Capitol, *Flesh and the Devil* earned nearly $250,000 and was seen by an estimated 400,000 people; in fact, its final week netted a larger gross than the first week of the movie that replaced it, Buster Keaton's *The General.* The picture also attracted Sweden's Prince Wilhelm, on a state visit to New York, who praised Garbo and Lars Hanson for their artistry.

What was the reaction of the film's principal players? John Gilbert called *Flesh and the Devil,* his seventy-sixth motion picture, "Mildly exciting because of its brazen display of sex lure, but only important for me because of my meeting with a glorious person named Garbo." His costar in "the supervamp outburst of 1927" was similarly unimpressed: "In the end I fall through the ice, so the play can go on. They want me out of the way," Greta explained to one reporter. "That is the kind of part I have. It seems too bad when there is nothing I love more than for everyone to like me— much!"

That January, Greta had a welcome visitor. Concerned about the depressed letters she was sending home, Lars Saxon traversed half the globe to catch up with his friend. "My first impression of Garbo was that she looked as though her eyes were sore from crying," Saxon recorded; "she looked care-worn." Though she had been absent from Stockholm for eighteen months, the editor felt that Greta had been Americanized "only to the extent that she drove a car." Her driving earned her another speeding ticket. "Always I must hurry here, always run—rush. I get arrest [*sic*] many time for the speed my driver makes," Greta confessed. This time, she would disappoint fans who had gathered at the Santa Monica courthouse; she forfeited bail and did not show up in court.

One evening, Greta treated Saxon to a festive dinner at the comfortably chic Ambassador Hotel near downtown Los Angeles. To decorate the meal, Greta brought along the crispbread and ginger biscuits Saxon had brought from Sweden and surprised him with a glass of decidedly contraband aquavit, a favored Scandinavian liquor, that a friendly employee at the Miramar had smuggled for her from a Norwegian boat.

Meanwhile, MGM indicated that the "Dove of Peace" was flapping its wings at the studio and that Garbo would be reporting for work on Tolstoy's *Anna Karenina* the week of January 24. But her salary was never reinstated. By the twenty-eighth of that month, Louella Parsons was again sounding the alarm. "Perhaps Greta Garbo has changed her mind once too often," she advocated. "Tests are now being made of Jeanne Eagels with a view to starring her in *Anna Karenina* . . ."

Having heard about Greta's Swedish visitor, Louis B. Mayer hoped to cultivate another sympathetic ear close to her and invited Saxon to his home. Saxon, unaware of the true nature of the invitation, apparently assumed that Greta was going to join them; he was wrong. As he served tea, Mayer spoke promisingly of a position that might be opening up as

MGM's Scandinavian representative before getting to the point. L.B. wanted Saxon's advice: What could they do to get Garbo into a better mood? How could they keep her at the studio? The executive admitted understanding neither Greta nor her moods.

Perhaps a little charity was in order, Saxon said. She should be allowed to go home and breathe Swedish air now and then. Once in Sweden, it wouldn't be long before she yearned to return to work. Saxon was thanked for his candor—though Mayer promptly disregarded the advice. It would be another two years before Greta retreated to Stockholm, and then only after she had forced the issue herself.

The uncertainty of not knowing what was up at MGM made Greta "terribly restless. I figured out that maybe the next moment I would be packing my trunks," she said. Had she pushed things too far? Greta packed her bags more than once. Only the restraint of friends such as Jack Gilbert and Mauritz Stiller prevented her from going through with it. "I was so low, as you say, that I thought I would break. But it's like when you are in love. Suppose the man you love does something to hurt you. You think you will break it off; but you don't do it."

The "premier de Luxe" of *Flesh and the Devil*, which took place on February 3 in Hollywood, was also an occasion of reconciliation. After weeks of speculation about whether or not Gilbert and Garbo were still a team off-screen, the couple arrived at the gala opening together. Jack, having recovered from a recent automobile accident, flashed huge smiles for the newspaper and newsreel cameras as he put his arm protectively around Greta and entered the Forum Theatre; Garbo looked rapturous. After the show, they took their bows from the stage and were greeted with a tremendous ovation. They joined their friends for a post-premiere party hosted by Clarence Brown at the Montmartre Café, a popular hangout for the movie crowd. There Greta "danced with Jack and looked like a doll in a pale pink dress." Then, according to a curious press, they disappeared.

"Jack Gilbert and Greta Garbo 'eloped' to Santa Ana to be married a short time ago, only to be halted at the altar by the chill, though beautiful, actress's exercise of a woman's prerogative," Dorothy Herzog reported two days later, "she changed her mind at the last minute . . ." It was hardly the kind of "good news" the studio wanted to hear. Suspicious minds were convinced that Garbo would marry—if not John Gilbert for love, then any American to stave off the ominous henchman wielded by the studio: deportation. On the thirteenth of February, Louella Parsons announced that the affair between Gilbert and Garbo had definitely gone cold. The very next day, she took it all back: "GILBERT WEDS GARBO, SAY FRIENDS."

According to unnamed sources, the couple had slipped out of town on the previous Friday, bound, it was believed, for Ventura or San Jose, maybe Tijuana.

Three days later, no one seemed to know where they were or if indeed they were married. When Jack showed up on the Metro-Goldwyn lot, he was confronted by anxious coworkers. Normally courteous and eager to converse with friends and colleagues, Gilbert was noticeably disturbed by all of the attention. He would not comment on the rumors, either to confirm or deny them. International gossips shifted into high gear, filling their columns with fanciful stories about the pair. When the actor checked into a hospital in Glendale "for observation," the rumor in hospital corridors was that he received a number of calls from his Swedish sweetheart on his private phone line.

Once back at home, reporters again tracked the actor down for comment. Were Jack and Greta married or not? "Well, if you must know, we are not," Gilbert replied in frustration. "No, we are not contemplating a marriage, either." Garbo was intercepted leaving her hotel. Once more, the question was posed: Did she intend to marry Jack Gilbert? Greta laughed. She denied that there was ever a romance and called the various stories speculating about them "ridiculous. We are not even engaged. I think a lot of Mr. Gilbert," she said. "I admire him very much indeed—as a friend. Not as a possible lover or husband."

As a friend, Gilbert was to provide a most valuable service: he introduced "Flicka" to his business manager, Harry Edington. Garbo's attorneys in New York and Los Angeles had not been able to put an end to the shell game. There was talk of George Ullman, Valentino's manager, taking over on her behalf. Edington, interestingly enough, was still an MGM employee. He had begun at Metro as an accountant and earned the respect of the front office when he accompanied the *Ben-Hur* production unit to Italy, where he became friendly with the film's harried lead writer, Carey Wilson. Back in Hollywood, Wilson referred his friend Jack Gilbert to Edington, and a business manager was born.

The fact that Edington preferred to stay on in his position at Metro did not constitute a possible conflict of interest until he became involved with Greta Garbo. With Garbo, he made the transition from being a business manager advising his clients on financial affairs to the agent who actually made the deals. Edington's competitive advantage was that he understood Garbo's needs as well as the studio's. He was sharp, quick-witted, and resourceful. After speaking with Greta at length, he learned—and accepted—that what she desired most was "no trouble and just a chance to make good stories."

MGM again put out the word that a number of actresses were looking at *Anna Karenina* with "covetous eyes" (one item would improbably suggest Joan Crawford).[3] Ironically, such coverage highlighted the difficulty of the studio in maintaining a hard-line stance. "The popularity that Greta Garbo has attained . . . in the short time that she has been in this country is a remarkable exhibition of her power to overcome any foreign prejudices an audience might hold," Whitney Williams stated in the *Los Angeles Times*. "I cannot recall any other European actress who has invaded Hollywood, and after three pictures still remains a genuine screen attraction."

A measure of her success, proof she would not repeat the failures of actresses like Lya de Putti and Jetta Goudal, was that Garbo's following was getting stronger; it was not diminishing. But, Louella Parsons noted, the Swedish diva's absence from movie screens was also risky. "Miss Garbo has surely started something in the movies. Whether or not her dizzy, sky-rocket career will be as permanent as those who have traveled slowly and more deliberately can be answered better in another year's time . . ."

Still wary of each other, both parties danced endless circles around one another, too mesmerized by the look in the other's eye to admit their fatigue and quit dancing. Metro would not allow a "neophyte" to dictate terms to them, yet they would not let anyone else claim her—nor did they want her to return to Sweden. Greta Garbo would have willingly gone home but had established ties in Hollywood and was unprepared to return to Sweden in defeat. Even Stockholm papers had reported her seemingly outrageous behavior without seeking confirmation from her side.

On February 26, just as Harry Edington was getting involved in the negotiations, Garbo was suspended for a second time. She had not shown up at the studio and had refused to sign a deal memo presented to her by Mayer. Four days later, she sent a note to L.B. denying that she had been given an order to report for work, but Mayer denounced her for not acting in good faith. Much of the problem in getting Garbo in sync with Metro related to miscommunication regarding terms other than money. The most important stumbling block—after money and the length of term had been settled—was how much of a rest she should be allowed between pictures. Greta wanted to make only two per year, with a minimum break of two months in between each project.

Disheartened by the beating she was taking in the press, she made a personal appeal to J. Robert Rubin, the general counsel for Loew's, Inc. whom she had met at San Simeon the previous year. Her voluminous six-page

---

[3]The story had originally been purchased for Lillian Gish, who chose to do *The Wind* instead with Victor Sjöström and Lars Hanson.

telegram of March 6, 1927, explained in detail the extent of her complaint. In a follow-up letter of the same date, she enclosed a copy of the proposed contract and urged Rubin to see for himself whether or not the contract properly represented their conversations. "When the new contract was drawn up, I was [to play] three roles a year. Because my constitution is not strong and if I were to play as many roles as they see fit I know I would break down under the strain and fail to do my work as it should be done," she stated.

On the sixteenth of March, *Variety* reported that Garbo had accepted a supporting role at her old salary. Mayer seemed determined to show Greta who was boss; he cast her as a chorus girl in *Her Brother from Brazil*, a romantic comedy featuring Lew Cody and Aileen Pringle.[4] Harry Edington advised his client not to protest; they would call Mayer's bluff. When a cooperative Garbo showed up for a costume fitting, it was Miss Pringle who rebelled. She knew perfectly well that she would have no chance onscreen with the most talked-about actress in Hollywood playing a supporting role. Louis B. Mayer called Greta into his office and accused her of being intentionally impossible. "For the first time I answered Mr. Mayer back," Garbo revealed. "I said I had all my clothes fitted and was ready to play the little part. What more did they want?" Her spirited defense only succeeded in escalating the pitch of Mayer's tirade, and she immediately regretted having talked back.

The mediation of Harry Edington and J. Robert Rubin, who came west to handle the negotiations personally, resulted in a settlement being announced on March 30. MGM would make most of the concessions. The twelve-page contract, signed on June 1 but back-dated to January, promised two films per year; the studio could not obligate Greta to perform in additional pictures without her express permission. Garbo was to be starred or costarred in all features. She would receive $2,000 a week during her first year; on January 1, 1928, the fee would jump to $4,000; $5,000 in 1929; $6,000 in 1930; and $7,000 per week in 1931, the fifth and final year of the new agreement. Unlike with most contracts, there were no layoffs built into Garbo's contract; she was to be paid whether she worked or not. A private arrangement between Edington and Metro freed her of paying commission; Edington received his bonus from MGM.

Principal photography on *Anna Karenina* was scheduled for the first week of April. By the time production actually began the following week, the

---

[4]The film was released later in the year as *Adam and Evil*; Gwen Lee played the blonde who "liked a cocktail and a millionaire for a chaser."

film had been given a new title: *Love.* The director: Russian émigré Dimitri Buchowetzki. The leading man: Ricardo Cortez. Jack Gilbert, although not officially on hiatus, was languishing at home waiting for *Twelve Miles Out* to start. At 3:00 in the morning of April 11, he was arrested by the Beverly Hills police. Gilbert had gone to the police station to demand the arrest of an unnamed third party. When he refused to leave, he was thrown into the drunk tank. There are several different accounts of the events leading up to the altercation. When seen as one, however, they provide an interesting composite of how Gilbert, Garbo, and Stiller interacted.

It started out as a quiet Sunday at Jack's. It was a strange, gray day. It had been raining on and off since early morning; there was six inches of snow on Mount Wilson, a hail storm erupted in Pasadena, and thunder resounded throughout the Los Angeles basin. Jack, oblivious to the elements, came bounding down the hill to the home of Colleen Moore and her husband, John McCormick. He was as happy as a puppy—Greta had finally consented to be his wife. "We're going to be married in the pine grove above my house," he said excitedly. The trio had a few drinks to celebrate. By the time Jack left to return to his house, Moore said, the liquor was showing its effect; he was "roaring drunk."

Back at the house on Tower Road, Greta was already having second thoughts. For one thing, she didn't know how to handle Gilbert's drinking. Jack was the type of drinker, Moore noted, who became more argumentative and belligerent with each drink. Jack's drinking had, in fact, been part of Leatrice Joy's divorce complaint against him three years earlier. "Garbo said he drank too much—for her," Leatrice Fountain says. "She did mention that to Eleanor Boardman and others. She hardly drank at all at that point. . . . But they all drank then. During Prohibition, it was a status thing."[5]

As guests began to arrive, Greta retreated to one of the secluded rooms downstairs. Jack pounded on the door, pleading with her to join their friends. "Go away like a good boy," she chided him. Sometime later, she left to meet Mauritz Stiller—her "big man" as she used to refer to him in Jack's presence, said Moore. To console himself, Gilbert went to visit Donald Ogden Stewart, who was renting a home in the flats of Beverly Hills. "After a considerable amount of horrible bootleg 'Napoleon brandy' . . . Jack decided to make one more assault on the Scandinavian fortress. He rushed away in his car with that wild look in his eyes which betokened that inter-

---

[5]To accommodate more serious thirsts, a part-time bootlegger named Rudy took care of employees from his office on the lot at MGM—an excellent way for the studio to keep tabs on problem drinkers.

nal emotional pressure was approaching the safety-valve point. We didn't quite know what was on his mind, as the conversation he so abruptly abandoned had been on the subject of a painting of the crucifixion by Pieter Breughel . . ."

Jack drove to the Miramar, but Greta refused to let him in. The well-fortified Gilbert would not take "no" for an answer. He attempted to climb an outside wall, scaling a vine-covered drainpipe. He fell. According to some reports, Mauritz Stiller was waiting for him on the third floor and pushed him away. Gilbert was stunned, but not hurt. "That son of a bitch tried to kill me," Jack reportedly told Carey Wilson.

One version of the story had Gilbert being taken away by the Santa Monica police at this point. Another had Wilson's girlfriend, Carmelita Geraghty, nursing his wounds at home. Before Geraghty was able to react, Jack had grabbed a gun, vowing to get his revenge with Stiller.[6] Jack tore out of the house before Wilson could calm him down. According to Colleen Moore and Sven-Hugo Borg, he was arrested speeding down Sunset Boulevard on his way back to the Miramar. However, newspaper accounts record that he was detained when he showed up at the Beverly Hills police station demanding that they arrest "someone" who had tried to kill him. "You better run along home and avoid trouble," he was told.

Gilbert went out to his car—and then came back, insisting that they listen to his story. The clearly intoxicated and increasingly indignant film star brought his gun back with him to show the officers that he was ready to make the arrest himself. He was quickly disarmed. "I don't know as I would go so far as to say that there was any great disturbance," Captain John McCaleb of the Hollywood division stated. "He was probably more excited than dangerous. They locked him up and he slept it off—and went home the next day."

Apprised of the situation by the captain on duty, Howard Strickling (newly stationed at the studio after a publicity assignment abroad) asked the arresting officers to keep Jack until he sobered up. The next morning, a twenty-five-dollar bail was posted on Gilbert's behalf; a studio limousine awaited him outside. Only Jack's close friends knew of the incident, "and they only told their close friends, so by noon the next day the story was all over Hollywood."

"GILBERT IN DUAL ROLE ON BLOTTER," the *Los Angeles Times* announced.

[6]According to Sven-Hugo Borg, this sort of violent behavior was hardly unusual. On at least one other occasion, Borg reported, Jack had threatened Greta with a gun; she hid in the closet. Samuel Marx recounted a similar story in *Mayer and Thalberg*, as did Cecil Beaton (quoting Garbo) in his *Memoirs of the 40's*.

"I must have been laboring under a hallucination and looking for trouble," the actor admitted. "I wasn't angry at any of my guests and I just went down to the station and the boys took care of me; very kind to me." On April 18, the city recorder sentenced John Gilbert to ten days in jail for disturbing the peace. Jack accepted his punishment without complaint—he even posed for photographs behind the bars of Cell #3, his new home. Louis B. Mayer wasn't amused. Thanks to the diplomatic intervention of Douglas Fairbanks and a Beverly Hills trustee, Jack was released less than twenty-four hours later.

Gilbert went straight to the studio to begin work on *Twelve Miles Out*, an action-adventure picture about bootleggers running afoul of government agents. Joan Crawford, who had yet to make her breakthrough, was his leading lady. Her initial excitement about being cast opposite MGM's top star turned to disappointment on the set. Gilbert wasn't interested in making the film, she discovered. "He was madly in love with Garbo, the love affair wasn't going well, and he was obsessed—a caged lion. After an evening with this exquisite woman, he'd stride onto the set in his stomping, military manner, rush to the phone to call her, only to find that her phone had been yanked out of the wall or her phone number changed—since last night! He fretted like thunder. He was impatient with the picture, the director . . . The moment he finished a scene, he'd rush to her set, to her dressing room, or he'd attempt again to call her. Thwarted, he was fury incarnate. He resented every minute on the set away from her."

Sven-Hugo Borg claimed that Greta continued to use him as a go-between. After Gilbert's return to the studio, she sent Borg down to Jack's dressing room to check and see how he was doing. "You go back and tell her she is the cause of the whole damn thing!" the actor shouted to the hapless intermediary. Borg closed the door and tried to talk sense with him. "I consider what you have just said unjust and unfair. You know you didn't mean a word of it," he reasoned. Jack glared and paced and gestured dramatically before collapsing into a chair. "She doesn't love me, it's Stiller," he cried with heartbreaking despair. He buried his head in his hands. "Oh, Borg," he said, "I'm awfully sorry, really I am. I do love her . . ."

That Jack Gilbert's affection had turned to obsession was obvious; Greta Garbo's true feelings were more impenetrable. Frances Marion had no doubt that Greta was "deeply in love" with Jack. Neither did Carey Wilson, who recalled a number of long, quiet talks—some when they were sitting idly around the pool or watching the sunset, many lasting late into the night—in which he and Greta discussed everything from radio transmission to Ibsen. "She never talked about herself, but she used to ask lots of questions about Jack," he said. "She wanted to understand him. 'Why does

Jack do this?' she would ask, or 'Why does Jack do that?' I knew that Jack wanted to marry her, but that subject never entered the conversation. It would have meant talking about her personal affairs, and that she refused to do."

Many of Jack's friends were critical of Greta's behavior and expressed concerns that such an "ice queen" was even capable of loving. Her romance with Jack seemed to them just "a matter of celluloid opportunity." Confronted with the question of whether she had ever been in love, Greta would laugh softly and then reply, "Of course, I have been in love. Love is the last and first of a woman's education. How could you express love, if you have never felt it? You can imagine, but it is not like the feeling . . . I am no different than the others." The unasked question was *whom* did she love?

> *Off again, on again—Greta and John again—*
> *How they have stirred up the news for awhile!*
> *Making the critics first sigh with them, die with them,*
> *Making the cynical smile!*

Years later, a beloved friend would concede that "Garbo was at her best with Jack. She came out in society, she laughed and went to parties. People will never forget how she was then, warm and vibrant and wildly beautiful." Why then would Greta continue to deny any romantic involvement with Jack Gilbert? Doubtless because she had an almost pathological need to keep her private life private—even from friends and family. "There are many things in your heart you can never tell to another person. They are you!" she would explain. "Your joys and sorrows—and you can never, never tell them. . . . You cheapen yourself, the inside of yourself, when you tell them."

As Greta's public self was subjected to increasing scrutiny, the need to protect her private self became incredibly important. Knowledge constituted power over her; better an evasion or white lie than anything resembling the truth. Throughout her relationship with John Gilbert, the deeper issues remained regarding her own feelings of inadequacy and unworthiness, as well as her insecurity about Jack's stability as a marital partner. Having acknowledged Moje's plans for her—her Destiny—Greta could not allow herself to succumb completely, finally, to the romantic fantasy of love.

The fact that Jack was continually attracted to women who were, to varying degrees, emotionally unavailable—whether by force of personality or ambition—sadly determined his fate. Eventually, each woman rejected him—just as his mother had. When things were going well with him in a relationship, he inevitably spoiled it. Jack Gilbert seemed doomed to repeat the most important and destructive relationship of his life: that of mother and son.

Still, Greta was as fascinated by the "brilliant, impossible and wonderful" Jack Gilbert as he was by her. He was a tender and considerate lover—and, for the time being, a forgiving one. Their affair would not end until it was fully played out. "The conventional thing to say is, 'Yes, we are going to be married and I am the happiest man in the world. But the brave thing to say is, 'No, we are *not* going to be married. Nevertheless, she is the most marvelous person in the world," Jack stated. "What does she want to do? I know—better than she does, I suppose. She wants to work with Mauritz Stiller. . . . Stiller discovered her; he taught her to act. And he understands her; knows what she is up against. She can be happy with Stiller. I don't think I was ever Stiller's real rival with Greta."

Having declared a truce—albeit a cool one—Garbo returned to work remarkably happy, calm, and seemingly undisturbed by the recent storm of controversy surrounding her. MGM made every effort to make their contemporary adaptation of *Anna Karenina* first-class, assigning a Russian director to the project and hiring former members of the Russian aristocracy and Tsar Nicholas's White Guard to add authenticity to the film. Frances Marion's screenplay telescoped Tolstoy's epic tale into the essential love story between Anna Karenina and Alexei Vronsky (missing from this adaptation would be the innocent young lovers, Kitty and Levin). Players cast in supporting roles included Lionel Barrymore, Helene Chadwick, ZaSu Pitts, and Dorothy Sebastian; Greta's favorite touch was the casting of an eleven-year-old boy as her son, which would have made her a mother at the age of ten.

Her relationship with Ricardo Cortez seemed on firmer ground the second time around. No longer the unchivalrous "pumpkin," he would tell Dorothy Calhoun that he genuinely liked his leading lady: "She never talks scandal, she never talks personalities, she never talks at all to speak of." Greta noticed the difference in attitude on the set immediately, writing to Mimi Pollak that she was being shown more respect at work. Unfortunately, she could not return the compliment as far as her new director was concerned, confiding to Mimi that she had little confidence in Buchowetzki and feared that she would not be good in the role.

Two weeks into production, she became ill. Garbo's lethargy had not gone unnoticed in the past. Watching her at work, Dorothy Calhoun noted that "The heavy-lidded droop of her eyes seems not provocative as the critics say, but weary; the languid grace they call seductiveness is merely low vitality." Though early interviews were full of such observations, the natural response of studio executives to her "alleged" illness was skepticism. After all, she had enough energy to spend extra time practicing ice skating for one scripted scene. A doctor's report convinced them otherwise. "The condition of Greta Garbo . . . was reported improved yesterday by Dr. Gustav Bjorkman, her physician," a local reporter divulged on April 30. "Her ailment was diagnosed as an intestinal affliction, probably ptomaine poisoning. Dr. Bjorkman stated last night that X-ray pictures were taken yesterday to determine the exact cause." Greta was given a week off to rest while the company shot around her.

She didn't get better. "There is general concern on the Metro-Goldwyn-Mayer lot over the illness of Greta Garbo. Reports from her sickroom are not as favorable as everyone has hoped," Louella Parsons wrote in her May 7 column, "and she is really, according to several of her friends, very sick." Greta's doctors asked for another two to three weeks' recuperation time. MGM had no choice but to call a halt to production on *Love*. "Fortunately, a good share of the Russian story has been filmed and there only remains a few scenes in which Miss Garbo appears," Parsons added. The truth would surface later.

The grim diagnosis was reported to be pernicious anemia, complicated by a case of the intestinal flu. The combination was potentially quite deadly. Anemia was one thing; it could have been caused by a poor diet, low blood sugar, or an excessive menstrual flow. *Pernicious* anemia was a more serious matter. This destructive condition differs considerably from the most common forms of anemia and relates to a problem Greta Garbo would battle the rest of her life. "I happen to have a very peculiar stomach department," she would tell Raymond Daum. "I haven't got enough things to digest food with." For someone suffering from pernicious anemia, the lack of an ability to fully absorb B_{12} can cause progressive disturbances in the muscular and nervous systems as well as gastrointestinal problems. Before a medical solution was found, pernicious anemia was considered fatal. However, according to Dr. Donald Reisfield, Garbo's lifelong problems did not relate to this affliction; she never suffered from *pernicious* anemia.[7]

For five weeks, Greta rested and followed a high-calorie diet under Dr.

---

[7]Years later, a more scurrilous "explanation" for this event emerged: that of a botched abortion. Incredibly, one source would credit Garbo with eight of these traumatic procedures over a period of two or three years. These claims are unsupported, undocumented, and absolutely untrue.

Bjorkman's supervision. Six months of pre-production and nearly $200,000 had been invested in the remake of *Anna Karenina* but, according to *Variety,* "M.-G.-M. officials found that the story as it was being made was unsatisfactory." After viewing the rushes, Irving Thalberg decided to scrap all of Buchowetzki's footage and find a new director and leading man. The production was officially suspended.

On May 21, while the rest of the world celebrated Charles Lindbergh's transatlantic flight, MGM welcomed Garbo back. Although pale and still looking far from well, she showed up at the studio for an hour "to let them see that her heart is in the right place." By the beginning of June, she was feeling well enough to socialize with friends. She went with Moje, Dr. Bjorkman, and his wife to a dinner party hosted by Einar Hansson and his roommate at their rented home on Ogden Drive in Hollywood. Like Garbo, Hansson was a Mauritz Stiller "find"—but where Moje nurtured Greta along after her discovery, Einar had insisted on plotting an independent course. After a falling out with Metro, Hansson (who used the name Hansen in America) went on to make films at several different studios opposite some of the top female stars in the business: Laura La Plante, Corinne Griffith, Anna Q. Nilsson, Pola Negri, and Clara Bow.

Despite these strong teamings, Paramount indicated that they might not renew Hansson's option. He had an appointment to discuss the matter the following day at the studio. Shortly after midnight, Hansson left his house in his roadster. A little over two hours later, on the morning of June 3, he was found on the side of the Pacific Coast Highway three miles north of Santa Monica. He was unconscious, his body crushed between the steering wheel and a ten-inch drainpipe which ran alongside the road; Bella, his pet Doberman pinscher, was lying beside the automobile guarding her master. She was lying near him when he died five hours later in a Santa Monica hospital. He was twenty-eight years old.

"I retired before his guests left and when I heard them go out they begged him not to take a drive," his housemate, Axel H. Hultgren, said. "He had been taking Veronal and long rides in the night to overcome his nervousness. I believe that he must have fallen asleep while driving along the ocean highway." Both Greta and Moje were devastated. Following a memorial service for Hansson, his body was shipped back to his parents in Sweden. Einar Hansson was the first one of Svensk Filmindustri's exports to make it back home.

"It's an ill wind that blows nobody good," Louella Parsons wrote. "If Greta Garbo hadn't been taken sick, [MGM] would not have dismissed the entire cast of *Anna Karenina,* and started all over again.[8] Now that they have been delayed so long they can get Jack Gilbert for the role of the prince. Isn't that enough to make everyone concerned happy?"

The new incarnation of *Love* assembled on a Metro-Goldwyn-Mayer production stage on June 22 under the direction of Edmund Goulding. The British-born Goulding smartly established a rapport with Garbo on the first day of production by helping her with her hair. The director was to guide Garbo and Gilbert through *Love* in twenty-eight shooting days, purportedly without a single retake or rehearsal. Expecting temperament, he found instead that there were few disagreements or misunderstandings. Members of the crew who had begun to take a proprietary interest in Garbo often noted Jack and Greta sitting in a quiet corner of the set, talking between takes. "Then, one day, we noticed that they were speaking very formally to each other," a coworker stated. But when the couple started playing the love scenes, "they forgot their quarrel and the romance was resumed."

Despite her repeated denials, Greta did write Mimi Pollak asking her for help in choosing some gifts for Jack. When word reached the press that Gilbert had bought a sailboat and renamed it *The Temptress,* elopement rumors began anew. "Is it that Americans have no love affairs themselves that they always want to hear about other people's?" Greta asked an American reporter. "God! If one looks at romance, it is bruised; if one touches it, it is broken. You think if I have a romance I tell everybody? No, I hide it! If you like, I tell you what Greta does after 6:00! Anything, everything to make me tired so I can sleep."

In *Love,* Greta Garbo would prove to Hollywood that she was more than an accident of beauty, personality or charisma. Here, the Garbo "destined for greatness" emerged, encouraged and supported by a generous costar. An item in the October 1927 issue of *Photoplay* intimated that Jack Gilbert had directed more than half of the film. This kind of intervention would have been discouraged by most directors, but Goulding supported his actors—as long as the emotional dynamics between Garbo and Gilbert remained intact. He described his star as "nervous, like a racehorse at the post. . . . She is superbly simple, shrewd, yet quite untouched by pettiness, jealousy, and other unimportant concerns."

In her first sympathetic American role, Garbo played Anna as an innocent inextricably caught up in the cruel workings of Fate. Surprisingly, the most evocative scenes would arise not from the love affair between Anna and Vronsky, but from the situation concerning Anna's son. Having

[8]Parsons refused to call the movie *Love* until it was finally released under that title.

deserted her child to be with her lover, Anna as played by Garbo shows the extent of her guilt when she sees a child who resembles Serezha; her pain is so intense she does not hear what Vronsky is saying to her, but helplessly curls up in a half-fetal position. Her poignant expression of deprivation forecasts the tragedy to come. Anna anxiously steals back into her house in St. Petersburg and enters Serezha's room while he is asleep. Her fragile delight in seeing her son again is reflected in the loving way she sets up the toy train she has bought for him. When confronted by her estranged husband, she pleads for a chance to see her son on occasion. Karenin's harsh response is indicated by the look of horror and despair she addresses to the audience before covering her face.

Though Garbo was still in need of refining her craft, the complexity of emotions she conveyed showed substantial growth from previous performances. Greta privately acknowledged that she was relying less on her training than on instinct; technique eluded her. "I know the person I am in the picture, and I feel that I am that person for the time being. How I get what you call effects, I do not know. I do not understand how I am here at all," she would say. "I do not know how I do it."

That July, Mauritz Stiller informed friends that he was planning to go home as soon as he was free of his contract with Paramount Pictures. Moje's career had not gone well since *Hotel Imperial*. Bad health had plagued him throughout his stay in Hollywood. Stiller's final effort behind the camera, *The Street of Sin* with Emil Jannings, put him at odds with the management at Paramount. The picture's release was pushed back in favor of Josef von Sternberg's film with Jannings, *The Last Command*—proof that the studio had lost confidence in Stiller's work.

Forces stronger than the both of them had finally succeeded in pulling Greta and Moje apart. The end result would not have the desired effect MGM once hoped for. Nobody won. No longer compelled to do Stiller's bidding, Garbo would, in fact, answer to no one completely for the rest of her life. Distrustful of studio politicians, Greta would also resist anyone she might gravitate toward in search of a new anchor in her life. In the future, many would seek to dominate her; they would be fooled by the intricacy of mirrors she set up around herself. They would effectively "dominate" a reflected image—but never again the true Greta Garbo *née* Greta Lovisa Gustafsson.

CHAPTER NINE

Captive Beauty

If she so desired, Greta could study her reflection in the wall of mirrors that had been installed in Jack Gilbert's home. At an estimated cost of $10,000, Gilbert and designer Harold Grieve had refurbished and redecorated one of his guest rooms with new paneling, Louis XVI furniture, and old Swedish prints. The most dramatic touch was saved for the bathroom, a shiny black marble room adorned with golden fixtures and full-length mirrors.

When the suite was ready, Jack invited Greta up to the house for the unveiling—"one of the bitterest disappointments a lover ever had," said Harry Crocker. Jack showed off the room "in anticipation of oh's and ah's," but Greta seemed to take it all in stride. It was a loving, extravagant gesture, but a pretty cage nonetheless; Garbo rarely stayed there. When she did stay at the house, she knew the cost.

Part of the price was acting as the unofficial hostess of Jack's Sunday brunches. "[Greta] tried to play that role as Jack wished, but it was hard for her," Carey Wilson admitted. "Sometimes, when the buffet had been prepared, Greta would become very nervous and uneasy if guests were slow in beginning to eat. She would go around to Jack and whisper anxiously that the food was ready but nobody was eating. 'Well, just go and tell the people it's time to eat,' Jack would say. But things like that she couldn't do. What was second nature for him was agony for her."

Gradually, as Greta got to know Jack's friends, she relaxed in their company, but she never got used to the near-constant socializing on Tower Road. "Never, until two months ago, do I go out in the evening," she declared in a 1927 interview. "I do not like to go. I would rather stay at home. Now I object and struggle, and say I will not go—and at last I go in spite of myself. I cannot work when I go to party and all that. . . . People take energy from me, and I want it for my pictures." Between projects she was decidedly more engaging. "She was, at this period, the most intriguing woman I have ever seen," Wilson stated. "She entered heartily and effectively into all the games, from tennis to murder mysteries. She could clown around with the best of them . . ."

Even as the couple survived their first year, it became obvious that the Gilbert-Garbo relationship had settled into something more comfortable for Greta. As the pursued mate, she retained nearly all of the power. She went sailing to Catalina with Jack on weekends, but stayed out of sight when guests came aboard. "I don't recall that she ever entered into that camaraderie that generally exists among sailors," actress Patsy Ruth Miller said. "It seemed that when we were in port, she generally stayed below. I do recall that once Jack did come aboard and had a few drinks with us— maybe more than a few—and had a little problem rowing back to his own boat. From a distance it looked as though she was a bit annoyed as he missed the ladder several times, but he finally made it on deck . . ." Jack sold the boat the following spring.

Sara Mankiewicz felt that the "illicit" nature of the Gilbert-Garbo affair, with Greta often living at the house and hiding away in secret rooms, added to the excitement for friends. Her casual demeanor around the house, sunbathing topless or even nude, shocked many people—not the least of which Jack's Japanese gardener—who assumed that being shy pre-cluded such "uninhibited" behavior. It was, however, a typically Swedish attitude that had little to do with either overt sexuality or lack of modesty about one's body.[1] As the status of Greta's relationship with Jack changed from week to week, the accepted rule was that friends were welcome at his home at any time—as long as they called first. Greta did not like being surprised.

Love wrapped production on the twenty-fifth of July. In August, Jack went to Washington, D.C., to begin his next feature, *Man, Woman and Sin,* with Jeanne Eagels. The sensational star of *Rain* and *The Letter* had often been courted by Hollywood, but was considered erratic and undependable. She was also seductive, intense, mercurial, incandescent—and soon John Gilbert was one of those caught in her spell. They entered into a brief affair. In the past, Jack had been involved in extramarital affairs with Lau-rette Taylor and Barbara LaMarr, thus destroying what chance he had of salvaging his marriage to Leatrice Joy. He was to be severely disappointed if he was expecting a jealous reaction from Garbo.

Greta often left Jack "on evenings when lovers should be together," he complained to Howard Dietz, Metro's head of publicity and advertising. Yet any attempt to make her jealous was doomed to fail. Even a rumored reconciliation with Leatrice Joy that fall and a subsequent flirtation with an old flame, Renée Adorée, during the following year didn't yield the desired result. "When I said 'I'm going out,' the only thing she said was 'I'll

---

[1]On the contrary, even today when Swedish women sunbathe in public parks, the unspoken agreement is that it is not an invitation for voyeurism. The body is considered private space, and one is expected to respect it as such.

leave the door open, Jack!' " Gilbert told Dietz. "What do you say to a girl like that?" Dietz wasn't sure. "I didn't know either, [so] I said 'I'm going out to sleep with Anna May Wong!' 'I'll leave the door open, Jack,' was all she said. What in the hell do I do?"

Mona Mårtenson arrived in Hollywood in August to make a screen test at MGM. The studio declined to give her a contract until they had judged the results of her makeover. Mårtenson went quietly home a few weeks later. Greta was preparing for her next film, *The Divine Woman*. Stiller had reportedly expressed a desire to work with Greta on this production; he was never seriously considered. Metro followed through on a promise they'd made to Garbo months earlier and assigned the picture to Victor Sjöström.

Despite her pleasure in this teaming, Greta could not help returning to work filled with anxiety. She found it difficult to sit still, she wrote Mimi Pollak, who continued to be a calming influence in her life. Again, she assured Mimi that she had remained faithful to her; she had no other companions to confide in. What's more, Greta declared, after this film she intended to go home.

The Divine Woman went into production on the twenty-eighth of September. Working under the direction of Victor Sjöström brought Garbo back home, in a sense. Like his star, Sjöström was sensitive and introspective—very much a loner, even at the height of his success in America. Though he was limited by the system in the United States, the director managed to adjust and continued to make films of excellence. Sadly, *The Divine Woman* would mark the beginning of a great uneasiness that was quietly overtaking his life.

After the script went through several rewrites, Irving Thalberg approved a version that Sjöström (uncredited) wrote with Dorothy Farnum. "This is the story of a woman who thought she could take Life by the tail and swing it about her head," the prologue stated. Although the story was loosely based on the life of "The Divine Sarah" Bernhardt, it also served as the first production to incorporate popular impressions of Greta Garbo into its storyline. Due to the standard plotting of its dialogue-heavy source (Gladys Unger's play *Starlight*), Sjöström was compelled to pare the story down to its most elemental force: the woman. Everything else would exist as background. "I do not think this is because the woman is Garbo, a star," critic Robert Herring opined, "because Garbo is handled much less as a star than she has been in America. [Sjöström] is not too impressed by her importance or her beauty, which is good for all of us . . ."

Listed by the American Film Institute as one of the ten most important "lost films" of the silent era, *The Divine Woman* deserves a brief synopsis here. Marianne, the daughter of Madame Zizi, a Parisian courtesan, has been secreted away in the countryside and brought up by peasants. One of her mother's admirers brings Marianne back to Paris as a surprise, but the joke backfires and Marianne runs away—straight into the arms of a handsome soldier named Lucien (Lars Hanson). A brief flirtation later, the soldier deserts his post to love and protect Marianne. She gets a job cleaning costumes at a nearby theater. The troupe's leading lady catches Marianne posing in her dressing room and threatens her with dismissal; instead, she is rediscovered by the company's producer, Monsieur Legrande (Lowell Sherman)—the admirer who originally brought her to Paris.

A desperate Lucien seeks to hide their dire financial straits by stealing a dress for Marianne; he is caught and goes to jail. In his absence, Marianne becomes a huge success on the stage. She has also acquired the necessary temperament expected of great stars. She is too nervous and tired to rehearse, and when her producer threatens to push her back into the gutter if she doesn't behave, she replies defiantly, "Push then—I don't care!" "I'm willing to end everything if you are—including our contract," Legrande reminds her. She looks at the electric sign spelling out her name, but says nothing as the producer exits. Legrande gives in. When Lucien returns from prison, he denounces Marianne for having betrayed him. She confesses her infidelity, but swears her love is true; Lucien doesn't believe her and leaves. Suddenly, the actress's success as the Divine One seems empty. "I can't go on," she complains. "God, I'm done for—I hate it all!" A final push and she is out the door—due to bad investments, she is also broke. "For a short time people wondered where the great Marianne had vanished to—Soon nobody cared!" the titles explain. After Marianne attempts suicide, Lucien, full of masculine bravado, rushes to her side and the lovers are reunited. "She belongs to me now," he says.

The script was obviously fashioned as a Garbo vehicle—her very first. And the first film to feature her name exclusively above the title. Even Victor Sjöström noted of the occasion, "Good-bye to the Gish-type. Garbo is now en vogue." In tandem with cinematographer Oliver T. Marsh, Sjöström sought to showcase Greta's youth and make her "a softer, more easy-going woman" than she had appeared in previous films. It was a happy collaboration. Garbo came well-prepared to the set, having memorized not only her lines but everyone else's. Sjöström praised her unusual dramatic sense—a quality of living and breathing each moment that helped to shape the natural, though sometimes offbeat, way in which a scene evolved.

Unfortunately, aside from a theatrical trailer, some photographs, and the reviews, there is very little record of their only collaborative effort. The master negative of *The Divine Woman* was destroyed in a catastrophic vault fire some time ago; no prints survived. In 1993, one reel of the film was unearthed in Moscow's Gosfilmofond archive and subsequently shown at the Pordenone Silent Film Festival in Italy. It was, according to film historians Kevin Brownlow and David Gill, "exceptional in every way. . . . A tantalizing glimpse of a very different Garbo: relaxed and girlish—her sexuality very simple and direct."

As *The Divine Woman* neared completion, Lars Hanson announced to friends and coworkers that he too planned to return to Sweden. Though the press was told he was going home for the holidays, Hanson's friends knew he had no intention of coming back. Hanson and his wife, Karin Molander, wanted to resume their stage careers. Principal photography wrapped on the seventh of November—inspiring Greta's last smile of the year.

Moje was leaving. "In Europe I enjoyed greater prestige while in America I have greater inducements," Stiller had written in a surprisingly optimistic article for *Variety* a few months earlier. "America is the place in which to do great things, the place in which to evolve great ideas and make them practical." Unfortunately, it was no longer the place for Mauritz Stiller. After months of deliberation, he was now packed and ready to go.

Nils Asther had arrived in Hollywood recently and was able to spend some time with Moje before he left. The night before Stiller's departure on the *Santa Fe Chief,* Asther remembered, they both "got drunk, cursing Hollywood and crying over our unhappy childhoods." In an amazingly candid moment, the director confessed to Asther that he had been an outcast in Hollywood from the moment he stepped off the train, and that the powers-that-be had wanted to get rid of him so badly that they spread a malicious rumor that he had forced Greta to become his mistress. According to this gossip mill, she subsequently became pregnant and the cruel, insensitive Stiller coldly demanded that she get an abortion. This he called "a damned lie," Asther reported. "Stiller urged me, time after time, to leave this hell immediately and go home while there was yet time. Here I would lose my soul."

But Garbo was staying behind. The following day, while Asther recovered from a bad hangover, Greta accompanied Moje down to the train station. It was, according to Victor Sjöström, a painful farewell, with Stiller seeking to reassure Greta that everything would be all right—perhaps not very convincingly—and Garbo promising that she would be home very soon, though both of them knew she had little say in that matter. More than two years before, she had sworn to her mother that she would return to Stockholm within a year—yet she was still in California, and now honor-bound to MGM for an additional five years. When she would be able to go home was more a factor of the studio's generosity—or disinterest—than her own yearning.

By the time Moje kissed her and boarded his train, both were fighting bitter tears. Greta was no longer his protégé; Stiller was no longer her pseudo-Svengali. Their paths were now separate, and no one knew when—or indeed if—they would converge again. Stiller's feelings on these matters were conveyed most vividly in a three-page letter he left behind. It is written on Ambassador Hotel stationery; at the bottom of the page a slogan suggesting "See America First" adds a touch of irony to the message. "My dear former Greta," it begins. "I am now leaving Hollywood, and the worst of it is I am leaving you here. Leaving you your freedom. Perhaps you—when I am gone—will blossom anew. Perhaps your face will get its peace back; your mouth, your lips will get their strength again. Perhaps your eyes won't tear as often—I am gone, obliterated from your life—you are free!

"But my thoughts are with you and I shall pray for you. You shall be saved from all evil, sleep well without the pain of guilt.—Life is terrible, but it's not going to be for you.

"I am teasing—you are free! As you have always been. And you shall not think about me. You don't even have to repeat 'poor Moje' every time we meet. You are free! And to speak in your new language—[*written in English*] Everything is all right. Moje."

Could anyone possibly believe such a letter would absolve the recipient of any guilt concerning their changed circumstance? Clearly, in directing that his dear, "former Greta" should not think about him, Stiller ensured that she would. His "forgiveness" was a silent recrimination. No woman could possibly feel as sad and inferior as she now felt, Greta wrote Mimi Pollak a few days later. She castigated herself for being bitter, mean, and mad—but she appeared resigned to what fate had decided for her. Seemingly devoid of emotion, she dramatically declared that something had died within her, and she faulted herself for selling out to Hollywood. Least of all, Greta admitted feeling nothing like a motion picture star.

She saved her most touching confession to Mimi for last: a fantasy about a "bachelor's" apartment in Stockholm, a good bottle of champagne, and Mimi by her side. Though life had changed for both of them, Greta resisted the inevitability of their changed circumstance. She still believed in a deep abiding friendship that bound them together.

The revolution began in New York one October afternoon in 1927. It was Al Jolson singing "Mammy"—not on the Great White Way but on-screen at the Warner Theatre. "Wait a minute," Jolson told an expectant audience, "you ain't heard nothin' yet!" Hollywood had found its voice. Most industry leaders, including MGM's Louis B. Mayer and Irving Thalberg, were convinced that the art of silent cinema was not lost, that sound would simply add a new dimension to their repertoire. They did not see the logical progression—or connect it with the growing popularity of radio—because films like *The Jazz Singer*, while capable of generating a great deal of excitement due to the addition of sound, were technically inferior to the great human dramas and comedies being produced around the world.

1927 alone saw the release in the United States of F. W. Murnau's *Sunrise* and William Wellman's *Wings* (the first films acknowledged for their creative achievement by the newly formed Academy of Motion Picture Arts and Sciences); Chaplin's *The Circus;* from Germany, Fritz Lang's production of *Metropolis;* and from Russia, Sergei Eisenstein's *The Battleship Potemkin*. Film, through the artful use of montage and pantomime, had developed into a powerful international medium. There was no business sense in taking several steps back before making a questionable leap forward. "We shall continue to rely on quality pictures to enhance our prestige and bring in the profit," Thalberg told reporters.

MGM didn't need to look any further than *Love* for proof that movies were better than ever. The photoplay made its debut on November 29, 1927, at Loew's showcase Embassy Theatre in New York, and quickly exhibited its strength across the country despite severe censorship in some regions. "The Embassy has finally got itself a picture that's going to do some business," *Variety* reported. "Try and keep the femmes away from this one. . . . Peculiar combination, this Gilbert-Garbo hook-up. Both sprang up suddenly and fast, Miss Garbo from nowhere. The latter isn't now as big as she should or will be, always . . . Neither has she been in enough pictures of late. [But] she's the biggest skirt prospect now in pictures."

Exhibitors were given a choice between an unhappy ending, with Anna tragically throwing herself in front of a train, or an imagined happy ending, with Vronsky and Anna reunited after Karenin dies. Most theaters chose Frances Marion over Tolstoy—the film, as many critics would point out, was not pure Tolstoy, but it was true *Love*. The final domestic tally represented a healthy 50 percent increase over the box office for *Flesh and the Devil;* a significant foreign gross was also added to the till. Metro's profit on the production was $571,000—the best performance of Garbo's silent period.

Very little is known about Greta's activities for the next few months. The day after *Love* opened, she was invited to Irving Thalberg's office and officially notified that MGM was picking up her annual option. "Her next picture is *Heat,* an original story by John Colton, author of *Rain,*" Louella Parson revealed. "Mr. Colton lays his drama in a tropical island of the Dutch East Indies, and Greta has a part that is said to give her a chance to be the same type of character that she played in *The Flesh and the Devil.*" The film was another project she had inherited from Lillian Gish. The announcement, however, was premature. Thalberg was looking at a number of stories for Metro's hottest property; there would be few scripts that came across his desk that weren't considered for Garbo first.

For a rarefied moment, MGM left Greta alone. But they would not let her go home, even for a brief vacation. "I have asked and begged to go home for Christmas," she wrote Lars Saxon in December, "but you cannot talk to these people here. My head is spinning when I think of the wonderful time you will all have at home." Without Moje by her side, she reminisced about having a holiday drink with old friends and watching children play in the snow or ice skating on a crisp winter day. Nothing appealed to her more than seeing the Strömmen and the familiar sights of Stockholm again. "Whether I work or not I am tired and unhappy and don't want to do anything. I don't go anywhere and just sit down staring. I will soon become a little old woman if I continue like this."

Demands for talking pictures did not overwhelm Metro-Goldwyn-Mayer until later in 1928. In the meantime, Irving Thalberg considered a different future. "Why are there so many writers and so few ideas?" he lamented in a meeting with his writing staff. "Perhaps you don't care about your work. You must realize that the studio cannot live without ideas." The studio's next idea for Greta Garbo was a spy novel by Ludwig Wolff entitled *War in the Dark.* Early story outlines and casting memos indicate that the project was initially intended as another Gilbert and Garbo outing. "The great difficulty in making this a man's story lies in the fact that a beautiful woman who is a spy is a much more vital and interesting character than a soldier who is merely performing his duty," scenarist Lorna Moon wrote in a memo to the production chief. "No matter how you change the situations *she* is the vital person." With Garbo's casting, the focus of the story did indeed shift from the young Austrian officer to the Russian spy, a change which was reflected in the film's new title: *The Mysterious Lady.*

"The flaming star of the North," as the publicity department now tagged her, had proven she could attract a sizable audience without Gilbert. *The Divine Woman* debuted at the Capitol Theatre on January 14, 1928, and opened around the country two months later. "Having made the most rapid strides of any foreign star, with the exception of Emil Jannings, it ceases to be any cause for wonder how she succeeds. The woman is *there*," Laurence Reid wrote in *Motion Picture Classic*. "Her particular screen technique is flashed in a story which is not so hot, but which is carried through by the Garbo style and personality." The feature was Greta's fifth consecutive success at Metro. While it would not last long in people's memories, one adjective would stick with Garbo for the rest of her life: Divine.

The next adjective she was anointed with also had a powerful resonance. With Louis B. Mayer devoting himself increasingly to Republican party politics, and Irving Thalberg away on a belated European honeymoon with Norma Shearer, *The Mysterious Lady* was assigned to supervisor Harry Rapf. Rapf preferred scouting talent to being tied to a desk, and with the approval of Mayer and Thalberg he made a number of safe choices. Fred Niblo, the man who had guided Garbo through *The Temptress*, was set to direct; Bess Meredyth, a trusted writer in Louis B. Mayer's stable before the merger, would write the treatment. But as late as March, executives were undecided about a leading man.

The construction of soundstages and a new commissary on Lot 1 was partially at fault for the slowdown in production. There were also new rumors about Greta's health. In contrast with the careless disregard that had clouded Greta's early relationship with the studio, memos between MGM executives now respectfully—even delicately—discussed the situation with Garbo. "Once she had been suspended; now she had to be rested," Alexander Walker remarked. Some in the front office worried that the actress had been dieting excessively, putting at risk an already fragile constitution. Evidence of Greta's resilience was that she had been spotted around town having a quiet lunch with Jack and flying in a small plane with Gilbert, Herman Mankiewicz, and producer Lester Cohen to survey a devastating flood north of Los Angeles.[2]

With Moje's disappearance from Greta's side, Garbo appeared less interested in continuing her romance with Jack Gilbert and more inclined toward friendship. A frustrated Gilbert seemed to take it all in stride. He did not accept the situation—but he had no choice but to comply if he wanted Greta involved in his life in any way. For the moment, he did. Even Jack appeared surprised about how little it now bothered him. When Joan Crawford worked with Gilbert on a gangster melodrama entitled *Four Walls*, he was a completely different person, she said. This time around,

[2]In March of 1928, the newly built St. Francis Dam (part of William Mulholland's ingenious plan to bring a sufficient supply of water to Los Angeles) collapsed, destroying virtually everything in its path from San Francisquito Canyon through the Santa Clarita Valley and on to Ventura. Hundreds of lives were lost.

Crawford witnessed the Jack Gilbert she had always heard about: "vivid, vital and dynamic." No longer tormented, he laughed easier, was less manic, and seemingly more interested in his costar.

On Sundays, Greta could still be found sitting by Jack's pool or tennis court, reading her Swedish newspapers while Herman Mankiewicz entertained the group with humorous discourses on life's absurdities. She rarely contributed to the conversation but often laughed at the jokes. "You don't understand one word. What are you laughing at?" Mankiewicz would tease her. "But I *do*. I *do*," she would protest, barely able to suppress her own laughter as she tried to explain the *dénouement* in fractured English. When she didn't understand the humor, she would ask of her companions, "Come on, I'm one of the boys. Tell me what it means."

Greta had heard appalling things about Moje's current state of health. According to Victor Sjöström, there was "something wrong with his chest" when he left Hollywood. The odds were against him if it was tuberculosis, then the nation's number-one killer. A highly contagious disease, TB had even managed to find its way to moderate climates like southern California.[3] So little was known about tuberculosis; there were many purported treatments or cures, but few successes. In the early stages, the infected rarely showed symptoms that would indicate their affliction; many carried it for years without knowing, and denied it—sometimes hid it—for as long as possible. With no definitive cure or means of prevention, even in the relatively enlightened 1920s the stigma of having tuberculosis was great.

Moje's doctors had begged him not to go back to Sweden. "Go to Davos [Switzerland], to high air," he was told.[4] But his desire to return home was stronger than his desire to get well. He arrived in Stockholm a few days before Christmas, staying with Axel Nilson until they could open up his home on Lidingö. "He was so glad to be home in Sweden again," Nilson recalled. "He found everything wonderful—except his own house, which he thought so much of before leaving for America. He became so unhappy at Bosön that now he was in a miserable mood. 'How dark and deserted it is here—and so cold! Oh, no!' he said. 'I am not going to be happy here.' "

Nilson helped him sell the estate—though Moje was so anxious to get rid of it that he took a loss of 50,000 kronor, half of what he originally paid for the property. The difference would have paid his future medical bills.

---

[3]At the time, Renée Adorée, Mabel Normand, Louella Parsons, and Louis B. Mayer's daughter, Edith, were among the Hollywood citizenry silently battling this disease.

[4]Common treatment for TB, although largely ineffective; the cold, damp air often made patients worse.

Stiller was primarily concerned with his work. He had signed on to direct a theatrical production, the Swedish adaptation of a hit play by George Abbott and Philip Dunning entitled *Broadway*. It would be a challenging, exhausting assignment, but with Gösta Ekman in the lead it was an excellent opportunity for the director to reassert himself.

When he made his dramatic departure from Hollywood, Moje had instructed Greta that she need not think of him, but of course she did. Sometime in early 1928 she wrote him a tender, slightly confused letter full of vague references that obviously demanded a response from him. Moje wrote his reply on the sixth of March; Greta received the letter two and a half weeks later. "Dear very missed Greta!" he wrote in his distinctive longhand. "So bad with this distance and this longing for you and those dreadful years in America. Those are now happily over and never again will be repeated—not for you and not for me.

"But why this letter to me? Was not everything supposed to be forgotten?! Why then do you write like this to me? Why not write plainly!—Your private thoughts and feelings you will not and perhaps cannot express in a letter to me—it is not a confession I am asking of you—but to write to me truthfully—give me some facts!" After reading her rambling letter, Moje professed that he was still in the dark about what she meant to say to him; "I don't know anything." He hastened to add that he wasn't asking about "some sort of forgiveness," though it was unclear who should forgive whom. "That you know very well," he assured her, "you are free and can act as you will—but if you mean something by what you have written me here, you must let me know it. Shall something new sprout from the old? Shall our feeling change skin? Is there going to be spring in our minds? What do you want? I would like to hear that!

"I feel so deeply for you something so unexplainable, wholehearted and holy, and yesterday when I saw you in the first rushes[5] I got so upset because it was you and I cried all night. Why? It is as if you were mine, my child, my love. Every step you take, every feeling you express, brings out unfathomable responses in me; I feel and hurt with you. Is it not the highest ideal we poor mortals could rise up to?! Or maybe my years play me this joke? Because I wanted to get away from you—mostly for your own good—but I cannot, my beloved Greta, not until I know how you feel, how you think . . ."

With a safe distance between them, Moje hoped that Greta would risk sharing her true feelings with him. "It should be easy for you," he urged, "let me know about it!" But then he dropped a bombshell. "If we shall stay together, we must—as I was against before—get married. If not, you don't

---

[5]Presumably of *Gösta Berlings saga*.

need to give me any explanation—I will understand and keep you in my heart forever—but then I want us never to meet again." Once again, he closed his correspondence with paternal instructions. "You shall take good care of yourself, it is in the long run the only right thing to do. I will not write about my illness, because I feel much better and in three or four weeks I am sure the doctors will grow tired of me and by then, my beloved Greta, perhaps you will let me know of your feelings about your Moje. Farewell!"

Tell me that you love me; if you don't, I don't ever want to hear from you again. Not surprisingly, Greta's response is not documented. Two continents separated by a great ocean ensured that she could not make any rash decisions; her commitment to MGM now protected her from that as well. When would she be able to leave? Immediately, if she was willing to give it all up and work exclusively with Stiller in Sweden. But could she?

"Greta Garbo, manless, heroless and hopeless, has waited for two whole weeks until Metro-Goldwyn-Mayer found a leading man to please her," Louella Parsons wrote on the fourth of May. Finally Conrad Nagel's name was mentioned and *War in the Dark* (still the working title for *The Mysterious Lady*) went into production on May 8, 1928. It was an uneventful shoot—though, on occasion, events seemed to conspire otherwise.

Marion Davies' latest film, *The Cardboard Lover,* shared part of the shooting stage with *War in the Dark.* During the first week of production, both Marion Davies and Louella Parsons showed up on Garbo's set hoping to watch her work. Both were "encouraged" to leave in not very subtle ways. The *War in the Dark* set was blocked off by a maze of black flats and screens, but Davies' productions were always open to visitors. The star had seen Greta watching her play a scene with Nils Asther and Jetta Goudal. Thinking she was repaying a compliment, she walked on to Garbo's set in the middle of a scene. It was not a welcome visit; the interruption had broken her concentration. Davies didn't take the hint and left only after Greta was quite blunt with her.

Davies' loyal friend Louella Parsons had "the curious experience of being completely shut off a movie set without a word of explanation" that same week. "Greta was in a temperamental mood. She ordered a screen placed in front of the script girl where I was standing. I stepped to one side. Then she ordered the screen placed in front of the musicians. Again I walked to another side of the room. Finally, the property boy placed a screen directly in front of me."

Both incidents were comparatively minor skirmishes that had no serious repercussions at the studio or in the press. They weren't part of the overall picture. There was a more important task at hand: MGM was building a star. Typical of most of her motion pictures from now on, Greta was needed on the set nearly every day of the thirty-one-day shooting schedule. At the end of each work day, the assistant director filled out a daily production report and turned it in to studio manager J. J. Cohn. Each report indicated how much footage had been shot; where they were in the production schedule, according to Cohn's calculations; and—if they were behind—whom to blame:

> May 8: Waiting for Miss Garbo. Had to have her hair fixed up on account of rain. Rehearsing 10:15.

> May 10: Miss Garbo 30 minutes late on set. [Called for 9:00 A.M.]— Filming in Tania's apartment.

> May 17: Miss Garbo 15 minutes late on set. Rehearsing 9:15—Interior train compartment.

> May 18: Miss Garbo on call. Scene—exterior railroad station.

> May 28: Miss Garbo 40 minutes late on set. Rehearsing 9:45—General's office.

> June 5: Miss Garbo 20 minutes late on set. Rehearsing 9:20—Interior ballroom and interior library.

> June 9: Miss Garbo 40 minutes late—Rowboat scene.

Near the end of principal photography, Metro put out the word that they were looking for a new title and offered a $50 bonus to the writer who came up with one. The winner was *The Mysterious Lady*. Once again, it was an idea that fed into a larger picture: the public's concept of who Greta Garbo was. William Daniels and his crew played an active role in this presentation. As the variables changed—different films, different directors—they were the constants in the equation that she relied on. The cinematographer continued to explore the contours of Garbo's face in *Mysterious Lady*, a veritable classroom on film lighting. She was introduced in silhouette, seen in stark relief next to a bust of Julius Caesar, illuminated by flashes of lightning, then by candlelight; mirrors were also used to great advantage, illustrating Tania's duplicitous nature.

Working toward the same ideal as Daniels, Metro portrait photographer

Ruth Harriet Louise thought her Swedish subject was "a wonderful personality," but as long as they worked together she remained elusive, difficult to photograph. "She has so many sides to her personality that one cannot do her justice . . . She is so young, and so sad; she has so many moods, and even when she smiles I always sense a great sadness." The industry's only major female photographer, Louise also was—perhaps not insignificantly—the only one who was Garbo's age (they were both twenty-two in 1928). She seemed less concerned with contributing to a manufactured image than capturing a real person. To accomplish this, she employed a little-used trick of the trade that allowed her to shoot some of the most open and revealing pictures of Garbo. Everything was photographed in long shot. Louise accomplished her miracles by the skillful way in which she cropped and enlarged; her close-ups emerged in the dark room.

The Mysterious Lady officially completed photography on the thirteenth of June. Nothing of Garbo's performance in the movie would give away the fact that she had only been working in the medium for five years. The difference between *Love* and *The Mysterious Lady* was that the rough edges have been polished. Garbo had arrived.

"Girls ashamed of their femininity are doomed for a final fade-out—cinematically and otherwise," director Fred Niblo stated in an article entitled "Masculinity Menaces Movie Maidens." "Moral courage and determination do not require a masculine outlook," the director proselytized. "Feminine fans, as well as the masculine majority, have little sympathy for the so-called heroine exploiting her boyish figure, mannish bob and usurped masculine ideas. I believe she is turning her own sex against her.

"Miss Garbo told me while we were making [*The Mysterious Lady*] . . . she had the secret ambition to impersonate a man on the screen. Several other feminine favorites secretly yearn to play roles of masculine flourish and force. But they are wise not to attempt this impossibility . . . Women are refreshing in business and in films chiefly for their femininity."

Niblo's argument was indicative of studio thinking, but not necessarily all of Hollywood. On a social level, the creative community was highly aroused by the less inhibited sexuality represented by their foreign artists. Beginning with the late Rudolph Valentino, this group now extended to include people like Ernst Lubitsch, Erich von Stroheim, Pola Negri, Dolores del Rio, Vilma Banky, Josef von Sternberg, and Emil Jannings. With much of the Scandinavian colony now preparing to return home, Garbo would find a peer in Jannings as well as compassion and friendship from his wife. Gussie Jannings was born in Germany, but learned English as a second language; she was not only fluent but articulate and often trans-lated for her husband during meetings with the press. She was small and slender, her blue eyes framed by curly blond hair that was carefully arranged in a stylish bob.

Greta had been introduced to the Jannings by Stiller and, with Moje's disappearance from her horizon, seems to have gravitated toward their rented home on Hollywood Boulevard. "I have some good friends. Mr. and Mrs. Jannings," she told *Photoplay*. "Mrs. Jannings is a real woman. She says what she means. Mr. Jannings is a real man. I do not mean feminine and masculine, as you say it. I mean the inside, deep—real people." As the celebrity world enveloped her, making Garbo's life more unreal, keeping in touch with "real people" would be essential.

Louise Brooks met Greta "one Sunday in the summer of 1928" at the home of Benjamin (Barney) and Alice Glazer. "Apart from the other guests clattering through lunch in the patio, Garbo and I sat with Alice drinking coffee in a little breakfast room," Brooks said. "The subject of the conver-sation, of course, was Alice's and therefore personal. I had divorced Eddie Sutherland in June, and while Alice poked into my private life with ribald questions and the worst possible assumptions, Garbo and I sat laughing and looking at each other. And it was then in that free and happy moment that Garbo seemed to condense, as it were, into a crystal of gracious joy in herself."

Brooks later described Greta's gaze as "so intense and so eloquent that I left after an hour although I had intended to spend the afternoon." She would tell archivist John Kobal that Garbo "made a pass" at her—surpris-ingly, Kobal neglected to follow through on that remark. Brooks privately revealed that she and Greta had spent a night together and that she had found the woman she considered the screen's greatest actress "charming and tender." The spirited young actress, then under contract to Paramount Pictures, would soon find success—and notoriety—abroad when she por-trayed the quintessential flapper, a high-living, fast-burning flame named Lulu in G. W. Pabst's *Pandora's Box*. Louise Brooks easily qualified as one of those in Hollywood who delighted in the sexual experimentation of the era. By her own admission, she was also a "keen gossip" who enjoyed "back-fence tittle-tattle" about the business—but she would not elaborate on her encounter with Greta Garbo.

Of course, Greta had female friends in Hollywood, among them Edith Sjöström, Karin Molander, Gussie Jannings, Alice Glazer, and Irma Stock-lassa. Through Jack Gilbert and his friend Edmund Lowe, she had also become friendly with actress Lilyan Tashman, a fashion leader in Holly-wood society and one of the founders of the Mayfair Club. Still, to Greta's way of thinking, there was no one who provided the unequivocal sustenance and emotional support that Mimi Pollak had when the two were fellow students at Dramatiska Teatern. She seemed torn between needing someone to take Mimi's place—and never wanting anyone to.

Michael Arlen's sensational novel *The Green Hat* was the *Peyton Place* of its time: modern, topical, and packed with sex. Readers identified with its condemnation of sexual (and social) hypocrisy. The story had been adapted for the stage, but Hollywood's moral conscience, Will Hays, didn't believe the revised scenario would make it past regional censors and refused to sanction the sale of the book to the screen. The studios could have circumvented Hays' authority—his power was based solely on their willingness to comply with his judgment—but they chose not to.

In December of 1927, after two years of sporadic negotiations, Hays and Irving Thalberg came to an agreement based on two important alterations: the film's title would be changed to *A Woman of Affairs* (character names would change accordingly); and the note of "impurity" would now revolve around the shame and degradation of someone embezzling money rather than having syphilis.[6] "Even eliminating what is censorable there is material for a great picture and a title of good publicity value," a June 1928 synopsis advocated. Garbo was clearly the first and only consideration for the female lead; she was the only actress who could get the material about a woman who "burns for love" past puritanical censors.

John Gilbert willingly subjugated himself to a supporting role; it didn't take a statistician to figure out that *A Woman of Affairs* was poised for box-office success. Gilbert knew that exhibitors wouldn't be measuring footage, they would be measuring results. In fact, during a script reading, when director Clarence Brown offered to strengthen his role, the actor turned him down. "I'd rather you didn't touch my part a bit," he told Brown. "My character *is* a weak character and he's got to be played that way."

A Woman of Affairs began filming on July 28. Cast opposite the tragic lovers, Garbo and Gilbert, was a trio of up-and-coming young players: John Mack Brown, Dorothy Sebastian, and Douglas Fairbanks, Jr. Both Greta and Jack took a liking to Fairbanks. The actor, then eighteen years old, was just beginning his career in films—much to the disappointment and disapproval of his famous father, who found it difficult

---

[6]In deference to Hays' ban of the story, correspondence between Irving Thalberg and Will Hays suggests that MGM intends to produce a photoplay entitled *A Woman of Affairs* and, because of the strong "resemblance" of its plot to *The Green Hat*, the studio was "obliged" to purchase the Arlen book.

to acknowledge that he had a son old enough to be making his own way.

On the set, Fairbanks played a much larger role than that of Garbo's younger brother. It began with a note Jack asked him to deliver to Greta. They had had another falling out and the atmosphere on the set was decidedly cool. "Here comes John simpering as usual," Garbo was reported saying. Lunch breaks were now spent in her dressing room with Dorothy Sebastian rather than Jack. In another instance of art imitating life—or vice versa—the scenes being filmed during the first two weeks of production were ones in which Diana Merrick and Neville Holderness were estranged. Offstage, Greta and Jack fluctuated between being "together one day, having rows the next . . . and sending notes back and forth when they weren't on speaking terms," Fairbanks remembers. Most of the correspondence seemed to come from Gilbert, who was arguing his case most fervently—without much success.

Garbo also used Fairbanks on occasion. "Greta would write something and say, 'Give this to Jack,' and I'd pass along the note. Then he'd write a little note and say, 'Well, give her this.' They were just lover's quarrels. They would last for about a day or so, and then all would be well again." The actor was under the impression that Gilbert and Garbo were still living together. "Maybe they weren't, but they were pretty chummy anyway. . . . It was definitely an intense love affair."

When the couple was arguing, Fairbanks filled in as Greta's escort outside the studio and took her to several parties at the homes of friends. He found socializing with Garbo an enlightening experience. Outside the stately gates of MGM, he revealed, "She is then, instead of the matured, sophisticated woman of mystery, a young girl of about twenty-three years who has a fresh clear face and is all enthusiasm. At such gatherings when she is among those who she knows well, she is animated and gay. . . . Although professionally her seeming aloofness does not encourage personal popularity, she is loved by her intimate friends." Through Garbo, Douglas Fairbanks Jr. (no stranger to Hollywood society himself) would become acquainted with the remarkably diverse German community, including Emil Jannings, F. W. Murnau, Fritz Lang, Conrad Veidt, and Ernst Lubitsch.

Encouraged that he had ingratiated, perhaps endeared himself to the star, young Fairbanks, in a moment of post-adolescent fantasy, decided to take the relationship one step further. "I remember how my deceitful heart bubbled when for a few days I thought I was well on the way to an underhanded conquest," he wrote in his autobiography. As the crew arranged the next shot, Fairbanks lured an unsuspecting Garbo into a dark corner of the stage, ostensibly to pass on a secret message from Jack. Once there, he lost his nerve and mumbled a nonsensical, rambling message that thoroughly confused his leading lady. Perhaps she suspected more than the aspiring young suitor knew, for Greta soon changed the subject to the rumors of a romance between Fairbanks and "that nice Joan Crawford." He had been put in his place without ever knowing whether she was wise to his game.

"I always found Miss G to be a happy person," Fairbanks states for the record. "Easy to laugh. Easy to get a joke. She was basically a very normal person. Charming . . . friendly . . . sincere. A talented Swedish girl who had been well-trained for her profession and wasn't an exaggerated exhibitionist."

The Mysterious Lady opened nationwide on the very day work began on the new picture. It would be the first of Garbo's films to employ a sound-effects track and a synchronized musical score. Critics, while acknowledging that the film was little more than a nicely photographed program feature—with an extraordinary star—were primarily concerned with talking pictures, then known as "talkers"; the absence of "that Gilbert man;" and the emerging Garbo "look." The fascinating duality of her cool exterior concealing a troubled, tempestuous soul appealed to moviegoers, especially in the urban areas. That Greta Garbo's cross to bear was her physical beauty—it brought her characters little happiness, only torment—made the struggle all the more intriguing. "The film presents encouraging evidence to prove that Miss Garbo can enact something besides fervid love scenes," Edwin Schallert wrote in the *Los Angeles Times*. "Her performance as the Czar's spy is really quite excellent, and as usual she radiates an uncanny magnetism every instant that she is on the screen."

August 1928. "Snapshots of Hollywood collected at random: Charlie Chaplin, Jack Gilbert, Buster Keaton, Harold Lloyd, Irving Thalberg and Fred Thomson gathered in a single group discussing the talkies." Even at this late date, industry executives optimistically predicted that silent films were not finished; 50 percent of motion picture production would remain in the silent arena. Chaplin, Gilbert, Keaton, and company weren't so sure. Studio rhetoric to the contrary, executives appeared to be hedging their bets.

During the first week in August, Garbo would be the subject of another camera's focus: that of renowned New York portrait photographer Edward Steichen. The photographer was in Hollywood to shoot pictures for *Vanity Fair*. Steichen watched her work through a crack between the flats surrounding the set. "The director was explaining to her some detail of action that he wanted.[7] It was a simple thing. . . ," he remarked. "She did it again and again, while the director, not satisfied, continually tried to explain. Finally she said, 'I think I'll go away for a while.' Going away meant going off the set and sitting on a chair while her maid put two screens around her." After some time, Garbo emerged from her cubicle and rehearsed the scene once more. Clarence Brown gave her the go-ahead and they shot the scene to everyone's satisfaction.

Steichen was given five minutes to get his photograph while the crew prepared the next camera setup. Garbo entered his work area and the photographer offered a chair. "She straddled it and used its back for resting her arms. I made five or six exposures, all more or less like her typical movie stills . . . but what bothered me most was her hair. It was curled and fluffy and hung down over her forehead. I said, 'It's too bad we're doing this with that movie hairdo.' At that, she put her hands up to her forehead and pushed every strand of hair back away from her face, saying, 'Oh, this terrible hair.' At that moment, the *woman* came out, like the sun coming out from behind dark clouds." Steichen remembered her scowling when she heard Clarence Brown beckoning her to the set. "Then she dashed up to me and put her arms around me saying, 'Oh you, you should be a motion picture director. You understand.' "

Neither temperamental nor dictatorial, Brown had an ongoing relationship with Greta Garbo that evolved principally from passivity rather than true empathy. Traditionally labeled Garbo's "favorite" director, he was simply her most frequent director because he was quiet, respectful, and didn't get in the way. Stylistically, Brown usually set the mechanics of a scene with a precision worthy of his background as an engineer—and left the discovery process to his actors. He was fond of telling people that he had to whisper directions to Garbo in deference to her well-known shyness (though this seems to have been his manner with everyone). Douglas Fairbanks, Jr. describes Brown as "very easygoing, soft spoken . . . He directed by the subtlest of suggestions. He never demanded, he just kept going until we got it right." Independent of a strong, opinionated director to challenge her, Garbo, with a few notable exceptions, would become a largely self-directed actress.

Fairbanks' most vivid recollection of Garbo was of the "shocking" amount of coffee she drank throughout the day, an attempt to keep her energy up and her weight down. Scarcely three weeks into production, she

[7]Most probably, the scene in the Deauville hotel room when Garbo, dressed in black, walks to the window and slowly focuses her gaze on arboretum below (where her husband had jumped to his death earlier).

was sent home by her director; Brown would report to the front office that Greta had been too ill to perform. Two days later, the studio sent out one of their doctors, Dr. Edward Jones, to examine her. The production crew was given a long weekend off, reassembling on Monday, August 20.

Once again, in a curious parallel, the big scene they were to film that week was the nursing home scene in which the emotionally distraught heroine confronts her former lover and his wife. The sequence begins with a semiconscious Diana in a French nursing home; she has recently suffered a miscarriage (which is only alluded to in the titles). In a profoundly moving sequence, she emerges from her hospital room in a delirious frenzy; her roses are missing. She spots them at the end of the hall—but does not see Neville, only the symbol of their love. With singular clarity, Garbo invests a passive object with a power representing, first, her memory and then her redemption. A myriad of emotions flashes across her face as she walks toward the flowers, takes them from the vase, and embraces them as she would a lover.

It is a "majestic transformation," critic Richard Corliss affirmed. Nothing less than a solo aria that takes Garbo's performance "from acting to being, from pulp to poetry. . . . Something beautiful has been created out of almost nothing . . ." The key was her extraordinary ability to focus emotional energy. "Garbo is often called a 'pallid anemic' type," William Daniels stated, "which is more than amusing to those of us who watch her work constantly. She uses up tremendous energy before the camera. I think the stage crew would collapse from exhaustion long before she would tire herself out, once she gets going in a dramatic sequence." The scene would be hailed as an eloquent culmination of Greta Garbo's silent film career.

John Mack Brown thought that Greta probably enjoyed the location days most of all. The former college football star who played a small part in *The Divine Woman* had a better opportunity to interact with Greta during *A Woman of Affairs*. "But even then our acquaintance was quite formal," he said. "She would sit around for a few minutes, talking or exchanging wisecracks with members of the cast, but all of a sudden I would look up and find that she had slipped out unnoticed. At first I thought she was shy or didn't like our company. Later, when I heard her tell of the beautiful drive she took or 'how green the sea looked yesterday' I realized that Greta Garbo was a dreamer—she must have felt very cramped there in the studio. She would stay and be sociable as long as she could stand it, and then suddenly disappear."

She dreamed of an escape. "I am presently working like mad on a new film," she wrote to Lars Saxon in August. "Immediately afterwards I am leaving the 'factory'—with or without permission." Greta had promised her mother that she was coming home, and she intended to keep that pledge. By the time *A Woman of Affairs* wrapped on the eleventh of September, Harry Edington had negotiated a deal on her behalf: If Greta completed one more feature before Christmas, she could return to Sweden for a visit. She did not make one film—she finished two.

The first was a simple cameo appearance that appears to have been shot in early October after Jack Gilbert returned from New York.[8] The film was a romantic drama starring William Haines and Josephine Dunn entitled *A Man's Man*. The scenario is worth noting because it is early evidence of Garbo's hypnotic effect on movie audiences. Remarkably, the story revolves around a young woman who imagines that she looks like Greta Garbo, and the man who fights to protect her from predators.

A group of fans waits outside Grauman's Chinese Theatre for a glimpse of Garbo and Gilbert. A movie premiere is in progress. The crowd goes wild when the couple finally arrives in a limousine together. "And here comes Greta Garbo . . . with John Gilbert!" Fred Niblo announces to radio listeners. Niblo greets the couple and brings Garbo up to the microphone. "Hello, everybody!" her title card reads. "I'm very happy to speak to my friends of radioland—" Peggy, the naïve heroine played by Josephine Dunn, is ecstatic; she is so close to Garbo she can almost touch her. The would-be actress sneaks under the ropes separating the crowd and approaches John Gilbert. When Greta walks back to Jack, Peggy extends her hand and Garbo takes it. The fans surge forward. Later on, Peggy tells her boyfriend (William Haines), "This has been the most perfect day of my life. Because I met Greta Garbo and John Gilbert."

Earlier treatments of the story had always put Gilbert's name first; the fans had come to see him and Greta Garbo was a bonus. By the time the film was released in 1929, Garbo took precedence.

As 1928 faded, the Gilbert-Garbo affair shifted from romance to friendship. The couple spent another weekend at San Simeon and were later spotted with Edmund Lowe and Lilyan Tashman cheering on the USC football team. But Greta was just as likely to be seen around town lunching with Nils Asther at the Roosevelt Hotel, shopping with Lilyan Tashman at Howard Greer's Sunset Boulevard salon, or sunning herself on the beach near Bebe Daniels' home. "The rumors of Miss Garbo's engagement to

---

[8]Gilbert and H. E. Edington had been in discussion with both Joseph and Nicholas Schenck, representing United Artists and Loew's Inc. respectively, regarding a new multi-million-dollar contract.

John Gilbert seem to have died a natural death," Louella Parsons reported. "One sees them together, but there is no longer any talk of marriage."

Near the end of October, the Sjöströms left Hollywood to share a real Swedish Christmas with their children. Greta made excited preparations for returning home, renewing her passport at the Swedish consulate in San Francisco, purchasing a new wardrobe (some would say trousseau) and an assortment of gifts. Whenever she saw something that struck her fancy, she would nudge her companion of the moment. "That is going back to Sweden," she would say.

Wild Orchids began as a story John Colton had written for Lillian Gish entitled *Heat;* it depicted a modern love triangle set in an exotic land: the steamy jungles of Java. Garbo's readiness to do another picture as soon as possible—even as she was being called for retakes on *A Woman of Affairs*— put *Heat* into her court.[9] Production commenced on the twenty-second of October, with director Sidney Franklin at the helm. The venerable Lewis Stone was cast as Garbo's husband, an older man who is oblivious to his wife's declarations of love; Nils Asther would essay the sadistic, womanizing Javanese prince who recognizes—and soon preys upon—the vulnerability of his young guest.

It was a casual, seemingly uninspired set. Garbo and Asther were frequently late. On the seventh of November, Greta received a disheartening wire from Edith and Victor Sjöström: "YOUR MESSAGE MADE MOJE HAPPY. HE SENDS LOVE. HIS CONDITION HOWEVER ABSOLUTELY HOPELESS DEAR GRETA. SEEMINGLY ONLY QUESTION OF FEW DAYS. NOW BECOMING MOSTLY UNCONSCIOUS—NO PAIN, LUNG TROUBLE. EVERYTHING POSSIBLE BEING DONE FOR HIM. MUCH LOVE, EDITH VICTOR"

Moje's friend Alma Söderhjelm later revealed that she thought Stiller regretted never marrying; he would have liked to have had children and a family life. That was not to be. According to Bengt Idestam-Almquist, Moje's medical problems included fluid in both lungs, poor circulation, and a skin disease akin to elephantiasis which had taken a turn for the worse. The skin condition was sometimes so painful he couldn't even bear to wear clothes. Unfortunately, a definitive answer to questions about his health cannot be ascertained, because Stiller's medical records have been misplaced in the labyrinthine maze of the municipal archives in Stockholm. These symptoms could also apply to a tubercular condition; TB is commonly associated with the lungs, but the disease can also attack the

---

[9]The studio soon realized that "Greta Garbo in *Heat*" would not be an acceptable banner for theater marquees. The film was retitled *Wild Orchids.*

skin, larynx, bones, joints, lymph nodes, and certain organs. Whatever Moje's affliction, the disease was considerably advanced.

The night that his production of *Broadway* premiered in Stockholm (April 28, 1928), Stiller was too excited to sleep. After a gala opening-night party at Oscars Teatern, Moje walked exuberantly around Djurgården with his friend Olof Andersson. He was so happy, Andersson said, he constantly seemed on the verge of tears. When morning arrived, they encountered a friend who was on her way out to buy a newspaper; Moje gave her an emotional hug. Finally, he got the courage to read the notices and learned that Stockholm had warmly welcomed him home. It was a gesture of confidence that the director had badly needed.

After the premiere, however, he no longer seemed to be making grand plans. Almquist reported that Stiller had thrown his back out and was confined to bed. Moje preferred to treat the problem with massage; he didn't believe doctors that he was only aggravating his condition due to the congestion in his lungs. By the time he agreed to see a specialist, it was too late. Stiller's lawyer, Hugo Lindberg, recalled taking an evening constitutional with him that fall. "When we were out in the night air, Stiller began coughing very badly. 'You can't go on like this,' I told him. 'Something must be done.' But he just passed it off. He said he'd be all right and started talking about something else. Three days later he collapsed and was taken to the Red Cross hospital." He was admitted in Röda Korsets Sjukhus on October 2.

Throughout the next month, Stiller was operated on several times by a Dr. Söderlund, who reportedly removed thirteen ribs to relieve the pressure on his chest after an opportunistic infection attacked the lining around his lungs. "He was a fine patient and took his pain as one believes a real man should," the doctor noted. Further operations were ruled out because they were too traumatic for the patient; by this time, the forty-five-year-old Stiller could only tolerate a local anesthetic. Yet through it all, Moje was surprisingly cheerful. His friends recalled with fondness that the Red Cross nurses all adored him. Concerned about his welfare, the staff tried to get him to write his will, but he refused to recognize the possibility that he might die.

By the time the Sjöströms had arrived in Stockholm, Moje's condition was considered grave. "When we passed London I heard that Stiller was ill but was not told it was anything serious," Victor Sjöström recorded. "Upon my arrival in Stockholm I went immediately to the hospital to see him. The moment I entered the room I saw a man marked by death. What a home-coming. What a reunion. . . . [Moje] had been expecting me impatiently. He cried like a child when he saw me, and I had to exert myself to the utmost degree to control myself. We had a long talk—he did most of the talking—we even drank champagne in small sherry glasses . . . and when I left him that day he was cheerful and in good spirits."

The director surrounded himself with memories; prominent among them: an Arnold Genthe portrait of Garbo that decorated his nightstand. Toward the end, he only allowed visits from Sjöström and Alma Söderhjelm. Sjöström visited daily, watching helplessly as his friend, once so robust and full of life, got weaker. One day, after returning from a visit lasting several hours, Sjöström received a call from one of the nurses; Moje had something very important to tell him. Thinking Stiller was ready to discuss his will, Sjöström hurried back to hospital—but Moje had long forgotten why he had been summoned. Both were quiet for some time. When Stiller spoke, he talked about how soft his undershirt was, how long he'd had it, and about a pair of skates that he hardly ever used and was anxious to try.

Sjöström took his hand. "The nurse said that you had something to tell me?" "Yes, yes . . . I will tell you in a minute," Moje responded before falling asleep. He awoke suddenly, again recalling "trivial, meaningless things," and lapsed in and out of consciousness until a nurse finally told Sjöström he must leave. Stiller suddenly became agitated and grabbed his friend's arm. "No, no. I haven't told him what I must tell him!" He had remembered his "grand idea." "The nurse separated us and pushed me toward the door. I tried to quiet and comfort him, saying that he could tell me tomorrow. But he got more and more desperate, his face was wet with tears."

"Tomorrow, Moje. I'll be back tomorrow," Sjöström promised. "No, no, no. It must be now. There will never be any tomorrow." Sjöström left his friend sobbing in the arms of the nurse. Tragically, it was to be their final conversation. The following day, Moje was too weak to talk. "I put my ear close to his mouth [but] I could not make out what he said. And I don't know if he understood what I said. He only kept staring at me." That evening, Stiller fell into a coma; he never regained consciousness. The Sjöströms, who had promised to let Greta know what was going on, wired her the news.

On Thursday, the eighth of November, Garbo was preparing for a scene in *Wild Orchids* in which Prince de Gace shows the Sterlings his palace. A postal telegram was delivered to her dressing room just as Greta was due to begin work. "MOJE PASSED AWAY LAST NIGHT QUIETLY AND CALMLY. LOVE TO YOU, EDITH VICTOR". The cause of death, according to an Associated Press report, was infective pleurisy.

Back on the set, the assistant director's production report stated, the cast and crew rehearsed the scene without Miss Garbo, "who did not arrive on set until 9:55, but she did not hold company up as they shot a dissolve without her." Although no one knew the reason for her tardiness, it would be one of the few times anyone at MGM bothered to make an excuse for her. Crew members recalled Garbo walking on the set dressed in an Oriental costume (for a later scene). She stood in front of a full-length mirror on the side of the set; people assumed she was checking out her costume and makeup. Suddenly, she turned "deathly pale." Concerned members of the crew, sure she was about to faint, rushed to her side. Greta waved them away. "She pressed her hands to her eyes, walked slowly across the set, and stood there for several minutes. Then, her composure regained, she returned and went on with the scene. She gave no explanation." Only later in the day would a property man find a crumbled telegram on the floor informing Garbo of Mauritz Stiller's death.[10]

One thing Greta Garbo would reproach Mimi Pollak for "throughout all these years—that I wasn't the one who told her that Stiller was dead. She took his death incredibly hard," Mimi said. Greta would be unable to speak about Moje's death—even to friends—only referring to her friend and mentor indirectly as "someone I have a great devotion for—and always will."

---

[10]If this story is accurate, the wire could not have been Sjöström's—which remains carefully preserved and uncrumpled to this day. Other reports have Greta reading the telegram on the set. Max Sarnoff, then a nineteen-year-old office boy, claims to have delivered it. Though his memory does not jive with the production schedule (his recollection is that they were filming the scene at the Java inn, not at the prince's palace), Sarnoff says that Greta got very quiet when he gave her the wire. She sat down with a sad look on her face, but never walked off the set as often reported.

CHAPTER TEN

Femme Fatale

It was probably the blackest day of Greta Garbo's life—more traumatic than the deaths of her father or sister, because Greta bore some of the guilt of Mauritz Stiller's painful and humiliating decline. Years later, she would tell Cecil Beaton that in her youth she had been "ready very early for life," but since that time her character had matured very little. "Suddenly, she found herself no longer a promising youngster," Beaton said. Moje's death was a defining moment for her, and the reverberations would be felt for years to come.

"You shall be saved from all evil, sleep without the pain of guilt," Stiller had written her in November of 1927, only one year earlier. "Life is terrible, but it's not going to be for you." Moje had foreseen an incredible future for Garbo. Before leaving Hollywood, he saw that the attendant celebrity and financial rewards of success were already hers. But it was wishful thinking that such an achievement would be enough to gratify or nourish her— Greta knew the cost of her Hollywood triumph to be someone else's happiness and success.

"You are free!" Moje had assured her. "As you have always been." But she had never been free emotionally. Though the choreography of events had not been of her making, Greta could still find fault in herself for failing the most important commitment of her life. "If I were to love anyone, it would be Mauritz Stiller," she once told Axel Nilson. Future commitments would be fraught with difficulty.

"You shall not think about me," Stiller instructed her. "You don't even have to repeat 'poor Moje' every time we meet." Poor Moje—unappreciated, ahead of his time, but his dreams never died. He would not be forgotten; Greta Garbo would privately honor his memory for the rest of her life.

A solemn Nils Asther walked back to his dressing room at the end of an emotionally exhausting day and was surprised to hear laughter coming from Garbo's quarters. An attempt to pass by unobtrusively was interrupted as Greta flung open her dressing room door. "I have something to show you, Nils," she said, inviting him in. "She was still trembling, but suddenly she laughed, holding a small perfume bottle in one hand. The tiny bottle was half-filled with brandy. Attached to it was a note from Louis B.

Mayer, saying, 'Dear Greta, my sympathy in your sorrow. But the show must go on!' "

The gesture, well-meaning in its intent but heartbreakingly conservative in scope, was a clear indication of Mayer's real concern: business. Hollywood barely acknowledged Stiller's passing. There was a brief obituary in *Variety*, nothing like the special memorial issue that had honored MGM founder Marcus Loew the previous September. At that time, Greta Garbo had fallen in line with other Metro stars and signed a half-page ad in memory of a man she hardly knew. There would be no reciprocation. For Moje, there had been a tiny flask of contraband whiskey.

The irony was not lost on Greta. "After Moje died, I could not sleep or eat or work," she told a close friend. "For me it was a time that was very black." She wanted to return to Sweden immediately and asked to be released from *Wild Orchids*. She had begun work three weeks earlier in such a state of excitement about going home that she admitted her mind had not been on acting; she now argued that she had neither the energy nor the motivation to maintain a consistent performance. Her grief had effectively compromised an essential component of her acting: her concentration. Greta warned the studio hierarchy that they would have "something dead on the screen. It will have no life." No one cared. "You must be faithful to us and to your work," she was told. Production continued on the Friday *and* Saturday following Stiller's death—contrary to previously published accounts, Garbo was occasionally tardy, but never missed a day of work.

Mauritz Stiller was interred at Judiska Församling Begravningsplats, a Jewish cemetery on the north side of Stockholm within walking distance of the Filmstaden at Råsunda. The funeral service was a memorable occasion attended by dear friends and colleagues. A string quartet from China-Teatern played some of Moje's favorite music, including "Suomis Sång" (Finland's Song); Alma Söderhjelm honored him with a poem. Victor Sjöström fought back tears as he gave an eloquent eulogy. "No one knew who you were," he said in a moving conclusion, "not even me."

The Swedish film industry was profoundly affected by Stiller's passing. After the release of *Gösta Berlings saga*, Stiller's final Filmindustri production, the once-spirited Swedish cinema entered a barren period highlighted only by the work of Gustaf Molander and Alf Sjöberg in the 1930s and 1940s. Victor Sjöström lost heart and worked only sporadically, primarily as an actor. Complacency and the loss of three principal players shook the very foundations of Svensk Filmindustri. Not until Ingmar Bergman's emergence in the late 1940s did SF begin to regain its footing and embrace a new cinematic vision.

"There were whispers that if Greta Garbo went to Sweden for Christmas she would remain and make a picture for Mauritz Stiller," Louella Parsons wrote on November 25, two days after Greta finished work on *Wild Orchids*. "Now the death of the Swedish director has changed any possibility of Miss Garbo's remaining in Europe. . . . she will only remain a few weeks." The columnist, who rarely had a kind word for Stiller when he was alive, now described the director as "an unselfish person . . . and a good friend to those who knew him."

Studio executives weren't entirely sure Garbo would return after the holidays. In a final, possibly unintended challenge, Irving Thalberg scheduled *Wild Orchids* retakes for Monday, December 3—the day after Greta had arranged to leave for New York. Would she stick to her schedule or comply with the studio's wishes? The answer was contained in an urgent cable delivered to the *Santa Fe Chief*, Train 20, Car 206, Drawing Room A: "THERE IS STILL TIME FOR YOU TO RETURN TO CULVER CITY . . . AND MAKE SWEDEN IN TIME FOR CHRISTMAS. RETURN OR GREAT LOSS AND DAMAGE WILL BE CAUSED US. LOUIS B. MAYER." On the fifth of December, Greta Garbo was again suspended. It did not matter. She was going home.

The *Chief* was the main rail connection between Los Angeles and Chicago, traversing eight states in two and a half days on its journey eastward. It was a route Garbo would come to know well. Indicative of her future routine, she out-maneuvered journalists by leaving Hollywood earlier than expected. Traveling under the name of Alice Smith, she got on— alone—at the Pasadena station wearing a disguise of black wig, floppy hat, and dark glasses, and remained in her first-class compartment for the entire journey east.

In Chicago, it was necessary to change stations in order to catch the *20th Century Limited* to New York. The switch almost proved to be Greta's undoing: she was recognized by a studio employee, who promptly tipped off the local press. Garbo managed to avoid a confrontation, slipping by reporters and boarding the next train without a fuss. Not to be outdone, the New York newspapers sent journalists to Grand Central Station to meet her train. Once again, Greta anticipated their reaction and disembarked at Croton-Harmon, a stop approximately one hour outside the city, then disappeared. Anxious cub reporters checked all of the city's well-appointed, luxury hotels—Greta Garbo was not to be found.

Greta had been met by Joseph Buhler and stayed overnight at his home in Greenwich, Connecticut, before venturing into the city. Sentiment weighed in on her choice of hotels: she spent her final night in the United States at the Commodore, where she and Moje had been sequestered during the summer of 1925. It was the first of many times during the trip she would attempt to reconnect with the past.

The SS *Kungsholm*, the newest steamship in the Swedish-American fleet, was moored in its berth near Fifty-seventh Street. The liner was set to complete its maiden voyage between New York City and Göteborg, weather permitting. Forecasts of the first snowstorm of the season did not dissuade its impressive list of VIPs from boarding the boat on the morning of December 8, 1928. Among the sailing Swedish aristocracy were two sons of the Crown Prince, Gustav Adolf and Sigvard; Count and Countess Carl Bernadotte, cousins of King Gustav V; Count and Countess Wacht-meister; and Baron and Baroness von Platen. All had just attended the Long Island wedding of Count Folke Bernadotte to an American woman. With society columnists focused on the royal party, "Alice Smith" was eas-ily secreted on board without attracting attention—and would have escaped unnoticed if it hadn't been for an enterprising journalist who stole on to the ship the previous evening.

Congested traffic in the windswept harbor delayed the *Kungsholm*'s departure by nearly four hours. Once at sea, the storm generated waves large enough to crash with some force across the front deck, slowing the liner down further and keeping many of the passengers in their cabins. But holiday cheer and the news of friends on board quickly brought Greta out of seclusion. Mimi Pollak had written to let her know that Nils and Märtha Wachtmeister were acquaintances of hers; Count Wachtmeister was a royal equerry and owned one of the oldest estates in Sweden. Greta also discovered that an old acquaintance was on the *Kungsholm*.

Lasse Ring had sent his card through a steward with a note offering his services. "Miss Garbo only wants to sleep," he was informed—but the next day, she was out on the main deck walking the promenade. "Good morn-ing, Captain Ring," she said. The man who had given Greta her first break in films soon learned that she had no interest in pursuing the phantom images of their common past; they spoke instead of Swedish films and the advent of sound.

At lunchtime, Ring accompanied Greta to the captain's table. The large dining room had been decorated with Christmas trees and festive orna-ments; a small orchestra played traditional holiday music while Swedish delicacies were served to guests. Suddenly, the veil lifted and Greta became a bright and cheerful companion, charming guests with her ani-mation and good humor. Asked by a crew member if there was anything she needed, she responded without hesitation, "Slightly better weather."

Garbo captivated an attentive audience, turning what up till then had been a shaky crossing into an unforgettable one. Prince Sigvard was clearly taken with her, as was Countess Wachtmeister (known to all her friends as Hörke). On evenings when she didn't eat in her cabin, Greta often dined and danced with the twenty-one-year-old prince. Sigvard was a direct descendant of Jean Baptiste Bernadotte, and third in line for the throne after his father and elder brother.[1] Royalty notwithstanding, Greta appears to have spent her fondest afternoons in the company of Hörke Wachtmeister. The countess was ten years her senior, but a kindred spirit nonetheless. An unpretentious woman who enjoyed a variety of physical activities, she like Greta relied on walking the promenade as an alternative to a normally vigorous routine. Over the course of the twelve-day crossing, a genuine relationship developed between the two women. It would be the most important friendship Greta had encouraged since that with Mimi Pollak.

Bad weather postponed the *Kungsholm*'s arrival in Swedish waters by almost two days. At last, on the nineteenth of December, the ship maneuvered through the straits between Denmark and Sweden and passengers saw land emerging from the mist. Soon, an island lighthouse pointed the way into the grayish-green waters of Göteborg Harbor. Greta put her handkerchief to her mouth and yelled triumphantly. A pilot boat brought the press out to meet her. This time, she patiently awaited them in the ship's library and politely answered questions until the liner neared its berth. "Yes. I am glad to be back, but not, as you may imagine, because I hate Hollywood. People say so many silly things about Hollywood," she said. "Let me tell you there are just as many temptations in Stockholm as there are over there. In Hollywood one is far too busy to be wicked! I have had to work harder than most, and I am very tired now. I have come home to rest."

Far too excited to remain inside, an "unspeakably happy" Garbo rushed back to the main deck. On the Svensk-Amerika docks, a military band was playing the Swedish anthem, "Du gamla du fria" (You old, you free). Greta waved her handkerchief, singing and cheering along with everyone else.

A crowd of several thousand people had gathered to observe the ship's arrival. Mimi Pollak and Nils Lundell were Greta's private welcoming committee. There was a formal one, as well. Variety performer Karl-Gerhard, a former Dramaten classmate, was among those chosen to welcome Garbo home. A full corps of security guards was needed to get her party through the crowd and into a waiting taxi—which was beset with admirers

---

[1]Bernadotte, one of Napoleon's most trusted commanders, gave up his French citizenship in order to ascend the Swedish throne as Karl XIV Johan.

jumping on the running boards and flinging themselves across the cab. One of the taxi's windows broke as they continued to press against the car. The receipt for damages read: "A hearty reception in Göteborg: 132.75 kronor—broken glass and dented wings."

Greta was overwhelmed by the homecoming. After a hectic pursuit by the crowd, she elected to stay overnight in Göteborg's Grand Hôtel rather than taking the train to Stockholm. Greta and Mimi stayed up and talked through most of the night. The next morning, they were awakened by the joyous sound of Christmas carols: Karl-Gerhard had dressed up as St. Lucia in the traditional white robe and festive headdress of lingonberry wreath adorned with lit candles. Now she knew she was home.

All along the train route, sightseers gathered to catch a glimpse of "the idol of the hour." Much to Greta's disappointment, a small army of reporters and photographers stayed close to her for the entire six-hour journey across Sweden. A witness to this chaotic scene noted that Garbo was now considered an *international* star—and "fair game." Each time her compartment door was opened, a picture was taken. Finally, it became too much to bear. "Man, think of my feelings!" she blurted out in frustration as another flashbulb went off.

Anna and Sven Gustafson met the train in Södertalje, less than an hour outside of Stockholm. Greta's immense pleasure in seeing her family outweighed any concerns about privacy; she hugged both hungrily on the station platform as the photographers snapped away. She had expected to drive the rest of the way into the city with Lars Saxon, but due to the extreme cold everyone now advised her against it. The group reassembled in the dining room car, posing for newspaper photographers, toasting family and friends—and the prospect of Greta's first Christmas at home in five years—with Swedish spirits.

"When I saw [Stockholm] for the first time in the early dusk of the winter afternoon, with all of its lights shining from a thousand windows, I could have cried—it was so beautiful," she reminisced. So much was different and yet nothing had really changed. A jubilant gathering similar to the one in Göteborg now awaited her at Central Stationen. More waving and more cheers—and more pushing as admirers surged forward. Before she got into a waiting car, Greta turned around and addressed the crowd. "Long live Sweden!" she proclaimed. Then, as she had done in New York, she disappeared into the city.

The press camped out at her mother's apartment would not find Garbo there. She leased a private apartment on Stockholm's quiet north side. The Gustafson residence at Blekingegatan 32 was no longer. Although parish records indicate that the family did not register their move until 1931, a city directory from 1928 suggests that Anna Lovisa had moved to a new apartment much earlier. After months of Greta and Sven trying to convince their mother she could afford a better place and that she wouldn't have to move away from her friends or the neighborhood that had been her home, Sven found her a nice one-bedroom apartment with a large kitchen at Ringvägen 155, a few blocks from Blekingegatan.

Greta's decision to find her own accommodations was a practical one, as she valued privacy over the pampering of a first-class establishment such as the luxurious Grand Hôtel. The modest apartment at Karlsbergsvägen 52 featured a studio living room, a kitchenette with a small gas stove, and a balcony overlooking a nearby park. It had all the amenities for someone who required few to make her happy, and what she wanted to do most of all was rest.

It would be a bittersweet Christmas reunion for the Gustafsons. Greta had arrived too late to participate in the joyous Festival of Lights or the annual celebration for the Nobel presentations.[2] Instead, the holidays reinforced sorrowful memories of everything she had lost in recent years. Returning home made those losses real. In Sweden, family members traditionally leave a "token of memory" at the graves of loved ones on Christmas Eve. But since reporters had no trouble following her to her "secret" apartment, tracing her phone number, or keeping track of everywhere she went around town, Greta was hesitant to do so. She decided to pay her respects at another time. On Christmas Day, however, Greta did allow herself to enjoy the privileges of her celebrity. According to Vera Schmiterlöw, both were guests of honor at a dinner given by Julius Grönlund at the Strand Hôtel.

Greta would admit to confidants that she was somewhat bewildered by all the changes that had occurred since she had last been in Stockholm. After the holidays, she arranged for a private screening of one of Alva's films.[3] There was little solace to be found in the fact that Garbo was now a year older than Alva had been when she died. She sat alone in the darkness—only the merciful clatter of the film projector would drown out her tears as she said good-bye to a loved one.

Vera Schmiterlöw recalled another incident in which Greta was bitterly

---

[2] A proud evening for most Swedes often accompanied by fireworks and late-night revelry. In 1928, the prize for literature was awarded to the popular Norwegian author Sigrid Undset.

[3] Variously identified as *En lyckoriddare*, the picture she appeared in with her sister, Alva, (as extras), or *Två konungar* (*Two Kings*); Alva had a featured role in the latter and made the film in Greta's absence.

reminded of Alva's suffering. Walking down a Stockholm boulevard with Mimi Pollak, she suddenly pulled down the brim of her hat. "I don't want to see that man walking over there," she said, motioning across the street. "He was the one who was courting Alva and hit her so hard on the chest it made her ill."

It was a disquieting time. If friends noticed any change in Greta, it was not her restlessness that stirred them but rather her relentless intensity. She smoked one cigarette after another, was alternately high-spirited or withdrawn, and, despite her exhaustion, was too anxious to sleep. She tried both conventional and non-conventional remedies for insomnia; the only thing that seemed to work was the comfort of friends—according to at least one source, female friends. After a hot bath or nightcap, an intimate revealed, she would "throw herself on the couch, weeping and bemoaning her tired state. With her head cushioned at last on the other woman's lap she would gradually calm down and slumber would steal over her. . . . This nightly ordeal went on for weeks."

Most painful of all were the memories of Moje. Gösta Ekman offered Garbo his box at Oscars Teatern so she could see Stiller's production of *Broadway*. Though one report had Stiller bequeathing one-half of his estate to "my ever-beloved Greta Garbo," in fact, no legal document had been produced. In the absence of a last will and testament, Swedish law stated, only family members would have inherited Stiller's estate (after his creditors had been paid).[4]

Hugo Lindberg, Stiller's lawyer and executor, received a call from Greta asking for permission to view Moje's personal belongings before they were sold. Lindberg escorted her to the storage facility. "I remember vividly how she walked about the room, touching this item and that," the attorney said. "She seemed very moved and talked about Moje in a hushed voice, almost a whisper. 'This was the suitcase he took to America,' she said, picking up the bag. 'And these rugs—I remember when he bought them in Turkey.' " The attorney never forgot that sober winter afternoon as Greta wandered around what remained of Moje's furniture and paintings making "sad little comments" about what it all meant to her.

Equally difficult to forget was what happened when Garbo was recognized by people on the street. Both she and Lindberg increased their pace

---

[4]The actual cash value of Stiller's estate was estimated between 400,000 and 626,000 kronor, with the larger percentage of Stiller's monies deposited in California bank accounts. Svensk Filmindustri claimed all of their former director's Swedish funds, and much of his American ones, due to previous debts. His brothers and sister divided the remainder of Moje's American savings.

as the crowd began to grow. "Finally it got to be enormous and we were practically running," he recalled. "When we were back in my office at last, Greta was very upset and nervous and seemed almost on the verge of tears. She sat down in a chair, took off her hat, and threw it on the floor. 'People are mad!' she exclaimed."

Before leaving the office, she asked for directions to Stiller's grave. This time, she wanted to go alone. On the first day, she bought a flower arrangement in the shape of a cross and placed it beneath the granite headstone. "The next day when I visited the grave again someone had torn the arrangement apart and thrown the flowers all over the place." Wounded by what she perceived to be a desecration of the gravesite, Greta turned to a bystander and questioned why this might have been done. The stranger patiently explained "what I in my ignorance had not understood—that the cross is a Christian symbol that has no place in Jewish life."

Moje's younger brother, Abraham, met Garbo for the first time in 1929. They were to become "good friends," according to Stiller. For nearly fifty years, journalists made the pilgrimage to Stiller's home in Helsinki to pose a key question: What was his brother's relationship with Greta Garbo? "I can only judge by what Greta said to me when we met shortly after Moje's death," Abraham Stiller replied. After their first meeting, Stiller asked Garbo to put her trust in him and emphasized that he regarded her as a niece. " 'I'd rather you said sister-in-law,' Garbo said. And I think that is quite a clear message," he stated. "She was deeply shaken by Moje's death and she made me swear to arrange for her to be buried in the same grave as he. Naturally, it would have been complicated, because she wasn't Jewish. Moreover, she was young—just twenty-three. I made her understand that a twenty-three-year-old girl should concern herself with the future and not bind herself to a dead man."

The two met several times during Greta's stay in Stockholm.[5] "We rarely spoke of Moje, but she grieved for him very much. Her depression was sometimes so strong that she couldn't pull herself [together] . . . one didn't hear her laugh many times that year." During subsequent vacations in Sweden, Garbo occasionally visited with Stiller, but always managed a solitary visit to Moje's grave.

Hoping for a respite from the frantic pace of Hollywood while in Stockholm, Greta found she was inundated by phone calls from former friends, acquaintances, local producers, journalists, and a host of people she had

---

[5]According to Fritiof Billquist, she also became friendly with Moje's sister in the United States.

never met before. In desperation, she had her phone disconnected until operators began intercepting calls for her. Returning to Sweden was not all that she had hoped it would be. "She enjoyed the reunion with her mother, brother, and old friends, but she was terrified of the crush of people who surrounded her, begging for autographs, mauling her clothes, craning to get a close-up view of the great Garbo," MGM publicist Howard Strickling offered. "Misunderstood in Hollywood because of her seclusion and fear of crowds, she was subjected to severe criticism in her native land. . . . Garbo was condemned on every side for being aloof, even to the extent of an editorial in one of the leading papers."

Carl Brisson was standing in the foyer of a local theater when an attractive young woman emerged from the crowd. "She was stylishly but simply dressed, manicured and coiffeured. . . . There could be nothing in common between the little Greta Gustafsson I used to know and this rare beauty," he stated. "Then as she came straight towards me she smiled, and complete recognition came in a sudden flash. I caught both her hands in mine and cried: 'Why, little Greta, how beautiful you have become. What has happened to you?' Greta stopped smiling and looked surprised. This was not the greeting she had expected. 'Oh, Carl!' she said, and broke into a laugh. Before I could recover from my astonishment she turned and darted through the crowd into the manager's office. 'So you know Miss Garbo?' said a voice in my ear."

But it was through a prince that Greta met a new comrade. Wilhelm Sörensen, a twenty-four-year-old law student, was the son of a wealthy Swedish industrialist. On the day before New Year's Eve, Sörensen received an exuberant telephone call from his friend and classmate, Prince Sigvard. "Guess who I'm going out with tomorrow night?" the prince said. Sörensen was invited to join the prince and Garbo at the winter palace in Stockholm. The trio planned to leave the palace festivities early and join the "hip" crowd celebrating New Year's at the Strand Hôtel.

Greta reserved a table at the Strand for the evening—no longer the starlet joining the great director at his table, she had earned her own table. The party broke up around 4:00 A.M. Garbo's Musketeers—Prince Sigvard, whom she irreverently called her "little prince," and Sörensen, now humbly referred to as Sören—adjourned to Sörensen's apartment for a chat. Greta's "Winter Apple" (another nickname) was tall, blond, a good conversationalist, and, unlike Sigvard, slightly older than Garbo. However, it was the girl from Södermalm who assumed the dominant role in this friendly group. At the end of their private celebration, Sörensen asked her to lunch. Greta was evasive, again unwilling to commit to even a simple lunch date. "Should I know?" she responded when

Sören inquired about her availability later in the week. "I'll call you back."

After the holidays, Prince Sigvard went back to the University of Uppsala to continue his studies. His attentions to Garbo had reportedly sent the Swedish court into a panic. On the *Kungsholm*, he had been ordered not to dance with her and he had complied—though he was quick to renew their friendship once they arrived in Stockholm. Sightings of the pair at a few harmless public events were enthusiastically recorded in the nation's press. Again Sigvard was advised to show more discretion. What palace insiders didn't know was that Greta Garbo had no designs on the son of the Bernadottes. Back in the States, she was asked about her relationship with the attractive young prince. Garbo, who was scarcely two years older than Sigvard, would assure the press that she didn't "play around with kids." And she wouldn't.

After recovering from a winter cold, Greta was seen around Stockholm with Sörensen at her side. They went on quiet strolls throughout town, met Prince Sigvard for at occasional dinner at Sörensen's house, and spent an afternoon at Skansen. Greta seemed to prefer having a male escort who was attentive and yet non-threatening—a person "without consequences," as Sörensen termed it. After the new year, she was also invited to visit the Wachtmeister's country estate with Mimi Pollak. "Oh, how exciting. It will be the first time I stay at a real castle!" Greta told Sörensen, who was a close friend of the Wachtmeisters as well.

The Wachtmeister manor, Tistad Slott, is located approximately fifty kilometers southwest of the Stockholm archipelago near the coastal village of Nyköping. In Sweden, a *slott* or castle is a residence where a royal suite of apartments is maintained year-round; the Wachtmeister family home consisted of seventy-five rooms, including several guest bedrooms. "Imagine our surprise—and our embarrassment—when on our arrival the servants . . . carefully unpacked the simple clothes we had hastily thrown together and arranged them neatly in the chests of drawers in our rooms," Mimi recalled with some amusement. "Our night clothes were laid out on our beds. Greta and I laughed—we'd never experienced anything like it before."

Tistad was a working farm with dairy cows, sheep, and chickens as well as the prize horses Count Wachtmeister trained and exhibited. Favored winter activities included cross-country skiing and ice skating. It was the perfect setting for long country walks, during which Greta and Mimi wistfully recalled a time that had past them by. Most of all, Mimi said, she would never forget "how Greta used to stroke the pieces of silver that were placed here and there throughout the castle. She had never seen anything so beautiful."

Back in Stockholm, their Dramaten classmate Alf Sjöberg described how the trio, now all successful actors in theater and film, used to revisit the old classrooms of their Dramatiska Teatern Elevskola apprenticeship. "The window, where we stood around [Nils] Personne, the same old locks are still in the window—the ones we hung on to, tired and yawning, before we went on stage. . . . I could see how happy Greta felt when her beautiful hands found the old well-known grip," he remarked. "Afterwards we would sit in Mimi's kitchen, just like we used to."

Surprisingly, she considered a theatrical outing while at home. According to Lars Saxon, Garbo rehearsed Tolstoy's *Resurrection* with a former employer, John W. Brunius, but panicked and backed out from the much-heralded performance the night before the dress rehearsal. She apologized to Brunius and costar Gösta Ekman, explaining that she was too nervous and agitated to appear on stage again. Another guest appearance she briefly considered was a cameo role as a prima donna in Karl-Gerhard's musical revue. "She had a sweet little singing voice and a wealth of humor that only those who knew her more closely had any idea of," Saxon noted. But Garbo's days of live performances were firmly in the past.

As her stay was drawing to a close, Greta announced that she would like to do something nice for Naima Wifstrand. Concerned that the once-cele-brated performer had been forgotten by her peers, she planned an intimate dinner at the Operakällaren, a stylish restaurant adjacent to the Opera House.[6] After dinner, the party regrouped at a friend's apartment, and, while Wifstrand sang in the parlor, Greta slipped into a secluded back room for some privacy. Away from the festivities, her mood immediately changed, artist Einar Nerman said. Her eyes filled with tears. "It feels so strange," she cried as Nerman comforted her. "It feels as if I have lost my footing . . ."

Lars Saxon's prediction that Garbo would be anxious to return to work once she had been allowed to go home proved to be correct. A New Year's call from John Gilbert did not bring her back to Hollywood; a telegram from Metro-Goldwyn-Mayer instructing her to return to the studio as soon as possible did. She wired back that she planned to return on or about the first week in March.

On the eighteenth of January, Greta appeared at the United States Embassy in Stockholm to apply for a visa allowing her to reenter the coun-try. Meanwhile, back in the States, *A Woman of Affairs* had opened in a

---

[6]As with *kyrka*, the *k* is soft. O-pær-a 'sha-lär-in: opera cellar. (The same rule applies to Nyköping on the previous page: Nē-shəp'-ing.)

select number of theaters nationwide. "If someone would promise me that all the silent movies would hold the interest and contain the excellent dramatic situations of *A Woman of Affairs* . . . I could do without the talkies all the rest of my natural life," Louella Parsons proclaimed in her syndicated review. "While Miss Garbo is on the screen she compels attention," Mordaunt Hall wrote in *The New York Times*. Hall was particularly struck by "her marvelous understatement in registering before the camera just the right expression, never exaggerating, always true to the mood of this intense young woman." It was the image of Greta Garbo as the complicated, heroic, tragically human Diana Merrick that most eyes followed.

With an extraordinary performance, a contemporary role, and a classic modern look (designed by Gilbert Adrian, her first association with the costumer), *A Woman of Affairs* would be the first of Garbo's films to withstand the brutal test of time and helped to catapult the actress into position as Metro's top female star of the 1928/1929 box-office season.

Hollywood studios typically measured a player's popularity based upon the amount of fan mail coming into their mailrooms. Mail from Garbo's admirers had increased dramatically since her arrival at Metro; she was now receiving 4,000 to 5,000 pieces a month.[7] Though talent, and most certainly beauty, played a prominent role in Garbo's success, it was her individuality that ensured the public's continued interest. Movie analysts of the era usually gave feminine stars the credit for attracting male patrons to the nation's theaters, and vice versa. It was a rather surprising oversimplification of the average movie audience, particularly for a dynamic new star creating the sensation that Greta Garbo did.

Garbo drew a strong masculine crowd, but she had an even more profound effect on her female audience. She reached beyond "the protective and romantic instincts in men" to touch women as well. Sex was undeniably part of it. Garbo's approach to lovemaking stimulated young teenage girls, even women in their twenties and thirties, who had been taught that pleasure was a man's prerogative. Her intimate posture and kisses suggested a woman—not a vamp—who was secure in her sexuality; Garbo often took the initiative and was allowed the right to have amorous needs and desires. Confident but never haughty, she challenged traditional roles with few negative consequences. "No actress, before or since, has combined the masculine and feminine wills so tightly in one embrace," one historian asserted.

As her cinematic presence spilled over into everyday life, Greta Garbo

---

[7]None of which she would answer personally. "These people do not know me," she said. "Perhaps I am very bad girl. Perhaps they would not like to get letter from me."

influenced the appearance of an entire generation. Glamour and style were tied in to this new idea of sex: the way she did her hair, the distinctive way she outlined her eyes—those deep, spiritual eyes that were supposed to be blue but always seemed much darker, shaded as they were under extraordinarily long lashes. Seeking to imitate this look, false eyelashes would become a staple in women's makeup. Garbo's effect on fashion crossed over in subtle ways. Part of "the look" would include sunglasses and certain hats, particularly berets and cloche hats. Both had been around for some time, but Garbo would give them new life.

Although her look was entirely natural, not all of the effects were unplanned. One movie "trick" involved the subtle highlights cameraman William Daniels brought out in her eyes and hair. The cinematographer had a small keylight mounted near the camera to illuminate what many acknowledged to be Garbo's most striking feature: her eyes. Daniels claimed that her eyes photographed darkly because of her emotional nature—but it also helped to have black flats around her. In close-up shots, dark blue or black velvet positioned near the camera showed as a dark reflection in her eyes. She had the opposite problem with her hair, which was honey blond but appeared darker in black-and-white films without Daniels' help.

Garbo's luminescence on screen wasn't just the divine manifestation of charisma. She used a light makeup base from Max Factor, Silver Stone #2, which was very popular among movie actors because it had a touch of silver in it. During the early days of the cinema, the clarity of film was so poor that players had to use every means at their disposal in order to avoid looking like old men and women. As technological advances improved the quality of the film emulsion, many actors continued to use this makeup, forcing cameramen to adjust the lighting accordingly. Anyone with a darker base suffered by comparison. Though it might not have been a calculated move, Garbo's decision to stay with the makeup she was familiar with reinforced her position as the technical center of each frame.

Because her holding herself apart from Hollywood was an essential element of Garbo's appeal, it was inevitable that there was a great deal of interest in her return to America. She was one of the few for whom absence would make most hearts grow fonder; the clamor for her films did not dissipate when there was a longer than usual delay—it was magnified. The Metro publicity department discovered this phenomena, first, due to Garbo's 1927 walkout; then a series of illnesses and delays throughout 1927 and 1928; and, finally, her 1928/1929 trip to Sweden.

The publicity machine was set into motion with the release of a movie featuring an MGM star. Typically, the cycle began in New York City; a Los Angeles engagement followed anywhere from two to six weeks later—add a few key cities and the run became a limited showcase. The general release concluded with international bookings later in the year. By the time the film was played out, the studio made sure their star had at least one new picture ready to exhibit. This strategy allowed popular actors to stay within public view—the theory being that most moviegoers had short memories. If one movie didn't do as well as expected, it mattered less because there was always another one on the way. Advertising, publicity, and promotion were intended to enhance the aura of success around established stars as well as to create new ones.

In Greta Garbo's case, the public couldn't wait. The press came to studio publicists for new stories. Normally, this would have made the publicist's job easier—but Garbo was uncomfortable promoting herself. "In my country the papers talk about the King and Queen and the royalty and otherwise about bad people," she said. "I do not want to have things printed about me, because I am not one of any of these people."

Garbo's conversation with Ruth Biery of *Photoplay* in December of 1927 (arranged by Harry Edington, not Metro publicity) was typically fraught with the anxiety of someone who never quite got used to the promotional aspect of her work. "When I first went to interview her she kept me waiting in the lobby of her hotel for fifteen minutes," the journalist recalled. "When she arrived she was all apologies—hesitating, nervous ones." Greta was polite but restrained, and highly sensitive to how she was being perceived. She began to speak somewhat haltingly, then stopped suddenly. "But you wouldn't understand," she said. "You laugh at me, maybe." The two were to meet on several different occasions before Biery felt she had enough material for the projected series of articles.

"[Greta] spent many hours giving me the material," Biery reported. "I was fascinated by her sincerity, her warm, earthy qualities; her utter lack of affectation." After the series had been published, however, she had one final encounter with her reluctant subject in which Greta told her quite frankly that she did not appreciate the revelations Biery presented in her story. "I do not like to see my soul laid bare upon paper," she stated. It was her last official interview.[8]

---

[8]This extraordinary series became the basis for countless magazine pieces and alleged new interviews which blatantly plagiarized Biery's material. Author Rilla Page Palmborg borrowed liberally from it, and Lars Saxon certainly used it as the basis for his 1930 serial in *Lektyr* (though Garbo herself validated Saxon's work). Even *Photoplay* got into the game, repackaging the interview with a Swedish update in Ake Sundborg's two-part article, "That Gustafsson Girl" (April/May 1930).

Swedish children absorb the concept of *Jantelagen*[9] from a very early age. *Jantelagen* is, basically, a generations-honored code guiding social behavior; specifically, how one relates to others. The underlying theme is humility and self-restraint. Of primary concern is anything that might be construed as an expression of vanity—any indication, regardless of its basis in fact, that one has excelled over others. It is a concept steeped in traditional Swedish folklore and superstitions that can also be viewed as an attitude of caring; one shouldn't take any unnecessary risks.

It is not a belief that is easily shaken. The more successful or independent the person, the greater the pangs of guilt and remorse. Needless to say, such an attitude is at odds with Garbo's chosen profession. There can be no dignity without privacy—and no privacy with celebrity. "Much has been written about Garbo's extreme reticence," her friend Harry Crocker wrote. "It has been called a pose. If it is it's the most consistent pose in cinema history." Even in the early days, Crocker confirmed, Greta rarely went out and was extremely diffident with people in general. "This always seemed too bad to me, because she is not only beautiful, but fun-loving, laughter-loving, and her shyness has stood in the way of her enjoyment of many things."

Louella Parsons scored a coup of sorts when she finally met Greta socially at a dinner party given by a mutual friend. "She was charming, delightful and pleasant," the columnist reported. "Then when she learned to whom she was speaking she ran and got her hat and dashed out of the house." Not meaning to be rude, she had run away "from what seemed to her a real danger."

Many Hollywood acquaintances viewed Garbo's reticence as that of an actress who wanted most desperately to receive attention for her work—and yet would do anything to avoid that recognition. They believed that everything she did was deliberately individual: every movement, every gesture, every look, even her clothes were designed to draw attention. Garbo was certainly the most unconsciously visible person the town had ever seen, but little acknowledgment was given to the language barrier, which easily separated her from her peers and made a foreigner struggling to express herself in a strange language the butt of unkind jokes. Many readers would find the phony, phonetic English used to transcribe her comments amusing; Garbo didn't, because it tended to trivialize anything she said.

Publicity chief Howard Dietz acknowledged that his Swedish star was hardly enchanted by all that went on in Hollywood. "She would wander

[9]Yôn-tǝ-lô-gin.

aloof among the two-dimensional buildings on the back lot, and she spoke the approximate truth in her interviews and panned Hollywood. I wasn't paid to pan Hollywood and it was important to harness this free spirit." As she became more important to the studio, Dietz insisted that a member of his department be present at interviews to help facilitate an often awkward—and sometimes painful—process. But Garbo was more opposed to the idea of being "handled" than of submitting to the interview itself. She told Dietz that she must be allowed to speak freely; if not, she would not speak at all. "This negative decision turned out to be the best publicity notion of the century," Dietz added.

What Garbo's absence had shown MGM was that articles continued to be written with or without their cooperation. In fact, many of the best promotional lines concerning her appeal and mystique were generated not by Metro but by the fan magazines. The phrase "Scandinavian Sphinx" was used in an August 1927 piece for *Motion Picture Classic;* mystery was conceded to her even earlier in Rilla Page Palmborg's "The Mysterious Stranger," published in the May 1926 issue of *Motion Picture.*

Over the years, many people have taken the credit for Garbo's "choreographed" withdrawal from publicity. No doubt, each would play a role. From Lon Chaney to Sven-Hugo Borg, they all reinforced an attitude that had been evolving ever since Greta Gustafsson first stepped into the public arena. The final decision to hold back on interviews was reached quite naturally, and while it might have appealed to Garbo for personal reasons, such an aloof stance never would have been accepted if it hadn't appealed to MGM on a business level. The uniqueness of her celebrity was vested in the realization that her reach extended beyond criticism from the press. Her independence suited everyone concerned; it generated good copy.

The "secrecy veil" was officially in place. From here on, most of publicity concerning Garbo underlined her isolation from the rest of the community. Ruth Biery's *Photoplay* series was published in April, May, and June of 1928. A few months later, Garbo's winter sabbatical made it a clean break in the public's mind, and although she had been part of the commercial scene in Sweden, endorsements would not be part of the package in Hollywood. Greta would return to the filmmaking community a new and, for the moment, silent Garbo.

She spent her last evening in Stockholm dining and dancing with Wilhelm Sörensen. The first time Sören saw Greta cry, he recorded, was the day he accompanied her on the train from Stockholm to Göteborg. Cognizant that her much-anticipated return to the United States would be monitored by the international press, she made a number of false rail and steamship reservations to confuse reporters. On the ninth of March, she boarded the *Drottningholm* bound for New York. Watchful eyes caught sight of Sörensen—who looked enough like Prince Sigvard to be mistaken for him—walking across the upper deck a few minutes before the departure time. A moment later, a tearful Garbo rushed after Sören and threw her arms around him; hundreds of passengers and well-wishers watched them say good-bye. Two days out to sea, Sörensen said, Greta sent a cable begging him to follow her. He claimed to have received three more telegrams over the course of the ten-day voyage.

The *Drottningholm* pulled into its berth on schedule on the morning of March 19. Greta moved quickly through customs accompanied by Swedish aviator Einar Lundborg and his wife, Margareta. Unlike her largely unheralded arrival three and a half years earlier, MGM's top executives now hastened to greet Garbo upon her return to America. Joseph Buhler was unable meet her boat, but had arranged for a friend, Robert Reud, to serve as his "fortunate ambassador." Loew's president Nicholas Schenck arrived at the down-bay docks bearing gifts and a Cheshire cat-like grin. "Every one of those persons who had conscientiously refused to meet her on her first trip, simply begged me for cutter passes," recollected publicist Hubert Voight. "I got Schenck one . . . I liked the irony of the idea . . . he brought her a huge bouquet of flowers and trotted alongside like a schoolboy. He could hardly speak when he met her."

Garbo was cool and collected at their meeting. Voight saw in her "a new sophistication—a polishing off of the rough edges—but there, underneath, not bothering to remain hidden, was the real Garbo." The publicist had procured a suite for her at the Hotel Marguery on Park Avenue, where a discreet staff spoke in hushed tones or by signals in order to avoid disturbing their guest. Voight arranged a brief interview with a *New York Times* reporter. "Let's not talk about me," enthused the star, now dubbed "The Hollywood Hermit" by the *Times,* "let's talk about New York and the skyscrapers. They look so beautiful from this window."

During her stay, Garbo was easily the most talked-about visitor in New York. "At the Ritz, at the theater and whenever she appeared she was pointed out and necks were craned to get a good look at her," said Louella Parsons. "The very fact that she refused interviews and that she did not talk over the radio seemed to only heighten the interest in her."

Greta would also see a lot of Robert Reud, an aspiring producer/entrepreneur who was then beginning his work in the trade as a press agent for prominent directors (Gilbert Miller, Max Reinhardt, Jed Harris) as well as stars of renown (Helen Hayes, Katharine Cornell). The debonair, southern-born businessman would be another complication in the disintegrating story of John Gilbert and Greta Garbo.[10] "Prince or no Prince—Jack Gilbert telephoned Greta Garbo as soon as she reached New York," Louella Parsons announced in her March 21 column. "She's still as reticent as ever about Jack Gilbert, but Jack will tell anyone who cares to listen that Greta is the cream in his coffee . . ."

Two days later, Greta left New York on the *20th Century Limited*. Despite a head cold, she hummed the refrain to "Can't Help Lovin' Dat Man" all of the way down to the train station. She'd heard the song the previous evening in a popular speakeasy. "THE SONG IS GONE BUT THE MELODY LINGERS ON," a chivalrous Reud cabled in a fond message of farewell delivered to her train compartment en route to Chicago. But it was a smiling Jack Gilbert, columnists eagerly reported, who was waiting to greet her in Los Angeles. Jack met the *Santa Fe Chief* at the Pasadena station and drove Greta to her new residence, the Beverly Hills Hotel. Early in April, the couple attended a private reception at Pickfair in honor of Prince George, the future king of England (following Edward's abdication). An elegantly attired Garbo danced with the prince as well as Douglas Fairbanks and Jack Gilbert. It was to be a last hurrah for Jack and Greta.

Changes were being made. By the time Garbo returned to Hollywood in 1929, the country had a new president (Herbert Hoover), and Louis B. Mayer and Irving Thalberg were embroiled in a vicious, albeit top-secret, boardroom battle for their movie company.[11] Publicly, while *Wild Orchids* was making its way into theaters at the end of February, Thalberg and Mayer were contemplating Garbo's debut in "talkers," now more commonly referred to as "talkies." Most of the Metro-Goldwyn-Mayer stable of stars had been tested, trained, and okayed for sound by the spring of 1929, and the remaining players were preparing to make belated debuts in the all-star *Hollywood Revue of 1929*. Garbo's participation would have been welcomed, but the front office didn't pressure her to move into the sound arena as long as her future in it seemed uncertain. The idea that the pub-

---

[10]Complication or diversion? Garbo's personal files reveal correspondence from Reud dated March 31, 1927, offering her the use of his good name "as a shield" in case she should need it during her contract dispute with Metro. "The only thing that matters in life is art," he declared. An introduction was finally made in December 1928 as Garbo passed through New York on her way to Sweden.

[11]After months of denying the rumors, it became apparent that Nicholas Schenck, a.k.a. "the General," had betrayed them and was, in fact, negotiating a sell-out of Metro-Goldwyn-Mayer to one of Mayer's arch-enemies, William Fox. The first inkling of this deal had been a private contract John Gilbert signed with Schenck in December of 1928 that prohibited Gilbert's nemesis, L. B. Mayer, from meddling further in his career.

lic might not respond to an audible Garbo was not an acceptable option.

Sound would change the typography of the film world. "During the first hectic, unsettled days of the talkies we were all swayed by the idea that only the experienced stage actor had a chance," Louis B. Mayer stated. "We know now that we were wrong. Who could we get to take the place of John Gilbert, Greta Garbo, Norma Shearer, Marion Davies, William Haines, Mary Pickford, Douglas Fairbanks, or any of the stars whose fame is international?" Yet, while talkies were no longer a novelty, Mayer still considered them to be in the experimental stage. "Only the public can determine whether we continue making our players speak or keep them silent, pantomimic artists," the mogul said. "If the map of the film world changes as many of us feel, it will not be because the stage players have come to Hollywood and have usurped the places held by our screen favorites. . . . [But] there is a possibility that we shall have many new names at the end of 1929."

Developing new names was exactly the point. Throughout 1928 and 1929, much of the panic throughout the creative community involved very real fears that the studios might use such a transition as a means of weeding out the ranks. "The word 'contract' has taken on a new and terrific significance in Hollywood," Louella Parsons chimed in a March 1928 column. "So many options on big stars have not been taken up that there has been considerable gossip in film circles that a movement is under way to quash all options with one fell swoop."

As Hollywood grew, many stars amplified their roles with lucrative production deals allowing them a creative and financial interest in the films they made. While the weekly salary for the average contract player remained stable, the money these stars extracted from the studios increased by staggering proportions. "Sound was a great disciplining force," Alexander Walker noted. It arrived at "the handiest possible moment" when many stars were demanding fees that most companies, following the box-office recession of 1926 to 1927, could not support. Talkies gave film producers and distributors the perfect opportunity to redefine their terms.

The possibility that management might use a technological revolution to affect a financial one had been the talk of the town for months. European producers were convinced that Hollywood accelerated this transition not because of public demand—a *Variety* survey published in December of 1928 suggested that the average talkie was no more successful than the average silent film—but for their own financial gain; specifically, to trim costly overheads. Two years earlier, major studio heads had met secretly and collectively agreed not to convert to sound production unless everyone was in accord. Suddenly, even the holdouts were declaring there was no turning back. Producers concerned about the cost now recognized the savings.

While fellow players struggled to prove themselves (with differing degrees of support), MGM had every intention of ensuring that Garbo's transition was a successful as well as a profitable one. "If they want me to talk I'll talk," she told *The New York Times.* "I'd love to act in a talking picture when they are better, but the ones I have seen are awful. It's no fun to look at a shadow and somewhere out of the theater a voice is coming."

Garbo's "gorgeous indifference" to work in general kept everyone wondering what she intended to do next. According to one report, she went before a camera and microphone and performed three test scenes for MGM: Margaret's monologue from Goethe's *Faust* in German; Solvieg's song from Ibsen's *Peer Gynt* in Swedish; and Ophelia's insanity scene from *Hamlet* in English. An ambitious undertaking, to say the least. Even before the pronouncement of that test's success, Irving Thalberg had purchased the property that would serve as Greta Garbo's sound entré: Eugene O'Neill's *Anna Christie.* A drama of a tattered soul and her attempts to relate to an estranged father, a feisty new lover, and "dat ole davil sea," *Anna Christie* was carefully sculpted to present Garbo in, undoubtedly, the most spectacular talkie debut since Al Jolson stirred things up in *The Jazz Singer.*

Jack Gilbert issued his final ultimatum. He was in love with Greta. He wanted to get married, build a life together, have children with her. Unfortunately, after nearly two and a half years on this emotional roller-coaster, Greta had learned to steel herself against Jack's demands for a definitive commitment. Her resolve was stronger than ever. She did not want to get married; she thought she would make a poor wife and an even poorer parent. She was too absorbed in her work.

Greta remained elusive to one of her most devoted admirers. She said no. "You are a very, very foolish boy, Yacky. You quarrel with me for nothing," she reportedly told Jack. She was determined to go her own way, but not part; she never removed the remainder of her belongings from the house on Tower Road. She soon found out how serious Jack was.

On the tenth of April, an item appeared in *Variety* announcing that Metro had "definitely decided" not to costar Garbo and Gilbert again. A blurb in the *Los Angeles Times* a few days later indicated that Gilbert was planning a trip to Europe. Alone. The team had ended. Again the story that Metro had selected for Garbo's next appearance had resonance. *The Single Standard* was based on a five-part story by Adela Rogers St. Johns published in *Cosmopolitan* the previous year. The essential conflict of the heroine, Arden Stuart, was a very modern one: Can there be a single standard for both sexes as long as women are mothers?

Even in the original *Cosmopolitan* piece, elements of Arden Stuart appeared to be modeled after Garbo: her charismatic presence, her distracted state of mind, her disregard for conventionality and dedication to a unique code of mores. "I'm not interested in boys," Arden tells an amorous admirer, foreshadowing Greta's subsequent statement regarding her Swedish prince. Metro writers embellished the scenario with personal details from Garbo's life. Walking alone in the rain, she admonishes a pesty suitor with the declaration that she is "walking alone because I *want* to walk alone." The boat that she and her lover, Packy Cannon, sail away on is called *All Alone*.

"I want always to play charming, interesting women who are natural, who are themselves," Garbo told the *Los Angeles Times*. "They do not show all they feel nor desire. They are carried on by what happens to them." At last, Irving Thalberg and his production staff had taken to heart Garbo's expressed interest in playing more attractive characters. There was enough mystery in her own personality to carry these women along without loading them down with melodramatic poisons. MGM would promote *The Single Standard* as presenting Garbo in her first "100 percent American" role.

Production commenced on April 15, 1929, under the tutelage of supervisor Hunt Stromberg and director John S. Robertson—but it was Mauritz Stiller who continued to speak to Greta's heart. "He says I must do this," she was overheard saying, or "He doesn't want me to do that." Above all, she remembered his emphasis on trusting her own instincts. "Don't try and be like Norma Shearer," he once admonished her. Shearer, the coquette . . . the flapper . . . the woman who followed tradition by marrying the man she wanted to be her protector and mentor—thus securing her position in the studio pantheon by a means that simultaneously earned her the enmity of many actresses on the lot and put into question her not inconsiderable talent.

John Mack Brown, working with Garbo for the third time in less than two years, felt she had changed considerably by the time they worked together in *The Single Standard*. He attributed her self-confidence to the therapeutic value of her vacation in Sweden. No longer taunted by homesickness, Garbo seemed happier in her work and more inclined to enter into a conversation or share a joke with the crew.

Away from the lot, she was also more comfortable socializing with friends and coworkers. When Einar Lundborg visited Greta at work, she posed willingly for publicity photos with the Swedish hero. At the end of April, she attended a masquerade ball thrown by Basil and Ouida Rathbone at the Beverly Hills Hotel. Few people apparently recognized her—including Jack Gilbert and his date, actress Ina Claire. Adrian had dressed Garbo as Shakespeare's melancholy Dane in black tights, boots, and black velvet doublet adorned with a gold chain and jeweled pendant (rented specially for the occasion). It was a friend of Jack's, Lilyan Tashman, who finally recognized the stealth-like Hamlet as Greta Garbo.

On the eighth of May, the *Single Standard* crew was transported to the isle of Catalina for location filming. Located a few miles off the California coast, the island has been the backdrop for countless motion pictures. In 1929, there were few phones on the island; most news was delivered via the ferries which conveyed passengers between Catalina and the mainland several times a day. Set lose in such a carefree setting, a seemingly content Garbo was seen running about Avalon Bay in the company's speedboat, the brisk ocean air streaming through her hair.

The following day, the company was working on board Packy Cannon's yacht, the setting for Arden Stuart to fall in love with the maverick artist portrayed by Nils Asther. An unidentified reporter arrived from the main-land with a Los Angeles newspaper and quietly handed it to Greta. "She turned white as she glanced at it," one crew member recalled, "then read with interest. Finally, she smiled, handed back the paper, and thanked the lender. Then she resumed her gaiety and was literally the life of the party." There was no comment.

Her stoic response masked what was, at least privately, a heart-wrench-ing moment. What Garbo had read was an account of John Gilbert's unex-pected marriage to beautifully articulate—and equally temperamental—Ina Claire. The couple had met at a Hollywood party scarcely three weeks ear-lier. They had taken the night train to the little desert town of Las Vegas because Nevada didn't require a three-day waiting period. "Who could resist her?" Gilbert told a crowd of locals gathered outside the courthouse. Rounding out the wedding party were Barney and Alice Glazer, and H. E. (Harry) Edington.

Greta showed very little emotion regarding Jack's marriage. Prior to the filming, everyone assumed that the lovers had quarreled—again—but would soon make up, as they always did. Crew members noted that the change of affairs hardly bothered Garbo. But a close friend of Jack's, Lenore Coffee, presented a different story. The writer had dropped in at Harry Edington's offices on the MGM lot the evening of May 8. Edington was on the telephone when she arrived. Realizing she could not negotiate an exit from Edington's inner office without disturbing him, she decided to wait. "Although I could hear only one end [of the conversation], some of the MGM telephones were very sensitive and I could tell that it was a woman's voice on the other [end]. I could almost tell which woman," Coffee wrote in *Storytime*. From this one-sided conversation she pieced together a dramatic scenario. The woman on the other end of the line was in "a state of great emotion," she said, and was pleading with Edington to stop the marriage of Gilbert to Claire—which, because she was in seclusion, the caller had just heard about. From what Coffee could make out, the woman made it clear that "Jack belonged to her—they never should have separated—what had been between them had been too real, too deep."

Edington's hand shook as he held the receiver, sweat poured down his brow. "You know that I'd do anything for you, but how can I stop a wedding which is to take place in a matter of hours?" he asked. "Please, you know how devoted I am to you, but you must be reasonable—you must not ask for the impossible! I'm Jack's manager, not his guardian." There was only one person who could stop the wedding—yet, Edington confided later, he knew that she would never do so. The storm had subsided.

"Any love affair which is thoroughly unhappy must die in time," Adela Rogers St. Johns wrote. "Myself, I do not believe there was ever any question of a marriage between Jack Gilbert and Greta Garbo. I think they both realized how impossible it was." According to her coworkers on *The Single Standard*, Greta often spoke about Jack "and said she wished both of them every happiness." In losing a lover, she had lost a companion and friend as well. A few years later, Gilbert would confess that there had never been a day "since Flicka and I parted that I haven't been lonely for her. And I think she has always been lonely for me."

CHAPTER ELEVEN

Okay for Sound: A Blonde with a Brunette Voice

On Catalina there was plenty of time to think; little time to be lonely. The *Single Standard* crew returned to Culver City on May 14, and promptly marched back to the beach where Greta, John Mack Brown, and the young child playing their son enacted an idealistic family scene. Brown's observations about her vitality and good humor contradict a feeling, then prevalent in Hollywood, that Garbo without Gilbert had lost her direction. "Since the marriage of Jack Gilbert, Greta is more elusive and more in her shell than ever," Louella Parsons suggested. "She seems afraid to trust anyone."

Although she cut herself off from many of Jack's friends, Greta was hardly without companions. Principal photography on her ninth film for MGM concluded on the fourth of June. Garbo left town after a single day of retakes. In his autobiography, Nils Asther wrote about a weekend trip he took with Greta to Lake Arrowhead, northeast of Los Angeles. Arrowhead is a man-made lake, but the mountain setting disguises its origin (a great dam prevents the annual spring thaw from being lost to the desert below). Greta and Nils, genuine Nordic spirits bound by their moods as well as their restlessness, fantasized about building "a Swedish log cabin high up on a hill, where we could withdraw from the rush of the film city." Without inspecting it in advance, Asther selected a small house in the woods surrounding Lake Arrowhead and invited Garbo to join him in inaugurating it.

After a long ride along the narrow, winding roads of the San Bernadino Mountains, they found the cabin—unfurnished. Greta slept on the floor in the downstairs parlor; Nils commiserated with the lumber in the attic. It was a confusing weekend. Asther, on the rebound from an on-again, off-again romance with Vivian Duncan (one-half of the vaudeville team of The Duncan Sisters), had determined to propose to Garbo "for the third and last time." The next evening, after a romantic walk in the moonlit woods, he did—and for the third and last time, she said no. "To myself, I cursed Mayer because I was convinced that he restrained his stars from marrying and bringing children into the world with all the means at his disposal," the actor wrote in his memoirs. He began to quarrel with Greta, who became sad, not knowing how to put a stop to it, and their weekend ended on this bittersweet note. A year later, Greta's moody "sailor" married Vivian Duncan.[1]

Garbo knew how to keep people, even those she cared about, at a safe distance. "Greta, if you had been born in the fifteenth or sixteenth century, they would have burned you at the stake," Ludwig Berger once teased her. "You are a witch." Her friend Jacques Feyder concurred with Berger's assessment. "She can sense people through her finger tips, and simply by touching them bind them to her will," he said admiringly. During the late 1920s and early 1930s, she won many friends in Hollywood with her unpretentious posture and unexpected sense of humor.

A party at the home of Emil Jannings provided John Loder with the opportunity to serve as an unofficial translator between Garbo and director Jacques Feyder, who spoke only French and German. Feyder, a European discovery of Thalberg's, had just arrived in Hollywood and was under consideration for a number of Metro projects. Greta liked Loder's English accent and Feyder's Continental charm; she would spend a substantial amount of time in their company. "Every Sunday morning I used to pick up Greta and Jacques at the Chateau Marmont Apartments, where Jacques lived, and drive them down for the day at the beach," Loder reminisced. "One Sunday I arrived to find Greta in the kitchen scrambling eggs. I crept up behind her and kissed her on the nape of her neck." The guest cook didn't miss a beat. "Don't be a fool, John," she laughed. "Make yourself useful. It's the table that needs laying."

English, German, Austrian, Belgian, French, Russian, Pole—all were becoming essential links in the Hollywood Greta Garbo embraced as she prepared to make the critical transition to sound. She met Salka and Berthold Viertel at a "black-tie party" given by Ernst Lubitsch during the spring of 1929. When they arrived, the Viertels found all the women at the party congregated in one corner while the men gathered in another. The one exception was Jacques Feyder, who had managed to be seated on a couch between two beautiful women. He got up to introduce the Viertels to one of his companions, the only woman who wasn't wearing an evening dress: Garbo.

"Oddly, when I met her I had not seen any of her films, with the exception of *Gösta Berling*," Salka recorded. "We talked about its première in Berlin; then she asked about my work in the theater. She was intelligent,

---

[1]"Sailor" was a favored term for her male, usually bisexual friends. "What kind of a sailor are you?" Greta asked Wilhelm Sörensen at their first meeting. On location in Catalina with Nils Asther, she was overheard berating the actor for grabbing her so roughly. "I'm not one of your sailor friends," she reminded him.

simple completely without pose . . . joking about her inadequate German and English, although she expressed herself very well." The next day, Greta showed up at the Viertel's Santa Monica home to continue their conversation. "She told me she was pleased that I had only seen her in *Gösta Berling*, as she did not care much for her other films. She was very funny, caricaturing the repetitiousness of the seduction techniques." After escorting her home, Salka and Berthold exchanged their impressions. "What had charmed us was her great politeness and attentiveness. She seemed hypersensitive, although of steely resilience. The observations she made about people were just, sharp and objective." They immediately saw that fame had prevented her from living a real life.

Salka Viertel was a buxom, turn-of-the-century kind of figure—an intense lady with dark auburn hair and dark eyes. A vivacious conversationalist and a lover of people, she was born Salomé Sarah Steuermann on June 15, 1889, in a country then known as Galicia, a small part of Poland that had been annexed by the Austrians (and later the Russians).[2] Though the Steuermann family was of Russian Jewish ancestry, many had owned land and maintained high positions in their respective communities. As a result, Salka, as she was known by friends and family, led a largely sheltered childhood fostered by private tutors, kindly servants, and a warm, loving governess.

But Salka Steuermann knew about heartbreak. She was sixteen when the man she loved died unexpectedly. She began a new life in Vienna, where she studied theater. Following her official debut in *Medea*, Salka signed on for short apprenticeships with theatrical companies in Teplitz-Schoenau and Zurich before winning a spot in Max Reinhardt's Deutsches Theater company in Berlin.

She met Berthold Viertel on the rebound from an ill-fated affair with an older, very much married man. Viertel was a promising young stage director then on furlough from the Eastern front—he was also married. Nevertheless, when they first met he announced with brazen assurance, "You know that I am going to marry you?" They were married on April 30, 1918. It was through her work with Berthold, who was also a poet, dramatist, and writer of philosophical essays, that Salka received much of her primary political education. Berthold got a job, first as a theater critic for a Prague newspaper, then as a director with the Royal Saxonian Theater in Dresden; she signed a contract with the Kammerspiele in Munich, later performing in Leipzig, Dresden, and Hamburg before returning to the frantic, wild pace of Berlin in 1922.

[2]Today, the town of Sambor is located in Ukraine.

Though it was a constant struggle to balance two actively divergent careers, the couple managed to have three sons in six years. Hans was born in 1919, Peter came along one year later, and Thomas arrived in 1925. In 1923, the Viertels founded their own theatrical company, Die Truppe; it was a short-lived venture. With economic conditions worsening in Europe, when Berthold received an offer from F. W. Murnau to write a film in Hollywood, he accepted with little hesitation. Like many of his peers, he hoped he could build a new life for his family on the money he earned in America.

Salka's recollection of New York City in 1928 was, not surprisingly, much like Greta's three years earlier. The city was "alien, frightening and extremely unreal," she wrote. Paradise was regained a few months later in Los Angeles when they found a house that was clearly home at the entrance to Santa Monica Canyon. Their new home at 165 Mabery Road quickly became a meeting place for an eclectic group of European intellectuals—witty, sophisticated expatriates who were nurtured by Salka's maternal concern as well as Berthold's unique analysis of world politics. "Salka was a Rock of Gibraltar," says actor Jack Larson. "You could have gone to her with any trouble you ever had. You felt like she was Mother Earth; she was a great cook, a wonderful hostess, and was knowledgeable on any level . . ." Her home would become a sanctuary for avant-garde filmmakers, writers, musicians, and scientists who had wearied of explaining themselves to their American friends. What possessed them, and who they were, was best expressed in their work. Within this stimulating enclave, Greta Garbo would find her real home in Hollywood.

After countless arguments with his father, Wilhelm Sörensen received permission to leave the university in Sweden and begin studying the movie business in California. The Sörensen family business was manufacturing boxes and Sören had been trained for the diplomatic service, but Garbo's words continued to haunt him. At age twenty-four, he recognized that he was not yet ready to settle down. "When Greta told me so many intriguing tales about Hollywood and the film colony, I was determined to come over and see what it was all about."

Without further delay, he wrote Greta to let her know that he would soon be on his way. Her response was less than enthusiastic. "If you really wish to come you are heartily welcome, but I must warn you that you may never understand me completely—*how* I really am, and *what* makes me so," she replied. "If I am working on a movie when you are here, we would not see much of each other, because then I must be alone." Undaunted by her seeming change of heart, Sörensen made plans for a transcontinental adventure. A round-trip steamship ticket to California via South America—a generous gift from a family friend—secured his passage, and by the end of June he was on his way.

In Hollywood, Garbo was becoming increasingly frustrated by the rigors of celebrity. When it became known that she was now a resident of the Beverly Hills Hotel (nicknamed the Pink Palace by locals), admirers began a daily ritual of gathering around the various hotel exits in order to catch a glimpse of her. Chaplin, Fairbanks, and Pickford notwithstanding, Hollywood had scarcely seen the likes of such unrelenting obsession. The barrage of publicity due to Jack Gilbert's marriage would complicate the situation even further.

"One morning," John Loder said, "a young girl came to the desk asking for Garbo. As directed, the clerk answered that she was not in. The young lady sat down and proceeded to wait." Later that afternoon, Greta walked through the lobby on the way to her car, but the girl had mysteriously disappeared. Garbo's Lincoln sedan proceeded down the circular drive in front of the hotel—however, just before the car reached Sunset Boulevard, the fan reappeared and threw herself with foolhardy zeal in front of the automobile. Fortunately, she emerged unscathed—her dramatic plunge had been orchestrated to get an autograph.

There were, of course, no rules about celebrity pursuit. Unsure of what so many strangers seemed to want from her, yet certain that, whatever it was, she didn't have it, Garbo would find it difficult to forget the desperate faces of her fans. Her only alternative was to begin her life "on the lam," as she would call it. Harry Edington found Greta a furnished three-bedroom house at 1027 Chevy Chase Drive in Beverly Hills. It was an attractive Mediterranean-style structure with a large fireplace, swimming pool, and a relatively secluded backyard framed by rosebushes and lemon trees. By Hollywood standards, it was a modest home; lesser stars would have wanted more—but Garbo didn't. With the assistance of the Scandinavian Employment Agency, Edington found a young married couple, Gustaf and Sigrid Norin, to tend to its upkeep. It was under the name of Norin that the telephone was listed, mail was received, and unwanted visitors were turned away.

With her household in order Greta could go back to work without further distractions. Production on her next film began on July 16, 1929, under the supervision of Irving Thalberg's executive assistant, Albert Lewin. Similar in design to her last three projects, *Jealousy* was based on an original story by director Jacques Feyder (credited as George M. Saville). Once again, the studio offered a bonus to the writer who came up with a marketable title. The winner was *The Kiss*. The story was developed with the foreign market in mind; technically, it would be a motion picture "with sound" but no spoken dialogue. "[Garbo] is one of the few stars in the country who would dare keep silent with this demand for talkies," Louella Parsons chirped. "I shall be curious to know just what the box office receipts are on this picture."

In *The Kiss*, Garbo would portray Irene Guarry, the unhappy wife of a prominent French silk manufacturer. Conrad Nagel was set to play the lover who defends her on a murder charge. Even more intriguing was the casting of an unknown actor to play Pierre Lassalle, the young man whose infatuation with Madam Guarry sets the tragic event into motion; he was a musician-turned-actor named Lew Ayres. Garbo had seen a test arranged by Paul Bern and immediately approved the handsome, boyish-looking actor for the juvenile lead.

According to Ayres, the first scene he shot with Garbo was The Kiss. Due to time constraints, no one had considered easing Ayres into the complicated, alternately playful and dramatic scene by introducing him to the star. After the first take had been completed, Greta turned to the assistant director. "I wonder if you would mind introducing me to this boy," she asked. "We have not met." Throughout the production, Ayres maintains, Garbo took secret pleasure in teasing him by inquiring—with a wink and a smile—"Have we met?"

Although there was a mere three-year difference in age between them, the actor felt his leading lady came across as being much older. She was more sophisticated, more cynical and world-weary. "To her . . . I was so naïve that she just always smiled at me in a motherly way, I suppose." Privacy was always an issue. During morning rehearsals, the black screens were always folded. But as soon as they were ready to shoot, the entire perimeter of the set was covered with flats, the crew was asked to step back—even the men positioned above were instructed to come down once the lights had been adjusted—and director Jacques Feyder took his station near the camera. Often during intimate scenes only the camera poked through the screens. Adding to the surreal and impersonal atmosphere on the set was Feyder's inability to speak English. Garbo conversed with him in German; the actors and crew received their directions through an interpreter.

Feyder described his star as a dream to work with: in costume, punctual, always prepared—and always ready to leave as soon as the clock struck 5:00. He believed her modesty to be sincere. She was rarely satisfied with her work and was always the hardest on herself, he stated. "Miss Garbo has a dramatic and emotional depth far greater than she has yet been called upon to use. . . . She was born with the true heart and soul of an artist."

Spying on Garbo at work or strolling around the lot was an irresistable temptation for coworkers. "About the studio she uses very little or no makeup," Conrad Nagel noted, "wears whatever is comfortable—soft-soled shoes, a cape when she feels chilled—in fact, whatever pleases her . . ." Whatever pleased Greta Garbo usually managed to please everyone else. Nagel referred to her as the "best and most natural comrade I've ever had. She isn't one of those who thump you in the back and say, 'Hello Mary—hello Dick,' that sort of naturalness is merely a sign of a deficient personality. Garbo had a very strong personality and she had the courage to show it."

When a break in filming occurred, Greta could be found sitting quietly off to the side waiting to be called. "I used to study her face as she sat there," Ayres recalled. "You couldn't tell whether she was plotting a murder, dreaming of her native Sweden, or figuring up her income tax." She was "a polite, gracious, lovely and removed woman," he says, but she was a wonderful artist whom he found to be very human in her emotional responses. Despite her contradictions, she was an easy person to work with. "She was far more than just a glamorous figure. She listened and heard you and responded."

On the twenty-seventh of July, *The Single Standard* began sowing "genteel wild oats" at the Capitol Theatre in New York. "The great Garbo bursts through the drab grey ashes of this inferior story like a clean, white flame leaping from volcanic vapors to the heights above," Laurence Reid extolled in *Motion Picture Classic*. Irrespective of the long lines outside the Capitol, *Variety* was more concerned with possible censorship. "The actress is almost unfeline in her brazen directness," they opined. "While censors probably expect to leap on this point . . . they will find no show. The star keeps well wrapped throughout and her intimate postures are so frequent and so matter of fact after the first dozen times that only once . . . do they come anywhere near getting an actual kick."

The single cinema standard was ticket sales. Loew's, Inc. cheerfully trumpeted an impressive first-week gross of $81,600 at the Capitol; the take during the second week declined a barely perceptible $600. It was the best showing of any motion picture since the previous Christmas. Garbo was still big box-office—with or without sound. The daring theme of an "unfeline" woman living by a man's rules (and, briefly, in his clothes) would go over with "the stenographer crowd" across the country. But, as *Variety* predicted, the film struggled with the threat of censorship. It was "pinked" by several review boards, meaning no children would be admitted.

In urban areas, the controversy only served to engender more interest in the picture. "Garbo, the pash, for adults only!" one paper enthused. *The Single Standard* set a house record at the Chicago Theater; two weeks later, it moved over to another first-run house for an equally profitable engagement. In trade terminology, "sunlight and moonlight lines" were reported in Pittsburgh, Seattle, Minneapolis, Los Angeles, and Boston, where extra shows were added to accommodate the crowds.

In rural America, however, where the presumably risqué storyline was deemed objectionable, the movie appeared to run out of steam. Louella Parsons articulated some of the small-town concerns: " 'What's happened to Greta Garbo?' ask our readers . . . 'She used to be the accepted vamp of Movieland. Now she goes and becomes a flapper,' [but] she doesn't look like one. She dresses like any girl in college and she wears low-heeled shoes. . . . Let's have Greta back as the grown woman. Leave the flappers for the other girls."

The HMS *Canada* docked at the Port of Los Angeles in late August. Prior to the ship's arrival, Wilhelm Sörensen sent Greta a telegram inviting her to join him at the captain's table for an authentic Swedish meal. "WILL COME IF NOT TOO MANY PEOPLE," she replied. Though she wasn't expected on board before noon, Greta arrived early. "You've traveled round half the world, but you don't seem to be in a hurry to get off that boat," she playfully chided Sörensen as she walked up the gangway. "I thought you'd come running to me as soon as you landed."

Greta broke one of her own rules by inviting Sören to stay with her until he found suitable lodging. "This is a very crazy place," she apologized as she showed him around the house. "It has rooms in all directions." The Norins had prepared a guest room for him upstairs; Greta's room was on the far side, away from everyone else. In contrast with the vivacious comrade Sören had enjoyed in Stockholm, Garbo in Hollywood was serious, dedicated, and rarely in the mood to share her adventures with others. The most exotic star of them all "lived a life apart from the film colony—an existence quieter than the most obscure shop girl. I learned that if I wanted to continue being Greta's pal, I, too, must live a life apart. That I must not allow outsiders to know that I even existed. It would be suicide for me if the world discovered that Greta Garbo had a boy friend."

Once *The Kiss* wrapped on August 26, Greta announced to her guest that she was going to Yosemite for two weeks, accompanied only by the driver from MGM, the script for *Anna Christie*, and a small stack of books. She wanted time alone to collect her energies before beginning her next project. She registered at the Ahwahnee Lodge under the name of Norin.[3]

---

[3]Located in Yosemite Valley, the Ahwahnee had opened two years earlier, offering rooms at the bargain rate of $6 a night including maid and chauffeur.

Wearing the standard disguise of dark glasses and wide-brimmed hat, she was able to walk around one of the nation's finest national parks without being noticed. Eventually, the initials on her luggage gave Garbo away, prompting her to retreat to her room and cable home for her car.

She returned to Hollywood in time to celebrate her birthday. The Norins made her a birthday cake and decorated it with twenty-four blue and yellow candles. Her gift from Sören was a comic sketch he had drawn of her dressed in a trench coat, derby hat, and men's shoes. That evening, they toasted the occasion with champagne and imported caviar at Ludwig Berger's.

"A thousand parrots couldn't have squawked louder than those first talkies," screenwriter Frances Marion remarked. "Everybody was chattering away as if they'd just discovered their voices." Considering the gravity of the situation, the last thing they expected was laughter from the audience.

Trade advertisements placed by Metro-Goldwyn-Mayer throughout much of 1929 listed John Gilbert as their top star. Gilbert was set to appear in talking and silent versions of *Redemption*. During this fragile period, literary or dramatic adaptations seemed like a safe bet for the great money-making stars of the silent screen. Musicals usually sold themselves, but dramas and comedies needed strong stories, many of which Broadway had already tested. There were no guidelines carved in stone, but there were many lessons to be learned.

Norma Shearer's first two talkies for MGM were stage vehicles, as were Marion Davies'. John Gilbert's one-two punch was literary as well as theatrical. *Redemption* was based on Tolstoy's *The Living Corpse; His Glorious Night* had been adapted from Ferenc Molnár's romantic comedy, *Olympia*. This time, words failed Jack. After an audience-pleasing debut as a hip-talking Romeo opposite Norma Shearer's Juliet in *The Hollywood Revue of 1929*, Gilbert stumbled in *Redemption*. Production had gone badly from the outset. The script, although approved by Thalberg and accepted by director Fred Niblo, was not finished.[4] It was a dark story, darkly told and darkly photographed. The report from the screening room was that the footage was static and muddy—even more important, there was "something wrong" with Jack's voice. This surprised many friends and coworkers who figured if anyone could talk on screen, it was Jack Gilbert. Attempts to

[4]Contrary to previously published reports that Lionel Barrymore directed half of the picture and was replaced, Niblo's name is evident in a number of pre-production materials, including early drafts of the screenplay. Barrymore was brought in for the retakes.

resuscitate the story failed and, in an uncharacteristic move, Gilbert begged Thalberg to shelve the film.

Late in July, Jack and Ina Claire left town on a belated honeymoon. As rumors of marital discord in Europe drifted back, MGM released *His Glorious Night*, the intended replacement for *Redemption*. Though a lack of concern for quality production values would be evident throughout *His Glorious Night*, the motion picture exhibited a shabbiness typical of early sound films. Concerns expressed by directors like Clarence Brown, King Vidor, and F. W. Murnau turned out to be painfully accurate—with motionless cameras trapped in sound-proof booths and actors limited by the placement of the microphone, there was less of an emphasis on imagination and feeling and more on simply hearing. The director of *His Glorious Night*, Lionel Barrymore, was not able to solve the problem of shattered silence.

Metro's poorly calculated effort to present their star in a bright romantic fantasy backfired due to a clumsy adaptation of Molnár's play, which was further complicated by Gilbert's stiff, melodramatic performance. Although he had a pleasant voice once described as "a cultured baritone," Gilbert's delivery of dialogue was more stage-bound than natural. He spoke in the self-conscious, over-enunciating fashion that many petrified screen actors were guilty of; there were few nuances.

One of his most ineffective scenes in *His Glorious Night* involved a confrontation with leading lady Catherine Dale Owen in which, for lack of anything better to emote, Gilbert was forced to repeat "I love you" over and over again. (The moment would later be parodied to great effect by Gene Kelly in *Singin' in the Rain*.) Although the initial reviews had been positive, word of mouth on *His Glorious Night* was increasingly grim. "Jack went to Europe the idol of millions of adoring women," Colleen Moore said. "He returned to America to find them laughing in his face." *Variety's* prediction that with "a few more talker productions like this and John Gilbert will be able to change places with [comedian] Harry Langdon," was borne out in the reports from exhibitors: "LAUGHED AT, NOT WITH, GILBERT'S GLORIOUS" . . . "GILBERT'S FLOP."

It was just the chink in Jack's armor that Louis B. Mayer had been waiting for. Privately, his daughters admitted, Mayer seemed to relish Gilbert's defeat and did little to help change people's minds. Over the years, their intense, brawling relationship had disintegrated from mild disgust to bitter acrimony. "It was very strange, this thing between Mayer and Jack," Howard Strickling said. "Like he'd made up his mind to hate the guy from the first time he saw him. As far as I was concerned, Mayer was way off base in his feelings about Jack, but you couldn't tell him that. Anything good about Jack Gilbert, he didn't want to know."

Poor audience reaction and the debacle of *Redemption*, released to equally hazardous effect in April 1930, gave John Gilbert's adversaries justification for withdrawing their support. Surprisingly, the man who could have helped him—his trusted friend, Irving Thalberg, who cast most of the films, assigned the producers, and supervised the writing staff at Metro— was mysteriously absent. By the end of 1929, it was Greta Garbo (soon to be joined by Joan Crawford, William Haines, and Norma Shearer) who received top billing in the MGM ads. Critics and columnists who knew better were suddenly writing about John Gilbert's "high-pitched, reedy voice," an unfortunate misrepresentation that escalated until even Jack's friends began repeating it.

"I have never believed, then or now, that it was Jack Gilbert's voice that ruined him," Colleen Moore wrote. "What ruined Jack Gilbert was three little words." Three little words, recorded and played back on primitive equipment, that didn't fulfill everything fans had thought, heard or felt about their idol. Tragically, as with many romantic stars, John Gilbert's screen image betrayed him. "Now, it shouldn't have, because John had a good voice," comedian Harold Lloyd insisted. "It was somehow how they used it, and how they presented him."

Many friends and associates came to believe that Gilbert's voice had been doctored. Could a studio, if it so desired, adjust recording levels to sabotage the performance of one of its stars? Yes—although any subterfuge would have affected other players as well. Did Metro-Goldwyn-Mayer intentionally destroy John Gilbert's career to satisfy a personal vendetta? That question can never be satisfactorily answered. If Gilbert had continued to make money for the studio, it seems unlikely that anyone would have allowed Mayer to manipulate the results. However, with Jack's ability to attract moviegoers compromised, even Thalberg was capable of coolly detaching himself in order to cut company losses. The future belonged to talking pictures.

Gone were the glass skylights, the musicians, and the portable partitions in between sets. In their place rose thick cement walls, motion picture cameras sequestered in booths affectionately known as "sweat boxes," and miles of recording cable buried beneath the new soundstages. To ward off air traffic, a number of red flags were placed above the MGM stages, along with a balloon requesting "Silence." With a little help from Bell Laboratories and Western Electric, department head Douglas Shearer, chief engineer Wesley Miller, and systems specialist A. N. Fenton put together a sound department where none had existed before.

Initially, soundmen were not well-liked on movie lots; in fact, they were despised. Much of the dissension was motivated by the sense that no one knew what they were doing. Most of these men were from radio, a comparatively new medium; they had never worked on feature films. But they assumed "all the dignity of their elders," actress Lila Lee said, "very self-important. The poor cameraman was in a horrible position because he knew how to film . . . and then this young engineer would say, 'But you can't do that because we cannot get the sound.' "

Opinions weighed in heavily during this period—and everyone seemed to have a different opinion about what Greta Garbo should be doing. Months earlier, she had expressed the desire to play Joan of Arc. "I would like to do something unusual, something that has not been done," she revealed to a *New York Times* reporter. According to Bengt Forslund, Victor Sjöström had been involved in preliminary discussions with Metro-Goldwyn-Mayer regarding *Anna Christie*. But it was Greta's *Woman of Affairs* director, Clarence Brown, who got the job.[5]

As evidence of the studio's interest in the project, Thalberg personally retained control as production supervisor. A newcomer named Charles Bickford was cast as Matt Burke, the "hard and rough" Irish sailor whose love for Anna complicates her relationship with her father. George F. Marion, who played Anna's father, Chris Christopherson, on Broadway and in the 1923 film starring Blanche Sweet, was set to reprise his role. Thalberg also brought in Frances Marion, a clever, skillful writer on tough projects, to adapt O'Neill's Pulitzer Prize–winning play. It was due to Marion's intervention that Thalberg agreed to test her friend Marie Dressler for the role of Marthy. The nearly destitute Dressler, a comic actress known primarily for her teaming with Chaplin in *Tillie's Punctured Romance*, had been bravely struggling in Hollywood for some time; *Anna Christie* would be a well-deserved break for an old pro.

Surrounding Garbo with veteran performers allowed her to focus on the challenges ahead. "What a superb Anna Christie Greta Garbo will make," Louella Parsons wrote in March of 1929, when the production was first announced. "Who better than Greta could interpret the moods of the unhappy O'Neill heroine?" In *Anna Christie*, columnists noted, Garbo could use her Swedish accent without "offending" the ears of the public. "It is a gorgeous story," the actress agreed, "and we will see to the accent."

---

[5]Sjöström had been unable to get a boat back to America before the latter part of August 1929. By the time he arrived in Los Angeles, *Anna Christie* was well into pre-production and set to go into rehearsal. Sjöström took on one more assignment at MGM—the English- and German-language versions of *A Lady to Love* (1930)—before returning permanently to Sweden.

Since Garbo rarely spoke publicly, the idea that she would talk in films took on added significance. For many admirers, it would be Greta Garbo, not O'Neill's Viking daughter, speaking. Irving Thalberg had little doubt that she would be able to transcend the difficult road laid out before her. "Garbo will fit into the leading role of a waterfront girl who speaks in a rasping, whiskey voice and no fake dubbing will be necessary," he confidently told Frances Marion. According to Wilhelm Sörensen, however, an unnamed studio executive did suggest that she take voice and elocution lessons. Greta declined. "What do I need lessons for?" she reasoned. "They know how my voice sounds, and I intend to talk English the way I do now!"

Her experience in Sweden remained an important influence. It was at Dramatiska Teatern that Greta and Mimi Pollak had marveled at Tore Teje's electrifying performance in the Swedish production of *Anna Christie*. Fellow students at Dramaten later reflected on how much pleasure "Gurra" seemed to derive from making her voice as low as Naima Wifstrand's—Wifstrand, the once-popular star of Greta Gustafsson's youth, was known around Sweden for her melodic, rich contralto voice. A husky timbre had always been a part of Greta's normal speaking voice; her ear for inflection and nuance would help to increase its natural range. Director Fred Niblo characterized her as "a blonde with a 'brunette voice.'"

Greta was meticulous in her study as the anticipation concerning her talkie debut built. On occasion, she read through the script of *Anna Christie* with Sören. "I was amazed at how easily she learned and her good memory," he said. "If I ventured once in a while to add some dramatic touch to my part in reading, she would quickly pull me down to earth, saying 'Don't fiddle-faddle, just read it straight!'"

Rehearsals began on October 7, 1929. Contrary to her previous posture with Sörensen, Garbo admitted being insecure about her ability to speak or understand English well, especially O'Neill's slang. Ironically, after she'd spent four years learning proper English, director Clarence Brown wanted her to affect a more stereotypical Swedish accent. Greta had learned her lines but often neglected to say words like "just" and "job" the same way twice; she might say "yust" and "job" or "just" and "yob" (although O'Neill himself varied the pronunciations in his play). She also had trouble with simpler words like "ain't" (ahn't) and "Matt" (Mott). It would be a frustrating battle: disguising enough of the guttural intonations of her accent to be understood and yet retain the classic "flaws" of a Swedish-American accent.

Principal photography commenced on the fourteenth. Wilhelm Sörensen furnished a perceptive eyewitness account to that fateful moment. "I did not meet Garbo so often during the days before the voice test," he would write in 1955. But on Sunday evening, Greta called him at home. "This is it, Sören!" she said, barely masking her anxiety. "Tomorrow's the day when silent Greta gets a voice." At 2:30 the next morning, she was on the phone again. "Come over here immediately," she commanded, and he obeyed. They sat in the living room drinking coffee and talking trivialities. "Then, before either of us had realized it, the clock had struck six, and a few minutes later the two of us were on the way to the studio."

A blanket of fog enveloped the car as Gustaf Norin piloted Garbo's old Lincoln through familiar city streets on the way to MGM. They drove in darkness—and interminable silence. Greta drew a wrap around her. Sensing her uneasiness, Sören remained quiet. After some time, he heard a little girl's voice come from beneath the blanket. "Oh, Sören, I feel like an unborn child just now," she exclaimed. Awaiting Greta in her dressing room at Metro were her maid, Alma, who also doubled as her wardrobe assistant, and Billy, who was assigned to help her with makeup and hair. "Both of them adored Garbo and on that morning their faces showed acute apprehension . . ." Sörensen said, "but Garbo would have none of this Doomsday atmosphere. Her manner had again changed, and she was now gay and lighthearted about the whole thing." Greta promised to meet Sören during the lunch break to let him know how things had gone.

It was a short walk from Garbo's dressing room to Stage 7, where Johnny-the-Priest's southside saloon had been re-created. It was a path littered with casualties from talkies. The exile from favor and the public ruinations of the Talmadges . . . John Gilbert . . . Emil Jannings . . . Pola Negri . . . Vilma Banky . . . Renée Adorée. Even Clara Bow, a screen natural, experienced problems transcending the sound barrier. With heartbreaking insensitivity, the new technology changed many lives for better or worse. Garbo could not avoid thinking about the actors who had fled—or failed—before her.

Clarence Brown and Marie Dressler were full of reassuring smiles when Greta arrived on the set. Acknowledging the importance of the occasion—and everyone's "mike nerves"—Brown agreed to shoot the master scene with Dressler uninterrupted. Garbo made her entrance on cue. With a resignation worthy of the role, she toted her suitcase across the room as if she could not bear to carry it one more step. Collapsing into a chair, she addressed Lee Phelps, the actor playing Larry the bartender. "Gimme a whiskey—ginger ale on the side." As Phelps was about to exit, she tossed him a weary look; a slight smile crossed her lips. "And don't be stingy, baby." Soon after, she invited Dressler to have a drink with her.

As soon as the take was completed, Brown and his players gathered around the sound booth to listen to the playback. "I'll never forget the look on Greta's face as she heard herself for the first time," said one crew member. " 'Does that sound like me, honestly?' she asked Clarence Brown and Miss Dressler, and there was a real smile on her face."

"I almost jumped out of my chair when I heard those lines played back to me," she told Wilhelm Sörensen. "But you should have seen how the others reacted. Alma makes a dramatic gesture with her hand towards her forehead and appeals to the Lord. Billy gets hysterics and runs out. Some of those tough boys on the set start clearing their throats." Despite congratulations from her director, there was one more hurdle to clear. Everyone waited for some indication from the sound engineer, Gavin Burns. Burns grinned and waved from the mixing booth. "Okay for sound." She was no longer an "unborn child."

Variety made it official: "GARBO TALKS O.K.," they announced in their October 23 issue. Alleging that Metro-Goldwyn-Mayer had been "dubious" about the outcome, the paper reported that doubt had been dispelled when the Swedish star "clicked with her first scene, running continuous nine minutes and using 850 feet of film. A record so far . . ."

The average Garbo picture to date had a shooting schedule of forty days and cost MGM between $250,000 and $350,000. *Anna Christie* was budgeted in the same range for twenty overhead days (not including rehearsals). The simplicity of the story allowed the filmmakers the luxury of shooting most of the script in sequence, with Daniels' cameras capturing close-ups and medium shots simultaneously. Frances Marion's screenplay deftly opened up a four-act play with two modest sets to allow for a more compassionate approach and show the gradual evolution of Anna's relationships with her father and Matt. To accomplish this, the camera went outside the ship's cabin—most successfully, in a new scene by Marion in which Anna and Matt encounter Marthy in a Coney Island concession.

"It was always fascinating to watch Garbo; her economy of gesture, constant changing of moods revealed by her luminous eyes that never played the little physical tricks used by so many actresses," Marion said. Greta wore her moods like a garment—and if she were bored by anyone, that showed as well. Then those eyes usually so full of feeling "burned dully like candles in daylight."

Interruptions during *Anna Christie* were few and, with the exception of a visit to the set by the Maharajah of Rapurthala, quite unplanned. There was a brief dispute regarding Garbo's characterization that was important enough to bring Harry Edington on the set. Shortly after, the company shot without her for two days when she was sent home due to illness. Her leading man didn't complain. Bickford had been reluctant to accept the role because he feared the movie would be thrown Garbo's way; he confessed that he had been wrong. Garbo wasn't one to upstage an actor during an important scene. "She's a regular fellow," he said.

The event that caused the cast and crew the greatest pause happened off the lot and was completely out of their control. Black Tuesday. On October 29, the United States Stock Exchange collapsed, leaving investors to scramble for cover. Like most of Hollywood, Garbo had put a great deal of money into bonds and shares. While the full amount of her investment cannot be substantiated, her bank—and most of her investments—were secure for the time being. Greta's loss on the stock market was later estimated at one-quarter of her earnings to date or approximately $100,000—a substantial loss but not a crippling one; her salaried earnings in 1930, 1931, and 1932 would exceed her combined earnings in Sweden, Germany, and the United States through 1929.

Principal photography on Garbo's first sound film was completed by the eighteenth of November. Three days earlier, *The Kiss* had opened at the Capitol.[6] Billed as a film with sound, it more accurately represented a death knell for silence. One sequence in particular would illustrate exactly what Hollywood had given up for sound. Irene Guarry must explain to detectives what happened the night of her husband's "suicide." She hasn't planned an alibi, and as she tells her story she must think ahead: What time was it when she went upstairs? Was the light in the living room on or off? Were her bedroom windows opened or closed? The camera moves throughout the scene—the tense situation illustrated not by words but action.

Though hindered somewhat by a surprisingly slight running time (sixty-four minutes, the shortest feature in Garbo's catalog), the picture managed to connect with moviegoers. "Golden silence reigns in the Capitol during the screening of Greta Garbo's latest film," *The New York Times* declared. "Miss Garbo's interpretation of this role is splendid. . . . It is as flawless a performance as she has ever given . . ."

However, a "haunting, beautiful" performance in a silent film—no matter how imaginative the storytelling—was no longer enough. "No figure in motion pictures, with the possible exception of Rudolph Valentino, has ever captured the public imagination and fancy like Miss Garbo," Pierre de Rohan wrote in the *New York Telegraph*. "She has a glamour and fascination for both sexes which never have been equaled on the screen. But a few pictures like this one will send her back to obscurity. And she is worth alto-

---

[6]Much of it hastily reassembled from alternate takes and a back-up lavender print (a protection master) after the master negative was lost in a laboratory fire.

gether too much to her producers for them to allow anything like this to happen."

The biggest dividend to be earned from the film would be the emergence of Lew Ayres as a young lead. Ayres didn't see Greta again for nearly five years. By then, he had scored in *All Quiet On The Western Front* and was making his way as an independent player. "One day, I was driving down Sunset Boulevard in my car—I think the top was down, and the top was down in the car beside me," he remembers. "As I passed it, I realized it was Garbo; she was driving alone." He honked his horn to say hello, but there was no acknowledgment. He drove a little bit ahead so he could look back and wave hello. Still no response. After two or three blocks of cat and mouse, he realized she must have thought he was just another admirer. "That's Garbo," her former costar says. "There was nothing I could do that would get her to look over. Not a thing."

With her cinematic fate in the hands of others, Greta retreated north, registering at a Lake Tahoe inn under the name "Gussie Berger." Meanwhile, Clarence Brown and editor Hugh Wynn prepared *Anna Christie* for an early preview. Irving Thalberg and his staff had worked to perfect the preview process at Metro-Goldwyn-Mayer. "He missed nothing at a preview," said David Lewis, one of Thalberg's associate producers. "I never saw anyone else with his clear analytical mind or his creative sense of doctoring. . . . He was like a surgeon, exploring, examining, and ultimately healing."

As soon as *Anna Christie* had been assembled, a special trolley was brought on to the Culver City lot. Metro had paid for its own spur on the Pacific Electric line. A special Red Car stocked with sodas and sandwiches took studio personnel to previews outside the city. During the ride back, they read the audience reaction cards, and everyone on board was invited to share his or her observations. Preview notes determined whether or not additional retakes would be needed.

Anna Christie was subjected to "the severest test a picture could possibly be given," Brown said. The audience in San Bernadino had come to see Garbo in *The Kiss* and had no idea of the bonus in store for them. The main feature was followed by a one-reel comedy, then *Anna Christie.* When the title flashed on the screen, Frances Marion recorded, there was an audible gasp in the theater. Surprise was followed by anxious titters—not a good sign, the nervous Metro contingent thought—but sixteen minutes into the movie, the audience settled down. Garbo had made her entrance. Its effect was not lost on Irving Thalberg. "Garbo is holding them in the palm of her hand," he whispered to Marion.

By the time the movie ended, the attending executives had been convinced that Greta Garbo would hold her following. "It's in the bag," Louis B. Mayer boasted. "Garbo's a winner!" Thalberg was continuing on to New York on the *Santa Fe Chief* and after the preview took possession of the film. "This is too good to touch," he assured Clarence Brown. "This goes right to New York with me and will be released exactly as it is."

Frank Whitbeck, then in charge of advertising for West Coast Theatres, was given the task of coming up with a publicity campaign. After a two-hour meeting with Thalberg in which both men "alternately hatched and discarded ideas of how to sell the picture," Whitbeck picked up an envelope from Thalberg's desk and wrote down two words: "Garbo Talks."

Greta wanted to re-create an authentic Swedish Yuletide celebration at her Chevy Chase home. Together with Gustaf Norin, she purchased a Christmas tree and "armfuls of flowers and holly." She went on a shopping expedition for more decorations and gifts with Sören and the Loders. They found many of the Christmas tree decorations at a five and ten-cent store on Hollywood Boulevard. Next on the list were the novelty gifts. A pair of lady's garters for Edington, an assortment of boys' neckties for Jacques Feyder . . . In one store, she found a pair of carved Buddhas, but thought the price was too high. She left the shop three times before the owner came down on his price. "You have to do it every time or they will cheat you," she told John Loder.

Back on Chevy Chase, the Norins had placed arrangements of poinsettias and holly all around the house. Christmas decorations were hung in the hall, living room, and dining room. Not even Greta's pets escaped being decorated. Sigrid Norin loaned her employer a holiday tablecloth and prepared the traditional Christmas Eve meal of lutfisk, julgröt, Swedish apple cake and coffee.[7]

Everyone was invited back for a late afternoon brunch on Christmas Day. It was a holiday John Loder would not soon forget. "She had drawn all the curtains tight to shut out the bright California sunlight," he recalled. This allowed for everyone to imagine snow outside. The living room was lit by an extravagant number of candles and the small, colored lights from Greta's Christmas tree. Yuletide logs burned on the fire, music was playing on the Victrola, and a delicious smörgåsbord was laid out before them. "After copious aquavits we sat down to a splendid traditional Scandinavian Christmas [meal] of roast goose," Loder stated. Though her guests were

[7]Julgröt is a Christmas pudding made from rice cooked in milk and seasoned with cinnamon. Before serving, a raisin, an almond, and a miniature doll are stirred into the pudding; each predicts a future for the recipient.

thoroughly stuffed after nearly four hours of eating and drinking, Garbo invited them to go for a swim in her pool. Most accepted her challenge—and quickly gathered in front of the fireplace afterward. "I thought the party would never break up," Gustaf Norin said. "Suddenly Garbo stood up, as she often did, saying in Swedish: 'Gå nu med sig,' which means: 'Out of here now, all of you.'"

Variety's first issue of the New Year reaffirmed that Garbo was Metro's top female star of 1929; once again, she was listed just below Lon Chaney and John Gilbert. Chaney's placement was due to his pictures being sold in advance; Gilbert's position was more tenuous. "It may seem strange that Greta Garbo trails Gilbert from the b.o. angle on the year," the paper reported. "Were her popularity taken from the last half of the year she would be far in the Metro lead." In her year-end wrap-up, Louella Parsons also "enlisted" Garbo for her All-American Team of Movie Players for 1930—Jack Gilbert was relegated to the "substitute" team.

"People say Garbo in one breath and love in the next. Yes, she loves—her work," Jacques Feyder stated. "It is her life. . . . The past performances of Greta Garbo are nothing compared to her future in talking pictures. . . . no one has yet seen Miss Garbo at her very best." Even so, Mayer, Thalberg, and Schenck were expecting Garbo to deliver. In the months since the stock-market crash, theatrical grosses for MGM, considered among the healthiest of the major studios, had declined significantly (representing a total loss of 40 percent in less than one year). Considering the high price the studio had paid for her, the time was ripe for Garbo to prove her worth.

The world premiere of Anna Christie was staged at the Criterion Theatre in Los Angeles on January 22, 1930. Declaring that Garbo "depicts and sustains the character with gripping fidelity," Monroe Lathrop of the Los Angeles Record pronounced her performance all the more surprising "because it is marked by a variety and skill we look for in players of long experience and training." Several critics expressed the hope that such talent would not be wasted on the trivialities that had consumed her in previous films. "Even those who are skeptical regarding the transition that Garbo might make to the talkies must admit the efficacy of her work in these moments of bitter and world-weary emotion," Edwin Schallert stated in the Los Angeles Times. "Her pleading for love and life is a very intense and real plea. It is reserved and restrained . . . and comes bitterly and with deep torture from the heart."

Although a seat had been reserved for her at the film's premiere, Garbo waited until a matinee performance to see it. She was escorted by Wilhelm Sörensen and Jacques Feyder. "We entered the cinema unrecognized and sat to one side," Sören said. Greta watched most of the picture without comment—though at times she seemed to be "suffering in silence," her friends observed. They left just before the film's end, but Garbo seemed to be pleased. According to John Loder, however, she wasn't satisfied with the end result and was particularly discouraged about her own performance. Loder had been told that she had moaned throughout the film. "Isn't it terrible!" she complained. "Whoever saw Swedes act like that?" But she was proud of Marie Dressler, who made a major impression in the picture, and sent the actress a tribute of yellow chrysanthemums.

MGM reaped the benefit of both actress's success in *Anna Christie*. The picture was held over for a record-breaking six-week run at the Criterion. Soon, it began to make its impact felt across the nation as well. Weeks before the film debuted in New York, it had been seen and heard in San Francisco, Seattle, Detroit, Cleveland, Minneapolis, Chicago, Pittsburgh, and Dallas.

Not all reaction was positive—some moviegoers were jarred by the unusual timbre of Garbo's voice—but people remained fascinated. Louella Parsons had been one of those who insisted that the actress's accent was perfectly acceptable. Five weeks later, she suddenly reconsidered her evaluation, though her reasoning clearly had nothing to do with the film. "Other stars who have been much more eager to please the public have received only half the consideration accorded Miss Garbo," she wrote in her column. "She remains aloof, cold and apparently unconcerned as to this almost fanatical interest in her career." While the critics and public continued to debate her future, Greta went away to La Quinta, near Palm Springs, to work on the German translation of *Anna Christie* with John Loder's wife, Sophie.

When the motion picture was shown at a February preview in Manhattan, Louella Parsons dutifully reported "an electric silence. All the critics in town rushed to the projection room to hear the Swedish siren talk." *Anna Christie*'s opening at the Capitol Theatre on March 14 was the most spectacularly anticipated event since the brothers Warner first challenged Hollywood. Early-morning lines in front of the theater left no doubt that when Garbo talked, people listened.

Sound added an unexpected new dimension to Greta Garbo's screen persona—much as it did for another established star, Ronald Colman; both possessed voices which were in "strange and beautiful accord" with their personalities. But talkies subtracted a dimension from John Gilbert. The bad news continued to accumulate for Jack. At the same time that Greta's triumph was the talk of New York, there were rumors circulating the film community that Metro-Goldwyn-Mayer was trying to buy out Gilbert's contract.

CHAPTER TWELVE

The Peasant of Chevy Chase

"The talking screen has taken its last and greatest toll from the glamourous personalities of the silent cinema," Pierre de Rohan mourned in the *New York Telegraph*. "It has taken Greta Garbo, the incomparable, indescribable, inscrutable enchantress [and] turned out a good screen actress. . . . She has matched speech with gestures, sound with symbols."

The alluring apparition of the former era, while not entirely gone, would indeed be missed; the latter, the Garbo that emerged as the 1930s arrived, was to be celebrated. Though critical opinion in New York was mixed, there was nothing tentative to be found in the public's support. This was the voice that shook the cinematic world. Fascinating. Seductive. Irresistible. To many, Garbo's intelligent performance proved once and for all that she did not need "seduction, sex and sets."

"Now that the Great Garbo of other days and other pictures is no more, I do not mind admitting that I was hypnotized by her personality," de Rohan continued. "I'm sure I never wrote a sober review about her, for I never had a sober thought concerning her. . . . I was aware only of someone trembling with a terrible nostalgia which could not be seen; of a turbulent storm of her inner discontent which found no phrasing in her calm and untouched face. I never saw and never expect to see a woman so unpossessed by outer things. . . . It was not so much what she did, or how she did it, but what she conveyed through some spiritual distinction of her own that set her apart."

Touted as a candidate for one of the year's best, *Anna Christie* set first ($109,286), second ($92,100), and third ($76,727) week box-office records at the Capitol with a facility that was becoming expected of a strong Garbo offering. The only apparent miscalculation was the failure of Loew's management to hold the film over for a fourth week. "Great artistically and tremendous commercially," *Anna Christie* was clearly "a wow picture" in all departments, noted industry pundits. Its final domestic gross was over $1 million—an extraordinary sum in a time of economic depression.[1] Another $486,000 was earned by the English-language version

---

[1] In 1930 ticket prices ranged from 25¢ to $1.50, with the majority of the fares falling between 35¢ and 75¢.

abroad; MGM claimed a net profit of $576,000. The film rose to become the top-grossing motion picture production of 1930.

Garbo's name had once again been attached to success. But it still had not been attached to a man's—at least, one that counted. Much to the dismay of the Metro publicity department, she was identified as one of the "Bachelor Girls" of Hollywood. In February, Louella Parsons revealed that Greta and French-Canadian actress Fifi D'Orsay—a.k.a. the "Parisian paprika"— had become "inseparable friends." They were spotted having lunch together, shopping, and playing tennis. "Greta stays in her shell and is so reserved that Hollywood has been greatly amused and interested in this alliance," remarked Parsons. "Just how long it will last no one knows, but the two 'gals' are certainly a colorful pair—so different and both so foreign."

It was a short-lived friendship. The publicity-savvy D'Orsay wasted no time in trumpeting the relationship to the press—in the process sacrificing Greta's trust. By the end of April, the Hollywood community was informed that Fifi's friendship with the Swedish actress "seems to have ended as suddenly as it started." As yet unreported was the presence of a more benevolent force in her life: Berthold and Salka Viertel. Even the genial Wilhelm Sörensen took notice that "It wasn't long before she was seeing more of them than she was of me."

By now, Greta's social life, independent of any romantic involvement, was unsurprisingly routine. She found no entertainment in hiding liquor under the table and stealing drinks as if one were drinking tea, and she did not like being on display. "It is all so silly," she would say. Garbo did not often visit the favorite haunts of the Hollywood elite. The Plantation Cafe, Brown Derby, or Montmartre were well-known to fans, but as a rule unknown to her. She would go out in public only when the crowds weren't intimidating. According to John Loder, one of her favorite clubs was the Apex on Central Avenue, just south of downtown. A garish place with checkered tablecloths and paper roses, Greta thought it "the most amusing place in L.A.," with the best music.

Another dimly lit, smoky room she frequented on rare evenings out was the Russian Eagle, where the owner was a former general in Old Russia and the headwaiter was a Tolstoy. Gypsy music was played while waiters in red smocks and fezzes served imported Beluga caviar and other delicacies. Greta always sat in the same booth in the far right corner. "When she is someone's guest, she always orders the dinner, table d'hôte, with no specialties. It is a flat sum," Theodor Lodijensky told *Motion Picture Magazine*. "But when she is alone or the hostess she orders anything she chooses because she will pay the check."

For a brief time, while designer Adrian maintained a dress shop near Olvera Street, the original center of town, Greta occasionally toured the sights of El Pueblo de Nuestra Señora la Reina de Los Angeles. She frequented El Teatro Torito, a puppet theater run by the Yale Puppeteers, and was apparently delighted with a Hollywood sketch in which she was a choice target. "With photography misty I did Anna Christie," her puppet announced, "and see what O'Neill did for me."

Another memorable outing involved a performance of La Argentina, a Spanish dancer of some renown, at the Philharmonic Auditorium. Greta's decision to attend was a last-minute one. She called Sören one evening and asked him to put on a dinner jacket. Sörensen found her still contemplating what to wear when he arrived at her home. Finally, she put together an evening ensemble using the top of her gold lamé lounging pajamas as a blouse. Concealing her hair under a stylish hat—and the rest of her costume under a mink coat—Greta looked "elegant and refined—but in a special way."

Harry Edington, Greta, and Sören shared Sid Grauman's private box; Garbo slipped in after the lights went down. It wasn't long before she was spotted. "There was a noticeable murmur of whispers," Sören recalled. Greta began to fidget. During the intermission, most of the audience remained in their seats and turned their opera glasses toward Grauman's box. "Let's get out of here," Greta told Sörensen. Stepping out into the narrow hall outside the box, they ran into Howard Greer, whose protective line of interference helped the star hide her unconventional garb and emerge with her glamour intact.

Once she had a home of her own, Greta took refuge in it. Her house was her fortress, independent of prying eyes. When something displeased her or she felt a need to restore her energies, she would insist with moody resolve that she didn't want to see or speak to anyone. Gustaf and Sigrid Norin were told to say she wasn't at home—even to Harry Edington, Wilhelm Sörensen, Nils Asther or the Feyders. "If any of her friends called at the door, I was instructed to give the same answer," Gustaf Norin reported. "After they had left she would call me to her and say: 'Who was that, Gustaf? What did he say? Do you think he believed that I was not here?' If I said I thought he suspected she was there, she would roll over on her side and laugh, as though she thought it a good joke."

Her favorite activity seemed to be inactivity: sitting on the couch in front of a fire, reading or listening to music. Adrian had helped her arrange the Spanish and Italian furniture in her living room. Interestingly, the only pictures in the room were a framed photo of her brother, Sven, and the sketch by Sören. Greta was fond of flowers and filled small vases in her bedroom with pansies and violets; elsewhere in the house she placed roses or generous arrangements of foliage.

The master bedroom was located on the ground floor in the back of the house. Garbo's bed sat on a platform in the middle of the room. A picture of Moje decorated a nearby stand. Embroidered Oriental panels, kimonos, and a handsome ceremonial robe hung on the walls; Chinese figures dotted the room—including one near her bed, which, the Norins reported, she often broke and they would find headless in the morning.

Greta's closets were filled with the clothes she had purchased before going back to Sweden; many of the gowns had never been worn. "I never saw her wear any of the evening dresses that hung in her closet," Sigrid Norin confirmed. In fact, Greta told her that she regretted buying them. But there was an old tailored suit that was carefully tended to: a plaid skirt and jacket that evoked memories of happier days with Moje. "She cautioned me to see that it was kept free from moths," Sigrid said. When Edith Sjöström came to the house, Greta brought out the suit and described how proudly she had worn it at work in Constantinople.

The Norins left Garbo's service in January of 1930. A well-educated couple characterized as "young adventurers," they had never worked as servants before and clearly didn't enjoy being in domestic service. "We found we couldn't please her, no matter how we schemed," Gustaf stated. "She scolded on general principles." Following their departure, the couple spoke with journalist Rilla Page Palmborg, the wife of a Swedish national. Sigrid and Gustaf Norin's personal revelations about their former employer would be published around the world.

"Don't let anyone tell you that Greta Garbo doesn't know how to handle money," they said. The Norins claimed that they had been allotted $100 a month for groceries and another $50 a week for Greta's personal items (cigarettes, medicine, magazines, and so on). Everything was duly noted in a little black book for Garbo to review. Gustaf served as the chauffeur, but also helped with the meals and did some of the gardening. In addition to her kitchen duties, Sigrid kept the house tidy, did the laundry, and maintained Garbo's wardrobe. Greta wasn't particular how her meals were served, they said. If she was in the garden, she ate there. When it was cold outside, she had dinner served in front of the fireplace in her living room.

The only schedule that was adhered to regarded work. On an average workday, Greta got up between 7:00 and 7:15 A.M. After her morning exercises, she would go for a swim and then get back in bed. Breakfast consisted of orange or grapefruit juice, creamed beef, a poached egg, fried potatoes, a sponge cake, and coffee; a favored standby was a more traditional American selection of ham and eggs. The morning papers always accompanied her meal. According to the Norins, Greta read the theater pages first, tearing out any articles she might want to send on to her family or discuss with Harry Edington later.

After everything was cleared away, the animals were allowed into the bedroom. Fimsy was a large red chow given to her by Emil Jannings' daughter, Ruth, when the family returned to Germany. Greta, while friendly with the dog, was never able to really bond with him. Her favorite pets were two black kittens, Pinten (half-pint) and Mira, and a talking parrot named Polly. "All of a sudden Garbo would realize that it was nearly 9:00," Gustaf Norin recalled with some amusement. Pets were hurried out of the room so that she could dress—then begin the mad dash to the studio. "But we were always late."

Keen about maintaining her weight (now a healthy 128 pounds) as well as her privacy, Garbo never ate in the studio commissary; instead, she carried a bag lunch. On alternate days, Alma brought her a green salad from the commissary, which Greta ate with Swedish crispbread. Lunch at home generally consisted of a small salad, a sandwich, and a glass of milk or beer; lunchtime guests were offered the same meal.

Greta diligently wrote her mother and brother once a week. Mimi Pollak was another frequent correspondent, Gustaf noted. Self-conscious about her spelling as well as her grammar, Greta talked through her letters as she wrote them. "She generally kept calling in to me to spell words for her while she was writing," he said. Norin remembered a particularly telling conversation when she was writing Mimi. Greta was anxious to post the letter as soon as possible and placed almost two dollars' worth of stamps on the envelope, asking Gustaf to drop it in the mail right away. Once a month, she sent all the latest magazines and clippings to her mother; her requests for solitude neatly coincided with the arrival of a reciprocal package from Sweden. According to the Norins, she was known to stay in bed "for days," reading and clipping.

Late afternoons were reserved for long walks or horseback riding. If it was raining, Sigrid and Gustaf could count on her bolting out the door before dinner was ready—it was her opportunity to wrap privacy around her for a moment. Though dinner was usually served between 6:30 and 7:00 P.M., many times Greta decided to start out on a walk instead and didn't return for two or three hours. Missing dinner, she often was heard rummaging through the ice box late at night.

Sometimes she returned home with a Loder, Feyder, or Viertel in tow. "Then she would be in high spirits. She would open the kitchen door," Gustaf said, "and call out, 'Bring in the dinner, even though it is spoiled. We are starved, we can eat anything.' " Despite the sameness of her routine, Greta never wanted to feel as if she must do something; she wanted to be in control. "In the year and a half that I have known her," John Loder said, "I cannot remember that she ever made one definite appointment, even a dinner engagement, a day in advance. 'Perhaps I will drop in to see you tomorrow night' is the nearest intimation of her intentions that we ever got."

They accepted this as a condition of friendship with a person they valued. A drop-in visit from Garbo was always welcomed. In return, their elusive friend showed her gratitude by helping in the kitchen with the meal and later with the dishes. She never overstayed her welcome. When ready to leave, she simply announced, "We must go." Yet the same courtesy or hospitality was not extended to surprise visitors at 1027 Chevy Chase. Uninvited guests—whether friend or foe—were inevitably turned away.

Feeding on a daily diet of movie magazines and gossip columns, the American public was beginning to see Greta Garbo as a young woman unspoiled by her success. At heart, John Loder noted, she was a simple person—he fondly referred to her as the Peasant of Chevy Chase—"Yet she has the divine flame which makes her the great actress that she is. Her dual natures are constantly at war with each other. As a result she is torn first this way and then that. . . . She has no routine, no set plans, is a law unto herself. She cares for nobody, is intolerant of bores, loathes interviewers, and will not be publicly exhibited."

Yet like many stars, Garbo was lured by the fan magazines. She pored through them at home and at work. Rilla Palmborg's two-part article was the first to reveal some of the trivialities of her life: that Greta liked to wear men's clothes (tailored shirts, silk ties, pajamas) and men's shoes (preferably oxfords) . . . that she used few cosmetics and rarely bothered with her hair . . . that she didn't use special lotions on her skin, and the only scents she liked were the lightest of gardenia or lavender . . . that she disliked the dry summers so much she created her own rain showers by turning up the garden sprinklers.

Within a matter of months, admirers discovered Garbo's home address. Anxious to make an impression on her comparable to the one she had made on them, the curious and the obsessed began showing up at all times of the day and night. A girl from Texas called, wrote, and finally showed up at Chevy Chase; a college student slept outside the front gate; a journalist from Sweden stalked her on the way to the studio demanding an interview; a group of Shriners woke her up with their boisterous serenade and pleas for her to come out; an ardent admirer from Wyoming sent her orchids twice a week, then beseeched her with phone calls until she changed the

number; a fan from St. Louis tried to persuade with candy. They even followed her on what was quickly becoming her legendary walks. Gustaf
Norin recalled the night Greta ran home with five young girls in hot pursuit, and another in which members of a local women's club hid outside the
gate—when Garbo came out, they tried to pressure her into joining.

Today, such stories about tourists, fans, and admirers would be deemed
a common affliction of celebrity; yesterday, in a world still shaking off Vic-
torian shackles, it was a fairly new phenomenon. The immediacy—and
intimacy—of motion pictures created a new level of international
celebrity. Garbo's complaint that she could not go anywhere without being
watched or bothered came from a genuine naïveté concerning the nature
of fame. She could not accept the fact that what was left of her private life
now had to accommodate a very public one.

Nothing was confidential. Lacking interviews with the star to console
them, readers of *Photoplay, Motion Picture,* and countless other magazines
about the silver screen grasped for the slightest bits of information. They
even knew that Garbo liked to sunbathe *au naturel* in what she believed
was a secluded area of her backyard. Few friends thought she was being
paranoid when she became convinced that an old man was observing her
from a clearing on a nearby hill. The final affront to Greta's sense of security was when she was surprised by a camera-toting fan as she swam in the
pool. "I don't like Chevy Chase any more," she told Sören.

Once again with Harry Edington's help, Greta inspected a number of
homes around Beverly Hills. She found a house in the "flats" of Beverly
Hills, but after a few sleepless nights decided the noise from the trolleys
running down Santa Monica Boulevard were too unsettling.[2] "I know how
strange the noises of the night can be: the laughter, people fighting in the
street below," she would say. "I sometimes lie with my heart beating like
mad—it's so awful, I feel life can't go on."

Not being able to sleep was a chronic problem. "She did lie awake a lot
at night. But anyone staying in bed as much as she did during the day
couldn't expect to sleep all through the night," Gustaf Norin complained.
"When Garbo wasn't swimming or walking or exercising she was usually
lying down." Her usual cure for insomnia was reading; Greta's bedroom
light often burned late into the night. That remedy failing, she might
request a glass of Swedish *glögg* (mulled wine). As a last resort, the doctors
on staff at Metro-Goldwyn-Mayer prescribed sleeping pills. The studio
needed her ready for work.

[2]Residents of Beverly Hills refer to the section between Sunset and Santa Monica boulevards as the "flats."

Within a month of moving into the house at 527 North Camden, Garbo was hunting for another property—this time searching between Brentwood and Santa Monica. A new home was found at 1717 San Vicente Boulevard in Santa Monica. There was no doubt about it being inconspicuous. Tall cypress trees stood between the main structure and the street, lining the long drive to the front entrance. The two-storied, cream-colored stucco house had three bedrooms and two baths. The grounds included a nicely tended garden with an arched walkway, an aviary, and plush, manicured lawns in the front and back. The backyard was perched on a rocky bluff overlooking the Riviera Country Club. Greta found a stairway winding down into the canyon. From here, it was only a short walk to the local stables—and less than a mile to the Viertel home on Mabery Road.

The staff at her new home would include—rather stereotypically—a French maid, a black chauffeur named James, and a Japanese gardener. Garbo moved into the house during the summer of 1930.

No sooner had *Anna Christie* begun its smash engagement at the Capitol Theatre than Garbo was called to report for her next picture. It wasn't the film she had planned on making, but she had been unhappy with the German-language translation of *Anna Christie*. With Irving Thalberg's permission, she worked on sharpening the screenplay herself; *Anna's* sets were struck and stored away for later use.

The change in plans was, in fact, more than okay with Thalberg. Aware that Garbo's voice had altered her onscreen personality somewhat, the production executive sought to remind moviegoers of the star's ethereal side. *Romance,* based on another theatrical warhorse, would present her in gorgeous period gowns and hairstyles. The combined effect of *Anna Christie,* where Garbo spoke the words of a respected dramatist, and *Romance,* where she was beautiful, sophisticated, and alluring, would demonstrate the breadth of her repertoire as well as reassure the audience that glamour had not been forgotten.

Garbo's name had been attached to *Romance* since June of 1928. On October 9, 1929, *Variety* announced that the popular Edward Sheldon play would be her next talkie. "Miss Garbo is reported to have rebelled at first but was finally persuaded to the studio's way of thinking," the paper reported. According to Wilhelm Sörensen, when discussions with Greta proved fruitless, Harry Edington brought scenarist Bess Meredyth to the house to sell her on the story. "They had a long conference. When it was ended, Garbo had agreed to make the picture," Sören said. "The next day, she regretted that she had let them persuade her to do it. She called the manager on the telephone and there was another argument. She finally banged down the receiver, saying: 'All right, I will do as I agreed.' "

Recalling the diva of Greta's first American film, the heroine of *Romance*, Rita Cavallini, is an Italian soprano. Neither operatic nor a soprano, Garbo would not sing, but she would lip-synch two arias for the film.[3] Like Anna Christie, Rita Cavallini speaks in an exaggerated style of fractured English—it was thought to be the play's most charming asset. Rita is cynical but lacks Anna's bitterness. Again like *Anna, Romance* would follow its original source meticulously, perhaps too rigidly, adding only a few exterior scenes.

An avid moviegoer who was known to hop in the car and drive to a preview on a moment's notice, Greta made a private list of artists she admired and hoped to work with; Gary Cooper and Rod La Rocque were current favorites. Unfortunately, neither was available for *Romance*. During preproduction, she was shown a screen test Gavin Gordon had made for a Norma Shearer feature and approved him as her costar.

"I will never forget our first meeting," the actor stated. "I was waiting in the studio office. The director, who was to introduce us, was busy at the telephone when Miss Garbo appeared at the door; he didn't notice that she had arrived." In anticipation of their meeting, Gordon had rehearsed a number of "pretty little speeches." He never got to use them. Garbo walked over to him and introduced herself. His awkwardness was immediately offset by her directness. "There was something in that friendly, informal little greeting that at once put me at ease," he said.

Rehearsals began on the thirteenth of March. The production had been allotted nine days rehearsal time (scattered throughout the film's schedule) and twenty-one days for principal photography. The first day of filming, March 17, was a long day, with Garbo, Gordon, Lewis Stone, and Florence Lake toiling in front of the camera until 6:30 P.M. According to Gavin Gordon, he was personally responsible for the delay. On the way to the studio, he was in a serious accident, but was so horrified at the thought of losing the role that he declined medical help. He went to the studio thinking he could grit his teeth and go on—then he fainted and was sent to the hospital anyway.

Gordon had broken his shoulder and was told by doctors it would be weeks before he could move without a brace. The studio wanted to replace him and, in fact, began shooting new screen tests; Garbo and Clarence Brown stood by their leading man. In his eagerness to please, Gordon again left medical care— and broke his shoulder for a second time. This time, he

---

[3]This action was later reduced in the movie to a pair of long shots (covered by Greta's stand-in).

refused to go back to the hospital. According to Sören, Greta offered to feign illness in order to get the studio to rearrange the shooting schedule. The point was made, and the actor was given the week off between March 29 and April 5 while the company filmed alternate scenes. Gordon performed the rest of his scenes with his shoulder and left arm tightly wrapped, removing his sling for the final takes.

He bore his pain admirably, but perhaps a bit foolhardily—his discomfort was clearly evident in many scenes. Despite a mutual regard between performers, Garbo had to do most of the work. "Some people insipidly prattle about the 'mystic barrier' with which Greta Garbo shields her exotic soul from the staring eyes of the world," Gavin Gordon later reflected. "What really lies between Miss Garbo and those who try to know and understand her is her greatness—a combination of unusual genius and plain hard work and study." For her own part, Greta was neither happy with her performance nor her attempt to affect an Italian accent, but she kept her opinions to herself.

Production was completed on the twenty-seventh of May, approximately ten days over schedule and at a final cost of $496,000. Just when it seemed appropriate for MGM to promote Greta Garbo and Joan Crawford as its top moneymakers, Norma Shearer made a commercial breakthrough in *The Divorcee* and *Let Us Be Gay*. She would become the principal focus of corporate publicity and advertising, making a quick ascent to the top in 1930. There was a more serious challenge across town. On the heels of a triumphant premiere of *The Blue Angel* in Berlin, Marlene Dietrich had arrived at Paramount Pictures in Hollywood, joining her director and mentor, Josef von Sternberg. Although none of her films had been seen in the United States outside of New York and Los Angeles, Dietrich was already being hailed as Paramount's answer to Garbo. She would make her presence felt with the release of *Morocco* a few months later. Interestingly, it was von Sternberg, not Dietrich, who was studying Garbo's pictures.

In June, Greta received word that Mimi Pollak was pregnant. On the eighteenth of that month, she wrote a letter to her illustrating her conflicting emotions regarding the news. First she scolded Mimi for not telling her sooner that she was going to present the world with a "little Mimosa." Then she joked. What would the baby be called? she asked. Was Garboni Pollak Mimosa Lundell too much? Still, she seemed to yearn for something that was lost along the way. She professed having neither the time nor the inclination to alter her course. She anticipated being alone because, she claimed, it was in her character—she could do nothing else.

Yet it amused Greta to ponder what "Nisse" (Mimi's husband, Nils) would think if he ever read her letter—would he think Greta a "jilted" lover?

Ofttimes, the things Greta wanted to change were irretrievably locked in the past. "I never will be able to understand my mother," she was overheard telling Nils Asther. "I send her money and ask her to buy herself some fine clothes. But she will not. I want her to move into a nice apartment in a better part of Stockholm, but she will not leave her old neighborhood. My money will never make my mother happy, no matter how much I make."

Her success made her brother happy. Sven went to Paris during the summer of 1928. Soon after, he was entertaining offers from film companies in Sweden, England, and France. In 1929 and 1930, he made three films in Stockholm and Paris—two as Sven Garbo and one as Sven Gustafsson. His name was changed for exploitation purposes without Greta's prior knowledge or consent. "Garbo was all upset the day she received a letter from her brother saying that the film company for whom he was working [Svensk Filmindustri] wanted to change his name to Garbo," Gustaf Norin revealed. "She said that she had made the name of Garbo herself, that it was her name, and there should be no one else using it." She sent a cable to her brother asking him to deny the company permission to use the name, but it was too late. It was to be Sven Garbo in *Konstgjorda Svensson* (Gustaf Edgren, 1929) and *Charlotte Löwensköld* (Gustaf Molander, 1930).[4]

Later in the year, Sven wrote Greta suggesting that he would like to come to Hollywood. Harry Edington was against it. So, for the moment, was Greta.

Metro's idea for Garbo's next motion picture was a throwback to another film from her silent repertoire. Like *Wild Orchids*, it was a love triangle set in the tropics—an African jungle instead of a Javanese one. *Red Dust* was announced in several trade advertisements during the summer of 1930. But Greta was more concerned with the upcoming production of *Anna Christie* in German. At the end of June, she returned to Yosemite to study her script—just as she had eight months earlier. The project was to be MGM's great experiment in the foreign arena. "In the days of the silents

---

[4]Sven received his most prominent exposure in *När Rosorna slå ut* (Edvin Adolphson, 1930), produced by Paramount Pictures in collaboration with Gaumont Studios/Paris. Here he was able to honor his sister's request and was billed as Sven Gustafsson—though he was heavily promoted as Garbo's brother.

we could ship our films all over the world, the only changes necessary being the translation of the titles," a studio executive noted. "With the advent of sound we had to reckon with dialogue." Before dubbing and subtitles had been perfected, the alternatives for Hollywood were importing all-star casts from foreign countries or tutoring American actors in German, French, Spanish, and/or Italian.

Ideally, a performer who could communicate in more than one language would have a distinct advantage in helping to increase the studio's market-share abroad. German audiences had been particularly hard on American talking pictures, laughing at the crude dubbing and inferior translations. With Greta Garbo speaking German in a film especially made for their market, Metro hoped to remedy that situation.

Paul Bern and Harry Edington were given major supervisory roles. At Garbo's request, Jacques Feyder was assigned the direction; Wilhelm Sörensen served as Feyder's assistant. It had been reported that Nils Asther's name topped the list of possible costars, but it was a relative unknown, Theo Shall, who won the assignment; Hans Junkermann would essay Anna's father.[5] Like Marie Dressler before her, Salka Steuermann— Salka Viertel—was badly in need of a job. Although twenty years younger than her predecessor in the role, she was awarded the part of O'Neill's besotted wharf tramp, Marthy. In the smaller role of Larry the bartender, Herman Bing, Berthold Viertel's personal assistant, won his second acting job in Hollywood.

Anna: "Whisky, aber nicht zu knapp." ["Whiskey, but not too short."]
Larry: "Soll ich nen ganzen Eimer bringen?" ["Shall I bring a whole bucket?"]
Anna: "Von mir aus!" ["All right with me."]

With its tough, no-nonsense script, the German Anna Christie began film-ing on July 9; production continued through August. "Playing Anna Christie for the second time, Garbo had to conquer the difficulty of still another language. She worked hard, with precision, and her German was almost without accent," Salka recorded. Her second Anna Christie was more cynical, more defeated by her circumstance, and, Greta thought, more realistic—from her demeanor to her clothes. The end result repre-sented one of the few times she would express satisfaction in her work.

While Anna Christie was again navigating a turbulent sea, Romance began its run in Los Angeles, opening first at the Loew's State Theater down-town, then moving to the Fox Criterion for two weeks, before settling at

[5]Junkermann replaced Rudolph Schildkraut, who died during rehearsal.

the Fox Pantages in Hollywood. The motion picture stole into first-run theaters with little advertising or promotional support. Despite this apparent lack of faith, the film was a success. Five weeks later, the premiere of *Romance* in New York City attracted the largest crowds to the Capitol since *Anna Christie* had established a new standard months earlier.

"Her performance is a thing of pure beauty," Norbert Lusk wrote in *Picture Play*, "an inspiring blend of intellect and emotion, a tender, poignant, poetic portrait of a woman who thrusts love from her because she considers herself unworthy of the man who offers it." A significant drop in attendance during the second week indicated that Garbo was drawing but the picture wasn't. Nonetheless, the picture made its mark—in fashion—with Garbo's "Empress Eugenie" hat an unexpected hit.

Having completed her second film in six months—and third in less than a year—Greta invited Sören to "escape" with her to San Francisco. They took a train up the coast and registered at the Fairmont Hotel as Mr. and Miss Sörensen. The next day was cool and foggy—a day incredibly reminiscent of Stockholm in the fall. They decided to take a private tour of Chinatown. Greta was fascinated by the notorious opium dens, with their underground passages and secret rooms. They also investigated the former scene of the infamous Barbary Coast. In the afternoon, they crossed San Francisco Bay and walked around the sprawling campus of the University of California at Berkeley. Throughout it all, Garbo managed to avoid detection—until the next day when she tried to cash a check. True to character, once her charade had been exposed, Greta left town.

At the end of August, a sharp tremor hit Los Angeles at 4:40 in the afternoon; Garbo and Sörensen were to suffer a temblor of a different sort. The reason for the rift was never explained. In later years, Sören avoided any mention of their falling out, speaking only of his heartbreak at the thought of returning to Sweden without Greta.

From the beginning, Sören had ignored any hints of trouble. Greta obviously didn't like him cultivating her friends, but he misinterpreted her comments; Sören believed that she was simply jealous. It should not have been surprising to him that Garbo could be proprietary in her attitude toward friends. One evening, Sörensen was invited to a dinner party at the home of Jacques Feyder and Françoise Rosay. Greta complained that she wanted to spend the evening with him and asked Sören not to attend. (Garbo had been invited to the party but had declined.) "I can't go on canceling engagements because of you," he told her firmly. Besides, he was looking forward to seeing "his" Hollywood friends. Greta was silent. Clearly agitated, she drummed her fingers on the armrest of her chair.

Then she spoke. "Call them and say I'll be coming with you," she said. "Call them yourself," Sören replied. "They're already offended at you for not coming the last time."

Greta defiantly made the phone call, "and was mildly snubbed for one of the few times in her life. . . . The rebuke stung Garbo to the quick. She started dressing for the event with a vengeance. On went her black tailor-made dress, as well as a little more powder on her cheeks and a little more mascara on her long eyelashes." When they arrived at the Feyder home, the lawn was so crowded with cars, it took Sörensen some time to find a space. "Garbo was fuming with impatience. Finally we made our entrance. . . . Garbo led the way, lovely eyes glowing, head held high, her lovely hair flowing over those handsome shoulders. And suddenly at the top of her voice she called out, in German, 'Ich bin ganz und gar besoffen!'—*I am stinking drunk.*" But Françoise Rosay, an actress of some reputation abroad, came forward and took Greta's hand. "Never mind, Greta. Sei herzliches wilkommen—*a hearty welcome*—to you, just the same." Greta looked deflated for a moment and then began to laugh. "She was, of course, as sober as a mule," Sören said.

To be Garbo's friend, said Jean Negulesco, was "to be simple and unde-manding and discreet in your judgment of her and of her moods." Sören had misjudged his position. In September, the first installment of Rilla Page Palmborg's "The Private Life of Greta Garbo" was published in *Photoplay*. Feeling betrayed by the revelations from Wilhelm Sörensen and John Loder, Greta soon removed herself from both lives. (Gustaf and Sigrid Norin had already left her service, so did not suffer the consequences of their indiscretion.) In November, Sören was called back to Sweden. Before he left, he spoke wistfully to Rilla Palmborg of a time, not long past, when Greta Garbo had favored him. This material would become the basis of the first full-length Garbo biography, published in 1931.[6]

There was more to come.

That October, the Academy of Motion Picture Arts and Sciences announced its nominations for 1929/1930. Garbo was recognized for her performances in *Anna Christie* and *Romance*.[7] By now, there was no doubt

---

[6]But not before becoming entangled in a mess of lawsuits: Edington threatened to sue Doubleday/Dorin if they published the book; Palmborg went to the press with charges that Doubleday had caved into pressure from MGM and only printed the contract minimum of 2,500 copies. (Even today, local libraries are much more likely to have the English edition on their shelves.)

[7]She would lose the Best Actress award to Norma Shearer, who was also double-nominated.

that Garbo's future was sound—but her contract was still a silent one. "In this respect, she is the one exception in our stock company," attorney Martin Greenwood apprised Louis B. Mayer. "The question of her signing was discussed with the advent of sound pictures, but she declined to sign, giving as her reasons, as I recall it, lack of confidence in the English tongue."

Since she had already spoken in three features, it seemed a moot point. On October 15, she began her fourth. The new production was based on *Sappho* by Alphonse Daudet, a dramatic story of a beautiful Parisian prostitute that had been updated to the modern era. Irving Thalberg assigned screenwriter Gene Markey to the project. Markey's heroine, Yvonne Valvret, is a fascinating creature who makes her living from men who can afford her company. Men also make their living from her: Yvonne is the inspiration for the most talented artists, poets, writers, and sculptors in France. Metro subsequently retitled the story *Inspiration*.

The film's cast included Robert Montgomery, Lewis Stone, Marjorie Rambeau, and newcomer Karen Morley. Montgomery, one of the studio's most promising actors, had been featured recently opposite Norma Shearer *(The Divorcée)* and Joan Crawford *(Our Blushing Brides)*. Eager to impress, Garbo's new leading man wore a new blue suit, white shirt, and tie on the first day of filming; Greta did not seem to notice. Years later, Montgomery would be credited with the opinion that "Making a film with Greta Garbo does not constitute an introduction." As was true of most of her costars, from Ricardo Cortez to Melvyn Douglas, few men felt that they knew Garbo any better on the last day of production than they had on the first. Most likely, part of the problem on *Inspiration* was that Garbo and Clarence Brown were at odds. According to Wilhelm Sörensen (who had not yet left the scene), Greta again felt that she had been talked into doing a picture she did not like—and she had tired of Clarence Brown, whom she thought old-fashioned.

Midway through production, word circulated around the Culver City lot that all was not well between Garbo and Brown. One of their disagreements reportedly revolved around the rehearsal schedule. Garbo felt that prolonged rehearsals needlessly spent her energy and creativity. She preferred letting the cast rehearse without her and then joining them at the end to nail the scene on the first take. There was no verbal battle between Greta and her director—both were too retiring for such an obvious confrontation—but the foundation for conflict was laid. "I would not direct Miss Garbo again under the same conditions that prevailed during the last picture," Brown admitted to a writer from *Photoplay*. "We would begin by having a completed script before we started. But for Miss Garbo, personally and as an artist, I have the greatest respect and admiration."

Scripts were always a problem. During a tense on-the-set conference, Greta walked over to Marjorie Rambeau and picked up the Pekinese dog she was carrying for the scene. "Excuse me, Miss Rambeau," she said, "but your dog must have some fresh air." With that, she walked off the stage with the dog. After an appropriate amount of time had passed, the assistant director appeared at the stage entrance beckoning her inside. "Not yet," she insisted, "not until the dog is all right." Several minutes later, Clarence Brown came out. "Greta, the script will be just as you want it," he assured her. Garbo picked up the dog. "The little doggie is okay now," she said.

Their conflict notwithstanding, Clarence Brown remained supportive in the press. It was hard to argue with Garbo's decisions as an actress, he maintained. "She is incomparable in the art of beautifying illicit love and passion. . . . She responds very easily to directions, although she will not hesitate to put up a strong argument if she feels differently [than] her director . . . Perhaps my success in directing her has been due to my recognition of her as a woman. I realize that the woman in her knows better how the woman character will react to circumstances in the story . . ."

Health was still a consideration. The intensity of the work often left Garbo nervous, tired, and susceptible to the elements. "Greta Garbo is not a strong woman," Brown told a journalist in 1932. "Her health is much better than it was two years ago, but she has not the physical strength many other players have for the long hours in the studio." The minute she felt a cold coming on, she would make an appointment at a Turkish bath in Hollywood where she would get a massage and spend time in the sauna or mineral baths—just as she had done as a theater student in Stockholm. "Temperamentally, Garbo is no different today than when she first walked in front of my camera," cinematographer William Daniels stated.

On November 24, the final day of production, Louis B. Mayer gathered his MGM family on one of his soundstages and, in an inspiring speech, sought to reassure employees that although times were tough, there would be no wage cuts at Metro-Goldwyn-Mayer. The mogul announced that he was meeting with other state leaders to ensure that the studio would not be imperiled by the current economic crisis.

The world premiere of the German *Anna Christie* took place on December 22, 1930, in Cologne. "GARBO SPRICHT DEUTSCH!" ads declared. The film was greeted with sell-out crowds from Berlin to Vienna. Equally important, it was embraced by nationalist critics who normally protected their local industry from outside, corruptive forces with patriotic zeal. In view of the film's cost, however, executives at Loew's and Metro-Goldwyn-Mayer determined that the experiment had not paid off. The studio put their plans for a Swedish language adaptation on hold (script files indicate that Wilhelm Sörensen was among those writers contributing to this translation) and released the English language version in the remaining markets.

According to Blanche Sweet, Eugene O'Neill never saw Garbo's Anna Christie. "He admired her work, but because he had been told by friends that the film wasn't very good, he never saw it." He would have liked the German translation. Eight minutes longer than the original talkie, it took more liberties with the dialogue but was truer to the weary essence of O'Neill's play.

At the end of January, *Inspiration* began making its appearance in theaters across the United States. For the first time in years, a critical reception met "The One and Only—The Divine Garbo" (according to advertising). "A sadly unconvincing talking pictorial conception of Alphonse Daudet's *Sappho*," Mordaunt Hall reluctantly reported in *The New York Times*. "It may be a handsome production, with fine photography and compelling settings . . . but for the most part [Clarence Brown's] work is as uninspired as the performances of all the players save Miss Garbo."

With its dimly lit interiors, *Inspiration* seemed to many to be a story that took place in the shadows. *Motion Picture Magazine* referred to it as "*Camille* without the cough." Theater attendance was less qualified. Domestic box-office kept pace with *Romance;* according to the studio's accounting, the final tally was over one million dollars worldwide, representing a fair to average profit of $286,000 for MGM. Garbo talking was still a novelty, but *Inspiration* would show her handlers how speech could increase the distance between the actress and her audience. It made her seem more exotic, less like one of them. "Garbo is the strangest personality of all of the freak or odd ones this extensive screen colony has been honeycombed with for years," *Variety* suggested to readers.

In February of 1931, rumors began to surface that when Garbo's contract came up for renewal, she would not re-sign with MGM. The talk of the town was that she intended to retire.

CHAPTER THIRTEEN

Chiaroscuro (Shadows and Light)

With rare exception, the light of the most gifted foreign artists burned brightly in Hollywood—and died out quickly. The flirtation with the American system soon became disillusionment. That Greta Garbo continued her work at Metro-Goldwyn-Mayer, surmounting obstacles that had turned many others away, surviving one heartbreaking disappointment after another, would bear witness not only to an extraordinary talent but also to her keen will to survive and her determination not to allow her creative spirit to be broken.

Greta met Sergei Eisenstein through the Viertels. The great Russian director, with his wild and shaggy hair accentuating his often brilliant provocations at Salka's, had been affectionately nicknamed "Eisenbahn" by Garbo; he called her Greta "Garbel." His first assignment in Hollywood was to adapt Theodore Dreiser's *An American Tragedy* for Paramount's B. P. Schulberg. But the director's political troubles abroad—he was banned from exhibiting his films in Western Europe because they were deemed Communist propaganda—appeared to follow him to the States. Calling the project "a glorious experiment," Paramount junior executive David O. Selznick urged Schulberg to pass on the picture, and "take whatever rap is coming to us for not supporting Eisenstein the artist (as he proves himself to be with this script) . . ."

What happened to Sergei Eisenstein perfectly illustrated how the Hollywood moguls' efforts "often made them bedfellows with the same reactionary groups that had attacked *them* for controlling Hollywood in the first place," Neal Gabler wrote in his study of the Hollywood studio system. "No sooner had Eisenstein—a Communist, a homosexual, *and* a Jew— arrived than he fell victim to an unrelenting campaign of anti-Semitism and anticommunism . . . [It] began with slanders in letters and pamphlets, but when it escalated to threats against the studio and against Eisenstein personally, his contract was terminated."

The financing on his next production, *Que Viva Mexico!*, was pulled while the director was shooting in Mexico. Unable to save his film from mutilation, a visibly shaken, disheartened Eisenstein returned to the Soviet Union, where he languished further under the Stalinist regime.

On the nineteenth of March, Greta attended a memorial service for F. W.

Murnau, the creative spirit behind such cinematic milestones as *The Cabinet of Dr. Caligari*, *The Last Laugh*, and *Sunrise*. Due to the salacious rumors surrounding Murnau's death, most of his Hollywood contemporaries had elected to stay away from the funeral parlor, fearing they might be "tainted" with the scandal.[1] But Greta, and Salka and Berthold Viertel, remained faithful and were among the few to honor their friend at the end. That Garbo seemed unconcerned about the scandal was evident by her gesture of commissioning a death mask. (Although this was not found among her effects in 1990, it was reported that she kept this memento on her bedstand for years.)

F. W. Murnau was the type of artist whose sensitivities doubtless reminded Greta of Moje. "During the period of mutual admiration between [Garbo] and the director Murnau . . . I remember them both sprawled in a lively tête-à-tête on the wide expanse of Ludwig Berger's billiard table," Sergei Eisenstein wrote in his memoirs. If Murnau's work recalled Stiller, his death in an automobile accident on the coast highway was strangely reminiscent of Einar Hansson's fatal crash four years earlier. Hollywood, it seemed, did not give up its prisoners easily.

Nor would they surrender Garbo.

"Let's get down to brass tacks about this mystery woman of the screen," Katherine Albert declared in "Exploding the Garbo Myth." Fully cognizant of the controversy she was about to create, the former publicist betrayed her alma mater by announcing that she was "bored with Garbo." Furthermore, she was not alone in her heresy. "At least I find company in Hollywood," said she. For fans and admirers, such a diatribe—which denied Garbo's artistry, intellect, and even glamour—would be nothing less than blasphemy.

Albert characterized her subject as stubborn, petulant, a shrewd businesswoman—and yet added, somewhat surprisingly, that "Garbo's a nice girl. . . . She's invariably lovely and kind to the new actors and actresses who work with her. She is touched by illness and sadness and expresses herself in flowers and gifts to those who are ill or sad. But the Garbo legend

---

[1]There were many conflicting stories and hints of strange, mystical warnings. The rumor that no one dared to discuss openly—but of course did behind glass doors—was that Murnau was "servicing" his young chauffeur when the chauffeur lost control of the car and it went down an embankment. According to Lotte Eisner in her biography of the director, Murnau was sitting in the back seat with a colleague. His regular chauffeur and a young Filipino boy who was learning to drive were in the front. As the car rolled down the embankment, Murnau was thrown from the car and hit his head against a post. The other occupants of the car, including the director's German shepherd, were not seriously injured.

is a myth . . . I have talked to many, many people about Garbo, people who know her intimately . . . and I have yet to have one of them give me the slightest evidence that her silences are a mask of deep thought."

Photoplay editor-in-chief James R. Quirk subscribed to the theory that "If a magazine doesn't make its readers mad, it has no vitality." Accordingly, his magazine received thousands of complaints over the next few weeks. "Greta can more thoroughly evoke an emotion of pity and defense than anyone I have ever known," a friend remarked. Many admitted wanting "to defend her, to protect her, to take her part." Harry Edington reported that Garbo received hundreds of letters and telegrams after publication of the piece. The "Garbo-maniac" was born.

It clearly bothered some industry-watchers that such unquestioning support gave the object of desire "license" to ignore the very people who made her success possible. Garbo's "indifference to all the recognized Hollywood values, her long silences, her brutal independence . . . have never deserted her for a single second," Clare Boothe Luce proselytized in *Vanity Fair.* "There is no chink in her magnificent armor of aloofness." Since Garbo neither catered to the lowest common denominator nor sacrificed the public's continued support, she did not appear to pay for the "sin" of her success. Her flight from publicity would be the most seductive element of her private persona that other luminaries would seek to embrace— with little success. "[Greta] seeks less, and gets more, publicity than anybody," Clarence Brown contended. "All sorts of silly stories circulate about her."

Her stubborn refusal to conform to "the Hollywood standard" frustrated unrelenting hosts and hostesses in a community where socialization was an instrument of ambition as well as a reflection of station. Paradoxically, because she held herself apart, Garbo's name was always on the "A" list. Non-attendance meant non-acceptance—who was *she* not to accept *them?* She was "a loner in an industry where people often react to insecurity by surrounding themselves with flatterers," Melvyn Douglas offered. "Garbo couldn't, or wouldn't, do that."

At the Viertels it was different. "Salka's salon," as it was increasingly known, was not an awkward congregation of sycophants—though even here respected intellectuals fell silent in Garbo's company. At the Viertel home on Mabery Road, a sympathetic gathering of friends helped to provide a protective shell around a fellow émigré. Contrary to the presumed profile of a neurotic, xenophobic movie star, Garbo pursued many friendships in Hollywood. As a fanatic international following developed around her, the friendly looking white house with green trim owned by the Viertels in Santa Monica Canyon became Garbo's anchor. Salka's home, friends insisted, was the only place in southern California with decent strudel and comfortable armchairs.

A somber portrait from *Inspiration* superimposed on the face of the Sphinx put a picture where there had only been words. When photographer Clarence Sinclair Bull showed the results of his experiment to Garbo, he was afraid that she might be offended. But Greta "roared with laughter and then begged my pardon, thinking she had offended me," he said. The composite was approved, much to the delight of the Metro publicity department. The "Swedish Sphinx" neatly capsulized the Garbo persona, becoming one of the most recognizable images in the world. "The more mask-like the face, the deeper the mystery," one fan magazine stated.

With the departure of Ruth Harriet Louise in 1929, C. S. Bull became one of Garbo's most important collaborators at the studio, astutely guiding her face into the light and exploiting its emotional depth in the shadows. They cemented their relationship with an extraordinary series of photographs Bull shot for *The Kiss*. Greta first walked into his gallery looking like "a frightened schoolgirl," he wrote. "What she didn't know was that I was just as scared as she." Over a three-hour period he shot her "in every pose and emotion that beautiful face could mirror," expecting that she would speak up when she'd had too much. She never said anything.

Finally he ran out of film. "I was quite nervous," Garbo apologized as she prepared to leave. "I'll do better next time." Bull patted her hand. "So will I." After a disappointing session with another photographer (George Hurrell), the actress informed studio management that there was only one man she wanted to shoot her portraits. C. S. Bull believed that as an actress, Garbo actually worked harder in front of his camera than anywhere else. She considered it an essential part of her job. "She comes in bounding—but with the air of a martyr. A sort of 'oh-how-I-hate-to-do-this-but-let's-get-it-going!' air. Not surly, merely resigned," a profile suggested. "It's always 'Mr. Bull' and 'Miss Garbo'; never 'Clarence' or 'Greta' . . ."

With a single session producing as many as three hundred portraits, Garbo learned to make herself at ease in the photographer's presence.[2] She liked to play popular music on the radio or phonograph, and walked about

---

[2]As did he. "There has never been anything false between Greta Garbo and me," he once said. But he was curious, as many were, about her famous eyelashes. "At the end of one long sitting . . . I thought I heard myself say, 'Are they real?' A slow smile drifted across her mouth . . . the lashes fluttered . . . a throaty giggle. 'What are you talking about, Mr. Bull?' 'Are your lashes real?' 'Pull them and find out.'" So he did—and they were. (Tallulah Bankhead and sculptor Carl Milles were among those who also accepted her challenge.)

the studio with such noiseless ease that he often wasn't aware of her. On one occasion, as Bull's assistant Virgil Apger was adjusting a baby spot, the light slipped and missed her by a few hair-raising inches. "Do I make you nervous, maybe?" Greta queried with a decided lack of temperament. But she never let the assistant forget the incident, teasing him each time she came to the gallery by first making sure it was safe to come in.

That May, an unidentified fan who was convinced that he was Greta Garbo's brother was arrested after days of stalking his subject around Los Angeles. Following a brief hearing, he was sent back to his home in Lewiston, Idaho. Columnists wondered if Garbo wasn't a myth, after all. Actually, the icon was back at work.

Susan Lenox: Her Fall and Rise was a dark tale of a woman's victimization by "society's wolves"—the father who deserted her unmarried mother, the uncle who raised her, the would-be husband she was sold to, plus a faceless chain of lovers. During her struggle, she rises to financial security but falls morally; her redemption is her love for Rodney Spencer and her willingness to trade her questionable security for his salvation. "This hurt that we have inflicted upon each other; it's become a bond. Nothing can break it," she tells him. "We're just like two cripples—twisted. Only together can we ever become straight."

Although the original novel by David Graham Phillips had been published years earlier, the story still had great significance for audiences in 1931. "By the third year of the depression, the economic independence of women, so newly won, so precariously held, had collapsed almost completely and they were thrown back on the immemorial feminine position," film historian Richard Griffith stated. "In the harsh world of supply and demand, they had nothing to sell but sex." Many MGM "heroines" during this period would, in effect, be women of the night—Susan Lenox was Garbo's third prostitute in eighteen months.

Robert Z. Leonard, who was assigned to direct the film, claimed two prior associations with Garbo. One was *The Torrent,* the production that introduced him to his second wife, Gertrude Olmstead. The second association was unheralded. "Soon after going with MGM, I was asked to make a test of a girl from Europe," he told *Variety* in 1944. Shrinking into the vast shadows of the Metro-Goldwyn shooting stage stood a nervous young actress who looked to be about seventeen, her hair unkempt, her face a blank. "She had, it seemed, done something in a small way in German pictures. This much I learned from a man with her. He did not tell me her name. She herself spoke no English, indeed was mute."

The director tried to show her what he wanted her to do, proceeding "with all the grace of my 225 pounds, to impersonate a flapper," he confessed. "As I turned around during my demonstration there was no Garbo! She had precipitately fled, leaving her companion [Mauritz Stiller] to explain to me: 'Watching you, Miss Garbo asked me, Am I supposed to do like that?' "

The theme of running away would be integral to the plot of *Susan Lenox*. More important still was the reintroduction of the concept of fate propelling Garbo's characters to an unhappy end. With increasing frequency, Garbo's "tragic fate" would take on added significance in her dramatic films, literally assuming a role as a third character in the story. The physical manifestation of this quality was evidenced most profoundly in the often-imitated "Garbo slouch."[3] This powerful dynamic would be in direct opposition to the raw, natural force projected by Garbo's new leading man: Clark Gable.

Scarcely one year into his MGM contract, Gable was already one of the busiest players on the lot. He made eight films in 1931, most notably as the gangster lover of Joan Crawford in *Dance Fools Dance* and Norma Shearer in *A Free Soul,* plus key appearances opposite Barbara Stanwyck (*Night Nurse*) and another up-and-coming player, Jean Harlow (*The Secret Six*). He came on so strong that the Metro mailroom had not been prepared for the volumes of fan mail they received. Vigorous and brutally masculine, his physical presence was undeniable. He had an air of sexual self-confidence that proved irresistible to most every woman he met. Clark Gable was "a new hero for a new era," the archetypal male for the scrapping thirties: tough, straight-shooting, an average Joe "who lusted after life and women [and] had no time for phonies." Much as Garbo had set forth a new image for actresses in the late-twenties, Gable established a new standard for the men on Depression-era movie screens. He wasn't the competition, he was the future; his success would irretrievably seal John Gilbert's fate at MGM.

"Does Garbo Tank She Go Home Now?" asked columnist Jack Grant. Harry Edington wasn't sure. "Naturally, I shall attempt to persuade her to remain in motion pictures, but the rumors of her retirement originated with Garbo herself," he explained as *Susan Lenox* was about to go into production. With less than a year to go on her contract, Greta frequently talked about going home. "And she can quit whenever she wants to,"

[3]Feet first, head and shoulders inclined slightly backwards, long gliding steps. According to fashion analyst Vernon Patterson, "It was an animal-like grace that, because it also accentuated the line and flow of one's clothes, was soon adapted on fashion runways in New York, Paris and Milan."

Edington added. "She has saved enough to be financially independent for life."

News about the demand for Garbo abroad—independent of MGM— drove executives at the studio wild. With the European box-office at an all-time low and an estimated two thousand movie palaces closing in the United States alone, the summer of 1931 had already gone on record as one of the worst seasons since motion pictures moved out of the nickelodeon.[4] Exhibitors were begging for good films. MGM needed "All the Stars in Heaven" out front and center. Those who could not be counted on to produce would soon be out of a job.

Susan Lenox began principal photography on May 25, 1931. Added to the cast were Jean Hersholt as Helga's uncle (Helga was Susan's name before the fall), Alan Hale as the crude brute who attempts to take her virginity before the wedding, John Miljan as the lecherous circus boss, and Ian Keith as the understanding "other man."

Although the majors had recently announced payroll cuts of 10 to 25 percent, Metro had again assured its players that it would not enforce the cutbacks. Instead, the front office proposed downsizing a number of departments—starting with the story department. The decision couldn't have been more ironic, given the score of writers who would make a variety of contributions to *Susan Lenox*. Six-day work weeks did not manage to make the script any clearer. First, the story opened in Indiana, then Iowa, and finally Minnesota's Swedish farming community. Rodney had a wife and child; a fiancée; then no one at all. Should Susan give everything up for him? Would Rodney sink into alcoholism and despair before Susan found him, or should his on-again, off-again wife make for a quick fade-out and die?

The threat of censorship solved some problems; others were less easily contained. "Plenty of turmoil at Metro during the production of *Susan Lenox*, which is still in the throes of production," *Variety* reported on the seventh of July. "Twenty-two writers worked at different times on the story before it went in, with some still working while production was on. Greta Garbo, topping, has done six walks off the set, at different times finding fault with the story. Several halts were made as a result to revamp, with the ending also changed several times."

"No one making films can be happy," Garbo said, the pathetic sigh in her voice a seeming redundancy. By now, however, she was sharing her melancholy with a new friend. It was an association that would forever

---

[4]Not all theaters closed permanently, but waited out the summer heat for the more prestigious fall lineup.

change the way Greta Garbo was viewed by Hollywood. Mercedes de Acosta would say that it was a predestined one.

Taking on the modern myth of Greta Garbo as illuminated by Mercedes de Acosta is a tricky proposition—for the illumination is translucent; one must navigate a minefield of fantasy, half-truths, and dramatic invention. Friends and acquaintances had just cause for renaming her memoirs *"Here Lies the Heart . . . and lies . . . and lies . . . and lies."* Yet at the core of this pseudo-fabrication was a relationship that—in and of itself—was real, vital, and absolutely undeniable. Mercedes de Acosta cannot be easily dismissed. Despite the numerous ups and downs of their relationship, she was one of the few people for whom Greta continued to make allowances. It was, in fact, with a poignant disregard for either history or human frailty that the insecurity and deep-seated need for attention that attracted Greta to Mercedes in the first place would betray them both in the end.

In a biographical piece prepared in 1942, Mercedes described herself as "an author and personality of international fame." An aspiring poet, novelist, and playwright, she was an American citizen who considered herself "by blood pure Spanish." She was proud that her mother, Micaela Hernandez Aloy y Hernandez de Alba, was born of a noble family and was a direct descendant on both her maternal and paternal sides of the Duke of Alba. Her father, Ricardo de Acosta, was the younger brother of the Spanish poet Ignacio de Acosta and, following his example, became a poet and a man of letters as well. "Although my father had little influence over me, we had much in common intellectually," his daughter would write.

The youngest of eight children, Mercedes was born on March 1, 1894.[5] In an early draft of her memoirs, she claimed to have been raised as a boy until the age of seven, when she was confronted with the awful truth. This contradicts her later portrayal of a sometimes idyllic, sometimes troubled childhood during which a precocious four-year-old so impressed an affluent theatrical producer that he attempted to adopt her. Though over-starched summer dresses were definitely part of that memory, Mercedes did admit to a brief obsession with playing a newsboy "with newspapers under my arms and one of my brother's caps pulled over my eyes."

She carried with her the "psychological contradiction" of being born in the United States to Spanish-Catholic parents who were, in effect, transplanted to Protestant America and who never completely adapted. "The feeling that my parents were unique and apart from other people made me

---

[5]This is her birth date according to her 1922 passport. Some sources indicate she was born in 1893—later passports stated 1898, 1900, and 1901.

regard myself as different too," she said, "as though it were only right that I be alienated from the common herd." This was one of many complex emotional issues Mercedes de Acosta shared with Greta Garbo.

Their mutual identification sealed their friendship. Both lost their fathers when they were teenagers; Mercedes' father committed suicide by jumping off a cliff in the Adirondacks. Both lost siblings a few years later; Mercedes' discovery was especially brutal—she was the one to find her brother Enrique's body. Both idolized their elder sisters; Rita de Acosta Lydig, a popular figure in New York social circles and a great patroness of the arts, was responsible for introducing Mercedes to an awe-inspiring list of international artists from Edith Wharton and Sarah Bernhardt to Enrico Caruso, Arturo Toscanini, Auguste Rodin, and Gabriele D'Annunzio (thus launching her on a career of "collecting" celebrities). Both were afflicted with an inner restlessness that was compounded by a chronic inability to sleep; Mercedes wrote of a deep disturbance she called her "moaning sickness," which could strike at any time during the day or night. Both were "desperately unhappy and unadjusted people" living in a near-constant state of melancholia. Owing to her Latin heritage, Mercedes' agitation was projected outward; Greta's turmoil was internal but no less stressful.

Since her marriage to artist Abram Poole in 1920, Mercedes had managed to keep their relationship an open and modern one. Before the civil ceremony, Poole agreed that Mercedes would keep her maiden name professionally and privately. "To the outward form of sex which the body has assumed, I have remained indifferent," she avowed. "I do not understand the difference between a man and a woman, and believing only in the eternal value of love, I cannot understand these so-called 'normal' people who believe that a man should love only a woman, and a woman love only a man."

As if to prove her point, Mercedes met one of the great loves of her life, actress Eva Le Gallienne, shortly before her marriage. It was with Le Gallienne that she traveled to Paris, London, and Budapest in 1922 before continuing on to Constantinople with her husband. Together with friends and lovers throughout the 1920s, Mercedes frequented Bob Chanler's legendary soirées on East Nineteenth Street, which attracted an intoxicating mix of artists and intellectuals of all races and sexual persuasions; and she partook in the illicit nightlife found in the speakeasies and clubs around Manhattan. "I suppose it was the newly found excitement of homosexuality," she wrote, "which after the war was expressed openly in nightclubs and cabarets by boys dressed as women, and was, like drinking, forbidden and subject to police raids, which made it all the more enticing."

When she wasn't suffering from one of her "indigo moods"—a near-suicidal depression that was sometimes so dark she kept a loaded gun near her bed—Mercedes projected an electric aura all her own. Five feet, three inches tall; jet black hair cut short and, in the spirit of a true Latin lover, usually brushed back from her face with brilliantine; chalk white skin (often made lighter by powder); thin red lips; deep-set dark brown eyes. Everything about her made a statement. She heightened that effect to nearly absurd proportions with her equally flamboyant attire: men's trousers, pointed shoes with large silver buckles, a black tricorn or round Cossack cap, and a full-length black coat with huge lapels, fitted waist, and full skirt. Her costumes were nearly always black—except if she was in love, when she might wear white. In a typically droll aside, Tallulah Bankhead characterized Mercedes as "a mouse in a topcoat"; other acquaintances referred to her as "Madame Dracula." "She is very mannish but charming, kind, clever & interesting," Cecil Beaton wrote in his diary; a "funny, thin, hawklike little woman" who talked in hollow tones, her sentences flowing in quick starts and jerks. But, Beaton added, she had "glorious enthusiasms" and "glorious friendships," and "could not be less like her outrageous appearance."

Mercedes told Beaton that, to her knowledge, Greta wasn't "so far a Lesbian but might easily be one." That knowledge was primarily based on what she read in newspapers and magazines or heard from friends of friends. It seems that she fixated on Garbo as soon as she saw her photograph. She wrote in the first draft of her autobiography that during her trip to Constantinople, she lived in anticipation of something extraordinary that was about to happen, "as though straining to hear a voice or catch a glimpse of a face . . ."

The photograph Mercedes would regard with wonder three years later was sent to her by Arnold Genthe. The first of his series of portraits, shot when Greta and Moje were in New York, was published in *Vanity Fair* in November 1925. With her relationship with Eva Le Gallienne now in shambles, Mercedes requested a copy of the picture from Genthe.[6] A few months later, *The Torrent* drew her in further. Once again, that mystic feel-

---

[6]This account intentionally disregards de Acosta's story of the Genthe photograph. After the humiliating failure of *Jehanne D'Arc* (written by Mercedes, and starring Le Gallienne) in Paris, both women were "exhausted, disilusioned and embarrassed" and returned to New York in late August. Their affair suffered another blow when Le Gallienne fell in love with Noël Coward's set designer on the boat. "By the time the ship docked in New York, Eva had replaced Mercedes with Gladys as the significant woman in her life," biographer Robert Schanke insists. Mercedes' excuse about not being able to go to Genthe's studio because she had been invited to Richard Le Gallienne's home is further suspect, because Eva had been estranged from her father since childhood—and Le Gallienne's home was in Connecticut, not Woodstock, New York.

ing was present. "I sat through the film twice and when I went out into the street I felt a great loneliness," she wrote. "I did not know then, as I know now, that there is such a thing as spiritually getting 'on the beam'. That there is a secret area of the soul which, when kept pure, can act as a magnet and draw to itself a desire—even an unconscious one."

One of the mysteries concerning Mercedes' first meeting with Garbo was how she contrived to make it happen in the first place. She had been in Hollywood for two months.[7] By her own admission, Mercedes knew of Salka Viertel through mutual friends (Hope Williams and Eleanora von Mendelssohn), and yet neither one of them appears to have been responsible for her invitation to Mabery Road. Salka called, seemingly out of the blue, introduced herself, and, during the course of conversation, intimated that there was a "surprise" in store if Mercedes came to Sunday brunch.

So Greta and Mercedes were introduced at Salka's. In her published memoirs, Mercedes addressed the physical impression of meeting Greta Garbo for the first time: how she looked, what she wore, what she said. In her original manuscript, however, she presented a more psychological rendering. She compared Greta to her mother, Micaela, and sister Rita. "There is some element which emanated from Rita which also emanates from Greta, a sort of despotic attitude—a tendency to overrule everyone while at the same time having in this attitude a certain tenderness and consideration," she stated. "Greta's high-handedness is like Rita's and also a certain aspect of her humour, as well as her tristesse."

Years later, Mercedes could not recall what they talked about that afternoon. "I was too overwhelmed to record the conversation. I remember discussing Duse with Greta and Salka, and then Salka went upstairs to telephone. . . . Greta and I were left on our own." Both fell silent—no problem for Garbo, who could always manage a silence. Mercedes waited and watched; but the object of her silent vigil did not stay long. "She explained that she was still shooting *Susan Lenox* and had made this visit as an exception. . . . 'Now I will go home to dinner which I will have in bed. I am indeed an example of the gay Hollywood night life!'" After she made her exit, Salka reported to Mercedes that Greta really liked her "and she likes few people."

The following weekend, Mercedes was again invited to Salka's—this time, for breakfast. She arrived exactly on time, but "Greta was already there, in white shorts this time, and again the visor. I noticed what an exquisite color her legs had become from the sun. At this second meeting

---

[7] Her friend Elisabeth Marbury, a prominent figure in literary circles on the East Coast, had secured a job for her as a writer at RKO-Pathé.

she was more beautiful than I had ever dreamed she could be. Her face was fresh and glowing. She was in high spirits and full of mischief." After break-fast, Salka suggested that the two go over to Oliver Garrett's house; Gar-rett, a writer at Paramount, was away on location and had left his home in the Viertels' care. In the privacy of a stranger's home, on a "brilliantly sunny day," they rolled back the rug and danced the morning away, singing along with the latest records. When the time came, Mercedes reluctantly got into a waiting car to go to a prearranged lunch at Pola Negri's. Garbo picked a flower for her from the garden and smiled. "Don't say I never gave you a flower," she said, laughing gaily and waving as the car pulled away.

Arriving at Negri's home, Mercedes soon discovered that Greta was right: she was just another face in the Hollywood crowd at Pola's. A phone call from a "Mr. Toscar" (Garbo) was all the persuasion she needed to drop everything and rush to Greta's home on San Vicente. Wearing just a Chi-nese black silk dressing gown and men's bedroom slippers, Greta awaited Mercedes at the base of her driveway. She motioned for the driver to stop. Mercedes thought the change in her look quite startling. "She looked tired and depressed," she recalled. "Only a few hours ago I had seen her radiant. When I came to know her well, I realized how easily her moods and looks could change. She could be gay and look well and within five minutes she would be desperately unhappy and apparently terribly ill."

The couple stayed in the garden; strangely, Greta did not invite Mer-cedes inside. They stretched out in the shadows of the eucalyptus trees, held hands, and watched the sun set late on that July evening. "Now you must go home," Greta said. Mercedes would not see her again until princi-pal photography on *Susan Lenox* had been completed.

Production wrapped during the second week of July. That evening, Metro previewed a rough cut of the film. The screening did not go well. With any-one else in the lead role, *The Hollywood Reporter* stressed, the film's box-office potential would have been questioned. "Garbo's gorgeous work, the presence of Gable and a perfect supporting cast—the love scenes—all these things help lift the story itself out of its rut, a very deep rut. Unfortu-nately, the star herself has never looked less attractive . . ." Gable's appear-ance was better received. "Heaven help the fan contingent when THIS picture gets out," the paper concluded. "As actor and lover—he's immense."

Irving Thalberg fervently believed that the making of a film was of less consequence than how MGM *remade* it. In the case of *Susan Lenox*, there was no doubt that extensive retakes would be in order. However, before the audience reaction cards were analyzed, new script conferences called, and retakes scheduled—in and around the ongoing preparation for *Mata Hari*—Garbo was promised a break.

Relieved to be finished with an emotionally draining role, she called her new friend. "My present prison term is over," she enthusiastically announced. This time Greta not only invited Mercedes over, she led her through the front door. Unlike the house on Chevy Chase, Greta had put very little of herself into the San Vicente house. The living room seemed "gloomy and unlived in," de Acosta said. Greta told her she lived mostly in her bedroom, but her room upstairs was equally spartan: a bed, a desk, a dressing table, and a few uncomfortable-looking chairs. For Greta, the basics were better. Fewer possessions meant fewer bonds—and more freedom to leave whenever she wished. A bed was just a place to sleep in.

As the sun faded behind the trees and the room grew dark, Greta shared some of her dreams, and fears, with Mercedes. It was a *sotto voce* confession that was offered, at first, hesitantly as Greta paused, deliberated, then continued on. "She told me about her parents, mostly about her father—then she spoke of her sister, her brother, her home. She told me in snatches little things about her childhood," Mercedes recollected. When she was finished, the couple sat on the floor, bathed in the serene light of a midsummer moon, and ate a modest feast.[8] Afterward, Mercedes suggested a late-night beach excursion. She piloted Greta's old car to a place she identified in her memoirs as "Casa del Mare"—most probably, Castellammare, the little-used name for the area between Pacific Palisades and Malibu, where fragile cliffs rise dramatically above the coastal highway. In this idyllic setting, they again conversed about matters both trivial and profound. A few hours later, as the dawn broke over the hills, they walked down to the car, blissfully picking rambler roses as they went along.

Early the next morning, Mercedes was again beckoned to Greta's home—but with less satisfying results. Pulling into the driveway, she observed James Rogers, Greta's driver, packing the car; he, in turn, gave her a curious, furtive look. Greta told her she was leaving town. Harry Edington had given her the keys to Wallace Beery's cabin in the Sierras. "I must go away and be utterly alone," she said. No one was to know where she was going or indeed that she was even gone. "Forgive me, I am just so terribly tired," she pleaded. With that, she put on her sunglasses and got into the car. James slowly pulled the Lincoln out of the driveway, leaving Mercedes speechless in its wake.

---

[8]Interestingly, Mercedes' story about this particular evening runs remarkably similar to another romantic evening she described in her autobiography. The hostess in the first encounter was Isadora Duncan.

Two nights later, after seeking solace where there was none to be found, Mercedes' despair disappeared when she received a long-distance call from Greta. She had decided that her mountain retreat was far too beautiful to keep to herself. "I am on my way back," she said. "Can you come to the island?" With seemingly all-too-convenient timing, RKO had reportedly dropped the option on Mercedes' Pola Negri project the very day Garbo left town. Mercedes was now free to do whatever she wanted—and what she wanted most was to be with Greta Garbo.

On the way back to Los Angeles, Mercedes stated, Greta called every few hours to let her know that she was getting closer. The final call came from Pasadena. De Acosta and her housemate, John Colton, had prepared a celebratory feast and offered the weary travelers a glass of champagne as soon as they walked in the door. That night, Greta slept on the "sleeping porch" of their rented Sunset Boulevard home. They set out the next day, making "a snail's crossing" through the Mojave as the heat rose from the desert floor. Mercedes recalled that the four-hundred-mile journey took nearly three days.

Their final destination was an island on the western shore of Silver Lake in the Sierra Nevadas. They found the lake, a sliver of water between two mountain peaks, midway through the third day. After loading a boat with provisions, Greta told James he could leave—and that he wasn't to return until the last possible minute. "If you turn up one second earlier I will throw you into the lake," she warned, reiterating that no one—not Whistler (her maid, Ettie) and especially not Mr. Louis B. Mayer—was to know where they were. As James drove away, Greta rowed Mercedes across the lake to their cabin on what is now known as Treasure Island.[9]

"How to describe the next six enchanted weeks?" Mercedes wrote in the most quoted passage of her book. She carefully presented a rapturous account of the time spent at Silver Lake. Devoid of any intimations of a sexual encounter, it was nonetheless a romantic story where a poor mortal realized her goddess on "bare Hellenic feet." During this time, she enthused, "there was not a second of disharmony between Greta and me or in nature around us. Not once did it rain and we had brilliant sunshine every day." When they swam in the ice-cold mountain water, Greta, with her long, sure strokes, always glided ahead; when they hiked in the mountains, it was Greta climbing ahead, with the wind blowing her hair back and her face turned toward the sun; when they ate, it was Greta, the hunter, fisher, and gatherer who cooked the meal. Sometimes at night, "with the dark moun-

---

[9]Presumably, a reference to one of Beery's most famous roles as Long John Silver in the classic screen adaptation of Robert Louis Stevenson's *Treasure Island*.

tains towering around us," they would take the boat out and drift in silence; they were "the merest specks in the Divine Cosmos."

"No one can really know Greta unless they have seen her as I saw her there in Silver Lake," Mercedes suggested. "She is a creature of the elements. A creature of wind and storms and rocks and trees and water. A spirit as hers cooped up in a city is a tragic sight." Once again, there was an unexpected element. "There in Silver Lake I never laughed more in my life and it was Greta who made me laugh," she said. "She kept me literally rolling on the floor with her sense of comedy. She told me amusing stories of her childhood, of her adolescence, and of her life in Hollywood. . . . The true essence of these stories is lost without Greta telling them. She is a born mimic and a true clown when she wants to be."

The time passed by quickly. In fact, Mercedes recorded, "There was no sense of time of all." Perhaps that would explain why "six perfect weeks out of a lifetime" were, most likely, in reality, less than two—if that much.

Garbo's schedule during this period was unbelievably tight. Principal photography for *Susan Lenox* had been completed on July 11, 1931. In an effort to keep Garbo in front of motion picture cameras as much as possible before her contract expired, MGM scheduled one project after another. According to a July 27 item in *The Hollywood Reporter*, Garbo was due back in town that day to discuss *Mata Hari*. Within two weeks, Irving Thalberg also had returned and ordered "extended retakes and revisions" on *Susan Lenox*. As soon as photography was completed, Greta was booked to go straight into *Mata Hari* and, following that, a yet-to-be determined third project.

To clarify this timeline further, later in the year Wallace Beery told reporters that Harry Edington had arranged for Greta to spend about three weeks at his cabin. "I gave [Edington] the keys. Two weeks later, he returned them," Beery recalled in another interview. "When I next visited the cabin, it looked exactly as I had left it. Not a book, not an ashtray had been moved. But her manager said she had been there and had enjoyed her stay."

By Mercedes' own account, more than a week was lost in travel—they were lucky to have six days together. In fact, the amazing thing was that they managed the trip without being noticed. Silver Lake is located in the High Sierras of northern California: north of Yosemite National Park, east of the Mother Lode district (a string of Gold Rush towns), and west of Lake Tahoe. The island where Beery's cabin once stood is situated in the narrow southern section of the lake and, unlike in Mercedes' description, is fairly close to the mainland. The Kit Carson Immigrant Trail, Plasse's Resort, a municipal campground, and a boys camp called Camp Minkalo (it was a girls camp during the 1930s) are all just a few minutes away. It is a public area which is secluded, but not completely private—especially during the summer.

Happily, while Greta Garbo's "un-American desire for privacy" didn't always hide her "bohemian" lifestyle, for the time being it did veil affairs of the heart.

Despite her complaint that she couldn't bear to go back to "that studio life," by the beginning of August Garbo was back at MGM. New writers were assigned to develop major sections of the film, including Susan and Rodney's first meeting and the critical final sequence, where censors insisted Susan's decline must be more obvious. One of the more interesting (ultimately unused) devices suggested for the retakes attempted to add an interior monologue similar to those employed in *Strange Interlude,* with Susan debating her conscience in a voice-over. Dissatisfied with the inability of a multitude of writers to find the proper words to suit the action, director Robert Z. Leonard managed to extract the most he could from an absence of dialogue.[10]

Clark Gable completed his work on September 15; Garbo was released from the production four days later. *Susan Lenox* had been in front of the cameras for forty-nine days, incurring a final production cost of $573,000—the most time-consuming and costliest Garbo picture since *The Temptress* five years earlier. A second preview over the weekend of September 19 proved that the effort had been worth it. "The *Susan Lenox* preview Saturday night was like one of those openings—everybody was there," stated *The Hollywood Reporter.* Even Garbo attended, sitting up front with the regular moviegoers.

There was no doubt who dominated the restructured film. *Susan Lenox* was immediately booked into the Capitol Theatre in New York and Loew's State in Los Angeles (traditionally Garbo's best houses) for the second week in October. "By far the most important thing in the film is Miss Garbo herself, beautiful, mysterious, world-weary, the envy and despair of debutantes, shop girls, and other movie actresses," Margaret Marshall wrote in *The Nation.* "Her range is not wide. In the present picture the early role of young innocence is not constantly sustained. Yet she never grows tiresome, even in tiresome roles, probably because, unlike most of her rivals, she has personality and intelligence as well as physical beauty . . ." Marshall was

---

[10]Most notably, in the opening scenes when Susan/Helga manages to evade the eternal question of who she is or where she comes from.

one of many critics who expressed the hope that Garbo would have better luck with future stories.

The much-delayed production of *Mata Hari* went before the cameras on September 30, with George Fitzmaurice at the helm. Wary of potential difficulties with the scenario, as well as unwanted comparisons with the similarly themed Dietrich/von Sternberg collaboration, *Dishonored,* Metro briefly considered not producing the spy story. But a curious thing began to happen: the publicity comparing Garbo to Dietrich only resulted in more fan mail for Garbo. Supporters believed that any comparison could never go beyond a cursory analysis of their exotic allure. "Anybody who knows them both would not mention Dietrich in the same breath as Garbo," Clarence Brown told *Film Weekly.* "Garbo gets her effects from herself. All the director has to do is to lead her gently along, and she will do the rest. But Dietrich is all director. Her work conveys the impressions of a man with a gun—standing over her, forcing her through every action, all the time."

Metro-Goldwyn-Mayer emphasized the difference in a glamorous, stylized presentation of Mata Hari. Historians have contemplated whether or not the former Margaretha Geertruida Zelle, the daughter of a Dutch plantation owner and a Javanese servant, wasn't set up by more cunning superiors—a half-willing participant in espionage duped into taking a tragic fall. MGM was less concerned with the factual accuracy of her life than with the simplicity of the original legend: romantic, seductive, and filled with intrigue. To this end, director George Fitzmaurice, set designer Alexander Toluboff (working under the supervision of art director Cedric Gibbons) and costumer Adrian gave *Mata Hari* a visual style that became the focal point of the picture.

Mercedes de Acosta subsequently took credit for encouraging Adrian's severe styles at the film's end. Though her published account errs in its placement of time, Garbo's long black cape and brilliantined hair do bear a striking resemblance to de Acosta's favored attire. Greta generally abhorred costume fittings, but seemed fascinated by these new designs. Adrian created an extraordinary array of ornate, bejeweled costumes— each of them more costly than anything the real Mata Hari could have afforded in wartime France—mixing gold lamé, velvet, and brocade with beaded cutaways and leggings that, for once, gave Garbo's boyish legs some feminine shape.

Dancer June Knight, who was hired to double for Garbo in the opening sequence, recalled Greta's keen interest in her costume when she modeled it for Adrian. "She'd feel a little here and then a little there and so forth. It felt strange and yet somehow familiar, the kind of thing boys were always trying," she said. "I didn't really mind it at the time because I was so young and dumb. I didn't figure out what she was doing until it was over."

Three weeks into production on *Mata Hari,* reports from New York indicated that *Susan Lenox* was approaching another house record for Garbo at the Capitol. The film was by far October's top money-maker. "The Garbo-Gable combination was too much for any opposition even to dent," *The Hollywood Reporter* indicated. Edited for the foreign market, the movie also enjoyed considerable success abroad. In the United Kingdom, Metro-Goldwyn-Mayer was forced to placate censors by dissociating the story from its original source. Though the new name was decidedly less pleasing on marquees, *The Rise of Helga* broke weekend records established by such recent successes as *A Free Soul, Min and Bill,* and *The Champ.* The film brought in $806,000 at the domestic box-office and another $700,000 worldwide.

Garbo's international prominence increased the pressure on MGM to reverse its no-interviews policy concerning the Scandinavian star. But the studio had reason to observe caution: local gossip columns were full of allusions to Garbo's new lifestyle that the studio didn't want to confront or explain.[11] "Greta Garbo has a new love," the Rambling Reporter hinted on August 21. On the twenty-third of September, the trade paper ran a blind item about an "ambidextrous" foreign star who was "using her wiles again." On October 7, *The Hollywood Reporter* offered the "real" lowdown: "Her recent associations are surely showing superficial effects at least upon a beautiful MGM star. Noted for her grace and 'softness' she has been appearing lately to show little concern for her appearance and is wearing her face 'bare'. Heavy, masculine tweeds and slouch hats complete the effect—with dire results. She is not the type to be a 'self-made man.' "

The following day, the news sheet's target was Greta's *gal* pal. ("Gal pal" or "best pal" was the frequently used terminology in fan magazines and columns.) "That 'sensation' on the Boulevard was Mercedes de Acosta, in wide, black satin pajamas, pale-grey sweat-shirt, white canvas gloves and an Empress Eugenie hat," the *Reporter* stated. Furthermore, the Rambling

---

[11]Studio "spies"—sometimes coworkers, underlings, outside vendors, or, more predictably, members of the MGM police department—were becoming increasingly adept at acquiring information. According to a February 4, 1932, item in *The Hollywood Reporter,* one of the major studios was so concerned about unseemly information leaking out about its artists that they had tapped telephone and telegraph lines to determine the source and plug the leak.

Reporter noted in November, "Greta Garbo buys men's suits for herself—from Watson, the tailor." Other times, another magazine divulged, the star could be seen buying her clothes from the Army-Navy store.

By the end of 1931, the undeniable stature and influence of increasingly malicious radio gossips caused additional problems; their vocal tone added much to seemingly innocent copy. Although some friends and coworkers were convinced that Garbo hung out with de Acosta because she loved hearing her speak English, few outside the community believed this. "The most talked-about woman in Hollywood is the woman no wife fears," one fan magazine proclaimed. Bisexuality was fashionably chic in sophisticated Hollywood circles during this period. "Everyone had to be a lesbian in the thirties," says Sam Green, "even if they didn't want to be. They certainly dressed up and went to lesbian bars—it was the thing to do. And it was the logical step in women's liberation."

For years, the Hollywood community had wondered about Garbo. Because she was rarely seen outside of the workplace (except in the company of her *outré* European friends), everything about her life was open to speculation. Unable to define Greta Garbo in terms of a man—and they did try for years—gossips, now by innuendo, attempted to define her in terms of women. Was it Greta Garbo's fate that women would pursue her more aggressively than men? Was her "mystery" simply a heavy cloak disguising her true sexual character? Or was Garbo, deemed one of the world's most desirable women, most mystifyingly of all—sexually indifferent?

Mata Hari was the first complete Garbo performance to communicate a coded message to gay and lesbian audiences. It is notable for Ramon Novarro's passive femininity as well as Garbo's more aggressive masculine posture. When Mata Hari approaches her quarry, Alexei Rosanoff, from behind, seductively commanding his forgiveness, the scene is nothing less than a homosexual love scene. There are elements of Garbo's insouciant, private persona sprinkled throughout. A maid announces the arrival of her hairdresser; Mata protests she is "too nervous" to see him. What if the Marquis should call? "I'm too tired . . ." And the Baron? "Oh, I'm not interested, really."

Garbo's presentation throughout the film appears to be an inside joke, and she plays the infamous spy with an uncharacteristic slyness—most notably, in her repartee with Lionel Barrymore. General Shubin, who has been Mata's principal source of information, discovers that she has spent the night with a young flier and tears apart his room in a jealous rage. Enter Mata Hari:

Mata: "What's happened? A private air raid?"
Shubin: "You cheat! You liar!"

Mata: "Good morning, liar, would be more polite."
Shubin: "Oh, be quiet, you—"
Mata: "We'll omit the pet names. Come to the point."
Shubin: "Rosanoff, that's the point. You were with him all last night. Dubois told me."
Mata: "How does he know—did he look through the keyhole?"

Once again, Garbo's love scenes challenged censors. Inevitably cut from the picture would be Rosanoff's first night with Mata Hari. "It's nice to be held by you," she says in a whisper. "Youth—adoration—desire." A second, highly provocative scene (also excised) was suggested by voices only—and the movement of a pair of cigarettes. Ironically, the moment that would defy censors most was one where the characters were fully dressed: Mata insists that Alexei prove that his love for her is supreme by extinguishing the votive candle burning beneath an icon of the Madonna of Kazan. It would be the first time since *Flesh and the Devil* that Garbo dared to test a religious ideal.[12] The sequence made it past some censorship boards, but not all. As a precaution, an alternate version was shot with a photograph of Rosanoff's mother in the place of the holy shrine.

In lieu of interviews, Metro publicity promoted a new Garbo romance: one with Ramon Novarro. Novarro was a confirmed bachelor. Though rarely seen in high-profile dates around town, fans believed this was due to his dedication to Catholicism (Novarro had once expressed a desire to become a Jesuit priest), not as a euphemism for his homosexuality. Pairing two vulnerable subjects with each other made the publicists' job that much easier, and the likable Novarro accommodated them by speaking generously about his costar. When her maid, Alma, showed up on the set at 5:00 with a glass of water, it was no act that Greta looked so tired, he observed. She would take her headdress off, shake the hairpins from her head, smile graciously, and then say good night. "No word of complaint or apology. She came to work early in the morning and worked steadily until five at night. That's all there was to it."

By the third week in November, principal photography had been completed, and *Mata Hari* was in the cutting room in preparation for its first preview. In the meantime, Garbo had moved into a new home on North Rockingham Drive in Brentwood. Mercedes de Acosta soon followed, moving into a house nearby. There are many indications that the enforced

---

[12]Not surprisingly, the main contributor to *Mata Hari*'s screenplay was the scenarist of *Flesh and the Devil*, Benjamin Glazer.

proximity was not appreciated by Greta, who left town instead with Salka Viertel to play "in the mountain snows." A couple of weeks later, a light snowfall in Los Angeles helped to put everyone in a holiday mood. All Jackie Cooper wanted for Christmas, Metro publicists intimated, was "a chance to play in a picture with Greta Garbo." All Metro-Goldwyn-Mayer wanted was to add Greta Garbo's name to the anticipated all-star cast for a project entitled *Grand Hotel*. All Mercedes de Acosta wanted was Greta Garbo's undivided attention—and Greta again resisted any such commitment. In fact, she had disappeared from the scene entirely.

In *Here Lies the Heart*, Mercedes would tell a touching story of a warm Christmas spent with candles lit and curtains drawn to nostalgically transport Greta and her back to Sweden. It never took place. "Mercedes was the kind of person who would take credit for a lot of things that didn't happen," says Jean Howard, an actress who was then about to make her debut in Hollywood social circles. The Mercedes de Acosta Collection, deposited at the Rosenbach Museum in Philadelphia, shows that she had been collecting newspaper and magazine articles about Greta from as far back as 1926. Presumably, she had read Rilla Page Palmborg's "The Private Life of Greta Garbo," published in *Photoplay* a few months before their first encounter, which included John Loder's Christmas story. Surely, Greta celebrated other holidays in this manner—but not in 1931. Whether by mistake or intentional misappropriation, Mercedes's touching Christmas story did not take place that year. Greta spent the holidays in New York . . . without Mercedes.

"New York is in a fit because it thinks Greta Garbo is secretly visiting there," the Rambling Reporter announced on Christmas Eve. Greta had managed to slip into New York City without being detected. Why she went alone can only be speculated about. The abundance of column mentions "coincidentally" linking Garbo's name to de Acosta's could have been a factor, inspiring a dramatic statement of independence from Greta. Mercedes could be a little overwhelming at times, admits Mary Anita Loos (who was named after her famous aunt). "That I experienced firsthand when she got stuck on me and wouldn't take 'No' for an answer. She used to pace in front of my apartment dressed like Napoleon, and the doorman would say, 'That woman is here,' and I'd say, 'Thank you,' and go out the back door. I can only imagine what Garbo went through."

A mutual friend, Luis Estevez, would describe de Acosta as "a very definite kind of person. She was very strong . . . very capable of battling for herself. She created her own myth, her own style," he says. "I think she thought of Garbo like a prized possession, a trophy." Cecil Beaton later concluded that Mercedes' infatuation seemed to get the best of her. She was often "at her worst in Greta's presence," he recorded. She could not resist the temptation to let others know of her intimate association with Garbo, bragging "in a rather too canny way" of their friendship. "This was not lost on Greta, who rather abruptly put her down," he noted on one occasion when the three were together. But she did not cut her off.

"To try and explain my real feeling for Greta would be impossible since I really do not understand myself," Mercedes wrote in a 1934 letter to Marlene Dietrich. "I do know that I have built up in my emotions a person that does not exist. My mind sees the real person—a Swedish servant girl with a face touched by God—only interested in money, her health, sex, food and sleep. And yet her face tricks my mind and my spirit builds her up into something that fights with my brain. I do love her but I only love the person I have created and not the person who is real."

If Mercedes' desire was not greater than Greta's, certainly her need was—and her possessiveness could have easily stifled a free spirit. Her touchingly neurotic, often hysterical personality could be dealt with—but in measured doses. In her work, Garbo had always chosen to work with even-tempered people who knew what they were doing and rarely, if ever, made her nervous—a Clarence Sinclair Bull over the exceptionally talented, more excitable George Hurrell, for example. That she would choose the same in her private life was natural. "When somebody like Dietrich or Bankhead went after her," Louise Brooks observed, "Garbo took it on the lam."

On December 28, New York reporters confirmed the rumors: Greta Garbo had been at St. Moritz on-the-Park registered as Gussie Berger of Chicago. "She tried to be completely anonymous by wearing black sunglasses and a black hat with a broad brim," states Fred Zinnemann, "and this sort of costume of course made people look at her with some curiosity. When people realised [sic] who she was a chase would inevitably start."[13] The following day's headlines told the story: "GARBO 'CAN'T SAY NOTHING,' SO SHE RUNS" . . . "GRETA, INCOGNITO, PLAYS TAG WITH N.Y. REPORTERS" . . . "GRETA GARBO ICEBERG? NO! SAYS FLORIST SHE PATTED". When "the exalted foreigner" came down into the lobby, "looking more like a prim New England schoolmarm made nervous by the big city surroundings," the throng had increased in size—and everyone wanted an interview. Lightbulbs flashed; the photographer's subject placed her hands in front of her face as if she feared the "evil spirit" of the camera. "No, I am not Greta Garbo," she insisted. "No, you must be mistaken. Go away—

---

[13]Zinnemann, who would later be acclaimed as the director of *High Noon*, *From Here to Eternity*, *Oklahoma!*, and *A Man for All Seasons*, was then working in New York as Berthold Viertel's assistant.

please let me alone!" They did not go away. "Oh, what's the use?" she said. "Yes, I am Greta Garbo. Now are you satisfied? . . . I came here from Hollywood for a rest, not to exhibit myself."

The gentlemen of the press were not gentle. Again, she was considered fair game, and their journalistic pursuit became an all-out safari. She walked to the exit; they stepped in her way. She hailed a taxicab; they got in their cars. She got out of the taxi at Central Park and Seventy-second; they chased her as she walked briskly through the park to keep ahead of the crowd, then faster, and faster. Greta again turned around to the reporters. "I can't say nothing," she declared. "I am not allowed to say nothing. I feel so sorry for you." She got into another cab, and this time eluded her pursuers, which enabled her to attend a matinee at the theater. When she returned with her escort, sixty reporters converged on her; she tried to hide in the florist shop. A chivalrous employee put his arm around her and whisked her safely up to her suite on the twenty-fifth floor via the servant's elevator.

In his essay on Garbo, Lindbergh, and the press, Berthold Viertel viewed a sinister side to the story. "Reporters and admirers pounce on a woman, encircle her, crowd around her, touch her, tear a pair of black glasses from her nose, stare and breathe into her face. The breathing is close and has a foul odor. The face pales, the lips quiver." The writer/director, who was also staying at the St. Moritz, took to heart Garbo's bad treatment and singled out the emperor of the nighttime airwaves, Walter Winchell, as the worst offender. "This purveyor of scandal which is fame and fame which is scandal initially attempted to approach [her] with an admiring poem," he wrote. "When ignored, he sought to set the police on her on the premise that she was an impostor posing as Greta Garbo." According to Fred Zinnemann, Winchell had wanted her to say hello to his listeners on Christmas Eve. When she failed to respond, the columnist—a "master of indiscretion," Viertel accused— threatened to savage her on his NBC radio show. He kept his promise.

After all of the press attention, the St. Moritz turned into a living hell for Garbo. "The lobby, all exits, the surrounding streets were occupied every day and night hour by storm troops—admirers and reporters—who chased the artist everywhere," Viertel recounted. "There was no lack of noble and discreet sympathy . . . even among the hotel personnel, although all of them—elevator boys, newsstand vendors, florists, ticket agents, room service waiters and telephone operators—had been induced with large tips to be private detectives. It is impossible to take this incredible affair lightly or as being humorous. Impossible to negotiate or pacify. Only one thing remained: flight, head over heels, through secret corridors, over back stairs, through side doors as in a mystery novel . . ."

"The story of my life is about back entrances and side doors and secret elevators and other ways of getting in and out of places so that people won't bother you," the beleaguered actress told Raymond Daum years later. Robert Reud, then the resident public-relations director at the St. Moritz, was responsible for getting Garbo most of her theater tickets; she attended several shows over the course of her stay. After she mentioned that she would like to meet Alfred Lunt and Lynn Fontanne, Reud arranged an after-show meeting at the couple's Manhattan apartment.

On other occasions, she met Ramon Novarro for dinner or a show. They sent messages back and forth under the guise of their character's names in *Mata Hari*, had early morning breakfasts at Reuben's, late luncheons at the Ritz, and even frequented the nightclubs in Harlem. Greta also went with Berthold Viertel to "21" (when it was still operating as a speakeasy)—but "the hottest speakeasy spot in New York" during the winter of 1931, according to *The Hollywood Reporter*, was a risqué establishment on Sixth Avenue, "with lavender boys serving the likker" and the top names in show business, including Greta Garbo, as its customers.

At the end of her vacation, Greta was invited for another late-night supper, this time with Katharine Cornell. She had seen the actress in *The Barretts of Wimpole Street* her first week in Manhattan. Backstage, all throughout the performance, the cast and crew had argued over whether or not Garbo was seated in the third row center, hiding behind a heavy tweed overcoat, tortoise-shell dark glasses, and wide-brim cloche hat. Twenty minutes after the final curtain, there was a commotion backstage. "Would Miss Co-o-ornell see a stranger?" a deep voice inquired. Garbo's casual appearance not only shocked the actors, but when she failed to introduce herself, Cornell began to feel that she must be an impostor. "So I became very haughty," she confessed. She turned Greta away. Ironically, the star who demanded that she must be in control of whom she met and under what circumstances had herself been rebuffed. "Miss Co-o-ornell, I see, does not like strangers," she remarked to the stage manager as she left.

Kit Cornell was greatly puzzled by the encounter—was it Garbo or not? She called friends in Los Angeles. No, Garbo was in California. She called other friends in New York. Yes, Garbo was in New York. Eventually, it was determined that Greta was indeed in New York City and a note of apology was sent to the St. Moritz. "I can't remember ever having a pleasanter, more *gemütlich* evening," Cornell would say of their conciliatory supper. Two years later, the women met again in Hollywood and, according to Mercedes, Garbo acted as if they had never met.

When she left New York, she still could not escape the reporters. Confronted by the press at Chicago's LaSalle Street Station, Greta repeated her mantra: "No, I am not in love. No, I am not ever to marry. No, I am not to stop playing in movies. They are my life to me. I am happy to be far away from New York. They are so impolite in New York." Was it possible that she was still in love with Prince Sigvard? she was asked. "No, I forget him," she insisted. "I love no one."

Extraordinary success would frame Garbo's trip to New York. She had arrived in the city on the wings of *Susan Lenox*'s nationwide success. On New Year's Eve, *Mata Hari* caused a panic at the box office when it opened at the Capitol. "Looks like a record week. . . ," *The Hollywood Reporter* announced, "with police reserves being required to keep the waiting mob in order." The benchmark for Greta Garbo at the cavernous Capitol Theater was a broken record.

Most of the national criticism of *Mata Hari* would call attention to its slow pace and melodramatic moments, yet echo *Variety*'s prediction of a smash hit: "Garbo, Novarro, Barrymore and Stone—the Metro Tragedy Four—are too strong a marquee combination of names to leave this film in box office doubt. With Garbo leading they dominate the whole affair making the picture, as a picture, very secondary. Through them *Mata Hari* becomes not only flop-proof . . . [but] manages to slide by as entertainment."

Three weeks into the film's run, exhibitors were reporting blockbuster business from Seattle to Chicago. Incredibly, a film Garbo had little feeling for and made more or less for the fun of it became the greatest success of her career to date. While its domestic box-office equaled the level set by *Anna Christie* ($1,012,000), *Mata Hari* was the first of her films to show a significant increase in its foreign bookings ($1,296,000); the final profit for MGM was $906,000, or nearly double the profit of any Garbo film with the possible exceptions of *Anna Christie* and *Love*.[14] The economics of Garbo-watching were too substantial to allow her to leave without a protest.

"GARBO ASKING FOR MORE MONEY IN NEW DEAL," *Variety* announced on December 27, 1931. According to the paper, thus far MGM had been "unable to reach terms with Greta Garbo." Now, as the studio extended her indenture another three months (by adding the time she was away in 1928/1929), the story was that the Swedish star was "desirous of increasing her weekly check to $10,000 if she enters into another agreement. It is not expected that Metro will assent." The extension that Metro imposed made way for Garbo's participation in the production that would most famously

---

[14]These figures, compiled from MGM's master list of films (now on deposit at the Academy of Motion Picture Arts and Sciences' Margaret Herrick Library), include a nominal amount earned during a 1941 reissue (United States only).

represent her ascendancy to movie icon. Her role as the fatalistic ballerina in *Grand Hotel* forecast, at the height of Greta Garbo's fame and popularity, what was to come. Although her craft would improve, she would never be more popular onscreen.

It began as a story entitled *Menschen im Hotel* (*The People in the Hotel*). Although a theatrical adaptation in Berlin closed less than a week after opening, MGM took advantage of the opportunity to subsidize the Broadway production. An investment of $15,500 secured a half ownership in the play and the option of a motion picture adaptation. From the project's inception, Garbo's casting as the Russian ballerina, Grusinskaya, was considered essential—though some people, including the story's author, Vicki Baum, continued to express reservations. "She's not a ballet dancer and she doesn't move like one," an executive advocated at an early story conference. "Don't worry," writer Frank Partos said, "the glamour of Garbo will bedazzle the audience."

What Garbo would bring to the role, as she did so many others, was a quality of wounded vulnerability: a world-weariness especially poignant in someone so young, tempered by her believability when she falls in love with a man she does not know. The actress Marie Dressler had described as living "in the core of a vast aching aloneness" was most alive when breathing life into a new part. Persistent arguments from Thalberg and company won Greta over, and she confirmed her participation in the film prior to her New York adventure.

Other actors under contract to Metro-Goldwyn-Mayer were less certain of their placement. Names mentioned for the production's "million-dollar cast" included Norma Shearer, Clark Gable, Buster Keaton, Jimmy Durante, and John Gilbert. Joan Crawford's name on the list soon replaced Shearer's; she was set to portray Flaemmchen, the stenographer whose presence at the Grand Hotel helps to tie the three main stories together. Lionel Barrymore, a recent Academy Award winner for his performance as an alcoholic lawyer in *A Free Soul*, secured the role of Kringelein, the accountant, over the luckless Keaton. In December of 1931, when Gable became embroiled in a contract dispute at the studio, John Gilbert was a rather surprising last-minute announcement for the lead role of Baron Felix von Gaigern, the "fascinatingly handsome, debonair" aristocrat with "a step as elastic as a tennis champion"—but the threadbare pockets of a pauper.[15]

[15]According to Samuel Marx, Thalberg had originally promised the role of Baron von Gaigern to Jack. "An immense amount of soul-searching went on in meeting between Thalberg and [Paul] Bern over the actor to portray the dissolute gambler," Marx recorded. "Gilbert, struggling with a career that plummeted with the coming of talkies, told his friends at the studio he was born for it . . ."

Unfortunately, Jack Gilbert, sitting alone in his palatial bungalow tucked in a corner of the main lot, was no longer the spirited comrade his friends and coworkers once knew. Following his divorce from Ina Claire, he seemed to be wallowing in one bad film after another. "His sunny personality had disappeared, he was morose, his nights filled with imagined dangers," Sam Marx stated. Most frightening of all, Jack's friends heard he now slept with a revolver near his bed. One good film—even one that did not rely solely on the tattered marquee value of Gilbert's name—might have reversed this cycle of doom. Instead, Thalberg acquiesced to pressure from the front office and agreed to consider other actors for the assignment.

John Barrymore, who could match Jack Gilbert "drink for drink and carousal for carousal," was awarded the pivotal assignment opposite Garbo. "Losing the decision embittered Gilbert," Marx said. "It seemed to him to verify Eddie Mannix's summation of Thalberg: 'He's a sweet guy but he can piss ice water!' " The door of the project formerly known as "Hotel Humanity" closed to Jack.

Thalberg had an idea that the multitalented Edmund Goulding would be an excellent choice as director. Described by friends (and foes) as "wonderfully erratic" and "delightfully corrupt," Goulding was admired for his imagination and despised for his inconsistency. "Eddie was a strange man," producer David Lewis acknowledged. "I liked him very much, but he was always either at your throat or at your knees." Louis B. Mayer had been so concerned about Thalberg's choice that he spoke with Goulding's former employer, B. P. Schulberg, at Paramount. Mayer cabled his report to Thalberg in New York: "ADVISED PICTURE HE MADE NIGHT ANGEL COST $600,000. HIS DIRECTION SO IMPOSSIBLE, UNBELIEVABLE DONE BY SOBER MAN. . . . URGE YOU TO ACT IN ALL MATTERS AS IF YOU OWNED THE COMPANY 100 PER CENT."

Rather than viewing the lost revenues of Goulding's most recent pictures as a peculiar form of leprosy—as so many had with Gilbert—Thalberg counted on the director's determination to prove himself. "He had a way of showing up with material to fill the void, a free-lance specialist much like a doctor or lawyer whose timely appearance saved a life or a day, winning gratitude and financial rewards," Marx, Thalberg's top story man, observed. Mayer worried that Goulding would skew the story toward Garbo and Crawford. To some degree, that was exactly what Metro's production VP wanted. "Thalberg was influenced by a belief Goulding's homosexuality would bring new dimensions to the performance of Greta Garbo and Joan Crawford," Marx continued. " 'Eddie thinks like a woman,' he said. 'He'll bring out their femininity. I want them to stand out over the men.' "

A transcript of a December 26, 1931, story conference sheds light on the contributions of both Goulding and Thalberg. The purpose of the meeting was to discuss Grusinskaya's attempted suicide and the problematic love scene that followed.

Goulding: "A closely guarded woman finds a man in her room and she knows that he has seen her naked and about to end her life. . . . Shall we cut out the suicide? . . . If this man is a criminal and knows women, he says to himself, 'Jesus, I have to tell this woman something.' He comes boldly out to stop a woman doing an awful deed. They play the scene—he's so calm about it, they might have been married for years."

Thalberg: ". . . I'd have her standing there next to the telephone. She says, 'What do you want of me?' Or anything. She is ready to yell out, holler. A close-up of him on the other side of the room. He says, 'I followed you because I love you.' Come to your close-up of her. 'You love me?' She starts to cry. Then from this moment on he gets serious. He's a nice fellow, and he comes in and says, 'Poor thing.' "

Goulding: ". . . She has the telephone in her hand. He says, 'I came here because I love you.' The thing that makes her cry is the irony of it."

Thalberg: "No, it's the sincerity of it. Then she explains why she cried. 'I was so alone.' "

Goulding: "She starts complaining to a complete stranger—where is her dignity? It's irony."

Thalberg: "I don't agree with you."

Goulding: "The thing behind the scene is that she's tired with life and is going to die."

Thalberg: "She says, 'I was so alone—always alone—nobody . . . and suddenly you were there' . . . that's what made her cry."

Goulding: "What a push-over."

Thalberg: "All right, that's what she is. Why does a woman want one man and another woman want another? Why does a man want one woman and another man another? That's the kick of it, goddamn it. To me, you've got a scene in which a man for about two pages lies like a so-and-so."

Goulding: "I'm not defending this."

Thalberg: "You haven't any sex in it."
Goulding: ". . . Wouldn't I bore you if I said I wanted to make a good picture?"
Thalberg: "No, not at all."

On January 11, 1932, the Immigration and Naturalization Service granted Greta Garbo an extension of her stay as a temporary visitor in the United States. Greta was still living and working in the U.S. as a non-resident alien, which meant more paperwork for Metro—as well as her own business people—and less money for her, due to extra tax monies levied on her income by the federal government. In 1930 she had decided that she wanted to become a permanent resident, but backed down when it became too complicated. MGM, along with most major studios, hoped to change the legal status of their valued foreign employees by effecting new legislation in Washington, D.C. In the meantime, Garbo's status remained unchanged; she was a visitor.

Rehearsals with "the greatest all-star cast ever assembled on the MGM lot" began on Monday, December 28, while Greta was still in New York. Rounding out the cast were Wallace Beery, Jean Hersholt, and Lewis Stone. The commencement of principal photography three days later launched one of Metro-Goldwyn-Mayer's most ambitious production schedules. As the premier film in their 1932 line-up, *Grand Hotel* employed the latest technology—via Bill Daniels' multiple camera stations—and the grandest budget (nearly $700,000 after star salaries and Cedric Gibbons' opulent art deco sets were factored in).

Garbo began work on *Grand Hotel* on a comparatively light note: a scene of Grusinskaya hurrying through the hotel lobby. She declined a run-through, joking that she had rehearsed it in New York. According to one source, there were fierce arguments between Paul Bern and director Goulding the first two weeks; the end result was that Irving Thalberg took control. The production troubles were widely reported in industry circles. "Enthusiasm has replaced discord on the *Grand Hotel* set," *The Hollywood Reporter* declared.

On the fourteenth of January, Greta acted in her first scene with John Barrymore. In deference to his leading lady, the actor reportedly showed up for work early. When 9:00 A.M. came and there was no sign of Garbo, Barrymore thought it to be a display of temperament until a propboy ran on to the stage. "I didn't know you were here, Mr. Barrymore. Miss Garbo has been waiting outside the door since 9:00 to escort you on to the set," he explained. "It was an honor she wanted to pay you." Greta was close behind. "This is a great day for me," she said. "How I have looked forward to working with John Barrymore!" The actor returned the compliment.

Late one night during filming, however, a clearly agitated Jack Barrymore showed up on Mercedes de Acosta's doorstep. "He was full of tales about *Grand Hotel*," she said. Professing a great reverence for Garbo, Barrymore admitted being frightened much of the time, but he was aware of her own deep wounds and pleaded with Mercedes not to tell Greta he had been to see her. "It might make her self-conscious with me." Mercedes kept her word (but couldn't resist telling the story later).

Public displays of anger, outbursts, or bad behavior were not part of her standard repertoire. "She has less temperament than any star I have ever handled," Edmund Goulding stated. In fact, Garbo's greatest difficulty would come in conveying a prima ballerina's temperament, having separated such temperament from her own mercurial moodiness. One famous incident had the actress refusing to work until Arthur Brisbane, editor-in-chief of Hearst's *New York Evening Journal*, left the set. An item in *Photoplay* would seem to contradict this: "When [Brisbane's] visit was over, Garbo seemed appalled at Barrymore's friendship with a newspaper person. 'Do you know him?' she asked curiously. 'Know him?' laughed Barrymore. 'Why I used to work for him!' " The actor explained that he had once been a cartoonist on Brisbane's paper. "Ah," Greta laughed, "that's better—much better!"

According to several sources, Greta was incredibly sensitive to Barrymore's private demons, protecting him on days when he showed up on the set with a bad hangover. During a lunch break one day, she reportedly helped rearrange the furniture in Grusinskaya's hotel suite so that the actor's favored left profile could be featured during love scenes. On January 25, the pair had a particularly difficult scene to film. At the end of the day, Garbo surprised the director and crew by impulsively kissing Barrymore. "You have no idea what it means to me to play opposite so perfect an artist," she exclaimed.

Inspired by his "divine madness," Greta often sat on the sidelines with Barrymore waiting for their next scene together and even allowed the unit photographer to shoot several candid pictures of the two of them together. There was, however, very little conversation between them. "Her interest in her work is absorbing and complete," Barrymore stated. "She hasn't time for desultory talk between scenes." Elsewhere, he characterized her as a real dynamo. "The physical power she expends in her work is amazing. Nothing is too much trouble. . . . She is a fine lady and a great actress and the rest is silence."

Under pressure to deliver *Grand Hotel* on schedule, Edmund Goulding put in sixteen-hour days balancing the different casts and crews working at different times on separate soundstages. Crawford and Beery. The two Barrymores and Joan Crawford. Garbo and John Barrymore. Each hotel room served as a prison for those who could not escape the past. Each story thread had its own drama and pathos—but Garbo alone added a new dimension by providing the film with its magical centerpiece. In four major (and four lesser) sequences in which Grusinskaya's only significant interaction is with Baron von Gaigern, Garbo filled each frame with her physical presence; her movement within the frame was as important to the scene as her now-famous close-ups. At work in the cutting room, Goulding raved about what he saw on film. "No director has any right to take any bows for any performance of Garbo's. She is director-proof," he enthused. Rehearsing in her dressing room, she would allow nothing to interfere with her total immersion in her work.

Sam Marx watched Greta pacing outside his office in the Story Building. Her walk varied in the speed and rhythm of the steps each time she passed his window. "Finally I got up to look and there was Garbo in the alleyway, deep in concentration. She would do a length, stop, put her hand on her chin and puzzle there for a while, then go at it again." Marx thought she was working on perfecting her character; specifically, the way she would float into the scene after Grusinskaya's love affair with the Baron has blossomed. There were other reasons for her restlessness as well. By February of 1932, she was considering another location change.

"Retaliation against foreign screen stars now working in American pictures as an answer to legislation against American players in European countries, especially England, was demanded yesterday by Representative Dickstein, of New York, at a hearing before the House immigration committee," trade newspapers reported on February 25, 1932. Backed by Actors Equity, the congressman from New York stated from the congressional floor that "There are one thousand movie actors and actresses in Hollywood who don't belong there! . . . Garbo, Chevalier, Dietrich and other foreign-born stars should be forced to become American citizens." Stating that only players of "distinguished merit and ability" should be admitted under the artist classification, Dickstein proposed a law which, if passed, could prevent Garbo from reentering the U.S. if she did not re-sign her MGM contract. Technically, as an "undesirable," she could be deported.

That Garbo would leave—sooner or later—seemed inevitable. Whether or not she *stayed* was also up to the host.

CHAPTER FOURTEEN

Dreaming of Snow

Greta looked out from her second-floor bedroom window toward a small dead tree in the backyard of her home. "This tree is my one joy in Hollywood," she told Mercedes. "I call it *my winter tree*. When my loneliness for Sweden gets unbearable I look at it and it comforts me. I imagine that the cold has made it leafless and that soon there will be snow on its branches."

As she fought off both nervous and physical ailments, the actress indicated to friends and associates that she was anxious to return to Sweden. Though her insatiable longing for home was not as feverish as it had been in 1928, when her emotions were complicated by a sense of hopelessness and loss, the sentiment was equally heartfelt and of late had acquired a brittle, almost neurotic quality. In 1932, for the first time in Garbo's film career, she was able to chose for herself the direction she wanted to move.

Mayer and Thalberg continued to press their suit at MGM, less concerned over new rumors of her marriage[1] than by their knowledge that Garbo's frugal ways and Harry Edington's wise investments had apparently paid off. Since 1927, Edington's role had evolved from that of business manager handling his clients' financial affairs to that of agent and personal manager negotiating contracts and voicing clients' concerns with studio management—all while maintaining an office at MGM. But when his contract as head of Metro's foreign department expired on December 31, 1931, the front office did not ask him to stay. As far as Garbo was concerned, it appeared that Mercedes de Acosta and Salka Viertel were providing most of the advice. Certainly, by 1932 their influence was increasingly felt in the corridors of Metro-Goldwyn-Mayer's executive building.

Mercedes and Salka—both educated, articulate women who were closer to each other in age than they were to Garbo—were often confused with one another in uninformed Hollywood circles. It was Salka who picked Greta up at the Pasadena train station when she returned from New York, and later compared notes with her on a biography of a seventeenth-century Swedish queen that both were reading. It was Mercedes who was hired to write an original script for Garbo.

[1] Several papers, including *The New York Times*, had erroneously reported that Garbo intended to marry Wilhelm Sörensen—a story she vehemently denied.

That Mercedes had not yet received screen credit for her work was partly due to her failure to fall in step with the traditional Hollywood dance. She continued to assert herself when it would have been more sound politically to "appear" to acquiesce. At MGM, she set her will against Thalberg at their first meeting. "Instead of sinking into my chair and allowing him to play the Emperor, I sat straight and as high up on the arm of it as I could, bringing myself almost on a level with him," she recollected. "What a mistake! For on an unseen level I had started up a resistance between us which lasted all the time I worked with him . . ."

To date, Mercedes de Acosta's efforts as a playwright and poet had been regarded as disappointing, uninspired, and hugely unsuccessful, but Thalberg recognized the wisdom of pleasing Garbo by giving her friend a job; he installed de Acosta in a small office in the writers' building. On the twenty-first of January, she presented the production chief with the result of her efforts. *Desperate* was a bizarre scenario incorporating fanciful bits of Mercedes' life into a globe-trotting narrative. The heroine is a confused soul named Erik Chanler. Her father (Sloane) is an American diplomat living in Paris; he is divorced from her mother (Erika), who was the daughter of the Norwegian ambassador to the Russian Imperial Court. As the story begins, Erik is going home to be with her mother on her eighteenth birthday—but her father delays her departure, and her distraught mother—believing she has been deserted—jumps into the nearest fjord (hanging on just long enough to die in Erik's arms).

A vengeful Erik begins her reckless adult life à la Diana Merrick in *A Woman of Affairs*. She is beautiful, polished, arrogant, wild, and now irrevocably estranged from her father. When her companion, Toto, is killed in a club in Harlem, Erik disguises herself as a boy to avert a scandal and leaves town. A scripted montage shows Erik making a spiritual ascent, giving up her old habits and purifying her life: "In making herself into a boy, shedding her skin as it were, she dissolves her whole identity." She winds up in a swank gambling club in Mexico City. "Dressed in immaculate and perfect evening clothes, her hair brushed straight back and varnished into smoothness, her face a mask, her hands slim and white and beautifully cared for, she is many times more a subject of interest among the feminine gamblers than the great wheel she operates with such superb dexterity. Each woman feels there is some unfathomable mystery in this beautiful, pale, Shelley-like boy—that no one can move to talk—whose eyes rarely leave the game—who has never been seen to smile—who is indifferent and disinterested in the life round him. Everyone wonders about him."

Her luck has changed. "Once I was afraid to be alone with myself," she says. "Now I no longer have that fear—and I am not lonely—ever." She is last seen in Wyoming as a "pretty new cowboy," able to tame wild horses—and men. Old wounds heal after an old lover reappears, and Erik wins a dramatic life-and-death struggle at the rodeo with the fiercest black stallion this side of the Mississippi.

Greta never read the completed manuscript, but Mercedes believed she was content with the scenario. According to the writer, even Thalberg had been fine with the story until she told him about the sequence where Erik passes as a man (in truth, a series of scenes that dominates nearly half of the story). Her recollection was that the executive put his foot down regarding Garbo wearing men's clothes on screen—this despite the fact that she had already appropriated Nils Asther's white shirts and trousers in *The Single Standard* two years earlier. What Mercedes never explained in her memoirs was that her *Desperate* scenario most definitely would have challenged the social mores of the times—not provocatively, as Mae West often did in her motion pictures or even as Radclyffe Hall had done four years earlier in *The Well of Loneliness,* but in a poorly conceived, surprisingly lame fashion. Irving Thalberg was hardly immune to the changing times, but he knew that controversial ideas demanded clever writing if they hoped to connect with mainstream audiences.

Mercedes didn't make the most of her first—and most important—opportunity to show Metro the stuff *her* dreams were made of. It was naïve to think that a movie studio firmly entrenched within the conservative establishment—in equally conservative times—would ever embrace her vision of a superwoman. Writing of their script meeting, Mercedes only remembered her supervisor's anger. "We have been building Garbo up for years as a great glamorous actress, and now you come along and try to put her into pants and make a monkey out of her," Thalberg railed. "Do you want to put all America and all the women's clubs against her? You must be out of your mind."

She got the point: Garbo must remain under cover. Later, when Greta expressed an interest in playing the title role in Oscar Wilde's *The Picture of Dorian Gray* (a role in which she would not "pass" as a man, but *play* a man), Mercedes responded, "You go and tell Irving that idea and have him throw *you* out the window—not me!" Still, both women appeared to enjoy shocking the public with their antics.

Keeping the couple out of the press would be the job of MGM's new head of publicity, Howard Strickling, as the studio prepared *Grand Hotel* for its roadshow engagement. Principal photography was completed on February 18, 1932. The following day, Mayer and Thalberg viewed a rough cut of the film and were "delighted" with the entire cast. At the suggestion of

Harry Edington, Metro promoted the star simply as "Garbo." As per the terms of their 1927 agreement, no more than one male actor could be featured above the title with her; a special waiver would be required from Garbo for the all-star cast. "I took this up with Miss G. and she tells me as follows," Edington wrote the legal department. "That the billing is all right as far as she is concerned and doesn't care anything about it."[2]

The trickiest territory to negotiate did not involve the three male costars, but a rather significant female one. By the end of shooting, the Hollywood rumor mill suggested that the balance of Greta Garbo's screen time to Joan Crawford's might be readjusted, depending upon the outcome of Garbo's contract negotiations. Once again, the studio resorted to a traditional ploy, using Crawford's enormous popularity (coming off her best year to date) as a way of pressuring Greta to stay. It didn't work. The actress, while ambitiously poised to take Garbo's place if she ever made good on her threat to leave, knew she could never replace the Swedish star in people's minds.

In fact, Garbo was her own role model as an actress, personality, and star. "Our dressing rooms were next door to each other," Crawford recalled, "and every morning that I went by when she was working I would just say: 'Good morning, Miss Garbo.' And *never* a sound from her. Never any sign of recognition . . . ," until the one morning Crawford was late for work and eschewed the usual greeting. Instead, Greta walked out to the landing and offered a shy "hello" as a surprised Crawford disappeared into her dressing room.

For as long as Garbo was at MGM, workers stood to the side while she independently navigated the studio walkways—often preferring to make her own path through the bushes rather than using the sidewalk, or entering the lot through the window of casting director Billy Grady's office near the east gate. Hedda Hopper, in the days before gossip became her business, was a featured player at Metro and vividly recalled the routine at the women's dressing room complex. "We rarely saw Greta except when she was violently disturbed over some part she didn't want to play or some lovers' quarrel she'd had the night before," Hopper reported. In such an agitated state, Garbo was known to pace the upstairs landing for a half hour or more, while eyes intense with curiosity and wonder viewed her moving back and forth, forth and back, "like a ship in full sail."

During the making of *Grand Hotel*, Garbo worked from 9:00 to 5:00; Crawford started rehearsing at 5:00 P.M. and shot her scenes between 6:00

---

[2]Since Greta refused to sign a letter to this effect, the studio was forced to take her at her word.

in the evening and 2:00 in the morning. Their separate worlds collided on the staircase of the women's building. Standing back with a friend as Greta came up the stairs, Crawford thought that she had timed everything correctly—and ended up bumping right into Garbo. "I got down two steps too soon, and she just came round and she *grabbed* me and this *magnificent* face looked into mine . . ." The actress was dumbstruck as Greta took her face in her hands and told her, "I am so sorry we are not working together. It's so sad; in the same film, and no scenes. What a pity!" The effect was so mesmerizing, Crawford admitted, her knees weakened.

Even as Metro-Goldwyn-Mayer continued its dialogue with Garbo, an independent theater in New York illustrated why she had little to worry about: *Die freudlose Gasse*, reedited to highlight Garbo's appearance and released in the United States as *Streets of Sorrow*, was doing turn-away business at the Lyric Theatre on Broadway. The trial engagement prompted an American distributor to prepare for the film's national release.

Whether or not Garbo might be deported was not a question MGM executives were worried about—whether she would choose to stay or not was. "Our contract with Garbo terminates April 24, 1932," the legal department notified the front office. "No further options, save for film completion . . ." With little protest, the company hurried Greta into her next motion picture. *As You Desire Me* was based on a drama by Luigi Pirandello. The focus of the story is on a lost soul referred to as "The Unknown One"—a woman for whom the past is so horrifyingly real she cannot bear to remember it, much less separate the truth from the fiction. She is a woman caught between two worlds.

In December of 1931, the studio set *Mata Hari*'s George Fitzmaurice to direct and Gene Markey (whose prior collaboration with Garbo had been the singularly uninspired *Inspiration*) to write the screenplay.[3] Though Nils Asther was a strong contender for the lead of the Italian captain who believes that "The Unknown One" is his wife, Maria, a newcomer named Melvyn Douglas slipped in to steal the assignment. At Garbo's insistence, Erich von Stroheim was cast as the sadistic writer, Karl Salter, who manipulates people as if they were chess pieces and creates a life for "The Unknown One" as a cabaret artist named Zara.

Production commenced the week of February 29. "I reported to the studio with much excitement, but the briefing by director George Fitzmaurice fell somewhat short of my expectations," Douglas wrote in his memoirs.

[3]An interesting alternative MGM chose not to pursue was writer/director Jacques Feyder, who was back under contract to the studio.

Fitzmaurice informed the actor that European military officers of the period always wore corselets and that he intended to personally make sure Douglas wore this undergarment whenever in uniform. However, apart from these instructions, the only other direction he offered Douglas was that "in pictures we expect emotion from women, but not from men."

If Fitzmaurice did not impress him as a director, Douglas admitted being "a little awestruck" by Garbo and was pleased to learn that her preeminence did not infect their working relationship. He found Greta to be "a very easy person to be with . . . She wasn't a trained actress—and she was aware of that herself—but she had extraordinary intuitions, especially in the realm of erotic experience," he said. "I've never seen anything like her sensitive grasp of colors and shadings. Her acting made you feel that here was a woman who knew all there was to know about all aspects of love." As their love scenes evolved, she proved to her leading man that "in the poetic intensity with which she gives voice to banalities, Garbo has no rivals . . ."

Behind the scenes, she gained a reputation for supporting the underdog—especially the veteran actors whose blood and sweat had helped to build Hollywood. Erich von Stroheim, the man Mayer and Thalberg loved to hate, was recovering from surgery throughout his involvement in the picture. Once celebrated for his genius behind the camera, von Stroheim was now reduced to playing secondary film roles. He was rude, ill-tempered, and plagued by self-doubt, but Greta—who had met the actor under friendlier circumstances at Salka's—was a model of forbearance as he stumbled and stuttered through countless takes. On the days when he didn't feel up to it, she often provided the excuse for the day's absence, thus taking responsibility for the delay.

On the eleventh of March, Irving Thalberg, Edmund Goulding, and company took a three-hour, rough assembly of *Grand Hotel* up the California coast to Monterey for a preview. The reaction at the Golden State Theatre was uniformly positive—with one important exception. "When Garbo sees the performance of Joan Crawford there will be some Swedish swearing," W. R. Wilkerson predicted in *The Hollywood Reporter*. "Not that the great Greta was not great . . . so far as the limitations of her part would permit. But Crawford has the feminine meat of the show and how she does take advantage of it." A headline in *Variety* a few weeks later underscored the real problem: "GARBO NO SIGN, JOAN MAY ROMP IN M-G'S *HOTEL*." But Greta's unique contribution to the film couldn't be ignored—in fact, her part was built up. Most of the retakes scheduled by Thalberg involved Garbo and Barrymore. Filming was rescheduled in and around production on *As You Desire Me* and was completed ten days later.

On April 12, scarcely two weeks after retakes had wrapped, Metro-Goldwyn-Mayer and Loew's, Inc. staged an all-star premiere for *Grand Hotel* at the Astor Theatre in New York. The excitement building around the film was immediately apparent; MGM had another hit on its hands. "You could not sit through *Grand Hotel* and not find it engrossing fare," the critic for the *National Board of Review* wrote, "but that much was destined; you knew it, even before a single crank turned, before a foot of film was recorded . . . Garbo is more elastic than she has ever been, achieving with—for her—amazing litheness, the sudden contrasting moods . . . Her face is photographed thought."

Though some critics judged her performance as a prima ballerina "an ingenious failure," most audiences connected with its magic. "Garbo dominates the picture entirely," John Mosher acknowledged in *The New Yorker,* "giving the tricky, clever film a lift, a spring, such as pictures without her, without that intense, nervous vitality she's got, cannot possess."

The roadshow extravaganza followed *Mata Hari* into Sid Grauman's Chinese Theatre in Hollywood on April 29, 1932. Among the extraordinary list of celebrities participating in the opening night gala were Marlene Dietrich, Jean Harlow and Paul Bern, Clark Gable, Marion Davies, Joan Crawford and Douglas Fairbanks, Jr., Norma Shearer and Irving Thalberg, Constance Bennett, Fredric March, Lew Ayres, Bebe Daniels and Ben Lyon, Laurence Olivier, Lilyan Tashman and Edmund Lowe, Robert Montgomery, Gavin Gordon, Anita Loos, and directors Fred Niblo, Michael Curtiz, and Cecil B. DeMille. It was an unforgettable evening made even more memorable by emcee Will Rogers' special announcement promising a personal appearance by Greta Garbo after the screening. What the audience got instead was Wallace Beery sashaying on stage in a tent-sized dress and long blond wig. The charade was a colossal flop, which provided an awkward ending for an evening that had been, up until that moment, an unqualified triumph. According to press reports, Greta spent the evening with "a foreign director and his wife."

During the darkest year of the Depression, *Grand Hotel* worked its way through a series of premium-dollar engagements (a lower-priced wide release followed later in the year) to earn $2.594 million internationally.[4] At the year's end, it would be ranked by critics as one of the best pictures of 1932; it is the only film in Garbo's catalog to be honored by the Academy of Motion Picture Arts and Sciences as Best Picture.

For moviegoers, *Grand Hotel* stands as the film where Greta Garbo finally voices the words that had long been attributed to her: "I want to be

[4]Posting a profit for MGM of $947,000.

alone." She speaks these words, first pathetically to her maid and manager, then as a plaintive cry; and, finally, as a futile declaration to a stranger. The stranger becomes her lover and she is no longer alone. In Vicki Baum's novel, Grusinskaya would utter "I wish to be alone" as often as "I want to be alone." Greta later declared that the sentiment wasn't hers. She never said she wanted to be alone, only that she wanted to be *left* alone. The subtleties in meaning were lost on her followers. To them, the public and private personas of Greta Garbo were one and the same—"being alone" was the operative phrase.

"Her face, this landscape of inscrutable loneliness, mirrored the alienation of her time . . . the existentialism of Sartre," her friend, actor Alf Sjöberg, wrote. "Her voice, the golden voice, that we thought was meant for our little corner of the world, had an echo . . ."

"The stories about Greta's shyness are incorrect," her *best pal* Mercedes de Acosta commented. "She is never shy—she is emotional and fears showing it." Director Edmund Goulding offered his analysis of the Garbo psyche to a *Los Angeles Times* reporter. When he first knew her, she was unbothered by the celebrity spotlight and lived "as others do, surrounded by a few friends and having a life of her own," he said. Fame had not only forced her to become cautious but, as others would confirm, extremely tentative when it came to social engagements. Goulding and his new bride, a delicate-looking ballroom dancer named Marjorie Moss, usually entertained Garbo alone. Independent of hangers-on, her opinions about her profession "and all her varied interests in the world of art" were freely expressed. "But she becomes restless if the bell rings and, with the advent of visitors, she will immediately leave," the director noted. "The curiosity of the public reaches out and hurts her as if it were a tangible thing."

During the spring of 1932, the Gouldings entertained a visitor from Great Britain. During a trip to Los Angeles two years earlier, celebrity photographer Cecil Beaton had spent a considerable amount of time pursuing Garbo for a possible *Vogue* sitting; the Metro publicity department offered him Joan Crawford or Norma Shearer instead. By 1932, studios sought Beaton out to arrange special photo sessions with their top stars. Still no Garbo. The photographer accepted the Gouldings' weekend invitation "with alacrity," knowing that Greta was an occasional visitor there. But when she phoned ahead one Sunday afternoon, she made it clear that she didn't want to meet strangers—especially ones who spoke to the press.

Despite the intended evasion, Cecil and Greta did meet. The erudite Beaton was then twenty-eight years old; his height and leaness emphasizing his highly manicured presence. That afternoon at the Gouldings', he was handsomely dressed in a white kid jacket, white shirt, and sharkskin shorts: he wasn't the person Garbo had expected *not* to meet. "But you are so young . . . and so beautiful," she remarked with discernible surprise when she accidentally encountered him. After an awkward start, they began conversing "without any of the polite preliminaries of strangers," Beaton recorded in his diary. "We talked nonsense as if we had known one another forever." A festive meal followed during which Cecil recalled Garbo scolding her director for making a vulgar joke that implied if she didn't behave herself, "he'd turn her upside down and give her a smacking where she sits upon."

According to Beaton, after the meal they went upstairs to the guest bedroom to look at photographs he had taken of his country estate in southern England. In an unpublished section of his journal, Beaton claimed that Garbo allowed him to kiss her. In the first volume of his memoirs, entitled *The Wandering Years,* the diarist was more discreet. "Are you happy?" Greta asked him when they were alone. "Yes," he responded, but she obviously felt it had been much too easy for him to say. Nothing was easy for her, she asserted. "Tomorrow I go to work with a lot of people who are dead. It's so sad. I'm an onlooker. I've passed being active in life. It's not a question of time and age—but it's just what you are yourself. One doesn't do the things one doesn't want to do."

Would she stay or would she go? Throughout production on *As You Desire Me,* rumors that Garbo was leaving the States for good escalated. She had been featured above the title in eighteen films at Metro and had been well compensated for it. But admirers were as concerned as studio executives that she might actually take the money and run. "I'm for a law that will bar Garbo from leaving the country," columnist Sidney Skolsky advocated. Even as her celebrity continued to grow into previously unexplored, seemingly combustible dimensions, the object of all this attention wondered at what point she had signed away her right to a quiet, happy life doing the thing she loved most: acting. It had happened not in 1925 when she and Moje agreed to come to Hollywood, but in 1927 when she agreed to stay. Now, as her contract came up for renewal, she had to decide whether to bring the devil on board—or set back out to sea.

On April 4, Greta applied for an extension to her Swedish passport (a necessary step if she intended to complete the term of her contract). *As You Desire Me* wrapped at the end of the month, retakes continued into May; the movie was scheduled for a June release. Garbo was now at the height of her popularity with American audiences. Even before 1932 was over, it was clear that she would be one of the year's top ten moneymakers. It was incumbent on Mayer and Thalberg to change her mind about leaving.

Years later, Greta described her feelings during the tortuous final days of her original contract. "I don't hate Hollywood any more than I hate Louis B. Mayer," she said. "[But] I don't like Mr. Mayer—although I see his point and I don't blame him for doing to me what he did." What did he do? Cecil Beaton inquired. "Well, he made me sign a long contract—five years—and I was terrified and very unhappy, for it seemed like a life term. When I had finished the contract I said to him: 'This is the end. I don't want to continue. I want to get out of pictures.' He and his minions were so worried! They had these long discussions with me, and we walked up and down outside the soundstage, and they said: 'You can't quit now; we won't let you. You're at the very peak of your career.' But I was all set. I was so unhappy."

As her servitude concluded, Greta longed to reconnect with her homeland; seven long years in the United States had not convinced her otherwise. She would always be, Mercedes de Acosta suggested, a Viking child "troubled by a dream of snow." On the twenty-ninth of May, industry papers carried an announcement that Garbo was indeed going home for what they termed an extended vacation. Whether or not she would return was unclear. "If she does go to Sweden, and comes back after six months or so, her return will be like a Second Coming—and will make a great story for the newspaper boys," Clarence Brown prophesied.

MGM took advantage of the publicity surrounding Garbo's anticipated departure and released *As You Desire Me* during the first week of June. The fact that *Grand Hotel* was still drawing crowds made for easy comparisons, although by now the twenty-six-year-old Garbo was treated so reverentially by most critics that any serious analysis of her films was rare. No one complained about the fact that the star's salary obviously devoured a significant portion of her movie budgets, or about the inconsistent production values or the preponderance of close-ups—such scrutiny of Garbo's veiled thought process was, in fact, what many admirers came to see. All moviegoers demanded of a Garbo production was Greta Garbo. Even by these standards, *As You Desire Me,* her shortest film since ending her silence, was a less than satisfying offering that left everyone begging for more. Historically, the picture marked the end of the third phase of her career, which took her from Europe to Hollywood and into the sound era; period fashions would dominate her screen future.

"If Greta Garbo's portrayal in the pictorial version of Pirandello's play, *As You Desire Me,* is her valedictory to the American screen, then the talented Swedish player has the satisfaction of leaving the Metro-Goldwyn-Mayer studios in a blaze of glory," Mordaunt Hall wrote in *The New York Times.* On a personal front, a less glorious blaze nearly obliterated her future. Late in the afternoon on Friday, June 3, after a week of secret meetings, the First National Bank of Beverly Hills was declared insolvent. With nervous customers lining up outside the bank on Saturday and early Monday morning, the institution formally closed its doors on Monday, June 6. "A marked shrinkage in security values in addition to general depressed economic conditions" was given as the reason for the closure.

Bank failures had become alarmingly routine by 1932. The fact that a large percentage of the bank's depositors were movie stars—among them, Jean Harlow, John Gilbert, Harold Lloyd, Will Rogers, Robert Montgomery, Marie Dressler, and Marion Davies—made it a national story. "I had in the First National every bit of cash I had," Harlow admitted. "It came at an exceptionally bad time for me because I had just made an especially large deposit." Constance Bennett was more fortunate. She had deposited a check for $20,000 into her account on Friday, which the studio immediately stopped and reissued.

The discovery that Garbo was among the First National patrons made international headlines. With an executive staff featuring some of the top financial officers in the business, the stalwart "pioneer bank" of the community had ridden out the early chaotic days of the Depression without a problem—a statistic that made it a logical choice for Harry Edington and his clients. Ironically, according to Wilhelm Sörensen, Greta had personally transferred all her holdings "of gilt-edged stock and other securities" from her bank in Hollywood to First National following the crash in 1929.

Exactly how much money she had deposited in various accounts at the bank is unknown. Her Metro earnings to date came to approximately $1.3 million. Her net worth after various taxes, levies, and modest living expenses was between $300,000 and $400,000. Harry Edington always maintained that Garbo's money was invested in "substantial American securities," but according to Carl Johan Bernadotte, she had purchased riskier bank shares and stocks—an investment that represented approximately two years' worth of savings.

Garbo had lost an undisclosed amount of money (believed to be no greater than $100,000) when the stock market first crashed and another disputed sum when Ivar Kreuger's empire collapsed in Sweden in April of 1932.[5] But nothing could have prepared her for such a catastrophe timed so close to her exit from Hollywood. As the days went by, a curious story

[5]Kreuger, known around the world as the "Swedish match king," committed suicide when his company, A. B. Kreuger & Toll, went bankrupt under the weight of massive debts and potential criminal prosecution. Swedish auditors reported Garbo's loss to be insignificant.

began to emerge: "Unofficial but reliable sources disclosed today that a client's demand for $300,000 resulted in the closing Friday of the First National Bank of Beverly Hills to protect interests of other depositors," *The New York Times* revealed on the seventh of June. That same day, *Variety* reported that "the bank officials were entirely willing to close as they anticipated that one of their heaviest depositors, a woman, and believed to be Garbo, was about to withdraw her money . . ." Furthermore, a *Los Angeles Times* columnist alleged, the source of this surprising information was none other than MGM.

Later information would absolve Greta of any "complicity" in the First National failure and suggest that the depositor in question was a widow in Beverly Hills contesting the bank's disposition of her late husband's trust fund. It is interesting to note, however, that with the publicity surrounding Garbo's imminent departure, bank officials had *expected* her to make a large withdrawal; when added to the widow's demand for accountability this helped to increase anxiety at the bank, sealing its fate.

Mercedes claimed that Greta was able to sneak into the bank through a back entrance and rescue securities locked away in her safe deposit box— but she was not able to avoid the immediate penalty forced upon depositors: all accounts were frozen until an examiner could determine the bank's ability to honor its debts. Garbo was particularly hard-hit; she had already booked passage on a boat home. With her accounts frozen for an indefinite period of time, her ability to return to Sweden was effectively compromised. "I'll wire President Hoover! I'll wire Dawes!"[6] Harry Edington was overheard angrily telling a bank official. "We'll see whether a foreign star who trusts her money to an American bank can be victimized like this!"

At the same time, the Immigration Department was believed to be "checking up" on the actress to make sure she left the country, "now that she is no longer under contract to Metro and out of the alien artist classification." Garbo wanted to leave, but couldn't without the money that misfortune had placed outside her reach. "It's slave labor," screenwriter S. N. Behrman said of Hollywood, "and what do you get for it? A lousy fortune!" The irony for Greta Garbo was that after several years in the United States she had no idea if she was any better off than when she came. "I have never been so poor in my life as I am now," she admitted privately.

Edington was furious, but there was very little he could do for her. Unbeknownst to Greta, however, Mercedes promptly sent a telegram to

[6]Former Vice President Charles G. Dawes headed the Reconstruction Finance Corporation, the Hoover administration's attempt to revive depressed businesses.

the White House. "PLEASE FORGIVE ME FOR BOTHERING YOU AT THIS MOMENT WHEN YOU HAVE SO MUCH ON HAND BUT MUCH IS AT STAKE," she wired Herbert Hoover on June 16, 1932. "AS YOU NO DOUBT KNOW THE FIRST NATIONAL BANK OF BEVERLY HILLS CLOSED LAST WEEK IN WHICH THE FILM STAR GRETA GARBO HAD ALL HER MONEY. I CONSIDER MUCH GRAVE DIS-HONESTY SURROUNDS HER. SHE IS A CHILD AND INCAPABLE OF TAKING CARE OF HERSELF. I HAVE WIRED THE SWEDISH AMBASSADOR MR. BOSTROM TO PRO-TECT HER AND HOPE YOU WILL COMMUNICATE AND ADVISE HIM."

The message was forwarded to the State Department, division of West-ern European Affairs. Whether or not any personal action was taken is unknown. The First National Bank of Beverly Hills was placed into receivership so that it might reorganize its business and reopen its doors. In the meantime, bank officers accepted jobs at various institutions around the country; within the year Bank of America took over the property. In a settlement, the bank agreed to pay fifteen cents on the dollar to patrons with unsecured accounts.

With so many conflicting stories, it isn't surprising that MGM was uncertain as to what Garbo's true financial status was. She had been dis-creet in the handling of her money, living the frugal lifestyle of someone who believed in saving money; publicly, she continued to act as if she were leaving soon. Yet behind the scenes, Harry Edington was discussing a pos-sible deal with Joseph Schenck of United Artists, and Greta's New York attorney, Joseph Buhler, forwarded an inquiry to Edington from Para-mount's B. P. Schulberg.[7] There were even rumors that Joseph Kennedy was involved in negotiations.[8]

But Garbo remained at MGM, where Edington eventually secured an extraordinary production deal for her. Autonomy was the key building block in her new contract—an unprecedented two-picture deal between MGM and Canyon Productions "for the services of Greta Garbo" that placed the star in the top salary bracket at $250,000 per film. The contract, dated July 7, 1932, proved that Garbo retained the power position by for-mally giving her director and costar approval. Most important, it secretly established a new production entity designed to help Greta deal with her tax situation internationally, amortizing her salary over a five-year period. Metro had no intention of letting its players (or indeed any of the film

[7]Garbo had expressed an interest in working at Paramount Pictures ever since Mauritz Stiller's association with the studio in 1926.

[8]Kennedy had met Garbo in 1931 at a dinner party hosted by *Photoplay* editor James R. Quirk in New York. The executive's aggressive pursuit of Greta at the party culminated with Greta locking herself in the bathroom until everyone had left.

community) know they had given in on this point. After much wrangling throughout the 1920s, the major Hollywood studios had effectively eliminated such costly setups during the transition to sound. Details about Garbo's 1932 contract were kept private for nearly fifty years.

That Greta had reconsidered her position due to the bank failure was undeniable. "Somebody joked that Mr. Mayer made my bank fail so that he could get me back," she explained to a friend. "He agreed to pay me for half my next picture in advance [and] wrote out the highest check I have ever seen. But I had nowhere to put it—no pocket, no bag, so I tucked it into my open shirt and went home to Sweden . . ." With a check for $100,000 in one hand and the traveling bag her coworkers had gifted her with in the other, Greta concluded her business and boarded an eastbound train on July 21. There were no farewell dinners, no flowers, and no official acknowledgment from the actress that she was coming back. Although there were reports that Garbo had re-signed with MGM, Edington and the studio continued to deny such stories. As far as most of Hollywood was concerned, she was leaving for good.

The public gathered at New York's Grand Central Station to greet her. Garbo had changed to a slower train in Chicago, but even her sidestep had been anticipated. When she got off the *Fifth Avenue Special* at 125th Street in Harlem, accompanied by Mercedes de Acosta and Robert Reud, she encountered an unwelcome committee of photographers and reporters. A magazine editor would invite readers to take a closer look at one of the photographs taken that afternoon: "You will see that she did not want to pose. . . . She makes herself face the cameras. See her clenched hand and defensively bent elbow. There is no ease to her figure. The most graceful woman in the world is taut and nervous."

In the confusion at the station, Mercedes was left behind with the luggage; Greta rushed into a taxicab with Bob Reud and led the chase through the Bronx to an obscure establishment called the Hotel Gramatan. How Mercedes even got on that train was something of a mystery. Garbo was alone when she stole on to the *Southwest Chief* in San Bernadino. Most likely, she met her en route. "The Garbo-Mercedes business has been too amazing. They had terrific battles," Anita Loos relayed to Cecil Beaton, "and Garbo left without saying goodbye. Then Mercedes flew to NY to see her and Garbo wouldn't. Mercedes flew back despondent—lost her job with MGM and is in the most awful state. Also says she is broke—can't get a break and it's too terrible. The story is as long as the dictionary . . ."

Mercedes made no mention of this farce in her autobiography. "Not long after this Greta sailed home to Sweden," she wrote. "After she left, Hollywood seemed empty to me." Greta's only reference to any trouble with her friend—code name "Black and White"—was typically subtle. "THANK YOU FOR EVERYTHING YOU HAVE DONE FOR ME BUT ABOVE ALL THANK HEAVEN THAT YOU EXIST," she cabled Salka Viertel the day before she boarded her ship. "AUF WIEDERSEHN LIEBE SALKA. HOPE TO GOD YOU HAD A CHANCE TO PAY BLACK AND WHITE."

Under the cover of darkness on the evening of July 29, Greta was escorted on to the *Gripsholm* by two Burns detectives. The Swedish-American liner was not scheduled to leave port until midday on the thirtieth. Neither Garbo's name nor any of her well-known aliases was on the passenger list—but news of her presence on board spread quickly. Passengers gathered in the hallways and on deck outside her deluxe stateroom. Two sentries were posted at the door, while the curtains of cabin 26, the royal suite, remained drawn. "I can't tell you that she is in there," a steward guarding the cabin insisted. "I can't tell you that she came last night and hasn't been out since. I can't tell you that she had breakfast sent in this morning. Somebody is with her, too. I can't tell you that I have orders."

Even after the *Gripsholm* cast aside its moorings, MGM preferred to let the public believe that Greta had left Hollywood without signing a new contract. Their continued effort to make the lack of PR pronouncements speak volumes kept her name alive in the press, but also generated much hostility. "Who is Garbo—that she could leave the town that has given her glamour, fame and wealth, without even saying 'Goodbye'?" one indignant magazine editor wrote. "Isn't it time now to wonder if her 'mystery' isn't just plain ingratitude?"

While some declared a crisis in Hollywood, others expressed no regret in seeing "The Divine One" leave. With jobs at a premium, America's growing xenophobia extended even to Garbo. Not only had she been outrageously successful, she had astounded industry-watchers with her stubborn refusal to flaunt her success or to bow down in grateful recognition for it. It was unusual behavior, which made skeptical nationalists believe that the actress, a foreigner, didn't appreciate what had been "handed" to her by what they saw as a more generous spirit. How did Greta Garbo get that way? a rising tide of journalists pondered in their respective newspapers and magazines.

Greta stayed inside her cabin until the ship was well out to sea and associated with few passengers on the voyage home. On occasion, she was seen with Ambassador Bostrom, Sweden's representative in the United States, and the Spanish consul general, Ambassador Matura, but generally restricted her visits to the dining room or to the deck for a game of shuffleboard with the ship's officers.

When the *Gripsholm* pulled into Göteborg Harbor on the eighth of

August, she was met on board by her brother. Greta surprised the reporters who accompanied Sven on the customs launch by agreeing to meet them in the smoking salon for an impromptu press conference. She was unprepared for the barrage of questions. "I am not exactly afraid of the press, but I do not like so much written about me," she explained. "My work is in the studio." Moreover, Garbo cautioned, she didn't think the public attached such great importance to movie stars. "People don't really want to see me in real life. All the public goes to the cinemas for is to forget its troubles," she insisted. "Surely the world doesn't care what soap I use to wash myself. . . . I am tired of picking up English, French, German and other newspapers sent to me in Hollywood and of reading my alleged views on love, cosmetics and health. I have never written a word in my life."[9]

She denied reports that she had purchased Ivar Kreuger's summer villa or that she intended to make a film in Sweden with Victor Sjöström. "I simply have no plans for the future. I can't even say when I am returning to Hollywood," she said. "What I should like would be to find some little place here in Sweden where I can hide. I want to use my freedom as I would like to—resting with my family and my friends. I do hope that people won't bother me." Greta was asked again about the rumors that she would make a film in Sweden or England. "Can't I make it clear that I have no plans? I hope I have convinced you I am not here as an advertising stunt. I hate publicity. I am very much in earnest about it." She refused to tell journalists where she was planning to stay. "Then there will be no peace," she reasoned, and it was her greatest desire to rest—"if there is rest for a restless soul."

A crowd estimated to be in the thousands waited patiently in the rain to cheer "*Heja,* Greta!"—Welcome home—as the ship pulled into the quay. "By the way, it is absolutely mad how many police are out," a reporter for *Dagens Nyheter* offered. "Even when we landed in Göteborg with King Alfonso and the dead moose a few years ago, there weren't so many people around." Garbo smiled for the crowd and waved her handkerchief while the newsreel cameras rolled. As she moved toward the gangway, the crowd surged forward and she became alarmed. "How dangerous this looks," she whispered to her brother. Once she got into her car, however, the newshounds lost the scent and Greta headed with Sven toward Stockholm, stopping overnight at a small hotel en route and then disappearing into the countryside.

By her own account, Mercedes de Acosta did not waste any time finding consolation after Greta left. She wrote of meeting Marlene Dietrich at a

[9]An allusion to recent "memoirs" published under her own by-line.

performance by dancer Harald Kreutzberg. Not so, according to Maria Riva, Dietrich's daughter. "My mother told me she found her sobbing in the kitchen during a party at the Thalberg's house. . . . This kitchen meeting had many versions but always ended with the 'cruel Swede' being replaced by the 'luminous German aristocrat,' " Riva said. It was the beginning of a new romantic adventure.

The next day, Dietrich brought Mercedes an armful of tuberoses and, with her soon-to-be legendary *hausfrau* intensity, determined to nurse her "White Prince" back to health. Marlene fussed over her in a way that Greta never did and commiserated in her despair; it didn't take Mercedes long to become smitten, overwhelming the object of her adoration with reciprocal flowers and gifts. A month later, when Dietrich was seen parading around town in men's suits, much to the dismay of conservative opinion-makers, the focus of their concern was obvious. Although Dietrich had built her Hollywood reputation on such controversial attire on screen, flaunting her sensational private life in public arenas—despite the comfortable cover of a husband and child—would be discouraged (but never controlled).

According to her daughter, it did not take long for Marlene to become bored with playing the role of the "Golden One." However, correspondence from Dietrich dated throughout 1932 and 1933 indicates the flame died out much more slowly—the shimmering façade was in place until it became inconvenient for Dietrich to maintain it. Mercedes continued to live in a fantasy world of drama and romance.

At last back in Sweden, Greta found a temporary refuge in a rented villa on an island outside of Stockholm. Days went by without anything but a silent, smiling midsummer sun and the lapping, temperate waters of the archipelago to distract her. At the end of the summer, she moved into a small house at Danderydsgatan 7 in Östermalm, the peaceful northeastern sector of Stockholm. Here she often gathered her new, extended family around her. In 1931, Sven had married Ethel Marguerite Baltzer; Peg, as she was known to her friends and family, was born in the United States to Swedish parents. Their daughter, Ann-Marguerite Gustafson (who later assumed the name Gray as her naturalized American name), was born during the spring of 1932. Greta had no problem with the idea of becoming an aunt—in fact, she seemed to enjoy it.

After reentering family life, Greta reintroduced herself to friends. Max Gumpel also lived in Östermalm. Since their courtship almost twelve years earlier, Gumpel had married, become a father of four, and was now separated from his wife. He was older, a little balder, but as friendly as ever.

"One day I received a phone call at my office from a mysterious woman who asked if I wanted to have dinner with an old friend," Max wrote in his fairytale-like memoir for his children. "She didn't identify herself, and though I wondered I waited for her to tell me who she was." He thought it might be a hoax, but was intrigued by the puzzle and asked "The Voice" to dress up in her nicest gown and have dinner with him at his home. "She said she didn't own a beautiful dinner gown so I told her, 'Just make yourself beautiful.' She arrived—it was She, and as her only jewelry she was wearing my little tiny diamond ring. On her it *was* the most glittering jewel in the English crown."

Gumpel became Greta's newest advisor, companion, and, according to some reports, renewed suitor. One of Max's best friends, Eric Erickson, recalled meeting Gumpel for lunch at the Grand Hôtel. "Max arrived at the hotel with Garbo arm-in-arm," he told Sven Broman. "He hadn't said anything about bringing her before. When the meal was over they announced to me their decision of becoming engaged, right then and there. With that, Max took a diamond ring from his coat pocket and slipped it on Greta's finger, saying to me, 'So now we are engaged, and you are our witness, but don't tell anyone about it.' " Greta even called Vera Schmiterlöw to announce that she and Max had become engaged and that he had given her a ring. "Greta told me that she was very happy about it," Vera confirmed, "but I don't believe that she took it very seriously because all the time she talked about it she was laughing and seemed to treat it like a big joke."

Her purported fiancé never wrote of the engagement nor of that second diamond ring, and Garbo subsequently denied any betrothal. What was important to her was a friend's guidance as a savvy businessman. As with the rest of the international community, Sweden had been struggling for survival throughout 1931 and 1932, but Max Gumpel (unlike industrialist Ivar Kreuger) had successfully steered his construction and real estate business away from the hazards and came out on top. "He was someone she could trust," notes his daughter Laila Nylund. "Dad would go out of his way to protect a friend, and he was particularly fond of Greta."

After having rested, Greta became more visible in and around Stockholm and was often seen playing tennis with Gumpel at an indoor stadium, shopping at PUB, or riding horseback in a nearby park during the early morning.[10] She hoped for a chance to get together with the Sjöströms, but hadn't been able to as yet. Instead, she met with Abraham Stiller and made an early-morning pilgrimage to Moje's gravesite with a wreath of roses in hand. Her most public appearance was a night at the

---

[10]One by one, she would give up each activity as it was reported in the press.

theater to see Karl-Gerhard's new musical revue. Her presence was discovered at intermission and the theater was soon inundated with photographers.[11]

Even at home, where Garbo had been voted Sweden's most popular national figure, people complained that she didn't dress or act the part of a star. During her 1932 sabbatical, Greta kept her social life simple and appeared oblivious to the idea of moving up in social rank. "To Garbo's credit, however, it can undoubtedly be said that she most likely doesn't care two whoops in Hades about the social register," stated one observer. The only titled peerage she was interested in was a count and countess by the name of Wachtmeister.

Gösta Ekman appealed to Greta to appear in a holiday production of *Grand Hotel* at the Vasa Teatern. The actress offered a "half promise" that she would consider his proposition, then slipped quietly out of town to Tistad Slott. The reigning movie queen was given one of the best rooms in the house, a guest room on the top floor of the castle with "the most enchanting view" of the estate. On warm days, she would climb from the attic to a skylight and sunbathe on the roof. She found a "merry playmate" in ten-year-old Gunnila Wachtmeister, helping Gunnila and farmhand Ernst Larsson gather stray animals in the meadow. "She was just 'Auntie Greta' to me," said Hörke's eldest child.

Greta and Hörke traveled to London during the first week in November. The countess found a discreet Mayfair hotel for them to use as a hideout; somewhat surprisingly, although she registered as "Greta Gustafson," Garbo's ruse was not exposed. Despite the raging success of *Mata Hari* and *Grand Hotel*, then making their way through European cinemas, the actress's "schoolmarm" disguise (a heavy blue coat, dark wig, and horn-rimmed glasses) was so effective, she was able to move on to Paris without incident. Once again, it was Greta Gustafson who checked into a modest hotel near the British Embassy.

She was in town for nearly a week before the staff of the Hôtel Castiglione discovered the true identity of their guest. As the public congregated in the streets, an extra detail of gendarmes was assigned to the perimeter of the hotel—not to ensure Garbo's safety, but to keep the traffic on Rue du Faubourg-St-Honoré moving. Hunted but not yet compromised, she still was able to sneak out and enjoy a promenade *incognito* down the Avenue des Champs-Élysées.

---

[11]Contrary to a previously published account, Greta's companion that evening was not Mercedes de Acosta; photos taken during the performance show Hörke Wachtmeister at her side. Mercedes was working in Hollywood at the time.

On her final evening in Paris, two days after her presence in the French capital had been revealed, Greta went out with friends to explore the bohemian life in the restaurants and dance clubs of Montmartre. The party was spotted at a scandalous nightclub reportedly "frequented by hard-boiled women of the Paris demimonde, who go there attired in mannish costumes to give lady tourists the shock they are looking for by asking them to dance." Hörke Wachtmeister danced with some of the female gigolos, said one eyewitness, but despite the efforts of several girls, Greta "did not appear interested, at least this evening, and instead remained at the table chatting with her boy friend."

The press caught up with her at the train station in Copenhagen, where she disembarked to meet with Victor Sjöström and learned that the art of pursuit was alive and well in Denmark. Back home in Sweden, Greta complained of the merciless persecution of the press that had turned her holiday into misery. Europe is dead, she proclaimed in a letter to Salka. "I have been so hounded I don't want to travel anymore."

Christmas that year was cool but not cold, and there was little snow in Stockholm—only melancholy and yearning. For Greta, there was bittersweet acknowledgment that she was a person without permanent roots. In the United States, she was a Swede; in Sweden, she was beginning to feel like an American. Wherever she went, she soon longed to be somewhere else. "The world is absolutely mad," she wrote to Salka on New Year's Eve. "If I were an American I would say: 'It is too bad.' But I am a wandering Jew, and we have no light expressions."

She anticipated returning to Hollywood by the beginning of March. Her ever-faithful maid "Whistler," now in charge of household affairs, had closed the Rockingham house and put her possessions into storage. "If only I knew [when] Berthold would be back," Greta wrote, "because if he is not I am going to ask you for a room in your house.[12] It would kill me if I had to go to a hotel." She planned to take a slow boat to the States that avoided the crush in New York by continuing south to the Caribbean and on through the Panama Canal to San Diego. "You will meet me won't you Salka? I will cable you from the boat the day of my arrival and of course I am going to try to go secretly again. God knows how well I succeeded all the time."

On January 16, 1933, after postponing the inevitable for several months, Greta went to the American Consulate in Stockholm to apply for

[12]Most recently, Viertel had been directing theatrical productions in New York, and films at Paramount's Astoria Studios. After the failure of a pet project in Germany, he accepted an assignment in London with Gaumont-British.

an immigration visa. Neither the demand for her services in the United States nor her artist classification had afforded her any special privileges. Since she had elected not to obtain a reentry permit prior to leaving the States, under the current immigration laws she now must appear in person at the American consulate to request a labor permit and non-preference quota number. In addition to the written application, she had to submit to a medical examination and present a copy of her birth certificate, accompanied by a statement from the local police department attesting to her model record as a citizen. News of her intention to return to Hollywood was relayed immediately around the world. Garbo's quota visa—number sixteen—was approved on the twenty-fourth of January.

Six months after the Canyon Productions deal had been set, Metro-Goldwyn-Mayer formally announced that Greta Garbo had signed a new contract, and that her next film would be based on the life of the controversial monarch Christina of Sweden. Early reports generously stated her salary to be $400,000 per film. "It is yet undetermined whether the picture will be made here or in Sweden, as it is not known whether Miss Garbo has been able to get a labor permit to return to this country," *Variety* disclosed.

On March 25, after another cunning series of false reservations and leaks to the press, Garbo set sail on the SS *Annie Johnson,* a small freighter bound for San Francisco. Her passage had been booked (in one of four passenger cabins) under the name "Emerson." "I don't know what made me go on that month in solitude," she confessed. "I was a young strapping boy and I didn't have anyone, so I went alone."

The voyage took five weeks. As one of the few passengers on a ship full of men, Greta would find this transatlantic crossing to be a memorable experience. The crew made an admirable effort to fulfill her most unusual requests. Each day, meals were served in the lifeboat of her choosing. "I liked being on the sea like that," she told Raymond Daum. She described walking the huge freight deck during a storm. "The ship went up and down and I adored it. Had I been in the cabin I probably would have been ill." At various ports of call, she even managed to go ashore without attracting attention.

There would be many changes—great and small—for Garbo to confront upon her return to Hollywood. Paul Bern, the production supervisor on *Romance, Susan Lenox, Grand Hotel,* and *As You Desire Me,* was found dead in his home, an apparent suicide.[13] In October, a spirited young

---

[13]The mysterious circumstances of Bern's death have never been satisfactorily explained. When his body was found by a servant, the studio was notified before the police department. It has been suggested that Bern's famous "suicide" note—"You understand

actress named Katharine Hepburn made an impressive screen debut in *A Bill of Divorcement*. The following month, Harry Edington formalized an alliance with an agent named Frank Vincent, creating an independent agency representing actors, directors, and writers.

The most profound change to take place during Garbo's absence would be Franklin Delano Roosevelt's election as president—a definitive signal that the times were changing. After his inauguration, Roosevelt asked Congress to repeal the 18th Amendment; Prohibition had succeeded only in funding a network of criminal activity across the country. In an effort to arrest further escalation of the banking crisis, Roosevelt declared a national bank holiday. The temporary closure affected many businesses, including several motion picture studios, but the end result was that many institutions began to show signs of stabilization. "It is foolish to say Hollywood is doomed," Irving Thalberg stated as he and wife, Norma Shearer, embarked on an extended European vacation. "A two-billion-dollar industry cannot stop forever. The only thing that can doom Hollywood is bad pictures . . ."

Least of all, Greta would not have minded missing the Long Beach earthquake in March of 1933, a substantial temblor that caused heavy arc lamps to pitch and sway from Culver City to Burbank.

From Cristóbal in the Canal Zone, Garbo sent Salka Viertel a detailed letter, written in German, regarding her projected arrival. A man would be calling Salka with the exact date and time of her arrival in San Diego. "I will take a little boat in," she wrote. "The *Annie Johnson* will remain out in the ocean because there's no harbor to dock." She fervently hoped she could avoid her manager, the media, and the fuss. "I have lied to Edington, and I hope he doesn't come [to San Diego]," she admitted. "Dearest, if you believe it is possible to get to San Pedro to meet me, please tell me.[14] I don't want the papers again. . . . It's such a peculiar wanderer who comes to you. The only thing that matters is that you're there. Otherwise—I don't know what."

It is interesting to note that all of these plans were made with Salka, not Mercedes. Yet, despite her caution, three days after Salka's letter was posted, a trade paper would report intercepting a wireless message from Garbo. According to the steamship's captain, C. O. Holmberg, Greta was

---

that last night was only a comedy"—was planted by Mayer and company to deflect any suspicion from alighting on Bern's wife, Jean Harlow. (Harlow had conveniently spent the night with her mother.)

[14]She may have confused the Los Angeles port of San Pedro (also on the *Annie Johnson's* schedule) with the southern-most port of San Diego.

fine until the day before they were due to arrive in United States waters—
then she became nervous in anticipation of the crowds and unnecessary
attention. She had been the perfect passenger, he said, "an excellent
sailor" who did not complain about inclement weather and was "the only
passenger who was not seasick at all."

Just before sunrise on April 30, the SS *Annie Johnson* steamed into the
port of San Diego. Greta was one of the first passengers to be processed by
immigration, and was given a certificate of arrival (necessary to validate
her application for permanent residency). After nine months, Garbo was
returning from Sweden a much more confident person, seemingly having
made peace with herself. Her eyes were bright, she was tanned, and she
looked much happier and healthier. She did not elude the press nor her
admirers who had been gathering since dawn. "I am very happy to be back.
As to how long I will stay," she stated, "I cannot say. One never knows
what tomorrow will bring, does one?"

"Today" brought a slight snag: although Greta got off in San Diego and
drove into Los Angeles with Salka, most of her luggage (five trunks and
three hat boxes) continued on to San Pedro, where a customs official
decided to hold everything due to what he believed to be Garbo's conflicting statements concerning her status in the United States. Was she a permanent resident or a quota immigrant? Spiritually, she was neither at
present; technically, she would soon be both.

PART THREE

*Child or animal, whichever you please, I prefer
to think of her as a deer, in the body of a
woman, living resentfully in the Hollywood
Zoo, suffering in the bonds of a complex civilization, startled by human contacts, disinterested in human things . . . Our generation's
loveliest woman is but a phantom upon a silver
screen . . .*

—Clare Boothe Luce

Drottning Kristina

hristina of Sweden (1626–1689)[1] was not, by any stretch of the imagination, a conventional queen. The woman who came to be known as one of Sweden's most controversial figures was also the daughter of one of its most popular kings, Gustav II Adolf—known to the English-speaking world as Gustavus Adolphus. She inherited the crown at the tender age of six when her father was killed in the battle of Lützen. Estranged from her mother (whom she believed to be weak, vain, and neurotic), Christina was raised in large part by her tutors, who were encouraged to treat her as a boy—Sweden needed a strong leader to step into the shoes of a king. Chancellor Axel Oxenstierna enthusiastically reported to the Diet that at age fourteen the queen "was not like a female, but courageous and with good understanding, so that if she escape corruption she will answer every hope."

As she matured, Christina was frequently the subject of conversation among her admiring court. "Despite her sex there is nothing feminine about her," wrote one observer. "Her voice is that of a man and likewise her manner of speech, her movements and gestures. . . . although she rides sidesaddle, she sways and bends her body in such a way that, unless one sees her from close quarters, it is easy to take her for a man." An Italian historian recorded that "Her lips, which were of fine red color, might have made a Venus of her, had it not been for so many other details of her physique and her bearing, which would have made one swear she was a Mars."

She ascended the throne in 1644 at the age of eighteen, taking the oath as Sweden's sovereign king. An advocate for the farmers and peasants against the flatulence of the burgeoning aristocracy, Christina was also a powerful force for introducing Sweden to the enlightening ideas of the Renaissance writers, painters, and thinkers. She established an academy, patronized the arts and sciences, commissioned ballets, and discussed complex intellectual questions at length with distinguished men of letters. One of her favored correspondents was the French philosopher René Descartes, whose *Cognito, ergo sum*—"I think, therefore I am"—defined many of their written dialogues. As reports of the erudition of the young

---

[1]More properly, Kristina.

Swedish queen spread throughout the European continent, royal courts focused their attention on the northern frontier.

There was within Christina the makings of an important world figure. Much to the dismay of her court advisors, however, she announced her intention to maintain her independence by carrying on the curious tradition of the virgin queen. For similar reasons, another great monarch, Elizabeth I of England (1533–1603), had decided not to "subjugate" herself to a man in marriage. The decorative standing of women in society served as a dismal reminder of the roles each queen would have been expected to play but for the fortune of their royal births exclusive of male heirs. Both women demonstrated their ability to affect history by failing to adhere to this standard; they demanded respect as the unquestioned rulers of their people without the comfort of providing a direct line of succession. "I tell you here and now that it is impossible for me to marry," Christina told her Privy Council in 1649. "So it must be, and I will not adduce reasons."

Still, her fiercest battle was not waged on a field of honor or in the Riksdag, but within her own mind—for Sweden was a Protestant nation and her father had died defending the faith. Martin Luther's Reformation had reached Scandinavia midway through the sixteenth century. Like many of his contemporaries, Christina's grandfather, Gustav Vasa, had used a popular religious movement to reclaim land and power from the Catholic Church; a new charter was written declaring the Lutheran Church to be the official church of Sweden. Scarcely a century later, the nation's new queen was secretly studying Catholicism with two Jesuits sent to her by the Church of Rome. "The free-ranging philosophical discussions jarred with the stiff, dogmatic Lutheranism which the daughter of Gustavus Adolphus and the queen of Protestant Sweden was expected to uphold," asserted one scholar. Christina became convinced that she would find in Catholicism, "a haven of free thought."

The queen's refusal to consider marriage precipitated a dynastic crisis, which was further complicated by growing social unrest; her leaning toward Rome threatened a constitutional one. In 1653, Christina began making preparations for her abdication in favor of her cousin, Karl Gustav. On June 6, 1654, in the great hall of the royal palace at Uppsala, she formally removed the crown from her head and left Sweden.[2] Most of her subjects had no idea why she was leaving, what she was taking, or that she had embraced Catholicism; even when her journey to Rome became known, Christina remained popular with the common people. But history, particu-

---

[2]After she had also removed the best paintings, tapestries, books, and manuscripts in the Royal Treasury.

larly Swedish Lutheran scholars, viewed her abdication as a betrayal, not the least of which because "Feelings of patriotism, a sense of obligation or of regard for the opinions of others . . . meant nothing to her, as against the gratification of her own bizarre desires."

Christina's final impact on Sweden was lasting one: in response to her abdication, the Riksdag passed a law denying women the right of succession.[3] But the drama of the queen's early ascent to the throne, the intriguing affairs of her court (including her well-documented attachment to one of her ladies in waiting, Ebba Sparre), her abdication, her extravagances as she traveled through Europe and was entertained by a curious aristocracy, her arrival in the Vatican City, her struggle to regain her crown—or any crown—and her unrequited love for the cardinal who was her inquisitor and protector have tempted writers and historians (most notably, Alexandre Dumas and August Strindberg) to tackle her story.

By the 1930s there had been a reinterpretation of the life of the Swedish queen by two female authors: Faith Compton Mackenzie in *The Sibyl of the North* and Margaret Goldsmith in *Christina of Sweden: A Psychological Biography*. Both books had been recommended to Garbo by friends and coworkers. Metro-Goldwyn-Mayer had, in fact, considered the story for Garbo as early as 1927 when Mauritz Stiller suggested it to Irving Thalberg.[4]

There were a number of fascinating parallels between the Swedish royal and the movie queen—several of which would become even more evident in the future: Both women were isolated socially; they were independent-minded, sometimes temperamental (certainly moody) women whose early course in life was directed by powerful men following the deaths of their fathers. On a more personal level, they shared certain habits in dress and manner which made clear their refusal to be defined by the company they kept or the clothes they chose to wear. A description of Christina's style of dress noted her scorn "of feminine lure as expressed in clothes." On several occasions of national importance, it was reported, "she appeared in garments so simple as to cause a sensation." She had no patience for most women. "I like men," she said in her memoirs, "not so much because they are men as because they are not women."

One of the unique strengths of MGM as a studio was its extraordinary

---

[3] The ruling survived for more than three centuries and was not struck down until 1980.

[4] *Filmjournalen*'s Inga Gaate first proposed the story to Moje before he left Sweden. "Allow me to remind you of our last meeting at the Grand Hôtel in Stockholm, where you very kindly said that you were interested in my idea of a film about Kristina," she later wrote. "As Kristina you can choose between Pola Negri or Greta Garbo! Both of them could, under your aegis, become Kristina."

ability to develop a definitive list of stars and personalities based upon its successful exploitation of their public and private personas. When a story was developed for Gable or Harlow or Crawford, bits and pieces of their own personal lives—as reported on the pages of *Photoplay* and *Motion Picture* magazines—were liberally woven into the scenarios. More so than at other Hollywood studios, at Metro-Goldwyn-Mayer a star's identity was irretrievably fused with his or her screen image. *Queen Christina* represented the most substantive—and provocative—fusion of Greta Garbo's private and public selves. "A fate and a life like Kristina's are like a fairy tale, an exciting adventure," an early proponent of the story assessed, "the arabesque of which consists of a woman's forceful and strange personality . . . tragic, comic, grotesque, poetic and grandiose." In short, it was a story Garbo lived to play.

"Why don't you write?" Greta had asked Salka Viertel when they first met. Upon reading the German edition of Margaret Goldsmith's biography, Salka found a topic she—and Greta—were interested in pursuing. With the help of Margaret Levino, Salka translated the outline of a screen treatment (which she had written in German) into English and presented it to Greta late in the spring of 1932.[5] Garbo sent it along to Irving Thalberg. Though he found the scenario to be a careful, studious adaptation—and "far from perfect"—Thalberg agreed that it was rich material for Garbo. In an impromptu meeting at his Santa Monica beach house, he assured both women he would personally oversee the project.

Garbo's new agreement secured the deal. According to the terms of her new contract, Greta selected the first script to be filmed. If the producers were in agreement, arrangements would be made to shoot the picture abroad. No sooner had she left for Sweden than Thalberg concluded negotiations on Salka's writing contract and brought in a new collaborator, Bess Meredyth. The film must be vivid and daring, he declared during an early story conference; the characters should be unusual, indelible, vulnerable. Thalberg asked if Salka had seen the German film *Mädchen im Uniform*.[6] "Does not Christina's affection for her lady-in-waiting indicate something like that?" he asked. Thalberg wanted her "to 'keep it in mind,' and perhaps if 'handled with taste it would give us very interesting scenes.' "

[5]According to the MGM script files, the first Viertel/Levino treatment was dated June 10, 1932.

[6]*Mädchen im Uniform* (1931), a disturbing story about a sexually repressed young girl's infatuation with one of her female teachers, had already caused a sensation on the Continent.

Much of the research for *Christina* was done by Garbo herself throughout her Swedish sabbatical. She visited the castle at Uppsala, the scene of Christina's abdication, as well as the Royal Library in Stockholm and the nation's fine art and history museums. For Greta, this was a chance to show something of her country's proud history, and she was tireless in her research. Many secret files and documents were opened to her for study. "Always clever with a pencil, the sketches she made at that time proved invaluable to the [MGM] research department when she returned," Howard Strickling reported. Her sketches of costumes, details of embroidery, furniture, and architecture were packed away and shipped on the *Annie Johnson.*

The actress "showed an enthusiasm that she had seldom displayed upon any occasion" toward a film project, Strickling observed. Her commitment and interest—so rare in the actress who almost left Hollywood due to disinterest—were among the reasons why her contributions and suggestions were welcomed at Metro. Garbo was "a daily consultant in matters of historical importance," said Strickling. "In every department, Greta Garbo was technical advisor as well as the star of *Queen Christina.*"

Greta's trip clarified for her the many benefits a "motion picture factory" offered over smaller European facilities. Salka Viertel, who had "ardently hoped" that the film could be made in Europe, now found Garbo reassuring her that "Metro was the best studio [and] Thalberg the most capable producer to deal with . . ." Greta wrote Salka about her decision less than six weeks after having arrived in Sweden. "I know that I am an impossible human being but I cannot make *Christina* in Europe," she stated, explaining that there were technical as well as emotional reasons why the film could not be made abroad. She apologized for changing her mind, saying only that, "When you have trafficked as much in film as I have then you would understand completely [what I mean]."

In their search for a solid Swedish anchor for the film, Metro representatives approached Victor Sjöström regarding his availability to direct *Queen Christina.* For reasons which were peculiarly his own, Sjöström was not able (or willing) to return to Hollywood. His refusal would be a disappointment to Garbo—but not a total loss. En route to the United States, the communications room of the *Annie Johnson* was inundated with radio messages keeping her informed of progress on the production. On March 29, she received a cable from the studio proposing Robert Z. Leonard or Edmund Goulding for director. Her response went out the following day: "GOULDING. REGARDS. GARBO." Two days later, Louis B. Mayer presented an interesting alternative: "THINK THERE IS OPPORTUNITY OF GETTING LUBITSCH. UNDERSTOOD YOUR FIRST PREFERENCE. ADVISE IF SO AND WILL TRY

BORROW FROM PARAMOUNT." Garbo's response was immediate and enthusiastic: "PREFER LUBITSCH. ALSO HAPPY FOR GOULDING."

Three weeks passed before the issue was resolved. MGM had not been able to free Ernst Lubitsch in time from Paramount. Edmund Goulding was also out of the picture, propelling Rouben Mamoulian's name to the top of the list; Greta expressed her approval. According to Mamoulian, the studio later tried to pressure Garbo into accepting someone else as director. Their last-minute alternatives included Clarence Brown, Jack Conway, Sam Wood, Robert Z. Leonard (resubmitted after Garbo's initial turndown), and Josef von Sternberg.[7] But she had already made her choice; she held out for Mamoulian.

A tall man with sensitive, dark brown eyes framed by black-rimmed glasses, the Armenian-born director was among the theatrical talent brought to Hollywood at the beginning of the sound era. Rouben Mamoulian effectively incorporated the revolutionary ideas of Stanislavski and the Moscow Art Theatre into his own creative work and, like Lubitsch, refused to acknowledge any rules regarding the making of sound motion pictures. Mamoulian's innovative ideas and fluid, rhythmic style would be evidenced in several ground-breaking films from *Applause* (1929) to *Dr. Jekyll and Mr. Hyde* and *Love Me Tonight* (both 1932). Most recently, he had directed a temperamental, unyielding Marlene Dietrich in *Song of Songs*. Greta was invited to Paramount Studios to view a rough cut of the film. The actress and the director made an immediate—and meaningful—connection. Aware that MGM had the power to spoil their film, Mamoulian, who insisted on shooting films his way, would become Garbo's greatest protection against any further compromise.

The 1932–1933 movie season went on record as the weakest season since Metro-Goldwyn's formation less than ten years earlier. Though Loews, Inc. was reportedly one of only five international film consortiums to have shown a profit during the fiscal year, the entire industry had amassed a $100 million loss. 1933 would be harsher still. The unique requirements of Depression-era audiences changed, for the time being, the way studio executives responded to the public. A midwestern exhibitor's assessment of *Grand Hotel* illustrated the conflict of producing the kind of "highbrow," quality projects Thalberg loved and the more direct, good-feeling mass

[7]Despite Metro's previous denial that they were in negotiations with von Sternberg—who had often expressed his desire to direct Garbo and had, arguably, modeled Marlene Dietrich after the kind of star he imagined Garbo to be—the director came closest to working with Greta on this, her most personal film.

entertainment embraced so vehemently by Mayer. He had reluctantly listed the film among the year's hits "because, from its box-office 'take', it deserves that classification. But from a 'popular priced' audience standpoint," he stated, "it deserves no such rating. The garden variety of fan came in large numbers and went away bewildered."

When Garbo returned to Hollywood during the spring of 1933, she found Irving Thalberg's position at the studio dramatically changed. On Christmas Day, 1932, Thalberg had suffered a mild heart attack. Concerned about his production VP, whom many considered the most talented producer in the business—and perhaps seeing the opportunity to cement his position as studio chief even further—Mayer brought in his son-in-law, producer David O. Selznick, from RKO to supervise and develop projects on an equal basis with Thalberg. Unlike other staff producers, Selznick would answer only to Mayer. Two days later, L.B. hired Walter Wanger, Hollywood's first Ivy League producer, away from Paramount Pictures.

When Thalberg learned of these changes, each made without first consulting him, a bitter quarrel ensued between him and Mayer. "The crisis came when Irving and Charlie [journalist Charles MacArthur] and Norma Shearer and I were going off to Europe for a holiday," actress Helen Hayes recalled. Thalberg's doctors wanted to get the tormented executive away from the studio and sent him to a resort in Bad Nauheim, Germany. One day, Shearer knocked hysterically at the MacArthurs' door. "Irving has had an attack," she cried. The trio raced back to Thalberg's hotel room where they came upon their friend, his face ivory white, his eyes half closed. "They knifed me in the back, Charlie," Thalberg said quietly. "They knifed me." Mayer had further weakened his position at the studio by elevating several of his assistants to full producer status. With Thalberg effectively decentralized, the supervision of MGM productions was now a committee affair.

Thalberg was still abroad when the critical pre-production decisions were made on *Queen Christina*, a project he had originally promised Garbo he would shepherd. (The actress had, in fact, already inquired about the possibility of getting David O. Selznick to work with her instead.) In Thalberg's absence, his top assistant, Albert Lewin, was one of the select inner circle temporarily overseeing the needed script changes and helping to plot *Christina*'s production course. David O. Selznick was given *Dinner at Eight* as his first Metro project; at the urging of director Rouben Mamoulian, Walter Wanger won the assignment of supervising *Queen Christina*.

In deference to Garbo's elevated position as an unofficial coproducer, most everything that concerned the script of *Queen Christina* was sent to her or Salka Viertel for comment; both women were actively involved in story conferences. As other writers were brought in (standard operating procedure at MGM rather than a sign of incompetence), Salka's role on the production evolved into the rather thankless task of being the keeper of historical truth—something Hollywood had little use for. Many of her ideas would be incorporated into the final script, some would be better articulated by others.

"If possible, one should show [Christina] as the proto-type of a modern woman who resents any of the feminine functions that tend to remind her of her dependence—and accordingly shrinks from both marriage and maternity," British playwright H. M. Harwood, suggested in an April 1933 memo to Walter Wanger. "Unconsciously, she resents the fact that she is not a man." Harwood subsequently wrote several interesting encounters between Christina and her court: "A queen who shares her bed may easily come to share her throne," she tells Count Magnus during one such confrontation. "Not you," her Minister of Finance responds, rather bitterly. "Your heart will never rule your head." "I hope not. Love is a poor counselor," Christina declares. "Love is a pretty enough game—when one is in the mood—but I have other things to be serious about. And so should you. A kingdom is not to be ruled by lovesick children."

Garbo had personal as well as professional issues to confront when she returned to town. It took no time for industry insiders to recognize that there had been a break between Garbo and manager Harry Edington. Some believed she hadn't approved of comments he had made to the *Los Angeles Times* and *Motion Picture* magazine prior to her departure; other tantalizing rumors suggested that she objected to Edington taking on Marlene Dietrich and Anna Sten (among other screen competitors) as clients. Inevitably, Garbo's financial loss from the bank failure determined that Harry Edington would no longer be handling her day-to-day business; she now sought decidedly non-exclusive advice from a number of knowledgeable businessmen in Los Angeles, New York, and Stockholm. But when she needed the man who had shown her the key to her own power at MGM, Harry Edington was there to protect her interests.

Another close associate currently in the proverbial doghouse was Greta's "Black and White" friend, Mercedes de Acosta, who—due to an unfortunate miscalculation on her part—now found herself unemployed in Hollywood. Mercedes had breached company policy by discussing the script of Metro's *Rasputin and the Empress* with two of the very much living Russian aristocracy. By divulging a significant change in the film's reporting of the historical drama, she provided the fuel for a libel suit (later filed in London). Irving Thalberg was furious. Her indiscretion would cost the studio more than $1 million; Mercedes had protected a friend, but had betrayed her employer and was fired.

Mercedes' ostracism by the studio precluded any significant involvement on her part in the development of *Christina*'s screenplay. Even her moral support would be difficult to offer to her adored "Scandinavian child." Contrary to the idyllic reunion with Garbo that Mercedes had indicated to friends (most especially Dietrich), Greta in fact seemed to keep her at arm's length, preferring instead to stay with Salka and her family for the first couple of months following her return to California. Until their relationship settled into something more comfortable for Greta, Mercedes went through another morose, indigo period.

By late spring, the mammoth task of casting *Queen Christina*'s principal characters was well under way. Finding a strong, charismatic actor to play Don Antonio Pimentelli de Parada, the Spanish envoy and Christina's principal love interest in the film, continued to elude producers. Leslie Howard was reportedly Garbo's first choice, but he passed on the opportunity. "She is a most intriguing personality. A peculiarly dominating personality on the screen and that is exactly why I declined the part," the actor frankly admitted. Franchot Tone was tested for two or three different roles; Bruce Cabot and Nils Asther (now enjoying renewed interest due to *The Bitter Tea of General Yen*) also filmed tests. Ronald Colman was offered the role—again, respectfully declined. By one account, at least eleven actors were approached, including Ricardo Cortez, Nelson Eddy, Ralph Bellamy, Fredric March, and Clark Gable.

The studio leaned toward a reunion with John Barrymore. After receiving a copy of the script, he wrote most enthusiastically to his most admired leading lady. "I read the manuscript and was delighted with the whole idea, not only for the very important reason of acting with you again, but because the part was definitely sympathetic to me and I had a distinct feeling that in the scenes between us, with your help and your artistry we could evolve something whimsical, touching and very lovely in the first part of the play, and something most significant and tragic in the latter part of it. . . . Naturally I would like to know what your reactions definitely are toward my playing the part, because that is of more importance to me than anything else," Barrymore wrote, assuring Garbo that whatever her decision was, it could "in no way affect my very great admiration for you as an artist . . ."

Garbo's response to Barrymore's poignant tribute is not documented. In May, he was both the studio's and director Mamoulian's early preference for her leading man. The actor was so anxious about the part that he kept calling the studio from his yacht, Mamoulian recalled. But Barrymore's age proved to be a drawback; soon both the director and star were looking elsewhere. Another prospect captured their attention: a young English actor named Laurence Olivier. "Everyone in Hollywood of any importance has been tested for the part, with no one so tested measuring up to the requirements," the June 2 issue of *The Hollywood Reporter* declared. On the twenty-eighth of June, after considering "just about everyone but Ben Turpin for the lead," Metro announced that Olivier had been signed. The actor was cast in such a rush, Hedda Hopper remarked, that his measurements had to be wired ahead so the MGM wardrobe department could work on his costumes while he was in transit.

With Garbo's formal approval of the *Queen Christina* cast, which now featured Ian Keith, Lewis Stone, and Reginald Owen in pivotal roles, rehearsals began on August 2, 1933. Despite Greta's preference for working on scenes cold, Mamoulian insisted on her rehearsing with the cast—even when the scene involved her alone. Garbo felt that she was at her best when she didn't plan everything in advance and could allow for momentary inspiration to add the nuances. "If that is true, I'll be the fastest director in Hollywood—we'll finish the film in four weeks," her director responded. Unlike Clarence Brown and others, Mamoulian had no intention of going for coffee while Garbo acted behind black flats. "I am on the set the whole time," he informed her. "Nothing happens that I don't supervise, direct, and witness." With the proper coaching, he felt that even Greta Garbo was capable of improving upon her performance. The director asked if she would work with him on a trial basis. She consented.

They rehearsed for an hour until Greta announced that she was "empty." Most actors "don't know when they're improving, because the minute you correct them they feel they're bad. And you correct them again, and they don't realize that they're getting richer and richer," Mamoulian said later. After eight filmed rehearsals, Garbo thought she had gone stale. The director instructed William Daniels to have the first and last take printed; both would be screened for Garbo in the morning. Greta started to leave the set and then came back. "Please don't print take one," she whispered. Definite, decisive, and direct, Mamoulian had won his point.

But when Queen Christina and Don Antonio went before the cameras to work on their first love scene, Garbo froze. Production was set to begin on the ninth of August—on the tenth, studio manager Eddie Mannix sent John Gilbert a surprising memo confirming *his* participation in *Queen Christina*.

* * *

Salka Viertel once described a chance encounter between Greta and Jack, former lovers now estranged for some time. She and Greta were driving down Sunset Boulevard when they came to the traffic signal at Doheny Drive. "Across from them was John Gilbert in a convertible going in the opposite direction," Jack Larson relates. "Garbo was transfixed looking at Gilbert—he didn't see her. The signal changed and as they drove on, Greta turned to Salka and said, 'Heavens, what did I ever see in him?' "

Things had not gone well for Jack Gilbert. Paradoxically, the extraordinary million-dollar contract that Harry Edington negotiated for him in 1928 had turned into a velvet-lined coffin. By the time the agreement went into effect in 1929, Gilbert's popularity had slipped considerably and, without attractive roles to reestablish his position, he continued to decline throughout the term of the contract. Good parts were dangled in front of him; with almost cruel consistency, he was awarded none of them. Gable won the assignment in *Red Dust*, John Barrymore was cast as the Baron in *Grand Hotel*. Sometimes Jack was called to a set only to find out he wasn't needed.

The actor's dream of a romantic studio life, where his luxurious two-story Spanish bungalow would become a gathering spot for the best and the brightest on the lot, crumbled away. "He would sit there and, instead of it being the happy place that he always thought it would be, with all of his friends coming around, he was there alone hour after hour, day after day," says his daughter, Leatrice Fountain. "He didn't see that what he had to do was to get away from MGM . . . Get away! Take the gamble, go to England, make another movie. It was a fixation that he was going to stay there and make Mayer pay him every last cent."

In retrospect, it seems clear that Gilbert was foolhardy in his determination to stay, regardless of the cost to him personally—though many friends saw his one-man struggle against the malevolent spirit of Louis B. Mayer as a triumph of will. Tragically, he was doomed from the beginning. Mayer "did everything he could to humiliate him," Colleen Moore indicated, "hoping Jack would do what we were all afraid he would do—tear up the contract and throw it in Mr. Mayer's face. Instead, Jack laughed in his face—something Mr. Mayer never could take—and the feud was on."

Irving Thalberg attempted to shift gears on Jack's career by moving him into the currently popular gangster genre. But his strongest character to date was one he wrote for himself: the devious, womanizing chauffeur in *Downstairs* (1932). Gilbert hung on until the bitter end, collecting $1.5 million in fees—and enough animosity and bitterness to destroy his spirit. By the time his contract ended in October of 1932, his acting career was virtually over.

*　　*　　*

Garbo found it impossible to relax in Laurence Olivier's arms. "I went into my role giving it everything I had. But at the touch of my hand Garbo became frigid," the actor stated. "I could feel the sudden tautness of her; her eyes as stony and expressionless as if she were a woman of marble." After a few words of encouragement from the director, the actors took a break and tried to talk themselves into some intimacy and passion. She was shy, he compensated with animated conversation; there was little rapport between them. Mamoulian despaired that their incompatibility would be all too obvious on screen.

"In Heaven's name, is there any man this woman *will* warm to?" he asked no one in particular. Olivier recalled one of the crew proposing "Jack Gilbert!" in jest. After a few days of this mismatching of personalities, producer Walter Wanger decided to call Gilbert in and ask him to rehearse with his former leading lady. Olivier's costume was still warm as Gilbert eased into it, Garbo's face softened, and before anyone else knew it Jack had completed a test for the role.

The reasons behind John Gilbert's return to Metro-Goldwyn-Mayer have been debated by Hollywood insiders and film historians for more than sixty years. According to Douglas Fairbanks, Jr., Olivier saw his test along with Gilbert's and it was "perfectly obvious" to him whose test was better. All of his impressive theatrical training had failed to make him more comfortable opposite Garbo. Prior to the debacle of the test, Olivier insisted, he had only been told how good he was. "And then endless obfuscation about my height vis-á-vis Garbo and my youth and my accent and all at once, it seems, I was back in London, realizing what had happened." Privately, studio executives blamed Garbo. "I suppose they thought that was the safe thing to do because they might—just might, some day—need me for something," Olivier said. But he never believed them.

The MGM legal and production files do not delineate the reasons for Olivier's rejection. "What they do is evince the sizable embarrassment even a major studio can suffer at the whim of a star backed by a cast-iron contract," Alexander Walker concluded. With Garbo's approval, Gilbert was offered a new contract (at a considerably diminished salary) with the studio that had been so happy to see him leave just a few months earlier.

There is a strong possibility that Greta was being purposefully difficult. She was, no doubt, aware of what had happened to Jack at Metro.[8] Reportedly, Gilbert was one of her early suggestions for Don Antonio and L.B. had

[8]Even Gilbert believed that Greta saw him as the victim of "a terrible wrong" that she hoped to set right.

ranted and raved until she backed down. With the production in progress, it was useless for anyone to argue with her further, writer Frances Marion offered, "so they raised the white flag and Gilbert's hopes at the same time." Further indication of the extraordinary nature of this turnaround was contained in an unprecedented statement from Garbo accompanying the announcement of Gilbert's casting, and in the actor's bewildered response. "Three years ago, I could have sworn that she would never look at me again, and now she has fought to get me this part, when I am down and most need encouragement. Incredible!"

Greta's acceptance—in fact, insistence—on bringing John Gilbert back into her professional life was all the more fantastic since both had surrounded themselves with new friends. Still, the old crowd loved her "for this last, wonderful gesture—to try to give Jack his career again," said Colleen Moore. Gilbert's casting was officially approved by Garbo on the fifteenth of August—but not before she dissolved her production agreement with Metro. Canyon Productions, initially seen as a means of sheltering the star's tax burden, was no longer deemed necessary. Garbo assumed the responsibilities of her July 1932 contract "both as to the benefits and burdens." Canyon Productions closed without producing a single film.

Principal photography began again on August 17, 1933. Christina's palace had been constructed, courtesy of Cedric Gibbons and his set designers, on one soundstage; a tavern and ship on another. As late as 1931, United Artists' Joseph M. Schenck had gone on record that he believed silent movies could make a comeback, and that as "the screen personality with the strongest drawing power," Greta Garbo could be the one to bring silents back. She nearly did in *Queen Christina*'s now-famous bedroom scene.

Actors often refer to "sense memories," moments from their past, as being emotional cues in their work. The memory of viewing Stiller's possessions in a Stockholm warehouse helped to establish a vivid sense of touching and remembering for Garbo. As she walked around the set, she seemed to transfer her feelings from one object to another: instead of Moje's desk, there was a dresser; a mirror in place of a Persian rug; a spinning wheel in place of a suitcase. Mamoulian had instructed her to move rhythmically (aided by a musical metronome which kept time off-camera) and she did so with an unexpected grace. Garbo was both photogenic and intuitive, he stated. She understood exactly the poetic quality the scene required and reproduced the emotion both physically and aesthetically.

Garbo "memorizing the room" projected Gilbert and the audience into the past as well. Ultimately, both actors were unable to separate themselves from their private histories. The leading man warmed to his love scenes, embracing his leading lady passionately—but Garbo turned out to be the film's most effective censor, tactfully suggesting that such intensity was not required. "Mr. Gilbert is a married man now, with a wife and baby," she reminded coworkers.[9]

One *Christina* crew member saw the film as a "dismal finish" to the Gilbert-Garbo relationship. Unlike the genial Gilbert who had been their comrade, Jack was by now nervous, depressed, and heartbreakingly unsure of himself. "I don't think Greta ever played a more thrilling scene than she staged for him—to illuminate his moodiness, she knocked herself out trying to be gay. Often we saw her watching him, when he didn't realize her eyes were upon him. . . . Gilbert never reacted to her efforts. He seemed like a man who had been floored by life, and was too tired to make the effort to get up from the canvas and continue the fight."

Word of an offscreen friendship between Garbo and Mamoulian quickly circulated through the ceaselessly curious Hollywood community. Over the Labor Day holiday, the couple was discovered at a dude ranch near the desert community of Victorville. An anonymous reservation had been made for them requesting "the utmost privacy and seclusion." Two days later, Garbo arrived with her chauffeur, maid, and Mamoulian. It was impossible for her to avoid recognition. Each time she wanted to go out for a walk, Greta would have her maid and the hotel manager run interference for her. Finally, the manager had enough. "If you insist that we should put blindfolds on our other patrons every time Miss Garbo wants to take a walk or a ride, you had better go some other place," he suggested. They arrived at the ranch on Saturday night—and left on Sunday.

Production moved slowly, almost fitfully on *Queen Christina*. Garbo struggled mightily with on-again, off-again ailments. "I have been and am still suffering the most sleepless anxious period I've had for ages," she wrote Hörke Wachtmeister. "I hope to God that the worst is over. I have just moved into a [new] house, and hope I will get a bit of peace behind my closed gates. Marvelous, 'wild' garden—it's huge. The only thing worthwhile here. . . . God help me if Hollywood finds out that I am a farmer."

Because she had been willing to take the heat before, many on the crew felt that Garbo's absences were choreographed to assist a comrade.[10] "Jack

---

[9]Divorced from Ina Claire in 1930, Gilbert had married actress Virginia Bruce two years later. Their daughter, Susan, was born on August 2, 1933.

[10]Stuntman Gil Perkins remembered Garbo's efforts on the crew's behalf when an important USC–Notre Dame football game fell on a shooting day. Several members of her regular crew had tickets to the game and when Greta heard this, she called in assistant director Charles Dorian. "Charlie, a lot of the boys are very unhappy because they can't go

Gilbert is back at work after being out of the studio for a couple of days again with a bad case of nerves or something," *The Hollywood Reporter* stated, adding that Gilbert "certainly makes it tough to determine whether he's ridiculously temperamental or whether the strain of how much this picture means to him is enough to keep the highly-strung Gilbert in a perpetual state of hysteria!" A week later, the publication reported on the trail of reporters which had followed Jack into Good Samaritan Hospital while he received a chlorine treatment for his nose and throat.

Admittedly nervous, raw and sick with excitement, Gilbert was responsible for several delays in filming. During one of these off-days, Greta and Salka showed up at S. N. Behrman's home for tea. Everyone seemed overwhelmed by the tortuous progress. Behrman, who wrote the final screenplay with Salka, blamed Garbo's leading man. "How could you have ever got mixed up with a fellow like that?" he complained. Not expecting an answer, he got one. "It was a considered reply, as if she were making an effort to explain it to herself. Very slowly, in her cello voice, she said: 'I was lonely—and I couldn't speak English.' "

There were light moments. "There's trouble afoot!" Greta solemnly proclaimed as she walked on to the set one day. Cast and crew members looked at each other in dismay. "What's the matter, Miss Garbo?" Elizabeth Young asked meekly. Nothing, said Greta, "I have just learned your delightful expression: 'There's trouble afoot!' " Young was the latest in a series of ingenues who played pivotal roles in Garbo's secondary relationships onscreen.[11] The actress had been hired to play Christina's favorite lady in waiting, Ebba Sparre—for the record, the recipient of some of the queen's most sincere declarations of love and loyalty.

Despite the authentication of Christina's attachment to Ebba by historians, a properly "moral" depiction of this relationship concerned the Production Code office. Dr. James Wingate of the Studio Relations Committee suggested that perhaps Ebba's lover, Jakob de la Gardie, should complain about the queen's unnatural fear that marriage would take Ebba away from her court. Wingate also recommended toning down Christina's

---

to the football game," she said. "So what?" he responded "Well, if I get sick and go home, can the boys go to the game?" she asked. The assistant director knew company policy all too well. "If you go home, we'll just shoot around you," he insisted. "We'll shoot something else." Garbo was disappointed. "Oh, all right," she said—and then, after a pause, "But if I could get them to the football game, I would!"

[11]This list would include Barbara Kent in *Flesh and the Devil*, Dorothy Sebastian in *A Woman of Affairs*, Cecilia Parker in *The Painted Veil*, Maureen O'Sullivan and Phoebe Foster in *Anna Karenina*, Elizabeth Allan in *Camille*, and the uncredited actress playing her friend Anna in *Ninotchka*.

renunciation of her lady-in-waiting for her seemingly false sympathy and concern. "Even with these changes we assume that you will be careful to avoid anything in the portrayal of this scene which might be construed as lesbianism," he informed MGM.

"I'm half-done with *Christina* now and half-done is what she's going to be when she's finished," Garbo wrote home. "It's impossible to try and achieve anything out of the ordinary here. This is the last time I'm going to try. . . . If only those who dream about Hollywood knew how difficult it all is. . . . The only thing I want right now is to have my head shaved and go skating on Lake Egla. To some extent this might be because I'm having problems with my hair at the moment."

Queen Christina's final, climactic scene occurs on board the ship that was to spirit Christina and her lover away from Sweden. Unbeknownst to her, Don Antonio has been mortally wounded in a duel with the evil, vindictive Count Magnus. Everything that Christina has given up her crown for is at risk. Antonio dies in her arms, and after a quiet moment Christina rises slowly. Her eyes have flooded with tears. Looking right then left, a crack in her veneer appears; Garbo's pale silver-toned makeup is juxtaposed against the rich texture of her cloak. It is her most exaggerated mask: near-white makeup, beaded eyelashes, eyeliner extended beyond the outside corners of her eyes.

"Directing Miss Garbo is like playing a fine musical instrument," Rouben Mamoulian said. "She is extremely sensitive to fine shadings." For the film's most intimate close-up, however, the director wanted audiences to supply their own interpretation of Christina's mask. For an actress whose greatest strength was an extraordinary ability to "project" thought, as if one could see the storm clouds moving across her forehead, it was a risky directive. Instructing her to act as a *tabula rasa*, devoid of emotion, could also come across as exactly that: no emotion. According to one crew member, Garbo listened to "None But the Lonely Heart" over and over during the final day of filming.[12] On movie screens, the moment—with Mamoulian's camera coming in tighter and tighter as the music built to an exalting climax—worked magically.

"In California I learned about people—how to really see what people are," Greta told a friend later in life. "The things that are striking about people are, first of all, their eyes and tone, those two things—their eyes and

[12]A popular song based on Tchaikovsky's Opus 6, No. 6. With lyrics by Johann Wolfgang von Goethe: "None but the lonely heart/Can know my sadness/Alone and parted far/From joy and gladness." The song had been a particular favorite of Greta's, and she requested it often when making the silent love stories with John Gilbert.

the sound of their voices. The way they move, too—you can judge a human being a lot by that. But mostly it's the eyes."

The production wrapped on October 25, 1933, several days overdue and at a final cost of $1.144 million—Garbo's first picture to break the million-dollar barrier. But the advance word was positive. MGM executives spread the word that *Queen Christina* was, without a doubt, "the best thing Garbo has ever done." Retakes were completed by the fifth of December, and the first preview was held the following Saturday in Santa Barbara. Theatrical trailers trumpeted the sensational speculation concerning Garbo's absence and her triumphant return in the story of a queen "whose affairs were as modern as tomorrow's tabloids." Any mention of the Gilbert-Garbo re-teaming was comparatively insignificant; a magnifying glass would be needed to find Jack's name in the advertising.

The movie's final obstacle would be Will Hays' Production Code office. Here, Mamoulian found a valuable ally in producer Walter Wanger, who consistently defended the film against objections from both Louis B. Mayer and the new Production Code administrator, Joseph Breen. Several scenes had been redlined by Breen's staff when they read the shooting script, but Wanger blithely ignored the dictates of the censors and allowed Mamoulian to shoot most of those scenes with minor changes.

Not surprisingly, the sequence at the country inn would inspire the most objections. "It seems to us that the explicit portrayal of any such liaison between these two characters is inadmissible under the Code and likely to endanger the story from a censorship standpoint," administrators warned. The erotic imagery of Garbo memorizing the room concerned them. "I think Miss Garbo should be kept away from the bed entirely," Breen wrote Louis B. Mayer. "The scene should be cut from the action at the spinning wheel, at least, and the business of lying across the bed fondling the pillow is, in my considered judgment, very offensive." The administrator refused to certify the film, hoping to enforce changes at the last minute. But Metro cut the film according to the recommendations of the New York censors (an astute studio representative worked with the committee for nearly two days before they approved reels five through seven: the sequence at the inn) and boldly released the film without a Production Code seal.

The gala premiere for *Queen Christina* was held on December 26 at the Astor Theatre in New York. "*Queen Christina* is a skillful blend of history and fiction in which the Nordic star, looking as alluring as ever, gives a performance which merits nothing but the highest praise," Mordaunt Hall declared in his *New York Times* review. While *Variety* complained about the film's lethargy, its crosstown competitor viewed it as a triple triumph for Garbo, MGM, and the film's creators. "How much of this artistic and dramatic excellence can be translated into the sensational box-office records that have been set up by earlier Garbo pictures depends on the success with which a reunited Garbo and Gilbert can sell their first screen romance in years," *The Hollywood Reporter* suggested.

Evidence that the "originality, daring and surprise" with which Garbo and Gilbert were brought together defied conservative censors could be seen in the near-breathless reaction to the scene at the inn. On the basis of the New York reception, Metro played its final card: they appealed to a select "Hollywood jury" under the Production Code's rules. A screening was arranged and on January 11, 1934, the specially appointed three-man jury wrote MGM executive Eddie Mannix. While commending Breen for his careful consideration, they voiced their unanimous approval of the film and overruled the Production Code administrator. *Christina* had passed her second test.

The public-versus-critical response to Garbo's performance represented an important juncture in her career. *Queen Christina* indisputably established her as the screen's premiere actress—she had already proven her preeminence as a motion picture star—and underlined her appeal to both men and women in the audience. "Her appearance in *Queen Christina*, along with the man she was earlier rumored to have been in love with, John Gilbert, creates a connection between image and life that is a powerful one," George F. Custen wrote in his study of how Hollywood has dealt with historical figures.

Subconsciously, the motion picture also pinpointed the moment when both sexes began to reevaluate what they saw in Garbo. Her powerful performance convinced many admirers that *Queen Christina* was her final statement on men, marriage, and her desire to live "a bachelor's life." Garbo's heterosexual male audience seemed especially perplexed, although largely unable to articulate their confusion. Did the bisexual subtext of the film provide an explanation of why she was so unattainable? If so, did this represent a "threat" to their own fragile sexual identities? After *Christina*, Greta Garbo films were consistently labeled "women's pictures," but prior to 1933 her pictures had been popular with both sexes; in fact, her early silent films were *believed* to have appealed almost exclusively to men.

Sex always sold more movie tickets than glamour or mystery. In her decision to restrain this side of her persona, Garbo would maintain her aura but not her domestic box-office. *Queen Christina* was the first of her films to show superior strength abroad. A gross of $767,000 in the United States represented less than 30 percent of the total box-office receipts; the foreign take was an incredible $1.843 million. Metro declared a final profit of $632,000.

Success also had its price. Three months earlier, a Long Beach laborer who claimed a "spiritual friendship" with Garbo had been arrested outside her residence at 1201 San Vicente Boulevard. Despite her pleasure with her spacious, seemingly secure home, Greta would soon look toward a new move. "On top of all the other absurdities," she now complained to Hörke, "they're marrying me for the 759th time. Can you think of anything lower than the people who are in charge of this 'beast' I am part of. . . . Out of nowhere comes long pieces about how I've gotten married, how I've disappeared, shot myself, gone to the moon, etc. And I never defend myself. However, I'm still not engaged, still unmarried, houseless, homeless and love walking on pineapples."

She was not, however, alone. Close attention was paid to the developing relationship between Greta and Rouben Mamoulian. Her inner circle insisted they were simply "great friends." His friends felt there was something more to it than that; he was definitely smitten. "Garbo is spending her days these days playing on the tennis courts and just playing—with Mamoulian," Hollywood's Rambling Reporter suggested. Two weeks later, the *Reporter* noted the increase of Garbo sightings, mostly with Mamoulian. And on January 6: "Greta Garbo and Mamoulian back in town from the Yosemite—or didn't you know they'd been there?"

The Yosemite trip indicated how badly things had deteriorated between Greta and Mercedes de Acosta. In her autobiography, Mercedes described in detail a winter trip to the popular national park. Although undated, the most likely time for this trip would have been winter 1933–1934. According to Maria Riva, Mercedes had expected to go on such a trip with Greta, had purchased clothes for Greta and herself from the Army-Navy store, packed the car . . . and waited. "Finally, de Acosta went to Garbo's house and there she found out that Garbo had gone away with Mamoulian instead of her," Riva's mother, Marlene Dietrich, told her.

Mercedes did not take Greta's friendship with Mamoulian lightly. "She drove Garbo nuts," Mary Anita Loos says. Loos recalls a story the director once shared about his romance with Garbo—diligently monitored by Mercedes de Acosta. "He told me about coming out of Greta's house and Mercedes was pacing up and down the sidewalk out front, waiting for him to leave." Garbo got in the car and ducked down in her seat. "Get me out of here. Get me out of here," she pleaded with Mamoulian. "Mercedes is there!" But the director was in no mood for charades. "You sit up, dammit, and we'll drive out. I will not let you crouch in my car because of this." So Greta sat up and they drove out, in full view of her distressed friend.

With Mamoulian at leisure, Garbo took him up on his offer of companionship. In January, they were stopped by the highway patrol at the California-Arizona border when their chauffeur mistakenly drove through a checkpoint. (In an effort to ebb the flow of migrant families into the Golden State, state law enforcement had placed a series of inspection stations near the border.) After accepting the blame for the error, Garbo and Mamoulian—alias Mary Jones and Robert Bonji—continued on to the Grand Canyon. News of their adventure sent journalists on the Garbo-Mamoulian trail.[13] Miss Jones and Mr. Bonji checked out of their three-room suite at the El Tovar Hotel on the edge of the Canyon; in Holbrook, Arizona, Robert Bonji became Robert Brown of Santa Fe, New Mexico; in Kingman, they were Miss and Mr. Brown of New York City. "To me, they were just a good-looking couple on a motor trip," said a hotel proprietor.

Rumors of an elopement were irrepressible. On January 18, the couple was reported to be back in Los Angeles; on the twenty-fourth they were discovered in the desert. Each time, local marriage licenses were checked to determine if they had declared their intention to marry. "All this fuss and stir was for nothing. We were not married and we have no plans whatever for marriage," Mamoulian told the *Los Angeles Times*—though even the *Times* felt compelled to note that the director had refused to confirm or deny whether or not he had ever discussed marriage with Garbo. Suddenly, Mamoulian was on his way to New York—and, despite frantic speculation, this time he was alone. "My son has not made up his mind yet," Mamoulian's mother said in response to endless speculation. But Greta had.

Knowing that the motion picture had consistently opted for drama over historical truth, Garbo worried about the reaction to *Drottning Kristina* in Sweden. Colonel Einhornung, the film's historical consultant, had complained vigorously about wigs, costumes, swords, candles, and fruit. Above all, he objected to the heterosexual love affair that had little basis in fact. "It is a gross insult to Swedish history and Royalty and Swedish womankind to picture the Queen as a 'light woman' who goes to bed with a complete stranger after having known him for a few hours," he chastised *Christina*'s producers.

Previously, the Hays Office had expressed concern that Swedes would be offended by such a "modern" interpretation of their queen. Garbo was

---

[13]One enterprising news service actually rented an airplane to help photographers get a picture of the couple—Garbo and Mamoulian waved, but never stopped.

otherwise concerned. "I am so ashamed of *Christina,*" she wrote mournfully home. "I often wake up and think with horror about the film coming to Sweden. It's really bad in every respect, but the worst thing is they'll think I don't know any better—just imagine Christina abdicating for the sake of a little Spaniard. I managed to believe for ages that it would look as though she did it because she was weary of it all and from a boundless desire to be free. But I am not strong enough to get anything done so I end up being a poor prophet . . ."

Yet the picture was an enormous success in Garbo's homeland. "It was a strange experience for the Swedish public to see her characterize a portrait of one of our best-known queens and to be able to observe that every feature of this portrait was a perversion of historical fact," Carlo Keil-Möller stated, ". . . and in spite of all this to bow before the might of the personal radiance that emanated from Garbo herself. [The Swedish public] simply rechristened the film 'Garbo' in their minds . . . Her acting was of such innate power and force that it could even gloss over the worst imbecilities of the film."

In 1933, the Academy of Motion Picture Arts and Sciences revised its voting schedule, extending the 1932–1933 season so that each succeeding period of eligibility reflected the calendar year. *Queen Christina* was caught in between the two ceremonies—too late for 1932–1933, too early for 1934. This situation was complicated by a mass withdrawal of actors from the voting academy due to a labor dispute. Neither *Queen Christina* nor Garbo's memorable performance would receive Academy recognition.

John Gilbert had already been forgotten. He had been required to sign a standard seven-year contract with MGM in order to guarantee his participation in *Queen Christina.* At the film's completion, he called L. B. Mayer to thank him for the second chance. Mayer, thinking the actor was about to make a pitch for more money, started screaming abuse without ever hearing Gilbert. The dynamics of their relationship never improved. Reports that Jack was being cast in several upcoming "A" productions—from *The Prisoner of Zenda* to a remake of *The Count of Monte Cristo*—came to naught.[14] Again and again, Gilbert's hopes were dashed. Although the studio exercised its first option in November of 1933, it appeared to be no more than an effort to secure his services should he prove to be a hit in *Christina.*

Contrary to his previous lack of publicly displayed anger over such treatment, this time Gilbert filed suit against MGM, asking the courts to

[14]Gilbert's name was allegedly used as a negotiating pawn to get Ernst Lubitsch to direct *The Merry Widow* at MGM. Once Lubitsch agreed, Jack was out and Maurice Chevalier was in.

interpret his contract and compel the studio to meet its surprisingly vague terms of employment. The suit, filed in December before *Queen Christina's* first preview, was subsequently dropped and refiled in January. After months of legal wrangling, Gilbert took out a full-page ad on the back cover of *The Hollywood Reporter:*

METRO-GOLDWYN-MAYER
Will neither
offer me work
nor
release me from
my contract.

JACK GILBERT

The suit—and John Gilbert's dreams of a triumphant comeback—were routinely dismissed. Gilbert made one more feature film, *The Captain Hates the Sea* at Columbia Pictures in 1934, then quietly faded from the scene. Hollywood seemed to breathe a collective sigh of relief. As long as he was working, Jack had been a painful reminder of a turbulent transition; once off the screen, he slipped into oblivion without further protest.

CHAPTER SIXTEEN

Ars Gratia Artis (Art for MGM's Sake)

The business of making movies is by nature, and arguably design, rife with conflict. In 1934, W. R. Wilkerson, publisher of *The Hollywood Reporter*, proclaimed motion pictures the fourth-largest industry in the world. Increasingly, the medium's power and influence made it vulnerable to attack from church groups seeking to curb the salacious sexual content and, to a lesser degree, gratuitous violence in films. The movement gained momentum throughout 1933 and in 1934 gave birth to the Catholic Legion of Decency, an organization that quickly established itself as a force for change.

Hollywood resisted any idea of a national censor. "Why should the picture business permit itself to be pushed into any corner that professional reformers and politicians may choose?" Wilkerson argued in a February 1934 editorial. But national Better Film Societies needed only to point to the phenomena of Mae West, the provocative *Red-Headed Woman* (Jean Harlow, MGM, 1932), or the shameless tale of a golddigger named *Baby Face* (Barbara Stanwyck, Warner Bros., 1933) to show that industry self-censorship had been careless, ineffective, and, at times, blatantly disingenuous. Working in conjunction with Roosevelt's National Recovery Administration, studio executives agreed to cooperate under the guidelines put forth by a restrengthened Production Code.

As *Queen Christina* played in movie theaters throughout 1934, the shift in Garbo's box office became abundantly clear. Her appeal to sophisticated, urban moviegoers was as strong as ever, but in smaller, more conservative towns—particularly those sprinkled throughout the South and Midwest—her popularity was in decline. Hollywood initially missed the big picture and viewed this disparity strictly in terms of the film itself. "It is a great disappointment that the Garbo picture is not going over in several sections of the country," stated one industry analyst. "The failure of audiences to grab that attraction in the big numbers we feel it deserved, sort of twists things up a bit. . . . Must we go back to that old wheeze, 'Audiences will not go for costume pictures?' "

If Greta Garbo's demographics had, in fact, permanently shifted, Metro executives believed that all they needed to do to reinforce her standing was to bring her back in a sensational new story. W. Somerset Maugham's *The Painted Veil* had been purchased in 1932 as a possible Crawford picture.

In May of 1933, even before *Queen Christina* went before the camera, the story had been reassigned to Garbo—an effort perhaps to remind moviegoers of her sultry past in such favorites as *Wild Orchids, A Woman of Affairs, Susan Lenox,* and *Mata Hari.*

In a surprise move, Garbo announced via Harry Edington that she would be ready to begin the second film of her contract as early as four weeks following *Christina*'s completion. This time, Metro wasn't ready. Neither Thalberg nor Selznick, Garbo's first choices for producer, were available; instead former sports writer Hunt Stromberg, whose most recent credits included *The Thin Man,* was brought in to supervise. John Meehan was assigned to the screenplay; his silent partners would include Dorothy Farnum, Vicki Baum, and Salka Viertel. In April of 1934, Richard Boleslawski signed on as director.

While the start date for *Painted Veil* continued to be pushed back, Greta recovered from a four-day hospital stay, and took advantage of the additional time off to go to a favored retreat: the Village Inn at Lake Arrowhead. Meanwhile, new concerns arose on the "Eastern front." Congressman Dickstein renewed his fire-breathing rhetoric regarding his proposed "Alien Actors Bill"—that the Congressman was still arguing his case in the media was an indication that the concept had gained momentum in the public arena. Louis B. Mayer was among the industry leaders who vowed to fight any such legislation in the courts. The studio mogul who claimed to have been born on the fourth of July didn't accept that opposition to Dickstein's bill was "unpatriotic" or "actuated by selfish motives."

June of 1934 came and went without Garbo stepping before the camera. She did manage a move to a new house on North Carmelina Drive in Brentwood; soon, the ever-watchful *Hollywood Reporter* would discover Mercedes de Acosta renting "a shack next to the Garbo menage." If Greta's idiosyncratic routine outside the studio involved a nomadic lifestyle in which she frequently moved to protect her privacy, inside the Lion's gates she stubbornly resisted any change. The area on the Culver City lot that had been most affected by the 1933 earthquake involved the wardrobe building and dressing rooms; executives decided to rebuild. Adrian designed a new suite for Garbo in soft gray highlighted by crimson trimming—but the star refused to move. She liked her old dressing room and enjoyed the fact that she now had the building all to herself. Greta remained in the old suite for another year before finally moving across the way.

Not everyone was enamored of her solitary routine. Salka's Mabery Road salon was a comfortable cocoon for her, but its very comfort often exacerbated Greta's problem by keeping her within a world of fellow Europeans. Instead of encouraging her to intermingle with her American coworkers, it magnified her seemingly pathological behavior. When actress Myrna Loy, a recent addition to the MGM roster, was given a dressing room suite next to Garbo's, her cheerful early-morning routine so intrigued her Swedish neighbor, that Greta often put her ear to the wall in an effort to determine what Loy and her friends were doing. The personable star of *Manhattan Melodrama* and *The Thin Man* made "several friendly gestures," via Greta's maid, but Garbo never responded (even when they ran into each other in the hallway). "I never knew what to do with her after that," Loy wrote in her autobiography. "I became intimidated, afraid to approach her, because she always put me off. She never encouraged anybody."

Loy's downstairs' neighbor, Jeanette MacDonald, had met Greta on numerous occasions at the home of Ernst Lubitsch, but she experienced a similar chill when both actresses were working at Metro. "It seemed a little childish . . . a little silly, I thought," MacDonald said, "but it was indicative of her peculiar anti-social attitude." At parties, she observed, Garbo preferred to stay in her corner with Salka Viertel and spoke almost exclusively in German.

The Painted Veil's director Richard Boleslawski had yet to meet "the glamorous one." Even as he sat in Adrian's office discussing the film one day, he discovered that the designer had excused himself to talk to Garbo in an adjacent room. She had expected to meet with Adrian herself, but— strangely, mystifyingly—when she heard that her future director was in the office, she decided not to come in. Upon hearing this, Boleslawski left a note with the designer: "Dear Miss Garbo, I am more scared of you than you are of me—so why did you run away?" When they finally met, Garbo continued to keep a respectful distance. She was pleasant, but there was "some inexplicable tension somewhere; we both seemed to be groping among rather meaningless terms," he admitted. "I soon realized that she was merely deliberating; dissecting every idea I put forward as though seeking some inner meaning . . ." The veil between them began to lift.

Another fell in its place. Joseph Breen's office was beginning to question the viability of the project. In a memo dated April 2, 1934, Breen expressed doubts about the story complying with the current Production Code, noting that it contained "some pretty strong sex situations." The Catholic Church's call for a boycott of movies on moral grounds added weight to Breen's concerns.

While screenwriters "polished" the W. S. Maugham story, Hunt Stromberg turned his attention to the cast. With Garbo as Katrin, the producer signed Herbert Marshall to play Walter Fane, the bacteriologist Katrin marries for reasons other than love; Jean Hersholt as her father, Professor Koerber; and Warner Oland and newcomer Keye Luke, the future team of Charlie Chan and number-one son, to head the "Chinese" contingent. But Stromberg had been unable to find an actor of equal weight to impersonate Katrin's equally married lover, Jack Townsend.[1] Principal photography commenced on July 2 without this important role cast.

Assembling the film's technical crew was much easier. With the exception of the director, assistant director, script girl, and sound engineer, they were the same faces Greta Garbo had worked alongside since *The Torrent*: cinematographer William Daniels; second cameraman Al Lane; assistant cameraman William Riley; set designer Alexander Toluboff; head electrician Floyd Porter; unit photographer Milton Brown, plus many of the same grips, propertymen, and electricians. Floyd Porter was Garbo's "good luck charm," assigned to follow her in each scene with a small key-light directed at her eyes. As soon as she finished an important scene, she ritually tapped him on the shoulder before leaving the set.

But the star continued to be plagued by very real security concerns. "The latest scarer-awayer on the Garbo front is a feller who stands outside her set with a gun," a trade paper reported when production began. Hollywood had become increasingly paranoid since the Lindbergh kidnapping and a series of extortion attempts involving well-known figures like Marlene Dietrich and Louis B. Mayer. Garbo's uneasiness was apparent in a letter she wrote to Countess Wachtmeister on July 28. "We've got to find me a place, Hörke. . . . I've never had a home. I think that if I had one, I'd be calmer." Perhaps, she suggested, the natural thing to do would be "to disappear from films and get people to forget totally that I ever existed"—except that she still wasn't "rich enough" to pull off such a plan permanently. "I ought to make another film," she reasoned, "I wouldn't be a good match otherwise."

A favorite game in Hollywood involved matching obscure film titles to prominent stars. It was an inside "joke," combining underground gossip and intriguing innuendo with movieland's top names. *The Hollywood Reporter* devoted at least two columns to the "game." Some of the connections were naturals and as such were rather benign: Irving Thalberg in *The Little Giant*; Jean Harlow in *Hips, Hips, Hooray!*; fan dancer Sally Rand in *We're Not Dressing*. Others bordered on the incendiary: Marlene Dietrich, *Male and Female*; Cary Grant, *One Way Passage*; Janet Gaynor, *I'm No Angel*; Ramon Novarro, *No More Ladies*; Myrna Loy, *Underneath the Red Robe*; George Brent, *The Warrior's Husband*; and Jeanette MacDonald, *Eskimo*. Garbo was matched with an insignificant Ramon Novarro feature entitled *The Son-Daughter*.

---

[1]Brian Aherne and Preston Foster were among the casualties of this search.

Although such gossip was restricted to the closely knit Hollywood community, it was further justification for Metro's publicity department to promote Garbo's genial relationships with her *Painted Veil* leading men. Herbert Marshall had only good things to say about his Swedish costar's generosity, professionalism, and concern for others. But even more satisfying from a publicity angle would be her comradeship with George Brent. Brent, who was borrowed from Warner Bros. for the project, did not report to MGM until three weeks into principal photography. Tall (6' 1"), dark (prematurely gray, he now dyed his hair black), and attractive (while undeniably masculine), he was also now single (having separated from his wife, actress Ruth Chatterton, several months earlier).

Brent was born George Nolan in County Galway, Ireland. In 1921, the teenager fled his homeland to escape British retribution for his involvement in Sinn Féin. He changed his name and began an acting career on Broadway, moving to Hollywood in the early 1930s to create his own niche as a "suave, if less than charismatic, leading man." Contrary to his cinematic reputation, George Brent was known as quite a ladies' man. According to his friends, Brent was the kind of man women found easy to be with. Bette Davis, his frequent costar at Warner Bros., described him as "a charming, caring, affectionate man with a wonderful sense of humor"— who often stained her pillows with his hair dye.

Scared, nervous, and tired prior to meeting his leading lady, Brent captured Greta's attention with his quiet loner stance. A proud man with something to hide during his early years due to his clandestine activities in Ireland, Brent respected privacy and knew the value of true friendship. On weekends, Greta played tennis and badminton at his Toluca Lake home, sunned in his secluded backyard, and even engaged in a couple of rounds of boxing. Despite the usual assurances in the press that the "George Brent–Garbo rumors don't mean a thing," the couple did enjoy a brief relationship. A blind item in *The Hollywood Reporter* published months later illustrated why Garbo's acceptance of Brent's friendly overtures were reassuring to MGM: "Everyone around one of the big studios is delighted over the fact that one of their femme stars is so smitten with a certain leading man—and vice versa . . . They all claim that it adds to her femininity and gives her a warmth in her work, which some claim has been sadly lacking in the past!"

The rest of *Painted Veil*'s production was characterized by disillusion, disinterest, and a series of illnesses, the worst of which required the crew to shoot around Garbo as much as possible to preserve her voice. While she privately referred to her current film as "rubbish," Greta had few complaints about her director. Richard Boleslawski, in turn, had nothing but praise for his star. "I found Greta consistently sympathetic and temperamentally even," he said. Working with her reminded him "of the days of the Moscow Art Theatre, where there was no fooling around, where every-thing was exact, and where we had to know and do our business without temperamental outburst."

After a three-day absence in mid-August, George Brent welcomed Greta back to work with an aerial salute, flying over her soundstage in his biplane. Production officially wrapped on the fifth of September, but pho-tography wasn't completed until the following week when the Chinese fes-tival was shot. "I have repressed the memories of *The Painted Veil*," Salka Viertel wrote; "I only recall that the producer, wanting to stress the Chi-nese background, insisted on scenes with a statue of Confucius under a tree. For some strange reason he always called him 'Vesuvius.' "

Midway through production, Metro began making overtures about Greta's next contract. *The Hollywood Reporter* suggested that producer Walter Wanger, now realigned with Paramount Pictures, was poised to steal the star away from MGM. The other shoe dropped when *Variety* reported that Garbo's asking price was an incredible $300,000 per picture. Though few doubted Garbo's worth, her public image was no longer enhanced by announcements of such unimaginable fees. In fact, American audiences were beginning to show a decided lack of interest in many for-eign imports. Weary of the Depression and anxious to reassert positive messages in motion pictures, by 1935 Hollywood was dominated by stars of a homegrown hue. Newly powerful at the box office were Shirley Temple and Bing Crosby, alongside the musical teams of Fred Astaire and Ginger Rogers, and Jeanette MacDonald and Nelson Eddy. Still popular were Will Rogers, Clark Gable, Joan Crawford, Norma Shearer, Wallace Beery, Mae West, and Gary Cooper; even Claudette Colbert, though French-born, was perceived as the archetypal young American sophisticate.

Garbo seemed oblivious to the significance of this change. If anything, she was relieved to be out of the center spotlight and appeared concerned only with the quality of her pictures. To ensure a continuing high standard, Harry Edington sought to align her with either David O. Selznick's or Irv-ing Thalberg's production units at MGM. Privately, however, Thalberg had begun to think of Garbo as a "superbly talented" actress—but "tiresome" in her complaints. With the boy wonder's attention waning and his power now effectively diluted, it was an appropriate time for Greta to be looking elsewhere for a producer.

David O. Selznick had MGM readers report to him with story ideas for Garbo. An August 1934 memo from story editor Kate Corbaley suggested

Garden of Allah, Sister Carrie, The Paradine Case,[2] and *Camille*—not to mention *Jezebel* and *Mary of Scotland*. A few months later, another Corbaley memo proposed filming *Hamlet* with Garbo as Ophelia and Leslie Howard as the Danish prince. There was some talk of Greta playing Isadora Duncan. By the end of September, Garbo and Selznick were leaning toward a remake of *Anna Karenina*.

"It may be hard for other people to believe, but my only diversions are my tomato field and a few scorched piles of sand," Greta wrote Hörke Wachtmeister as she basked in the sunlight of her "so-called garden." The tomato field, located on a plot of land below the Brentwood house, was a refuge for Greta "when the cottage feels too cramped. Sounds like a poem, doesn't it?" she joked. She wrestled with the fact that she'd only made two films in the time she had been back. "I don't suppose you, Mrs. Hörke, have any idea that you have to pay half of what you earn in taxes. I say that so that you will understand why I have to make a new film." Longing to return home to Sweden, Greta looked into various possibilities, but encountered many of the same old problems trying to find a secluded country home to rent there. "I wish Tistad was my cousin," she confessed.

During these inactive periods, news regarding Garbo's activities became so scarce that newspaper columnists and fan magazines grasped for the tiniest morsels. The *Los Angeles Times* published a story about the new windshield wipers, tires, and engine Greta had installed in her aging 1927 Lincoln. *The New York Times* announced that she was hospitalized for several days with an undisclosed illness (but was recovering nicely). At the end of October, Greta and George Brent were observed at a favored retreat in La Quinta, *The Hollywood Reporter* stated. What went unreported was her reconciliation with Mercedes de Acosta.

Irving Thalberg had rehired Mercedes to work on an adaptation of *Camille* for Garbo—but the writer had other ideas. One of them was the story of George Sand, the nineteenth-century French novelist. A brilliant, provocative writer, Sand (in real life a member of the French aristocracy) would be remembered for her bohemian lifestyle, fondness for cigars and masculine attire, and a series of scandalous affairs—most notably, with poet Alfred de Musset and composer Frédéric Chopin.

Even more to the point, Mercedes hoped to revive *Jehanne D'Arc* at MGM. "I believe that Greta was worth much more than all the glamour

---

[2]"I think the only way we will ever get this story on the screen is to use it for Garbo," Corbaley wrote Selznick. Garbo's Swedish background was believed to have been an inspiration for some of the story.

and sex films she had been forced to play in. I had always wanted to see her play a peasant role in which she could brush her hair straight back off her face and wear simple clothes . . ." Nature is Greta's element, de Acosta told Thalberg; she should be allowed to play roles that were closer to the soil. Thinking of the simplicity, purity, and drama of their stories, Mercedes suggested that the lives of several Catholic saints might suit her.

On August 4, Mercedes delivered her notes on *The Life of Jehanne D'Arc*, including her analysis of other dramatic works, to the story department. "I personally do not like the Shaw play, except for some passages, but think the preface tremendously interesting," she wrote. She received approval to go forward with the story. By her own account, Mercedes spent nine months working on the screenplay. "Greta complained during these months that I was 'not there.' In a certain way I wasn't and yet in another way . . . I was never for a second separated from her . . ."

When she completed her first draft, however, Mercedes didn't share it with Greta; she went directly to Thalberg. It was not a wise move. Thalberg "praised [the script] extravagantly and said it was the best 'one-man job' he had ever seen," de Acosta claimed. "After reading it he actually came out of his office and with his arm around me walked with me to my car." Later in the day, she received a call from the executive. Garbo did not want to do the story. "Have you discussed this with her?" Thalberg asked. Mercedes still had not. "Greta is being influenced by someone," he concluded. "She would not make this decision on her own. But don't be discouraged. . . . She is not the only pebble on the beach."

To Mercedes she was. Why then had she neglected to consult Garbo first before showing the story around at MGM? If she was gambling that Thalberg's approval would carry more weight with Garbo, she missed an opportunity to hear what she really thought. "The following day I saw Greta. She did not mention the subject and for some unaccountable reason I could not bring myself to mention it to her. . . . For some time after this when I was with Greta a ghost seemed to stand between us—the ghost of Jehanne d'Arc. But I never again mentioned a word to her or to anyone else about it."

Except to her new circle of spiritual advisors. In her letters to them, she explained in detail her fanatic devotion to Garbo and her deep unhappiness at not having that devotion returned. "If she has not yet come to you nor desired to do your picture now, *she will* in the near future," M. S. Irani assured her.[3] Irani urged her to send a message through a mutual friend. Mercedes

---

[3] Irani was better known among seekers of truth as Sri Meher Baba, a Hindu holy man who took the vow of silence.

tried another tack, writing director George Cukor in the hopes that he might intercede with David O. Selznick regarding the project. Cukor, a new arrival at MGM, was now set to direct Garbo's next film, *Anna Karenina*.

On October 23, 1934, Greta Garbo signed a one-picture deal with Metro-Goldwyn-Mayer guaranteeing her a salary of $275,000, plus a substantial bonus if her services were required beyond the twelve-week production schedule. As Cole Porter would soon declare in *Anything Goes*, Garbo's salary was again the top. Hollywood believed that she would take the money and run home for Christmas, but Greta's commitment for one more motion picture precluded this. Surprisingly, she was considering an even bigger commitment. "Larry Beilenson, Garbo's attorney, was in to see me today about some matters in connection with the picture," Selznick informed Louis B. Mayer. "During the course of conversation, he stated he thought it was time to open negotiations for pictures with her beyond this one and that they were waiting for us to take the first steps."

The first week in November brought a disastrous preview of *The Painted Veil* in Glendale. While MGM publicity touted the Garbo who "electrifies . . . fascinates . . . allures . . . intrigues . . . and enchants," the preview audience found the whole enterprise less than "captivating." "The chief fault seemed to be with the story structure, although the picture has gone back to the retake stages several times for corrections and additions," *The New York Times* reported. Equally distressing, Garbo's clothes were considered "so—well—distinctive" that at one point the audience "burst into gales of laughter upon her entrance."

Though Joseph Breen okayed the cleaned-up film immediately following the preview, MGM elected to hold it back for six days of retakes. W. S. Van Dyke was brought in to supervise the new shoot. It was Greta's sole opportunity to work with "One-take Woody," and his quick-paced, efficient mode of working amused even the normally meticulous actress.

Ultimately, an early reader's report that *The Painted Veil* had "some good character portrayals but lacks dramatic strength" would prove prophetic. "Miss Garbo's new film is a conventional, hard-working passion-film which manages to be both expert in its manufacture and insincere in its emotions," *The New York Times'* Andre Sennwald opined when the film opened at the end of November. *Variety* termed *Painted Veil* "a bad picture" from any standpoint. "It's clumsy, dull and long winded. In spite of that, of course, it will do some business on its cast pull. But it won't be what Garbo should get."

As preview audiences had noted, the movie made its most extreme statement in terms of Garbo's wardrobe and décolletage. Fashion accomplished visually what the writing had only alluded to, isolating an exotic star from the "feminine norm" throughout the story. But, this time, Adrian's styles were deemed too bizarre. Despite the careful image manipulation—with all advertising and publicity, even the film's credits, distilling everything down to the singular participation of *Garbo*—studio executives had not been prepared for the negative reaction. Again, the international audience demonstrated its strength, pulling in more than two-thirds of the film's box-office take. Without the increasingly important foreign market, neither *Queen Christina* nor *The Painted Veil* would have gone into profit.

The domestic disenchantment with Garbo represented a real problem for MGM. After consecutive disappointments, her next motion picture had to recapture some of that disenfranchised American audience or the studio risked damaging their own considerable investment. *Anna Karenina* placed her in yet another adulterous tale—a silent picture cycle she had nearly broken until *The Painted Veil*. In a memo to Louis B. Mayer, Joseph Breen strongly recommended that Metro adhere to the changes they had once made in the silent film scenario, *Love*. "In a story such as this, where transgressions result in suffering, in tragedy, and in death . . . acceptability under the Code depends pretty generally upon the flavor created by the atmosphere, and the handling of details," he stated.

Atmosphere and details were part of David O. Selznick's significant contribution to the development of *Anna Karenina*. The producer assigned Salka Viertel to collaborate on the screenplay with Clemence Dane, an English playwright, painter, and sculptor. Salka liked her immediately. "She wore long, trailing, chiffon dresses, had never been married, and told me that she had never had a love affair. 'So we shall rely on *your* experience, my dear Salka,' she announced when we began to work on the script. 'I have very little understanding for Anna Karenina. What *does* she want?' "

An October 23, 1934, meeting involving Selznick, Dane, Viertel, and two Production Code representatives proved to be pivotal. PCA administrators indicated there might be a problem with the sequence involving the illegitimate child Anna has by Vronsky and called everyone's attention to the difficulty Goldwyn Pictures was having clearing *We Live Again* (based on another Tolstoy story) past censors. "We did not leave the impression that it was an impossible story, but advised them to give it rather careful consideration before going too far with it," Dr. Wingate reported.

Selznick was especially concerned that the elimination of the scene in which Vronsky and Karenin meet at Anna's bedside negated an important plot point. "This decision was so heart-rending," he alleged, "that we were sorely tempted to abandon the whole project." The producer appealed directly to Breen for support, assuring him that "we will give no offense" in the production. Two months later, after Viertel and Dane delivered script revisions, Breen gave a tentative approval to the production.

In the meantime, George Cukor lost interest. The director, who was able to maneuver through Hollywood "with the skill, political savvy, and discretion of a courtier in the court of the Borgias," had recently completed *David Copperfield* under Selznick's supervision. He met Garbo at Salka's house. "I hear you are at work on the immortal, ever boring Anna," Cukor's friend (and *Copperfield*'s scenarist) Hugh Walpole ribbed him. "How are you getting on with the Garbo? . . . Is she rude to you? Boley and the other people who have directed her tell me that the only thing is to be rude to her.[4] But you are so charming to everyone and probably Garbo now bullies you like a trouper."

Cukor couldn't get a handle on the material and opted instead to do *Sylvia Scarlett* at RKO; his collaboration with Garbo was put on hold. In a Christmas letter to Walpole, the director confessed that he "just couldn't face all the suffering, agony and rat-killing" of *Karenina*'s story. While the project had afforded him the opportunity to meet with "the Great Garbo," he found her to be a bit depressing, "very nice, sweet, completely without humor, arty and rather pretentious," he confided to Walpole. "I think Lesbians—real Lesbians—are a little heavy in the hand, don't you? They are so god-damned noble, simple and splendid. I'm so glad you're not one any longer." Cukor left the production in January of 1935; his friendship with Greta Garbo wouldn't be realized for another year.

In all likelihood, Greta was not at her best when she first met Cukor. Winter still weighed heavily on her. Another Christmas spent in Hollywood instead of Sweden. Another Festival of Lights with only Salka to ask her to play the joyous bearer of light (and gifts), St. Lucia. Another diet for another film that was only partially relieved by Dr. Bieler's revolutionary new ideas.[5] Another movie she was motivated to make for money rather than art.

In anticipation of roadblocks ahead, David O. Selznick kept the door open for a last-minute replacement of *Anna Karenina*. His first priority was to do a comedy; second, a contemporary drama. To this end, he brought in story editor Val Lewton to assist him in the search. Edmund Goulding submitted a three-page treatment of a story he called *The Flame Within* about a female psychiatrist falling in love with one of her patients. The producer had a better idea. *Dark Victory* told the story of spoiled heiress who bravely comes to terms with her terminal illness due to the love of her doctor; the drama was set to open on Broadway with Tallulah Bankhead.

Selznick was investigating buying the film rights for Garbo when he discovered that she had slipped out of town. He immediately enlisted Salka's help, arming her with a letter for Garbo and a synopsis of *Dark Victory*. On Monday, January 7, 1935, Salka drove into the desert to enact the role of Garbo's Scheherazade.

Miss Greta Garbo
La Quinta, California

Dear Miss Garbo:

I was extremely sorry to hear this morning that you had left for Palm Springs, because we must arrive at an immediate decision, which, I think, will have a telling effect on your entire career.

As I told you the other day, we have lost our enthusiasm for a production of *Anna Karenina* as your next picture. I, personally, feel that audiences are waiting to see you in a smart, modern picture and that to do a heavy Russian drama on the heels of so many ponderous, similar films, in which they have seen you and other stars recently, would prove to be a mistake. I still think *Karenina* can be a magnificent film and I would be willing to make it with you later, but to do it now, following upon the disappointment of *Christina* and *The Painted Veil*, is something I dislike contemplating very greatly.

. . . Therefore, since you feel that you must leave the end of May and cannot give us additional time, we have been faced with the task of finding a subject that we could make a picture comparable with your former sensations and one that would, at the same time, meet my very strong feeling that you should do a modern subject at this particular moment in your career. The odds against our finding such a subject were very remote . . . Now, however, I find that if I act very quickly, I can purchase *Dark Victory*, the owners of which have resisted offers from several companies for many months. The play is at the top of the list at several studios and if we do not purchase it, the likelihood is that it will be purchased at once for Katharine Hepburn. The owner of the play, Jock Whitney, is leaving for New York tomorrow and it would be a pity if we were delayed in receiving your decision concerning it . . . Therefore, I have asked Salka to see you and to bring you this letter and to tell you the story—which I consider the best modern woman's vehicle, potentially, I've read since *A*

Bill of Divorcement and which I think has the makings of a strikingly fine film.

... As far as the character goes, it is our thought to make you the daughter of an American heiress who has married a foreign noble-man ... The play is so moving and the tragedy so inevitable that I am sure audiences will accept it; and the great value of the excitement of the girl's life, both before the blow falls and afterwards, will, I think, have enormous added values through being underscored and back-grounded with the pathos of her situation.

I intend engaging an outstanding dramatist on the rewriting of the play and believe I can secure Philip Barry, who is undoubtedly at the top of the list of American dramatists today ... [an] expert construc-tionist; a man who has devoted his life to writing of people of this par-ticular milieu and who is unquestionably America's finest dialogue writer.

Further, Fredric March will only do *Anna Karenina* if he is forced to by his employers, Twentieth Century Pictures. He has told me repeat-edly that he is fed up on doing costume pictures; that he thinks it a mistake to do another ... Mr. March is most anxious to do a modern picture and I consider his judgment about himself very sound. We are doubly fortunate in finding in *Dark Victory* that the male lead is also strikingly well suited to Mr. March.

For all these reasons, I request and most earnestly urge you to per-mit us to switch from *Anna Karenina* to *Dark Victory* and you will have a most enthusiastic producer and director, respectively ... [We] will be very disappointed, indeed, if you do not agree with our con-clusions.

Most cordially and sincerely yours,
David O. Selznick

For years, the legend has been that, despite Selznick's impassioned plea, Garbo turned down the chance to do *Dark Victory*. The villain in this sce-nario was understood to be either Salka, because she was unwilling to relinquish her role as scenarist—or the intractable Garbo, because she was unwilling to alter her schedule and insisted that her next picture be *Anna Karenina*. Selznick's own correspondence contradicts this.

On the ninth of January, Louella Parsons received word of a substitution for *Anna Karenina*. Selznick responded quickly, urging the columnist not to publish the item—yet. On the fifteenth, the producer composed a telegram to J. Robert Rubin at Metro's home office in New York: "LOOK [*sic*] LIKE *DARK VICTORY* STOP GARBO REFUSES EXTENSION AND WHILE SHE WOULD BE

WILLING DO EITHER *DARK VICTORY* OR ISADORA STORY FEEL IT IS SAFER UNDERTAKE *DARK VICTORY* WITH LIMITED TIME STOP ALSO FEEL THAT DESPITE HARD WORK AND PRESSURE THAT WILL BE INVOLVED PREFER DOING THIS STORY AT THIS TIME RATHER THAN *KARENINA* . . . " The producer went on to question Jock Whitney's asking price. "ADVISE HOW YOU WANT NEGOTIATIONS HANDLED STOP FRANKLY SEEMS GREAT PITY PAY SO MUCH MONEY FOR IT IN VIEW OF FACT WE WILL UNDOUBTEDLY REWRITE AT LEAST SEVEN-EIGHTHS OF IT. . . . [BARRY] IS WILLING TO DO *DARK VICTORY* AND ONLY QUESTION IS WHETHER HE FEELS HE CAN UNDERTAKE IT IN REQUIRED MAXIMUM OF TIME."

In spite of his enthusiasm for the project, Selznick was already questioning the prohibitive cost of acquiring it and whether or not the production could be put together without Philip Barry's participation. But, according to Selznick's records, this cable was never sent and there is no further indication what happened to the project at MGM. It would be four years before former Metro associate producer David Lewis coproduced the film adaptation with Hal Wallis at Warner Bros.; Bette Davis and George Brent starred.[6]

Neither Garbo nor Selznick gave up exploring other last-minute replacements. As late as February 22, she was expressing interest in a comedy about a Russian duchess and her consort who hire themselves out as domestics in Paris after the revolution. "For your information, Miss Garbo is very enthusiastic about *Tovarich*," Selznick reported to Samuel Marx. "I, personally, am still a little afraid of it, but would like to withhold a final expression of my opinion until I get a chance to read the script."

A note of stability was introduced when Greta approved Clarence Brown as her director; it would be their first collaboration since *Inspiration*. Work on *Anna Karenina* continued irrespective of the search for other stories. Val Lewton was given the task of assessing the different scripts and recommending which writers should continue. In a memo dated February 25, 1935, Lewton wrote that he favored the Clemence Dane/Salka Viertel adaptation because they had a better ear for dialogue. With no substitution in place, principal photography on *Anna* was scheduled to begin the second week of March.

Two new treatments of the Tolstoy novel by United Artists and RKO suddenly gave the Production Code office cause to reevaluate MGM's script. "As we see it, [Vronsky] is a seducer, who lives openly with an adulterous woman who he finally deserts to return to his former social and military life," Breen informed L. B. Mayer. "We feel that the present treatment

---

[6]Interestingly, it is believed that Brent was with Garbo in La Quinta when Salka arrived. His interest in the story—if any—has been lost to posterity.

leaves the picture open to the accusation that it sets up a double standard of morals." The administrator was also concerned about the scenes of Anna and Vronsky living together—and any scene displaying intimate physical contact. "The cumulative effective of such scenes, if retained in the picture, is likely to prove highly dangerous from the point of view both of public reaction and political censorship."

Selznick was taken aback. "I was surprised and distressed by your letter of March 5th to Mr. Mayer, concerning *Anna Karenina*," he wrote Breen two days later. "I was surprised because the criticisms of the script are so much more extensive than they have been formerly. . . . I am distressed because your comments come too late to do anything but give us the alternative of making a completely vitiated and emasculated adaptation of Tolstoi's [*sic*] famous classic. Miss Garbo leaves for Europe, willy-nilly, the middle of May, which gives us just enough time to make the picture allowing leeway for scoring and preview. . . . Had you, in December, the same objections as now to the script, I would most certainly have abandoned the whole project . . ."

Quitting the production at this late date, Selznick argued, would mean a loss of thousands of dollars—and for no reason, since *Anna Karenina* was an acknowledged classic and its scenario well-known to readers. To make any substantive changes would be to lose the story. "*Anna Karenina*," the producer affirmed, "is solely and simply a love story and an adulterous love story. To try and make it anything else is utterly impossible. . . . As to the physical contact between Anna and Vronsky, I don't know how love scenes can be played, particularly in a story of this kind, without physical contact." Without a strong producer to fight the tough battles, the project might have been sunk. Selznick might agree to compromise, but he would never lose sight of the story.

On the eleventh of March, Garbo cosigned a letter requesting a two-week postponement on *Anna*. Casting continued despite the setback. Reginald Owen, who had played Garbo's princely cousin in *Queen Christina*, revealed that the actress fought for his casting in *Anna*—even after another actor (Alan Mowbray) had been hired to play Stiva. "The moment she knew that I wasn't playing her brother, she went to Selznick and she said, 'You promised me that Reginald Owen would play my brother. Why isn't he doing it?' And some excuse was made to her. 'Well,' she said, 'that's not good enough for me. You promised me and that's what I want.' " The substitution was announced less than a week later.

Costume fittings were perhaps her least favorite chore. "I had to fight with her every time she came and had a fitting," Adrian would complain to a friend. This was especially true following the public reaction to his work in *The Painted Veil*. But the designer surpassed himself on *Anna Karenina*—and even Garbo, no fan of elaborate period costumes, was pleased with the result.

Selznick was given the green light when Joseph Breen notified MGM that the most recent *Anna Karenina* revisions were open to "no reasonable objection from the point of view of the Production Code." Anna made her fateful entrance at the railway station on March 25, 1935. With extra security guarding the soundstage, Anna's doom was sounded very early on. According to Clarence Brown, Breen and his staff watched the production "like hawks," each new scene having to be passed by their office in advance.

David O. Selznick made his presence felt both on and off the set, guiding the cast and crew through the patchwork script (comprised of different scenes from different screenplays in order to balance the story with the requirements of the new Code). "We had to eliminate everything that could even remotely be classified as a passionate love scene; and we had to make it perfectly clear that not merely did Anna suffer but that Vronsky suffered."

Battling a "watered down" adaptation of Tolstoy further complicated the impersonal relationships on the set of *Anna*. Having been informed of Fredric March's reputation as a womanizer, Greta reportedly chewed on garlic prior to their love scenes as a deterrent against unwanted advances.[7] The actor admitted that he never really got to know Garbo well. He misunderstood her preference for addressing him as "Mister March." Even when making small talk about March's trip to Tahiti, the distance was there. "She was always so afraid, shy, everything bothered her," he said. After observing her in a particularly poignant scene, the actor offered his congratulations. "She looked at me. 'You were looking, Mr. March?' 'Yes, Miss Garbo.' 'Really, you were looking at me, Mr. March?' 'But yes, Miss Garbo.' 'Please you should not look at me, Mr. March. It is embarrassing.' She had many complexes, poor dear."

Basil Rathbone failed to establish the genial relationship with Garbo that he had expected given their prior acquaintance. Rathbone had been introduced to Greta at Jack Gilbert's house years earlier and was put off when she failed to acknowledge this. "Our reintroduction was formal and as though we had never met before," he said. "Never during the entire time of the making of the picture . . . did she give the slightest indication that we had ever met before." Rathbone recalled that she remained alone in her dressing room and never talked with anyone "except Miss Constance Col-

---

[7]Though, according to information from David Lewis, this may have been an unintentional slight. Garbo's "garlic kick" was part of a new diet she was on.

lier, with whom it would seem she shared the secret of some disturbance that might be troubling her."

Rumors about Garbo's temperament, her uncooperative attitude, and her haughtiness had been so persistent that even Clarence Brown appeared uncertain what to expect. He was prepared for the worst, but got the best. "She has a zest for hard work and long hours that is truly amazing," he stated, contradicting the impression that the star never worked late. Yes, her maid, Alma, still appeared on the set at 5:00 with a half-full glass of water, but as often as not Garbo stayed to finish the scene they were working on.

But Greta had changed, Brown stated. "Formerly, it disturbed her to have me sit in front of the camera, now it doesn't distract her. And her diction is greatly improved. She thinks in English now, and she's becoming more Americanized." A relationship characterized by a silent understanding between director and star was made even easier. "She knew just what she had to do and how she expected to do it. . . . She listened respectfully, sometimes arguing quietly but never angrily. She always wanted to give the best she had. Everything was for the picture's sake."

Worthy of its million-dollar status, *Anna Karenina* was the next Garbo production to commandeer two separate soundstages; the train station scenes—Moscow, St. Petersburg, and the small water stop somewhere in the Russian tundra—were shot on the back lot. A bit of humor was introduced when an April windstorm blew *Anna*'s snow on to the summer garden set for Joan Crawford's *No More Ladies*. Two weeks later, Greta was dancing the Mazurka with eighty ballroom extras. Dance director Chester Hale had rehearsed a double to replace Garbo in the long shots. She was not needed. Hale found Greta to be "the most pliable and adept pupil I had ever trained."

Interestingly, while in movie theaters it was women who now responded most ardently to Garbo's allure, the reverse was often true on her movie sets. Reginald Owen saw her as "a very, very simple woman." In the morning, he watched her arrive at her portable dressing room attired in nondescript clothing, comfortable shoes, and thick stockings. After a comparatively short time with makeup and wardrobe, she would reappear on the set dressed in full costume and was "absolutely the most magnificent-looking woman you've ever seen . . . absolutely beautiful," he extolled, "and I really liked her as much as any actress I'd ever played with . . . She had a charm about her and an almost Rabelaisian wit. . . . I enjoyed her enormously."

Maureen O'Sullivan, who played Princess Kitty Shtcherbatsky in the film, found Garbo's economic approach selfish but effective. "I did not have very much contact with Garbo during the making of *Anna Karenina*. I liked her;

she was nice, very beautiful," the young contract player, then beginning to make a name for herself, stated. "As an actress, she gave you very little. . . . In fact, when working with her, one felt she was doing nothing really, that she wasn't even very good, until you saw the results on screen and you realized the love affair she had with the camera . . ."

Working on *Anna Karenina*, Garbo seemed to particularly enjoy the company of two veteran character actresses: Constance Collier, an imposing theatrical grande dame (and private tutor for actresses such as Katharine Hepburn and Norma Shearer), and May Robson—both of whom were as protective toward the film's star as she was toward them. The youngest member of the principal cast was eleven-year-old Freddie Bartholomew, who played Anna's son, Sergei. *Anna Karenina* would be Bartholomew's first showcase since *David Copperfield,* and Selznick hoped to capitalize on his favorable reception by American audiences. Greta marveled at the young actor's ability to ad lib and even joke before launching into a serious scene, yet she struggled valiantly with the precocious youngster. According to S. N. Behrman, the only time he ever saw her cry was when she worked on a difficult scene with Bartholomew. But her effort to establish some kind of maternal bond showed in her work.

Even before filming had been completed, word leaked out that Selznick would be leaving MGM. Despite Louis B. Mayer's machinations, Metro was still Thalberg's studio; Selznick felt he had been "a mere interloper." *Anna Karenina* was one of his final projects at the studio. On May 14, after Anna jumped in front of an oncoming train, production officially wrapped on the twenty-fifth film of Greta Garbo's career. Two weeks later, a rough cut of the motion picture was assembled for a preview in Riverside.

Contrary to popular opinion, Garbo often attended the previews of her films—though she viewed each picture in agony due to her dissatisfaction with her own performance; the magic of her persona was lost on its creator. Sam Behrman was deeply affected by "the delicacy and distinction of Garbo's performance" when he attended the screening with Greta, Salka, and the Selznicks, but remembered Greta sitting quietly in the back seat of the car on the ride home. "She spoke once, in reply to a query from Selznick as to how she felt. 'Oh,' she said, 'if once, if only once, I could see a preview and come home feeling satisfied!' " Once back at the Selznick's, she felt the urge to work off her nervous energy and challenged a friend to a nighttime game of tennis. Lacking the proper shoes, she played—and won—in her socks.

In the midst of production on *Anna*, Greta laid plans for an extended visit home. On the sixth of April, she applied for a United States reentry permit, and on the eleventh was issued a new Swedish passport by the Royal Consul in San Francisco. At the end of May, she signed a new contract at Metro guaranteeing her $500,000 for two films. If principal photography on either production lasted more than twelve weeks, she was to be paid a bonus of $10,000 per week—moreover, she was to be kept on salary until her services were no longer required; there would be no unsalaried breaks between principal photography and retakes.

"Betcha Garbo furnishes the local photographers with a real picnic within the next ten days!" *The Hollywood Reporter* predicted as the time for her to leave neared. They weren't disappointed. On the evening of May 31, she boarded the eastbound *Santa Fe Chief,* accompanied by Carter Gibson (variously described as an MGM employee, her manager, or George Brent's stand-in). Outside Chicago on the morning of June 2, Gibson convinced the *Chief's* conductor to let them off before the Dearborn Street Terminal in order to avoid the inevitable media crush. Gibson hailed a cab to take them to Union Station. On the *Manhattan Limited,* they repeated their performance, exiting at Newark and continuing into New York by car. At Washington Square, Garbo called a truce and posed for a few photos while sitting in her taxi.

Gibson escorted Greta to her refuge in the captain's cabin on the SS *Kungsholm.* With a piercing blast from its whistle, the ship left New York harbor promptly at noon on June 4. Among its fourteen hundred and fifty passengers, the *Kungsholm's* most illustrious guest—alias "Karin Lund"— was absent from view for most of the voyage. She exercised in the morning, ate a Spartan lunch in her cabin, and occasionally appeared later in the day for a swim, a walk, or a deck game. Passengers observed that she seemed to be fond of the ship's second officer, Ewert Eriksson, who had been born a few houses away from her childhood home. On the voyage's final evening, she appeared at the captain's table dressed in a striking black velvet ensemble and ate a hearty Swedish meal.

The *Kungsholm* arrived in Göteborg Harbor on the thirteenth of June after an uneventful crossing. Garbo met the press in the ship's library, skillfully avoiding giving anything more than a glib answer to most questions. Her work was available for public consumption, she suggested, but she was not. "You know, my sister has never deliberately granted an interview in any other place than Sweden for years," Sven remarked when he arrived on the scene. "So—when she has loved so much to see you—I know you will not mind, if I take her away now." Greta smiled. Outside, the crowd was treated to a breathtaking moment when she stepped on to the gangplank ahead of her brother. Suddenly, a breeze blew her hair away from her face and onlookers were magically reminded of the final close-up in *Queen*

Christina. "Well, here I am now—wild and uncombed," the star said with a quiver in her voice.[8]

In anticipation of Greta's departure, Mercedes de Acosta sought the guidance of Sri Meher Baba, writing the guru at length regarding her relationship with and concern for the star. Baba responded with a full mediumistic profile of Garbo, explaining that "the extremes of agonies" of her present state would "grow so terrible at times that they may lead to excesses of mad behaviours or even insanity or suicide." The profile could hardly have appeased his already disturbed correspondent.

After Greta left, Mercedes applied for a new passport and consulted with Baba regarding the wisdom of following her star to Europe. Her spiritual guide continued to reassure Mercedes that her difficulties were transitory, "in spite of disappointments all around . . . and even if Greta has gone away without seeing you. For that will all adjust itself automatically in time . . ." He advised patience; she couldn't wait. On the twenty-second of June, Mercedes set sail for Europe on the SS *Normandie.* Even *The Hollywood Reporter* made note of her sudden exit: "Mercedes d'Acosta [*sic*] is in Europe divorcing her husband, Abram Poole—or didn't you know she had one?"

Lacking the invitation to join Garbo in Sweden, de Acosta remained in a holding pattern on the Continent, waiting for a word—any word—from Greta. She spent part of June in England; then used France as a base to travel between Austria, Switzerland, Germany, and Italy throughout the rest of the summer. It was in an old monastery near Assisi, above the Umbrian valley, that Mercedes met Sisters (Sorella) Maria and Amata, two new spiritual guides. Yet her obsession did not diminish in Greta's absence, it grew. She determined that she *must* see the object of her adoration in her native environment—she must see Greta in Sweden.

There was no doubt that Garbo was finding more changes at home. In 1933, the first Tunnelbana station had opened in Södermalm; by 1935, there was an entire subway network linking together the vastly divergent neighborhoods of Stockholm. The city she knew as a child was growing up. After a few days of shopping and meeting with friends, Greta retreated to a

---

[8]The consistency of such dramatic comings and goings would soon be lampooned in Paramount Picture's *The Princess Comes Across* (1936), the story of a Brooklyn showgirl (Carole Lombard) who masquerades as a Swedish royal in order to further her career—but encounters a whodunit twist during the Atlantic crossing. Arriving on board, she is confronted by reporters about an upcoming film debut. "Who is your favorite movie star?" Lombard is asked. "Mickey Moose," she replies in a faux Swedish accent.

summer house the Wachtmeisters had found for her. Ånga gård was located near the coastal community of Nyköping and owned by Elisabeth Palme, the mother of Sweden's future prime minister, Olof Palme. The estate's access to Lake Ången, which emptied into the Baltic, allowed Greta to swim in a coastal freshwater lake—and, despite strong currents and brisk temperatures, she did. Nothing could deter her from enjoying her first Swedish summer in years.

In July, she received word that Salka had arrived in London. "Can not believe that you really are in Europe," she hailed in a letter from Tistad, typewritten on Loew's/Metro-Goldwyn stationery. "I hope it is not going to hurt you to come back to former things; I know how dreadfully sad it can be at times." Surprisingly, scarcely six weeks into her vacation, it was Greta who brought up the subject of work. "As I do not know if you keep on working while in Europe, I might just as well tell you now that I was thinking about the Napoleon story [*Marie Walewska*] and was going to ask you something that you probably would not like. I have a great longing for trousers, and if I ask you in time maybe you can put in a little sequence with the trousers, maybe her dressed as a soldier, going to Napoleon's tent, at night, or some thing. I am sorry, not to contribute anything more, but it is merely to remind you about the trousers—/ trousers, girls in trousers, pressed trousers, girls, trousers, trousers. / By G. Stein. I hope, poor Salka, that you do not have the black and white running after you and making your life miserable or the oposit [*sic*].[9] It is amusing and still I wish I had some of her persistency and your energy and I would be more than Napoleon to day."

On August 30, *Anna Karenina* opened across the United States. "A classic love story told magnificently pictorially," the *Hollywood Reporter* critique read. "Garbo's pedestal is not only restored, but is made to look unbreakable in this picture." *The New York Times* saw that Garbo, "always superbly the apex of the drama, suggests the inevitability of her doom from the beginning, streaking her from happiness with undertones of anguish, later trying futilely to mend the broken pieces, and at last standing regally alone as she approaches the end."

There was a potential flaw, however, in what was once seen as the glamour of being melancholy. "The problem confronting operators of theatres out of the deluxe class," the *Motion Picture Herald* articulated, was that there was "little, if any, hoorah in the picture. Patrons who look for 'whoop

[9]In a letter from M. S. Irani dated July 16, 1935, the guru refers to Mercedes meeting Salka on a boat and the talks they had about Greta.

it up' won't find any here. Instead they will see the sincere presentation of a moving and heart-touching story." Given the constraints of censorship, the story lacked the dynamics of true sexual tension and thus missed out on repeat business. The first week's gross at the Capitol Theatre in New York was not up to the old Garbo record-breaking standard. In Chicago, the film received a pink "adults only" tag.

Elsewhere around the country, *Anna Karenina* opened respectably, but wasn't always a strong holdover. Although the movie attracted the largest American audience since another Anna, *Anna Christie*, the general perception of *Anna Karenina* was that it was further proof of the widening separation between Greta Garbo's domestic and foreign box-office.[10] In the United States, the year's top film was the Astaire and Rogers musical *Top Hat*. But Garbo's preeminence abroad—where, Clarence Brown noted, she was first, second, third, fourth, and fifth—secured her the #2 position under Clark Gable on Metro's list of luminaries.

Anna Karenina was honored by the Venice Film Festival as "a work of undoubted artistic value" and the year's Best Foreign Film. At the year's end, the recently organized New York Film Critics cited Garbo for giving the finest female performance of 1935. But there would be no corresponding recognition from the Academy of Motion Picture Arts and Sciences.

Greta returned to Stockholm as fall alighted on the Swedish countryside. Julius Carlsson, manager and maître d' at the Strand Hôtel, had often let a promising young theater student named Greta Gustafsson eat without charge in the hotel restaurant. When she returned to Stockholm as a successful actress, Greta Garbo often stayed at the Strand. "She was content with a simple room, never anything elaborate for her," Brita Ahlström commented. "I served her several times in Bakfickan [the popular hotel restaurant] . . . I remember one time when she sat alone and ordered a smörgåsbord. 'This we don't get in America,' she said." Although she ate what she wanted, back in her apartment she still weighed herself with the bathroom scale she had brought from California.

Encouraged by her spiritual advisors, Mercedes sent Greta a birthday gift. There was no response. Finally, with her funds dwindling, she reluctantly returned to New York. Garbo had frustrations of her own. On the eighteenth of September, she passed what was surely a major milestone for any actress in 1935: her thirtieth birthday. Greta was more concerned with Salka Viertel's silence. "This is my last attempt to try and get an answer

---

[10] The film grossed $865,000 in the United States and $1,439,000 abroad, representing a net profit of $320,000 for Metro-Goldwyn-Mayer.

from you. Are you ill—or has something else happened?" she wrote. "Perhaps my letters havent reached you, or you are perhaps angry at something. If you will let me know, I shall try and correct it." Though clearly puzzled by Salka's failure to respond, Greta had no qualms about keeping another friend dangling. "Yesterday I got a wire from 'Swartzweise' who wants to come here and wait and accompany me back. She is indeed amazing. I shall not answer," she vowed.

She had a change of heart. With Mercedes safely on American soil, Greta finally wrote her. It was a short letter but—as she might have feared—its very existence was apparently a signal to set an anxious friend into motion. "In her letter she said jokingly, *I will meet you for dinner a week from Tuesday at 8:00 in the dining room of the Grand Hotel.* I got this letter Tuesday morning," Mercedes later claimed. "I figured that if I could get the necessary ship passage, I could then fly from Bremen to Malmo, Sweden, that same day, take the train from there to Stockholm and arrive late that night." She booked passage on the SS *Europa* and cabled Garbo that she would meet her as per her "invitation."

Logistically, there are a few problems with this story. A cable from Sri Meher Baba dated October 11 supporting her decision to "GO SWEDEN" indicates that Mercedes received her communication from Garbo that week. A crossing by boat would take approximately nine days—putting her well past the "week from Tuesday" scenario. Obviously, time was less a factor than accepting a less than half-hearted invitation. According to her 1935 passport, de Acosta arrived in the historic coastal city of Malmö on the twenty-third of October. She journeyed to Stockholm, where she checked into the Royal Suite at the Grand Hôtel.

No sooner had Mercedes fallen asleep than the phone rang. "It is not possible that you are here," Greta declared, promising to come right over. They walked to Djurgården for breakfast. Later, they wandered around the city zoo at Skansen; Greta's playful mood was effectively deflated when she got too close to one cage and was scratched on the cheek by a monkey. Her spirits picked up when she and Mercedes dined that evening in the elegant waterfront restaurant of the Grand Hôtel.

After an unpleasant confrontation with fans outside a theater, Greta resolved to take her companion to the Wachtmeister's. Here Mercedes won the much-desired glimpse of Garbo in her element. "In Hollywood Greta did not seem to me to belong so much to Sweden as she did when I actually saw her there on her native soil," she observed. "When we tramped past typically Swedish, red-painted, farm houses and saw the cones of fir trees piled high in their courtyards, I realized that in some mysterious way she had an affinity with them which I, as a stranger, did not and never could have. I suddenly felt her in the countryside as though she were part of it."

Mercedes prayed for snow—and an early Christmas—as her final gift from Sweden. On her last day at Tistad, she was surprised with a roaring fire in the library, a large, brightly lit Christmas tree in the dining room, a traditional holiday meal, and an abundance of the Yuletide spirit—capped by a light snowfall. On this occasion, Mercedes saw another side of Garbo, the one who enjoyed living well and being spoiled by those who could afford to do so.

Before she left Stockholm, Greta took her to see the house where she was born. "She made no comment as we stood looking at it—nor did I." They bid farewell in the city. Mercedes began her return trip to the States via Malmö and Bremen on the second of November. She had not been able to convince Garbo to come back with her—nor was she invited to stay longer. But she couldn't suppress her sense of triumph and pored her heart out in letters to Sorella Maria and Sri Meher Baba. Letters of congratulation and support awaited her when she arrived in Los Angeles. "Yes, I accompanied you on your journey, and I am happy to have received your two letters," wrote Sorella Maria. "I was very interested in the story of your trip to Sweden, and I'm sure that your friendship—so sincere and so strong—will have touched Greta."

Garbo revealed contrary feelings in a letter to a true friend and confidant. "So you have had troubles. . . . I have no lovers but I have troubles just the same. It is maybe from all the wrong done to my poor body," she wrote Salka on November 22. "Mercedes has been here as you know by now. I took her to Tistad as I didnt know what else to do. She is more quiet than before but otherwise the same. She didnt see much of [Stockholm], I was afraid to let her stay there. I was a wreck after she went and I told her she must not write me. We had a sad farewell . . ."

As winter descended on Stockholm, Greta looked forward to traditional winter sports activities: skiing, ice skating—and a holiday favorite, sleigh riding. Her treasured Scandinavian winters were all about cuddling in front of fires, bundling up for long walks down romantically lit streets, snow crunching crisply beneath one's feet, and the nostalgic smell of pine. Years later, Greta would tell the story of a return visit to Sweden during which she had gone for a walk on a frozen lake with Hörke Wachtmeister. Suddenly, the ice cracked and they found themselves neck deep in the water. "Her terrified companion implored her to keep calm while Greta first hiked out her walking stick, pulled herself, and then her companion, to the icy surface," Cecil Beaton recorded. With clothes dripping wet and freezing in the sub-zero weather, Greta and Hörke considered going to a nearby house and calling a doctor. But they could imagine the headlines, so they risked pneumonia and ran all of the way home.

When Nils Wachtmeister arrived home, he found Garbo in bed with his wife drinking hot whiskey—and, according to Greta, he laughed.

CHAPTER SEVENTEEN

Tragic Muse

In Nyköping, a doctor by the name of Bengt Gullberg received a phone call from one of his patients. She wanted him to prescribe some cough medicine. But Hörke Wachtmeister sounded as healthy as ever. Was anything wrong? No, she said, "but I have a friend with me who has a cough and she doesn't want a prescription in her name." The medicine was for Greta Garbo.

Greta was, in fact, sick throughout most of the winter of 1935–1936. "I am in bed most of the time and so stupified [sic] I cannot even get myself to write. I have been in bed for years, I feel," she wrote Salka. Illness did not prevent her from thinking about the work ahead. Salka had been working on the story of Marie Walewska, the nineteenth-century Polish heroine, since May. Four months later, when she submitted a treatment to MGM, the front office surprised Garbo and Viertel by putting the project on hold. "I do not understand why they are not going to do *Waleska* first," Greta asked incredulously. "And are you not doing anything on *Camille?*"

If Thalberg was having a problem, she suggested, perhaps Mayer should let Selznick produce instead. "I shall write another sheat [sic] of paper and if you wish you can show it to Thalberg. Please ask Thalberg to think very carefully about *Camille*. Its so like *Anna* that I am afraid. . . . Its devastating to do the same story again." She argued that the *Waleska* story was "a newer thing—because Napoleon isnt a usual figur [sic] on the screen, like my other fifty thousend [sic] lovers. . . . I am very nervous as you see in my silly letter. But every time, the studio goes thru [sic] the same misstakes [sic] and ones heart goes fluttering again."

It did not take long for news of Garbo's poor health to reach the halls of Metro-Goldwyn-Mayer's executive building. Late in the fall of 1935, she wrote to L. L. (Laudy) Lawrence, head of Loew's/Metro office in Paris, concerning a job for her brother. Shortly thereafter, Lawrence met with the Gustafsons at their apartment on Klippgatan in Södermalm. On December 3, he reported back to Louis B. Mayer: "Sven is a nice boy, but that is all . . . his health is very bad. Incidentally, the entire family is in bad health, including Garbo. . . . [She] is rather seriously ill."

A network of Loew's/MGM associates soon confirmed Lawrence's bleak report. Finally, on the eighth of December, in response to a direct inquiry from the studio, Greta wrote a touching letter to L. B. Mayer. She addressed him as "Sir" and promptly thanked him for Metro's efforts on Sven's behalf. She had been fighting a bad cold since September, she admitted—much of the time, she had been confined to bed. But Garbo's most startling news concerned the possibility of an operation, which she confessed dreading.[1] She asked for a month's recuperation time so that she could be at her best when she returned to work.

Officially, the mysterious malady that threatened her was variously described in the press as a "nervous ailment" or "throat infection" that had caused problems previously; unofficially, friends believed, Greta was suffering from bronchial catarrh (an inflammation of the nose and throat), the beginning of the chronic bronchitis which plagued her throughout her life.

That didn't stop her from reentering Stockholm's social scene over the holidays. "On one of my on days I met Noël Coward who was very charming to me," she wrote Salka. Garbo was introduced to the multi-hyphenate entertainer at a party hosted by the Wachtmeisters. Later, the pair were seen walking around Djurgården. Although rumors of a "blossoming romance" between England's gay blade and the solitary diva from Sweden quickly circulated in the international press, a source close to the actress labeled them "pure fabrication." What was really happening, Coward's friend and biographer Cole Lesley agreed, was that Noël Coward could not be coerced into meeting a friend at an obscure location wearing dark glasses and a turned-up collar. He wanted to see and be seen. So he wheedled and coaxed and bullied Garbo until she agreed to more public meetings, including a party given by Gösta Ekman attended by Stockholm's fashionable elite, and a private New Year's Eve party thrown by Prince Wilhelm.

Regarding the possibility of a romance tryst, however, Lesley was never completely sure whether the rumors were true or whether Greta and Noël simply found it more interesting to continue the charade. "I do know that they exchanged affectionate telegrams and telephone calls for some time after, calling each other 'My little bridegroom' and 'My little bride,' and that she had said she 'wished the newspapers was right.' "

On January 9, 1936, Greta attended a performance of Schiller's *Maria Stuart* at Dramatiska Teatern. During the intermission, she was greeted by a rush of reporters blurting out the news that John Gilbert had died. Too stunned to comment, Garbo reportedly received the news with great self-control, returning to her seat briefly before exiting hurriedly out of one of the side doors. She got into her car unescorted and was driven away.

---

[1]No further information is available regarding this operation. It most likely involved a gynecological problem.

The news, while surprising due to Gilbert's age (he was thirty-six), was not totally unexpected. Gilbert had been on a steady decline since his unsuccessful attempt to revive his career with *Queen Christina*. According to Leatrice Fountain, the last time her father spoke with Garbo was on the telephone following a *Christina* preview.[2] Virginia Bruce filed for divorce in 1934; Gilbert's reaction is clearly seen in Lewis Milestone's *The Captain Hates the Sea*, in which he started out cold sober and ended struggling to remain stationary. Formerly healthy and robust, his skin often nicely tanned, Jack lost weight and his face took on a gray pallor. The suspicion that he might be drinking himself to death was confirmed, said Bruce, on the occasions when he actually coughed up blood.

For a time, Marlene Dietrich took Gilbert under wing and he seemed to bounce back; he looked thin, but happy and healthy, in a color screen test he did for Dietrich's next film at Paramount. But even the sympathy and concern of one of the world's most alluring women could not manage Jack's demons, and he soon turned back to the bottle. He cut himself off from the social circle that had been so important to him as a star.

In November of 1935 Jack again became ill, and in early December he had a mild heart attack, followed by a more serious one on the second of January. When she discovered that a series of doctors had done little more than medicate the patient and suggest private nurses, Marlene Dietrich insisted that Gilbert see one of her private physicians, but a battery of tests revealed nothing conclusive. In the predawn hours of January 9, he had a massive attack; a shot of adrenaline administered by the nurse failed to revive him. Leo J. Madsen, the attending physician, pronounced Gilbert dead at 7:50 in the morning, attributing the cause of death to an acute phase of heart disease aggravated by chronic alcoholism and a hardening of the arteries. Significantly, the latter conditions he dated back to 1929.

John Gilbert's funeral was a Hollywood affair—possibly the greatest showing of support the town had given him since the debacle of his talkie debut. A misty-eyed Dietrich arrived, dressed in black and sobbing to friends that she blamed herself for not being able to save the man once known to the world as the Great Lover. "He was always an enigma," his second wife, Leatrice Joy, reminisced. "I never solved him—I wish I had. Many people, I guess, have been likened to mercury, but Jack Gilbert was mercury: you'd touch him and he'd vanish."

[2]In Fountain's biography of her father, *Dark Star*, Leatrice related a story about a visit Garbo made to Tower Road—with a jealous Marlene Dietrich steaming at the front door while Jack and Greta talked in her car. This encounter, Fountain admits, was unconfirmed and had been erroneously added to the manuscript by a collaborator. Gilbert's daughter now believes it to be nothing more than "a romantic fabrication."

Garbo's response to Jack's death, according to the press, improbably ran the gamut from indifference to despair. More likely, it was a contributing factor to her continued sickness and depression. Responding to her request for more time to recuperate, Mayer sent a cable on the tenth of January stating that he was "terribly distressed" regarding news of her illness and assuring her "all contract negotiations would be suspended for a month." Relieved of the burden, Greta appeared to show immediate improvement. Her January 15 cabled reply was brief and upbeat: "AGREED. THANK YOU. FEELING BETTER. GREETINGS. GARBO."

"Why must it be that ones closest one, make ones inside so heavy, heavy, heavy," Greta asked Salka rhetorically in a letter. Back in California, Mercedes de Acosta was comfortably but unhappily settled in her rented Hollywood home. "I'm worried about you," Sorella Maria wrote her in February of 1936. "Not only because of your loneliness and your difficulties which pain me. But because of the state of slavery in which you live." In the clearest indicator of how things stood between Greta and Mercedes, the sister offered that Garbo's recent behavior revealed her true feelings. "Since she scorns all you've done for her out of the extreme generosity of your heart; since she acts so indifferent and obstinate in her silence; one must respect her way of being and what she wants. You in turn must become absolutely reserved. Otherwise, you would lack the dignity of your human conscience."

Indifference and obstinance did not characterize Greta's relationship with Salka Viertel. In direct contrast to her vacillating relationship with Mercedes, Greta encouraged Salka's involvement in her professional life. Equally important, she demonstrated that she cared what Salka thought of her, as evidenced in another letter written that winter: "Salka lilla," it began, "Only a few lines. God knows how I struggle 'through'. I dont write in English as you know and not in German. And life's difficult, I have no dictionary here . . . I know that you have to struggle with a little and big Napoleon.[3] Poor little Salka. Can it help you in any way that I tell you again that I am glad God mad [sic] me so intelligent that I can understand 'wie begabt sie sind' [how gifted you are]. You dont like me as mutsh [sic] as you should because you dont understand me (sounds like Mercedes). . . . What I really wanted to say was, even if you do not like me mutsh, if you think of the moment when I read you *Walewska,* and my sad face registers nothing but a little later when I have a chance I shall grab you and say 'blessed be the God that made you'. I dont suppose that is mutsh of an inspiration to

[3]Mercedes being one; the script for *Conquest* being the other.

give you, but its all I have for the moment." In closing, she made a veiled request for Salka to "gossip" to her if she heard "anything wrong" about Mercedes' activities.

There were no signs of anything wrong in mid-February when Greta was discovered tobogganing with her three-year-old niece in a local park, or in March when she paid her respects to Selma Lagerlöf. She met with the ailing writer at the Karlavägen home of a mutual friend. "I promised to pick her up in an hour's time," Einar Nerman recalled. "But I had to wait a long time before Greta returned." When she finally came out of the building, she was silent at first and quite obviously agitated. "How strangely I must have behaved—what will Selma think of me?" she said as they drove away. "Think if I could have met Selma Lagerlöf when she was young. What good friends we might have become! She must have been wonderful then. Little Selma," she sighed again. "She must have thought I was crazy."

Reports that Garbo planned to end her vacation soon were contradicted when she applied on March 12 for an extension to her reentry visa. Her request was denied; she was told she must return to the United States as planned. On the twenty-first of April, Greta was issued a 4(b) non-quota visa at the American Embassy in Stockholm. Two days later, "Miss Mary Holmquist," a reclusive passenger bearing a remarkable resemblance to a well-known Swedish movie star, embarked on the SS *Gripsholm* bound for New York. The Swedish-American liner slipped into its West Fifty-seventh Street berth on May 3.

Eschewing her normal routine, Garbo sent word that she would meet with the American press en masse. She entered the ship's smoking lounge dressed in a black twill suit and wearing very little makeup; observers thought she looked unnaturally pale. Greta's hands moved constantly—in her pockets, out of her pockets, brushing aside her curly hair, clutching her throat—as she answered questions. She stated that she was happy to be back in the States, suggesting that she had not enjoyed her stay at home because she'd been sick with "something like" the grippe. Anxious to slip away, whenever there was a momentary lull in the proceedings she would politely ask no one in particular, "Can I go now? Are you through with me?" An assistant held a match behind her head to allow photographers to adjust their camera lenses for the dimly lit room. "This is awfully strange. I don't know what you're doing," Greta said, keeping a nervous eye on the match.

Before the ten-minute press conference concluded, Fifi D'Orsay rose from her seat. The former star had accompanied a radio crew on board, hoping to record a few words for their listeners. "Hello, G.G. Do you remember Fifi?" she said breezily. "I am so happy to see you." Greta acknowledged her with a "How do you do." D'Orsay nudged forward. "It's so nice of you to talk to the press. Won't you speak over the radio?" But the rest was silence as Garbo left the room without further comment. Two unidentified companions spirited her off the ship and took her to a private apartment that had been acquired for her stay in New York.

One year later, Robert Reud wistfully wrote Garbo about their May 4 "anniversary" and reminded her of the little church on Fifth Avenue where she once sat beside him, rescuing him "from a desert of desolation." As time passed, the publicist became increasingly nostalgic about the time they had spent together on this trip. But Garbo, it seemed, was again just passing through.

Greta returned to Hollywood in a "back-to-the-earth trance," telling friends that she intended to go off and raise carrots and potatoes. "The things which have to do with the soil are the only things which are pure, fine and wonderful," she would declare enthusiastically. She wanted to establish roots. But in California, Garbo's routine of lengthy, biannual visits home—and a new house every time she returned to Los Angeles— often meant disturbing those roots. She lost most of her personal staff, even her personal maid Hazel, to more consistent employers. Once she was back on the MGM lot, she continued to be treated like a queen. She moved into her new dressing room, which had been attractively furnished with a plush antique sofa and modern French furniture, as well as several prints chosen by Garbo herself; gardenias and white heather grew in the newly planted private garden outside her suite.

With her screen appearances becoming rare, each new Garbo production took on added importance at Metro-Goldwyn-Mayer. As per their most recent contracts, Metro deferred to a production schedule dictated largely by their star's health. Each agreement delineated an intricate series of steps whereby Garbo would be put on "full, munificent salary." Furthermore, her 1935 contract stated, once she had reported for work, the motion picture must go into production within two weeks or the company would pay a financial penalty. Even before she arrived in town, the studio had made tentative assignments concerning their next project.

Greta Garbo's face was said to be the model for the *Tragic Muse* mosaic on the steps of the National Gallery in London—and there was no more tragic figure in drama than Marguerite Gautier in Alexandre Dumas fils' *La Dame aux Camellias*. First published in 1848 and adapted for the stage four years later, the theatrical world's most spectacular actresses immediately embraced the role of the French courtesan whose fatal flaw was her great capacity for love. On the Continent, Marguerite was brilliantly illuminated by Modjeska, Sarah Bernhardt, and Eleanora Duse; in America, she inspired Ethel Barrymore, Tallulah Bankhead, and Eva Le Gallienne on the stage, and Theda Bara, Nazimova, and Norma Talmadge on screen.

By December of 1935, Irving Thalberg and his staff had shifted their focus from Garbo's preferred project, *Marie Walewska*, to a remake of *La Dame aux Camellias*, more popularly—although mistakenly—known in the United States as *Camille*. "The great weakness of the story for a modern audience is, of course, the self-sacrifice theme; and the chief reason for this is not so much the difficulty of believing that Camille's self-sacrifice was really necessary, but of believing that Armand was even to a slight degree worth making any sacrifice for," James Hilton, the author of *Goodbye, Mr. Chips* and *Lost Horizon*, wrote in a critique for Thalberg. "In both the novel and the play he is such a spineless weeping willow that Camille's love for him becomes not only incredible, but a thing that seriously detracts from the sympathy any modern reader or playgoer can feel for her." Hilton and Frances Marion suggested changing Armand's profession to that of the diplomatic service. In that case, if Armand were to marry Marguerite, she would never be welcome in the world he moved in.

Thalberg was concerned about how best to contemporarize yet another theatrical warhorse for his star. "We have to live within the mores of the day," he told his writing team. "Men marry whores in our present society— women who have been promiscuous—and they very often make marvelous wives. In this town you find them all over the place." The producer conceded that audiences would find Armand "an awful little prig" if he rejected Marguerite for this reason. David Lewis, who had been assigned to the project as an associate producer, hit upon the idea of having Armand poisoned by jealousy: he might forgive Marguerite for her past but could never forget the men who had shared her favors.

Finding the right tone proved to be exceedingly difficult for the screen-writing team. "Frances Marion was having fun," Lewis recalled. "In writing *Camille*, she was dramatizing her current 'love affair' with Jimmy Hilton. She was the pale, frail Marguerite and he was the charming, delightful young Armand." Lewis was horrified by the Marion-Hilton collaboration. "It was ludicrous—flowery, overblown, and just downright badly conceived and overwritten. . . . I remember Armand's pet name for Marguerite was *ma petite choux* ('my little cabbage'). Frances thought it adorable and the name was all through the script—even in the death scene."

Thalberg soberly agreed with Lewis's evaluation—as did George Cukor, who was "even more dramatic about being appalled than either of us." Cukor had been given his choice of Garbo projects and had chosen the romantic fiction of *Camille* over *Marie Walewska*'s historical backdrop. But the director agreed that something must be done to revitalize the screenplay and suggested that poet and playwright Zöe Akins work on the adaptation.[4] Akins was officially brought into the project by May of 1936. An extravagant, wildly generous woman with exquisite taste in everything except the right man, Akins was as interesting as any of the people she wrote about. "She had a tender understanding of life," David Lewis said. Greta took an immediate liking to her.

Zöe Akins' flowing poetic verse galvanized the screenplay of *Camille*, making it possible for Cukor and company to begin production even as she continued writing. Principal photography commenced on July 29, 1936. Neither Akins nor Lewis could resist sneaking into *Verboten* territory; Garbo immediately called them over. Instead of chastising the pair, she thanked Akins for her "beautiful script," then turned to Lewis. "I expected someone a little older and a little uglier," Greta jested. "You are both welcome on my set at any time."

Conversely, Garbo respectfully declined to meet her new leading man, Robert Taylor, before filming began, indicating that she wanted to keep her romantic illusions intact. The newest incarnations of Marguerite and Armand were finally introduced on Stage 23, which had been expertly transformed into the Théâtre de Variétés. Taylor arrived before Garbo. "An hour sped by before a lithe figure in silk pajamas came on the stage," the actor noted. "She paused to scan the set-up. Eventually, she detected the presence of cameraman Bill Daniels . . . she tip-toed up behind Daniels and poked him playfully in the back." Cukor took care of the introductions, though Greta continued to shy away from any lengthy conversation. "She was polite but distant," Cukor acknowledged. "She had to sell herself on this picture of an ideal young man. She knew if she became friendly, she'd find out he was just another nice guy."

Taylor, a former medical student whose good looks netted him an MGM contract, had recently made a major breakthrough as a romantic lead opposite Irene Dunne in *Magnificent Obsession* (Universal, 1935). Prior to that assignment, his film experience had been limited to less challenging fare. Admittedly intimidated by Garbo, he found consolation in the unwavering support of his girlfriend (and soon-to-be wife), Barbara Stanwyck. "Just be natural," she told him. "Treat her as you would anyone else."

A freak occurrence nearly undid them all. When the cameras first started rolling, the company was surprised by a blinding flash, followed by a glitter-

---

[4]Among her stage-to-film credits: *A Bill of Divorcement, Morning Glory, Christopher Strong,* and *The Old Maid.*

ing shower of sparks. A central fuse box controlling the key lights on the soundstage had blown out. Taylor gallantly pulled his leading lady under the protective awning of their theater box.

George Cukor's greatest strength as a director was his keen attention to the specifics surrounding each actor's characterization: dramatic costuming, historically authentic music, decorations, and sets—anything that might help frame and enrich their work. Having seen many classic interpretations of the Dumas story, he agreed with Thalberg that the drama must move beyond the social mores of the time and address Marguerite's and Armand's "hot impatience" for each other. Cukor found Garbo "wonderfully suited for the part" as well as sensitive, charming, and cooperative, although even she was capable of deliberately spoiling a take—an old trick which she used "quite a lot" if she sensed something wasn't going well.

Garbo and Cukor always met on equal ground, a crew member noted. "It was apparent when they worked together that there was a deep admiration and friendship between them." Much has been made of Cukor's designation as "a woman's director"—a label he fought throughout most of his career—yet he would admit that he had a special empathy with most of the actresses he worked with. "I suppose it is foolish to admit you like to direct women more than men," the director stated. "But I have a fundamental reasoning back of it." A pretty woman needed "no more excuse than her beauty to have a reason for being before the public," he suggested. "Therefore, I can overlook stupidity in a woman with far more ease than a man." Despite this simplistic view, the actresses Cukor worked with most brilliantly were intelligent, creative women known less for their time in front of the mirror than for their distinctive screen personalities.[5]

Joseph L. Mankiewicz, who would soon assert himself at MGM as a producer, writer, and director, felt that there was a valid reason why women especially responded to Cukor. Actresses adored him "because they felt at ease. And women by and large did not feel at ease [in that era]." Associates believed that Cukor's sensitivity—read homosexuality—made him a nonthreatening presence on most sets; there would be no demands on his actresses aside from that of delivering a solid performance.[6] "I think women,

---

[5]Interestingly, in the same films in which Cukor directed Ina Claire, Tallulah Bankhead, Jeanette MacDonald, Constance Bennett, and Katharine Hepburn to great success, Fredric March, Maurice Chevalier, John Barrymore, Basil Rathbone, W.C. Fields, and Cary Grant—no slouches on screen—were also starred.

[6]On the other hand, it made him a threatening presence to some actors. Clark Gable's inability to relax with Cukor during the making of *Gone With The Wind* cost the director his job after months of hard work on the film.

in the earlier days, before they became important, had a pretty tense time with the very masculine directors," Mankiewicz added. "A woman could come on his set and be absolutely safe."

Privately, Cukor was also someone whom women found fun to be around—the kind of person, says Jean Howard, who rolled up the rugs and danced with the ladies at Hollywood parties while the men adjourned to smoke their cigars. He was a good friend and loyal confidant: funny (though sometimes wickedly catty), well-read (within the scope of subjects he enjoyed), and fascinated by many of the same things as his female friends. The son of Hungarian immigrants, Cukor had learned about the theater on the streets of New York. Like Garbo, he "always had been excessively secretive about himself—determined to blend in, not to be perceived as any kind of 'hyphenate'—at the same time that, perversely, he enjoyed throwing out clues," Patrick McGilligan, undoubtedly the director's most perceptive biographer, stated. Cukor saw "beneath the façade, [Garbo] was high-strung and nervous, her droll patter of conversation and jokes a smoke screen for her insecurity. She needed reassurances, and Cukor could have had REASSURANCES printed on his business cards."

By the time they met, Cukor had filled out his homely looks with a cherubic countenance. Greta described him as "extraordinarily nice . . . [but] so funny, with his huge hips and woman's breasts." The director's respect and liking for Greta Garbo really began on the set, McGilligan says. "Although she teemed with ideas, Garbo kept her own counsel and had a working method unique to herself. Her rehearsals were sketchy; her real acting was saved for the camera. . . . Cukor's principal role was to do as little as possible, to establish a relaxed and friendly (yet intensely concentrated) mood on the set. Garbo did the rest."

Cukor observed that Garbo referred to anything in danger of becoming boring or stale as "government business." She had a reason behind her "so-called shenanigans" on the set, he explained to columnist Hedda Hopper. "There are eight thousand intrusions while a picture is being made. All acting is concentration [and] she had real intensity. . . . She allowed no disturbances or distractions."

One of Cukor's first surprises from his leading lady was a request to move out of her line of sight whenever she was filming a particularly difficult scene. The director had a habit of acting out scenes as they progressed, which often provoked a comic response from his actors. Now, however, Garbo explained to him "in a very nice way" that his facial expressions were just "too depressing." He proposed that her acting, while brilliant and intuitive, might also be termed primitive because it was devoid of the tricks and the technique of many trained actors. "She lives parts in a curious way," he remarked. "Her unwillingness to tamper with the illusion she created in her mind carried over into her attitude towards other people."

Although she had secretly viewed rushes of *Anna Karenina* in Marcella Bannett's office (adjacent to Selznick's office in the Metro executive building), according to Cukor, Garbo never watched the dailies on *Camille* because "She believed in real illusion; she was never pleased with what she saw on the screen." But Irving Thalberg watched the rushes and was tremendously pleased with the results, commenting to Cukor that this was a new Garbo: vital and unguarded. By the end of the first week, he was predicting that *Camille* was going to be something special. "He told me Garbo had never been so good," associate producer David Lewis reported. "She was showing a certain vulnerability she had not [exhibited] before. . . . 'If we can catch it,' Thalberg said, 'Garbo will be the great Camille of our time. No one can touch her.' "

In an interview twenty years later, Cukor articulated that enthusiasm. "The public is interested in that beautiful face and her unconventional way of thinking. . . . Remember [Robert Jordan] in *For Whom the Bell Tolls?* The hero's erotic dream was always Garbo bending over him brushing him with her hair. It was always Garbo. She has a curious hold on the public. They think that under that ice there's nothing she wouldn't do."

Garbo knew that there was a price to be paid for a screen image tied to physical beauty. In the midst of production on *Camille*, David Lewis recalled being beckoned to her dressing room with a plaintive cry. He ran upstairs, where he found Greta sitting in front of a magnifying mirror. "These lines, these lines, I'm getting old," she stated quietly. "Greta, you've had them ever since I can remember," he assured her. "It's the way you smile." But she kept repeating, "I'm getting old." Garbo, Lewis then realized, wasn't entirely immune to an actor's conceit regarding their looks. "She constantly examined her face; that was why she had the magnifying mirror," he said. "I don't think it was vanity—she knew what her values were."

Assistant directors at Metro were especially attentive with actresses in their charge, keeping track of anything that affected their health, looks, or ability to perform, including drinking, drug usage, insomnia, and especially menstruation cycles. The legend surrounding *Camille* suggests that a real-life illness added dimension to Greta Garbo's performance as the terminally ill heroine. The fact was, assistant director Eddie Woehler learned, that Garbo had an ovarian infection that on occasion flared up painfully (some believed this to be the result of a botched abortion) and her menstruation cycles were irregular at best, heavy and absolutely incapacitating at their worst. "Her periods were irregular," David Lewis confirmed, "and she might look like hell for a week. You'd have to shoot around her or not do close-ups. She would get very thin-faced and gaunt."

In Mercedes' opinion, there was no doubt that her friend was truly ill, "but there was also a psychological factor involved. She had so much identified herself with the character of Marguerite Gautier that even off the set and out of the studio she was conscious of the illness of this tubercular woman. Sometimes when we walked in the hills or on the beach she would stop and put her hand to her heart as though her breath was coming too fast. . . . It was not a happy time and I was glad when the shooting of this film was over."

In her autobiography, Salka Viertel recollected she had never seen Greta more "happy, glowing and inspired" than during the making of *Camille*. But the memories of those who worked on the film were more in line with those of Mercedes. Actor Rex O'Malley, who played Gaston, Marguerite's frivolous but nonetheless intensely loyal friend, attested that Garbo was "a very sick woman" throughout much of the shoot. "We got on, I think, because I was very ill, too, shortly after I started working, and had to have an operation. That delayed production three weeks. When I returned, she always came over to ask how I was feeling. We had lots of fun discussing our aches, pains, and symptoms together."

"I've got no time for anything other than 'the lady' [*Camille*] and my health," Greta wrote Hörke Wachtmeister that summer. "I have never worked under conditions like these before. I sometimes start crying from tiredness. . . . I've been feeling out of sorts the whole of last month and still had to work." She described getting treatment for her troubles at the studio after hours, "but don't know if it helped or made it worse. At the moment, I'm lying in bed—as usual when the moon is walking about."

"It's a funny thing, I'm probably the only person in the world who was not an ardent Garbo fan. Her work on the screen always left me cold. I never could understand what everybody raved about," Rex O'Malley said. Acting opposite Greta Garbo inevitably placed the burden of working out the personal dynamics on the other actor. Though O'Malley found it difficult, at first, to respond to her restrained presentation, he soon learned how to modulate his own performance—and in the process discovered Garbo's true fascination. "She doesn't act; she lives her roles," he explained. "She was 'Camille' during the entire filming of the picture. . . . Beautiful beyond words of description."

A rare few might view the filmmaking process as a twisted manipulation of Garbo's personality, labeling the result "method acting by ambush," but coworkers characterized her as always being in control. She was "an uncanny craftsman with a playful sense of humor," said Robert Taylor. On location in the Hollywood Hills, Greta surprised the crew by lunching with them and kept everyone laughing with stories about her adventures with the press in Europe. Riding back in the studio car, she inquired about a newly installed device that allowed for communication between the driver and passenger. After an assistant demonstrated its use, she picked up the microphone with a look of delight. "Hello, hello! This is Greta Garbo speaking. . . . The first time Greta Garbo is on the air."

If privately she felt that her life was in turmoil, publicly nothing seemed to phase her. Others suffered the slings and arrows of outrageous misfortune. George Cukor's beloved mother died just before production commenced. Later that summer, it is believed he was arrested in Long Beach on a morals charge—although, according to Patrick McGilligan, with discreet encouragement from Metro's front office, the charges were mysteriously "erased." Lionel Barrymore's wife was gravely ill, and cinematographer Bill Daniels disappeared for three days toward the end of production. It was later discovered that he had gone on a drinking jag.[7] Greta agreed to a temporary replacement, Hal Rosson. Finally, Karl Freund, the renowned German cinematographer, took over.

Dark clouds were looming overhead. On Friday, September 11, within two or three weeks of wrapping principal photography, the star's health again sidetracked production. Studio manager Eddie Mannix "could be ruthless and violent, but he adored Garbo," Salka Viertel would write. Although unsure of what the problem was, he agreed to put the production on hold until the following Wednesday.

On Monday, the fourteenth of September, Irving Thalberg died. A late summer cold had developed into lobar pneumonia, and before anyone knew just how sick he was, the executive had expired. Grief-stricken employees walked around in shock, David Lewis said. They were "absolutely devastated . . . No matter what, he was much respected and loved by the ordinary people at the studio. I doubt if much work was done at MGM that day."

In fact, all of Hollywood mourned. Many blamed Louis B. Mayer for the coldhearted manner with which he treated the man he had once credited with being the shining light behind MGM's finest films. Industry analysts pondered whether the studio would ever be the same. Writers and directors began to drift away before they were even missed, but for artists like Garbo who had aligned themselves exclusively with Thalberg's production unit, there was no one in whom they could vest a similar trust. George Cukor and Edmund Goulding (now preparing *Maytime*) had the foresight

---

[7]According to Hedda Hopper, Daniels' father passed away during the making of *Camille*.

to insist on an "out" in their contracts if something happened to Thalberg. But Garbo's current agreement had been negotiated while David O. Selznick was still a viable force at the studio; she did not have this option.[8]

Proof that Greta was "very much affected" by Thalberg's death was evidenced on September 17 when she attended his funeral, a rare public appearance for her. It took weeks for things to settle back to normal at the studio. Naturally, the projects that suffered most were those under Thalberg's supervision: the Marx Brothers' *A Day at the Races*, the MacDonald and Eddy musical, *Maytime*, and *Camille*. It had been Thalberg's idea to develop *Camille* for Garbo; on his advice, the project took precedence over *Marie Walewska*, and he had been instrumental in the evolution of the screenplay. "[Garbo] must never create situations," he emphasized. "She must be thrust into them; the drama comes in how she rides them out."

But *Camille*'s fate was now complicated by its new production supervisor, Bernard Hyman, who took it over under protest from Thalberg assistants Albert Lewin and David Lewis. The film's problems were directly related to the subsequent power struggle. "Everyone in the studio had some idea or other. Things were tried that almost sank the film," Lewis stated. "Bernie Hyman couldn't keep his hands off. All of his ideas were based on not knowing the care that Irving had put into the development of the script. . . . [He] didn't think she had been properly set up in the beginning [and] made extensive—and expensive—retakes before the first preview." Protecting Thalberg's vision would be the challenge of *Camille*'s final days.

"If you're going to die on screen, you've got to be strong and in good health," Greta advised. During the making of *Camille*, Garbo was neither—yet she persevered. Three different versions of the final scene were filmed. At Thalberg's suggestion, the bedside scene had been rewritten and the actors were moved to a chaise lounge. In another version—filmed later—Marguerite had a long speech; in a third, the dialogue was kept to a minimum. The loss of friends and family members would provide the emotional thread to weave together the subtle nuances of a fully realized performance from Garbo. Here, more than ever, what wasn't said was as important as what was. The third version of the death scene made it to the final cut.

"If I hadn't been so out of sorts *Camille* would have been one of my most entertaining memories thanks to the director," Greta wrote Hörke Wachtmeister. The production officially wrapped on the twenty-seventh of Octo-

---

[8]However, Garbo was understood to be among the handful of stars who were set to move over to Thalberg's independent production outfit when it started up in 1939.

ber. Metro's legal department was already investigating the future: "G's contract provided for a rest period of five weeks between pictures. What would happen if we made retakes and then let her go? . . . If we call her back, does her rest period start all over again? Would it be an advantage to let her go, then make up our minds if we wanted her to do a retake? Would we be any the worse off?"

Returning from a business trip, David Lewis was informed by Cukor that *Camille* had a disastrous preview in Santa Barbara. Soon after, the associate producer saw the film for himself at a preview at the Golden Gate Theater in Whittier. "I was horrified. Hyman had screwed the picture to hell and gone. The opening went on forever and didn't set her up at all," he reported. "The picture had suddenly become a heavy-handed costume drama." According to Lewis, without support from the front office Cukor had been forced to scrap the one thing Thalberg had fought so hard for: Armand's all-consuming jealousy. "It was the same old dreary Armand Duval from the novel," he said. "Garbo was there and the audience applauded when the Baron [Henry Daniell] slapped her. They hated her. I was furious."

The next day, both Lewis and screenwriter Zöe Akins met with Eddie Mannix. They told him what Thalberg's attitude had been toward the love story and how that vision had been emasculated. Mannix announced that they would be having a special showing of the film in Palm Springs on December 12. "If you can get the retakes done in time, I'll okay it," the studio manager promised. Akins had a new scene typewritten and on his desk in twenty minutes. "She had already written it in her mind," Lewis remembered. "She came back with the scene, and it was brilliant. It was the scene in Armand's apartment with Garbo's haunting line, 'Once I had a little dog . . .' "

Final retakes on *Camille* were shot during the last week of November and the first week of December. "GRETA GARBO CATCHES FIRE IN LOVE SCENE WITH TAYLOR" the *New York Herald Tribune* blared a few days later. In the midst of filming the new scene, an ember from a nearby fire ignited the skirt of Greta's dress. This time, Robert Taylor pushed her away in time for two members of the crew to douse her with a bucket of water. With her makeup, costume, and hair effectively ruined, Garbo asked to go home. She finished the scene without interruption the next day. "*Camille* never ends," Greta complained in a letter to Hörke. "We have to shoot retake after retake and are going to do some more in a couple of days. . . . Nothing new has happened apart from Mercedes wanting me to ring. But I am going to have to think about the matter first. Poor Mercedes—she has got an extraordinary ability to make people nervous. Even people who are not quite as unkind as me."

Following an afternoon preview for *Camille* at the Four Star Theater in

Los Angeles, the film's editor, Margaret Booth, went to David Lewis's office and gave him a big hug—the preview had been a success. The motion picture received its Production Code certification without any threat of censorship.

Across the Atlantic, a real-life romantic drama was taking place in England during December of 1936: Edward VIII had abdicated the throne of England for the woman he loved.[9] In Hollywood, the closest MGM publicists could come to such a story was to fantasize that George Cukor was Greta Garbo's "new sweetie." She was among the group of friends who saw him off at the train station when he went to Sun Valley for the holidays. But she took *her* rest cure in Palm Springs alone.

On December 30, Greta received word that she had been awarded the blue ribbon of *Litteris et artibus*, Sweden's highest acknowledgment of the arts. She was the first motion picture actress to be so honored.[10] Unable to attend an official presentation and obviously overwhelmed by the very idea, she wired her appreciation to Sweden's ambassador to the United States, Wolmar Bostrom. "THANK YOU FOR YOUR TELEGRAM. MAY I ASK THE AMBASSADOR TO PASS ON MY MOST PROFOUND GRATITUDE TO HIS MAJESTY THE KING."

Preparation for *Marie Walewska* recommenced in December. According to Salka, Irving Thalberg had thought its political background "too complicated for American audiences, but became interested after I had suggested Charles Boyer to play Napoleon." He gave the go-ahead on the story after hearing her well-informed pitch to representatives of the Production Code Administration. Charles R. Metzger, one of Breen's associates, discussed with them "the advisability, or otherwise, of putting Miss Garbo in three pictures in a row in which she would play the role of an adulteress," but his argument only made Thalberg more determined. After *Camille*, it would be four.

While historical fact has often been called the greatest stumbling block in the construction of a good drama, for an industry threatened by censorship it also presented a glimmer of hope in loosening the censors' constraints. How much of a well-known historical story would censors dare to tamper with? And if a true story could make it past the guardians of good taste, establishing a new precedent, perhaps a fictional story could make it past the next time.

---

[9]"Dear Mrs Simpson," Greta wrote home in a letter to Hörke Wachtmeister, "now her quiet days are over. She'll be pursued now wherever she goes. Hope the camera-hunters will scare her so much that she'll leave my king in peace."

[10]She had been mentioned for this award as early as 1934.

The current popularity of biographical films made this scenario not only attractive, but eminently possible—as seen in an internal PCA memo dated December 5, 1935: "The story deals with adultery not only condoned but urged upon Marie by her elderly husband and the Polish statesmen. It deals with Napoleon's divorce of Josephine. It deals with diplomacy in which women's favors are used as pawns for securing advantage, nothing new but a bit unsavory for the average middle class motion picture audience," Metzger reported. "Since the characters and the events represented in this story are all historical facts and this illegitimate child survived and became a rather important person in France . . . it is not possible to 'clean this story up' under the code and have no intimate relationships between Marie and Napoleon or the industry makes itself somewhat a laughing stock by its treatment of historic facts. . . . The story looks dangerous to me."

In response, Joseph Breen stressed the need for more voices of morality, less urging of the sin of adultery upon Marie Walewska by the Polish patriots, and specifically condemnation, not support, by her husband. After reading Salka's November 1935 screenplay, he was "particularly pleased" to note that "there is little physical contact suggested between the illegitimate lovers and, likewise, a conspicuous absence of bedroom scenes, scenes of illicit fondling, etc. This, in our judgment, is going to add much to the worthwhile flavor of the story."

Potential problems with legal clearances (reminiscent of the *Rasputin* controversy) encouraged the producers to withhold a final go-ahead on the project, thus moving *Camille* into the forefront. In an effort to "liven up" the story, Thalberg and his successor, producer Bernie Hyman, involved a series of writers—eighteen in all, including Robert Sherwood, Zöe Akins, Carey Wilson, S. N. Behrman, Charles MacArthur, Donald Ogden Stewart, and Samuel Hoffenstein.

Garbo formally approved the dependable Clarence Brown as her director for a seventh (and final) time.[11] Brown was not her first choice—but actor Charles Boyer was. Like Robert Taylor, Boyer had recently made a breakthrough as a Hollywood leading man. Ironically, the actor had first come to town in 1929 to act in French-language versions of MGM's early sound films; one of these was slated to be Garbo's *The Kiss*. When the studio opted not to continue producing foreign translations of their films, Boyer went back to France. In 1932, he returned to Metro on a six-month option and was cast in a secondary role in *Red-Headed Woman*. Again, Irving Thalberg passed on keeping the actor because "nobody can understand

---

[11]"I dont know if Brown is the man to do it," she wrote, "as a matter of fact he isnt . . ." But, she claimed, he had been the only one available.

the guy's accent," he complained. Language differences notwithstanding, people understood his characterization of the carnival barker in *Liliom*. When Boyer was summoned to Hollywood in 1935, this time he stayed—and prospered.

Concerned with how he would fare in an under-written role opposite Garbo, not to mention the challenge represented by a Frenchman playing Napoleon, the actor initially turned the project down. But MGM was persistent. After heated negotiations, producer Walter Wanger, with whom Boyer had signed a non-exclusive contract, and Charles K. Feldman, Boyer's agent, skillfully secured a fee for their client nearly equal to Garbo's. Rounding out the supporting cast for the film to be called *Conquest* would be veteran actress Maria Ouspenskaya in her second American film, Reginald Owen (in his third with Garbo), Leif Erickson as Greta's proud brother, Henry Stephenson as her elderly husband, and Scotty Beckett as the love child of Napoleon and Marie Walewska.

By January of 1937, while many of these casting decisions were being finalized, *Camille* had opened in theaters across the nation. "No more tragically appealing lady of the camellias has ever graced stage or screen than the one here projected by Greta Garbo," *Daily Variety* advocated. "Rich acting role is made to order for Garbo's personality and talents and she dignifies and exploits it with fine sincerity, moving pathos and emotional power." Frank Nugent applauded her restraint. "It is because her emotions do not slip their leash—when you feel that any second they might—that saves her parting scene with Armand from being a cliché of renunciation," he wrote in *The New York Times*. "And, above all, it is her performance in the death scene—so simply, delicately and moving played—which convinces me that *Camille* is Garbo's best performance."

Although much of the film's success depended upon Garbo's beautifully modulated performance, each of the artists and craftsmen involved also rose to the occasion. "This is a guiltily rhapsodic film, an infuriatingly honest film, a deviously discreet film," Ethan Mordden offered in his treatise on Hollywood studios; "it depends on your mood the day you screen it. It is the motion picture many call Greta Garbo's greatest . . . [but] It is also Laura Hope Crew's—the perennial Aunt Pittypat at last given some meat to bite on as a greedy hanger-on. . . . The picture is as well Lenore Ulric's—a great David Belasco star in a rare historical preservation. But surely *Camille* is, above all, Cukor's greatest picture, for the way he brings the Parisian demi-monde to life, far more persuasively than one would have thought possible after the 1934 reinforcement of the Production Code."

The overwhelming majority of critics praised lavishly the emotional power of Garbo's Marguerite Gautier—flirtatious in her first meeting with Armand; ruthless in her self-scrutiny; breathless, though dismissive of her own poor health; and graceful even in death. Oscar would see things somewhat differently. After Academy of Motion Picture Arts and Sciences president Frank Capra declared that the organization would no longer involve itself in labor union matters, he brought in a substantial number of new members, swelling the ranks from eight hundred to over fifteen thousand potential voters. Twelve thousand of these were screen extras who would be allowed to cast ballots for Best Picture, Acting, and Song for the first time. No longer controlled by company politics, the Academy Awards became more of a popularity contest, albeit among "peers."

There was little doubt who the odds-on favorite for Best Actress was. Luise Rainer, a winner the previous year for her performance in *The Great Ziegfeld,* was so sure the statuette would go to Greta Garbo that she was not planning to attend the ceremony.[12] Neither did Irene Dunne (*The Awful Truth*), Janet Gaynor (*A Star is Born*), or Barbara Stanwyck (*Stella Dallas*) hold out much hope. An audible gasp reverberated through the hall when C. Aubrey Smith announced the winner for the Best Actress of 1937: *The Good Earth*'s Luise Rainer.

Camille did succeed in reviving Garbo's domestic box-office. Though its $1.154 million take in the United States and Canada didn't offset the production's overhead of $1.485 million (inclusive of the delays incurred due to Thalberg's death), when combined with an additional $1.688 million from the foreign market, the film sailed into profit. MGM continued to list Garbo as the company's "most potent coin-getter" outside the American market. Ironically, *Camille* was her last motion picture to get a full European release. It was also, rather notoriously, one of Hitler's favorite movies; the Führer reportedly "retained" a private copy of the film confiscated by his customs officers.

Conquest, formerly known as *Marie Walewska,* went before Karl Freund's cameras on March 3, 1937. After several delays pushed back the January start date, producer Bernie Hyman was encouraged to rush the company into production in order to avoid losing Boyer and to cover the loss of a new film from Thalberg's widow, Norma Shearer. Principal photography began with an incomplete script; new pages were delivered to the set on a daily basis. Lacking his predecessor's taste and judgment, Hyman's solution would be to spend more money—enhancing the motion picture's opulent appearance but not its quality overall. It was not the way Garbo liked to work.

[12]Garbo's nomination was her first since *Anna Christie* and *Romance* in 1930.

According to Cecil Beaton, when Mercedes drove Greta to the studio on the first day of filming, her unhappy passenger was in tears all the way to Culver City. "This is prostitution," she cried. In an earlier conversation, Greta despaired that she didn't have "the slightest idea what this story is all about or who the hell Marie Walewska is."

Again, views of Garbo contradict each other. "She seemed a lot happier when we started *Conquest* than at any time since her first days in Hollywood. We all noticed it the first day," Ralph O'Dell, an MGM guard, told the *New York Post*. "She used to drive in, say good morning to the gateman, and drive through to that half-hidden entrance [to her dressing room]. We never saw her about the lot . . . But when she and Charles Boyer started in *Conquest*, it was all different. She stayed on the set to gossip with Boyer or Karl Freund, the cameraman. . . . When [Clarence Brown] played catch with a baseball to limber up a broken arm, she joined the game and got a lot of fun out of it."

O'Dell humorously recalled how stages emptied to watch Garbo whenever she walked across the lot for a meeting at the producer's building. David Lewis was given the task of bringing Greta to the Chief's new all-white art deco office for one such meeting. "She had never been in his office," Lewis said. "I talked to her and she said, 'Sure.' I walked her up to his office and he slammed the door in my face. Two minutes later, she came out and said, 'That was an experience!' " Lewis never learned what happened in that office, "but to her it was not only ludicrous, it was funny. . . . Garbo was the only one in my experience who saw through [Mayer] and got away from him as fast as possible."

Another close call was an unexpected meeting with a former costar. Greta arrived at the studio to find John Barrymore outside the dressing room complex talking to a director. Barrymore rushed to her car, helped her out, and greeted her with a kiss, ecstatically throwing his arms around her. Garbo reportedly took it all in stride, laughed easily, and then walked to her dressing room—where she locked the door.

Conversely, when Clark Gable showed up on the set uninvited, she not only came out of her room to visit, but told studio guards he was welcome back any time. She reverted to her old routine when Clarence Brown tried to sneak Jack Gilbert's daughter on to the set. Garbo was too involved in her own work to concern herself with the drama of dealing with Gilbert's former wife, Leatrice Joy, or his clearly adoring teenage daughter. She retired to her refuge behind the black flats until the pair left the soundstage.

One month into production on *Conquest*, Greta sat down and wrote Hörke Wachtmeister that she was "incredibly tired of being a 'star'," and was most anxious to return home as soon as possible. "My last hunt was at

Tistad," she remarked. "But that time it was a fox that was shot. There are only lions here at MGM so I'm not interested." She confided that she was seeing a new doctor, "a little hunch-backed man who I am dragging down into the abyss of pessimism. . . . We sit there fencing with words and keeping a watchful eye on one another." She believed that the doctor, clearly a psychologist, saw her as "an interesting case of depression."

On film, the star appeared thinner—and more beautiful—than ever before, a mature variation on her look in *Gösta Berlings saga*. Try as she might, she could not avoid the past. In August of 1936, producer David Schratter, formerly of Trianon-Film A.-G., resurfaced in Los Angeles, filing a lawsuit through an intermediary charging that in 1924 he had loaned Garbo sums in excess of $10,000 and had never been paid back. A previous suit had been dismissed due to a lack of proper showing. When it was refiled, Greta adroitly dodged Schratter's process servers for weeks before a traffic signal held her car up long enough for them to toss a summons in through the window. A new hearing was scheduled for May 3, 1937. As the court date neared, MGM lawyers filed a motion to delay the proceedings, citing the company's concerns about their investment in *Conquest*. Schratter's suit was abruptly dismissed on June 16 without any indication of its resolution (though it seems likely that, rather than waste additional time in court, MGM settled on Garbo's behalf). Greta Garbo's deposition would stand as her only comment concerning the matter.[13]

Stuntman Gil Perkins found an unusual place to "hang out" with Garbo: they sat in an old whaling boat, waiting for the fog to clear in the Catalina Channel so that they could shoot a sequence for *Conquest*. "She sat out there and talked to us about our lives, our wives, our children," Perkins remembered. "I thought to myself, 'Boy, if this had been Crawford or Bette Davis, they'd have been screaming: What the hell are you doing keeping me out here?' Because she was there from about 8:30 until noon before we ever got a shot. She just sat there and talked; it didn't bother her."

Technical snags, illness, and inertia sent the budget of *Conquest* spiraling. Garbo was absent for nineteen production days between March and

---

[13]She denied ever borrowing money from Schratter. As to whether or not Mauritz Stiller might have asked for an advance on her behalf, Greta stated that she was unsure exactly what business had been conducted—only that the film she and Moje were hired for was never made. "I was merely a young actress working in a picture, and the people in it, like me, were merely put on a train and taken along," she testified. "How we were paid, I don't know. Mr. Stiller was handling all my business affairs." Because of her absolute reliance on and devotion to Moje, Greta had no idea that she never collected a salary for her time on location in Constantinople.

May due to miscellaneous illnesses; Boyer and the second unit continued work without her. *Conquest* would be a perfect illustration of "the difference between cost with quality and cost without it." Neither producer Hyman nor director Brown truly understood the material, Salka Viertel lamented. At times she felt that Brown actually obstructed the production's progress with his uncertainty.

The frustrated cast and crew began to feel eternally bound to a project where there was no end in sight. In 1926, Stiller's replacement had forced *The Temptress* to continue on for a grueling eighty-three overhead days. Indecision and misdirection sent *Camille* into a merciless schedule of retakes, adding up to seventy-five days. Now, an incredible one hundred and twenty-seven days—approximately twenty-two weeks—would be charged to *Conquest*. By July, the joke on the Metro-Goldwyn-Mayer lot was that workers were forming a "*Walewska*-Must-End" society.

The budget on the production exhibited a life of its own, taking on a near-epic status that was not justified by the script. On July 16, 1937— $2.732 million later—the cast and crew celebrated the completion of principal photography. Previews and retakes continued into October, with Garbo and Boyer collecting generous paychecks for each day of overtime (according to tax records, Garbo's compensation at the end of the year was a whopping $472,499). *Conquest* earned the brief distinction of being MGM's costliest venture since *Ben-Hur*, making it the fourth-most expensive motion picture in cinema history to date.[14]

Gottfried Reinhardt, who had made a lightning-quick rise through the executive ranks at MGM, urged his companion, Salka Viertel, to "keep [Garbo] away from historical topics and convince [her] to do a comedy for once."[15] That summer, Salka ran into a writer named Melchior Lengyel at the Brown Derby in Hollywood. During the course of conversation, she mentioned that they were looking for a comedy for Garbo and asked Lengyel if he had "a story up his sleeve." The writer promised to consult his notebook when he got home. When he did, he found a possible scenario and called Salka back. A charming, amusing man with a contagious smile, Lengyel pitched the idea to Greta as she swam in George Cukor's pool: "Russian girl saturated with Bolshevist ideals goes to fearful, capitalistic, monopolistic Paris. She meets romance and has an uproarious good time. Capitalism not so bad after all."

[14]That record would be inherited by *Gone With The Wind* in 1939.
[15]Salka and Berthold Viertel had come to an understanding regarding their marriage, and began accepting other companions into their lives. Salka met Gottfried Reinhardt, then an assistant in Irving Thalberg's office, in 1933.

The idea not only captured Greta's attention, it won the favor of Bernie Hyman and various executives at MGM. Lengyel was asked to develop the story further.

Joseph Breen was pleased to note that when *Conquest* was previewed for the trade on October 21, the film's sexual content had been admirably repressed—as was any chance for its survival in a world of screwball comedies, frothy musicals, and adventure pictures. "If you can't make an audience forget the costumes in the first five minutes, you're doomed," the late Irving Thalberg often told his staff. Failure to adhere to these principles could be seen in several post-Thalberg projects, including *Parnell* (Clark Gable, 1937) and *Marie Antoinette* (Norma Shearer, 1938).

Conquest was released during the first week of November. Amazingly, most of the critical reaction reflected the superlative hype over the paying public's more realistic response. John Mosher had become bored with "Madame Garbo's elegant anemia," he confessed in his review for *The New Yorker*. "Beautiful, fragile, and tired, she stands in the first scene among the Cossacks invading her husband's house; and quite unchanged, fragile, and tired still, she waves her last farewell to Napoleon, as though she would assert and try to prove that loyalty is but a symptom of exhaustion. I think that for the first time Madame Garbo has a leading man who contributes more to the interest and vitality of the film than she does."

Boyer would be nominated for an Academy Award in the same year Garbo competed for *Camille* (he lost to Spencer Tracy). Interestingly, given its strong foreign cast, the motion picture encountered its greatest censorship roadblocks on the international front, especially in Italy and Japan where anything resembling a political speech was deleted. More than $2 million would be taken in worldwide box office, but that was not enough. According to MGM's accounting, *Conquest* lost almost $1.4 million—an extravagant sum that, Louis B. Mayer could later point out, represented the total negative cost of three or four highly profitable *Andy Hardy* pictures.

In October of 1937, as Hollywood insiders played a guessing game regarding Garbo's next project, a far more intriguing story hit the national press. "DIVORCE RUMOR LINKS GARBO AND STOKOWSKI," the front page of the *New York Post* proclaimed. Leopold Stokowski, the renowned classical conductor, had met Garbo at Anita Loos's Santa Monica beach house the previous February. Stokowski (or Stoki, as many of his friends referred to him) had expressed an interest in meeting the Swedish diva ever since he arrived in Hollywood. Loos was the first of their mutual acquaintances to accommodate his request. She invited both to a Sunday brunch—and

Greta surprised them all by showing up. "Stoki didn't waste much time on the overture," Loos said. "He got straight down to business, laying on the charm. He told Garbo they were destined to have a history-making romance, like Wagner's with Cosima. It was written in the stars. There was no use in their trying to escape it. The gods had made their decision. Mere mortals could only obey."

CHAPTER EIGHTEEN

Distant Thunder

Greta purchased her first home at the bargain price of 276,000 kronor, just in time for her thirty-first birthday.[1] Hårby gård was a working farm which included a modest selection of livestock, a large garden, and approximately one hundred and sixty acres of farmable land. Located sixty kilometers southwest of Stockholm near the town of Gnesta, the original estate dated back to the sixteenth century when it was owned by a noble family. It was an idyllically secluded piece of land. The main house, a typical Swedish manor, faced Lake Sillen and was hidden behind a wall of birches, poplars, and oaks that lined Hårby's private road. The estate also encompassed a series of smaller lakes, one of which produced crayfish. During the winter, a herd of elk often sought shelter in a section of wooded land Greta bought separately called Torsnäset.

She found the property with the help of her brother, Sven, and the Wachtmeisters. "I want to thank you from the bottom of my heart for all your help," Greta wrote Hörke. "It's as though a huge weight has been lifted from my chest." Sven was appointed caretaker and moved his family, including Anna Lovisa, to the estate when the main house was ready for occupancy. A local antique dealer helped to furnish the rooms. Mrs. Gustafson was given her own three-room suite within the house; guests stayed in a nearby summer house. To show that he took his new role seriously, Sven went to Tistad to study how Nils Wachtmeister ran his farm.

Throughout much of 1937, Greta worked toward making her way to her new Swedish home—while Leopold Stokowski set his sights on Garbo. "G.G., what do you do when you go home?" cameraman Karl Freund once asked her. "I rest a bit, the maid brings me dinner, then I study the next day's script and go to bed," she replied in German. "I've been in my new house for three months and would you believe it, I've never seen the living room." Feeling bolder, Freund inquired about her love life. Garbo's response was equally frank. "Many of the men who ask me out go crazy about my Swedish maid, who is very pretty. They pat her on the cheek and flirt with her, but for me, at the end of the evening they say, 'Thank you,

---

[1] Although Sven Gustafson signed the contract, there was a provision allowing him to assign the property rights to his sister without any further formality.

Miss Garbo,' and they tell me how wonderful it was but not one ever says, 'Let's go to bed.' " It was the price she paid for celebrity.[2]

Any idea that Greta was either alone or celibate was contradicted by Raymond Daum, a walking companion. "Walter Wanger, who produced *Queen Christina,* told me in the 1960s that Garbo was the most sexually alive woman he had ever worked with, and added, 'There is nothing she doesn't know about sex!' " An entry in Cecil Beaton's diary offers further illumination. "Of course she's a sensuous woman, will do anything, pick up any man, go to bed with him, then throw him out," Beaton recorded George Cukor telling him, "but she reserves her real sensuousness for the camera."

She could not deny her attraction to Stokowski, a dynamic personality twenty-three years her senior. Although married since 1926, Stoki had been unabashedly enamored of Garbo for some time. "Ah, she is beautiful," he told a friend in 1931, "and I would like to meet her. Perhaps I can if I go to Sweden . . ." He didn't have to go any further than Hollywood. While working on *100 Men and a Girl* at Universal Pictures, the popular Philadelphia Symphony Orchestra conductor prevailed upon friends—from Adrian and George Cukor to L. B. Mayer—to introduce him to the Swedish star. But it was Anita Loos who succeeded in getting them together. Loos did not remember much of their encounter. "It didn't strike me as a romance because everybody was busy working and he was making film tests concerning sound," the diminutive writer told Oliver Daniel, Stokowski's friend and biographer. She believed that the affair didn't last more than a few weeks. "On that score," Daniel remarked, "Miss Loos was quite wrong. It was of much longer duration and, at least on Stoki's part, of considerable seriousness."

There has always been more to Greta Garbo than her extraordinary good looks, David Lewis noted. "She was magnetic, more so than anybody else I ever observed. She could imply a great sense of intimacy, all the time keeping a cool distance." Though perfectly capable of applying this technique in her relationships with either sex—and successful with both— Greta still "did not want to be captured, either mentally or in bed, and resolutely evaded all attempts," added a female friend. What made Leopold Stokowski different from other suitors was that he was a peer; he had his own life and work. He was fascinated but not obsessed, and he car-

---

[2]Katharine Hepburn underscored this in a story about one of their first meetings. George Cukor brought Greta over for a tour of Hepburn's new house. "Went upstairs—showed her the bedroom," the actress wrote later. "She walked over to my bed. There was a lump on the bed (obviously a hot-water bottle). She looked at me, patted it, and sighed. 'Yes, I have one too. Vat is wrong vid us?' "

ried himself with total assurance. Stokowski was very much aware of his own sexual power—married or unmarried, attractive women constantly decorated his life. Garbo was easily led into a relationship.

Greta seemed intrigued—and bewildered—by the earnestness of Stoki's pursuit. "He was a very glamorous and handsome man. He dressed beautifully, often in black silk shirts, and was something of a Don Juan," actor Jack Larson says. Although he got to know both Garbo and Stokowski—separately—later in life, Larson is certain that the couple had an intimate, sexual relationship. "Why wouldn't they?" he asks. In fact, why would the maestro bother with Garbo if he wasn't being satisfied sexually? "Stokowski was out to have fun and romance and love and go to bed with beautiful women," Larson says. "Yes, I'm sure they did." Yet there were other friends who believed that Stoki was too vain to set himself up for the sexual rejection they assumed was inevitable with Garbo. For the record, all Leopold Stokowski would ever say about Greta Garbo was that she had "great imagination and great humor."

An active imagination, perhaps, which allowed her to get caught up in a fantasy. Privately, Greta now referred to Stoki as her "boyfriend"—and on this count, many of her friends took her seriously. The larger-than-life romantic aura had seemingly swept her into the "world-shaking romance" friends and associates had often hoped for. The underground buzz on the couple was that they often could be found dancing together or in romantic tête-à-têtes at private parties, where Garbo appeared to snuggle contentedly in the conductor's arms. Gottfried Reinhardt recalled an intimate afternoon at Salka's, "where Garbo knelt before Stokowski and listened, enraptured, to such tales as when he spent an entire day—from sunrise to sunset—with a native sage on an Indian mountaintop . . ."

Such a relationship could not be hidden from MGM—hence the press—for long. This time, they said, it was Garbo who was smitten. Rumors about the pair first surfaced during the production of Conquest. When Evangeline Stokowski and her children returned from Japan in late July, she was surprised to learn that her husband had decided not to meet them. The conductor still drove to Santa Barbara to be with his family most weekends, but his "busy schedule" kept him in Hollywood during the week. "No one close to [Garbo and Stokowski] denies any longer that they have been seeing each other, and often," one journalist offered. "The attitude now is, 'Certainly they see each other, so what?' On that point, the film colony's gossip corner is stumped."

The Stokowski children came home with one burning question when they returned to school in the fall: "Who is Greta Garbo?" For the sake of their children, Evangeline Stokowski had insisted on keeping their names out of the papers—"for a few years at least." Her husband's refusal to make such a promise had more to do with his career than any recent romantic attachment. *100 Men and a Girl* was a hit, and he was talking to several studios about future musical projects; neither had the demand for Stokowski's services as a conductor abated.

In October, Evangeline Stokowski established legal residence in Nevada and filed for divorce. Though Garbo was not named as a corespondent, she was understandably unhappy about having her name dragged into the press in conjunction with the suit. A divorce was granted on December 1, 1937. Mrs. Stokowski wasted no time finding a new husband, wedding an exiled Russian prince in February of 1938. "Now that Mrs. Stokowski herself has married, there is nothing to keep Garbo and the orchestra leader apart," Louella Parsons wrote. Nothing except the Atlantic Ocean.

Both Greta and Stoki labeled stories that they might marry absurd. "I will not deny Mr. Stokowski and I are very good friends. But as for marriage to him—no," Garbo told a stringer for Hearst newspapers when confronted in George Cukor's driveway. Stokowski responded from Philadelphia. "There is really no occasion for me to answer," he protested. "She said quite plainly there was no truth to those rumors." Prodded further, the conductor stated that "Miss Garbo has a group of friends in Hollywood and I am one of that group. There is actually no question of marriage. All those stories are absolutely without foundation and are mistaken in every way."

As December dawned, Greta slipped quietly out of town to meet Stokowski in New York before boarding her ship. She was not completely successful in evading attention. If attendance on her pictures had fallen, the mystique of Garbo was stronger than ever; she was mobbed. "I guess I cant complain," she concluded in a letter to Salka Viertel. "After all, I'm only a circus lady." She signed off with a drawing of a tightrope-walker carrying a parasol.

Garbo and Stokowski defied the gossip patrol and, on the night before she was scheduled to leave, were seen out on the town drinking "a fond farewell" at a New York night spot. On December 8, Stoki and Bob Reud accompanied her to the *Gripsholm* and filled her suite with gardenias and roses. As usual, Reud was rapturous in his admiration toward his sailing siren. "NO CABLE I MIGHT EVER WRITE COULD DO JUSTICE TO MY FEELINGS SINCE LAST WEDNESDAY," he wired the reclusive occupant of Cabin 1-A. "THE MIRACLE OF THAT ONE MOMENT BLINDS ME STILL. PLEASE DEAR GODDESS CABLE TWO WORDS, WELL AND LOVE. ALL THAT MATTERS ON EARTH EVER TO ME."

Apart from the romantic speculation, Garbo's departure in December

KAREN SWENSON

of 1937 was noteworthy for being the first time MGM had allowed her to return home without a signed contract in hand. She was free to come or go as she pleased. The *Gripsholm* arrived in Göteborg Harbor on the eighteenth. As he boarded the liner from the pilot boat, Sven was nearly knocked down by a wave washing over him. While he dried off in his sister's cabin, Greta met a small group of reporters in the lounge—this time, with an agreement in advance that there would be no pictures. "I don't look nice enough to be photographed today," she professed.[3]

She claimed to have traveled under the name Jonas Emerson and was emphatic in her denial of any intention to marry Stokowski. "We are only good friends, you understand? All this gossip is very idiotic." When asked if she considered marriage a hindrance to an actress's career, she replied that it would depend on whom one married. Suspicious journalists observed that she had removed only one of her gloves, her left hand glove remained on; Greta explained that she had injured her hand closing a porthole in her stateroom.

Regarding her plans for work, she indicated that her next picture would probably be a comedy. "Will I be allowed to keep my lover in it? Certainly I am hoping so! Don't you think it is high time they let me end a picture happily with a kiss? I do. I seem to have lost so many attractive men in the final scenes!" She expressed the hope that she might work with the director of *It Happened One Night* and *Mr. Deeds Goes to Town*, Frank Capra.

As Greta and her brother disembarked, a crowd waited to greet them and wish Garbo *"God Jul"*—Merry Christmas.

Torches lit the way to Hårby gård as Greta's car pulled into the snow-covered lane on a picturesque winter evening. A heavy mantle of snow framed the house, its cream color highlighted against the turquoise blue, green, and scarlet trim of its wooden shutters and pointed gables. The curtains of each window were drawn back so that welcoming lamps could shine out. Inside the house, Anna Lovisa Gustafson greeted her daughter with a festive candlelit dinner and decorated her holiday table with fragrant boughs of evergreen.

Greta's life at Hårby gård began just the way she might have imagined. Each morning, she bundled up and went on a walking tour of the farm with Sven, checking in on the cows, chickens, horses, and pigs. In order to further secure their privacy, Greta and Sven also visited neighboring estates hoping to purchase the headland surrounding Lake Sillen. Such visits went unannounced and had predictable results: clearly taken by sur-

[3] Of course, one was taken anyway.

prise—by Garbo as well as the generous offer—most of their neighbors agreed to sell.[4]

At midday, Anna Lovisa and Peg Gustafson, Sven's wife, prepared a smörgåsbord for the family. Dinners were also large and featured many of the foods Greta missed in Hollywood. Anna Lovisa was determined to put some color back in her daughter's face. Greta often spent her quiet time around the communal stove poring through European and American magazines—a scene reminiscent of similar winter days around a much smaller stove in Södermalm.

After the holidays, she ventured back into Stockholm to meet with friends and partake in the winter sports. Thus far, she had managed to keep her presence in the city comparatively quiet, despite her increased visibility due to the critical and popular triumph of *Kameliadamen (Camille)* in Sweden.[5] Early in January, Garbo's performance in *Camille* was acknowledged as the year's finest by the New York Film Critics. During the live radio broadcast, presenter Robert Benchley asked for "a period of silence" in lieu of a speech from the absent winner.

Garbo was still in search of peace. *Conquest* was due to open in Stockholm soon and Greta was not happy that it was. In a revealing letter to Salka Viertel, she wrote poignantly of her life in Sweden: "I do not believe in sorrow. Having been my companion all my life, I definitely do not believe in it. . . . I live in my brothers place which is a 'mess.' I tryed [sic] to find something that would have helped him in life but it is not right. He cant take care of it and now I dont know anymore what to do. I have been trying to find furnitures [sic] for the house, otherwise I go nowhere, see no one. Just like in Brentwood and I am not much of a hausfrau."

That routine, she noted, was due to change. "Soon I am going to see Stoky [sic] with the help of divine power. God help me if they [the press] catsh [sic] me. But I must try. I always sit in a corner somewhere and I dont see anything. . . . Is Gottfrid [sic] still with you or have you sent him away from you? It is hard and sad to be alone but sometimes its even more difficult to be with someone. Its strange that most things in life have to be such 'government business' . . . But somewhere in this world are a few beengs [sic] who do not have it as we have. Of that I am certain. And if I would stop making film I could

<hr />

[4]A protective measure only. Despite Garbo's desire for privacy, her homeland weighs a landowner's claim versus "Everyman's Right" of access to public and private property differently. Swedes insist on their right to enjoy the flora and fauna of the countryside and Swedish law supports this. *Allemansrätten* allows citizens to walk where they please in the fields and forests of Sverige—even camp on private property as long as they keep a discreet distance away from the owner's home and garden.

[5]Which Garbo managed to see with Hörke in Nyköping.

go and see if I could find out a little about it. . . . Live well, dear sir—and will you greet your children and my and your Hardt."[6]

Leopold Stokowski set sail for Europe on February 5, arriving in Naples two weeks later. Speculation began anew. While the maestro was en route, Hedda Hopper, in her first syndicated newspaper column, concluded that Garbo "must be serious" about marrying Stokowski. Before sailing for Sweden, she was told, Greta had visited Stoki's relatives in Philadelphia and they had approved. But the fledgling columnist's story was later discredited—Stokowski didn't have relatives living in Philadelphia. Another unsubstantiated story discussed the new "trousseau" being designed for Garbo.[7]

By February 24, after a ski vacation with the Wachtmeisters in the mountains of Jämtland, Greta traveled alone across Europe. It was her last peaceful moment. She joined Stokowski in Rome and they drove south to the village of Ravello, where the formality of presenting their passports to the town's mayor made it possible for the media to find them. Within a few days, the whole countryside knew about their famous guests; Garbo was staying at the flower-decked Villa Cimbrone under the name Margaret Luisa Gustafsson. The centuries-old Cimbrone was built on a cliff overlooking the coastal city of Amalfi and the Gulf of Salerno. Despite a "Keep Out" sign posted on the front gate, the congregation of fans and reporters continued to multiply; tourists mingled with locals and the media. Four carabinieri and three police dogs were assigned to protect the villa's occupants.

Villagers dubbed Garbo "La Donna Misteriosa," "with as much affection as curiosity," a friend of Stokowski's observed. They gathered in strategic areas near the balcony and behind the garden wall, hoping to get a glimpse of the mysterious one. What they got instead were snippets of innocuous banter as Greta and Stoki did their morning exercises. At one point, Garbo was overheard giving instructions to have a doctor ready in case anyone was hurt.

Every mood of Greta Garbo's most public relationship since John Gilbert was gleefully reported in the press. Her influence over the maestro abroad was as profound as his had been over her in Hollywood—here, it was Garbo who was clearly in charge. One reporter noted that the couple favored a restaurant at the Hotel Caruso, where they usually ate vegetarian lunches of beets, carrots, and lettuce. "He certainly must love her to eat that

[6]Etta Hardt was a German refugee whom Salka had helped to sponsor and, when Garbo was in Hollywood, a valued keeper of her home and hearth.

[7]Any new clothes in Greta's wardrobe no doubt represented a gesture she had made in deference to Stokowski, who once asked Anita Loos to take Greta to Bullock's Wilshire to select a more attractive wardrobe.

stuff," a waiter said. "Before she came he used to eat plenty of meat and spaghetti."

Greta's trip with Stokowski was a perfect illustration of her free, nomadic style on the road. "I live like a monk with one toothbrush, one cake of soap, and a pot of cream," she explained to a friend. "I simplify life like mad!" Villa Cimbrone's housekeeping staff was amazed at how literally she took this credo. A single worn suitcase reportedly contained a pair of blue flannel trousers, sweaters knit by her mother, a pair of coarse flannel pajamas, blue espadrilles, sunglasses, an assortment of veils, and several pots of jam. The only request Garbo made to the staff was to have her pajamas washed and ironed every morning and a bottle of olive oil and some salt available before she went to bed; presumably, the salt was to brush her teeth and the oil was for her skin. Even more surprising, she had brought very little Italian currency with her.

With their every move carefully monitored, the couple remained unwilling to compromise their idyll and ventured forth to the isle of Capri. They managed the drive to Sorrento without being noticed—that changed when they hired a boat to take them across the bay. On the island, they visited the world-famous Grotta Azzurra, the Blue Grotto, and had tea with Dr. Axel Munthe, whom Greta had met years earlier in Sweden.[8] A crowd awaited them upon their return to Amalfi.

Italy was undeniably enraptured by having the Divine One in their presence. Mountains of mail addressed to her arrived daily in Ravello. Even so, MGM had no way of gauging how the American public would receive news of her unconventional relationship with a twice-divorced, older man. However real or imagined the romance, the fact that Garbo and Stokowski were seen traveling together—as well as living under the same roof—was generally considered unacceptable. Unbeknownst to either party, studio executives were concerned that a scandal would be a significant obstacle to Garbo's application for reentry into the United States. To ensure an unimpeded return, Metro lawyers kept informed about press coverage of the affair.

Marriage rumors circulated with all kinds of improbable scenarios: in Sweden, it was reported that Max Gumpel would attend the nuptials; in the States, another story suggested Wallace Beery would. Rumored guests depended on the country of origin. A leak to the media—some claimed Stokowski himself was the source, others insisted it was a zealous Metro publicist—indicated that the conductor hoped to marry Garbo in northern

---

[8]The writer's home, Villa San Michele, was an imposing modern structure built atop an ancient Roman ruin near the village of Anacapri.

Italy's historic city of Turin sometime between March 15 and 17. This was promptly denied by both. "Marriage? I wouldn't know," Greta stated. "There seems to be a law that governs all our actions, so I never make plans."

At least one of Garbo's friends believed the stories. "DEAR GODDESS," Robert Reud hailed in a telegram dated March 7, 1938. "AM I COMPLETELY LOST, PLEASE GIVE ME SOME WORD OR SIGN SO I MAY HAVE CAUSE TO LIVE STOP DESPITE CURRENT AMERICAN NEWSPAPER HEADLINES AM STILL PRAYER- FULLY HOPING THAT AT LAST YOU MAY BLESSEDLY DECIDE TO MARRY ME IN THE END . . ." Given Reud's usual effusiveness in his correspondence with Garbo, and the chivalrous proposal that had begun their relationship in 1927, the seriousness of his despair remains a subject for debate. But he had reason to believe Greta was still entertaining offers—despite protesta- tions otherwise.

That March, the German army marched across the Austrian border; Hitler formalized the annexation and met with Benito Mussolini in Italy. Still, the events that would soon affect everyone's lives were often pushed off front pages in Italy by the latest reports of Garbo and Stoki—which hardly elevated Greta's mood. "I am really very sad," she wrote Hörke Wachtmeister on the sixteenth. For once, she expressed regret that she had not stayed in Los Angeles, "but I am so polite to friends and acquain- tances once I've gotten to know them. And when they have plans like going to Italy, I can't say no. . . . One thing is clear, I have to stop making films. I cannot go on this way. . . . The only way out of this current prison I'm in is to meet the press and with God's help I shall do so tomorrow."

A truce was struck with the press. In exchange for a promise to leave them alone for the remainder of their stay, Garbo and Stokowski agreed to a March 17 press conference at their villa. Stokowski appeared first. He was smooth and well-prepared for the barrage of personal questions, making a poignant appeal for people to leave them in peace "so that Miss Garbo can see something of Italy—at least more than I can see from my window."

Greta entered the library and sat near the fire. She wore a subtle combi- nation of Swedish colors: a blue gabardine suit, Norfolk jacket, yellow sweater, blue woolen scarf, flat suede shoes, and gray gloves; her hair was straight and she had limited her makeup to mascara and a trace of face pow- der. Reporters were no longer distracted by the view of the bay. Again, Garbo maintained she was quite unwilling to change her single status. "I only want to be let alone," she reiterated. "There are some who want to get married and others who don't. I have never had an impulse to go to the altar."

Regarding her trip, she said that she had seen very little of the world. "I wanted to see some of the beautiful things of life with my friend, Mr.

Stokowski, who has been very much to me. He has seen so much and knows about the beauty of life and . . . I optimistically accepted. I was naïve enough to think we could travel without being discovered and without being hunted. . . . It is cruel to bother people who want to be left in peace. This kills beauty for me."

Within a few days, the *New York Journal American* reported, "The film star and the orchestra conductor left their vacation villa at Ravello as secretly as they had gone to it early this month." Believed to be en route to Sicily, they instead bypassed media scrutiny by driving to nearby Naples and visiting the ruins at Pompeii. They arrived in Rome on March 23 and were seen holding hands as they toured the city's historic sights. Five days later, Greta and Stoki were again on the move. An advance report indicated that they would go to Vienna—predictably elusive, they emerged from the confusion bound on an Italian steamer from Assisi to the African port of Tunis.

Returning to the Continent, Stokowski endeavored to show "La Divina" the places he knew and loved. What they found instead were the echoes of something far more sinister: a Europe preparing for war. Germany had mobilized; France was calling up its reservists; and British Prime Minister Neville Chamberlain met with Hitler in a futile attempt to ensure "peace in our time." Although she professed not knowing much about what was happening in the world (other than what she learned at the Viertels), Garbo's tour with Stokowski through Italy, France, and Germany underlined the alarming nature of these events—and the inevitability of the catastrophe before them.

"I was wondering whether you would be kind enough to have me and another person to lunch when we 'travel through Sweden,'" Greta wrote Hörke from Paris. She hoped Wachtmeister could meet them in southern Sweden when they crossed the Baltic strait by ferry. The plotting began. "If I wire you the name and date of the meeting place, you'll know it is from me and then you can do as you like. With 'God's help' it'll be around the beginning of May or maybe a little bit later."

The couple arrived in Sweden early in the morning of May 5. They had driven their rented Lincoln Zephyr to Sassnitz, Germany, where they boarded a ferry to Trelleborg, Sweden. A scenic drive on a lovely spring day quickly turned into a comedy of errors with Stokowski the driver and Garbo the map reader. The sight of the pair stirred up the countryside as they wandered through southern Sweden, gradually making their way to Nyköping. "I'm a rather unreliable human being," the would-be navigator later admitted to a friend. "As a traveling companion I don't recommend myself—I'm too much of a menace." Greta and Stoki didn't arrive at Tistad Slott until well after midnight. The next day, they drove to Hårby, and Stoki met the Gustafson family. For appearance's sake, he rented a flat on Stockholm's Djurgården—but for all intents and purposes, the conductor lived at Hårby gård.

By the end of the month, there was a call to work: Greta's lawyers were negotiating a new deal at Metro, Stokowski's representatives had aligned him with a project at Disney. Postal worker Sven Strengnell claimed that Garbo practically saved his life during the summer of '38. "My first post was with the post office in Gnesta," he explained. It was a last-minute assignment and Strengell arrived in Gnesta with very little money. Garbo bailed him out. "There was an express letter to her almost every day," he said, requiring that he bicycle to Hårby gård. "I received ten kronor in tips each time from Garbo." And, on one occasion, an invitation to dinner; the postal worker spent the evening talking to Leopold Stokowski about music.

Most affected by Greta's ongoing relationship with the maestro was Mercedes de Acosta. Again Mercedes timed her vacation with Greta's. She traveled abroad from May through December 1938. For the most part, she lingered in France, later adding side trips to Germany, Poland, Italy, and, finally, Egypt and India.

She cabled George Cukor from Paris trying to confirm newspaper reports about the "Viking child." Cukor, honoring Garbo's wishes, did not give Mercedes any definitive information. But he did send a telegram to Greta on June 1, discussing the pros and cons of proceeding with a comedy or the story of Marie Curie next. That Aldous Huxley, the author of *Brave New World*, had been asked to write the latter made Cukor more excited about the prospects for *Curie*. "HE IS AN INSPIRATION AND A GODSEND," the director wired Garbo. "HE WILL MAKE *CURIE* HUMAN AND IMPORTANT." Greta responded to Cukor's telegram on June 7. "WONDERFUL PLANS," she affirmed. Alluding to the problems on *Anna Karenina* and *Conquest*, she asked only that they start with a finished manuscript this time.

While Cukor ironed out the details at MGM, Greta considered retreating to an even more secluded location and contacted Wilhelm Sörensen about his villa on Sweden's rocky western coast. During last week of June, a story emerged from Sweden about a smash-up Greta and Stoki had on a rain-soaked, muddy road outside Södertälje. Stokowski had lost control of the car and it overturned in a field. "The maestro had suffered such a severe shock that he did not dare to venture on any more extended automobile trips in Sweden," Sörensen concluded. "Indeed he abruptly decided to cut his trip with Garbo short." Stoki continued on to London and Paris for business; Greta canceled the holiday at Sören's villa in Svinevik.

* * *

"DIDN'T WE ALWAYS TELL YOU NOT TO DRIVE RECKLESSLY," George Cukor and Salka Viertel joked in a cable to Garbo. "SHALL WE SEND JAMES OVER TO DRIVE YOU?" Her most intimate circle of friends might make light of the situation, but Mercedes de Acosta was losing her perspective. It is noteworthy that in her extensive collection of personal letters, there isn't one piece of correspondence from Greta to Mercedes between the years 1937 and 1945.[9] The apparent estrangement propelled de Acosta into a familiar pattern of acquiring information about Greta through mutual friends.

On the tenth of July, Mercedes again wrote "Lorenzo" Cukor from Paris: "It may amuse you to know that some weeks ago I saw Stokowski walking in the street with Dick Hammond. I was in a taxi and he did not see me. Two days later I went to London. I was sitting in my Pullman seat wondering who was going to share the empty one opposite me when suddenly in walks Stokowski and had this seat! He nearly died when he saw me—you can imagine. . . . I asked him 'How is Dick?'—he answered he had not seen him for three years . . . just shows what a liar he is. I saw Dick later in London who told me he had seen Stokowski every day in Paris. S was very afraid apparently that I would think some break had come between him and Greta since he was on the continent . . . Have you heard anything about Greta's return to Hollywood? . . . Stokowski told me that he was returning in August to work with Disney but as he lies so much to me perhaps this is not true. I did not ask him anything about Greta except about her health. . . . I believe he only stays there in Sweden to save his face."

Stokowski returned to Stockholm in July, as promised. Åke Bonnier met Greta and Stoki at a lunch arranged by a friend, music publisher Lennart Reuterskiöld. He subsequently invited the couple to his parents' estate, though his father made it clear he wasn't interested in film stars. Garbo and Stokowski arrived on a fabulous summer day: a good sign. "On days like that the table would be set on the terrace. Garbo arrived in long white trousers, which were considered rather startling in those days," Bonnier recalled in a private memoir. Greta charmed her way out of any ill feeling for her unintended faux pas. "My father was obliged to have Garbo sit next to him. She turned out to be in a very lively and pleasant and talkative mood." After dinner she took her host under the arm and asked for a tour of his garden and greenhouse. In the wee hours of the next morning, Åke

[9]The Garbo letters are sealed until the year 2000. However, a count of sides (pages and envelopes) is contained in the museum's listing of Mercedes' papers. There are 34 pieces dated between 1931 and 1937; 50 items between 1946 and 1950; and an additional 97 from 1952 to 1959.

Bonnier was startled by a phone call from his elderly father. "Thank you, dear Åke, for forcing me to have Greta Garbo to dinner," he said appreciatively. "You see, I have fallen so dreadfully in love with her."

According to Sven Broman, the Wachtmeisters felt that Greta and Stoki were "very attached" to each other, "but they also knew that Garbo found it difficult to make up her mind." If she hadn't yet, it was doubtful that she ever would—at least, to Leopold Stokowski's satisfaction. On July 24, she accompanied him to the train station. When Greta phoned Wilhelm Sörensen to tell him that Stokowski was gone, she was in a nostalgic mood. She asked for his help in setting up a screening of *Gösta Berlings saga*. Hörke and Sören remained outside the theater while Garbo watched the film alone; she emerged from the screening looking emotionally drained.

Later in the evening, they met at the home of Marguerite Wenner-Gren, the wife of Swedish financier and diplomat Axel Wenner-Gren. After an elegant meal, with Mrs. Wenner-Gren feeding partridge to the two Chihuahuas seated in her lap, Greta cajoled her hostess into taking them out on her husband's yacht. At the end of the evening, Mrs. Wenner-Gren gave Sörensen a pair of silver cuff links with a Siamese elephant insignia; Greta received a crystal perfume ampoule. "When we set foot on dry land once again Garbo asked me what I'd been given. I obediently showed her the cuff links. Without a word she thrust the perfume bottle into my hand and said peremptorily: 'All right, let's change!' That's the last I ever saw of those cuff links!"

In August while Stokowski was crossing the Atlantic, Greta joined the Wachtmeister family on a trip to Norway. On the twentieth of September, she applied at the American Embassy in Stockholm for permission to reenter the United States. The visa was granted without the objections anticipated by MGM. By the end of the week, Garbo was on her way to Göteborg. Stoki and his assistant, Reggie Allen, worked diligently to facilitate her return; Allen met the ship in New York, arranging with the Swedish-American line and U.S. customs to board the *Kungsholm* from the cutter sent to meet it.

Garbo's arrival in New York on October 7 generated a new controversy. Some of the media, including the increasingly influential *Life* magazine, suggested that her "sloppy" appearance at the onboard press conference was so distressing that MGM made sure newsreels of the event were suppressed. Surviving footage proves otherwise, with Garbo typically—albeit unglamorously—dressed in a smartly tailored outfit. She was nervous, but animated and intent on giving thoughtful answers. She encountered her most stinging criticism for her straight, shoulder-length, decidedly uncoiffed hair, condemned as "wholly unsuited for wear" by the Coiffure

Guild of New York and the International Master Ladies Hairdressers Association (which just happened to be holding a joint convention that week). Metro publicity would take the unusual step of protecting the fragile image of womanhood by explaining that, while such a severe style was suited to Garbo, women should not attempt this at home.

Following the press conference, Greta gave Reggie Allen "a perfectly enormous number" of baggage tickets. "There were so many bags that I had two officials checking them. One man had opened a case that contained nothing but shoes . . ." he recorded, "suddenly I heard him say, 'Why, this ain't so big!' I turned around and he was holding one of Garbo's shoes in his hand just like Hamlet with the skull in the graveyard scene."[10]

The chase began again when she disembarked from the ship. Despite an offer from Bob Reud for a quiet rooftop apartment with a "wonderful Hungarian woman" to help out, Greta elected to stay at composer Richard Hammond's spacious apartment on West Fifty-fourth Street. Hammond was a frequent theater date, escorting her to several "after dark" parties. Once she allowed herself to relax in this social setting, the composer observed, the real Garbo shone through the manufactured myth. Richard Rodgers met her at one such gathering at the Waldorf-Astoria. She was "exactly the opposite of everything we'd all heard about her," he said. Rodgers played piano while Greta sat alongside, requesting his songs by name. "I played them and she sang along with the other people . . ." As the party wound down, Greta stood at the elevator with Rodgers and company. The door opened and the group piled into the elevator. "I tank you go home now," she said, leaving a new group of admirers with a wink and a smile.

The star couldn't make up her mind about when to return to Hollywood. "You know how she is," Richard Hammond told a mutual friend. "So I said, 'Would you like to come up to the country?' And she said, 'Yes, I'd love it.' So we got a drawing room on the *Merchants Limited* and we went up to Gloucester. Nobody knew where she was. Walter Winchell was guessing all over." By the time she returned to Manhattan a week later, everyone knew where she had been. "GARBO GOES CRUSIN' FINDS IT AIN'T AMUSIN'," the New York *Daily News* heralded readers. She was also discovered lunching at the Hotel Marguery "with two swains"—one of which was Robert Reud.

"I am sending tickets and ask if you would be kind enough to take my trunks over to your house. I hope you have some space left," Greta wrote

---

[10]Interestingly, the stories about Garbo's shoe size increased in direct proportion to reports of her escalating salary. If her talent was not to be denigrated, her feet were "fair game."

Salka from New York on October 19. "I cannot tell you now but I am horribly (cant spell) tired. If I had a reason for staying in New York . . . God, how people can live this way I dont understand. If you have my trunks I can take some things and go right to Stokis place." Strangely, though she planned to have lunch with Cukor, she requested that Salka not tell him where they would meet. "And ask if he will be silent about my coming if it is not in the newspapers. . . . I will wire 'meet Bieler'—that means Pasadena."

Three days later, she finally—reluctantly—boarded a train to California. "Poor Reggie Allen was getting a drawing room on every train out of New York," Hammond recalled. "But she couldn't make up her mind to go." Allen made arrangements for Garbo to bypass Chicago entirely by getting off the *Broadway Limited* in Gary, Indiana, and boarding the *Santa Fe Chief* at Joliet. Stokowski complimented his assistant for a job well done. "I am deeply indebted to you for all the trouble and thought you have given to this," he wrote.

Prior to finding a new rental home on North Amalfi Drive (near Topanga State Park), Greta moved into a guest house on George Cukor's property. She also visited Stoki at his Santa Barbara home. Confusion about her whereabouts helped deflect an overture from director Leni Riefenstahl. Riefenstahl, who claimed to be apolitical but had aligned herself successfully—and cinematically—with the Nazi regime, had hoped to follow up her *Triumph of the Will* in the world's film capital. But her visit to Hollywood made most people nervous, especially after a filmland tour by Mussolini's son the previous year had backfired badly in the press. The horrific news from Germany of the terrifying *Kristallnacht* sealed the director's fate in Hollywood.

Greta and Stoki's romance did not survive the holidays. But the publicity continued. "What poor imaginations publicity men have," Garbo complained. "Their only idea to attract attention is to say that I am going to get married, when there are so many other interesting possibilities in life." Greta's final word on the subject was contained in a May 1939 letter to Hörke Wachtmeister. "My friend will be coming to Sweden soon. Although by the time you get this note at Tistad he may already have been there. I haven't seen him for a long time. He has been staying in New York for the last few months. Perhaps you'll go and hear him—in that case do let me know what it was like. I've never 'seen' him conduct. . . . Us poor moderns (though perhaps it has always been like this) we have to live with so much anxiety inside ourselves but maybe in a couple of million years things will be as they should be . . ."

Among friends, circa 1930: on the left sipping tea is actress Françoise Rosay, Salka Viertel is on Greta's immediate right; Wilhelm Sörensen and André Berley are in the background.

For a time, throwing a medicine ball around an outdoor set or at home was a popular recreation in Hollywood. Greta often had to retrieve hers from the garden.

Sound engineer Gavin Burns adjusts the microphone while Garbo talks with director Clarence Brown. "I remember going to *Anna Christie* and everyone waiting to hear Garbo's voice," Bette Davis recalled later. "Her first talking picture. You just held your breath, praying. Finally, she had her line and there it was—every kind of voice you wanted her to have." (Courtesy Academy of Motion Picture Arts and Sciences)

(Above) In the German language version of *Anna Christie*, Garbo's makeup and costume in the opening scene clearly indicated Anna's previous occupation. (Courtesy Bibliothèque du Film)

With Salka Viertel as the drunken waterfront hag, Marthy. (Courtesy Bibliothèque du Film)

Garbo returns to glamour in her second film of 1930, *Romance*.

One of the few highlights in *Inspiration* (1931) were the scenes conducted on the staircase leading to Robert Montgomery's apartment. Cinematographer William Daniels is seated to the left of the camera; Clarence Brown controls the action from his seat at the center of the platform. (Courtesy Åke Fredriksson)

Greta's "black and white" friend, Mercedes de Acosta. (Courtesy Rosenbach Museum & Library)

(Right) Garbo's playfulness in her early scenes with Clark Gable in *Susan Lenox* helped to offset the dark theme of an abused child who grows up to become a high-priced prostitute, and then gives up everything for the man she loves.

Under the watchful gaze of Bill Daniels and director George Fitzmaurice (next to the camera), Mata Hari meets her Russian aviator, Ramon Novarro.

Since Garbo only interacted with John Barrymore in *Grand Hotel,* MGM's solution for placing her pictorially within the all-star cast was to paste her into the group photo.

(Above) "Garbo still belongs to that moment in cinema when capturing the human face still plunged audiences into the deepest ecstasy, when one literally lost oneself in a human image," essayist Roland Barthes wrote. Here, as the tragically doomed Grusinskaya, she is lost in her own world.

In her *Grand Hotel* hairstyle, Greta poses for Clarence Sinclair Bull in an *As You Desire Me* costume. Due to Greta's desire to leave as soon as possible, a single portrait session was scheduled to accommodate both films.

Avoiding public scrutiny during her 1932/1933 sabbatical.

Garbo wins: After months of lobbying, MGM finally acceded to Garbo's request to cast John Gilbert in *Queen Christina*. Greta was more beautiful than ever and decidedly more confident in her work; time had been less generous with Jack.

(*Above*) *Christina* was Garbo's first opportunity to wear masculine clothing since *The Single Standard*. The scene at the Swedish inn slyly capitalizes on the star's androgynous persona while winking at audiences (who know the "young man's" secret). Greta is pictured here with Gilbert and director Rouben Mamoulian.

Christina ponders her future as queen of Sweden.

Fashion trend-setters believed that only Garbo was capable of pulling off such exotic styles as those featured in *The Painted Veil*, 1934.

In describing Garbo's acting technique, Basil Rathbone would declare that Greta was "the screen's greatest economist. Yet she never economizes to the extent of defeating an emotion." A perfect example of this is the beautifully modulated scene in which Anna Karenina is torn between her love for her son and her love for Vronsky (Fredric March, pictured).

On board the *Kungsholm* on her way back to Sweden in 1935. (Courtesy Åke Fredriksson)

A nature girl at heart: Greta frolics in the snow with the Wachtmeisters. (Courtesy Åke Fredriksson)

Her romantic illusions intact, Greta's express-es her desire for Armand in *Camille* by deli-cately smothering Robert Taylor with kisses —without ever actually touching him with her hands. (Courtesy Academy of Motion Picture Arts and Sciences)

(Right) Cinematographer Hal Rosson was a tem-porary replacement for Bill Daniels during the idyl-lic sequence in the country. (Courtesy Academy of Motion Picture Arts and Sciences)

One of the finest death scenes ever put on film: Garbo as Mar-guerite runs the gamut from resignation to disbelief to excite-ment, agitation, a pathetic plea for help, breathless impatience and, finally, pure joy. She is pictured here with Rex O'Malley and Jesse Ralph.

A light moment with Charles Boyer
on the set of *Conquest*. (Courtesy Culver Pictures)

"Garbo is the hippie of the world," her
costar Leif Erickson offered, "surveying
the scene, never partaking of it, not even
active enough to pass judgment. She
becomes a mirror . . . Garbo's quiet
makes people see themselves in her, and
finally they want to become like her."
(Courtesy Bibliothèque du Film)

A *Ninotchka* rehearsal with costar Melvyn Douglas and director Ernst Lubitsch.

The irrepressible Count d'Algout turns a simple request for directions to the Eiffel Tower into a romantic flirtation . . .

. . . and eventually wins Ninotchka over.

(Below) Clearly uncomfortable, Greta still manages to hit her mark with director George Cukor on the set of *Two-Faced Woman*. (Courtesy Academy of Motion Picture Arts and Sciences)

(Above) At times, she even appeared to be having fun, while cinematographer Joseph Ruttenberg struggled valiantly to keep her from revealing too much in an ill-fitting dress that was not originally designed for her.

Swan song: During what was to be their final photo session together, as Greta gathered her things and got ready to go, Clarence Sinclair Bull asked if he could shoot one more portrait.

Garbo and Leopold Stokowski outside the walls of the Vatican City in Rome, 1938. (Courtesy Svenska Filminstitutet)

(Above) Relaxing with Gayelord Hauser circa 1940.

(Above) With George Schlee (following in his "rear guard" position) in London, 1947. (Courtesy USC/University Archives)

In 1951, Cecil Beaton finally succeeded in getting Greta to visit him in England—and found himself protecting her from the constant vigil of the press. (Courtesy Topham Picturepoints)

"Try to figure out where you've been the happiest," Greta would say. "I'm still attached to California, because I was there for so long. I will never get out of that feeling. But you have to leave Hollywood." (left photo only: Cecil Beaton/Sotheby's London)

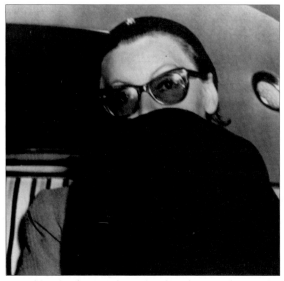

Many times, when confronted with a photographer, Garbo
would shield not her eyes but her mouth—the single feature which betrayed her age. She is pictured here in 1955,
shortly after her fiftieth birthday. (Courtesy USC/Univer-
sity Archives)

Captured by Cecil Beaton's lens. (Cecil Beaton/Sotheby's London)

CHAPTER NINETEEN

Box-Office Poison: Garbo Laughs

"WAKE UP! HOLLYWOOD PRODUCERS," a full-page advertisement in *The Hollywood Reporter* read on May 3, 1938. "Practically all of the major studios are burdened with stars—whose public appeal is negligible—receiving tremendous salaries necessitated by contractual obligations." Having paid out such enormous sums, the studios were obligated "to put these box office deterrents in expensive pictures in the hope that some return on the investment might be had," the ad charged. "Among these players, whose dramatic ability is unquestioned but whose box-office draw is nil, can be numbered Mae West, Edward Arnold, Garbo, Joan Crawford, Katharine Hepburn . . ." Kay Francis and Marlene Dietrich were also pronounced deadly "poison at the box office."[1]

The uncredited author of this controversial advertisement was Harry Brandt, writing on behalf of the Independent Theatre Owners Association. Brandt's purpose had not been to tear down stars, but to put the studios on notice. With movie grosses in a slump, small-town exhibitors resented being forced to take product they didn't want ("prestige" films) in order to get movies they did (Andy Hardy, Charlie Chan, comedies, westerns, adventure pictures). The exhibitors' wake-up call started a public debate just as producers and distributors were getting together to discuss product for the upcoming season. However, the industry rallied in defense of the studios. Independent theater owners would not win their point regarding block booking until the Department of Justice intervened a decade later.

It was the *studios* that took up the standard of "Box-Office Poison" and used it to their advantage at contract time. Paramount had already bought out the remainder of Marlene Dietrich's contract. Katharine Hepburn was now a free agent as well. Much of this deselection process, though painful, was a timely changing of the guard similar to the talkie conversion ten years earlier. This time, however, the consequences were less devastating for the stars involved; there would be no public humiliations. Most of those on the list would find success at new studios—Garbo being the exception.

All of this was allowed to happen, Anita Loos advocated, because there

---

[1] Fred Astaire's name would soon be included in the discussion—with little objection from RKO.

were no Irving Thalbergs to protect a Garbo or a Crawford from the expensive debacles of their recent cinematic efforts. *Anna Karenina, Camille,* and *Conquest* strengthened a doomed romantic image, but did little to reestablish Greta Garbo's reputation at the box office. Even her front-office appeal due to a superior international standing diminished when Loew's/Metro-Goldwyn found itself unable to get its funds out of Germany and Italy.[2]

MGM needed a steady glamour girl to fill the void as Garbo moved into more mature roles. In late 1937, while their Swedish star prepared for another long sabbatical, Metro initiated talks with Dietrich regarding a contract. The studio was also developing a number of potential new stars. Dietrich found work elsewhere; the Garbo replacements would come later.

Garbo would concede with her critics that the tone of her career had become one of seduction and repetition; that her screen image was in serious danger of being enshrouded in celluloid amber. Two projects awaiting her when she returned proposed different solutions to this problem. The story of the Nobel Prize–winning husband-and-wife research team of Pierre and Marie Curie was based the 1936 biography *Madame Curie,* by their daughter, Eve. Though the story was originally purchased for Irene Dunne, Bernie Hyman "moved heaven and earth" to secure the film rights for MGM; Garbo's interest would make the project hers.

After preparing some notes on a treatment, Salka Viertel discovered that Aldous Huxley had been given the script assignment. The novelist was extremely reticent about his ability to write a screenplay for Garbo. Even as he was debating her role, Huxley caught fire with an idea and talked himself into writing the narrative. He envisioned glowing glass tubes in a dark shack, scenes in the Belgian Congo and Russia depicting how radium was used in hospitals. "Now Aldous is taking it all so seriously that I'm afraid he'll suffer horribly if there is a disappointment," his wife, Maria, wrote. "He wants to project the passion of scientific curiosity, and the nobility of such a life . . . The great advantage of having Garbo is that she passionately wants to play that part; she admires Aldous and would do a bit more under his direction . . ."

By the time Greta arrived back in California in late October 1938, several productions at MGM were about to undergo the Hollywood shuffle. It began as George Cukor reluctantly gave up Garbo and *Madame Curie* to

---

[2]American film exchanges received early warning of the escalating problems abroad, but ignored the signs and continued yielding to fascist demands until their bank accounts were frozen and they were thrown out.

direct *Gone With The Wind.* In Cukor's absence, Metro producers pressured her to do a comedy first; everyone was determined that Garbo should laugh. The promise of a top director made her acquiescence a victory for both the studio and star.

Ninotchka had come a long way since its genesis in the mind of Melchior Lengyel. His original story, *Love Is Not So Simple,* played out the corrupting influence of a "capitalistic" romance against the unromantic backdrop of negotiations for the exchange of Russian furs and French machinery. There was little comic relief; the plot wreaked of revenge. In January of 1938, Gottfried Reinhardt had taken over stewardship of the project. Among the writers he brought in to develop the story was Jacques Deval *(Tovarich),* whose contributions included changing the fur deal to the purchase of a French-Afghan coal company, and having Leon follow Ninotchka to Moscow where he is "tricked" into a state marriage in which divorce is accomplished by sending in a postcard.[3]

A fifteen-page outline by Ben Hecht and Charles MacArthur incorporated casting suggestions into its scenario: Ina Claire in a supporting role as the duchess and Cary Grant as her indolent, charming consort, "a boy of the boulevards . . . with an unbroken record of failure as a member of the French government trading company." Production Code administrator Joseph Breen immediately advised Bernie Hyman that he could not approve the story due to the "illicit sex affair" and suggested that the screenwriters fashion a story without the hint of an affair between Garbo and Grant. Such affairs were unsuitable for comedy, the administrator emphasized; sex must be proven to be wrong.

Suppressing the sexual chemistry between two such charismatic performers would have negated the reason for pairing Greta Garbo and Cary Grant in the first place. Garbo did not need to repeat the failing of indifferent teamings in *Anna Karenina* and *Conquest;* she needed to re-create the excitement of her chemistry with Gilbert and Barrymore, or at the very least, Taylor.

Doubtless the hottest independent actor in Hollywood, and one of the few who didn't appear to be intimidated by working opposite strong women, Grant couldn't make a wrong move—in front of the camera. "I was on the set one day when Noël Coward, who was staying at my house, called and asked me to come home right away," the actor recalled. "He said that Garbo was there having tea. She had a film she wanted to discuss making with me. I was very

---

[3]This device, contained in Deval's September 27, 1938, draft, was later employed in the similarly themed *Comrade X* (1940) with Clark Gable as a fast-talking American reporter and Hedy Lamarr as an idealistic Communist trolley conductor. The film was produced by Gottfried Reinhardt.

nervous about meeting her." In fact, he was nearly "out of his mind" after receiving the call, actress Phyllis Brooks said. "He called me and tried to get me to leave work to accompany him to meet Greta Garbo."

But Brooks couldn't go and Grant went alone to the bachelor pad he shared with Randolph Scott on the Santa Monica beach. Garbo was just leaving. "In my nervousness, I thrust out my hand and heard myself saying, 'Oh, I'm so happy you met me,' " Grant said. Unfortunately, previous commitments put an end to the dream screen team.

As a direct result of her "poison" status, Greta signed a new contract with MGM at a considerable (though unpublicized) drop in salary, one-half ($125,000) her former fee. However, she lost none of her privileges regarding director and cast approval. The day after her re-signing, Metro came to terms with the man who would be responsible for shaping *Ninotchka* into a successful motion picture comedy.

Gottfried Reinhardt and company had struggled throughout the fall to find an appropriate comic balance for *Ninotchka*. Conference notes from late October and November with production supervisor Sidney Franklin, writers S. N. Behrman, Claudine West, and Samuel Hoffenstein show a variety of changes in plotting and situations, but very little growth or invention. It was Ernst Lubitsch, with his native German wit, acquired Gallic charm, and fondness for off-beat, ironic Central European comedies, fantasies, and satires, who opened the door to inspiration.

Lubitsch was not an outwardly sophisticated man, but he knew what he liked and his sense of showmanship played to the heart of what Americans expected to see in movies. Garbo's request for his services effectively knocked him out of consideration for the screen adaptation of Clare Boothe Luce's *The Women*. *Ninotchka* became the first production in his new two-picture deal with the studio.[4] He reported for work on February 8, 1939.

It had been over ten years since Lubitsch was first introduced to Garbo. As an actress, she especially admired the ease with which he had transcended the clumsiness of early talkies. "Garbo had a wonderful time chuckling at Lubitsch's subtle wit," Wilhelm Sörensen revealed. She had been so moved by the elegance and charm of *The Love Parade*, his first picture with Maurice Chevalier and Jeanette MacDonald, that she insisted on buying an armful of roses after the movie and taking them to Lubitsch's home.

Three years later, she again showed up unannounced at his doorstep—the scene this time was his beach house and she wanted to introduce him

---

[4] Ironically, the Hollywood shuffle was completed when George Cukor, dismissed from *Gone With The Wind* in February 1939, suddenly became available to take over *The Women*.

to Mercedes de Acosta. "When Lubitsch entered the living room and saw Greta he let out a great yell of joy," Mercedes said. He seized Garbo in his arms and kissed her wildly. "*Mein Gott, Mein Gott,* Greta!" he exclaimed. "Greta, Greta, sit down and never go away." They sat down on the sofa and Lubitsch made an earnest appeal. "Greta, why don't you tell those idiots in your studio to let us do a picture together?" he asked. "*Gott,* how I vould love to direct a picture for you."

Garbo's response was equally direct—but much less positive. "Ernst, you tell them. I am far too tired to have a conversation with any studio executive," she said in a sad voice. Most everyone laughed; Lubitsch shook his head. "What fools they are," he noted of the powers that be.

After several missed opportunities, MGM turned the fantasy into reality for Garbo and Lubitsch. Greta prepared for her comic makeover by retreating to the desert at the beginning of 1939; Ernst Lubitsch focused his attention on the screenplay. Writer Walter Reisch made the first contribution, turning the trade negotiations into a deal concerning the sale of imperial jewelry. The collaboration was expanded to include Charles Brackett and Billy Wilder, and together the writing team reinvented the trio of fumbling Russian negotiators named Ivanoff, Buljanoff, and Kowalski.

It was Lubitsch who—with a recent visit to the Soviet Union still burning in his memory—injected much of the pathos into the story concerning Ninotchka and her comrades in Moscow. "I feel it is wicked that Billy Wilder and Walter Reisch and I are even mentioned in connection with *Ninotchka,*" Charles Brackett insisted; "it was so much Ernst Lubitsch's own baby. He was a director in a creative frenzy at the time, and everything he did was to me wonderful and funny and stimulating. . . . Walter Reisch made a great contribution in the pattern of the picture, and I got Ernst's ideas into English, but I give him the full credit for the picture."

Billy Wilder offered further insight into Lubitsch's work method. "He wasn't just a gagman, he was the best creator of toppers," he stated. "You would come up with a funny bit to end a scene and he would create a better one. . . . He would look at our stuff and go, 'Ho-ho, very good,' and scratch out the next line. He'd read a bit more, go 'Ho-ho,' and scratch out another line." Alternating between various drafts, Lubitsch "purified" the script down to its finest comic moments.

Joseph Breen, who received an incomplete draft of *Ninotchka* in May, pronounced the story "acceptable under the provisions of the Production Code"—provided that "the greatest possible care" be used to delineate the relationship between Leon and the Grand Duchess Swana (there should be no sex implied); Ninotchka's acknowledgment of a simple biological need common to all men; and, most importantly, her drunk scene.

Garbo offered one further objection: she thought one of Ninotchka's early speeches crude and unnecessary. "The class system is crumbling," she tells her comrades. "How can a civilization survive which is still running trains with first, second and third class? The first class compartment is upholstered with the finest springs and covered with velvet. In the second class they have leather. In the third class the people have to sit on hard wooden benches. There must be a change . . . a change from the bottom up!"

In fact, Greta felt so strongly about this speech, as well as her ability to do the subsequent drunk scene in front of dozens of extras, that she drove to MGM to meet with Lubitsch privately. The director got into the passenger seat of her car and discussed the story with her for two hours. The drunk scene and its follow-up represent the moment when Leon proves that his affection for Nina Ivanova Yakushova is no longer an act. Although she had acted intoxicated in *As You Desire Me*, those scenes had a dramatic twist; *Ninotchka* required a lighthearted approach that intimidated her. As a compromise, Lubitsch promised to postpone the scene as long as possible—but he was unable to convince Greta about making changes in her speech "from the bottom up"; after several alternatives proved unworkable, Lubitsch agreed to cut the objectionable line.

"Is she back yet?" would-be Garbo-watchers inquired at the studio. The actress's return to MGM after an absence of a year and a half was warmly anticipated by coworkers as well as new players on the lot. By the end of spring, the answer was yes; she was back. Garbo reported to the studio for costume fittings, which were followed by a ten-day rehearsal schedule. According to Hedda Hopper, Hedy Lamarr (disguised as a wardrobe mistress) and hairstylist Sydney Guilaroff (who tried to pass as an electrician) joined the list of unrepentant gate-crashers when they tried to sneak in on her fittings with Adrian.

"Dear Lady," Greta wrote Hörke Wachtmeister, "My studio is starting to collapse because everything is in chaos." She admitted that she should have started work the previous November "but nothing gets finished," and she felt guilty about spending her time in such an unproductive way. "How is Yorken's mother?" she continued. "I think about her sometimes too and wonder whether she looked up that doctor in Göteborg I told her about. As for me personally, I take pills as well, though under protest. . . . I have so many wonderful memories of Tistad. . . . Dear Hörke, do write me and tell me about everything, about the trees and the water and the animals and Larsson[5] and what you've got in the cellars and in the apple shed."

[5]Tistad's handyman, Ernst Larsson.

If she was taking medication for insomnia or depression, as she alluded to in her letter to Countess Wachtmeister, Greta might take solace in Robert Reud's forthcoming astrological report. "AM HAPPY TO SAY THAT THE TENSION WHICH PERHAPS HAS EXISTED RECENTLY IN YOUR STARS WILL BE GREATLY LESSENED AFTER MAY TWELFTH," he predicted, "AND THE MONTHS OF JULY, AUGUST, AND SEPTEMBER WILL BE VERY WONDERFUL IN MANY WAYS IN YOUR LIFE."

Having completed an acting assignment opposite Norma Shearer in the *outré* sophisticated comedy *Idiot's Delight* (once mentioned for Garbo as well), Clark Gable was briefly considered for the role of Count Leon d'Algout, *Ninotchka's* rakish bon vivant-turned-negotiator. *Gone With The Wind* would take him off the employment list for the year. William Powell came very close to signing but wound up chasing another *Thin Man* instead. Finally, Lubitsch suggested an actor he had worked with on one of his last films at Paramount: Greta's former costar in *As You Desire Me*, Melvyn Douglas.

Now Garbo was ready to laugh.

Principal photography commenced on May 31 under the watchful eye of William Daniels. It was to be Greta's final turn in front of his camera. It was also her last fully realized collaboration with Adrian—and one of their best efforts. Freed of the oppressive costuming of her most recent films, Garbo would shine in the simple lines of his new styles, beginning with Ninotchka's severe, almost militaristic garments and graduating to a lighter, freer wardrobe as the story progressed.

Conversely, Ernst Lubitsch got more formal, donning his suit jacket to pay his respects each morning before filming began and at the end of the day to wish his star a good evening. Though Garbo may have been the most inhibited actor he had ever worked with, she was not unreasonable. She depended heavily on Lubitsch's guidance and support. If she became agitated about an upcoming scene, it was up to him to help her relax and confront whatever fears she might have: first, by listening; second, by making tactful suggestions. "Now you go away and think it over," he would tell her, and she obeyed. "She would go into a corner, all by herself, and brood," Lubitsch said. "Then she would do the scene again."

It took a little time for Garbo to adjust to her director's gregarious style. Lubitsch was a man of enormous energy. But he was an easy man to like— exceedingly clever, his assistant Joseph Newman said, and "the actors all loved him." He had "a very human quality about him. He was the type of man that became your friend after you met him once." Looking back on the experience, Greta confessed that she thought it strange she got mixed up in such a business. "I remember, one morning, going in and seeing

[Lubitsch], cigar in mouth, with my big leading man, running through a scene on the sofa that I was to do. He was being so funny! But underneath he was a vulgar little man, and he made such a noise on the set, always shouting. One day I said to him in German: 'Please, when you speak to me, please speak more softly,' and he was so surprised that from then on, whenever he looked at me, he became quieter.' "

Patience yielded a reward. In spite of tremendous insecurities, Garbo could be a surprisingly trusting actress at times; her best performances were not created in a vacuum. "I love to work with her," Lubitsch told a reporter for the *New York Post*. "She's got no phoniness, no star allures. She is the only star I ever worked with I did not have to drag away from the mirror."

As the end neared, Ernst Lubitsch admitted there had been one thing that worried him. "I wondered if she could laugh, because I didn't have a finish if she didn't have a laugh," he explained to Garson Kanin. "She had the most beautiful smile. What am I saying? She had a whole *collection* of smiles. . . . Warm, motherly, friendly, polite, amused, sexy, mysterious. Beautiful smiles. But a smile is not a laugh." When they first began to talk about *Ninotchka*, Lubitsch asked her if she could laugh. He gave her time to think about it and when Greta came back the next day, she gave him a "beautiful" laugh.

However, according to Melvyn Douglas, when they filmed the scene in question, Garbo acted the moment but did not give it a voice. "In spite of *Ninotchka*'s billing as the film in which 'Garbo laughs,' she was unable to articulate so much as a titter during the shooting of the restaurant scene. I never learned whether the laughter, which must have been added in the dubbing room, was Garbo or not."[6]

Because American comedy has its own cadence and English was not Greta's native language, Melvyn Douglas believed that Garbo wasn't able to pick out "the most important phrases in a speech or color individual words for subtle shades of meaning"; she did not underline the same words most American actors learn to. Paradoxically, this was exactly what made her line readings so natural as a dramatic actress. She reproduced "an extraordinary comic effect in *Ninotchka*," Douglas acknowledged, "not so much because of any comic sense she may have had as through the genius of the director, Ernst Lubitsch; he knew just how to make use of the stolid Scandinavian in her."

Her love scenes left them all astonished. "In the scene in *Ninotchka* in

---

[6]A careful analysis of the scene at Pere Mathieu reveals that it probably was not—or, at the very least, higher-pitched laughter was added to her largely silent guffaws. Consider the realistic, almost silent laughter in *Queen Christina* (the scene with the carriage in the snow) and *Camille* (with Henry Daniell at the piano).

which we come back to the hotel after drinking champagne and she behaves like a girl in love, she achieved a quality and feeling that were literally breathtaking," Douglas commented. "She was utterly superb." As promised, Lubitsch delayed the scene as long as he could. Five weeks into production, the sequence was rehearsed and shot. Crew members thought Garbo's stamina, as she gamely executed numbing pratfalls take after take, especially admirable.

Ernst Lubitsch became especially alarmed when Garbo's weight plunged below 125 pounds. According to the director, she was on a strict diet of raw carrots and cabbage when *Ninotchka* started. "I convinced her that her screwy diet was no good," he said. " 'Roses I got to have in your cheeks!' I told her. 'One nice thick juicy steak is more important to this picture than all the dialogue!' " She finally took his advice and returned to work a different girl, Lubitsch remarked. "Nice pink cheeks! Nice bright eyes! Beautiful!"

It seems that advice had come from another corner, as well. Vegetables, fruit juices, and protein-rich health foods were the cornerstone of Gayelord Hauser's philosophy of how to "Eat and Grow Beautiful." The popular diet guru wrote in his *Treasury of Secrets* that Garbo had heard all about him from Leopold Stokowski and asked if she could see him. Hauser invited her to the home atop Coldwater Canyon that he shared with his partner, Frey Brown. She arrived alone, Hauser remembered, "a vision of breath-taking beauty, with her long hair and fresh golden complexion. . . . She was at that time following a diet consisting mainly of boiled vegetables and thou-shalt-nots. In spite of her radiant beauty, this diet had had a marked effect on her vitality; she was suffering from overtiredness and insomnia, and was in danger of serious anemia."

The dietitian fed her wild rice and nut burgers, with broiled grapefruit (topped with blackstrap molasses) for dessert. "I made it my task to wean her away from strict vegetarianism, and coax her back to intelligent eating—no easy chore with a woman who has a will of steel," he stated. "Finally she consented to try my suggestions." She was encouraged to continue eating vegetables but to fortify them with bits of protein: ham, chicken, cottage cheese, wheat germ.

This high-vitality program was the primary reason for her newfound energy during the making of *Ninotchka*. Dr. Benjamin Gayelord Hauser—"Doctor" being a title he assumed rather than earned—would become a major force in Garbo's life.

Ina Claire, the woman John Gilbert had married on the rebound in 1929, shared Greta's interest in diet, health, and Bieler's broth. To the amazement of some, both women were not only cordial during production, but remained friendly and even met occasionally afterward. Surprisingly, it was Claire who did not like talking about Jack. A mutual friend, interior decorator Billy Baldwin, recalled one such occasion; Garbo was amused by the stories about Jack, Gilbert's third wife was not. "I could see that little foot of hers tapping on the floor," Baldwin noted, "and I can still hear that strong little voice saying to Garbo, 'Shut up, you damned fool. I married him!' " That sense of rivalry, however cordial, would give their verbal sparring the desirable edge on screen.

Production wrapped on July 28. Less than one month later, a rough cut of the film was readied for the important preview process. At first, it appeared that the experiment had failed. "That howl of discontent could be heard all the way from Pomona after the preview of *Ninotchka*, teaming Garbo, who's never done comedy, with our own Ina Claire," Hedda Hopper wrote on the twenty-fifth of August, ". . . and unless the film is slashed and parts redone Ina steals it." The film would be sent back to Lubitsch and editor Gene Ruggiero for adjustment.

Aldous Huxley arrived at Greta Garbo's house late one afternoon and found it "as silent as the grave. There was absolutely no indication that it might be occupied," he told his friend, Basil Rathbone. Huxley was about to leave when the door opened and he was ushered into the living room by a servant. The room "was a large, dark, monastic type of room sparsely furnished, with little indication that the sun was shining brightly outside. On a very large sofa sat a very small woman, a small but most exquisite woman both in features and figure and in the manner of her dress. . . . She introduced herself as Mercedes de Acosta. I sat opposite her and we maintained a polite conversation until Miss Garbo entered the room. She was dressed like a boy, a very beautiful boy I grant you, but I was somewhat startled by the transformation."

Greta told Huxley that she wanted him to write about St. Francis of Assisi—and that she intended to play the sainted Jesuit on screen. How serious she was about this request is debatable. There certainly was a tug of war between the women of history Salka guided her toward and Mercedes' vision of Garbo playing venerated saints, particularly Joan of Arc and St. Brigitte, Sweden's only Catholic saint. Years later, the subject of a film about St. Francis resurfaced in a conversation between Greta and director Jean Renoir. The introduction of such an extraordinary concept confused Renoir, who envisioned Garbo in more romantically idealized roles. "What was she talking about?" an elderly but still perplexed Renoir asked Salka repeatedly at a meeting toward the end of his life. Viertel avoided giving him a direct answer, but confided to a friend that it had been Garbo's way of ending an awkward conversation—and thus the project.

Given the fragmented history of projects like *Madame Curie*, Salka spoke from experience. In August of 1939, she sailed for Europe, apparently unmindful of what was about to happen, while MGM, in a rather odd choice, quietly assigned F. Scott Fitzgerald to the story.

Within a few short weeks the script would become historically irrelevant. On September 1, Germany invaded Poland. Salka was in Paris and did everything she could to get her family out of Eastern Europe before catching one of the last boats to America. At the same time, MGM made preparations to get the Gustafson family out of Sweden. The urgency of this mission was vividly illustrated two days later when Britain declared war on Germany and the RNS *Athenia* was struck by a torpedo from a German U-boat two hundred miles off the coast of Ireland. Among the United States–bound passengers were Ernst Lubitsch's infant daughter, Nicola, accompanied by her nurse; thankfully, both survived.[7]

The outbreak of another war in Europe motivated *Ninotchka*'s director to add a whimsical preface to the film regarding "those wonderful days when a siren was a brunette and not an alarm and, if a Frenchman turned out the light, it was not for an air raid." The changing perception of Russia after it aligned itself with Nazi Germany concerned MGM even more. A second preview was held in September at a Long Beach theater and attended by Lubitsch, Brackett, Wilder, Reisch, several studio executives—and Garbo. According to an MGM publicist, while her handlers waited for Greta in the theater lobby, the star of the show patiently stood in the ticket line, surrounded by a happy group of sailors, before she was discovered by a theater employee and escorted to her reserved seat. "She was *so* excited," Lubitsch reported. "When people started to laugh, it was a most amazing thing! She looked around like she heard thunder claps!"

The director too had been nervous. He "swooped down" and took the preview cards before anyone else had a chance to look at them, reading them in the privacy of his limousine on the way back to the studio. "He had this very serious expression as he was reading, and you could tell that it was pretty positive," Billy Wilder recalled. "Well, he gets to this one card and he just stares at it for a while and then he breaks into this howl of laughter. He was rocking back and forth on the seat and pounding it with one hand. We were looking at each other and wondering what the hell was so funny. Finally, he

---

[7]One of the heroes of the day was Axel Wenner-Gren, whose 330-foot yacht, the *Southern Cross*, was conveniently within range of the *Athenia* when it was torpedoed. The Swedish industrialist and his crew rescued more than two hundred survivors.

hands me the card and this is what it said: 'Great picture. Funniest film I ever saw. I laughed so hard, I peed in my girlfriend's hand.' "

After testing a number of different titles—from *Intrigue in Paris* to *A Foreign Affair*—MGM settled on *Ninotchka*. "If you can't pronounce it, sneeze it," one columnist jested. Metro's advertising and publicity departments were less concerned with moviegoers being able to pronounce the title of the picture than with getting people into theaters. To that end, they orchestrated an entire campaign around another catchy slogan from Frank Whitbeck: "Garbo Laughs." The tag line would be used prominently in all advertising—often in larger print than the film's title.

Success at last. *Ninotchka*'s world premiere took place on October 6 at the Chinese Theatre in Hollywood. With this film, the screen gets a new Garbo, *The Hollywood Reporter* proclaimed. Warm, human, beautiful—"a Garbo whose grosses will hit a higher mark in this domestic market than she has ever registered in the last seven or eight years."

As *Ninotchka* made its debut in theaters from coast to coast, the movie was declared a triumph for all concerned. Audiences were reportedly laughing so hard, there were complaints from patrons who couldn't hear the dialogue. "[*Ninotchka*] finds the screen's austere first lady of drama playing a dead-pan comedy with the assurance of a Buster Keaton," Frank S. Nugent wrote in *The New York Times*. "It must be monotonous, this superb rightness of Garbo's playing. We almost wish she would handle a scene badly once in a while just to provide us with an opportunity to show we are not a member of a fan club. But she remains infallible . . ."

Final affirmation was contained in a letter written by the managing director of Radio City Music Hall to Joseph Breen. The film had followed the year's biggest hit, *Mr. Smith Goes to Washington*, into the Music Hall. After playing to an astounding 426,890 people, *Ninotchka* closed out its third week at the 6,000-seat theater with a total gross of $306,441. "We could easily have run the picture another week or two, maybe three. There did not seem to be any let-up," reported W. G. Van Schmus. The manager noted that one of the most interesting phenomena was the amount of applause Garbo received when her name appeared on screen and, seventeen minutes later, at her entrance in the film.

All of this fuss confirmed what Greta's friends had always known: that Garbo had a marvelous sense of humor. Couldn't you see how funny she was? Lubitsch asked Garson Kanin. How she would make quirky, insightful comments about people she had known? The director shared with Kanin the memory of a visit Greta and Gayelord Hauser paid him. As they walked the grounds, "for some reason, she started to tell me about her affair with Stokowski, about traveling with him . . . [and] how Stokowski would try to play the idea of wanting to hide from the crowd, and then becoming furious when no one recognized him . . . She was funny [but] she was light, light always, and for comedy, nothing matters more."

Ninotchka yielded Garbo a fourth (regrettably, final) Oscar nomination.[8] It also vaulted her to the top of the female contingent at MGM, returning her to the profit category with domestic billings of $1.187 million and another $1.092 million from foreign sales.[9] As expected, the picture was banned in many Communist countries—a minor point since it received limited European exposure due to the war. In Mexico, *Ninotchka* was passed by the censor but opposed by labor unions, which successfully suppressed its exhibition in 1940. Even more surprising, it was rejected by French censors as late as 1947.

It should have been a time for celebration, but Greta was filled with apprehension. "I was just on the point of leaving for home when the war broke out," she wrote Hörke Wachtmeister. Although the United States was not yet in the war, MGM vigorously opposed employees making the Atlantic crossing. Greta's family was reluctant to make the journey—but afraid not to. In the meantime, Garbo had no alternative but to pray for better news. "The whole time I believed it would quiet down again, but now I have my doubts," she admitted to Hörke.

True to their word, Metro-Goldwyn-Mayer threw its corporate resources behind getting the Gustafson family out of harm's way. On October 24, Anna Lovisa, Sven, Peg, and Ann-Marguerite Gustafson set forth from Oslo on the Norwegian steamer *Stavangerfjord;* also aboard were Einar Nerman and his family. They arrived safely—and happily—in New York City on the third of November. Bernie Hyman ("Mr. Heineman" on the Passenger Manifest) vouched for the family with U.S. Immigration. The family flew straight to California (another luxury that MGM had not permitted Garbo, since they considered planes too dangerous). Greta had purchased a home in Inglewood under her mother's name. It was a short-term residence. When L.A. didn't work out for them, Sven and his family moved to Tucson, Arizona, where they

---

[8]Though produced during Hollywood's "golden year" 1939, *Ninotchka* still received nominations for Best Picture, Best Original Story, and Best Screenplay as well. With the exception of Original Story, *Gone With The Wind* dominated each of these categories.

[9]Yet, according to studio records, the film's profit before a series of reissues in the late 1940s and early 1950s was a modest $138,000.

remained through the spring of 1940. Never completely satisfied with the climate due to health concerns, the Gustafsons moved around more than their famous relative, settling briefly in Montecito, California (near Santa Barbara), before wandering back to the East Coast to live in Manchester, Vermont, then Bronxville, New York.

As MGM began its search for new romantic comedies to follow *Ninotchka,* Greta was looking into her future as well. "I still don't know what I am going to do about filming," she confided to a friend. "I find working more difficult than ever. I don't know why that's so, but I am so embarrassed when I'm in the studio."

Elsa Maxwell, the doyenne of society columnists, described attending a party Cole Porter had arranged in honor of newlyweds Clark Gable and Carole Lombard. "Garbo was uncommunicative, as usual, and no one noticed that she slipped out of the room after dinner," said Maxwell. "I went to the powder room, opened the door, and stood there transfixed. Garbo was staring so intently in the mirror that she did not hear me enter. I have no idea how long she had been studying her reflection, but she shuddered suddenly and buried her head in her arms. Only she could have found a flaw in that exquisite face. . . . Garbo was thirty-five [actually just shy of thirty-four], and all she could see were middle-aged roles in her future."

But the fear of aging wasn't the only thing that could have inspired such a reflective mood in Garbo. With her family on the West Coast, her private life had turned on its end—as had her professional life. Even a woman lacking in an actress's traditional vanity would have been aware that, after thirty, age was a factor to be considered *because* it mattered to others. Most producers believed that audiences preferred young faces on the screen. Stars remained stars as long as the camera was kind and audiences continued to "vote" for them.

The appearance of Gayelord Hauser on the scene could not have been more needed or opportune. Ten years Garbo's senior, the tall, solid, always immaculately dressed Hauser had emigrated to the United States from Germany when he was sixteen years old. Two years later, he became afflicted with tuberculosis of the hip. After traditional medicine had been unsuccessful in easing his pain, Hauser followed the advice of a naturopathic doctor and checked into a decidedly unorthodox clinic in Europe, where he learned the value of special diets, herbal teas, and "living" foods rich in vitamins and minerals to combat disease.

Once back in the States, the fully recovered, now healthy and robust young man launched into a personal study of nutrition and natural sciences. He opened one of the first health food stores in Chicago and, at the suggestion of a business student named Frey Brown, bought the Milwaukee company that produced many of the products and supplements he sold.[10] The self-styled nutritionist billed himself as Dr. Hauser and began lecturing on diet across the country, attracting a heavily female audience from upper-class communities. Celebrities followed society, and Hauser soon had a devoted clientele from Palm Beach to Hollywood.

As Garbo's advisor and friend, Hauser assumed custody of her physical as well as spiritual well-being, reintroducing her to foods that had been lacking in her diet, forbidding her barbiturates to sleep, and ceremoniously banning "complacency and routine" from her life. Greta was a frequent visitor to his Palm Springs home. "That skinny Swedish actress and her fancy boyfriend are always running around naked in their backyard," a neighbor complained. Hauser even managed to drag her to parties she had no interest in attending, insisting that her melancholia was simply the result of being out of the mainstream for too long. She responded in kind, declaring herself his most "ardent admirer, 'protector' and friend—most loving friend."

Hauser was the conduit through which Garbo now said yes or, more likely, no. It was through him that Mercedes attempted to reconnect with Greta in the late fall of 1939. "Life has been rather hectic, working constantly. The lady went through one of her 'depression weeks,' and hasn't been able to do a thing, which may explain why she has not called you again," he explained in a letter dated November 9. "I hope that by the time you receive this she has gotten in touch with you. Do take my advice and not write to her at her address, as that is one of her 'pet peeves.' "

Small wonder that insiders thought that Greta and Gayelord, despite the complications of prior relationships, might be a match. The Gustafsons had arrived in California amid a flurry of rumors regarding Garbo's impending marriage to the affable nutritionist. "But as usual nothing happens," she assured Hörke Wachtmeister. "I remain a 'maid.' "

Garbo once expressed a desire "to travel to India and become wise." She settled for a picnic in Tujunga Canyon, which Anita Loos later described as a fractured version of *Alice in Wonderland*. There was the Hindu holy man Krishnamurti, with his Indian assistants, all elegantly dressed in saris and carrying an assortment of pots and pans to cook their brown rice and vegetables; the tall, lean Aldous Huxley, with his strangely vacant eyes (due to near blindness) and shock of unruly hair; his equally dramatic looking wife,

---

[10]Among these, an herbal substitute for salt he called "Spike" (still a best-seller for Modern Foods).

Maria; poet and philosopher Bertrand Russell, dressed like "a naughty pixie on a spree . . ." And then there was the Hollywood contingent: Anita Loos, the world's smallest former flapper; Garbo, attired in men's trousers, an old battered hat, and carrying bunches of carrots slung over her belt; Charlie Chaplin, in a Mexican peasant-style outfit, followed by his paramour, Paulette Goddard, who carried the champagne and caviar. Compared to this odd assembly, writer Christopher Isherwood and the Viertels must have appeared almost "normal."

The party eschewed the public picnic areas and found a nice spot near a stream. After eating, they crawled under a chain link fence and wandered on to private property. "Doesn't anybody in this gang know how to read?" an exasperated forest ranger asked, sternly pointing to the "No Trespassing" sign. Berthold Viertel tried to introduce the illustrious members of his party, but the ranger was unimpressed, citing him instead for smoking. "I've seen these stars in the movies and none of them belong in this outfit," he charged. The circus meekly moved on.[11]

Neither self-discovery nor her recent enlightenment concerning diet and health had quieted Greta Garbo's inner anxiety about her life, her family, or her work. As the year drew to a close, she began seeing psychologist Eric Drimmer for "relief from nervous tension." Drimmer, a fellow Swede, was specifically hired to work with MGM players. (Clark Gable, Robert Taylor, and Mickey Rooney were among his regular clientele.) "As I became familiar with her problems, I grew increasingly convinced that Greta Garbo suffered from a shyness *vis-à-vis* the world around her that bordered on the pathological," the doctor remarked. "During our many long conversations, I also came to realize that the first step toward a change for the better in her health had to come from within herself. She had to reveal openly her fear, not hide behind it or call it something else. . . . It would be only then, I said, that she would be able to live like a normal person."

Greta told the psychologist that she occasionally attended lectures given by an Indian swami at a temple in the Verdugo hills above Glendale. "She was naturally drawn to prophets—genuine and otherwise," Christopher Isherwood confirmed. Dr. Drimmer thought of her as a serious student of Eastern religion who "spent a great deal of time with me talking

---

[11]On another occasion, Garbo convinced a group of friends to search for a certain spring on the top of a hill overlooking the desert. She had heard it had medicinal waters. After a long trek, they discovered the "spring" to be an iron pipe sticking up out of the ground with a faucet attached. "Underneath the faucet was a battered old tin bathtub," Anita Loos recorded. "But, alas, in the bathtub lazing away was a bewhiskered tramp."

about Indian and Yogi philosophy. More than anything else," he said, "she wants to know the secret of life." The fact that Greta was looking for answers in unusual places was undeniable; she consulted with at least one astrologer, a psychic, and a fortune-teller. It was equally hard to deny that she wanted to learn the meaning of life in one easy lesson, Isherwood observed—"before her butterfly attention wandered away again."

The Virgo astrological profile is a virtual blueprint of Greta Garbo's personality: reserved, modest, practical, discriminating, devoted, loyal, highstrung. According to those who study the stars, outwardly the quintessential Virgo woman may appear serene and remote—but she keeps her passions under tight rein while dark emotions surge underneath. Emotions represent the unpredictable, the unknown. To observe that before she enters into a long-term relationship, such a woman is careful to take note of "where the exit doors are" would be an uncanny characterization of the private Greta Garbo. She knew where all the emergency exits were—and had invented a few of her own.

CHAPTER TWENTY

A Celluloid Grave

In December of 1939, after being stung by criticism for not demonstrating her support earlier, Greta made a $5,000 donation to the Finnish Relief Fund. Although Sweden had proclaimed its neutrality in the European conflict, history and practicality demanded that they back up their Finnish neighbors in their struggle against unprovoked Soviet aggression. Sweden sent arms as well as food, and needed money for both. As one of Scandinavia's most prosperous exports, Garbo still worried that she really hadn't done her "bit" for Finland, the beloved homeland of Mauritz Stiller.

It had been fourteen years since she first came to Hollywood. During this time, Greta had managed to convince everyone—including herself—that acting so consumed her, she was unable to deal with anything that might distract her while working. "People go like mad in California," she would say, "up early, out late, going like mad, even if they don't know what they're doing." The energy required to sustain such an intensity in front of the camera left Garbo totally depleted at the end of the day; Hollywood parties were definitely not on the schedule. "There are always dinners and parties at people's houses," she later told Ray Daum. "To mingle with the world, that can be lovely. But I don't seem to be like normal people . . ."

For the first time in years, someone challenged her to partake in a more active, stabilizing personal life. As part of her coming out, in January Greta went with Gayelord Hauser to New York, where she was seen dining with him at Manhattan's posh nightspot "21", attending a gallery preview at the Museum of Modern Art, and walking unbothered through city streets. Privately, the woman who never dwelled upon her image in the mirror made her first visit to cosmetologist Dr. Erno Laszlo, "the Svengali of the Skin," at his Fifth Avenue salon.

Unbeknownst to most everyone, while she was back east, Greta missed out on an opportunity to work with Bette Davis on *All This and Heaven Too* at Warner Bros. According to producer David Lewis, Davis had suggested switching roles and playing the Countess to Garbo's lead as the long-suffering governess, Henriette. "Although an interesting idea, I knew it would never happen," Lewis said. "I recalled for Bette that Garbo had once complained to me about working with Freddie Bartholomew, whom she referred to as 'a monster,' on *Anna Karenina*. She swore she would never play against another child again . . . I also knew the superstitious Garbo wouldn't touch any picture not made on the MGM lot . . ."

At the moment, she wasn't contemplating *any* motion pictures; she was looking for refuge. During the first week of February, she drove south along the eastern seaboard accompanied by Gayelord Hauser and Frey Brown. Their destination was the Hotel Whitehall in Palm Beach. On the seventeenth, the threesome flew from Miami to the Bahamian capital of Nassau, where they boarded Axel Wenner-Gren's yacht, the *Southern Cross.* Their party was temporarily detained when customs officials discovered that Hauser's papers identified him as German, prompting a demand for proof that he was a naturalized American citizen.

It was well-known that Wenner-Gren enjoyed mingling with celebrities and high society; the Duke and Duchess of Windsor were two of his most recent conquests. However, according to an undisclosed source at the FBI, he was also suspected of including arms and munitions dealers on his passenger list. Wenner-Gren had been one of the "amateur diplomats" who tried so desperately to negotiate a peaceful alternative to war by placating the Nazis; instead, he slowly—and painfully—discovered how brilliantly he had been manipulated by them. Now he wandered between countries, unofficially accused by both British and American intelligence organizations of collaborating with the Germans. How much of this Greta knew in February of 1940 as the *Southern Cross* sailed through the West Indies is unclear. In a letter to Hörke Wachtmeister, she appeared to see only the poignant longing for home of a fellow traveler. "They certainly feel bitter at Sweden," she wrote. "But I've no idea what happened so I can't judge."

News of Garbo's surprise cruise resurrected the usual wedding rumors. Ignoring the fact that Hauser's "constant companion" was also present, Hollywood gossip suggested that the nutritionist planned to "hijack" the elusive Swede in a valiant effort to nudge her toward marriage. In spite of information from tipsters that Hauser himself was responsible for the leak, Greta's "beau" continued to deny any such marital scheming. What Garbo needed—and valued—was his friendship.

The movie star and her consorts returned to Miami on February 27. A few days later, Greta was on her way back to Hollywood—there was nowhere else to go. "The family is living here only a day's journey away. Peg is having a lot of trouble with her joints and my brother and Mum want to go home," she wrote Hörke. "I've seen the Nermans a couple of times and they're finding things difficult as well. . . . If peace comes, what I most want is to go home and not to make another film. I don't even want to think about it."

She filled her time with meaningless pursuits, lunching at the Sycamore Tearoom in Bel Air or dining at the Cock 'n Bull, a private restaurant near her home. Even these activities were open to criticism. An evening out at Dave Chasen's new eatery earned her some harsh words for failing to acknowledge Ernst Lubitsch and Clarence Brown at nearby tables. In Palm Springs, she attended a charity circus with Frey Brown and socialite Mona Harrison Williams ("one of the world's ten best-dressed women") and made the columns because they reportedly tried to sneak a peak for free. Garbo was on view a few days later at Ciro's, the popular Sunset Strip nightclub, with Hauser, Brown, Mona Harrison Williams, and Greek shipping magnate, Andre Embiricos.

The unthinkable happened on April 9, 1940, when Germany invaded Denmark and bombed neighboring Oslo. Sweden hurriedly mobilized its modest forces. Denmark was overrun in a day, but Norway courageously—though ultimately unsuccessfully—resisted a similar invading force. Perilously short on supplies due to its recent support of the Finns and cut off from its allies to the west by the German advance, Sweden elected to re-declare its neutrality and, in doing so, reluctantly declined to support its occupied neighbors. In a controversial, not easily forgotten decision, they banned the shipment of arms and supplies to Norway—but later allowed the Nazis to transport troops to Norwegian locations via Swedish rail. Though there were distinct advantages in having Sweden remain neutral—and unoccupied—many Norwegians never forgot this capitulation.

As wartime censorship descended upon them, Greta thanked Hörke for keeping her informed about what was going on in Sweden. "I read the papers for news, but not everything they print is true." It had been months since she last set foot on the Metro lot, she stated. She remained a restless wanderer, "still lazy or looking for peace within."

The escalation of the war in Europe affected Greta tremendously. Like thousands of expatriates, she was isolated from her homeland in a way she had never been before. By May, in order to protect her status in the United States, MGM attorneys sought to obtain the proper papers in her first step toward citizenship; she signed a preliminary Declaration of Intention form on June 10. That same day, she joined a group of employees gathered around a radio in Gottfried Reinhardt's office to listen to President Roosevelt condemn Italy's invasion of France. "Victor Saville, Sidney Franklin and Walter Reisch were present," noted one source. "Suddenly Garbo walked in; the men rose but she said, 'Please, sit down. I just want to listen to the broadcast.' When the speech was over, Garbo burst into tears."

According to Charles Higham, approximately one month later she was initiated into the world of espionage. "On July 16, Axel Wenner-Gren, now under the gravest suspicion of Nazi sympathies, arrived in Los Angeles aboard the *Southern Cross* with his wife and sister-in-law," Higham stated. "Garbo met them at the docks and took them with her in her Buick sedan, Wenner-Gren sitting in front with the driver, FBI agent Frank Angell following them, to Paramount Studios. . . . She was keeping an eye on Wenner-Gren, as she had on the previous yacht voyage, looking for indications of admiration for Hitler."

It is true that Garbo met with the Wenner-Grens several times during their visit to Los Angeles. However, any conclusion drawn from this circumstance would be highly speculative. According to Leif Leifland, formerly Sweden's ambassador to Great Britain and author of a book on the blacklisting of Axel Wenner-Gren, the industrialist knew that he was under investigation by the FBI and British Secret Service. Leifland believes that Wenner-Gren "wasn't intelligent enough to be a good spy. He was a simple businessman who made the mistake of trying to mediate between Germany and Great Britain."

The idea that Greta Garbo—an actress who rarely, if ever, involved herself in political discussions—would consent to share information about a friend or acquaintance with an unnamed intelligence network is doubtful as well. Contrary to Higham's account, Garbo did not sever relations with the Wenner-Grens at this time. She would meet with the couple one more time in Los Angeles and again in New York.

A far more revealing alliance was made during this period, as indicated in a Hedda Hopper column of July 29, when it was reported that Greta had recently entertained New York fashion designer Valentina and her husband, George Schlee. This acquaintance soon evolved into an important friendship that was vigorously pursued by all parties.

"My life is much the same as usual, mostly on my own. Sometimes not on my own. Very rarely the latter," Greta wrote Hörke Wachtmeister. "I see my family once a week and the Nermans once a month, if that. Quiet flows the river and yet is never still."

The momentum of the river of public opinion that flowed through Washington, D.C., was neither quiet nor still. A congressional committee had been established to expose unattractive foreign elements and "un-American" activities. Now, an Alien Immigration Law required all alien residents—including celebrated ones—to register with the Immigration and Naturalization Service. Garbo submitted her Alien Registration form on September 4, 1940. In return, she acquired yet another number for identification: #1 367 702 mg.

The perceptible shift in Hollywood's attitude toward its "Swedish enigma, spinster star" was apparent in an October 1940 column by Hedda

Hopper, who claimed to be one of her biggest admirers. The columnist reminded readers about the time Garbo made the news by snubbing Hearst editor-in-chief Arthur Brisbane. As time passed, the "charm" of such idio-syncrasies began to wear off, Hopper suggested. Garbo's silence was "a great act . . . It helped make her a star. . . . Then it became usual—and a bore—and she's conceived no other plan to bring back the prestige which she's lost."

At the end of the month, Greta signed her name to a new form at the Federal District Court in Los Angeles: a Declaration of Intention to file for United States citizenship. She listed her address as 165 Mabery Road in Santa Monica. Salka Viertel, her family, and friends remained Garbo's anchor in Hollywood. Evidence that she was fearful of the turbulent tran-sition before her is contained in the night letters Robert Reud sent her dur-ing this period. The wires had changed in tone from romantic overtures to lengthy discussions of her future according to the stars.[1]

The fact that Garbo was seeking such guidance is significantly tied to another event: on November 20, she signed a new contract with Metro. Between 1925 and 1940, the arrangement been MGM and Greta Garbo had progressed from agreements in which the studio maintained all the controls to unique one- and two-picture deals that kept the actress on the MGM payroll as their premier prestige artist, but with no obligation on her part beyond the contracted film. Her latest commitment called for a base salary of $150,000—a modest increase from her *Ninotchka* fee (and still one of the top fees in the industry)—for a yet-to-be-determined project.[2] While it has been reported that she was offered the remake of a Swedish film starring Ingrid Bergman, *En kvinnas ansikte* (*A Woman's Face*), produc-tion notes show Joan Crawford's attachment fairly early on. No other names are mentioned in the script files.

In a Christmas letter to the Wachtmeisters, Greta confirmed that neither she nor the studio was ready to go to work on a new picture. "I've had a cold for over five months, so I haven't been very cheerful," she admitted. "Just now I'm lying on a bench out in the desert all on my own. I'm the only guest where I'm staying. . . . I was invited to our friends in Nassau, Axel W., but I can't travel. I'm off to New York soon for some kind of treatment. . . . Then with

---

[1]Garbo wasn't the only star Reud was guiding at this time. A number of his Broadway friends had turned to him for readings. Later in the year, he started inner circles buzzing with his advice to Gertrude Lawrence not to sign a contract for a play she had been offered and to wait six weeks before making a decision; six weeks later, she was offered *Lady in the Dark*.

[2]As with the previous contract, Garbo's exact arrangement went unpublicized. The media would improbably speculate figures between $10,000 and $25,000 per week.

God's help I'll start working again. They're in no hurry nowadays when our films are not being shown in Europe." Interestingly, this letter, with its reference to Axel Wenner-Gren, would be her only correspondence known to have been opened by wartime censors.

Her mood had improved by the time she reached New York, where another glimpse of Garbo could be seen in Wenner-Gren's diaries. Greta and Gayelord Hauser met the industrialist for tea at the Ritz Tower. They had, according to Wenner-Gren, a "quiet and pleasant afternoon and delightful conversation." The following day, they attended a cultural demonstration together. On the fourteenth, there was "Dinner at Valentina's with Grand Duchess Maria [of Russia], Greta and Hauser, Greta tried on dresses. Nice and pleasant evening as usual, spirits ran high."

Wenner-Gren and Garbo dined alone on their final evening together. Although they discussed reconnecting in Nassau, Greta never saw the Wenner-Grens again. "My guess, but it's only a guess, is that she was given a discreet warning by the FBI or MI-6 [British Intelligence] not to go to Nassau again," Leif Leifland says, "and that she was told Wenner-Gren was suspected of being a German spy." The industrialist lived out most of the war in Mexico; he did not return to Sweden until well after Germany's surrender, by which time his reputation and business were effectively ruined.

The Garbo/Hauser friendship continued in a very public fashion. "Now that Garbo and Gayelord Hauser are motoring through the State of Maryland, those marriage rumors are again being revived," Hedda Hopper announced in her January 15 column. "I do know that they took a picnic lunch and spent a whole day together sitting on a piece of land in Brentwood, trying to make up their minds whether a home should be built on it."

Privately, there had been some changes. "Fur will fly if it's true Garbo has taken Marlene Dietrich's best beau, Erich Remarque, away from her," Hopper intimated in a column ten days later. Erich Maria Remarque, the acclaimed author of *All Quiet on the Western Front* and *The Road Back*, had followed Dietrich to Hollywood in 1939. Exiled from his native Germany, where the Nazis had condemned his work, Remarque lived in France and Switzerland throughout the 1930s. He was brilliant, moody, and legally bound to—though definitely estranged from—another woman as he openly conducted an obsessive, almost masochistic affair with the German film star. When Dietrich moved on to younger lovers (most notably, James Stewart, John Wayne, and Orson Welles), Remarque also sought comfort from others.

He met Greta in New York at the home of theatrical producer Gilbert Miller. Garbo first caught his attention with her "beautiful dark voice," he recorded in his diary. Though she left the party early with her companion, Gayelord Hauser, Remarque believed that they had exchanged a look that indicated she had noticed him. Two weeks later, she called. Initially, theirs was a brief flirtation. "It is strange to think of Garbo as being an interlude for Remarque," biographer Julie Gilbert offered. "He was puzzled why she pursued him, but willingly allowed himself to become 'slightly infatuated'. . . . He found her accessible, caring, and candid."

An avid art collector, a connoisseur of fine wine, good food, and, most importantly, someone who understood something about the conflict and pain involved in being torn away from one's homeland, Erich Maria Remarque was just the kind of teacher Greta would have appreciated. The couple saw the sights of New York together—the galleries, the parks, the anxious refugees—"and she would advise him to cut down on alcohol, to stay away from nightclubs, and out of Harlem," Gilbert stated. "He promised her he would try."

Garbo lingered in Manhattan while Metro put off making a decision about her next project. That was fine with her. "It never pleased me to act all the time," she would tell Cecil Beaton. "I don't like to work for months on the film before shooting. I don't want to go to the studio except when I'm necessary; I'm not one who must be performing in front of a camera in order to feel good."

Madame Curie, as far as Garbo's participation was concerned, had fallen by the wayside. "Anita [Loos] couldn't understand why [Huxley] was so upset," Christopher Isherwood said. "She didn't understand that we thought writing something for Greta Garbo or Ingrid Bergman was more glamorous than winning a Pulitzer. She had been around Hollywood so long that she couldn't understand the magic it held for outsiders like Aldous and me. She thought Hollywood had failed Huxley where I'm pretty sure Huxley felt he had failed Greta Garbo." *Curie* resurfaced in 1942 as a possible story for Katharine Hepburn before being assigned to Anglo-Irish actress Greer Garson.

The appearance of Garson and Bergman on the scene—both arrived on the Metro lot in 1940—posed a double threat to Garbo, inasmuch as they projected certain qualities that moviegoers had previously only seen in Garbo. Additionally, the public appeared more "comfortable" with, and less threatened by, both women; as far as motion picture executives were concerned, both actresses were younger, more ambitious, and under contracts that promised a regular output of films for their respective studios.

MGM executives were, no doubt, torn between their English and Swedish GG's—both fell into the category of "great ladies" on screen. But

Garbo seemed more threatened by her Swedish compatriot. American journalists openly invited comparisons between the two; they shared similar backgrounds, friends, associates, and sponsors. Bergman had been brought over to the United States in 1939 by David O. Selznick; Gottfried Reinhardt produced her first film at MGM.

"The destruction of stars is a very subtle process. You scarcely notice that it is happening," Irving Thalberg warned in a 1933 memo to Nicholas Schenck. "After all, commercially pictures do fluctuate up and down. Sometimes what seems to be quite a good picture somehow tends to destroy the background of glamour and interest that has been built up in the star. Stars are not that much more beautiful or that much more talented than the ordinary players . . ." The difference was the hot-and-cold perception of personality. Bergman was hot; Garbo was cooling.

The publicists at Selznick International had lobbied to get their young protégé invited to meet Garbo during the making of *Ninotchka*. After a series of admiring flowers and telegrams—and no response—an answer arrived a few short days before Bergman was due to return to Sweden. "I remember telling George Cukor about this some time later . . . and saying how sad I was that we'd never met and how kind she was to have sent the telegram," Bergman related. "George laughed and said, 'But of course Greta wouldn't have sent the telegram unless she were certain you were leaving.' " By the time Garbo was ready to meet, Bergman had lost interest.

The actress without a film wandered from coast to coast looking to fill her time. In May of 1941, Greta asked Richard Griffith of the Museum of Modern Art if he could arrange a private screening of *Gösta Berlings saga*. The museum's copy of the picture was in Swedish with a limited number of English subtitles. Greta translated for her guests, Gaylord Hauser and Erich Maria Remarque. "At one point she lost the thread of the story completely," Griffith recalled, "and when this became apparent to the others she set her head back and howled delightful Ninotchka laughter."

"REGARDING BIRTH DATE IN LETTER, PLEASE TRY VERY HARD TO KEEP HIM FROM MAKING TRIP AT THIS TIME," Robert Reud wrote Greta. The soothsayer continued to offer advice regarding her next film. "FRANKLY, IT WOULD BE PRACTICALLY IMPOSSIBLE FOR [SAM] BEHRMAN TO DO A SOUND, WORKABLE SCRIPT WITH HIS PRESENT STARS. FORTUNATELY, HOWEVER, BEHRMAN DOUBTLESS WILL NOT BE NECESSARY, AS YOU ARE NOW PRACTICALLY AT THE VERY HOUR WHEN DESTINY WILL BLESS YOUR LIFE WITH A GREAT, MIRACULOUS AND UNEXPECTED CHANGE. AND LATER ON, IN NEXT FEBRUARY, YOU WILL TOUCH A NEW AND EVEN GREATER PEAK OF GLORY . . ."

That June, the Gustafson family seriously considered returning to Sweden—with or without Greta. They stocked up on rationed food items and booked passage on a Finnish boat scheduled to depart New York City on June 15. It never showed up. "It seems so odd whenever I hear anything from home," Greta wrote Hörke. "I'm still thinking about leaving, but then I get frightened again. Not of the explosions at home, but of all the crazy things lying in the sea . . ."[3] Sven and his family settled in the suburban community of Scarsdale, New York for the duration of the war.

Finally, in June word leaked out that MGM had settled on *The Twin Sister* by Ludwig Fulda for Garbo's next film.[4] The plot followed the popular comic scenario of madcap ex-wives and their husbands—*The Ex-Mrs. Bradford* (Jean Arthur, William Powell), *The Awful Truth* (Cary Grant, Irene Dunne)—in this case, modified to portray a simple, uncomplicated woman who creates a nonexistent, more outgoing twin sister in order to win back her husband. Gottfried Reinhardt was set to produce; George Cukor to direct; Salka Viertel, S. N. Behrman, and a new collaborator, George Oppenheimer (best known for his work with the Marx Brothers), were responsible for the screenplay. "As nothing divides people more than difference in their sense of humor, it was a miracle that my friendship with Gottfried survived the severe test," Salka wrote. "Sam Behrman's authority and intervention prevented many bitter feuds."

Joseph Breen received an incomplete script on June 12, the story had been re-titled *Two-Faced Woman*. The Production Code administrator promptly communicated his concern about suggestive dialogue. "Due to the fact that this script is coming in segments, it is very difficult to render any kind of an intelligent opinion as to the final acceptability of the various sequences," he wrote, allowing that "Such an opinion will probably have to wait until we can judge them in reference to the whole story."

It was the same conflict producers had been struggling with for years. If anything, the mood of the country had become less tolerant. "In those days, cinematized sexual intercourse was—well, it just wasn't," Gottfried Reinhardt stated. "The script of *Two-Faced Woman* was turned down by the Breen Office on the grounds that it conveyed implications of a premarital carnal relationship. What, I proposed as an alternative, if the lovers were not illicit lovers? What if the cad *marries* the girl of high principles and then abandons her? And what if she, through her masquerade stratagem, wins him back?"

---

[3]According to Gray Reisfield, some family members did manage to make it home—briefly—before returning to the States.

[4]The story had previously been used for the silent screen comedy *Her Sister from Paris* starring Constance Talmadge, and a sound remake featuring Constance Bennett.

Breen liked this twist. The Production Code administrator approved an interim script while the offending scenes were rewritten.

Greta reported for work on the eighteenth of June. She was, in accordance with Bob Reud's prognostication, in great spirits. "I've started work on a film, which probably won't amount to much. In any event I don't feel too ashamed," she relayed to Hörke. For her, these were downright euphoric sentiments. It was the studio that appeared unsure. "But these are such strange times that they are worried that if [the movie] isn't a tiny bit vulgar it won't do well. It's strange that I should be writing about films when war is on our doorstep."

Melvyn Douglas's casting should have signaled a problem to anyone who was looking. Among his many industry pursuits, Douglas was a director of the Screen Actors Guild and on the board of the Motion Picture Relief Fund. He was also active in the Democratic Party and spoke forcefully against fascism. After the release of *Ninotchka*, the actor had fought with Louis B. Mayer regarding his right to express his views publicly.[5] According to author Ingrid Winther Scobie, when Douglas refused to tone down his political stance, L.B. tried to bribe him with a contract for his wife, actress Helen Gahagan Douglas. The actor again refused and was discreetly removed from consideration for the studio's top assignments. It was in the midst of this fall from grace that Douglas was cast in *Two-Faced Woman.*

In a rather ironic touch of symbolism, the most definitive sign that something was awry could be seen in the development of the film's wardrobe. In a July 1941 column, Hedda Hopper described the innovative fashions Adrian had designed for Garbo, complemented by the finest furs and jewels: "One gown, which she wanted to wear but the Hays office banned, is so beautiful. It's made of suntan soufflé over the same shade of lining, gathered skirt, gold-lace belt with lace coming up the front. . . . Strange, isn't it, that a girl who cares nothing about clothes has created so many outstanding fashions?"

A disagreement over this very costume precipitated a conflict with its designer. Production executive Bernie Hyman, backed by the front office, wanted to scrap the glamour and bring Garbo down to earth; Adrian objected. However, George Cukor, still wounded by his experience on *Gone With The Wind*, went along with it. Tampering with Garbo's screen persona—an impossible-to-define mixture of elements which were securely rooted in her own personality—was a dangerous proposition for everyone concerned.

---

[5]An example of Mayer choosing commercial expediency over humanity. Douglas's name had begun to represent a problem on foreign marquees.

* * *

Greta Garbo had become a cultural icon—as significant to her era as Chaplin had been to his. Director Ernst Lubitsch had satirized that image, magically turning the statue into something real and attainable. With confounding logic, Metro executives sought to homogenize this most ethereal of stars still further by proving she could be as much fun as any flippant American comedienne with painted red nails. They demonstrated their faith by slashing the film's budget, refusing George Cukor sufficient time to work with the writers on the screenplay, discarding Adrian's initial designs, and substituting more "plebeian" garments. How would an actress who reacted emotionally to the costumes for each film have judged the "committee work" on *Two-Faced Woman?* Not well.

A description of the first days of filming by cinematographer Joseph Ruttenberg gives a clear indication of the disintegrating fortunes that surrounded Garbo during the making of the film. "I don't know why she took *Two-Faced Woman.* . . . It wasn't a good story to begin with, and it wasn't a Garbo picture. Poor woman," he empathized, "she didn't have a very good bosom and during that picture they spent months making gowns for her to make her look beautiful and dressed up." Yet the day before shooting the nightclub scene, producers still had not agreed on a gown for the star. Cukor summoned Ruttenberg to the wardrobe department where he and Adrian were assessing a décolleté dress. "Isn't that beautiful?" Cukor said. Ruttenberg didn't agree. "Well, it's a beautiful dress but . . ." Garbo finished his thought. "You don't think it's very good looking for me." Ruttenberg nodded. "Joe, these things here," she said, "this is God's. I'm not responsible."

The gown had not been designed for Garbo and had already been worn by another (unidentified) actress. In desperation, Adrian hoped to mask its deficiencies with jewels—but the next day on the set, it was obvious they had a problem. "Every time that Garbo would bend over, the dress would come out and you'd see the bosom," Ruttenberg recalled. "If she was sitting still during a scene I could do something . . . I'd get a low shot set up and have a wine glass cover it up. This was fine . . . but when she was dancing there wasn't anything you could do." Watching the rushes the following morning, Gottfried Reinhardt admitted it had been a terrible mistake. "My God, you can't use anything here," he told Cukor and Ruttenberg. Garbo wore tailored clothes beautifully, but evening gowns with plunging necklines, and off-the-rack fashions were definitely not for her. Still, the powers-that-be persisted in staying with this "new" homegrown image.

Adrian decided he'd had enough; his resignation was tendered by the first week in August. "When the glamour ends for Garbo, it also ends for me," he told friends before departing the studio. Greta would interpret his departure not as a showing of support, but with a childlike sense of betrayal and abandonment. "I'm very sorry that you're leaving," she told her former comrade with uncharacteristic coolness, "but, you know, I never really liked most of the clothes you made me wear." The cruelty was in her unexpected candor where formerly she had kept silent. Adrian had been an integral part of her support system at work; she relied exclusively on his fashion sense. Although the designer's credit remained on the completed motion picture, *Two-Faced Woman* also featured garments produced by other costumers, including a sexless bathing suit designed by Valentina.

Following Adrian's exit, it was rumored that the producer and director consulted with Greta's rival in the film, Constance Bennett, for further guidance. Garbo had already agreed to a bob and perm by stylist Sydney Guilaroff after seeing Bennett's new hairstyle—an attempt to "modernize" her coiffure that only succeeded in dating her. In both instances of hair and dress, Bennett, a well-known fashion-plate whose star once shone nearly as bright as Garbo's, did her no favors. "Garbo was exceptionally nice to me," says actor Robert Sterling, who had been hired to play the handsome young Lothario in the film. "Constance Bennett was just the opposite. She was very difficult and was always concerned about messing her dress or her hair or some damn thing. . . .

"I had met Garbo before, but when we were introduced [on the set] she made a big fuss about me and was very sweet. I leaned down and gave her a little peck on the cheek, and she seemed to like that. She took my hand and squeezed it. 'You are so rosy,' she told me." At one point, a break was called and Constance Bennett announced that she was serving tea in her dressing room. "And she looked around and invited everybody: Melvyn Douglas, Roland Young, Ruth Gordon—but she went right past me. It was such a noticeable kind of a slap in the face because we had had a few words coming in. Much to my amazement, they all turned her down. Then Garbo took my hand and she said, 'You come with me, darling. We'll have tea in my room.' . . . She didn't throw her weight around, not that I could see. She just was a loner."

There were moments of humor, Sterling added. "I was clowning around the set one day and fell down. I had a ski suit on and I picked up all the lint and the dust and the dirt on the floor, so the guy was laughing as he brushed me off. And she came by and said, 'Nobody ever tells me anything funny.' I said, 'You're always hiding!' I just said it, you know, like that—and she laughed. She thought that was funny. We got on very well."

Even with an incomplete script and wardrobe troubles, the day-to-day routine of *Two-Faced Woman* did not appear abnormal. Fellow workers remembered Greta walking to and from her set with long, easy strides—her car always trailing behind carrying her maid, makeup, and clothes. When they filmed on the back lot, she traversed that route four times a day without complaint, seeming to revel in her time alone in the sun. "If she starts down a street on the shady side, she automatically gravitates to the sun," Ruth Gordon observed. Gordon, a seasoned New York actress, turned down several theatrical contracts for the opportunity of working with Garbo. "It is difficult to describe what it is she gives her fellow actors. So many players read their lines well, but then they stand and wait for you to speak. Garbo does something quite different. After she speaks the line there is a sort of projection that carries over from her to the other person which creates a wonderful continuity. It is rather like the follow-through in golf. It is something that you feel without being able to analyze."

Greta continued work on her twenty-sixth film at MGM in an upbeat though restless frame of mind. "I'll soon be finished with my latest baby and have no idea what it will be like," she wrote Hörke on the twentieth of August. "I'm only very sad that the story was changed so much. Salka had a much better story to begin with. But since I would rather go walking in the country than fight for stories, it will have turned out like it has."

Principal photography wrapped two days later, sort of. By mid-September, Greta was back in front of the camera for extensive retakes. She was still working on the picture when her thirty-sixth birthday slipped by almost unnoticed. "No one had remembered it," said Kenneth Brown. Brown was an associate of Paul Flato, the Beverly Hills jeweler who provided most of the jewelry for the film. Recalling a pair of pajamas Garbo had considered buying at a shop in the Ambassador Hotel, Brown special-ordered them and had the pajamas delivered to the set of *Two-Faced Woman*. During a lunch break, she walked over to Brown and put her hand to his ear. "They fit," she said. Brown noted that there was a big smile on her face as she walked away.

When he returned to Los Angeles, Erich Maria Remarque renewed his friendship with Garbo. "They went for long walks along the beach at Santa Monica with his two Kerry blue dogs," Julie Gilbert reported. "They laughed, talked, hugged, kissed, and to top off the walk, Garbo would show him a handstand in the middle of the road. 'Every dog on the road knows her,' Remarque wrote affectionately. They went to the movies—*That Hamilton Woman*—and Garbo sobbed when Lord Nelson died. They visited the Botanical Gardens, went for a long walk afterward, and then back to Remarque's house, where they cooked hamburgers, ate ice cream, and sat in front of the fireplace listening to records."

Remarque's journal entries read like the notes for a scene in one of his novels: "She rolled up her sweater. The smooth brown skin. Brought her back to the house. Leaned over the gate. She slowly moved backward toward the house. The beautiful face under the hat. The silk ash-gray blond hair. She wants to go to India." Another entry describes their first sexual encounter. After a leisurely stroll, the couple returned to his house in Westwood. Greta was nervous and animated, but calmed down as they listened to gypsy music and shared an intimate candlelit dinner. Later, they went upstairs. "She entered the bedroom, the light of the dressing room behind her, softly flowing over her shoulders, enchanting her outline, the face, the hands, the trembling, something imperceptible shook her, then the voice . . . the absence of any form of sentimentality or melodrama—and yet full of warmth."

She seemed uninhibited when she was alone with Remarque. He wrote about a walk in a field; Greta, the sun-worshipper, took off her blouse. "The most beautifully tanned back and the most beautiful straight shoulders, more beautiful than Puma's, whose shoulders are a bit too high.[6] Farewell in the car. Garbo seems soft and opens up. And, idiot that I am, called her a little fool. She froze. I had frightened her. She called later. Thank God." Dietrich, interestingly enough, had been so focused on her pursuit of Jean Gabin that she had not paid much attention to the blossoming relationship between Remarque and Garbo. Once enlightened, she called her former lover—whom she refused to let go—and was pleased to have interrupted a romantic rendezvous. But Remarque did not come to her and Dietrich "began to blackmail Garbo," he recorded in his journal. "Says she has syphilis and breast cancer, can be arrogant and ugly, etc. A bombardment of jealousy, and then, confirms her love for me. Finally, I go to her."

Inevitably, there were to be no commitments—either from Dietrich or Garbo. There was a minor confrontation at the Café Gala, a hip gay-and-lesbian "couples" club on the Sunset Strip. Dietrich took over the stage and, according to Hedda Hopper, "sang her entire repertoire of songs" while Garbo watched with her companion, Gayelord Hauser. This strange dynamic remained a constant throughout much of 1941 and early 1942. Though Remarque expressed an interest in developing his relationship with Greta further, he admitted being impatient with her. "I tell her that to Puma, men are like hotels; some are better, some are worse, but it makes no difference in which one she lives." Ultimately, indecision would overrule emotion and the relationship quietly faded. "Garbo, all the nights with her, sitting in the dark. Never liked to switch on the lights. A strong solitude," he wrote. "Take her as an example, soldier!"

---

[6] "Puma" was Remarque's nickname for Marlene Dietrich.

* * *

In October of 1941, *Two-Faced Woman* was previewed in New York. Ruth Gordon reported to George Cukor on a screening she attended with Michael Redgrave, Gabriel Pascal, Thornton Wilder, Dorothy Kilgallen, and Valentina and George Schlee. "All laughed quite a bit and seemed to have sunny faces at the end and said fine things indeed. . . . No one who didn't read that lousy script will ever know what windmills you had to fight and what worlds you conquered." *Variety* labeled the movie "a daring piece of showmanship"—but an experiment that wasn't entirely successful. "Had the script writers and the director, George Cukor, entered into the spirit of the thing with as much enthusiasm, lack of self-consciousness and abandon as the star, the result would have been a smash hit."

Garbo, safely tucked away in her cocoon, acknowledged the criticism but appeared resigned to it. "I have finished with my 'latest' and sadly it's just nothing," she wrote Hörke Wachtmeister. "Maybe you'll see it soon and then you'll be able to see for yourself what's missing from my art. It sounds heartbreaking for Salka and me." There were more important things to consider. "We're all afraid of being drawn into the war soon and then there'll be panic. It seems crazy that millions are being killed instead of a few thoughtful people getting together to try and sort out what's wrong. But then there would have to be give and take and no one wants to give."

She wrote about looking for a house to buy. She really didn't want to, she contended, but "rents are likely to rise so much that it would be stupid not to own your home . . ." The idea of owning her own home soon consumed her. "You said I would buy a house is that really so? I thought a house would fly to me, but no house," she playfully chided Bob Reud. "Can you also see in the stars if I should buy . . . so called paying real estate. I have one offered to me, but God knows what to do. Maybe if you looked closely at your planets, that this could tell! Everything is so uncertain one becomes afraid of everything. Do you know if I am coming to N.Y. I have sort of vaguely thought of it. But I dont know. . . . If you cannot tell where I am going, I will just have to leave it to the Lord. Whenever it is I shall always be glad to see you again. Besides all that is there going to be peace?"

According to Los Angeles County records, Garbo finally purchased a house (the former home of Anthony Quinn) on the third of November. More investments would follow.

Greta was already planning her escape. When advised of Garbo's wish to vacation in Mexico—then considered a hotbed of Nazi activity on the Continent—MGM executives sought to talk her out of the trip. "I learned that it would be impossible for her to leave until toward the end of this month, and that she planned to take a vacation of something from a month to a month and a half," Metro's lead attorney William A. Orr informed the INS Travel Control Division. "I explained the uncertainties that might arise in the meantime, and it now seems very likely that she will change her plans and follow the suggestion."

Her escape was put on hold while the promotion surrounding *Two-Faced Woman* heated up. MGM publicists went so far as to describe the star as "the greatest oomph girl of all time"—though, in fairness to her employer, the unique choreography of Garbo's career to date nearly demanded such efforts. "Her pictures are so far apart that Metro starts off each publicity campaign with a broadside, as if she'd been buried and dug up for the occasion," Hedda Hopper remarked. "We've had 'Garbo Talks,' 'Garbo Sings,' 'Garbo Dances' and 'Garbo Laughs.' No doubt her ultimate picture will be 'Garbo Retires' and do terrible business from a public expecting a bedroom farce." Fateful words.

On November 23, just as MGM prepared to release the motion picture in first-run theaters, it became the focus of public scrutiny. An innocuous comedy became the first movie in the recent history of the Production Code office to be passed by censors but condemned by the Catholic Legion of Decency. The film received a "Class C" (condemned) rating for its "Immoral and un-Christian attitude toward marriage and its obligations; imprudently suggestive scenes, dialogue and situations; [and] suggestive costumes." In an unprecedented move, Archbishop Spellman, the powerful leader of the church in New York, published a pastoral letter urging faithful Catholics not to see *Two-Faced Woman*; other church leaders would follow suit.

The movie was banned in Boston and in Providence, Rhode Island, without the formality of a preview. Representative Martin J. Kennedy of New York entered his protest into the *Congressional Record* when he called such films an affront to Congress and "a danger to the public morality." The Knights of Columbus joined in the attack, denouncing it as "a challenge to every decent man and woman." Joseph Breen and his staff scrambled to explain the discrepancy between their view of *Two-Faced Woman* versus the self-appointed censors. "[At] no time did we ever have a completed script on this subject, from which we could actually judge the moral values of the picture," an internal PCA memo stressed. "The script kept coming in in sections, always without an ending . . . By actual count, we read and reported on 23 sections of script for this picture, including retakes."

The compromise on the script Metro had arranged with the Breen office had not satisfied "the cinematic watchdog of the Catholic Church." Gottfried Reinhardt's argument that the sister-in-law in the story was, in fact, the philandering man's wife was dismissed by church elders as "Hollywood sophistry." Reinhardt would recall the furor that overwhelmed his picture with some resentment. "[Archbishop Spellman], even more incensed than his minions, took time off from shepherding X-million souls to wage a one-man crusade—in a world torn by strife, with his own country on the brink of it—against my sinful *Two-Faced Woman*. He whispered his caveat into the ear of his proselyte, Louis B. Mayer, and Mayer thundered into mine to 'flush the filth down the drain where it belongs.' "

It was the ultimate act of betrayal of Greta Garbo, an actress who once had been prized for her ability to reach beyond the censors. She was hurt and frightened. "They are trying to kill me. . . . They've dug my grave," she reportedly told friends. She knew the pendulum had swung.

"There is surprisingly little wailing in the high places of MGM over the condemnation by the Legion of Decency of the new Greta Garbo film," Paul Harrison wrote in the *New York World-Telegram*. "I have talked with several studio people who saw it, and some said frankly that it is a poor and generally disappointing effort. Two said that it should have been shelved for the preservation of Miss Garbo's artistic reputation. All said that as far as morally objectionable aspects of the picture are concerned they were mystified as to why it was singled out from among many recent racy comedies for condemnation."

Indeed, the Legion had passed a similarly themed story, MGM's *The Chocolate Soldier*, scarcely a month earlier. Neither had the sexually provocative comedies of Preston Sturges, Gregory La Cava, or Frank Capra drawn much fire. *Time* magazine termed the campaign against *Two-Faced Woman* an opportunistic appeal to increase the Legion's strength at the expense of a high-profile star. While a small group of theater-owners urged Metro-Goldwyn-Mayer not to cave into pressure—recalling the negative effect the Legion had on the box office in 1934—Louis B. Mayer and Nicholas Schenck agreed to pull the beleaguered film from release and replace it with a Rosalind Russell comedy, *Design for Scandal*.

Most of the changes the Legion demanded would be a simple matter of editing. The only retake involved Melvyn Douglas and was based upon a suggestion from Archbishop Spellman: the husband should discover almost immediately that Katrin, the "twin sister," is really his wife, Karin.

Gottfried Reinhardt was in a Metro dubbing room working on the alterations when the first news of Japan's December 7 bombing of Pearl Harbor disrupted a radio broadcast. "Every last one of us in the room, as everyone in America listening to the radio, realized instinctually that life and its pursuits had been radically changed. Everyone save New York's Prince of the

Church," Reinhardt believed, "who, undeflected by earthy cataclysm, fought on to redeem the soul of MGM's evil daughter. Up until the very day of Los Angeles's first air-raid alarm, when he flew in and asked for a viewing of the expurgated version. I ran it for him and gained the sanction my employers set such store by."

Greta's whereabouts during this period aren't known. Against the advice of the MGM legal department, she had proceeded with her application for a reentry permit to allow for her journey into Mexico. The application was withdrawn by William Orr on her behalf two weeks later. One report stated that she was ill and had hidden away in a New York sanitarium for two weeks.

On the seventeenth of December, the Legion of Decency announced it had reclassified *Two-Faced Woman*, bestowing it with a "Class B" rating that indicated it was "objectionable in part." The picture achieved its belated release on New Year's Day. "Having seen the original version and the amended motion picture, it still strikes me that the Legion was causing a tempest in a teapot when it gave *Two-Faced Woman* a black eye with its original condemnation," Howard Barnes wrote in the *New York Herald-Tribune*. Many critics viewed the film as clumsy but harmless.

Or was it?

"For a woman who never rehearsed the emotions of a scene on a film set, but only the mechanics, this was a film that was all mechanics and no emotions," Alexander Walker concluded. Shattering the illusion of mystery and glamour effectively destroyed Greta Garbo. Playing two distinct characters usually gave less idiosyncratic actors an opportunity to explore the depth of their talents—but Garbo's "magic fascination" had been to layer simplicity on top of complexity, purity with passion; she was cinema's first existential heroine. To separate the flesh from the spirit was to lose her entirely, and—as Elinor Glyn once predicted—the artifice showed.

The over-zealousness of the wizards at MGM erasing all traces of "European decadence" in Garbo was her undoing. Image-makers had intended to "homogenize" her uniqueness; instead, much as what had happened to John Gilbert twelve years earlier, Metro unwittingly subtracted a dimension from her. "The wickedness in *Two-Faced Woman* was not in its careless disregard of what are supposed to be public morals," Cecelia Ager stated in *P.M. Daily;* "it had no more contempt for the conventions than a half-dozen recent movies whose transgressions it was made an example of—its wickedness lies in its vandalism. . . . It makes Garbo a clown, a buffoon, a monkey on a stick. The fact that it's a comedy doesn't excuse its confused motivation, its repetition, its distasteful heartlessness."

Garbo's decision to stop work after *Two-Faced Woman* was due to her disintegrating relationship with Louis B. Mayer, opines Douglas Fairbanks, Jr. She was convinced he was trying to ruin her. "My father used to say jokingly that stars when they reached the top should be shot, so that they could be remembered at their best," he says. Thus they were spared the humiliation of failure. Garbo took responsibility to the extent that she allowed others to push her into working in a different manner. "She shouldn't have let one bad picture upset her," Charles Boyer remarked. But most friends and coworkers understood that she had responded much as any sensitive artist would have. "People who've been sacrosanct are often unable to handle a flop—especially their first—the mocking and making fun of them," said Roddy McDowall.

Contrary to its dismal reputation, *Two-Faced Woman* was a modest success. Surprisingly, it performed best in areas where the controversy had been most heated. The foreign and domestic box-office (minus a full release in Europe and Japan) totaled $1.8 million; MGM charged a loss to the film of $62,000—less than the cost of the final round of retakes. The National Board of Review took the unusual step of sending out a special press release entitled "The Garbo Film and the Legion of Decency," which urged industry leaders to "challenge in the courts the right of public officials to overstep their proper functions" by arbitrarily censoring films. It was a moot point. As the United States entered World War II, motion picture producers voluntarily yielded to censors and remolded American film to project the image the U.S. government wished to project abroad.

"In this harsh new world there is no place for me anymore," Garbo prophesied in the film that proved to be her swan song. Poisonous Hollywood pens predicted that she would be among the year's unfortunate casualties. "To adults she is a violet-shaded memory. To the current generation of flaming youth she is just a legend," John Rosenfield advocated in the *Dallas Morning News*. "Unless Metro-Goldwyn-Mayer and Miss Garbo are earnest about rescuing her career, she will soon recede into history and become one with Theda Bara and Betty Blythe." Meanwhile, her contemporaries at MGM were also raging against the dying of the light: Melvyn Douglas went straight into *We Were Dancing*, one of Norma Shearer's last motion pictures; Joan Crawford stumbled after previewing her future in *A Woman's Face* and would leave Metro in 1943; and many of the studio's dependable male stars—Gable, Taylor, Stewart—put on real-life uniforms and went to war.

"Even while we were doing [*Two-Faced Woman*], it had a chill, a portent of failure," George Cukor said. Even so, he disputed the contention that his film had finished Garbo's career. "That's a grotesque over-simplification," he protested. "It certainly threw her, but I think what really happened was that she just gave up . . ."

* * *

Greta made frequent pilgrimages to New York, as if remaining on the East Coast would bring her the news from Sweden she longed to hear. Her lengthy visits fostered a renewed association with designer Valentina and her husband, George Schlee. According to a mutual friend, antique dealer Joseph Lombardo, Gayelord Hauser brought Greta to Valentina's showroom at the Sherry-Netherland in January of 1942; they were accompanied by publicist Eleanor Lambert. The designer—typically grim, usually turbaned, draped to the heels, and unsmiling—was the epitome of "Rraashun pairrsohnality and pretentiousness," as Ruth Gordon would say. Her husband, George, was just the opposite. Friends characterized him as a man of the Old World and the old Russian manner—"a cosmopolitan of immense knowledge, charm, kindness and understanding." The only thing he seemed to have in common with his wife was the dark, soulful eyes of their native land.

"Valentina was not on show in her shop," a journalist friend related. "She was hidden away, but if some lady came for a fitting and Valentina agreed to see her, she would ask her to move a bit so that she could get an impression of her. She had an uncanny instinct about how clothes move on the body." During their first fitting session, she wanted to see how Garbo moved. Valentina was busy at work when Schlee, who had been in the back office, walked into the fitting room to say hello. According to several reports, Schlee walked in on a nude Garbo and was immediately struck by her lack of false modesty. Joe Lombardo, who met both a year later, could not confirm this story—only that "as soon as George saw Garbo and Garbo saw him, it was an instant love affair."

George Matthias Schlee was born in St. Petersburg, Russia; some sources say as late as 1900 or 1901, another states that he was twenty-five in 1920 when he first met Valentina. George's father owned considerable land in the southern province of Crimea, where the farms were blessed by fair weather and rich soil. During the summer, affluent families flocked to the region and one of their favorite gathering spots was Sevastopol's Grand Hotel, which was owned and operated by the Schlee family. As a young man, George published the local newspaper and helped to found the free people's university in Sevastopol.

In 1918, Valentina Nicolaevna Sanina—whose birthdates also vary, from 1901 to 1904—left her home in Kiev, a city torn by war (as it was surrounded by the Germans advancing into Russia) and soon Revolution. Her story resembles a real-life version of *Odalisken från Smolna*. She went to study drama and design at a school in Kharkov. When her mother and brother were killed during the early days of the Revolution, she fled with the family jewels across the Ukraine and down the Crimean peninsula to the port of Sevastopol on the Black Sea. It was here that the teenage refugee encountered the young Russian officer at the Sevastopol train station. She was tall, blond, and possessed an air of aristocratic elegance despite the chaos and poverty around her. George Schlee, now an captain in the White Army, took the frightened young woman under wing. When the army fell apart in 1920, he escaped with her to Athens.

In deference to social propriety, Schlee offered to marry Valentina and swore to take care of her for the rest of her life. "I can't give you love," she replied, "but if you want friendship, then I'll marry you." They were wed shortly after arriving in Greece. The Schlees made and lost a small fortune along the way to America via Rome, Paris, and points in between. At times, Valentina acknowledged, in order to survive, "we ate our diamonds." The couple emigrated to the United States in 1923. They spent their first night sleeping on a park bench. Within two years, George helped Valentina to secure financial backing and open her first dress shop on Madison Avenue. In 1928, when that business collapsed—their "angel" had absconded with the funds—they launched Valentina Gowns; she designed, he managed. Her shop at the Savoy-Plaza on Fifth Avenue was established with thirteen dresses from her private wardrobe.

Valentina was her own best advertising. She was known for her long, elegant dresses and skirts (when women were wearing short flapper styles) and considered herself an "architect of dress," using shadows and light and colors to achieve effects rather than extreme designs and cuts; she believed in free movement in clothes. The designer saw that her best opportunity lay in creating fashions for women who prized individuality above all. Accordingly, she developed a client list that included artists: Gloria Swanson, Irene Selznick, Norma Shearer, Joan Fontaine, Paulette Goddard, Vivien Leigh, Rosalind Russell, Gertrude Lawrence, Mary Martin, Lily Pons, Gladys Swarthout, and Fleur Cowles; as well as society: Mrs. John Hay Whitney, Mrs. Robert Watt Miller, Mrs. Edward Pitcairn, Mrs. George R. Hand, and Lila Bell Wallace. The names Astor, Vanderbilt, Mellon, and McCormick could also be found in her appointment book.

By 1938, Valentina had risen to become "the most talked-about dressmaker in New York." Among the plays that featured her gowns were *Come of Age* (Judith Anderson), *Idiot's Delight* (Lynn Fontanne), *Herod and Marianne* (Katherine Cornell), *The Philadelphia Story* (Katharine Hepburn), *Venus Observed* (Lilli Palmer), and a Metropolitan Opera production of *Carmen*. "Valentina has designed clothes that act before a line is spoken," Brooks Atkinson noted.

In the fall of 1940, the Schlees purchased a four-story building off Fifth Avenue as the new home for Valentina Gowns. Here Valentina personally oversaw a staff of sixty-five seamstresses and assistants. Two years later, the principal modeling chores would temporarily shift from the company's owner to its newest client. Garbo was the ideal model, Valentina told columnist Sheilah Graham, because "she has an innate simplicity and a good feeling about clothes and her own beauty."

It appeared that she also had a good feeling about the Schlees.

Greta enjoyed stepping out in New York. She lunched almost daily with Gayelord Hauser at the St. Regis, went to the movies to see a new Soviet film imported "direct from the front," *The Girl from Leningrad,* and dined at the Cotillion Room at the Pierre.

On January 24, 1942, the Hollywood Victory Committee presented a live radio broadcast featuring a host of celebrities speaking on behalf of the Infantile Paralysis Fund. One of the show's anxious writers had hoped to snare Garbo and announced her participation to the press. A report later surfaced suggesting that no less than Eleanor Roosevelt had appealed to the Swedish star for help. According to the Victory Committee, however, Garbo was never asked. The person brought in to write the charity show was under the impression that he was to cast it as well, but the committee had already assembled an impressive all-star cast: Bob Hope, Bing Crosby, Humphrey Bogart, Marlene Dietrich, Tyrone Power, Deanna Durbin, Claudette Colbert, James Cagney. Disappointed, the writer waged his own campaign to get Garbo, and the story soon took on a life of its own.

The ploy backfired. With the uncertainty of the first dark days after Pearl Harbor, Greta didn't even know when she would be returning to the screen, let alone attempt radio. The shelling of an oil field off the coast of Santa Barbara by a Japanese submarine in February and the sinking of a German U-boat on the East Coast the following month seemed to confirm the worst: even the once comfortably isolated American continent was vulnerable to attack. The latest "invasion" of refugees to Hollywood included scientists, artists, musicians, writers, and expatriate Americans who had lived and worked abroad. Culturally and economically, the Second World War would permanently change the face of Los Angeles.

That March, one longstanding member of the disenfranchised was looking at real estate in Milwaukee, Wisconsin, where Gayelord Hauser's brothers were local realtors and one of their housing projects was available for investment. Whenever she was away from Hauser during this period, Greta seemed to be a torn sail flapping in the wind; she was obviously embarrassed about the debacle of *Two-Faced Woman* and no longer knew whom she could trust at MGM. Hedda Hopper reported a friend running into her at Valentina's salon. Asked simply where she was staying, Garbo gave her inquisitor a hurt look and turned away. "I don't know," she said.

Gayelord Hauser announced that he would like to bring a visitor for Sunday brunch. His hostess was radio singer Jessica Dragonette and her sister, Nadea Loftus. "A series of half hourly telephone calls ensued in which Gayelord announced the *status quo*. 'Yes, she will come.' Then, 'No, I don't think she can make it.' Again, 'She has changed her mind.' And finally, 'She will come if you can assure her that no one but yourselves alone will be there.' It all added up to a kind of frenzied suspense until at last I went to the door myself in answer to the bell," Dragonette wrote in her autobiography. "I found Gayelord standing on the sill alone. Where was his guest? She had evaporated into thin air, playfully hiding. Suddenly, from back of the door leading to my outer hall, she emerged with a laugh that was like a chime of bells. Then in a burst of full glory, with the out-of-nowhereness of her cinema entrances, I saw Greta Garbo . . . standing in the center of my doorway, her eyelids hooding her soft blue gaze."

Dragonette's first encounter with Garbo was memorable, less for its display of the woman than of the child. Greta "fought" with Hauser over their respective places at the table and kept asking "Why?" to every question; she announced that she only ate poached eggs and gave a package of Postum (a decaffeinated drink) to Dragonette's maid. Before leaving she asked for a rubberband and was given a red one. "I hereby give you the Légion d'Honneur," Dragonette said.

"This was a signal for her improvising humor again. She came back and jumped up on the bench before the fireplace. 'Will you vote for me as President of the United States?' she said. Then patting herself on the chest and flashing her white teeth in a broad smile, 'I'm a good man. Besides I'll have to do something important after having been in the films.' "

CHAPTER TWENTY-ONE

Transition: The War Years

Perhaps, in time, she could allow herself to be philosophical about everything. Yet, in time, just as the public had become convinced that John Gilbert's voice had been high-pitched, so too did Metro-Goldwyn-Mayer persuade journalists—as well as Garbo and the moviegoing public—that a Swedish Sphinx without her foreign cache of theaters was of little value to American studios. "As long as I'm head of this studio, Greta Garbo can go on making pictures here," Louis B. Mayer proclaimed to shielded ears. The truth was that MGM no longer knew what to do with her.

Despite the uncertainty, none of this damaged Garbo's rarefied position in Hollywood. Wherever she went, she moved freely between the elite "A" list and the decidedly less mainstream "refugee" list. "It was a most wonderful time in Beverly Hills," says James Pendleton. Hollywood's eccentric wartime recruits were "highly sophisticated and knowledgeable people of the arts." Blackouts and curfews increased the importance of cultural gatherings and weekend brunches within the creative community. Suddenly, there wasn't "a" salon, there were *many* salons—and many rivalries.

Sir Charles and Lady Mendl were particular favorites in many circles. A former actress, sometime interior decorator, personality, and hostess, Elsie de Wolfe Mendl was also one of the legendary "Four Horsewomen of New York".[1] She astonished everyone by marrying—at age sixty—Sir Charles Mendl, a charming diplomat attached to the British Embassy in Paris. Forced by war to leave their palatial villa at Versailles, the Mendls managed to bring several servants, their car, and their chauffeur with them to America. In Beverly Hills, a town that valued European aristocracy—real and imagined—the Mendls became major stars. Mary Pickford choreographed their introduction to the Hollywood social set; it was at Pickfair that Greta was first introduced to Sir Charles and Lady Mendl.

During subsequent visits to their home, Harry Crocker observed, Garbo was most intrigued by her vivacious, septuagenarian hostess. She wrote to Gayelord Hauser about a party she had attended alone. She had been invited after viewing a few of the art treasures Elsie rescued before leaving

---

[1] The other riders were represented by her former lover, Elisabeth Marbury; banking heiress Anne Morgan; and Anne Vanderbilt.

France. "Axel [Wenner-]Gren wrote me a threatening letter than I mustnt [sic] fail her and her other 13 guest [sic]," Greta related. But it turned out to be a typical Hollywood party after all. "It must have been 100 trailing in wüst!"[2]

In the city, among movie stars and heiresses, Greta led "an unnatural life," friends believed. Yet it was in the borough of Manhattan that she sought refuge throughout much of World War II. One important reason was the anonymity she found within the crowd. Fans continued to be a problem for her in Los Angeles. In 1939, a postal employee had been sent to a federal hospital for treatment after sending her a series of obscene letters. Three years later, another in a long line of ardent admirers was arrested after attempting to scale the garden wall of Garbo's Beverly Hills home.

With many of her friends, as well as her immediate family, relocating to New York, Greta had both the time and inclination to explore its distinct environs. During short stays, Bob Reud or Sam Behrman usually arranged for her to take over the apartment of a friend. Eventually, she settled into a suite at the Ritz Tower on Park Avenue and began a daily routine that included walks in Central Park, complemented by frequent visits to local galleries.

She began her art collection in a spectacular manner—not surprisingly, many acquaintances would take credit for guiding her in this direction. Journalist-turned-actress-turned-interior-decorator Barbara Barondess MacLean—the woman who broke the "story" of Garbo's true shoe size—claimed that she helped to secure Greta's first two Renoirs at a November 1942 auction that featured several pieces from Otto Preminger's private collection.[3] Another possibility is that Erich Maria Remarque nudged Garbo in this direction. Already a collector of some renown when she met him, Remarque had recently directed the Swiss art dealer guarding his collection—which featured works by van Gogh, Degas, Delacroix, Renoir, Picasso, Utrillo, Daumier, and Cézanne—to ship the bulk of his collection to the United States.

But, according to David J. Nash, Sotheby's expert in Impressionist painting, Garbo alone went into a gallery on Fifty-seventh Street and inquired about a painting on display. As she admired Pierre-Auguste Renoir's study of his nephew Edmond, entitled *Enfant assis en robe bleue*, she was joined by Albert Barnes, one of the world's foremost collectors of Impressionist painting and a major force behind the Philadelphia Muse-

---

[2]*Wüst*: desert, waste.

[3]However, Preminger did not sign with 20th Century-Fox until 1943; he amassed his collection of *objets d'art* as films like *Laura, The Moon Is Blue,* and *Anatomy of a Murder* brought him to prominence.

um of Art. "Young lady, you won't go far wrong with that painting," he assured her.

Sam Green heard a slightly different version. Greta had been told that the best paintings were always displayed on a velvet easel in a back room of the exhibition. She walked into the back room of a prominent gallery and told the owner just what she had been told to say. "Without turning around, a little man sitting in front of the picture smoking a cigar said, 'Lady, you don't know a thing about painting.' " Barnes insisted that the painting was an inferior Renoir and allowed her to buy a Renoir that he had set aside for himself. Then Garbo's new benefactor offered to take her to the best galleries in town; later, she visited his private gallery in Philadelphia. In two days, she learned most everything she needed to know about buying art.

During a remarkable two-week initiation into the world of fine art, Greta purchased Renoir's *Confidence* at Sam Salz's Manhattan gallery (November 9); *Léontine et Coco*, a portrait of the artist's youngest son, Claude, with his governess, at the Bignou Gallery (November 11); and *Enfant assis en robe bleue* from Jacques Seligmann & Co. (November 16). On the twenty-fifth, she acquired Pierre Bonnard's vibrant still life *Les Coquelicots* from Paul Rosenberg & Co. It proved to be one of her favorites. "Just before he painted that, he thought color had turned his head and he was sacrificing form to it," Greta shared with a family member. "Look at it. It makes you feel like you've had a glass of champagne—the brink of dizziness."

At first, she did not choose to display her art, says James Pendleton. Most of her paintings were stored back to back on the floor of a closet in her Beverly Hills home. Investing in art was a safe place for Greta to put her money during the war—and she did have a need to protect new income. Officially, as of December, there was more film money coming in.

Several projects had been developed at MGM with Garbo in mind. Topping the list were *The Paradine Case*, Robert Hichens' tale of a lawyer who falls in love with the woman he's defending on murder charges; and *Scorched Earth* (retitled *Song of Russia*), another story which focused on the male lead: an American conductor visiting the Russian village where Tchaikovsky composed most of his symphonies. One screenplay hoped to capitalize on Garbo's mystery quotient, the other on her highly publicized romance with Leopold Stokowski. She turned down both.[4]

---

[4]Four years later, she was tempted to reconsider *The Paradine Case* when director Alfred Hitchcock and leading man Gregory Peck signed on. But, producer David O. Selznick noted, she "has always had an aversion to the story."

Sticking with the Soviet theme, producer Bernie Hyman suggested something "new": turning the love goddess into a morale booster. Garbo goes to war. *The Girl from Leningrad* would cast her as a courageous leader of the Russian resistance. "It was a moving, simple story about a wounded soldier and a nurse, made during the Russian-Finnish war, but changed into the Soviet-German conflict," Salka recalled. "The menacing presence of the Nazis was not so much seen as constantly felt . . ." On December 20, 1942, Garbo signed a one-picture contract with MGM offering her the same basic terms as her *Two-Faced Woman* agreement.

Within a few short months, however, Metro canceled the project. One could only speculate about the reasons. "Perhaps Garbo's enthusiasm was not emphatic enough, or they did not want to make a film sympathetic to the Soviets," Salka offered. With Bernie Hyman's passing (the producer died before the *Leningrad* deal was finalized), there no longer was anyone in the executive office actively pursuing Garbo stories. Greta had collected a payment of $70,000 before MGM decided not to make the film. Due to the bailout, according to the terms of her contract, she was entitled to full payment. Louis B. Mayer had a check for $80,000 prepared, but much to his amazement, Garbo refused it. She could not accept what she had not earned. Even when it would have been to her financial advantage, the actress refused to play games, said producer David Lewis. "She simply existed within what she really was."

According to Sydney Guilaroff, Mayer was less generous when it came to Garbo's dressing room. One afternoon, Guilaroff received a call from Greta at the studio. She sounded depressed. Someone—she wouldn't say who—had informed her that all of her belongings had been packed in boxes and moved out of her dressing room in order to make way for Lana Turner. Greta tearfully asked Guilaroff to find out if it was true. It was—and, according to the matron in charge of the women's building, Mayer himself had ordered it.

As Mercedes's relationship with Greta teetered on the delicate line between disfavor and accord, Mercedes finally turned to the Office of War Information for a job. She received an assignment editing a magazine called *Victory*, which necessitated a move to New York. Mercedes found a small apartment on Park Avenue—not far from Greta's wartime home.

Given the dreadful anxiety and turmoil of the previous two years, it would have been understandable to discover Garbo trusting nothing and no one. Paradoxically, she had no choice but to trust *someone*. Despite her highly valued independence, she needed a guide through this new world she was moving into and increasingly found one in the person of George Schlee. Well known in New York circles for his personable manner, shrewd business sense, and European air, Schlee wasn't a particularly attractive man, but he seemed "the ideal companion for Garbo," David Niven observed. "She seemed completely happy in his company . . ."

By most accounts, the relationship began on a business level, with Schlee helping Greta make appropriate wartime investments. "I suppose everybody who meets Garbo dreams of saving her—either from herself, or from Metro-Goldwyn-Mayer, or from some friend or lover. And she always eludes them by going into an act," Christopher Isherwood noted in his diary. "This is what has made her a universal figure. She is the woman whose life everyone wants to interfere with." The more George Schlee interfered, the more he was drawn in by Garbo—and she by him. Friends in Sweden who met the couple years later suspected that Greta was attracted to Schlee because he reminded her of Moje Stiller. But there was nothing overtly businesslike in Schlee's assessment of his newest and, some would say, dearest friend. He would tell a reporter that she was "a flawlessly cut gemstone in the show-window of womanhood—hard and cool on the surface, yet forged in fire and everlasting."

Friends and associates were equally divided on the subject of how intimate the relationship became, and when. Viewed purely as an aspect of his need to control, it seems likely that Schlee pushed to solidify a relationship very early on. Greta was generally the aggressive pursuer in inconsequential relationships, but passive with people who would soon wield the greatest influence in her life. "George Schlee overpowered Garbo," states Joe Lombardo.[5] "He was a fantastic man . . . but he demanded that all of the attention go to him."

Another friend, Betty Spiegel, believes that Greta's relationship with George Schlee was "one of the most overtly eccentric things in her life. How she managed to get him away from Valentina remains a mystery because G. wasn't the manipulative sort of person. Maybe she really did love him." Schlee's behavior when potential competitors came on the scene certainly were the actions of a jealous lover: suspicious, overprotective, demanding, possessive.

Where did this new state of affairs leave Valentina Schlee? Less than enamored, yet a willing participant in this social ménage à trois. Whether or not theirs was a sexual ménage was the subject of bicoastal speculation; Valentina's friends denied it. A devoted threesome on the town at New York restaurants, parties, and the theater soon evolved into a less conve-

---

[5]Joe, the younger brother of orchestra leader Guy Lombardo, was finally introduced to Garbo in the early 1940s when Mercedes de Acosta brought her into his antique store in Manhattan.

nient pair of twosomes: George and Valentina, Greta and George. Accord-ing to an employee of Valentina Gowns, "Valentina never liked the arrangement, but she put up with it. We could never figure Garbo out."

Discussing the situation with his wife, Schlee reportedly reassured her that divorce was not an option. "I love her, but I'm quite sure she won't want to get married. And you and I have so much in common." Yet these progressive ideas—mutually defended by both parties—did not diminish his wife's suffering. "I think Valentina was a little hysterical and liked the drama of it all," Betty Estevez, a mutual friend, says. "George actually felt he had two crazy women in his life."

Summer always brought Greta back to California. Previously unrevealed is the existence of another man in her life during this period: actor Gilbert Roland. The two had been aware of each other since their early days in Hol-lywood when Roland gained a reputation for his eerie resemblance to his act-ing namesake, John Gilbert. He and Greta had many friends in common, but only saw each other in passing. In 1943, when Roland was on leave from the Army Air Force, they happened to meet on an empty street in Beverly Hills. "We walked toward each other, stopped a moment, our eyes met," he wrote in an unpublished memoir. "She pulled her hat down, walked away."

Roland confessed that he had often dreamed about Garbo. "I desired her in silence," he said. A couple of days later, he got up the courage to leave a note with Salka, explaining that he was leaving the next day to return to the war and wanted to see Greta for a moment. She appeared at his door that evening and, according to the actor's memoirs, the two shared a romantic din-ner on his patio under a full moon. Then they went upstairs. "She touched the holy gold medal and chain around my neck, touched the gold identifi-cation bracelet with name and serial number, the gold ring. 'You are the golden one,' she said. On parting I gave her the gold ring, and took her silk panties with the initial 'G'. We kissed goodbye. I boarded the Army Trans-port plane back to the field, her panties still inside my coat pocket."

There is an interesting connection here. Recorded in Cecil Beaton's journals is a story Greta once shared with him about a serviceman who acquired her address and phone number. Thinking he intended to sell his house, she decided to go see him. "He answered the door. They talked. They saw the garden together, the downstairs room. And Greta thought to herself: 'Why not?', so she asked: 'Have you a very beautiful view from your bedroom?' Next day he went to war."

Gilbert Roland received his commission as a lieutenant in the U.S. Army Air Force and was variously stationed in North Carolina, Alexandria, Virginia, and Washington, D.C., during the war. He was still married to Constance Bennett at the time—quite obviously, not a problem. In his memoirs, he wrote that his relationship with Garbo continued when she returned to New York that summer. He described an idyllic day they spent strolling through Central Park, an elegant dinner out on the town, and two intimate encounters at her New York apartment.[6] "We were together frequently," he stated. "Some days she was happy, smiling, laughing. Other times she was silent, moody, morose."

According to his former son-in-law, Scott Harrison, Roland kept over a dozen letters Greta wrote him between July and December 1943. Typical of her intricate subterfuge, none of these letters was signed with her own name or dated. When she did include a signature, she used one of her nicknames ("M—Boy" or "H.B.," for Harriet Brown); dates can only be verified from the postmarks on each envelope. In the correspondence, she referred to Roland as her "Little Soldier," "Little Spaniard" (the actor was born in Mexico), or her "golden one." As for herself, Greta took on different personas for different moods: "Mountain Boy" (M—Boy) denoted her contradictory, secret, but gentle masculine side; "Eleanor" her wistful feminine one. Interestingly, it was Mountain Boy who required—in her words, "craved"—the greatest amount of affection. If "Eleanor" received too much attention, he became the jealous, needy one.

In perhaps her most revealing letter, Greta noted the peculiar way in which she conveyed her feelings without actually spelling everything out and expressed the hope that her lieutenant might be able to share his feelings with his captain over a glass of whiskey. How was it possible, she wondered, to miss someone she scarcely knew? Finally, she wrote to say that she was going away. "This is going to make you sad, but it must be done," she said. "Please dont be too unhappy and try to understand. I cannot see you for a while. And you must not call me, if you do it will be more difficult. It takes too much out of me to see you, and I will not get well . . ." She promised to write "as soon as I am big and strong and Spanish . . ." After a few weeks, Roland begged to see her, but Greta remained resolute. Her final message, written just before Christmas, was a virtual "Dear John" letter.

Gilbert kept her monogrammed silk boxer shorts in his army backpack until the day he died. It is not known what Garbo did with his gold ring, a family heirloom, inscribed with the last words Roland's mother had said to him before she died: *Hijo mio, No te apuras, no te asustas*—"Do not worry, do not be afraid."

* * *

[6]She had registered at the Ritz Tower under the name Harriet Brown.

Like everything else in her life, Greta kept her feelings about the war to herself. She did not attend rallies choreographed to sell war bonds; she did not appear on the USO circuit or at the Hollywood Canteen. Harry Crocker and Salka Viertel often found themselves defending Garbo in the press regarding her "silent support" of the war effort; Crocker even hired a clipping service to keep track of what was being said and to correct "any mistaken ideas."

To many observers, being pro-Swedish or neutral was tantamount to declaring oneself pro-German. The problem for Swedes was far more complex. The Queen of Sweden, the wife of Gustav V, was a German princess. However, her son, the Crown Prince, had married a member of the British aristocracy, and both Gustav Adolf and Princess Louise were vehemently pro-British. With Norway and Denmark to the west and south occupied by the Nazis, and Finland to the east absorbed by the Soviet Union, Sweden alone was "successful" in remaining neutral during the war. They accomplished this partially through the continued sale of iron ore, their number-one export, to Germany. As the Axis weakened, the Swedish government felt strong enough to stop the "leave traffic" of Nazi troops to Norway.[7] But the nation continued to be economically dependent on Germany. It would take persistent and severe threats from the Allies throughout 1944 to compel Swedish businesses to halt the shipment of ball bearings and iron ore.

Much of the Swedish population expressed remorse when they compared their efforts against the heroic legacy of the Norwegians and Danes, whose resistance was highlighted by the Norwegian schoolteachers taking a public stand against the Nazi invasion, the sabotage of heavy water factories in Norway, and the courageous citizens who smuggled thousands of Jews and other political prisoners to safety. But there were acts of valor in Sweden, as well. One of the nation's finest moments was defined by the Swedish diplomats Raoul Wallenberg and Count Folke Bernadotte, whose efforts were central to the refugee escape plan. Another moment involved a Swedish-American businessman named Eric Erickson and his friend, Max Gumpel. Erickson, with the silent backing of Gumpel, helped the Allies locate key munitions sites in Germany. Part of his "proof" to the Nazis that he was willing to betray his friends involved a public snubbing of Gumpel (who was part Jewish). Erickson's story was later dramatized in *The Counterfeit Traitor*.

Former ambassador Leif Leifland believes that both Greta Garbo and Ingrid Bergman "were anxious to show their sympathy with the Allied force." Garbo wasn't a spy, he says, but she cooperated with the Allied

---

[7]Many Swedes would refer to the money earned by the Swedish railway for the transport of Nazi occupation troops as "blood money."

effort. "America was her second home. I don't find it surprising that Greta Garbo was anxious to prove her allegiance." Yet MGM correspondence shows that—despite the urging of the State Department, Swedish diplomats, and friends such as Einar Nerman—she refused a request to tape a patriotic radio message to be broadcast to Scandinavia. Neutrality would not have been the issue, but rather Greta's belief that it was not her place to articulate what other people must do; Sweden and America had their own political leaders who were better equipped for that.

Conversely, Garbo revealed to friends that she had actually received a "fan letter" from Germany's ruthless dictator. "I wonder how it would feel to stand face to face with a man like Hitler," she mused, later admitting to Einar Nerman and Sam Green, among others, that she had fantasized about the perfect assassination plot. Who would dare to search Greta Garbo on a special invitation from the Führer? If she couldn't convince Hitler to stop the atrocities, she would shoot him. Considering her abhorrence of brutality of any kind, the scheme was uncharacteristically bold—especially from a woman who fretted that nothing she might do could possibly make a difference.

Some acquaintances would later take this intriguing suggestion as proof that Garbo had agreed to spy or carry messages for the Allies. It was a romantic notion. Nevertheless, MGM's Mata Hari was typically sly when asked to comment on such rumors; she neither confirmed nor denied them.

Most of these stories emanated from a book about the British Secret Service entitled *A Man Called Intrepid.* Canadian William Stephenson—code name Intrepid—helped to set up a special office coordinating activities between the British Secret Service and its counterpart in the States, and was known to use key entertainment industry figures as covers. Charles Higham, author of several books on wartime espionage, maintains that Garbo was asked by Stephenson to help keep an eye on Axel Wenner-Gren. Her first assignment would have been the trip to Nassau from Miami in February 1940. "For the rest of the war, she would devote herself to the allied cause," he declared. "She would risk her life involving herself in the mass rescue of Jews from Denmark, and would bring to bear a strong influence upon King Gustav of Sweden . . ."

Stephenson's original claim was much more vague. "As a member of the Stephenson-Churchill group, [Garbo] provided introductions and carried messages," his *Intrepid* biographer recorded. "When Stephenson called on her royal admirers, he was quietly arranging escape routes—especially for [Denmark's pioneering nuclear physicist] Professor Niels Bohr . . ." For his part, Stephenson made no connection between the actress and "tainted" Swedish businessmen such as Axel Wenner-Gren or Axel Johnson.

"I would have died of shame if I had ever had anything to do with spying," Greta said later. But would she have carried messages? First, there is no indication that Garbo ever left the United States between 1938 and 1946. However, in the 1960s, after meeting U.N. secretary-general Dag Hammarskjöld, she would confide that there were "some things that happened a long time ago that we had to talk about. We spoke Swedish to each other," she told Raymond Daum. "It was very painful for me . . . but I can't tell you that story."

What did the war really mean to Garbo? Learning to drive secondhand cars, using ration cards for food and gas, coping with air-raid scares, planting Victory gardens, house-hunting (again) with Sydney Guilaroff and his two adopted sons. Yet while many American women were obtaining their first jobs, there still was no wartime work for a glamorous, soon-to-be forty-year-old actress.

It wasn't for lack of trying. Metro readers submitted several new story ideas, including Eugenie Leontovich's *Dark Eyes*; a new screenplay by Michael Arlen (which became *Heavenly Body*, with Hedy Lamarr); and a Norwegian play entitled *Victoria*, by Knut Hamsun. Katharine Hepburn, who was now firmly entrenched at MGM thanks to the back-to-back successes of *The Philadelphia Story* and *Woman of the Year*, told Garson Kanin that she was "absolutely besotted" by Eugene O'Neill's *Mourning Becomes Electra* and wanted to do it at Metro with Garbo and director George Cukor.

Hepburn arranged a meeting to pitch the project to Mayer with Garbo and Cukor in attendance. The studio boss listened to the story, as told by Harriet Frank, his talented storyteller.[8] "I thought this [arrangement] was idiotic until I heard Mrs. Frank do [her job]. . . . She was brilliant," Hepburn recorded in her autobiography. "I was absolutely riveted and fascinated when she told *Mourning Becomes Electra*." It took almost two and a half hours to present a detailed synopsis, and Hepburn could tell by the end of act 1 that they had lost Mayer. The trio left Mayer's office without further comment. Greta was obviously perplexed and wanted to know what had happened. There was some discussion about taking the project to Warner Bros., but all three partners preferred keeping in alignment with their adopted alma mater.

During the summer of 1943, before she left the studio for good, Salka Viertel was summoned to the Chief's office. Mayer accused her (and, by

[8]Garson Kanin says Mayer's assistant at that time was Lillie Messenger, whom L.B. stole from RKO; Harriet Frank assumed the role of chief storyteller after World War II.

indirect inference, Garbo) of being a hopeless, heartless highbrow. "He went on telling me that Joan Crawford blindly followed his advice and had fared very well by it, and 'that poor little girl, Judy Garland, she always does what I tell her; even Norma listens to me—only Garbo is difficult. I am her best friend. I want her to be happy—she should come and tell me what she wants—I'd talk her out of it!' " When Salka related this conversation, Greta admitted that it seemed "pointless" to return to the studio. There was nothing left for her to do.

It was Mercedes de Acosta's dream project—but Mercedes wasn't invited in. "Greta Garbo has finally got the role she's been waiting for. She'll sail sometime in September for England to play Joan of Arc in George Bernard Shaw's *Saint Joan*, under the direction of Clarence Brown," Hedda Hopper announced in a May 1943 column. David O. Selznick had planned to produce *Saint Joan* with Gabriel Pascal directing, but George Bernard Shaw didn't like any of the prospective names placed before him to play Joan. "The Californian suggestion of Miss Garbo for Joan is—well, Californian," he wrote in a September 1938 letter to Pascal. Privately, the playwright labeled Garbo "a mere sex appealer." Joan "should be a simple, real down-to-earth peasant, without false eyelashes and typical movie make-up," the director concurred.

Shaw, having put his faith in Pascal after he successfully brought *Pygmalion* to the screen, was beside himself when he learned that the director had reconsidered Garbo. "It was finally decided between Gabriel and myself that G.G. was out of the question for various reasons. . . ," he wrote a friend. "Joan must not be an old Hollywood star no longer in her first youth." On the strength of Garbo's casting, however, Pascal secured the interest of producer J. Arthur Rank in financing a package of Shaw adaptations; *Saint Joan* would be the first to go. Sure that he could allay Shaw's fears once Garbo arrived in England, the director offered Salka the unenviable task of fashioning the screenplay in tandem with Gottfried Reinhardt's brother, Wolfgang.

By July, according to Cecil Beaton, Greta was all set to travel on a Portuguese boat to England to shoot the film. Germany's horrific buzz bombing of London put an end to those plans. On the other side of the Atlantic, the British government put pressure on Pascal and Rank to postpone the production, arguing that it would be "injudicious" to present a film in which modern-day allies were in conflict, with the British burning a French patriot at the stake. The project was put on hold indefinitely. "That was the first serious disappointment in my career—a hefty blow," Greta told Beaton; "after that nothing has happened."

* * *

In March of 1944, Greta bought Loretta Young's former home on Bedford Drive in Beverly Hills. Her first contribution would be to plant a pair of orange trees in the backyard. As for the interior of the house, she sought the advice of decorator Barbara Barondess MacLean. "Garbo is simple and thrifty in her tastes," MacLean noted. "[She] likes French and English furniture of the eighteenth century, the 'elegant country' type. . . . Mostly she just broods or makes slip covers."

She continued to need a base in Los Angeles. David O. Selznick was intent on being the producer to bring Garbo back to prominence and had his readers on a continuous search for material; he was currently developing a screenplay concerning the sensational life story of Sarah Bernhardt. Harry Edington had offered Garbo a new home at RKO. Edington, now in charge of production at the studio, had purchased *Lena Storme* with her in mind and was seen "huddling" with Greta regarding a contract.

Producer Lester Cowan, whose recent credits included the popular war film *G.I. Joe,* commissioned Salka to write *Women of the Sea,* a tale of a female skipper in the Norwegian merchant marine. Dutch filmmaker Joris Ivens was hired as a technical advisor, and former Warner Bros. writer Vladimir Pozner was brought in to punch up the Resistance angle. The stakes were increased when the Norwegian Ambassador to the United States made a personal appeal to Garbo to make the film. But she refused to sign a contract without a finished shooting script. "After two-thirds of the script was finished," Salka recalled, "Cowan decided that this and a synopsis of the rest should be sufficient for Garbo to make up her mind."

The star said no. It was then that Salka made a stunning discovery. "I had been concentrating so completely on my work and my personal conflicts that I was only superficially aware of the red-baiting which began to occur in Hollywood. To my utter amazement, I learned that Greta had been warned that it was only a matter of weeks before Norway became a communist country, and also that I was 'under the influence of the Reds.' Her agent, Leland Hayward, first enthusiastic about the story, declared that war films were 'outdated and nobody cared to see them.' "

There was no indication of this from Hedda Hopper, soon to be one of the town's most flagrant red-baiters. "The Garbo–Lester Cowan situation over the Norwegian picture she had agreed to do . . . is by no means settled," she announced in her column. "Lester's being very fair about it. He's placing the matter before a committee of the Screen Actors Guild . . ."

Lena Storme also ran into troubled seas at RKO. When Harry Edington left the studio, Garbo lost interest in the project entirely. By one journalist's count, she had turned down twenty-six screenplays to date.

* * *

On June 6, 1944, Allied forces landed on the beaches of Normandy. Years later, historians discovered that the success of D-Day had been dependent on a clever deception code-named "Operation Garbo." The most success-ful double agent of the Second World War, Juan Pujol Garcia, was known to the Allies as "Garbo" and to the German intelligence service as "Ara-bel." His spy ring, based in wartime London, was so highly regarded by both sides that he had been decorated by both for his achievements. Pujol explained that he acquired the code name "Garbo" because MI-5, the British Security Service, considered him to be "the best actor in the world." The name reflected MI-5's high regard for the agent "and also offered some cover," stated military historian Nigel West. "If the Germans ever discovered that MI-5 were operating a double agent with the name of a famous actress, they might assume the agent to be a woman."

While the D-Day landings were being planned, the master spy kept the enemy supplied with reports from a bogus organization of twenty-four sub-agents. In a daringly conceived plan, Pujol led the Nazis to believe that the invasion force would land near Calais. Even after the beachhead had been established at Normandy, his "network" continued to assure the Germans that the operation was a diversion—thus encouraging them to keep their forces spread out.

Sir William Stephenson was right, Garbo *was* a spy. But "she" was a he and *he* never met she.

Two events occurred while Greta was still in Los Angeles that irrevocably changed her life. One July evening, she opened her bedroom door and saw "the shadowy form of a man" in her hallway—it was a toss-up who was sur-prised more, Greta or the prospective burglar. She locked the door hastily, and climbed out the window and down a drainpipe. The police arrived just after the man fled the house and climbed over a nearby fence, leaving Garbo to pick up the valuables scattered in his wake. Greta was so unnerved by the incident that she moved temporarily into Minna Wallis's house and didn't return to her Bedford Drive home for weeks.[9]

On the eighteenth of October, Anna Gustafson died in Scarsdale, New York. According to medical records, the cause of death was coronary throm-bosis. Garbo's loss was kept private. Other than the standard listing in the obituaries, there was no press attention; even family friends were kept in the

---

[9]The sister of producer Hal Wallis, Minna was a top agent at Charles Feldman's agency. A clever, capable woman, Wallis was well-liked in the community; she fussed over Garbo in much the same way Salka did.

dark. As late as 1948, Mercedes de Acosta believed Greta's mother was still alive. Einar Nerman recollected that whenever he received a letter from Sven and Peg, Anna Gustafson always added her greeting: "Love, Anna." During a walk with Greta sometime later, Nerman told her that he hadn't heard from the family in a while. Did Anna still miss her home? "Greta looked up to the sky. 'How would I know?' she said quietly."

Greta lingered on the East Coast for several months, passing up potential projects as the news from Europe got increasingly optimistic. While the Allies were rushing toward Berlin, Greta was taking a tour of the New York Stock Exchange, studying how her money could work for her. Then came the joyous news that the war in Europe was over and Garbo, like many expatriates, began making plans to go home—at least for a visit.

"Spent my time chewing over whether to go home in June or July," she wrote Hörke Wachtmeister on the fifth of June. It was the first letter she had posted to Sweden in about two years. "Would you mind asking Grönlund at the Strand Hôtel if there are any rooms available. . . . If they have nothing free there, maybe Max [Gumpel] knows of an apartment I could rent for a while." She couldn't wait to visit her friends in Sweden. But the passenger liners would not be running until 1946; it would be another year before Greta was able to go home.

In spite of the disappointments, Hollywood wasn't dead for her. Selznick proposed a new project based on *Scarlet Lily* by Muriel Elwood; Elsa Maxwell suggested *Anna Lucasta;* and Bing Crosby was paging her for *The Emperor Waltz,* written by the *Ninotchka* team of Brackett and Wilder. Garbo also considered generating her own projects. In November of 1945, George Cukor wrote W. S. Maugham on her behalf. "Your friend, Miss Garbo, has a notion. In my opinion a pretty good one—and it all depends on *you!* She thinks an extraordinary picture could be made about Duse." Though Cukor pointed out the pitfalls involved in dealing with such a "high-falutin'" legend, he agreed that "it could be dramatic to see a romantic and noble creature done in by an ego-maniac like D'Annunzio."

If Maugham responded to the story, Cukor wrote, Greta wanted to meet with him when she returned to New York. "In the meanwhile, George Schlee, who knows a good deal about the project, could talk to you about it. . . . In fact, it was Schlee who brought the whole subject to her attention.[10] You probably know him. He's nice, and intelligent. He is married to Valentina, the dressmaker, and by way of being a beau of Miss G's. Now don't be shocked, those things do happen."

---

[10]Actually, according to Einar Nerman, Salvador Dali brought up the idea at one of Schlee's parties.

Unfortunately, Maugham was not available. "I think the fair Garbo's idea is quite a good one, but I have far too much work on hand to undertake anything else," he replied. "Why doesn't she approach Andre Maurois?" Cukor downplayed their disappointment. "Garbo was pretty let down when she realized how intransigent your love for her was. Apparently under the influence of soft lights, Viennese waltzes and liquor, you gave her to believe that your heart, your fortune, your pen, were at her feet," he jested. "Now you turn her down! Actually, she was very sweet about it. She was grateful for your suggestion of Maurois. She is following that up." The subject was added to David O. Selznick's growing list of dream projects.

It had been four years since Garbo had been in front of a movie camera. She shared her true feelings in a letter to Hörke Wachtmeister. "I have been considering a film I might try making, but I don't know. Time leaves its traces on our small faces and bodies," she suggested. "And it's not the same any more, being able to pull it off. . . . I have no idea how I would arrange the world if I had the power to do so. . . . I am still just as lonely. Nothing changes. I spend my time wondering why I don't have some marvelous person who would scamper around with me . . . And so it goes."

PART FOUR

*Things happen. We can't always arrange our
lives as we want them or even try to explain
why we arranged them . . . so strangely.*
                              —*Garbo in* The Painted Veil

Comeback

The word "comeback" has an ominous ring in Hollywood. One makes a comeback from failure, hopefully—but how does one recover from an absence? If Garbo had made a picture directly after *Two-Faced Woman*, few admirers would have remembered the misstep. Even without a film, if she had remained active, performed on radio, or made personal appearances, the pressure on her would have been minimized. But this behavior would have been out of character. "I don't believe she'll ever make another picture," Billy Wilder told Louella Parsons as 1946 rang in. "She's as frightened of pictures as she is of personal appearances and everything else that brings her in contact with people."

The actress was foremost among those critics who had begun to doubt whether people really wanted her back. Many disagreed with this thinking. "Greta Garbo? The top movie actress that ever was," Ruth Gordon asserted. "Looks, talent, everything. She could not make a wrong move, then did: she left the movies." The bigger question was, to paraphrase silent screen actress Mae Murray, did Garbo leave the movies or did the movies leave her?

Some moviegoers already considered her retired; a rare few thought she should stay that way. When columnist Jimmie Fidler heard that MGM proposed bringing Garbo back, he wondered what induced executives to believe that she could be "re-sold to the American public." His primary concern was her lack of visibility during Hollywood's significant wartime effort. "Being a great actress isn't enough; it's also necessary for screen stars, if they are to have fan followings, to be attractive personalities. And I believe Garbo long since lost the attraction she once had for theater-goers. . . . Her persistent discourtesy to the public, which, in the final analysis, paid her every cent she owns, now excites resentment instead of curiosity."

According to Hedda Hopper, Garbo was one of three major entertainers who failed to show at the Hollywood Canteen (the other two were James Cagney and Charlie Chaplin). Other columnists would join in the chorus that the star "had better offer an explanation of why she had refused to join the Victory Caravan" if she had any intention of continuing her film career. The effect of such negative campaigning was felt all the way to Washington, D.C., where the Immigration Department received correspondence from a handful of irate citizens demanding that "if she does not approve of our country," Greta Garbo should be deported.

Whether or not she had completely alienated her fan following depended on one's perspective. George Schlee was confident that there would be no problem. "She reminds me of Duse," he said. "She had been in retirement eleven years and returned to greater triumphs than ever. This will happen to Garbo." Rumors about her return were certain and irrepressible. Ernst Lubitsch reportedly wanted her for *A Royal Scandal*; MGM was again touting a George Sand biopic; producer David Lewis tried to snag her for the lead in Erich Maria Remarque's *Arch of Triumph*. The possibilities were overwhelming, yet nothing progressed to a stage that would have made Garbo secure in the knowledge that her commitment meant a "go." At times, it appeared that the producers' intentions were as halfhearted as her own.

Nothing was secure. "Dearest, darling Hörke," Greta wrote on the sixth of February. "I am wondering once more why we never write. Maybe you're going through the same feelings as I am at present. Or maybe you're still the same, old cheerful Hörke. . . . I have bought a home here after all these years and am trying to furnish the blessed nuisance, and it's not easy. Everything I do is wrong. I have never worked as hard as I am doing now. And nothing happens." Curiously, although she hesitated to say as much to her friends in the States, to Hörke she confided that she had tried "to get away from this place so often because I [will] never work again at my former job."

This did not stop people on both coasts from working on her behalf. George Schlee concentrated on getting Garbo to "come out" socially. He did this in an unusual way: the couple had been inviting themselves to the homes of friends to drink vodka and share a tin of imported Russian caviar they'd bought at a local gourmet shop. In March of 1946, they attended a party at the apartment of *Vogue* magazine's society editor, Margaret Case. It was in this glamorous setting that Greta was reintroduced to photographer, designer, and sometimes actor Cecil Beaton. "At the sight of Garbo I felt knocked back, as if suddenly someone had opened a furnace door onto me," he remarked. "The warmth of her regard, her radiance, her smile—robbed me of equilibrium . . . and I was flattered beyond belief to be the object of her attentions as she spread a piece of caviar on a biscuit and offered it to me pronouncing the word 'kahr-vee-yeyarr' with histrionic flamboyance."

How should we interpret the words of an unrepentant diarist? According to his biographer (and now literary executor) Hugo Vickers, Cecil Beaton compiled more than 145 volumes of letters, essays, and personal memories between 1922 and 1974. When he began publishing highlights from these journals in the 1960s, Beaton took some liberties with the material. "An historian should always mistrust a diary edited by the diarist himself," Vickers offered. "In *The Wandering Years,* the first volume, entries were rewritten with hindsight, some extracts were added that do not exist in the original manuscript diaries, events were kaleidoscoped and dates tampered with." Similar allowances were made when later journals were published; some entries were sanitized, others were embellished.

Although the material was sometimes manipulated, two things remained constant: Beaton's uncanny depiction of Garbo, and his compulsion to reaffirm his importance in her later life. In order to understand the psychology of this relationship, it behooves us to review its genesis. As with Mercedes de Acosta, it began with an obsession. During Beaton's first trip to Hollywood in 1930, the photographer admitted making a desperate appeal to Howard Strickling regarding a photo session with Garbo. The answer was no. "No advice or pressure would be of avail; she could never be won by flattery," he wrote in his published memoir.

But, according to his diary, Beaton's initial response was far less civilized. After having his hopes raised by Strickling, the photographer called the publicity office one last time. "What about getting Garbo?" he asked. "Not a chance," the dean of publicity said. "Hell. Damn. Blast the bitch. I almost wept with fury, exhaustion, pique. . . . Bloody Hell to Garbo—the independent and foolish bitch. Perhaps some day she may wish she *had* been photographed by me. . . . She'd got nothing else to do."

Having vented his wrath privately, it was a different story upon his return to Hollywood a year later. Inevitably, conversations with friends "always seemed to revert to Garbo: her hermit-like independence, her unconventionality in this most conventional of all worlds." With the able assistance of Edmund and Marjorie Goulding, Beaton found that the image that had haunted his dreams became real in March of 1932. Beaton would write of an encounter abounding in romance and poetry. A vase of yellow roses had been sprayed with a mist of water and placed on the Gouldings' bar. "Garbo picked up a rose and kissed it, fingered it with an infinite variety of caresses and raised it above her head," he recollected. "As she looked up at it, she intoned, 'A rose that lives and dies and never again returns.' " The moment was reminiscent of a scene from a film—one of hers, in fact.[1]

"Suddenly the dream was over," Greta's would-be suitor recorded. "It was time for Garbo to leave." Beaton wanted to meet her for lunch. No.

---

[1]In *Romance,* Rita Cavallini compares her philosophy of life to the roses that we love and smell and throw away. They are so fresh and beautiful, why should we take them home with us and watch them die? she asks a would-be suitor. "Oh, I wish I knew a flower that would never die."

Would they ever meet again? Who knows? "Then this is Goodbye?" he asked while still in a daze. "Yes, I'm afraid so. *C'est la vie!*" As if to prove to himself that the evening had been real, Beaton kept the yellow rose and later had it preserved and mounted in a frame.

After two years of silence, he wrote an essay about the star in a London paper, *The Sketch*; an expanded version was published in *Cecil Beaton's Scrapbook* in 1937. In addition to his own impressions, both articles were based in part on Hollywood gossip retrieved for him by a circle of friends, including Mercedes de Acosta. "She has a sense of humor, a sense of fun, but she is unhappy, neurasthenic, morbid, for she has become . . . something she never wished to be," he opined. "A healthy peasant girl has been publicised as an exotic spy." It would not be his last word on the subject.

When they met again more than a decade later, Beaton observed that Garbo had changed in appearance. "Then she had been like a large apricot in the fullness of its perfection . . . Now the apricot quality had given place to vellum. Her eyes were still like an eagle's—blue-mauve and brilliant, the lids the color of a mushroom—but there were a few delicate lines at the corners." Yet her allure had not diminished for her admirer. With a nervous, edgy companion hovering about, Beaton pulled Greta out to the roof garden for a private moment. "The sudden cold outside went through the body like a succession of knives, but I was determined that she should remain there until I struck a chord of intimacy," he stated. "She talked, talked, talked, gabbled ever harder, like an excited child, in order to cover her embarrassment at the things I was blurting out to her while discovering the knobbles of her spine and smelling the new-mown hay freshness of her cheeks, ear and hair."

She promised to call, but it would be several days before she did. Beaton was soon initiated into her ritual of briskly paced walks on the streets of New York or around the Central Park reservoir. "We 'steppe outte' for miles very fast, around the reservoir, then all the way home from Ninety-Sixth Street to Fifty-Ninth. During these walks over the grass, under the early springtime trees, her mood becomes euphoric," he wrote. "To be part of nature gives her the same elation as champagne to a novice drinker. She strides, leaps, laughs, becomes as lithe as a gazelle."

Cecil Beaton won the assignment many photographers coveted. Greta needed a picture for her new passport and he skillfully turned her tentative request into an impromptu sitting in his hotel suite. "At first she stood stiffly to attention, facing my Rolleiflex full face as if it were a firing squad. But, by degrees, she started to assume all sorts of poses and many changes of moods. The artist in her suddenly came into flower," he recorded. Once she relaxed, Beaton brought out some prop clothes—a pierrot's ruff, various hats—and shot approximately two dozen photographs of Garbo in various reflective moods.

On May 9, 1946, the Swedish Consul General in New York issued her a new passport; on it, Greta continued to list the Wachtmeister estate, Tistad gård, as her home in Sweden. She also used one of the Beaton photos for her reentry permit. Contained in the application was the seemingly hopeful declaration of her current occupation: movie star.

Greta slumped into an armchair in Cecil's room. "Phew! I've been three hours listening to a story! Why don't people cut it short?" she remarked in a clearly exasperated state. She had spent the afternoon with Clare Boothe Luce discussing a film scenario, but described her meeting to Beaton without mentioning names. "I got so tired," she exclaimed. At the end of the pitch, she was asked if she liked the story. "Yes, it's all right, but it isn't written yet," Greta said. "How do you know what it will be like when it's written?" She hesitated to encourage anyone to work for months when it was doubtful that she would like the end result. "So it's better if I say now: 'I ain't going to do it.' "

Garbo was so careful about what she should do next that she obviously preferred a simple "no" to the agony of "maybe" or "soon." But she couldn't say "I ain't gonna do films." Every summer, Greta would show up on Salka's Santa Monica doorstep to share the dreams about films and the future that everyone thought she had long ago abandoned. On the twenty-first of May, she went west to wrap up some business before returning to Sweden. Harry Crocker, who was now her neighbor on Bedford Drive, met her at the train station.

The wartime machine had left behind a new order of producers, directors, stars, and even executives for Greta to deal with at Metro. "I think the biggest thing I could sense was the fact that it had become more assembly line instead of the individual thought given to pictures [by men] like Irving Thalberg," said director Joseph Newman. "Now it had become more of a committee approach. . . . And it had become an era where the agents were gaining more and more power." Salka had once lost her job at MGM because she dared to bring the "enemy," an agent named Paul Kohner, on to the lot. By the late 1940s, the Charles Feldmans and Leland Haywards and Paul Kohners of the industry controlled the greatest talent in Hollywood.

As the movie industry changed, Greta continued to rely on the people she could count on as being constant. During the transitional postwar years, this meant Salka Viertel, Gayelord Hauser, and Harry Crocker. In spite of her hard work and effort, Salka was perpetually labeled a "Garbo specialist." Her writing assignments were few and far between and almost always attached to the prospect of bringing Greta Garbo in. "The high command of the industry was prone to typecasting actors and actresses and, as it turned out, scriptwriters as well," her son, Peter Viertel, noted. "My mother's old friends remained loyal to her in spite of this change in her fortunes, but the groups at her Sunday tea parties at Mabery Road became noticeably smaller."

After the war, Salka's position was complicated by the political perception of her. The home that friends had affectionately dubbed "the New Weimar" was constantly under observation by the FBI. Officially, the investigation began in March of 1942 when Berthold applied for a job at the Office of War Information and the agency was asked to do a standard security check. Unbeknownst to Viertel, he was identified as an "alleged" Communist; he resigned from his position at the OWI shortly thereafter. Salka's name was added to the FBI Watch List the following September— she was reported to be "anti-capitalistic and communistically-inclined." The bureau monitored Berthold's political activities and read articles he wrote that were published in key left-wing newspapers and magazines. The Viertels' participation in the Anti-Nazi League and the League for Peace and Democracy furthered their reputation as Communist sympathizers.

Although an FBI report of April 22, 1943, concluded that there was "no indication that either subject has important Communist Party connections," Salka's continued humanitarian efforts to get jobs for European refugees were viewed with suspicion in Washington. The fact that so many of her friends now populated the FBI's watch list gave the agency cause to extend its "discreet inquiry" to reading mail coming to and leaving from 165 Mabery Road. This included most of Garbo's correspondence, since Greta used Mabery Road as her principal mailing address.

Finally, in 1944, after years of professional separation and personal entanglements, Salka and Berthold divorced. Unfortunately, informants assigned to keep tabs on the Viertels reported nothing of their changed marital status. Berthold remained the subject of an FBI watch throughout the war and well into peacetime. In March of 1945, he was placed on a National Censorship Watch List due to his contact with the Free German movement (also considered a Communist front). Chaplin, Bertolt Brecht, Thomas Mann, and Lion Feuchtwanger—all gods in certain intellectual circles—were highly suspect in government ones; as was Salka's membership in the Screen Writers Guild. For the time being, Salka's activities were viewed as more social than political; nonetheless, she continued to be observed. After looking into her bank account, agents revealed that Salka was not "in a good financial position." She had requested numerous extensions on loans and usually had a low bank balance.

Money problems Salka rarely shared with her best friend; her problems with the government would soon become abundantly clear—but talked about even less.

On July 6, 1946, amid delicious rumors of a Garbo/Beaton romance, Greta "scampered" to Sweden with George Schlee. She boarded the SS *Gripsholm*, moored in its westside berth at Pier 97, three hours before sailing time. Captain Sigfried Ericsson brought her to the bridge to avoid the press. Just before the ship left, Greta had a change of heart and agreed to pose for a few photos, even managing a smile. "I had to get up very early this morning," she stated, adding that she was going to Sweden "just to take it easy."

For once, she made no effort to hide during the voyage, having booked her stateroom under her own name. She often mingled with Schlee and other passengers on board, including Swedish sculptor Carl Milles and his wife, and the sisters Gish, Dorothy and Lillian. After a brief stopover in Liverpool, the *Gripsholm* arrived in Göteborg Harbor on the morning of July 17.

Greta was overwhelmed with emotion as she witnessed the hero's welcome that greeted her at the pier. The crowd chanted her name as mothers and fathers lifted their children up for a better look; she had been away far too long. Garbo and Schlee were whisked away by Swedish Consul General Axel Johnson to a private coach on a waiting express train. At Stockholm Centralen, they were met by Max Gumpel. There was more cheering as Garbo stepped into her old friend's elegant automobile and was carried "like the wind" through the streets of Stockholm.

Gumpel had arranged to take the couple to his country estate of Baggensnäs, hidden near the summer resort of Saltsjöbaden and guarded by trained dogs. "I have promised Miss Garbo and her friend that their visit will be an undisturbed one. They will enjoy the summer as private persons," Gumpel told the press waiting outside his gate. Inside the manor, a festive homecoming was celebrated with wine and champagne.

They stayed at Baggensnäs for about two weeks, Laila Nylund, Gumpel's youngest daughter, remembers. Then Greta went away to visit an uncle, Axel Johansson, on his farm near Kalmar. The party returned to the Gumpel estate for another week before moving on to Tistad. "She didn't stay long in Sweden," says Nylund. "The people were awful; they really clobbered her." Underneath it all, many countrymen felt, was a deep resentment of Garbo's success. "Some [Swedes] denounce their own when they move out and become stars—and then when they return, they act as starstruck as everyone else," Nylund offers. "There were newspaper photographers and reporters hiding in the bushes and trees across eleven acres of land . . . they were all over the place. My sister and I sent the dogs after them and thought that was really funny." The children, too, had become her protectors.

Greta related to children in a rather unique way, Nylund says, not condescending or juvenile but as an adult who talked and played with them on their level. "She was always good with kids. It wasn't just that she related to you, but that she was a child within herself." During her visit, Laila Nylund vividly recalls the sight of Garbo on the children's swing and her attempt to best them in lawn acrobatics. Though nearly forty-one, she didn't hesitate in trying cartwheels or anything else the kids were doing. "She tried. We thought she was such a good sport. She would laugh if she didn't make it, and we laughed. She absolutely idolized us; kids feel that."

Laila, who was then about fourteen years old, recalls being fascinated by another side of their visitor's personality. "The Swedes have a number of fairytales about trolls, especially trolls in the forest," she explains. "And Greta always talked about trolls—even the last time we saw her. 'My best subject is trolls,' she would say. We would ask her what it was that intrigued her with trolls. 'Oh, I don't know. They're kind of spooky and you really don't know about them—but they're friendly,' she would say in her deep, dark voice. She said they had mystique. . . . I think she wanted life to be a fairytale, and sometimes she had a hard time coping because it wasn't. Ultimately, she was very, very lonely because there was no one to whom she dared to admit that she was that child in her way of looking at things."

"I think she was happier reading make-believe stories with happy endings," Nylund adds. "Dad used to like that. He was something of a philosopher and kind of liked that she was drawn to those stories. He'd look at me as if to say, 'Do you see why I like her?' He thought it was a side of her that was very profound."

From the adult perspective, observing Garbo with George Schlee, Nylund believes that their relationship was a loving one—but not a passionate affair. "You never saw them walking hand in hand or him with his arm around her shoulder . . . nothing whatsoever. It looked very platonic, but—what should I say?—a friendship that was deep and lasting and respectful. I mean, you could tell they respected one another just by the way they talked to one another, and the way they dealt with one another. It was a true friendship—more than any of the other ones." Interestingly, Laila also remembers another beau visiting Garbo at Baggensnäs: an exotic-looking man, perhaps Egyptian. Like Schlee, he seemed to idolize her.[2]

[2]According to Jean Howard, this person may have been Raymond Hakim, a close friend of Charles Feldman's. "Charlie told me that Raymond had quite a long affair with Garbo. He was an Egyptian Jew, very attractive—and he played around with all the girls."

Sadly, there were friends who had once understood Greta better than anyone else from whom she now seemed to be withdrawing. She reconnected with Mimi Pollak and Alf Sjöberg in Stockholm. Sjöberg recalled telling Greta about a book by Hjalmar Bergman, *Chefen fru Ingeborg,* in the car on the way back from Mimi's house. "I always dreamt that she would come home and that together we would make the greatest love story in the Swedish language," he said. "A Phèdre tragedy. . . . I could see a new road open up for her." Their car stopped in front of her hotel on Djurgården and both passengers sat quietly in the back for several minutes. "Greta was sitting in her corner, her face even more beautiful than in her youth. But she did not say anything, she just looked across the water . . ."

Finally, she told Sjöberg to send her the book and she would read it on the boat home. "And then she was gone." Sjöberg stayed in the car and watched her walk away. Though his pitch had been persuasive, he knew Garbo would never do the film. "Times change, and no one knew that as well as she. Behind that inscrutable face is a consciousness that knows exactly when the time has come."

The trip to Sweden also represented some kind of closure to her relationship with Hörke Wachtmeister. The war had precipitated much of this estrangement. Separated by treacherous waters and the constant threat of danger, Hörke concerned herself with the men in her family and her wartime work, while Greta had been caught up in the trials and tribulations of a fading career. When she returned to Sweden, Garbo told Cecil Beaton, she felt uprooted, "knowing no one except a certain friend on whom I daren't call under the present circumstances." Why not? "It's a tricky subject," she stated. "But the U.S. uproots one: I have been here so long."

Through the years, Greta had grown to depend on her correspondence with Hörke. "Your messages always give me new hope," she hailed in one letter. Each letter from Tistad was accompanied by an assortment of newspaper and magazine clippings, as well as greetings from the Wachtmeister children and their friends. To show her thanks, Greta often sent along items that were difficult to get at home, especially coffee. As the war dragged on, her letters to Hörke became more desperate ("Not a single word from you, what's the matter? Don't you like me anymore?") . . . demanding ("When are you writing me a letter?") . . . and, finally, resigned ("I am once more wondering why we never write"). The final break, Sven Broman suspects, was an unexpected one: Greta had fallen for Nils Wachtmeister, Hörke's husband. "I don't know how far it went or if the feelings were mutual, but eventually their friendship came to naught," he says. While it is possible that the reverse was true—that one of the Wachtmeisters was attracted to her—there is a spark of truth in the idea of Garbo pursuing a friend whom she felt she could trust with her money.

Five weeks into her stay, Garbo and Schlee were joined by Lillian and Dorothy Gish. On the twenty-fourth of August, they boarded the *Gripsholm* for the return trip to the States. Ironically, when freed of contractual demands, Greta enjoyed the least amount of time in Sweden. "Dockside roofs and windows were crowded with spectators when Greta Garbo, under a heavy police escort, boarded the liner *Gripsholm* which sailed for New York tonight," *The New York Times* reported. It was the ship's first nonstop voyage since the war.

The *Gripsholm* arrived in New York on September 3. Greta stayed on board while the ship was cleared and reporters were ushered onto the main deck. She was "at first tolerant and later gracious" as the flashbulbs popped and she was inundated with questions. "I haven't been elusive," she maintained. "Being in the newspapers is awfully silly to me. Anyone who does a job properly has a right to privacy. You'd think the same if you were in the same boat." It would be far better, she said, if everyone went home and had a cup of coffee. "I have no plans, not for the movies, not for the stage, not for anything," Greta added, "and I haven't even got a place to live. I'm sort of drifting."

At the Ritz Tower, she registered under the name Harriet Brown; Greta Garbo was not available—especially to photographers named Beaton. Cecil Beaton had been unable to resist the opportunity to command some attention with his photographs. With Greta's permission, he sent the pictures to Alexander Liberman, the art director at *Vogue*. Liberman "could hardly believe his eyes," Beaton recalled. "Here was a precious windfall of a dozen different pictures of someone who for ten years had resolutely refused to be photographed." The actress had given permission to use one photograph. Disregarding their agreement, Beaton talked Liberman into publishing a full series.

There is little doubt that Beaton's motives were self-serving ones. His primary desire had been to reestablish his reputation at Condé Nast.[3] "I think he bought his way back into a career there by selling [Garbo] out," stated Sam Green. "He was desperate to get published again in the United States." While in Sweden, Greta sent Beaton word that she expected to see only one picture published in the magazine—but it was too late to change. Frantic, the photographer cabled, sent flowers, and placed telephone calls to Stockholm, New York, and Los Angeles; Greta refused to listen to excuses.

---

[3]Beaton had been blacklisted by the publisher because of an illustration he did in 1938 which contained hidden anti-Semitic slurs. The drawing was published in *Vogue* before anyone was alerted to the problem.

Finally in October, she accepted his phone call—but not his apology. She was in Beverly Hills and alone. "She said she had received a letter from me but that she couldn't decipher my handwriting; there was cruelty in that, so I said it appeared that she enjoyed making me suffer," he wrote. Garbo protested. "I wouldn't do anything to any human being to make him suffer," she answered. It was far from a reconciliation. "By your action you have deprived me of a friend," she told him during a subsequent conversation. There would be many frustrating days ahead before they again met face to face.

There seemed to be no shortage of provocative movie ideas for Garbo. The top prospect on David O. Selznick's list was *Sarah Bernhardt,* with a sharp script by Ben Hecht and the lure of a dynamic young leading man named Gregory Peck. Then Cukor had an even better idea: he invited Salka to lunch. "As always, he was bubbling with ideas and good humor. He began telling me how disgraceful it was that in six years MGM had not been able to find a story for Garbo." The director had been reading about George Sand. "I had never thought of Garbo as George Sand but Cukor's enthusiasm was infectious," Salka reflected. "Nevertheless, I thought that most of George Sand's biographers were biased, condescending and ironical. Only a few condoned her many lovers, her trousers and her socialism."

There were plenty of reasons not to proceed with the screenplay, not the least of which was a recent albeit archaic adaptation of Sand's affair with Frédéric Chopin in *A Song to Remember* (with Merle Oberon as a glossy version of Sand and a dandified Cornel Wilde as the composer). There were equally compelling reasons why they should do it. Doubtless Garbo was attracted to Sand's cavalier lifestyle and refusal to adhere to what other people expected of her. Through such a character, she could explore creativity and sexuality without concern for Hollywood glamour. Cukor proposed an international production shot on European locations, and both Greta and Salka were in favor of it.

As the New Year approached, there was a discernible undercurrent of public sentiment in favor of a motion picture—any motion picture—starring Greta Garbo. Selznick, in particular, sensed that her screen return could be a huge success. But Greta was in no hurry to make a decision. Due to timely investments, she was spared the financial pressure of needing to get back to work. By the war's end, a significant portion of her money had been funneled into premium real estate, stocks, bonds, and art. With the help of Gayelord Hauser, she had been investing in property from Los Angeles to Milwaukee since 1942—both directly and indirectly through title transfers and real estate partnerships. Within a few years, these investments were working for her and she no longer needed to touch the principal.

At the same time, she was gradually divesting herself of property in Sweden. Greta's brother, Sven, journeyed to Stockholm in March of 1947 to make arrangements for their mother to be buried in the Gustafson family plot. Hårby had already been put on the market and Greta's antiques placed in storage. While Sven was back home, he arranged for the remainder of their furnishings—clocks, bureaus, and Chinese sculptures—to be auctioned off anonymously.[4]

By 1947, Valentina and George Schlee had turned their Russian Easter party into a yearly event, inviting New York's finest to indulge their gourmet palates. Here Garbo made quite an impression on actor John Gielgud. "[She] is the most extraordinary individual—little girl face and now quite short hair tied with an Alice ribbon; hideously cut dress of beautiful printed cotton to her calves and then huge feet in heel-less black pumps," he noted. "Lovely childlike expression and great sweetness—she never stopped talking but absolutely to no purpose—said her life was empty, aimless, but the time passed so quickly there was never time to do anything one wanted to do! All this with twinkling eyes and great animation, not at all the mournful tones of her imitators . . . But I couldn't make out whether her whole attitude was perhaps a terrific pose."

From New York, Greta wrote Salka Viertel about their film project. "I spoke to Hayward and told him to talk to you of S. Bernhard [sic] story. Did he? . . . I am so sorry that it is so difficult for us to get started. Perhaps 'they' dont like us!" "They" were looking for a way to pull the rabbit out of the hat. Caught up in a whirlwind of debt compounded by a bitter divorce, David O. Selznick had a diminishing cash flow and he needed a commitment from Garbo. "I SHOULD LIKE TO HAVE ANOTHER CHAT WITH [HAYWARD] ABOUT GARBO, WITH A VIEW TO MEETING WHAT REMAINS OF HER ECCENTRIC DEMANDS AND WORRIES[5] BY OUR AGREEING TO A DEAL FOR THE TWO THINGS ABOUT WHICH SHE WAS EXCITED, *BERNHARDT* AND *THE SCARLET LILY*, PLUS ONE MORE PICTURE," the producer cabled his legal liaison, Daniel O'Shea. Although chivalrous enough to show Garbo the respect she had earned, Selznick wanted her to recognize the extremes to which he was going to meet her concerns, "WHILE AT THE SAME TIME TREATING HER AS

---

[4]The first day of the auction, held on May 14, 1947, brought in over 60,000 kronor. Only after the sale did the new owners learn of the seller's true identity.

[5]According to Paul Kohner, one of these "whims" was Greta's insistence on her standard 9 to 5 workday.

THOUGH SHE WERE STILL A GREAT DRAWING CARD, WHICH NO ONE IN THE INDUSTRY WILL CONCEDE . . ."

Privately, Greta confessed that she lacked the emotional fortitude to jump into the fray with producers—in her mind, this was the very reason why Salka's contributions to her films had been so substantive. "If there was ever any argument about a script I always had this woman to fight for me," she told Cecil Beaton. "She was indefatigable and worked on them to saturation point and always found something good that others would not bother about."

One month after Selznick's memo, there still was no answer from the Garbo camp. On the twenty-ninth of May, the producer got one he probably didn't like: she had committed to do *George Sand* with someone else. By her own account, Salka spent more than six months putting together a film treatment based on various source materials concerning George Sand, Alfred de Musset, and Frédéric Chopin. Jack Larson read the completed screenplay years later. "It was like seeing the film, this script was so crafted for what Garbo would do," he remembered.

British producers showed the strongest interest in the story. With motion picture production severely threatened in Hollywood by the breakup of the studios' theatrical alliance, as well as by the uncertainty posed by the coming of television, international backing became not only attractive but the only way independent producers could survive. With this in mind, Peter Cusick, an agent at William Morris, assembled an international partnership for the production of *George Sand*. The United States partner was to provide the star, director, story, partial financial backing, and a distributor; in exchange for his financial participation, the French production partner would guarantee the studio facilities, costumes, sets, and production crew; Britain would furnish the remaining cast and technicians, including the production designer. Cusick proposed bringing Laurence Olivier into the project and optimistically plotted an April 1948 start date.

On August 9, 1947, Garbo and her faithful companion, George Schlee, embarked on the HMS *Queen Elizabeth*, arriving in the English port of Southhampton seven days later. "Why, when and where I go to in London I cannot say," "Miss Hansen" a.k.a. Greta Garbo told the assembled press, adding wistfully, "I don't think I shall return to Sweden." The couple went straight to Claridge's, where Greta registered under the name Harriet Brown. According to Salka, she specifically requested that she be shielded from any communication regarding motion picture projects. Instead she toured the Cabinet War Rooms with Winston Churchill and made arrangements to accept an unusual bequest.

Back in the States, a reclusive Michigan farmer named Edgar H. Donne had willed his entire estate "to Greta Lovisa Gustafson, whose stage name is Greta Garbo." Furthermore, it stated, if she should become his wife, the estate would go to "Greta Lovisa Donne." Donne had been estranged from his family for some time, owing to a youthful love affair. He reportedly had written Garbo on numerous occasions and even traveled to Hollywood in order to get in touch with her. Now the loner offered his favored actress the ultimate tribute: an estate which included $15,000 in English securities, one hundred and sixty acres of land, U.S. war bonds, and jewelry. Since the will had been written in England, it was in that country that the estate was probated. To everyone's amazement, Greta accepted the inheritance.[6]

Garbo and George Schlee flew to Paris on their way to the French Riviera, where they had been invited to stay at Villa la Reine Jeanne, Commandant Paul-Louis Weiller's home in Bormes-les-Mimosas. Greta had met the French industrialist through Elsie Mendl and jokingly referred to him as "Paul-Louis Quatorze." Douglas Fairbanks, Jr., recalls meeting Garbo, Chaplin, and a host of others at Weiller's home. On one memorable occasion, the group took a motorboat out; as they turned into one of the alcoves, they noticed a group of nude bathers on shore. Seemingly ignorant of who their visitors were, several unembarrassed bathers started waving, others swam toward the boat. When a few portly swimmers turned to float on their backs, Greta couldn't contain herself any longer and broke out into peals of laughter. "She was just roaring," Fairbanks remembers.

Later in the month, Garbo and Schlee continued their journey along the Côte d'Azur, through colorful communities that wore their café society status like a badge: St. Tropez . . . Cannes . . . Cap d'Antibes . . . Monte Carlo. One report intimated that before returning to London, they also met with Thomas Mann in Switzerland. However, according to Betty Estevez, Greta went to Switzerland for more personal reasons: to get off the sleeping pills prescribed to her years earlier at MGM.

While Greta and George traveled abroad, Mrs. Schlee, cast off in New York, indicated to friends that she definitely was not amused. When Noël Coward met Valentina for drinks, she "bared her soul a little over George and Garbo. Poor dear, I'm afraid she is having a dreary time." So was Cecil Beaton. "It was no good your being here [in London] and yet not here," Beaton charged in a letter written the day after Greta sailed for New York, "for under the auspices of that Russian sturgeon I could have no chance. I think it was mean of him, though, to allow you so short a time in England, and of course it was intentional." Beaton, frustrated by the miscommunications and canceled meetings, urged Greta to forget America and return

[6]News reports suggested that she was considering a charitable donation, such as the Sister Kenny Foundation. This was never confirmed.

to Europe, where she would find herself in "much more sympathetic surroundings."

Hollywood's witching hour had arrived. In May of 1947, the House Committee on Un-American Activities (HUAC) met in a closed session with a group calling itself the Motion Picture Alliance to discuss the perceived Communist threat in Hollywood. The Alliance's prominent membership—which included Walt Disney, John Wayne, Robert Taylor, Gary Cooper, Adolphe Menjou, Charles Coburn, Ward Bond, Hedda Hopper, and Sam Wood—became the Committee's first "friendly witnesses" decrying the use of their industry to further anti-American propaganda. Within a matter of days, worried studio executives began examining employee rosters and considered weeding out potential problems. Because the industry's most misaligned trade union, the Screen Writers Guild, was accused of being "lousy with Communists," writing staffs topped the list of "problems" to investigate.

Salka Viertel was one of many politically visible writers caught in the margins of this confrontation. Many of her problems actually resulted from government surveillance of her former husband. FBI correspondence from 1947 indicates that Berthold Viertel was identified by a known Russian agent as a "favorable person" who had mixed with some "bad people" in New York during the 1940s. But Salka was also described by "an informant of unknown reliability" as a Communist, although Party members denied this. Internal bureau memoranda show a determined effort to establish Salka's Party membership; they could not, but remained unwilling to clear her. No doubt her association with Hanns Eisler and Bertolt Brecht hurt her the most—Eisler's brother, Gerhart, a suspected German spy, was an acknowledged Communist in the postwar era.

Despite the perception of guilt by association, a review of HUAC transcripts reveals that Salka Viertel's name never came up in actual testimony. "She wasn't a Communist," Jack Larson says, "she wasn't even a socialist; she was a humanist." Perhaps outsiders did not take her political opinions as seriously as she had. No longer on a studio payroll, she was a small fish in the pond for J. Parnell Thomas and his committee. Technically, she avoided the blacklist, but not J. Edgar Hoover's unofficial "pink" list of suspected Communist sympathizers; the FBI remained in the background as long as Salka remained in Hollywood.

For Greta Garbo, the ruthless political persecution of many of her Hollywood friends, as well as the prevailing puritanical climate in the United States, most definitely contributed to her feelings about wanting to make a film abroad. In October, Peter Cusick finalized his plan for the multi-international financing of *George Sand*. The motion picture would be produced in association with Pathé Cinema in France and Laurence Olivier's production company in London.

But Leland Hayward, Garbo's agent and manager, was not impressed; Cusick complained that he ridiculed the money offered his client until he was informed of her profit participation. Cusick spoke with George Schlee "at great length" about the problem with Hayward. "[Schlee] wants to have Miss Garbo do this film," he wrote George Cukor. "He claims that he is trying to get her down to the fact of it all and that she must do some things or it will all blow up . . . I really think that he would like to take Leland's place as her manager, but does not know quite how to effect that." Even with Hayward's involvement, Schlee would exert considerable influence over Garbo—but neither one would be successful in getting her to do what she was not prepared to do. Over the next two years, this would be their most difficult lesson to learn.

With athletic grace, Cecil Beaton miraculously surmounted the obstacles that typically befell others attempting to penetrate Garbo's inner circle. An assignment from *Vogue* brought him to New York at the end of October. Greta, who was safely ensconced in her tower at the Ritz, evaded his phone calls at first. When they did speak, she expressed an interest in a rendezvous, but maintained that she must be free for Schlee (whom Cecil mischievously referred to as "the little man"). Finally, Greta indicated that she would come to his rooms at the Plaza. This time, there were no delays or postponements; she arrived on schedule. "Her practical side came out when touring the apartment she suddenly drew the mustard velvet curtains," Beaton recorded. "I was completely surprised at what was happening. It took me some time to recover [from] my bafflement. Within a few minutes of our reunion . . . we were suddenly together in unexplained, unexpected and inevitable intimacy."

When the rumors of a Garbo/Beaton romance began circulating in show-business circles, Hollywood was understandably cynical. Insiders had previously referred to Beaton's connection with Garbo anonymously: he was the man "whose name would slay you." Skeptics doubted that Cecil—who was often accused of being "as regal as the Queen of England, as elusive as Garbo, and as prissy as the fussiest Edwardian"—even liked women. Clearly, he adored them, but was he capable of being intimate with them? Significantly, before he contacted Greta in New York, Beaton had spent time with his latest male infatuation.

"My attitude to women is this," the nineteen-year-old diarist wrote in 1923, "I adore to dance with them and take them to theatres and private views and talk about dresses and plays and women, but I'm really much more fond of men. . . . I'm really a terrible, terrible homosexualist and try so hard not to be." He learned the value of artful cover. When designer Charles James accused the young man of trying too hard to be part of the heterosexual world, Cecil confessed that he found himself making rude remarks about "fairies" because "they frighten and nauseate me and I see so vividly myself shadowed in so many of them . . ."

Yet, according to Jessica Dragonette's husband, Nicholas Meredith Turner, Greta confided that she enjoyed Beaton's company—he practically killed himself trying to do little things for her. As for the rest, she said, "He can't do anything. He's just a fairy." (Like Beaton, she preferred this quaint term to other more accepted ones.) Cecil recorded a similar, though somewhat gentler, put-down when the couple met Constance Collier and her companion, Phyllis Wilbourn, at the Farmer's Market in Los Angeles. "Why don't you two settle down?" Collier asked. "But you don't think he's that sort of man, do you?" Garbo responded.

It is possible that these "winking" retorts were a convenient means of evading the truth. Jack Larson believes that Beaton never would have risked writing about the relationship during Garbo's lifetime if the basic facts weren't true. "Cecil definitely was obsessed with her," he says. "He loved beauty and he was crazy about her . . . I don't doubt [they had an affair] at all." Even so, when magazines containing excerpts from his journals arrived at the Klosters newsstand years later, the absence of emotion from Garbo was a statement in itself. "With frozen face, she bought all the magazines and, without a word, went quickly home," Gore Vidal recalled, "leaving me and Ratzski [Vidal's pet terrier] to read the Italian version of the love affair that, she assured me later, never took place. 'And people think I am *pair*-annoyed,' she observed with a scowl."

Was it a fantasy?

"I knew Cecil Beaton and I knew Garbo, and I don't see either one of them doing any such thing, particularly with each other," another companion, Sam Green, offers. "I think he was capable of [having sex with women] in a kind of fumbly way . . . and she might have acquiesced because she wasn't prudish at all about her physical self. She was downright seductive, if you wanted to take it that way. She was always grabbing one's hand, putting her hands on one's knees . . . If I was standing in a museum, she'd come right up behind me and rub all over me. But it had nothing to do with sex. It's just that she was a big strapping Swedish girl, and it didn't bother her at all to be physical.

"Cecil Beaton made up a lot of stuff. He operated a great deal with his imagination. . . . I think she and Cecil were very good friends, and I think he probably did put the make on her. But she didn't go for the mush and he talks about mushy romance and deep kissing and fondling. . . . She wasn't the type; she wasn't romantic. And he was gay—she may have been, too. I don't see the energy there."

When the memoir revealing Beaton's affair with Garbo was published, "Everyone in Hollywood was laughing about it," actress Coral Browne told Hugo Vickers. "It was a trip down memory lane so far as I was concerned." Browne admitted having a brief, intimate encounter with Beaton in the 1930s. "Many of Cecil's friends took the line that he would have had no idea what to do with a woman," Vickers acknowledged. "Even today his detractors and some of the homosexual community with whom he associated refuse to believe it. Yet many of those who knew him well attest to his involvement, and there is evidence that, in a curious way, he had more success with women than with men."

Beaton's mistake, Jean Howard thinks, was to write about the relationship or even let on he'd known Garbo that well. "She really liked him enormously, saw a lot of him and admired what he could do. . . . Maybe it didn't last long, but I really am quite sure they probably did go to bed a couple of times." Howard confirms that Beaton certainly went through a phase of "pouncing" on women. When he decorated a suite at the Sherry-Netherland, he invited Howard, then married to Charles Feldman, to view it. As soon as they got upstairs, Beaton excused himself. "He came out in a dressing gown and made a beeline for me, shoving me back on the bed. I had on a brand-new dress that I liked enormously and my one thought was, 'The dress!' I laughed, really laughed hysterically." She pushed him away and got up from the bed. Beaton was furious. "I've never seen a woman so disinterested in a male body," he exclaimed. "Good night, Cecil," Howard said as she calmly straightened herself up and exited with her pride intact and his in shambles.

Emotionally, Cecil Beaton was Garbo's complete opposite; his energy and enthusiasm could be overpowering. "Perhaps she is attracted to the violence in others that she lacks in herself," critic Kenneth Tynan suggested. "Yet sustained violence wearies her, makes her shrink from it and return to the remote security of her own being." What intrigued—and repelled—her most was Beaton's constant proposals of marriage. Cecil was nothing less than an ardent pursuer. When Greta began to withdraw after a few rapturous days, he became desperate and sought the advice of a mutual friend, Mona Harrison Williams. "Don't be a dope," she chided him. "You've got to get her mind. And her mind's got to worry about what's going on in your mind . . ." In order to avoid losing her, he must change her way of thinking.

The tactic worked. Cecil suddenly became unavailable, filling his schedule with dinners and weekend invitations—now Garbo became interested. According to Beaton, she was jealous of his friends and intent on throwing a wrench into whatever plans he made. "So you are stepping out in both directions," she inquired after showing up unexpectedly at his door. Greta tried to talk him out of going to a cocktail party, but Cecil was determined to go. He clearly enjoyed turning the tables on an elusive lover. "Why though did it make her smile so much?" he wondered. "Was it because she was no longer bored by the faithful admirer?"

There is no doubt that Beaton was serious about capturing the Divine One in marriage, and that he sincerely believed Garbo might be rethinking her stand in this regard. "I couldn't ever marry you," he once told her. "You are not serious about me." Greta laughed. "What a rebuff! And I adore you, Cecil—I love you—I am in love with you!" She would confide that she had never thought of anyone in particular when it came to marriage. "But, just lately, I have been thinking that as age advances we all become more lonely, and perhaps I have made rather a mistake—been on the wrong lines—and should settle down to some permanent relationship." Beaton claimed that most recently she had entertained a marriage proposal from the head of Columbia Broadcasting, William S. Paley.

On the thirteenth of December, Cecil received an important call. "It was such a strange voice speaking in pathetic, plaintive tones that I was worried. . . . She sounded utterly dejected. 'I'll meet you on 58th Street by the cinema,' she said, slurring her words. . . . I ran along the street and in the distance saw a very forlorn figure dragging towards me. As she approached her face was turned somewhat sideways with an expression of great sadness. Weeping, with large tears coursing down her cheeks, she was *in extremis*, unmindful of passers-by."

The gist of her predicament was this: Greta had gone outside to get some fresh air, misjudged the freezing temperature, and returned to her room to warm up. "To overcome her numbness she had taken a swig of vodka which, because of low resistance, had gone straight to her head. She became dizzy, then lachrymose. Even now she made little sense and kept throwing her head back and flicking her hair. Her eyes were dazed. I wanted to give her hot milk and cover her with a rug, but she said 'no' to every suggestion."

Even goddesses could be childlike and vulnerable. Later, after she calmed down, Greta lay on the sofa while Cecil read a letter from home to her. It was at moments like this that her willfulness and his haughtiness dissolved into the natural impulse to protect and defend a friend and lover.

Contrary to Beaton's characterization of Greta wasting her life with "boring people," she continued to meet some unabashedly eccentric and interesting ones. She was introduced to playwright Tennessee Williams in California during the summer of 1947. "She goes under the name of Harriet Brown and sneaks around like the assassin of Bugsy Siegel," Williams wrote his lover, Donald Windham. "The meeting was arranged very carefully and privately like an audience with someone superior to the Pope." Garbo drank straight vodka and told Williams she wanted to make another film "if the part was not male or female." Dorian Gray was one of the roles she mentioned. "In appearance she is really hermaphroditic, almost as flat as a boy, very thin, the eyes and voice extraordinarily pure and beautiful," Williams wrote, "but she has the cold quality of a mermaid or something. . . . She scares me to death."

That December, Greta attended a performance of A *Streetcar Named Desire* in New York. After the show, much to Williams' surprise, he alone was invited back to her sanctuary at the Ritz. "We sat in the parlor drinking schnapps . . . and I began to tell her the story of *The Pink Bedroom*." The scenario, which Williams hoped she would consider for a future film, wasn't finished and doubtless contained too many biographical similarities—and bizarre twists—to suit Garbo. Yet as he told her the story, he recalled that "she kept whispering, 'Wonderful!' leaning toward me with a look of entrancement in her eyes." He thought he had convinced her to return to the screen. But an hour later, when he had finished "she sighed and leaned back on her sofa. 'Yes, it's wonderful, but not for me. Give it to Joan Crawford.' "

Garbo denied making any such comment. "We talked about nothing—the weather," she told Cecil Beaton, "and after a bit I said: 'Well, I've got an appointment . . .' " She offered him a drink before he left. "But that didn't loosen him up—we hadn't got anything to say. He's not an interesting person: he is just a little man with a mustache."[7] According to Beaton, Williams harbored the fantasy of casting Garbo as Blanche Dubois in the movie version of *Streetcar*. Precisely how he envisioned the intrinsically European Garbo as a neurotic Southern belle has never been explained, but Greta saw the pitfalls. "I couldn't bear to tell lies, and see things round corners, like that girl in the play," she said.

Whether or not she played the role, she certainly could identify with Blanche Dubois's fragile sense of self and deepening melancholia. "You must realize I am a sad person," Greta would say. "I am a misfit in life." The theme of "nobody must know" pervaded most aspects of her life. Garbo's friends were expected to be friends without comparing notes. This was nearly asking the impossible of Cecil Beaton and Mercedes de Acosta. Greta and Mercedes' relationship was "on" again—though seemingly patched with Band-Aids, as Cecil was to discover when de Acosta's name

---

[7]Beaton was not an admirer of Tennessee Williams. Much of his account of Greta's continuing litany of complaints seems to have been filtered through his own prejudices.

was mentioned in conversation. "Greta said there must be something wrong, otherwise she wouldn't be so alone, so unpopular and miserable. 'But she's done me such harm, such mischief, has gossiped so and been so vulgar. She's always trying to scheme and find out things and you can't shut her up.' " Cecil revealed that Mercedes had asked recently if he and Garbo were having an affair. "That's just like her," Greta said. "It's so vulgar."

The trio met for breakfast on Christmas Day. "Mercedes, unable to hide her anxiety, was extremely preoccupied with the thought of having to prepare a meal. Greta, sensing the climate, at once took control and entertained us all with a most amusing and adroit performance," Beaton recorded. Part of her repertoire: a medley of Salvation Army hymns, including "Nobody Knows the Troubles I've Seen But Jesus." After such "random, higgledy-piggledy outpourings," Greta tied a towel around her waist and cooked ham and eggs for everyone.

Cecil observed the two women together with keen interest; there was much to be gleaned from their personal dynamics. "Greta has a paralyzing effect on her best friend, who becomes tactless and silly in the presence of her high priestess," he noted. "This is a pity, for Mercedes, at her best, is capable of conversing on a wide range of subjects . . ." Loyal to both, in his own fashion, Beaton was perfectly capable of playing "Miss G" against "Madame Alba," commiserating with each about the other. "Typically, when on good terms with Garbo, he saw Mercedes as a threat. When on bad terms, he saw her as an ally," Hugo Vickers stated. At all times, Mercedes was an important source of information.

Information would not be easy to glean from George Schlee, but Cecil hoped to disarm him by assuring him of his good intentions. He invited Garbo and Schlee for cocktails in his hotel suite on Boxing Day. It was a purposefully small gathering; included among the other guests were Salvador Dali, Natasha Paley Wilson, and Allen Porter. In the center ring: George and Cecil. " 'The little man' seemed ill at ease, and his eyes never met mine with any confidence or honesty," Beaton declared. "Throughout he emanated a troubled, electric aura. Even the drinks did not give him any false faith in me, and he was quite correct in his surmise."

When Greta showed up at Beaton's door on New Year's Eve with a grave look on her face, Cecil had every reason to believe his campaign was gaining momentum. She admitted being cruel to Schlee, reacting defensively because she felt caged. "Oh, I've said such wounding things to him, but I couldn't help it," she said. "I became quite hysterical, and I laughed and I cried, and all my mascara ran and I looked such a sight."

Did they fight about Beaton? Greta wouldn't say. "He's been such a good friend to me, none better," she explained later. "Before you came along I never used to go out anywhere: now he knows I see you and he's worried." Clearly unhappy, Schlee told a mutual friend he'd made "a great mistake" letting Greta and Cecil get together; that he was in a position to do him great harm. Beaton remained confident of his position, but an unplanned encounter illustrated exactly what he had to contend with. He saw his adversary rush to the telephone—just as he had—to check in with Garbo during a theatrical intermission. Thinking about it later, Beaton realized how "dreadfully devoted" Schlee must be to her. He knew he had "a real tough battle" ahead of him, "but," he said, "the reward is worth it."

In January of 1948, MGM prepared for the re-release of *Ninotchka* in the United States. The studio received "help" from an unexpected source. Labeling the film "a nine-year-old slander against the Soviet Union," the Communist paper *The Daily Worker* accused Metro of using *Ninotchka* to prove its "true loyalties" in the wake of the HUAC hearings. The controversy only focused attention on the movie and served as a launchpad for its first-run exhibition across Europe, reportedly sponsored by the U.S. State Department.[8]

The path to success for Garbo's next picture was less certain. When Greta showed up with a new escort, French director Jean Cocteau, at a party given by James Pendleton and his wife in New York, there was renewed talk of a foreign production. A few weeks later, she was seen on the arm of Leland Hayward at the Broadway opening of *Mr. Roberts* (which Hayward produced).

Greta was at an important crossroads in her life. Should she go back to Hollywood, sell her house, stay in New York with her new circle of friends, or return to Europe? Whatever her decision, her career could not be put on hold indefinitely. She must reconcile herself to work or risk damaging her career irrevocably. "If she doesn't work, what is there in store for her?" Mercedes wondered. "What will happen to her in ten years' time? What is her life now? Hunting around Third Avenue shops for junk, waiting for orders from [Schlee]. She has only a handful of friends, and some of those are pretty suspect."

The irony of this situation, Cecil and Mercedes agreed, was that Greta, "the most suspicious person, should often find herself on friendly terms with those least suited to her by temperament. Terrified of being exploited, she was always being victimized." Mercedes included Gayelord Hauser on

---

[8]Despite protests from the Soviet Embassy, the film attracted turn-away crowds in an unprecedented number of theaters in Rome and Milan. According to the *Motion Picture Herald*, Garbo and the film were given credit for turning the tide against the Communists during the Italian elections.

this list, but gave no credit to either Hauser or Schlee for Greta's improved state of health and mind. "When we lived together in Hollywood she used to come back from the studio in tears most nights, abysmally unhappy," she said, "and she would sit alone locked in the cellar and for days on end she wouldn't talk." She still brooded and never seemed completely happy in her life, but at least she was stable, Mercedes conceded.

Having become a screen personality before she had fully developed as a person, Garbo often thought about working behind the camera, where "velvet gloves" weren't required. "It's such a waste of energy not to be able to say: 'I want the thing to be done in this way,'" she told Beaton. She spoke enviously of living the life of a painter or writer and being able to enjoy the fame of such artists independent of the public dissection of personality, and expressed a desire to put on film "some of the things she had been impressed by: the strange groups of people that people naturally fall into—not just the conventional line-up that fills the screens today . . ."

Greta's possessive, dependent relationship with George Schlee may have nullified Cecil Beaton's quest to bring his beloved to the altar—but neither gave up easily. Both men made getting their star back in front of the camera a priority. As part of his comeback scenario, Cecil took credit for setting up a meeting between Garbo and British producer Alexander Korda to discuss an English adaptation of Jean Cocteau's *L'Aigle à deux têtes* (*The Eagle Has Two Heads*).[9] Beaton saw many similarities between Garbo and Empress Elizabeth of Austria. "Each lives a part of her life in a world of dreams and fantasies; each has her own eccentricities—so baffling to more ordinary people." There was also talk about filming Anton Chekhov's poignant tale of *The Cherry Orchard*. Either one would accomplish Cecil's objective of getting Garbo to England.[10]

While Korda considered the possibilities, Greta returned to Los Angeles. Anxious to avoid a showdown with Schlee, she asked Cecil not to follow her. Beaton, however, was determined to make his winter's conquest complete. He knew he must capture Greta within the "Vatican" walls of her own home, and he followed her to Hollywood on the pretext of a "meeting" with Alfred Hitchcock. She appeared more than happy to see him. "I was on the point of sending you a telegram," she said. "Suddenly I get so restless." Due

[9]Actually, Korda was in town to discuss a joint production deal with David O. Selznick.
[10]Soon after, Greta received a telegram from the producer stating that, due to prior commitments, he would not be able to do *The Eagle Has Two Heads*. Though unable to disguise her disappointment, she could not be talked into the Chekhov piece, which she thought dull and dreary.

to the war, little work had been done on her house. Greta preferred spending her time in the garden, a sunny area enclosed by white walls and filled with geraniums, oleanders, and white lawn furniture. She gradually showed Beaton around the house. Here she lived oblivious to the movies "and Miss Parsons," he wrote. "Here were her bookshelves, the cupboards with tennis racquets and old mackintoshes, the pad with telephone numbers written in her square, capital lettering. So this was where 'the *Divina*' lived."

In his diary entry dated March 4, 1948, Beaton claimed that their reunion had been another intense affair—at least, *one* version of his journals indicates this. But, according to Hugo Vickers, this passage was copied on to a separate sheet of paper and then erased from the regular journal. In his fourth volume of memoirs, *The Strenuous Years*, Beaton kept the specifics to a minimum, acknowledging only that after this encounter he would feel "Olympian while the lives of others were as pigmies."

Cecil spent an eventful fortnight in Los Angeles, frequenting many of Greta's favorite haunts with her. There were long, quiet walks along the beach watching man and nature collide—but now, instead of retiring to the security of her hotel suite, there was a house in Beverly Hills that she still felt unsure of. "A noise of dry leaves scraping together was heard from outside in the alley. Like a frightened animal Greta was on the alert," Beaton observed, "then in a flash was peering through the slats of the blinds. . . . Ever since her house was burgled, her nerve has gone, and she is in a bad state of restlessness. We went through the empty rooms to see that no one was hiding in them." When he left that evening, he looked back to see Greta peering through the Venetian blinds.

His finest moment occurred on March 12, when he got Garbo back to MGM for a private screening of *Anna Karenina*. "Well, well, it takes Beaton to get me to the studios for the first time in six years!" she declared. Greta became increasingly flustered as her car approached Culver City. The reason for the screening was more than idle curiosity: Beaton had designed the costumes for Korda's production of the Tolstoy classic starring Vivien Leigh and wanted to see the Garbo film for comparison.

Greta passed through the gates and into the projection room without being recognized by studio personnel—a rather sad commentary on transitive celebrity, Beaton thought. Throughout the movie, she added her own narrative: her remembrances of the Russian extras, how they used feather bits in place of snow, Adrian's costumes, the troubles with her hair. Time had allowed her the luxury of showing pleasure in the final result.

Three days later, Cecil departed on the *Super Chief* for New York. "It had never struck me quite how much I would mind this parting," he recorded. "I knew that, in some ways, I had scored a victory over Greta: I knew that I had made her love me. Yet I had failed to give her the strength to act, to have the ability to take a more positive stand with herself. . . . She had for so long designed her life to protect herself—locked up in her walled garden, with 'the little man' on duty as Cerberus to keep reality at bay . . . Greta had conquered again by sheer stasis."

For various reasons, there had been little activity on *George Sand* since the fall of 1947. Now with a first draft of Salka's screenplay (entitled *Intimate Journal*) in hand, Peter Cusick began making arrangements to produce the motion picture in London in a joint venture between British Lion (Korda) and MGM; the French were no longer part of the equation. Time was ticking away. "I know if I don't do a picture this year, I never will again," Greta told Cecil Beaton with some resignation.

At the end of March, she was notified by the INS that her 1940 Declaration of Intention no longer was valid; she must begin the application process again. Within two weeks, she had re-signed and re-submitted the preliminary paperwork. In April, she attended Sir Charles and Lady Elsie Mendl's Easter party, "looking better than I have ever seen her and much friendlier to everyone," Louella Parsons reported. "If she had any doubt of how she stands with Hollywood, she must have realized how many admirers she has, for everyone made a point of seeking her out."

Suddenly, a new film subject was thrown into the mix by George Cukor. "I read the story of Ruth," Greta wrote Salka when she returned to New York. "You know, I suppose it is a very beautiful story but I wonder if it would hold interest enough for the public . . . I think Cukor said I was to play the old woman. That I wouldnt care to do either so will you give those little peculiar statements to Cukor please and give my best regards." She was equally confused about what was happening to the film she had agreed to do. "Cusick wants to see me again. I still cant figure out what he has. Have you or Cukor any clear idea yet? Whatever he is talking about it is something for an agent to figure out. Legal matters, after all, are not our strong points."

Yet another complication emerged when Cusick received a cable from London informing him that Korda had "some difficulties" to straighten out. "What is back of all of this is the problem of Alex's last three pictures," he divulged in an accompanying letter to Cukor. "They have not nor are they expected to do very much business in this country. Hence he is not riding very high." Cusick hoped to have everything worked out within the week. Garbo was less sure. "*George Sand* could make a wonderful story, but it's eight years since my last film; the war came in the meantime, and there are such difficulties in the world today," she said. "My mother country is in such a poor state—everyone's money frozen there—and in France and

England there's so much unrest and lack of responsibility—perhaps the same here."

But she felt there was little left for her in California—"just an unfurnished house with dreary rayon curtains that are too short and the ugly, ready-made sofas."

CHAPTER TWENTY-THREE

Man Proposes . . . God Disposes

Greta Garbo had been off movie screens for the better part of seven years—a relatively brief period of time, but in Hollywood it represented the average span of a career. As filmmaking changed, each new prospect of work became increasingly frightening for her. "If I disliked it all then, what would I feel about it now?" she asked. Camera angles and lighting had never been her concern. Now, she said, she'd feel lost with everyone watching her, studying her. "I'd be conscious of all the things in my face that weren't there before. . . . I'd be humiliated."

Age had become a factor; Greta knew she risked her reputation with anything less than "divine." Despite her discreet efforts to slow down the ravages of time, she equated her smile lines and crow's feet with the double chins, droopy eyelids, and wrinkled flesh of actors much older than she. Sitting next to a young actress at a party, she suddenly saw her reflection in a mirror. "I appeared so old," she said, "and I realized how quickly youth has gone—it has gone in a flash."

Garbo still possessed an inner youthful glow that would have translated into magic on screen—but she wasn't secure in this. "Even if the public didn't notice these things, I would," she said. "No—in certain ways I miss the life, but I'm not an actor who must go on in any circumstances . . . and I don't have to do it, so what's the point?" Ironically, the apathy that characterized her early years in Hollywood and had won her the respect of movie moguls now worked against her achieving anything as substantial in her later years. "It is impossible to bind Greta," Cecil Beaton noted. "She is a virtuoso at delaying tactics, shelving decisions and leaving a situation in the air." How could she convince investors she now cared?

Clearly, indecision was a disease that plagued all parties during Garbo's postwar "comeback" efforts. In a little over a year, *George Sand* had jumped from the hands of David O. Selznick to Peter Cusick; the United States distributor was to be either MGM or 20th Century-Fox or Columbia Pictures; in England, the mantle passed from Laurence Olivier to Alexander Korda or, maybe, J. Arthur Rank; in France, Pathé-Cinema was a major production partner and then it wasn't involved at all.

After a year of frustrated finagling, a new name entered the mix during the summer of 1948. "I have been busy like a beaver from morning to night running around in circles, doing all kind [sic] of tedious jobs and even having conferences with such prominent people as Mr. Walter Wanger," Salka wrote George Cukor. She had run into her former *Queen Christina* boss at Romanoff's; Wanger told her he was interested in meeting with Garbo if she was serious about making a film. Greta responded "immediately and wholeheartedly" to his offer.

By the mid-1940s, Walter Wanger was one of Hollywood's top independent producers. Although Garbo reportedly had not been very impressed with him during the making of *Christina*, she agreed to a meeting. "There was a lot of chat and bantering," Salka recalled. "He asked her if this is the story she wanted to do—she said yes." Like Selznick, Wanger warned her "that he wouldn't be interested in making only one picture with her and then see her return joyously and forgivingly into L.B.'s arms."

After a long *"hin und her"* in which Wanger's only other suggestion was casting Robert Cummings as Alfred de Musset, Greta and Salka went home encouraged . . . and confused. The producer had been gracious but cool and decidedly vague. A few days later, he informed them his bankers had determined that a costume picture would be too expensive. Instead, he sent along a book entitled *The Ballad and the Source*.[1] Greta did not like the story.

But Wanger didn't give up and encouraged an associate, Eugene Frenke, to pursue Garbo and Viertel. Salka dodged Frenke's phone calls, thinking that he and Greta were "an utterly impossible combination." Finally, she told him the Sand story and was surprised to hear that Frenke, a former director turned manager and producer, loved the characters, the background, and the possibilities her story offered. Above all, he offered criticism that was both perceptive and hard to argue with. "From then on everything began to move rapidly. Wanger called again, Frenke called five times a day, and I spent hours and hours on the telephone," Salka wrote George Cukor. "Then we dined in his house, Greta, Wanger and I—and during a most phantastic [sic] dinner everything was set, you were signed, the story bought, Greta happy, etc. etc."

A few days later, Leland Hayward entered the equation. "You can have Garbo," he reportedly told Wanger, "nobody wants her. I don't give a——" Salka didn't know what to do. "I couldn't tell Greta this because it would have hurt her pride and ego terribly, but I implored her to get somebody else to represent her—Minna Wallis or anybody, only not Leland who would again ruin the deal." Tortured by the possibility of making a mistake, Garbo suddenly became mysterious about signing an agreement; every-

---

[1]Wanger had already purchased Rosamond Lehmann's best-selling novel for an astounding $195,000.

thing ground to a halt. "Somebody is coming and then we'll see what happens," she told Salka. So the two friends reverted to their old routine, "but we talked very little about the story," Salka said. "Finally the mysterious 'somebody' arrived and I was not at all surprised to discover that it turned out to be George Schlee."

Unfortunately, Garbo's appointed protector had ideas that didn't include Salka Viertel. "The one thing which came out clearly from my conversation with Schlee was that he disliked George Sand, de Musset and my story intensely," she shared in her letter to Cukor. "Alas—George Schlee's world is the narrow and snobbish world of Valentina's customers. . . . This is not a personal matter—I know how devoted he is to Greta—but I have no respect for his artistic abilities."

Nevertheless, Schlee was effective at the negotiating table. On the fourth of August, Garbo signed a deal memo with United California Productions and Walter Wanger–International, the soon-to-be incorporated partnership between Wanger, Frenke, and financial manager George Mercader. Her salary was structured on a multitiered pay scale: $50,000 would be paid in installments during the course of production; another $50,000 was due after Wanger-International paid off its first $200,000 loan; the final $50,000 payment would be paid when the picture had earned $2 million. In addition, she would receive a 15 percent cut of the producer's net profit. Principal photography must commence within the year. In a special rider, Garbo and Wanger also agreed on a short list of directors: George Cukor and Carol Reed.

News of the agreement was released to the media two weeks later. "Greta Garbo, the woman who couldn't make up her mind, has ended seven years of indecision by signing a film contract," the Los Angeles Times announced. The final contract was officially signed the following week. Dated August 26, 1948, the agreement offered Garbo an extra $25,000 as part of the third payment; overtime was to be compensated at the rate of $10,000 per week. She was guaranteed script, director, and cinematographer approval, as well as a leading man of equal stature. Surprisingly, though the project was to be the cornerstone of Wanger's new company, she was not guaranteed top billing, only that she would be the star or first costar. It was a one-picture deal with no promises for the future—but it was a start.

"Greta is impatient to work and on the other side she is afraid of it," Salka acknowledged. "I understand this very well after all these years of idleness. Work is a habit and she lost it."

The topic of conversation in Hollywood throughout the fall of 1948 was Garbo's movie deal. "I thought it extraordinary good news when I heard that you and Miss Brown had decided to make Cinema History together. It will put an end to the terrible waste of Miss Brown's wonderful gifts and valuable time," George Cukor wrote Walter Wanger from London.[2] And then he struck an oddly pessimistic note. Though he hoped that nothing would interfere with his doing the picture, he advised the producer that "From time to time, the project is sure to run into difficulties and discouragements that will be pretty tough to cope with. Also, at the risk of sounding Mittel-Europaische or melodramatic, I shouldn't be surprised if obstacles were deliberately put in its way." Still, it would be to their credit if they succeeded in bringing Garbo back.

Leland Hayward quietly receded from the scene; in his place, George Schlee eased into his new business role with complete assurance—many would say too much assurance, as producer Walter Wanger was to discover. Schlee went to Europe that fall to discuss the project with potential writers and investors. Eugene Frenke, carrying Wanger's letters of introduction, joined him a few days later. Schlee, who was convinced they could not make a deal without him, accompanied Frenke on meetings with Cukor in London as well as with key British and French production executives, writers, and financiers.[3]

Making a great European film was as important to Wanger as it was to Garbo and her friends. He was particularly obsessed with finding the right people to work on the screenplay. The announcement of Garbo's signing generated an avalanche of story and casting suggestions. Though most were unsolicited, it seems clear from the ideas that were pursued that Wanger hoped to steer their star away from *George Sand*. "HAVE [JEAN] ANOUILH, [MARCEL] ARCHARD, [JEAN] COCTEAU, SASHA [GUITRY] WORKING IDEAS. ALL WOULD NOT TOUCH *SAND*, DON'T LIKE IT," Schlee cabled Wanger on September 15. "HAVE ONE SCRIPT COCTEAU. HE WILL COME NEW YORK OCTOBER . . . TALKED [NOËL] COWARD AND [TERRENCE] RATTIGAN. THEY WILL THINK." The majority of these ideas were rooted in the same milieu of storytelling that Garbo and Cukor had established in *Camille*. Anouilh suggested *Victoria* or *La Duchesse de Berry*; Archard liked *Madame Sans-Gêne* and *Elizabeth D'Autriche* (based on the same story as Cocteau's *L'Aigle à deux têtes*); other literary possibilities included works by Henry James, Gabriele D'Annunzio, and Honoré de Balzac.

Cukor spoke with a number of writers as well, including Jean Auranche and Pierre Bost (Wanger's first choice as collaborators due to their work with Claude Autant-Lara on *Le diable aux corps*). The director believed

[2]Where he was directing *Edward, My Son* for MGM.
[3]Another alliance they investigated involved Harald Molander and Svensk Filmindustri.

that Daudet's *Sappho* was especially worthy of reexamination. "Don't you think it would be wise if Garbo did not take up her career at the same point at which she left off—if she struck a new and bold note," he asked Wanger. "She would achieve the desperation, the pathos, through her performance. The part has such great power and humanity. It should be as distinguished a success for her as *Camille*."

But Cukor was informed that Greta had said no to *Sappho*. Wanger remained qualified in his enthusiasm for *George Sand*. "My great concern about *Sand* is that it be bright and really entertaining. I don't think our leading lady should be made into a female Paul Muni," he wrote "To date, I am not at all impressed with any of the material . . ." It was, however, the only project that continued to interest his star.

On September 9, Greta filed a new Declaration of Intention with the Immigration and Naturalization Service. At last, there was some momentum pulling her life forward—and she had work to do. Walter Wanger compiled a reading list of collateral materials concerning George Sand and arranged several movie screenings for her to look at possible cinematographers and leading men. Because of the problems he was having extricating Cukor from MGM, the producer also assembled an alternate list of directors for Garbo to consider; among them, Charles Vidor, Victor Fleming, Carol Reed, Jean Cocteau, Réné Clair, and G. W. Pabst. Although Greta had been deeply moved by Pabst's film *Der prozess*, that collaboration would have been too risky for her to undertake. The director's reputation in France—after he was "forced" to return to Germany—was nearly as bad as Sascha Guitry's; the general public considered both "tabu."[4]

By the end of the year, Salka was pretty much out of the loop as far as a Garbo film was concerned—a definite indication that the momentum had swung away from *George Sand*. With the institution of loyalty oaths just about to cut off her income permanently, Salka was looking for a fallback position of her own and half-seriously contemplated opening a restaurant, "Chez Salka," across from Romanoff's. Publicly, Wanger and his associates assured everyone that it was the *Sand* story they would begin shooting in Rome the following April; privately, he hired Dorothy Parker to add her own twist to the script while he investigated purchasing the film rights to Balzac's *La Duchesse de Langeais*.

Greta had troubles of her own. In December, after returning to New York, she was questioned for two hours by a federal district attorney regard-

---

[4]Guitry, who was high on George Schlee's list of preferred writers, had collaborated with the Nazis in wartime France.

ing a fraud case in which her name had been used, without her knowledge, to sell phony stocks. She was met by a friendlier welcoming committee in the person of George Schlee, and during the holidays was glimpsed strolling arm in arm with him around Manhattan.

The holiday season also brought a tentative reunion with Cecil Beaton, who had managed to fill the eight-month gap between their meetings with lengthy letters. It was a largely one-sided correspondence, though occasionally Greta did acknowledge his letters with a brief response indicating that she was tired or wishing she were somewhere else and that she was thinking of him. Anything more would have been too personal. "There's not much point in trying to find out if you've been seeing Constance Collier's companion [Phyllis Wilbourn], or more of [Azadia] Mamoulian," Beaton complained, "if you've altered the pink lamp shades . . . if Madame Alba [Mercedes] has been cribbing your shopping lists or if you are now enjoying the rewards of putting down all those sacks of manure . . ."

According to Hugo Vickers, Cecil began writing "covert" love letters: an outside letter written in more formal language which Schlee could read and assure himself there was nothing to worry about—while an inside envelope contained a more intimate message for Greta. Yet when Beaton arrived in New York, once again there was a careful distance between them. He was frustrated that she didn't take his calls; she claimed to have been out. "Do you swear?" Beaton asked. "I never swear," she replied. "Stop behaving like Mercedes." The source of the tension between them was obviously George Schlee. "It's very unkind just to see me when you feel like it and whistle me along," Cecil pleaded on another occasion. Perhaps, he suggested, it would be kinder not to meet again; Greta did not disagree. Things were just becoming too complicated, she said. "It's giving me a nervous breakdown."

Hurt about being told he was second in line, Beaton couldn't fault Garbo for her loyalty to Schlee and eventually apologized. And there was a happy ending to his visit: Christmas shopping in Chinatown, an afternoon appointment with astrologer Nella Webb, a romantic dinner at the Colony.

As the astrologer predicted, the New Year brought still more changes. Walter Wanger succeeded in convincing all parties involved that proceeding forward with *George Sand* would be "a dreadful mistake." On March 15, 1949, Garbo signed a new letter of agreement with Wanger-International, formally switching the focus of their efforts to *La Duchesse de Langeais*. The current plans, Wanger notified Schlee, were for exteriors to be shot in and around Paris "so that we can benefit from the beauty of the city in the spring," followed by interiors in Rome "where we have the advantages of better stages and better equipment."

As for finding an actor of equal stature, the producer confirmed that he was negotiating with James Mason. Significantly, Wanger also developed an important European contact to help simplify the financial negotiations abroad. Leopold Schlossberg was put at Wanger's disposal "through the kindness of Baron Élie de Rothschild," having been associated with the Rothschild family in their motion picture ventures.

La Duchesse de Langeais, part 2 of Honoré de Balzac's trilogy entitled *Histoire des Treize* (History of the Thirteen), is a story of romance, revenge, and redemption. Scholars believe that its inspiration was Balzac's rejection by the woman he hoped to make his mistress, the Marquise de Castries. He avenged himself by writing about a heartless coquette, Antoinette de Navarreins, the Duchesse de Langeais, who moves about in the vapid, pleasure-seeking world of the French aristocracy. Unhappily married and successfully separated from her husband, the Duc de Langeais, Antoinette encounters a newcomer to the court of Louis-Philippe, the Marquis, Armand de Montriveau, and is poised for an amorous adventure. He suffers with the knowledge that he is being toyed with. She learns to love at the moment of her greatest humiliation: when de Montriveau calls upon a secret group called the Thirteen to help him abduct her, intending to brand her as a temptress. Her desperate change of heart dooms both of them.

It is easy to see what attracted Garbo to the piece—though it seems unlikely that she read the novella.[5] What grabbed her, and indeed what moved the project along faster than *George Sand* (with its demands for historical research), was the 1947 French film, which provided Greta with a clear idea of what to do with her part. Wanger even explored the idea of opening up the story to include a song by French chanteuse Edith Piaf.[6] In March, he hired two American writers, Henry Garson and Robert Soderberg, to prepare a screen treatment. One month later, a new screenwriter was brought in. Sally Benson, best known for her screenplays of *Meet Me in St. Louis* and Hitchcock's *Shadow of a Doubt,* was considered MCA's top writer. Having recently provided emergency assistance to Wanger on a troubled film, no one questioned that she could deliver a script within the contracted ten weeks.

Meanwhile, MGM pulled George Cukor out of consideration for director by assigning him to *Adam's Rib.* The expanded list of candidates now included Robert Siodmak, Max Ophuls, Mervyn Leroy, Henry Koster, William Dieterle, Curtis Bernhardt, Irving Rapper, and, briefly, Vittorio De Sica. Rapper was busy at work on *The Glass Menagerie* and spoke with agent

[5]Cukor had and begged her not to do it.
[6]The final screenplay contained two pivotal scenes in a nineteenth-century café with a world-weary singer acting as a sage.

Charles Feldman regarding the project. He did not expect Feldman's frank response. "Irving," he said, "Garbo will never get off first base with this story, so forget about it."

But it was too late for Greta to turn back. Instead, she concerned herself with cinematographers. During the first week of May, subject to an approved screen test, Wanger signed Joseph Valentine as director of photography. Valentine's recent work had flattered two of the industry's top stars, Joan Crawford (*Possessed*) and Ingrid Bergman (*Joan of Arc*), but Garbo needed celluloid assurance—as did Wanger and his investors—that she would shine in front of Valentine's camera. Although the records concerning this event are incomplete, a test was most likely conducted on May 5, 1949.[7]

Valentine shot 490 feet of black-and-white film (approximately twenty minutes). The test begins with a close-up of Garbo in natural makeup and hair. She is wearing a light-colored blouse and has tied a generous scarf around her neck. By turns, she is nervous, wary, shy, and somewhat serious as she displays her right and then left profile. Behind the scenes, the crew is obviously joking with her to put her at ease. She smiles and laughs—with her left eyebrow arching as it often has in so many films before. She looks down demurely; the lines around her mouth, chin, and neck are barely perceptible. In the next close-up she is a little more relaxed, but still uneasy in the spotlight. Next, she puts on a hood and pulls her hair away from her face— there are glimpses of Grusinskaya, Mata Hari, and Susan Lenox. Finally, she adds a bit of casual glamour with a simple black jacket. She takes off the hood and runs her hand through her hair; her hands do not betray her age.

Like many things about *La Duchesse*, there has been considerable confusion about this test—possibly because immediately afterward the forty-eight-year-old cinematographer became ill and on the eighteenth of May succumbed to a heart ailment. It was the second unexpected death that Greta had been confronted with that spring (a stroke had felled Harry Edington two months earlier). Wanger and company didn't waste any time. The following week, they introduced Garbo to James Wong Howe, the cameraman whose artful chiaroscuro set the mood for countless black-and-white *and* color cinema classics.

It has been erroneously reported that Garbo's contract guaranteed that the movie would be shot in black-and-white. There was no such clause. However, there was no argument that what was known as the "Garbo mystique" benefited greatly from the moody contrasts of black, white, and gray.

---

[7]Sources differ on the location of the shoot. The marker on the footage on file at the Library of Congress and the State Historical Society of Wisconsin (where Walter Wanger's papers are located) indicates it was shot at Universal-International, Valentine's alma mater.

According to James Wong Howe, the purpose of the new screen tests was to compare his work with that of other cameramen. On May 25, Howe met general manager Roland Totheroh at the United Artists/Chaplin Studio lot in Hollywood. Together, they assembled the required electricians and camera crew.

Garbo arrived an hour later without the typical Hollywood entourage of agents, managers, hairdressers, and makeup artists. "I remember she had a big black [straw] hat on and a pair of slacks and a white blouse," Howe reminisced. "She was very gay, 'Hello, hello, hello.' " Greta asked where her dressing room was and Totheroh offered to take her to makeup. "Oh no, I can go and do my own makeup, fix my own hair. I don't need any costume," she insisted. "You're just going to do close-ups, aren't you, Jimmy?"

Forty-five minutes later, she appeared on the stage with her makeup and hair fixed, wearing a checkered jacket and black scarf. Howe had improvised a setting with a plaster Grecian column and a table. He asked Greta to sit on the table and lean on the column while he analyzed how to assemble the lights and compose the shot. "Can I smoke a cigarette?" she asked. Howe nodded and she put an Old Gold into her cigarette holder. Admittedly nervous, Howe finally turned on his camera just to get started.

"The minute the cameras started rolling, she took on, oh, a wonderful feeling," he said. "You could see this creature just come alive. And then I began to get a certain inspiration of lighting . . . I could see what was required . . ." He killed all the lights except for one baby spotlight, "and I lit that and moved it around as she stood [with] that sculptured face of hers . . . it was just wonderful. [Her face] just seemed to reflect the light." A simple gesture of Garbo looking up, with her cigarette smoke filling the space in abstract patterns, translated into an extraordinary moment on film. Howe did three setups, modifying his lighting as his subject relaxed in front of the camera. After about an hour, Greta turned to him. "Sufficient now?" The cinematographer agreed. "Good," she said, "I think I go home."

However, according to film records, she had one more test to do: in the evening, she stepped in front of Bill Daniels' lens.[8] "She seemed timid and afraid of how she would look, but seemed quite happy with the test," he told Hedda Hopper. Throughout the six setups they did together, Daniels scarcely modified the way he lit Garbo. She wore the "same old-fashioned makeup," he said, but "other than a few laugh wrinkles, her face was the same."

The following day, the Pathé laboratory in Hollywood developed 817

[8]The identification accompanying Daniels' footage indicates that it was also shot on May 25; possibly at Universal, where Daniels was currently under contract.

feet of film that included highlights of both men's work. Where Daniels took a standard approach to Hollywood glamour with no rough edges, Howe's footage was far more interesting; it had a soft focus, *film noir* look akin to his work in *Nora Prentiss*. Walter Wanger soon initiated contract talks with Howe's representatives. George Schlee ran into Cecil Beaton in Paris and announced that the results of the tests were excellent. "Greta admitted that they pleased and reassured her, for she felt that her eyes had a depth that had not been conveyed in earlier pictures," Beaton recorded.

Walter Wanger was not concerned about the outcome of the tests. He was already in Europe ironing out the details of a complicated financial venture. James Mason still hadn't signed, but seemed committed to the production and promised he would be available after June 15. After years of kicking about in bit parts, Mason had made the leap to full-fledged stardom two years earlier in *Odd Man Out*. Though the actor was a sound choice for the moody tamer of the Duchess's heart, Garbo wanted to make sure she wouldn't tower over him. Wanger arranged for them to meet at Mason's Beverly Hills home. "Don't scare her off by talking about the film unless she brings it up," Mason instructed his wife. He need not have worried. Greta talked about everything except the film and, in fact, spent more time playing with his children.

That June, Wanger returned from Europe to discover that Sally Benson's completed first draft was "barely a script at all." According to biographer Matthew Bernstein, "Benson had been neglecting her work and drinking heavily." Her meager attempt to revise her script was equally appalling. Wanger began looking for a writer who could deliver a shooting script in time for a projected September 1949 start.

Irrespective of these problems, on July 1 Wanger-International officially notified their star that she was expected in Rome by the fifteenth of August for costume fittings and other pre-production activities requiring her approval. Principal photography was set to begin the first week of September. Wanger and Frenke had arranged to finance the film in United States dollars, French francs, Italian lire, and English pounds. Their partnership was responsible for the first $300,000, which Wanger expected to be partially secured through a distribution agreement with either Columbia or RKO Pictures; an additional $200,000 in deferred salaries would be due after a repayment of the first bank loan. The Rothschilds would help "thaw" $50,000 in frozen French funds for the location work in and around Paris. Giuseppe Amato and Angelo Rizzoli, partners in Scalera Films, were expected to raise approximately $170,000 for production in Rome. Finally, Wanger-International turned to Rank Films to finance the additional

$95,000 needed to pay the English supporting cast and editorial department.

Completing *La Duchesse de Langeais* would require an act of faith to keep the elements together. Garbo had once made pictures under the protective wing of MGM that cost more money without the risk now involved in this financial high-wire act. On July 15, she sailed with George Schlee for France. The *Queen Elizabeth* arrived in Cherbourg six days later; Greta was the last one to go through Customs. Although she didn't escape having her luggage—marked "Schlee"—opened, she managed to avoid paying a duty on the two hundred packages of American cigarettes she brought with her (claiming a fifty cigarette per day habit).

After a short stay at the Hôtel George V, the couple met with director Joshua Logan outside Paris. At the time, Logan had the top drama *(Mr. Roberts)* and musical *(South Pacific)* on Broadway. Although he later claimed that he was asked to direct *La Duchesse de Langeais*, Logan didn't get any further than his luckless predecessors. His recollection was that while he pleaded for more time to work on the scenario, the project fell apart. In fact, another writer/director had already committed to the picture.

On the eighteenth of July, before Garbo and Schlee had arrived in France, Wanger signed Max Ophuls to polish Benson's screenplay. Born in Germany, now a French citizen, Ophuls worked occasionally in the United States and had acquired a reputation as a writer and director of elegant, romantic films.[9] He had also collaborated with James Mason in two of his most recent films, *Caught* and *The Reckless Moment.*

The key elements were in place. Now it was up to Garbo to deliver—or so it seemed.

While everything was being finalized, Garbo and Schlee journeyed to Aix-les-Bains in the French Alps to partake of the waters and rest before filming began. The couple arrived in Italy on August 26 amid a whirlwind of publicity—for *Lover and Friend,* the new American title for *La Duchesse;* for Ingrid Bergman and Roberto Rossellini, who were making gossip columns due to their affair during the making of *Stromboli;* and for Garbo and her lover/protector/friend. "Miss Harriet Brown" was hidden away at the Hotel Hassler.

Like a tightly wound clock, the intricate financial plan for *La Duchesse* began to unravel. Even as Garbo went on salary, the projected start date was pushed back to October—and still no agreement on the leading man's terms or salary; Mason elected to stay in Los Angeles with his family. "After

---

[9]The most recent example of this was 1948's *Letter from an Unknown Woman* (Joan Fontaine, Louis Jourdan).

a rather careful reading of the script, I am somewhat at a loss to understand why you wish to make this picture in Italy," Henry Henigson, MGM's top executive in Rome, wrote Wanger. The answer was money. The production company desperately needed the influx of cash expected from the Italian partnership and also hoped to save money with cheaper (though potentially less efficient) Italian labor. Although there was no money in the bank, Greta was given daily assurances that the producers were ready for her to begin work.

Garbo *was* needed in Italy—to help the company get the additional money they needed to start. On September 1, she went to Le Grand Hotel et de Rome, the production's temporary headquarters, and learned the true meaning of harassment. The paparazzi swarmed around her as she made her way to a meeting she was supposed to have with Scalera Films producer Giuseppe Amato and publisher Angelo Rizzoli. Incredibly, Walter Wanger had been traveling and was not present for an event which would prove critical to the project's existence. The encounter was most upsetting to Garbo. "Here she discovered they wished her to smile at rich Italians so that they would put up the necessary cash," Cecil Beaton divulged. "But no—she would not do that." She would not be their circus horse. Things quickly went from bad to worse. Amato was upset that Greta thought he had arranged for the photographers; Rizzoli was simply upset.

By press time, the print media had the story. "Signor Rizzoli, Rome newspaper magnate who was to put up finance for the Italian end of the proposed Garbo–James Mason film, *The Duchess of Langeais,* today refused to go on with the venture until the American parties put up their funds," the *London Daily Express* announced. Neither Wanger-International nor United California Productions had enough capital to make substantive guarantees of their own. Wanger had recently received word that Banker's Trust would deny his loan unless he was willing to pledge worldwide film rentals as collateral—but this he could not do, since his production partners had used potential European income to secure *their* loans.

Another blow was the lack of available production facilities. Ironically, Metro-Goldwyn-Mayer, having booked all the studios at Cinecittà for *Quo Vadis,* was having its own problems and reportedly offered Wanger their facilities—providing he was ready to go. Without Rizzoli's additional support and without a leading man in Rome, this seemed impossible. Although he'd agreed on a fee, James Mason did not want to be paid in pounds or lire and insisted on having his $75,000 guarantee put into escrow before he left town. Attorney Greg Bautzer was working frantically to get Howard Hughes and RKO to bail the company out in time to meet a September 8 deadline. "The Greta Garbo–James Mason picture is off unless Howard Hughes saves it by putting up more than $500,000," Hedda Hopper reported on the day of reckoning.

By the time Max Ophuls and James Wong Howe arrived in Rome, everything was in chaos. Howard Hughes, still reeling from his battles with Congress over his flying boat (nicknamed the "Spruce Goose"), was mired in his own financial woes as he tried to keep RKO afloat; he agreed to finance part of the film, but not all of it. Wanger's proposal to bring an English backer in to secure Mason's salary was declined by the actor's representatives, who wanted to avoid losing that money to taxes. "WISH TO ADVISE THAT AS OF TWELVE MIDNIGHT CALIFORNIA TIME TODAY THERE HAS BEEN DELIVERED ONLY PART OF DOCUMENTS AND ITEMS REQUIRED," Abe Lastfogel of the William Morris Agency cabled Wanger at the Grand Hotel. "FAILURE TO DELIVER THESE ITEMS . . . LEAVES NO ALTERNATIVE BUT TO ADVISE YOU ALL NEGOTIATIONS DEFINITELY OFF."

In anticipation of such an event, Wanger and his associates put out feelers with representatives of Errol Flynn and Louis Jourdan. The bad news continued. Sally Benson filed suit against Wanger-International charging breach of contract, and Production Code chief Joseph Breen regretfully informed the producers that the Benson/Ophuls script was unacceptable, "BECAUSE IT IS STORY OF ADULTERY WITHOUT ANY VOICE FOR MORALITY."

If someone had asked the tough questions earlier on Garbo's behalf, perhaps she wouldn't have seen herself repeating the debacle of *Odalisken från Smolna*. More than anything else, Wanger had wanted to be a success in Europe—partially because he wanted to be a trailblazer where the major studios and major independents, including David O. Selznick, had failed. By the end of September, he was willing to make almost any deal in order to keep *La Duchesse de Langeais* alive. Where before he saw that his prestige in Europe would be greatly enhanced by a picture with Greta Garbo, now he could see that he would be hurt irreparably if he fumbled her comeback effort.

In the meantime, the star at the center of this fracas was "at leisure" in the Eternal City, besieged by head-hunting newsmen and photographers. Greta described her stay in Rome as absolute misery. She tried three different hotels in two weeks, with none providing sufficient security; each move invariably ended in tears. On the tenth of September, she gave up the struggle. "Visibly indignant, Greta Garbo left Rome for Paris today in her blue DeSoto, driven by her companion, George Schlee," the *London Daily Mail* reported.

The Italian press sneeringly suggested that Garbo's trademark broad-brimmed hat and "droopy clothes" were a sign that she was "no longer glamorous and beautiful and had lost her charm and sex appeal." Furthermore, they stated, she was sullen and uncommunicative, and her demands had been impossible. Suddenly, blame for the breakdown in negotiation was being laid in the star's lap. Friends of Angelo Rizzoli claimed the publisher had been asked to make an investment of approximately 300 million lire (over $500,000), but it was Garbo who had brought a list of demands to their meeting.[10] The actress's latest conditions allegedly included her insistence on full payment up front and that her work must be completed in seven weeks, with no more than thirty days of filming in Rome. Her friends explained that Greta suffered from "slight attacks of rheumatism" and that it was because of her desire to avoid a cold, damp winter in Paris (where principal photography was to wrap) that she had wanted to make the film quickly.

Walter Wanger's changing attitude was apparent in a telegram he and Eugene Frenke composed to inform Roy Myers, Garbo's agent at MCA, one of the top agencies, about the current situation. "SCHLEE'S POSITION SINCE ARRIVAL ROME EMBARRASSING AS CONSTANT COMPANION OF BROWN IN HOTELS AND TRAVELLING AS REPORTED IN PRESS HAS FORMED BARRIER FOR DIRECT CONTACT," it began. The producers complained that Schlee was interpreting the contract his own way, criticizing them for involving foreign production partners, taking charge of wardrobe arrangements, and advising Frenke that Garbo would not accept Errol Flynn or Louis Jourdan as her costar. Wanger charged that Schlee made it virtually impossible for them to continue. "HE NOW ADVISES FRENKE SHE UNABLE TO WORK DUE TO HER PHYSICAL CONDITION AND WANTS POSTPONEMENT TILL SPRING," the wire continued. As failure loomed before them, the producers agreed to a postponement, promising to "HOLD [SCHLEE] AND BROWN RESPONSIBLE FOR ALL DAMAGES."

On the twenty-second of September, Garbo and Wanger met in Paris and signed a new letter of agreement. The four-page agreement, negotiated by MCA boss Jules Stein, offered Garbo compensation ($16,125) for the two-and-a-half weeks she had been available to producers in Rome and Paris, and full reimbursement for her transportation expenses between Los Angeles and Rome. It was mutually agreed that any public pronouncement regarding the venture to date should be "favorable and complimentary to all parties concerned." Most important, by January 1, 1950, Wanger consented to provide Garbo and her representatives with documentation concerning his ability to fully finance the production.

The producer called a press conference to officially announce the film's postponement to spring 1950. True to his word, Wanger didn't blame Garbo for the delay, saying that she had "graciously assented" to his request and that the rumors about her looks fading were totally unfounded. "She is

---

[10]No mention was made of the fact that Rizzoli was now demanding control of the negative or that the Italian partners initially balked at Mason's price, not Garbo's.

now more beautiful in every way and more fluent in her English, and she will enchant more than ever," he proclaimed.

When Cecil saw Greta in Paris at the end of September, he expected that "her sufferings from the chicanery of film crooks" would leave her a nervous wreck and was surprised to hear "a very bright and chirpy voice" on the phone. When they met, Beaton thought she looked thin but lovely—and relieved that *La Duchesse* had been shelved. It had been "a bad day" when she signed a contract for the picture, Greta told him. "These picture people are a tough lot, and they lie—they lie—they lie all the time. And by their lying they've wasted a year of my life; they've prevented my doing other work," she complained. "Eventually I've got to go through with the picture; but it isn't very pleasant knowing that, sometime in the future, you have to work for people you don't like."

Schlee later bragged to Beaton about how clever he had been in extricating Garbo from the project. "As he tried to justify himself I was convinced that he is partly responsible for the fiasco of the film not coming off," Cecil wrote in his journal, ". . . & the way he has managed to take control of Greta's interests is quite alarming . . ." But she was touched by his efforts on her behalf; she saw Schlee as a "martyr" to her cause—"and thus they are bound to each other . . ."

Over the weekend, they were invited to Lady Diana Cooper's Château de St Firmin and visited the great château in nearby Chantilly. Cecil would describe the outing as idyllic and Greta as "a person possessed" as she frolicked in country gardens and fields of freshly stacked corn. The day's activities had exhausted Beaton, but Greta seemed revitalized. A few hours later, he inadvertently witnessed a moment of sweetness and intimacy between her and George Schlee as they drove by in their car. "They seemed very much interested in one another, and Greta was looking at him with a smile of affection and his head was close to hers. This was a revelation."

On Monday, the third of October, Garbo and Schlee boarded the *Île-de-France* in Le Havre. According to a report from the ship, Greta was less elusive than she had been on previous crossings, even taking meals in the main dining room. Her mood, however, again changed, and by the time they arrived in New York one week later, reporters thought Garbo looked tired, sad, humiliated. She remained in her cabin for two hours after the luxury liner reached quarantine. When she emerged from her stateroom, she raced with George Schlee down the gangway and across the pier to an elevator that took them to the street. Then the woman who could jump into a taxi faster than anyone again slipped out of the public's reach.

* * *

At the recommendation of Mercedes de Acosta, Greta began seeing a New York osteopath, Dr. Max Wolf.[11] By November, she had relaxed into her Manhattan routine. One evening, she would appear at a Broadway opening with Schlee; the next night, while he was out with his wife, she was content to have a drink with friends and retire early. Occasionally, she would receive word of efforts being made on her behalf by Wanger and Frenke to reposition their film.

Wanger's frustration grew into a genuine feeling of betrayal by the partners he had trusted. He believed that Frenke and Ophuls had let him down, because they supported Garbo's unspoken contention that the entire operation had been conducted haphazardly. In November, he released Ophuls to make another film in France. (One of his best: *La Ronde*.) Frenke continued to work toward bringing new backers on board, despite a flurry of angry notes from his partner.[12] On New Year's Eve, Wanger personally delivered a preliminary proposal to Jules Stein concerning the new financial arrangements for *La Duchesse*. The most surprising aspect of the new proposal was that Garbo was being asked to defer her entire salary—in effect, becoming a major investor herself.

But Wanger never delivered full documentation, and thus Garbo had her "out." "I was very much surprised to hear Miss Garbo and Mr. Schlee had injected legal advice into this situation. I thought our arrangement made in Paris was made in good faith," Wanger wrote Stein on January 3. The producer considered Schlee's negative attitude idiotic. He argued that it was counterproductive to expect the stability of Metro-Goldwyn-Mayer or Paramount from an independent producer. The only thing that counted, he wrote, was a good picture, "and I agree with you completely that the first problem is to find out whether she wants to make a picture or doesn't want to make a picture." In a postscript, Wanger undermined his own cause by noting that the producers had pursued RKO, Paramount, Columbia, Warners Bros., and 20th Century-Fox—"but to date, no interest."

When Wanger's plan was finally, inevitably rejected, he would accuse Garbo of deliberately scuttling their agreement by maliciously interfering with the negotiations. The rumor in Hollywood was that she had instructed MCA to disapprove any financial plan that was submitted and that she had no intention of rendering her services in the film; Wanger believed that she was

---

[11]Although her initial complaint concerned her wrist, Wolf worked on her back and hips as well.

[12]In all fairness, there is no evidence that the partnership ever cost Frenke anything more than a few out-of-pocket expenses—unlike Wanger's extensive personal investment.

the source of these stories. On January 17, 1950, MCA officially repudiated the contract on their client's behalf. The producer threatened to sue for breach of contract—but continued in his effort to lure Garbo back with copies of loan agreements and supporting financial statements.

On the seventeenth of February, he wrote her directly in an attempt to appeal to her sense of fairness and professionalism and perhaps even to reforge their bond of "truthful understanding." "Maybe we would all have been better off if we had gone ahead with the original George Sand deal and made a quick and profitable film," he advocated. "However, when you said to me that you had waited eight years and you did not wish to make a mistake, and that I give you my word not to let you do anything I did not believe in, I took you at your word . . . Although this has been a most unfortunate venture, so far you have been protected. You have not made a bad picture." It seemed a small consolation. Wanger hoped to make a new beginning, but it was The End.[13]

Undoubtedly, Greta Garbo flirted with the idea of restarting her career just as she had flirted with the idea of marriage: the next morning, after she'd had an opportunity to rethink things, she could see only the negatives and would invariably say no. Her struggle was reminiscent of the Swedish monarch she had re-created with such verisimilitude seventeen years earlier. Like Kristina, she had tried to keep her negotiations for a new throne secret and was foiled by the political machinations of others. Like Kristina, her humiliating trials were conducted in the glare of a public spotlight. Failure for both would have endless repercussions—and encourage endless comment.

Nicholas Turner recalls visiting Greta shortly after she came back. "What happened to the movie?" he asked. It was a disaster, she told him, she was finished. "She grabbed me and pulled me to her," he remembers. "I could see tears coming out of her eyes; it had upset her. She said, 'I'll never make a movie again,' and she never did."

"People who have climbed a cliff and are resting peacefully on the summit have been known to glance casually down to the void below and for the first time realize to their horror that they suffer from 'vertigo,' " David

---

[13]Wanger's fortunes went steadily downhill after the release of *Joan of Arc*. Tragedy erupted on December 13, 1951, when he shot and wounded Jennings Lang, his wife's lover, in the MCA parking lot. The producer pleaded "not guilty by reason of temporary insanity," waived a trial, and was convicted on a lesser charge of assault with a deadly weapon. He served four months in a state prison—and turned that experience into his first hit in years, *Riot In Cell Block 11*.

Niven wrote in *Bring on the Empty Horses.* "I often wondered if something of the sort had overtaken Garbo at the pinnacle of her career . . ." So he decided to ask her one rainy afternoon. "Why *did* you give up the movies?" he inquired. "She considered her answer so carefully that I wondered if she had decided to ignore my personal question. At last, almost to herself, she said, 'I had made enough faces.' "

CHAPTER TWENTY-FOUR

Introducing Miss Brown

"The result of our lives should bear witness to what we are, what we will do, what we can achieve. And our work tells this best in its own language. Mine happens to be the language of the motion picture screen," Garbo had stated in 1928. At heart, she was still an actress—it was an essential part of her being—but the forum for her to express her creativity had changed. The legendary actress receded from public view while privately channeling her energies into a new life of leisure on the international social circuit, and an unassuming persona she called Miss Harriet Brown.[1]

It has been said that a person who adopts a pseudonym is telling the world a fiction about himself—but like most façades, the fiction reveals much about the teller. This was certainly true for Greta Garbo. At the height of her movie fame, she expressed a heartfelt longing for "two faces, one for the screen and one for my private life, so I could live quietly without being followed and hounded." Unpretentious to a fault (if fleeing the spotlight could be considered a fault), Garbo had been expected to behave like an obedient servant in Hollywood. That she could not do so guaranteed her emotional separation from the community. "She is decidedly a woman apart," Adrian stated in 1935. "Because she so consistently lives her life the way she wants to, regardless of criticism or the suggestions of her friends, she cannot help but be different—*because she is.*" The designer believed that from childhood, Greta "yearned for as much solitude as she wanted. And she has succeeded in having it against the great odds of human nature which surround her and fight her at every turn."

Like most great artists, she was a mass of contradictions. Garbo saw herself as a simple, direct person; friends saw an ordinary woman working under extraordinary pressure—but Hollywood could only see the complexities, the iron will, the skillful evasions. "Greta Garbo the screen star was a concept almost physically beyond Greta Gustafsson's sympathy and, perhaps, understanding," film historian Alexander Walker submitted. "The greater Garbo became, the more strain was put on Gustafsson till in the end she resolved the dilemma by denying us Garbo."

---

[1]Occasionally Mrs. Brown, sometimes abbreviated in correspondence as Harry, Brownie, or simply H.B.

Much as she had accomplished with her screen incarnation, Greta assumed the identity of the person she imagined to be Harriet Brown, a simple woman closer in character to her true self. As far as anyone can recall, she first used the name on a trip to Yosemite National Park in 1934. As time went on, she would also use it as an alias on trips to Paris, London, Rome, Côte d'Azur, Barbados, Palm Springs, and Palm Beach, as well as on hotel registers in New York and Los Angeles. "We never travel," she explained to Betty Spiegel. "Miss Harriet Brown travels."

The fact that she took on another identity when traveling was not unusual. Many celebrities choose *noms de voyage* based on favorite romantic characters or songs; others select names that will help them fit more comfortably into the crowd. The names Karin Lund, Mary Holmquist, Jonas Emerson, Margaret Gustafsson, Emily Clark, and Mary Jones all found momentary favor on Garbo itineraries. However, by the mid-forties, she began to insist that friends use Harriet Brown, not only as a code when leaving phone messages wherever she was staying, but also in introducing her to acquaintances.

Why did the name have such staying power? "It was just a dumb, don't-pay-any-attention-to-me name," says Sam Green. Sven Broman believes that the Swedish poet Harriet Löwenhjelm was a partial inspiration; Greta once told him that she thought Harriet was a beautiful name. When Cecil Beaton became reacquainted with her in 1946, he recorded that Greta was intrigued by a biography of Löwenhjelm, a brilliant, troubled young woman who often referred to herself in masculine terms. As for the second part of her assumed name, many people believe that she chose "Brown" because it is a fairly common name in the United States. Other friends have suggested that Harriet was a nod to Harry Crocker and that Brown alluded to the original "Brownie," Gayelord Hauser's lifelong partner, Frey Brown (also one of Greta's favorite companions).

There is one more possibility. In 1933, shortly before she began using the name, Warner Bros. released a provocative pre-Production Code film entitled *Female*. Its heroine, played by Ruth Chatterton, is a ruthless, highly driven owner of a major auto manufacturer. George Brent portrayed the confident designer who challenges his boss's list of priorities and ends up winning her heart; Johnny Mack Brown had a brief bit as one of Chatterton's discarded lovers; Gavin Gordon played a male secretary. Interestingly, Chatterton's best friend from college, introduced in the first reel, was named: Harriet Brown.

If Greta Garbo was the quintessential movie star and legend, Harriet Brown was her alter ego—the private person that Garbo inhabited who was, arguably, her most magnificently sustained performance. Through sheer force of character, she was able to do what few actors (once they have become celebrities) are allowed to do: reenter the mainstream and observe life. The isolating factor of fame contributed to her childlike wonder in even the most mundane things; nothing escaped her inquiry.

To many of her friends, Garbo was ever the Viking child "troubled by a dream of snow." Yet, after fulfilling the prophecy of her mentor, Mauritz Stiller, she appeared quite happy to live out the rest of her life in the comparative obscurity "Harriet Brown" offered her. In essence, she assumed the identity as well as the name and in so doing declared her independence from the shackles of her Hollywood existence. Though she had the courage to be herself—to stay true to her own code of social conduct—she was not brave enough to compete with the Garbo legend once she had reluctantly separated from it.

She did not have to compete with Harriet Brown. Miss Brown went shopping and roamed the streets of New York. She wore comfortable clothes, sneakers, or flat-heeled shoes (her favorite style was a dancer's slipper) and pulled her hair back in a rubber band. She did not have to be exotic or glamorous; she didn't care what people thought. The twist that Greta Garbo, the actress, added to this plain, rather nondescript character was that Harriet Brown could be a witty conversationalist, tell amusing stories, and be flirtatious and charming—when she so desired.

"She didn't impress me, but she fascinated me," says Patrice Hellberg, a Swedish journalist who met Garbo at the Manhattan home of Zachary Taylor and Ruth Ford. "She had an air about her: she knew she was Greta Garbo. You could feel it when she walked into the room that she knew who she was." Equally fascinating was the fact that Greta didn't seem to mind that people generally knew Harriet Brown to be her concealed identity—but in this acknowledgment she succeeded in instantly, albeit silently, declaring the terms under which she would proceed with social contact. People who did not respect this unspoken creed were dismissed from the circle.

Friends quickly fell in step, realizing that Garbo's desire not to call attention to herself was genuine. Still, some could not resist winking back. "Miss Brown," Ivor Novello, a popular British playwright and performer, said upon meeting Garbo at a party, "now that we know each other better, do you think I might call you Harriet?"

Greta Garbo, the former movie star, was not looked down upon by the elite, well-cushioned members of the upper class; she was embraced as an aristocrat. Interesting, educated people from New York and European social circles vied for her attention. When Ruth Ford and Zachary Scott hosted a party in honor of Danish author Isak Dinesen, Garbo's attendance was part of its success. She was a frequent guest at the East Side home of Jane and John Gunther, as well as the country estates of Maud and Eustace Seligman, and Fleur and Gardner Cowles.[2] Among world leaders, Winston Churchill was a well-known admirer, as was Adlai Stevenson and the Brazilian ambassador to the United States.

"What she had was incredibly instinctual—and dazzling," said Gottfried Reinhardt. "She could walk in a room and talk absolute *rot*, but she dazzled you." Sam Green viewed Garbo from a different perspective. "She was the best conversationalist of anybody I knew," he says. "She put things in a kind of prose, which I daresay she thought about a good deal because she had a lot of time alone. . . . She made up her own rules and, of course, there were special codes. There were references to things that happened in the past that we developed a whole kind of strange dialogue and vocabulary [for] . . . She loved making up codes. You'd tell her something and three days later, she'd come up with an entirely different version which was very funny. She was a comedienne, and it was worth seeing what her take was and how far her imagination would take her. . . . She was more playful than anybody my age."

Of course, there were many subjects that one dared not broach with her. Friends learned that Garbo talked about herself only in the most indirect terms. "I think she thought if she never referred to herself, no one could quote her," says Betty Spiegel. In the twenty years that Sam Green knew her, she rarely used the words I, me, or mine. In effect, she viewed her past in much the same way as she looked at her movies: removed, impersonal— almost as if it had been *someone else's* life.

Over the years, Greta developed many effective ways of disassociating herself as a subject of conversation. "It was understood that she was never to be considered someone who had formerly been in California or the films," Green continues. "Her conversations were elaborately disguised to remove herself from being a movie star or a former movie star or a person from Hollywood or anyone in that despicable show business. She would refer to herself in the third person. She would say, 'A young man in California . . .' just to remove herself from being anyone who might be a celebrity."[3]

[2]She had first met journalist John Gunther in Hollywood during the war. Gunther was separated from his first wife and dealing with the tragic circumstances of his son Johnny's terminal illness, later memorialized in *Death Be Not Proud*. Greta was introduced to Jane Perry in 1946; the Gunthers were married two years later. Eustace Seligman was George Schlee's attorney and was instrumental in freeing Garbo from her contract with Walter Wanger. Schlee also introduced her to the trend-setting writer, editor, and painter Fleur Cowles.

[3]Many of Garbo's friends viewed her usage of masculine terms as a clever put-on, a way of playing with people as well as words. "She thought it was cute," says Betty Estevez.

Using good manners was one way of keeping people at a respectful distance. Another defense mechanism was Greta's ability to instantly turn a conversation around. "She was charming, but she would talk about *you*," James Pendleton remembers. "She'd say, 'Now tell me about you. What do you do? Oh, isn't that interesting? Now tell me more.' "

More than one acquaintance marveled at her ability to jump "from one conversational orbit to another." "To talk to Garbo in any vein—tender, sad, flirtatious, lugubrious—is to find oneself talking film-script dialogue, with the slightly disconcerting qualification that now there is no film to go with the dialogue," said one observer. She especially liked American slang. She once confessed to Nils Asther that she had had "an awful row with God this morning," meaning, he thought, that she had been depressed and unable to sleep. Her "usual state of cursing" was to use the word "hell." She also had a great facility for making up words. "Geler Lilla," she wrote to Gayelord Hauser. "Just wondering how you are. 'Fussling?' And if you should wonder how I am—also fussling."

How much of her humor was intentional? Elizabeth Young, the ingenue in *Queen Christina*, vividly recalled how Garbo "always waits mischievously to see whether you get her double entendres and if you do, she's as pleased as punch." Greta called singer Jessica Dragonette "Dr. Nightingale," a reference to her fussing over the health of a friend as well as her vocation. During one memorable gathering, as the conversation veered into the strides being made by Turkish women, Dragonette caught a poignant look from Garbo that indicated they were getting into unfamiliar territory. "Oh," Greta said, "shall we have to use the dictionary?"

The minority opinion that she was an uneducated peasant was contradicted by Dragonette, who recounted Greta reading a poem from Walt Whitman's *Leaves of Grass* in her eloquent contralto; and also by Raymond Daum, who spoke with her about an assortment of books she'd read, from Emily Brontë to Hemingway and Fitzgerald.[4] Cecil Beaton recorded many instances of Greta quoting modern writers such as Joseph Conrad, as well as classical thinkers: Goethe, Heine, Sappho. She was fond of reciting dramatic passages in their original languages. In a revealing moment, he recalled her reciting a line from a sonnet about Michelangelo in which he admitted liking "only the things that would destroy lesser people."

Garbo's intricate use of language was a significant reason why many of her hetero- and homosexual friends remained confused about her true sexual

---

[4]Though the novel is short, Garbo admitted she couldn't finish *The Great Gatsby*, Daum said. "Dangerous things started to come up."

identity. Wilhelm Sörensen, who knew her at the height of her fame in Hollywood, wondered why Greta never exerted her power to captivate men with any seriousness outside the range of movie cameras. "Any mortal being with whom she came in contact would have succumbed to her potent powers of attraction," he advocated. "Yet she has decided instead on the lonely life in which she lets her enormous sex appeal lie dormant." For Sören, she had left no clues.

Twenty years later, Beaton wrote about a confessional conversation he had with Greta in which he confided some of his bleak family history. "Parents make it so difficult for us," she nodded in sympathy, adding that "it must be terrible for parents, who only wish for their offspring to lead sheltered, conventional lives, to find them being so strange." Ideally, she felt that people should be allowed to lead their private lives and guard their personal secrets from unwanted exposure. But she warned that "in general the homosexual life is a 'cut up' without a sense of responsibility. . . . that she herself was always intrigued by paths that were slightly fantastic, but public flaunting of these things was obnoxious." So Cecil spoke of marriage instead.

"If the press would lay off her personal life," Edmund Goulding once said, "[Garbo] and the press could make up. The thing she balks at is people going into her bedroom." Rumors about her preference for female companionship continued unabated irrespective of her public attachments to men. During one visit to Erno Laszlo, for no reason in particular she broke down and began to cry. The cosmetologist attempted to calm her by inquiring about her personal life. "Have you got a boy friend or a girl friend?" Greta was taken aback and stopped her sobbing as suddenly as it had begun. The next time she saw Laszlo, she asked, "Did you think I was a lesbian?" "Good Heavens, no," he responded. "I meant any sort of friend. You're too much alone."

A comment from James Pendleton perfectly illustrates the confusion within her interconnecting circles of friends. "I think of her at times as being asexual," he begins. "You hear so many tales. But you never heard tales about her and her romances except that she was going with these men. That's all. . . . I don't know if she was a lesbian. She could have been, she could have been very easily—but she could have been bisexual. That's more likely the story."

Nicholas Turner seems more secure in his assessment—but not by much. "People are trying to make her an abnormal or some strange person, and she wasn't," he says. "Number One—she loved men. Now whether she also liked women, it could be possible that maybe in her life she had an affair. But she didn't go after women as far as I know."

Interestingly, her male friends were more likely to see Greta as bisexual. "I believe she was known to go to lots of lesbian bars in New York during

the fifties with Mercedes de Acosta or somebody or other," Sam Green suggests. "I don't think, however, that she was going in the back room and
groping the girls." Her female friends did not see the obsession with sex. "I
just don't think G. was sexual. Although I will say this," Betty Spiegel adds,
"she did like to hear about other people's exploits. There again, I think she
lived vicariously through us."

Raymond Daum vehemently protested the characterization of Garbo as
"technically bisexual, predominantly lesbian, and increasingly asexual as
the years went by." "I think it is fair to say that a same-sex relationship was
her obvious choice, despite numerous affairs with men," he voiced in a letter to *The New York Times*. "She once told me, 'Homosexual love without
discretion and dignity, if flaunted, is sordid.' Garbo was haunted by a private code of conduct, trapped by the mores and traditional old-fashioned
values of her generation."

Most everyone in Hollywood had something to hide during the 1950s.
Leftist leanings, fondness for alcohol, and bedroom secrets were prime fod-
der for a new twist on tabloid journalism perpetuated by magazines. Lesbianism, in particular, was highlighted in publications like *Confidential*
magazine as revelations about Hollywood's "double-standard dollies" and
"baritone babes." No target was considered sacred, even Greta Garbo.
Over the years, there would be plenty of insinuations, but no definitive
proof. "I don't know what I can tell you," Betty Estevez states with understandable frustration. Estevez would be one of the few female names publicly attached to Garbo's. "She may have had something occasionally with
a woman, but one doesn't know about that," she insists. "I certainly don't
know—although people think I should. When I became friendly with her,
she was really not interested in sex."

Mercedes de Acosta notwithstanding, most of the modern-day assessment of Garbo as a lesbian is based not on factual accounts of Greta with
women, but in an interpretation of her body language on screen. Beyond
this, people like Laila Nylund don't believe anyone will ever find definitive
evidence of Garbo's lesbianism. Nylund's reminiscences are reflected
through the eyes of a young teenager watching a famous star relax on her
father's estate in the Stockholm archipelago. "I will say that, in person, she
looked more like a man than a woman," she concedes. "At the time, neither my sister nor I knew anything about things like bisexuality. . . . She
wore slacks; I never in my life saw her in a dress—I'd seen her in a nicely
tailored suit, but no frills, nothing to show off her figure . . . and flat shoes
that you wouldn't be caught dead in. She asked us one time, 'What do you
think of my clothes?' 'Oh, they're different!' we said. But we meant that
they were different because they were so mannish-looking. And that's the

kind of relationship we had with her. When she came over she wanted to curl up in the sofa and be comfortable."

The public's curiosity didn't wane once Garbo retreated from Hollywood. A *Daily Variety* poll in February of 1950 reaffirmed her position as motion picture's Best All-Time Actress: #1 in the Silent Actress category, #2 in Sound. A *New York Times* survey abroad continued to rank Garbo at the top in each of the thirteen countries polled—and she would remain in the #1 position through 1951.

While Betty Grable, June Allyson, Esther Williams, and a teenager named Elizabeth Taylor all vied for a place in the new world order, the spectacular stars of Hollywood's golden era were being remembered with a tinge of sadness by the writers and directors who survived them. According to a number of sources, Greta was deeply wounded when Billy Wilder and Charles Brackett included her in Gloria Swanson's famous "We had faces then" soliloquy in *Sunset Boulevard.*[5] Being included among the remembrances of things past followed *La Duchesse de Langeais* too closely for comfort—especially since she was still entertaining film offers.

Late in the fall of 1950, Greta was in Los Angeles awaiting word regarding her application for United States citizenship. "I still havent been called to the flag," she wrote Allen Porter. "I have been ill for a while and also in a state of nerves which is rather frightening. My girl in my house left me . . . and I thought the world had come to an end. I almost wired you to come and save me, but what would have happened to the Museum if you had left. Truman should give me a medal for not having upset one of the institutions of [the] U.S.A."

Pragmatism and not patriotism eventually pushed Garbo toward changing her national allegiance. Sweden's Gustav V died in 1950. Worsening trade conditions and rising unemployment had characterized much of his later reign. Even more alarming in the late 1940s and early 1950s were the legitimate concerns about Russia's postwar domination of the Baltic; thus far, the Iron Curtain had stopped in Finland (a few short hours away from Stockholm by boat). If the Soviet Union moved a step closer, Greta feared that her Swedish investments—and conceivably some of her monies in the States—would be in jeopardy. During the early days of an uncertain Cold

---

[5]"Still wonderful, isn't it?" Norma Desmond ponders as she watches the silent screen. "And no dialogue. We didn't need dialogue—we had faces. There just aren't any faces like that any more. Only one: Garbo. Those idiot producers, those imbeciles! Haven't they got any eyes? Have they forgotten what a star looks like?"

War, she became convinced that American citizenship would protect her interests best.

Greta signed a preliminary Petition of Naturalization on her forty-fifth birthday, describing herself as an "unemployed motion picture actress." Whether or not she would become "a member of the USA" was Garbo's primary focus for the next few months. The fateful test occurred on the twenty-first of November when she was called to the Federal Building in downtown Los Angeles to answer questions posed to her by Naturalization Examiner Barney F. Potratz. Potratz quizzed her thoroughly concerning her feelings about Communism and, in particular, her connection with Salka Viertel. "Miss Garbo has never lent her name or support to any organizations, least of all to Communism," the examiner wrote. "The report that a Mrs. Salka Virtel [sic], who approves Miss Garbo's stories, is a Communist, and that her son lent his home to Fritz Eisler, was discussed . . . and Miss Garbo states she does not know anything about Mrs. Virtel [sic] and her political beliefs, and only has dealt with her in connection with possible stories for picture making."

Greta's witnesses, Harry Crocker and Minna Wallis, backed up her story. Although given the current political climate such a declaration was deemed necessary if she were to become an American citizen, Garbo's private denial of Salka was a troubling break in the veneer of her usually admirable sense of honor and integrity. By 1950, Salka was aware that she was under surveillance, and occasionally asked friends and associates to check with the studios to see whether or not she had been "officially" blacklisted. This was always denied. Yet, according to the Department of Justice, she was made the subject of a FBI Communist Index card on January 29, 1951. "Subject's name is recommended for inclusion in the Security Index because of her statement [in an intercepted letter to her former husband] that any government, including a Communist one, would be preferable to the type of government the United States now has," an interbureau memo indicated.[6]

* * *

[6]Ironically, one of her strongest links would come through her son Peter's first marriage to Virginia (Jigee) Schulberg. Like many young idealists looking to change the world, Jigee was a member of the Communist Party in Hollywood during the 1930s and with her first husband, writer Budd Schulberg, was active in a number of leftist causes. Years later, Jigee and Peter would serve as the models for Katie Morosky and Hubbell Gardiner in Arthur Laurents' *The Way We Were*; Salka was memorialized as Katie's friend and mentor, veteran screenwriter Paula Reisner. According to Jack Larson, Salka did not appreciate the tribute and referred to the film as *The Way We Weren't*.

While waiting for her citizenship papers to be processed, Greta flew to New York for another treatment with Erno Laszlo. It was, reportedly, her first commercial flight, and the turbulence due to bad weather left her so shaken she immediately retired to a friend's home in the country. Once back in Manhattan, she returned to her seventeenth-floor suite at the Hampshire House. In December, she was joined briefly by Cecil Beaton, who was on the verge of conceding defeat on the marital front. "She seems more than ever in a muddle and can't help herself out of it, and I don't think even I could influence her not to do the wrong thing for herself," he admitted in a letter to Clarissa Churchill. "The emptiness and pointlessness of her life, as it is, is monumental . . ."

The New Year would bring forth even older acquaintances. Max Gumpel and Eric Erickson had come to the States to visit Gumpel's son at Cal Tech. They were accompanied by Laila Gumpel, who was just out of high school and had agreed to be her father's translator. They visited with Garbo at her home in Beverly Hills. Now an ambitious, poised young woman, Laila was able to talk to Greta for the first time as an adult. "We could see that she was unhappy," she says. "I think she felt used. She warned me against an acting career. 'Don't do it, Laila,' she said, 'because you don't just get the accomplishment and the fulfillment . . . You have to take all the other baggage. It's overwhelming and it doesn't pay and you will have no privacy whatsoever. . . . Promise me you will never let money or fame or other people control your life.' "

Laila's father also noticed that Garbo had become cautious and distrustful. She had been charming during their visit to Hollywood, Max Gumpel told his daughter, but her eyes did not sparkle. She seemed to have lost the fire.

After verifying that Greta Garbo a.k.a. Greta Lovisa Gustafsson had no criminal record, her Petition for Naturalization was approved by the State Department. On February 9, 1951, she repeated the standard oath of allegiance along with 150 other participants. Several top officials of the Immigration and Naturalization Service insisted on attending the ceremony. Garbo stood out in her somber attire; a spotted black veil discreetly hid her face from the ruthless examination of news cameras as she signed her citizenship papers. After the ceremony, she agreed to pose for cameramen. "All right, go ahead," she said, while privately telling her companion, Minna Wallis, "I don't think I will ever change to the extent of liking to have my picture taken."

Garbo's disassociation with her past was nearly complete. She celebrated her new citizenship by selling her house to director Jean Negulesco and applying for her first American passport. As soon as the house went into escrow, Greta had her belongings packed and shipped. "It's rather frightening to think that that is all I possess in the world," she told Beaton. "I have no trace of my existence: no papers, no love letters, no relics involving any human beings." Most of her furniture was put into storage; some was shipped to her brother who had relocated to Santa Fe, and the rest to New York. Yet giving up her California base seemed to bring on a new feeling of melancholy. In April, she wrote Cecil that she was going through a particularly sad period. George Schlee had been in and out of the hospital and she was spending her afternoons keeping him company; she was also battling a persistent cold of several months' standing. Greta invited Cecil to send her his own list of complaints so that they could compare notes.

That summer, Garbo and Schlee went to Bermuda where, she confided to friends, her companion scared her by going straight to bed upon their arrival at the hotel. After two days, the most she had seen of the island was the view from her terrace. Garbo and Schlee, minus Valentina, were becoming more and more like a husband and wife. According to passport records, they were in Bermuda together between July 2 and 20. At the end of September, they made what was becoming an annual migration to France. Although Schlee still was not well, he was distressed to hear that Greta might be traveling to Europe without him—most especially, to meet Cecil Beaton. Inevitably, he insisted on accompanying her.

The couple arrived in France on September 22 and were met at Orly Airfield by John and Jane Gunther. Two weeks later, with the press still tailing her, Greta arrived in Southhampton on the French liner *La Liberté*. Cecil met her in the ship's restaurant. Neither Garbo nor Schlee offered Beaton a smile upon seeing him. "It was as if I was coming to make the final transaction of a business deal," he noted. In full view of everyone, Beaton whisked his visitor away before Schlee had a chance to object. Cecil had made plans for Greta's stay in England and they did not include her companion. For once, Schlee didn't have the strength (or will) to protest; he stayed on the ship and returned to the States alone.

For five years, Cecil Beaton had dreamed of bringing Greta Garbo to Reddish House, his estate near Broadchalke in the Wiltshire district. In fact, according to Hugo Vickers, Cecil had Greta in mind when he bought it. "He knew enough about Garbo to be aware of the likely appeal of a Queen Anne mansion in a sleepy English village." She responded positively, wandering around the countryside for the next six weeks. In the afternoon, she and Cecil would take off for Salisbury Cathedral, the Roman town of Bath, the schools at Eton and Oxford, or to see the changing of the guard at Buckingham Palace.

Despite the constant intrusion of the Fleet Street press, Beaton managed to protect his charge, denying even family members who lived at Reddish House—as well as his best friends—access to Garbo until she was ready to meet them. His elderly mother was not impressed and often referred to their guest as "that woman"; Cecil's sisters and his secretary were like-minded. The reactions of Cecil's friends were predictably mixed. Clarissa Churchill, Winston Churchill's niece, was enchanted by her. Cecil's former lover, Peter Watson, was amused. Stephen Tennant, the reclusive poet and artist, thought she was "very lovable." But the Marquess of Bath failed to recognize her, and painter Pavel Tchelitchew announced, "She's got a lovely face, lovely looks, but *elle est si bore, Mon Dieu, elle est si bore!*"

Indeed, Garbo and the man better known in England as the photographer to the Court of St. James were the talk of the town that fall. Beaton had hoped to entice Greta into staying in England for Christmas, but a letter from George Schlee propelled them to the Continent. In Paris, they were joined by Mercedes, who lived with her current lover, Maria (Poppy) Kirk, in a small flat near Notre-Dame.[7] With Greta no longer exclusively his own, Cecil began to feel more and more like an escort; the weather was as bad as his mood. He disliked the Hôtel de Crillon, eating in restaurants, and everything about the routine. Under stress due to the complexity of the situation, he would describe the past two to three months as "a long and emotional autumn . . . Greta was a full-time job and an anxiety as well as a pleasure."

The infamous "Mademoiselle Hamlet" encounter began with Mercedes meeting Alice B. Toklas on a Paris bus and receiving an invitation to Toklas's apartment at 5 rue Christine. In concert with Cecil, she lured Greta to the apartment with the intention of showing her the late Gertrude Stein's impressive collection of art. Garbo appeared "a bit shy—quite Vassarish—unpretentious but very criminal," Toklas later wrote. "She asked me with simplicity and frankness—Did you know Monsieur Vollard [Paris galley owner, Ambroise Vollard], was he a fascinating person—a great *charmeur*—was he seductive. She was disappointed like a young girl who dreams of an assignation." She earned the tag "Mademoiselle Hamlet" when she took a cursory look at the panorama of Picassos seated on a bench in the middle of the room, then pronounced herself ready to leave. "*Mystére c'est devoileé,*" said Alice.

---

[7]Mercedes met Poppy Kirk, the American wife of an English diplomat, during the fall of 1948. Their relationship was a tempestuous one, complicated by long separations, Mercedes' poor finances, and Kirk's uncontrollable jealousy concerning most of Mercedes' friends—especially Greta. She was particularly concerned that Mercedes still planned her schedule around Greta and was bold enough to confront the star herself when she visited Mercedes in Paris. The ensuing fight reportedly ended in a draw.

On the fifteenth of December, Garbo returned to the States on the Pan Am Clipper. After another nerve-wracking period of silence, when Cecil arrived in New York a few weeks later, he "tricked" Greta into lunch at the Colony. Beaton gained courage as both downed a couple of strong drinks. "I daresay I am a very bad-tempered wretch," Greta offered in response to a question about her failure to acknowledge his recent phone calls and notes. She was sure he'd fallen out of love with her in Paris. In fact, she said, "I don't think you've ever really loved me." Beaton protested interference from a "rather sinister little Road Company Rasputin," but Greta denied that George Schlee had anything to do with her feelings. "I had made up my mind before you came," she said. "You see, you have such vitality—you can't keep quiet or relaxed. One has to be on the run with you all the time. And I'm going through a bad period in my life . . . I don't feel up to seeing you."

Her feelings of uneasiness and depression Cecil attributed to "the change" (menopause)—although there was a more logical reason for her change of heart. On Valentine's Day, someone gave her a copy of *Cecil Beaton's Scrapbook,* with Beaton's penetrating words about a Garbo he scarcely knew in 1937. The piece described her as difficult, selfish, and full of tragic regrets; a person who did not know the meaning of friendship and was incapable of love. Miraculously, Cecil once again transcended a potentially disastrous moment. By the time he returned to England in April, he had not only been forgiven for his prior indiscretion, but also received an apology of sorts from Greta for her aloof behavior.

Even so, the misunderstanding represented a new turn in their relationship. By the end of the year, Beaton would begin writing shorter letters, and less often. Now it would be Garbo's turn to provide the balance by writing more frequently (much the same as her correspondence with Mercedes had changed as their relationship had evolved).

Between 1951 and 1952, there was a final burst of activity concerning Garbo's film career. After a positive meeting with the star during the spring of 1951, Dore Schary, who took over stewardship of MGM from Louis B. Mayer, assigned John Gunther to work on developing story ideas. But Gunther's best attempt at a screenplay wasn't good enough; Garbo passed on the project. Gunther realistically accepted defeat. "You know, there's something about this woman that people just won't concede," he said. "This woman wants to be left in peace. Everyone is saying, 'When will you do this?' 'Why don't you do that?' And what does she want? To be free of this constant tugging at her."

Writer/producer Nunnally Johnson had better luck when he got 20th Century-Fox mogul Darryl Zanuck to option Daphne DuMaurier's *My*

Cousin Rachel. The fact that the author had heard the studio was considering Garbo for the lead carried considerable weight with DuMaurier in the sale of the property. But Johnson began to have doubts. "Personally I would rather not go into the matter," he wrote a few short weeks after the purchase. Unsure of what Garbo looked like now, he admitted that he "would rather go on remembering her as she looked in *Camille.*"

George Cukor's introduction to the project in early 1952 revived Garbo's name on the list of casting possibilities. "[Cukor] says he couldn't get Garbo out of his mind while reading the book," Johnson confirmed in a March 11 memo. "He thinks she has the mystery as well as the quality that is needed for the part. . . . It is his belief that she is still stunningly beautiful . . ." When Cukor approached her with the idea, however, he was told, "No murderesses." Yet her response was worded in such a manner, Johnson reported to Zanuck, "that an interpretation could be that she wanted to do it very much but was fearful of a return to pictures. George, knowing her and her way of thinking, believes that this possibility justifies an effort on our part . . ."

At Cukor's behest, Nunnally Johnson flew to New York to pitch *My Cousin Rachel* to Garbo. He spent his time talking to her on the phone. "The passion was so evident in my voice and manner that she quite prudently avoided any suggestion of a meeting in person," he wrote. Greta was sorely tempted—"but as she went on talking, it was almost as if she were arguing with herself. She began to think of how she looked in her last pictures . . . She talked to me about the difficulties of photographing her . . . about angles, about her arms, but what it all amounted to in the end was that she couldn't do it. She repeated her several emotional reasons for not wishing to come back into pictures and did this so winningly," the producer remarked, "that I was presently enthusiastically on her side . . ."

My Cousin Rachel would represent the last serious attempt to bring Greta Garbo back to the screen. Many producers would fantasize about it—none would come close. "The goddess has gone and . . . she will never come back," Cecil Beaton remarked.

Garbo arrived in Paris on May 11—without George Schlee—and was met by her caretaker for the summer of 1952: Eric Goldschmidt-Rothschild. Friends saw Rothschild as a good companion for her. "He has infinite leisure—in fact nothing to do—is quite a delightful person with knowledge of objects d'arts and cultivated tastes," Cecil wrote Mercedes de Acosta. "She might learn from him if she applies herself . . ." Greta and the baron went on a motor tour of Europe, traveling first to Austria to visit with Rothschild's wife and mother-in-law and continuing on through Switzerland to

France. In Cannes, they met up with George Schlee, whose presence must have eased the minds of the reportedly worried Rothschild clan.

Garbo and Schlee rented a yacht and sailed to the harbor city of Portofino in Italy, where Rex Harrison and his wife, Lilli Palmer, owned a villa. In her memoirs, Palmer described her impressions of a meeting between Garbo and the Duchess of Windsor that summer: "The two women sat face-to-face and sized each other up from head to toe. Looking at them, I thought that life casts people in roles that a good scenario would never assign them. The woman for whom a man would be willing to give up his throne should obviously have been Greta Garbo, forever the world's most beautiful woman, unique and unattainable. . . . Yet there she sat in old blue slacks and a faded blouse, a lonely woman."

A trip out to Garbo's boat afforded Palmer the opportunity to observe the factor of her celebrity. "Their rented yacht could dock only at night. During the day it drifted half a mile or so from shore, the deck shielded by canvas awnings, as though they were expecting a cloudburst," Palmer stated. "Photographers and reporters circled the yacht in rowboats and dinghies." Onlookers waited, not for autographs, but simply to applaud her presence.

Back in Paris, Greta ran into Clark Gable at the White Elephant Café and surprised everyone by happily chatting about the past with her former costar. She returned to the States on September 30, but was such a wreck, she later wrote Cecil Beaton, that he should be glad they never married. "Greta still complains of sinus—and not being able to get rid of an interminable cold," Cecil informed Mercedes. "I think the real trouble is she can't get rid of an interminable bore—but she is resigned—and more than ever is content to wait for 'orders.' "

Following an indifferent encounter that winter, Beaton also appeared resigned. His friend Truman Capote offered the opinion that Garbo was so dissatisfied with herself that she no longer seemed to believe in anything except her own limitations. Beaton recorded an incident illustrating this in his journal: "[Gayelord] Hauser had telephoned to her: 'You're not still just wandering the streets,' he asked her. 'Haven't you taken a house? Haven't you done anything about anything?' 'No,' and she laughed at her inability. But it is no laughing matter." Without new interests in life, Beaton feared that Greta faced "a very empty, lonely and unhappy old age."

In March, she departed for Hollywood, checking into a $100 per week apartment at the Chateau Marmont under the name Harriet Brown. Although located on the noisy Sunset Strip, the Chateau is nestled up against one of the Hollywood hills, thus offering its clientele considerable privacy. From her fourth-floor suite, Greta looked directly on the hill and often wandered up its side to gather wildflowers. She was an undemanding guest, employees said, who preferred moving her bed herself into another room rather than registering a complaint about noise in a neighboring suite.

The main reason for Garbo's stay at the Chateau was that Salka's home was no longer available. In the spring of 1953, she gave up the valiant struggle and sold her beloved home to producer John Houseman. Salka moved into a Santa Monica apartment—and, following that, into the Los Feliz area of Los Angeles—without Greta ever being aware of the dire straits she was in.

During the summer, Garbo and Schlee again traversed the Atlantic to luxuriate under the warm Mediterranean sun. According to passport records, Greta was in Italy and France between July 12 and September 21, 1953. Whether they were in Paris or on the Riviera, it was quite obvious to outsiders that Schlee was back in control. "When he didn't want to do something, they didn't do it, no matter how she felt about it," said a mutual friend. "He was as jealous as the devil. I don't think he could tolerate having her exposed to other people, especially to interesting or attractive men. Whenever that happened—and it happened several times—he would invent some excuse for cutting the trip short. . . . She never objected, never spoke a contrary word. Schlee dominated her completely."

The couple booked return passage on the *Queen Mary*, arriving in New York on the twenty-first of September. Here Greta met up with Salka Viertel—but not Mercedes. "The night before she left for Europe in July she made a remark about you which I defended," de Acosta informed Cecil Beaton. "We got into a row and I told her one or two truths. She was angry and left without calling me the next morning or saying good-bye. So, no, on her return, she has not called me. . . . It is really so idiotic and unnatural that after years of friendship, one has to still go on handling her with absurd 'kid gloves,' or else suffer a falling out of some kind."[8]

That fall, Greta purchased a seven-room apartment on the fifth floor of the Campanile at 450 East Fifty-second Street. After years of wandering between two continents, it was time to settle down. "I had a hard time getting this apartment," she told a friend. "They don't like actresses in this building." Yet she had an unbeatable inside connection: George and Valentina Schlee lived on the ninth floor.

The building that Dorothy Parker termed "Wit's End" when Alexander Woolcott and Edgar Kaufman lived in it is located in mid-town Manhattan at the eastern end of Fifty-second Street. Turning on to the street as it pro-

---

[8]What Mercedes didn't say was that Greta believed she had furnished some of the information contained in Cecil Beaton's essays.

ceeds from First Avenue to the East River, one is reminded of similar neighborhoods in Stockholm; it is, at once, secluded and at the center of things. The Campanile's newest tenant would take great pleasure in watching the river traffic from her living room window. The quiet cul-de-sac is dotted with high-priced cooperative buildings. Greta's investment of $38,000 in 1953 would be worth well over $1 million today.

Furnishing and decorating the apartment to fulfill Garbo's concept of comfortable elegance would take time. Over the next few years, she would enlist the support of many creative people, including Cecil Beaton, Gayelord Hauser, and interior decorator Billy Baldwin. By the time Baldwin visited the apartment, Greta had already devoted a considerable amount of time to its realization. "A large L-shaped living room was filled with sunlight from two long walls of windows facing south and east. All the colors were rosy and warm; there were beautiful curtains of eighteenth-century silk, a Louis XV Savonnerie carpet, the finest quality *Régence* furniture, and wonderful Impressionist paintings," he observed. "The bedroom, which overlooked the East River, was a nice square room, practically empty, waiting for its background. Miss G. picked up a small candle shade of shirred mulberry-colored silk and held it up for us to see. 'This shade,' she said, 'was on a candle in a dining car in Sweden—in the first train I was ever on.' Then she lit a candle and held it beneath the shade. Our job was to paint the room the color that resulted from the candlelight shining through the silk!" After several tests, Baldwin and his assistant accomplished the impossible and received Greta's thanks for a job well done.

"She knew just how to use color to energize space," offered design director Roger McDonald, who worked with her between 1962 and 1966 on a series of colorful, geometric rugs she designed especially for her bedroom, closet room, and hall. Greta was nothing if not definite about what she didn't want in her home. When Gayelord Hauser sent her several decorative pieces, including a French commode, she wrote him thanking him, but added "Better not get anything more at the moment. Besides Mushkla wants to be along. Mushkla wants to go through the agony of trying to deside [*sic*] on the wrong thing. . . . What's the use of spending hundreds and hundreds of dollars without having the fun of spending it. *Mushkla wants to go along.*"

Her mood was decidedly less upbeat over the holidays. Greta and Salka spent a lonely Christmas Eve together. It had been a bitter year, Salka said. Still, she found her friend "compassionate, unchanged, and very dear." Following their modest Christmas Eve celebration, Salka went to Switzerland to visit her son, Peter. Greta spent Christmas Day at the Schlees. It was pure torment, she told Cecil Beaton. She suddenly wondered what in

God's name she was there for and had several martinis to drown such wonders. She was in a peculiar state of mind, she admitted, more so than usual. But it was late at night and she was feeling terribly alone.

"Dear Darling Sir—Imagine I never called you to thank you. But I have moved in the meantime and I dont know if I am on my head or feet anymore," Greta wrote an old friend, Robert Reud. "I thought virgos were rather good at fixing things, but all I do is move." She proposed that they meet for a drink. "I can call you friday at 4 to see if it is all right. If you dont feel like it just tell operator to tell Miss Brown [it's] not possible. If you feel like it come to the phone. I know how we are!!!"

Meanwhile, Cecil Beaton was in London trying to reconcile Greta with Mercedes by mail so they might join him in England. He was unsuccessful. "It's sad that Greta wouldn't come over and get out of her rut—but I have no influence in the face of the Valentinas." Unfortunately, Beaton noted, she had no sense of time being important. "To her it hardly exists . . ." Cecil also responded to a bit of gossip Mercedes had shared with him. "Apropos the [Harry] Crocker story, it makes me annoyed that he, who is such a good friend of Greta's, should have repeated the adventure to anybody. Greta told me that . . . they had had a little of red wine on top of two cocktails, and as a result— wasn't it awful!!—she'd gone to sleep at the play. . . . It is a ridiculous exaggeration to use the story as an indication that she is seriously drinking."

Greta appeared to friends as restless as ever. In May of 1954, she went to Palm Springs as the guest of television producer William Frye. Throughout the fifties and sixties, she would often use the desert as a retreat; its sunny, arid climate providing temporary relief to real and imagined medical ills. Later that summer, she visited her brother in New Mexico. Due in part to the top-secret work being conducted in nearby Los Alamos, as well as its rich Native American tradition, Santa Fe was one community where privacy was respected. For Sven, the aspiring artist, the area offered an extraordinary view of mountains and desert set against moody, colorful skies.

The Gustafsons had fallen in love with an old adobe ruin and purchased their first property on Cerro Gordo Road in 1946. They gradually expanded further up the hill, dominating the entire end of the canyon road.[9] Sven dabbled in developing the land, but was basically known as "a man of leisure," says Carlos Martinez, a local resident. Memories about the family are mixed: some knew Sven was Greta Garbo's brother, insisting

---

[9]Garbo set up a trust for her family in the early 1940s. Sven studied art at the Art Students League and exhibited several paintings in local galleries. He was variously identified in city directories as A. Samuel or S. A. Gustafson, artist.

that he told nearly everyone; others never knew, although today a plaque on one of the homes proudly declares its heritage as the "Casa de Garbo."

Few knew when Greta was in town—and she preferred keeping it that way. According to Hugo Vickers, she lasted only a few days and went straight back to New York. Correspondence seems to indicate otherwise. She wrote Salka from "Desertland" that she had "dissapeared [*sic*] in the wilderness . . . I am practically a prisoner because I dont want anyone to know I am here." She instructed her friend to address her letters to "Occupant."

The Hollywood press devoted a fair amount of attention to Garbo that summer. Ironically, while many of the great female stars of her era were struggling to maintain flagging careers, the one star who would have been happier being left in peace was still in the news. Only Marilyn Monroe basked in a hotter spotlight. The *Los Angeles Mirror*, a pioneer in the new fifties' style of tabloid journalism, launched a weeklong series of features updating aficionados about "Garbo—The Eternal Stranger." It was the first story to reveal that Greta's advisors had established a trust fund on her behalf that would soon provide her with an estimated annual income of $100,000. "She has plenty of money," an unidentified friend divulged. "But she has so little of the other things that count."

The news, as far as Cecil Beaton was concerned, was not good. "Greta returned three weeks ago from New Mexico . . . She has been ill for four months—has got very thin—but I don't know what's wrong," he wrote Mercedes in December. Greta and Cecil spent an afternoon at her apartment drinking vodka martinis and reminiscing. "When she philosophises she is on sure ground—her instincts are very strong & she speaks with a conviction that she lacks in everyday life," he stated. The conversation turned suddenly when Greta referred to Cecil as a flippant person; Beaton's emotions were quickly aroused. The discussion devolved into a full-fledged argument in which the subject of the by-now notorious *Scrapbook* was reintroduced. Cecil lashed out at her obsessive concern with an old grievance they had already discussed and, he thought, forgotten. "Have you no feeling for the way I have protected you from the world since I've known you?" he asked. "Have you no feeling of loyalty, gratitude or fondness for my devotion—Have I ever let you down by ever saying anything indiscreet? Have I ever exploited you like your intimate friends?" Beaton certainly didn't think he had.

Normally, it was impossible to best Garbo in an argument, but Cecil had struck a nerve. She tried to kiss him; he turned his face away. "I was angry—disenchanted—wanting to leave. I called for the elevator & the old man who answered my summons caught Greta in the act of hanging on to my coat collar." The balance in their relationship had shifted, with the awkward, uncomfortable moments starting to outweigh the best of times. Yet because the person at the center of this was Greta Garbo, it would be difficult for Beaton to give up.

There were many distracting forces at work as Greta Garbo approached fifty. In March of 1955, she found professional validation taking place on two very public fronts. After she had consistently turned down one movie project after another (most recently, the part of the Dowager Empress opposite Ingrid Bergman's Anastasia), the motion picture industry recognized the finality of Garbo's decision to withdraw. In acknowledgment of her "luminous and unforgettable screen performances," the Board of Directors of the Academy of Motion Picture Arts and Sciences voted her an honorary Oscar. Jean Negulesco, who was assigned to produce the show that year, was one of those who had lobbied for giving her the special award. Next he lobbied for her cooperation. "I knew that Garbo would never make an appearance to accept the Oscar, but would she let me come to New York and make a shot of her in her apartment, on her balcony, or any location she would chose?" he inquired. He offered her a writer to help her prepare a brief thank-you speech and, most important, the right to destroy the film and negative if she didn't like what they shot. "Let me call you in two days," Greta told him. But her answer was "No."

Instead, at the end of the March 30 telecast—an evening remembered primarily for Grace Kelly's surprise Best Actress win over favorite Judy Garland—the industry audience was shown a scene from *Camille,* after which the award was dedicated to Garbo and accepted by actress Nancy Kelly on her behalf. Minna Wallis inherited custodianship of the statue after the show. It would be two years before Greta saw the award, which she temporarily gave to George Schlee for safekeeping; Oscar was put away in a closet with the rest of her movie memories.

March also saw the publication of the first full-scale biography of Garbo, another sign that Mercedes and possibly other friends had been indiscreet. According to George Schlee, Greta was given a package containing the book, but tossed it into the ocean without ever opening it.

Goddess Emeritus

The Mediterranean villa that the world came to know as Le Roc was purchased by George Schlee in 1955. Located in Cap-d'Ail, three miles southwest of Monte Carlo on the Basse Corniche, the lower coastal road, the
imposing structure stands solidly on its own rock peninsula beneath the
cypress-lined lower cliffs of Tête de Chien. With its price tag of $50,000,
Garbo-watchers immediately assumed that the palatial villa, built by King
Farouk of Egypt for one of his mistresses, had been purchased with the
star's money. Although this was rumored for years, there is no documentation to support the assumption; in retrospect, the scenario seems unlikely.
Real estate records in Los Angeles, New York, and Milwaukee show that
Garbo did not hedge in buying property under her own name or as a partner in investment ventures; when transfers in ownership were necessary,
they were usually made within the first year. But Villa Le Roc remained in
George Schlee's name until his death, and no arrangements were ever
made to publicly declare her as a co-owner.

This is not to say that Greta didn't think of it as home—she certainly
treated it as such. She viewed the villa for the first time when she arrived
on the Riviera on the tenth of July. Curiously, she did not spend much time
there her first summer, accepting instead an invitation from Aristotle
Onassis to cruise the Mediterranean on his yacht. Onassis had spent over
$4 million converting the *Christina*, a 322-foot Canadian frigate manned
by a crew of fifty to sixty-five. Equipped with a modern radar system, radio
telephones, hydroplane and helicopter pad, the ship epitomized the Greek
tycoon's gregarious style. Other amenities included a screening room, a
swimming pool for those who didn't like saltwater, and a sunken blue
Sienna marble bathtub surrounded by Venetian mirrored walls. Guests
could choose from nine luxuriously appointed staterooms.[1]

Onassis spoke some Swedish, having commissioned his first big ships in
Stockholm and Göteborg. His pet name for Greta was "Vackra svenska flicka"
(beautiful Swedish girl); she called him Ari. As generous a host as he was

---

[1]Each was named after a Greek island. According to biographer Peter Evans, most guests
(including Garbo) selected the opulent Itháki; but another guest, director Jean Negulesco,
says Greta usually chose Lésvos.

ruthless a businessman, Ari loved to play practical jokes. Nearly everyone had been short-sheeted or pushed into the pool at one time or another. Not Garbo. "He didn't dare have a go at me," she said. He did test her humor: "Madame, you are sitting on the largest penis in the world," he gleefully announced when she sat down on a barstool covered with whale foreskin.

That summer, the *Christina* visited the isle of Capri and the Sicilian port of Palermo before heading up the Adriatic to Venice. By August, they had found a home off the island of Itáki. Greta celebrated her fiftieth birthday on board the yacht. She returned to Nice via a plane from Athens, with George Schlee at her side; Onassis joined them on an October 4 flight to New York.

On an evening out with Greta and Ari, Jean Negulesco recalled being struck by Garbo's varying moods: a burst of gaiety, then caution and reserve; she was also jealous—another surprise for the director and his wife. When Onassis suggested going to see a Rumanian singer, Greta snapped that he only liked her "because she sings all her songs to you and only to you." She did like being the center of attention after all.

The comfortable routine of 1955 became the framework for Greta's activities over the next decade. Her schedule revolved around an eclectic group of friends. During the spring, she would venture on her own to California, ofttimes with brief stops in Palm Springs or Santa Fe. She spent most of the summer in Europe with George Schlee, usually in and around Cap-d'Ail. After her birthday, Greta would return to New York, where she enjoyed watching Central Park change colors throughout the fall and experiencing the near-ebullient mood as Manhattan dressed for the holidays. "New Yorkers are so friendly in the snow," she said.

In late March of 1956, she had a health scare. Greta checked into New York Hospital to undergo a complete physical examination and was relieved to learn the illness wasn't serious. Because information was doled out on a need-to-know basis, many friends didn't even know she had been ill. "Garbo works with her friends much on the theory of the underground—one cell doesn't know the next cell," stated Harry Crocker.

Over the years, she carefully widened her circle of friends in New York. Decorator Billy Baldwin met her at the home of Allen Porter. "Garbo was crazy about her ballet lessons from [choreographer] John Butler," he said. "She was so strange and complicated and, in a way, heartbreaking, because you wanted to be a warm friend, but she simply wouldn't let you." Yet when Baldwin was hospitalized with pneumonia, Greta was one of the few friends who showed up, carrying a small bouquet of flowers in hand.

She methodically filled her time with people and travel. By the first week in July, she and Schlee were back on the road. Again, they spent the summer on Onassis's yacht, soaking up the sun in ports along the coasts of Italy, Greece, and Yugoslavia. From Monte Carlo, she wrote Cecil Beaton that she would be at the Hôtel de Crillon in Paris by September 20—possibly with a new friend: Cécile de Rothschild.

Cécile de Rothschild was the sister of Élie de Rothschild[2] and one of Eric Goldschmidt-Rothschild's many cousins—she represented the Paris branch of the family, he the Viennese. It was through the baron that Cécile met Greta. Although "Mademoiselle Cécile," as Greta affectionately called her, was eight years her junior, their friendship clicked—motivated somewhat by self-serving purposes on both sides; Cécile was an unabashed admirer and Garbo could always use a facilitator.

People who could manage the nagging details of travel and entertainment were a necessity in life, Greta confessed. More than the status afforded her by such an acquaintance, she obviously enjoyed the hospitality, comfort, and security offered her by people like the Rothschilds or Aristotle Onassis. Along with George Schlee, they defined her later years as profoundly as Mauritz Stiller and MGM had her youth.

Cecil Beaton arrived in Paris in mid-October and found, happily, that he got on extremely well with Greta's new companion. He believed Cécile to be "a person of complete integrity and lack of vulgarity . . . Certainly an improvement on all that cheap Russian baby-talk and Second Avenue junk shop level—and she has nothing to do but make things easier for Greta . . ." Despite the easy beginning, they had a rather difficult week. When Beaton successfully negotiated their departure to England, Greta— or, more correctly, Harriet Brown—checked into Claridge's instead of staying with him at Reddish House. She spent the first few days with the Gunthers and the rest dodging the press.

The highlight of her visit was a tea Beaton had arranged at 10 Downing Street on the seventeenth of October. Clarissa Churchill had married the prime minister of England, Sir Anthony Eden. Although preoccupied with the Suez crisis, Eden managed to set aside state business long enough to spend a half-hour with their guest. "I've admired you ever since I first saw you in a silent movie of *Anna Karenina*," he said, almost gushing. Greta smiled nervously. "Does that take you back into another world? Does it make you think how strange it was that you should have been that person?

[2]Along with his cousins Guy and Alain de Rothschild, Élie ran Compagnie du Nord, the main link in the family's investment empire.

Did you enjoy being a great movie star?" Garbo claimed not to think about the old days anymore. "They don't mean anything to me," she said. The subject was changed to Sweden.

Despite the momentary awkwardness, Greta appeared to enjoy herself as she toured the prime minister's residence. Her visit became news when photographers waiting to get a picture of the president of Costa Rica caught Garbo instead. After a pleasant weekend in the country, she decided to return to Paris with Cécile. Once again, Beaton was unsuccessful in convincing her to stay over for Christmas. The fact that she might actually want to fly back "to that dreary Schlee-ridden routine" was beyond his understanding.

Greta renewed her passport and returned to Cap-d'Ail in June 1957 with flags waving and spirits high—Aristotle Onassis had arranged to have a Hungarian orchestra meet her at the railway station. Being Garbo—not to mention an intimate friend of Onassis's—also got her admitted to an exclusive Monte Carlo casino wearing a "scandalous" pants ensemble amid the formal dress of other women. (Curiously, Marlene Dietrich had been turned away from the same club a year or so earlier when she attempted to make a similar entrance.)

She returned to the States early due to an undisclosed medical problem. "Garbo began to complain of her health when she arrived in Paris about ten days ago from the Riviera," the *Sunday Dispatch* reported on October 6. "She complained of severe intestinal pains and two doctors were summoned to her fourth-floor apartment at the Hotel Crillon." She was later taken to a Paris hospital, but the doctors could find nothing wrong. The following day on an outing with Schlee, she again complained of pain and insisted on consulting with her own doctors in New York.

In a letter to Mercedes, Cecil Beaton indicated that her concerns were very real. Not only had her kidneys been "out of order"—echoes of her father's infirmity—but there had been a reoccurrence of her chronic and debilitating pelvic infection.[3] "She really has been feeling ill," he wrote. "She has gone from one doctor to another. Suddenly she started to feel better when she was given insulin injections by a quack." According to Jean Howard, the doctor in question was an Austrian psychiatrist named Menford Sakel, one of the doctors credited with "inventing" shock treatments.

Howard had recommended the doctor to Greta after he successfully brought her out of a deep depression with his controversial insulin treatment. For a period of time, Sakel saw Garbo seven days a week, allowing her to enter and exit through a separate entrance so as to avoid the waiting

---

[3]Possible early signs of a diabetic condition.

room. One day, however, she stepped into the elevator only to find out that Sakel had passed away the previous evening. "She turned and walked out of the building without saying a word," Howard says. "She was devastated."

Cecil thought the doctor's death "a blessing in disguise" because friends had told him "he reduced his clients to such a nervous state with these shots that they all got to the condition known as the 'shakes.' " Beaton confirmed Garbo's poor state when he saw her in New York later in the year. She looked like "a terrified creature," he wrote in his diary, but he managed to get her laughing, chasing the blues away with vodka—"although she should abstain."

Eleven years Garbo's senior, Mercedes de Acosta had suffered many of the same physical and emotional pains, sought the same homeopathic cures, and yet received scant support from the woman she considered the love of her life. When they met on the street, Greta would nod at her "in the most cursory manner," said Beaton. Though oblivious to Mercedes' recent health problems, worries about her own health helped to forge a reconciliation between them. One night, after nearly two years of silence, Greta showed up on Mercedes' doorstep and burst into tears. "I have no one to look after me," she cried. "You don't *want* anyone to look after you," Mercedes responded.

But she was not immune to Greta's pleas of being frightened and lost. She quickly (and presumably happily) reverted to the role of protector. Even Cecil had to admit that Mercedes was a good friend, who "for thirty years has stood by her, willing to devote her life to her." When Greta complained about a shop owner who told her she didn't look well, Mercedes ran to the store and scolded the woman. "Don't you ever tell Miss Garbo she doesn't look well again. However badly you think she looks, tell her she looks fine."

At the moment, she felt—and looked—a wreck. As did Mercedes. Due to her diminished income and mounting medical bills, Mercedes moved from Park Avenue to a smaller apartment on East Sixty-eight Street. She had a serious eye infection in 1957 that forced her to wear a patch over her right eye, thus exaggerating her decidedly unique appearance. In response to another problem, her doctor prescribed cortisone, which made her irritable, depressed, and nearly suicidal. One day when she was having a bad time she sent a note to Greta via a friend. "Soon a reassuring telegram arrived, which began, 'Darling Boy—' " Hugo Vickers reported. "Mercedes put her gun away."

For the most part, it was Mercedes who did the nurturing. She checked out the doctors and made referrals. But when one of Garbo's doctors asked for her phone number, she made him promise he wouldn't pass it on to Mercedes. Greta was, Mercedes and Cecil agreed, a perplexing mixture of greatness and pettiness. Although she suffered dreadfully at what Beaton saw as Garbo's cruelty, Mercedes managed to keep her sense of humor.

"Well, we really must admit she's a character, if not a real eccentric," she told Beaton.

At the end of the year, Greta suddenly left New York to consult with yet another doctor in California. She soon seemed to forget her problems and became immersed in those of others. On March 22, 1958, producer Michael Todd was killed in plane crash. His beautiful young widow, twenty-six-year-old Elizabeth Taylor, was inconsolable and went into a seclusion that lasted for weeks. Though Garbo and Taylor had never met, Greta braved the gauntlet of press outside the Todd home to pay her respects.

She had also recently been caring for an ailing Harry Crocker. Crocker lost his syndicated column in 1951 when his boss, William Randolph Hearst, passed away. After that, a friend noted, he seemed "a rather sad, philosophic and ailing man." Hollywood's most genial society reporter died in May of 1958 unnoticed by all but a small group of friends. According to Joe Lombardo, it was Greta who looked after Crocker until the very end.

Back in New York, she visited Montgomery Clift after his catastrophic car crash. She had known the actor for several years, and although they were not close friends, Greta had become "permanently fond" of Monty, says Jack Larson. "She often asked me about Monty." Larson recalled one late afternoon meeting in particular. Greta met Salka Viertel and writer James Bridges at Clift's Sixty-first Street townhouse. "She arrived with a bandanna on her head and dark glasses and went straight out to Monty's garden terrace." Clift always fussed over Garbo, making sure she could be seen to her best advantage—whether it was at a candlelit dinner or cocktails under the soft light of a waning sun. After drinks in the garden, Greta followed him into the kitchen where the two of them conversed over a tin of caviar. "Here are two of the most glamorous people in the world and what are they talking about?" Salka laughed. "The dishwashers they never use because they never entertain."

During the summer, Greta and George Schlee again availed themselves of Onassis's hospitality. On occasion, Winston and Clementine Churchill joined them on board the *Christina* for lunch and a leisurely game of cards. Garbo, Onassis, and Churchill were seen around Monte Carlo with increasing frequency. Later in August, they dined together at the Château de Madrid, a world-class restaurant perched high up the mountainside. "Churchill was very interesting, but he only wanted to talk about war. He offered me a cigar," Greta told Sven Broman. He also offered her advice about her career, urging her to make a screen comeback. "It's never too late," he said. "Look at me, I didn't become prime minister until I was over fifty . . ."

Garbo, Schlee, and Onassis received an invitation from the Churchills to attend their fiftieth wedding anniversary celebration. Although unable to attend (the *Christina* was already on its way to Greece), Garbo and Schlee later reciprocated by inviting everyone to Greta's birthday party. Strangely, they ended up spending the day alone. In fact, the couple had returned rather abruptly from Athens four days earlier. "There was much comment in Paris about Schlee's behaviour aboard the Onassis yacht this year," Cecil reported to Mercedes, clearly unable to suppress his delight. "It seems he's not likely to be invited again."

The cause for the trouble is unclear, but Schlee's jealousy appears the most likely prospect. Garbo had received another proposal. What Ari proposed— given that he was already married and she was aligned with Schlee—is not known, but it was not the first, nor would it be the last, entanglement she had with a married man. Watching Garbo interact with her husband, Leland Hayward, "Slim" Hayward often wondered if there had been something between them. Jean Howard (Greta always called her Mrs. *Field*man) had a similar feeling. "It crossed my mind once, long after I was divorced from Charlie [Feldman]," she says. "Knowing how much she liked him, I wondered, 'Did he?' But I never asked."

Like Leland Hayward and Charles Feldman, Aristotle Onassis enjoyed chasing beautiful women. Though Greta certainly enjoyed the game, being caught was not an option. Garbo and Schlee returned to the States on October 17, seemingly without making much of an attempt to see anyone else. It would be some time before Greta saw Ari again. In November of 1958, he began his courtship of Maria Callas.

Greta also had a falling out with Eric Goldschmidt-Rothschild. Director Herbert Kenwith, who lived nearby on Fifty-fourth Street, witnessed an incident where the couple got out of a car near the Campanile. They were having an argument, he recalls. Suddenly, Rothschild slapped her and walked away, leaving a stunned Garbo in his wake. The breakup was never explained; even Beaton admitted being puzzled by the sudden turn in events.

In January, Cecil dined with Greta in New York. More than anything, he was dying to ask what that inextricable link with George Schlee was; why she always seemed to turn to him first. Anxious to elicit some kind of response, Beaton announced that he was thinking of getting married. "Well, well, well. So you've got a girl, have you?" Greta teased. "I'll be right over to stop it— I'll come to cut her head off." She correctly anticipated his next statement: that he wasn't "in love" with his intended, an attractive widow named June Osborn; he only felt that he should get married.

New social acquaintances were cultivated during the summer of 1959. Principal among these would be that with independent producer Sam

Spiegel, whose yacht, the *Malahne*, was moored near Onassis's in Monte Carlo Harbor. Garbo was one visitor Spiegel never kept waiting. Luis Estevez recalls lounging on the yacht one bright summer day as Sam came rushing in, having just arrived on a flight from London. Soon they heard a car pull up and everyone looked toward the dock. At the top of the stairs stood a woman in a dark blazer, white flannel pants, large straw hat, and sunglasses. Garbo took off her glasses and looked at Estevez. "Sam, darling," she said in that unmistakable voice. "I thought I would find you with a beautiful girl. Instead I find you with a beautiful boy."

Contrary to impressions from others, Estevez remembers both Sam and George Schlee deferring to their illustrious companion. On a short cruise to nearby Villefranche, Luis suggested inviting his friend Alice Thompson to lunch. "We don't do anything unless that's what *Miss G* wants," Spiegel replied. After a few basic questions, Garbo agreed. "Let's invite Mrs. Thompson to lunch."

"Garbo has this effect on people," Estevez acknowledged. "They don't act normal, they're just in a paralyzed state of ecstasy. I mean, that was my problem. She was fifty-two, fifty-three . . . and she was quite spectacular looking. When Sam introduced Alice to Garbo, she could hardly talk." Greta extended her hand to greet Mrs. Thompson. Nearby, Estevez was dripping wet, having water-skied back to the boat. "And Garbo grabs a big white towel and she comes over and wraps it around me. 'You must not get a cold.' Then she goes back to the lounge and sits in the midst of all these pillows, motioning for me to sit beside her. Well, I knew right away that she was playing a game, you know, but I loved it. I was fascinated and Alice was fascinated. . . . She knew exactly how to grab the scene."

Drinks were served, and Alice was still staring. Greta turned to Luis. "Oh, you have salt on your eyelashes," she said. He started to wipe his eyes, but she stopped him. "Don't touch them. I love the salt on your eyelashes." When they returned to Thompson's villa, Estevez was inundated with questions. "Luis, you're not having an affair with Garbo," Alice exclaimed. Even after Garbo and Schlee returned to the States during the second week of October, there were questions. Valentina became very curious about George and Greta's relationship with Luis and Betty Estevez. Not wanting to be left out, she contacted Luis and asked him out to lunch; Garbo heard about it soon after. "Oh, you met Valentina," she said. She looked at him intently. "Luis, being my friend is not going to be an easy thing for you."

Greta's reconciliation with Mercedes was destined to be temporary. Desperate to resolve her financial situation, de Acosta had been secretly working on her autobiography since 1954. As she considered publication, many friends offered their support, advising Mercedes against letting a "cat" rule her life. In March of 1960, *Here Lies the Heart* was published—replete with a photo section that featured the topless pictures documenting Mercedes' trip to the Sierras with Garbo in 1931. Although she had been notified of the book's release, Greta appears to have been one of the last persons to see a copy of the controversial memoir.[4] Despite several attempts by Mercedes to explain or apologize for her "transgression," Greta never spoke to her again.

In the years to follow, the memoir would acquire an underground reputation, largely due to its documentation of the gay subculture in New York and Los Angeles. It would be considered a pioneering work. Published works usually present something of a problem for gay historians, because the hidden subtext of these stories involves characters that have been combined, sexes changed; years, dates, and places switched to avoid harassment from disapproving heterosexuals. Surprisingly, Mercedes did little of this in *Here Lies the Heart*. She may have veiled sexual encounters behind poetry, but for the most part she took great pains to name names—and in Garbo's case: years, places, and films—in order to firmly place herself within a circle of celebrated friends. Her identity was entwined with theirs. Was the author capable of exaggerating her importance in the lives of Eleanora Duse, Isadora Duncan, Nijinsky, Nazimova, Igor Stravinsky, Picasso, and Edna St. Vincent Millay? Many former friends thought she was.

Unfortunately, the book neither relieved the pressure on her financially nor brought her comfort. "I have always thought that Greta would end her days with Mercedes—a sort of desperation solution for two lonely people," Cecil wrote. "But it seems Greta is really 'through' with Mercedes—not for the reason that Mercedes imagines . . ." The real reason, he thought, was that apart from being chronically irritated and bored, Greta felt Mercedes brought her bad luck. Previously, de Acosta had the misfortune of referring her to not one but two doctors whom Greta felt had done her great harm: an osteopath and a physiotherapist, both of whom specialized in manipulating muscles and joints. One "made her bones float about her body, put her hip out, & caused her mouth to go lopsided," Beaton stated. The experience permanently scarred the relationship between the women.

After her first operation to remove a brain tumor, Mercedes sold her jewelry to pay her bills. Before making contact with the Rosenbach Museum in Philadelphia, she also tried (unsuccessfully) to sell some of her art to friends. Museum director William H. McCarthy, Jr., became her unofficial benefactor, arranging to have the Rosenbach buy her collection as well as

---

[4]De Acosta sent bound galleys to several friends—including Cecil Beaton and Marlene Dietrich—for their comments and approval.

extending several personal loans. Mercedes managed to make the transfer with notable discretion. "I hope you did not mind too much my not letting you read Greta's letters," she wrote McCarthy after one meeting. "You see, they mean a lot to me and I just could not take it to sit there and to have some one just carelessly reading them. You should have understood and I think you did."[5]

In October of 1960, Greta visited Klosters for the first time. The Swiss mountain community was the home of Peter Viertel (now a successful author and screenwriter) and his second wife, actress Deborah Kerr. Following the tragic death of his first wife, Jigee, Viertel brought their daughter Christine to live with him, and Salka insisted that there was no way she would allow such a distance to separate her from her granddaughter. Klosters soon had a grande dame. Cécile de Rothschild's chalet just two hours away in St. Moritz made Salka's new home a logical stopping place for Garbo.

That November, "Harriet Brown" traveled to London to visit Sydney Guilaroff while he worked on *Cleopatra*. She spent the rest of the year nursing George Schlee, who was in and out of a doctor's care. Though briefly hospitalized, Schlee was well enough by late summer to make the annual trip to France. Valentina was a country away, spending her summer with her lover in Venice before taking over Cap-d'Ail in the fall of 1961. The once-celebrated ménage à trois had unraveled into less than a ménage. There is, in fact, sufficient evidence to conclude that by this time it was Greta who was asking for (and not getting) a full commitment.

It was left for Cecil to tell her that Mercedes was seriously ill and might not recover from a second major operation. He urged her to send a note, a postcard, anything; that she would be plagued with feelings of guilt and remorse if Mercedes died and she had made no gesture toward forgiveness. Although she was obviously "deeply, deeply upset," Greta did not relax in her judgment. Neither did Cecil relax in his judgment of her. "I am a swine not to unbend completely, not to dissolve into tears; but I cannot. . . . I'm resentful of the continued waste, the continued regrets, the lost opportunities sighed over and the new ones never faced."

He never took Mercedes' wrenching experience to heart. During the fall, *The Wandering Years (1922–1939)*, the first of several Beaton journals in which Garbo was at first a minor, then a major character, hit the book stores. "It was hard to decide to 'publish and be damned' but I thought it

---

[5]Garbo's letters were sealed along with those of Eva Le Gallienne and Marlene Dietrich—ostensibly until ten years after their respective deaths.

no good giving a watered-down version of the original diaries," the author stated. "God knows what will happen if I ever bring them more up to date!"

A "death" in her homeland reportedly brought Garbo to Sweden for the first time since 1946.[6] She flew to Sweden alone on the seventh of December. It would be her first Christmas abroad in over twenty years—and, sadly, her last visit to the once-bustling Wachtmeister estate at Tistad. She spent much of her time with Carl Johan and his wife, Kerstin Bernadotte, who turned over their eleven-room apartment in the heart of Stockholm to her. Count and Countess Bernadotte (the prince had given up his royal title to marry a commoner) also entertained Greta at Båstad, their estate on the southwest coast of Sweden.

However, according to her old friend Mimi Pollak, it was at the Grand Hôtel that she received a surprising telegram from Paris: "VALENTINA WILL NOT AGREE TO DIVORCE BECAUSE OF RELIGION. SADLY WE CANNOT MARRY. GEORGE." This conflict was the most likely reason for her unscheduled trip to Sweden. Greta was immediately cheered by the reunion with Mimi and Vera Schmiterlöw at Mimi's home. They reminisced until the wee hours of the morning. "Greta repeated many times that our theater school days were the happiest period in her life," Vera revealed. "She spoke with regret of the mistakes she made in later years. Not getting married, she said, was the greatest of them all. A close second was her failure in ever being able to conquer her shyness."

History was made late in the afternoon of January 4, 1962, when Garbo met with Ingmar Bergman at the Svensk Filmindustri studio. Greta was an admirer of Bergman's work, particularly *Wild Strawberries* (1957) and *Through a Glass Darkly* (1961). She declined a formal reception at Råsunda, asking only that the director escort her around her old stomping ground. She arrived in a limousine, accompanied by Countess Bernadotte. While Bergman's assistant entertained Garbo's companion with brandy and the latest gossip, Greta and the director adjourned to his office.

Bergman presented her with a small wooden bear carved by one of his children. "The room was cramped, a desk, a chair and a sagging sofa," he recalled. "I sat at my desk, the desk lamp switched on. Greta Garbo sat on the sofa. 'This was Stiller's room,' she declared at once, looking round. I

---

[6]Passport files do not identify the deceased, only that Greta made an application for an emergency renewal of her passport. Interestingly, Ingmar Bergman heard she had come to Stockholm to see a doctor—but, according to Kerstin Bernadotte, the real reason for the reported "emergency" was that Greta had gone all of the way to New York airport only to discover that her passport had expired.

didn't know what to say, so replied that Gustaf Molander had had this room before me. 'Yes, this is Stiller's room, I know for sure.' We talked rather vaguely about Stiller and Sjöström . . . Silence fell. Suddenly she took off her concealing sunglasses and said, 'This is what I look like, Mr. Bergman.' Her smile was swift and dazzling, teasing. . . . In the half-light in that cramped room, her beauty was imperishable. If she had been an angel from one of the gospels, I would have said her beauty floated about her. . . . She immediately registered my reaction, was exhilarated, and started talking about her work on Selma Lagerlöf's *Gosta Berlings saga.*"

They went on an informal tour of the studio, visiting the area where the fire at Ekeby had been staged nearly forty years earlier. Greta moved around energetically as she talked about the electricians, assistants, and other members of the crew she had worked with. When they returned to Bergman's office, she seemed cheerful and relaxed. She lit another cigarette and spoke of how Alf Sjöberg had wanted to make a film with her. "He was so persuasive, he was irresistible. I accepted but changed my mind the next morning and refused. That was awfully stupid of me. Do you think that was stupid, Mr. Bergman?" This time when she leaned across his desk, her face was illuminated by the desk lamp. Bergman was startled by what he had not seen before. "Her mouth was ugly, a pale slit surrounded by transverse wrinkles. It was strange and disturbing. All that beauty and in the middle of the beauty a shrill discord. . . . She at once read my thoughts and grew silent, bored. A few minutes later we said goodbye."

According to Sven Broman, Greta did not fault Bergman for his frank assessment; the transverse lines above her upper lip had been the focus of her efforts to hide her face from photographers over the years. "I was shocked to see all those lines above my mouth show," she acknowledged, "I know I have them and I asked [Erno] Laszlo if he couldn't get rid of them; he can't."

Those who had hoped that the break with George Schlee was permanent were, no doubt, disappointed to hear that by February, Greta was back with him. In the spring, she began going to the New York University Medical Center for treatment of acute arthritis. "When I dont feel very well, I go more tightly in the corner," she wrote Sydney Guilaroff. Apparently, making a determination of which malady to treat had not been easy. "The last [doctor] said there is nothing serious that he could see but said if pain persist [sic] to come back in a week. It is very depressing the whole thing."

Increasingly, on her walks about town with Joe Lombardo and Nicholas Turner, Greta ventured into neighborhood churches, often making long detours in order to light a candle under a favored saint. "I am going to a church were [sic] there is a saint called Jude, and I stand and stare at him and ask him to remember me," she wrote in a letter to Salka. "There is a guardian there and since I dont cross myself or do anything but stare and ask without words, I am sure he thinks I am some sort of lunatic."

She still didn't feel well. When George Schlee began making plans for their next trip to Europe, she told him she didn't want to go. But she had been thinking about visiting a friend. "You would never know that I love you when you never hear anything from me, but I do—and forever," she wrote Salka in July. "[I] would give anything to be back in the days when I could take my buggy and drive to Myberry [sic] Road and see you—the vibrant, wonderful person that is you. Now I am almost afraid to face you because I would be ashamed for many, many reasons, but the longing to see you is there, as always." Owing to her health, she wasn't making any definite plans for the summer, "but if all turns out well and I can travel, I shall try to come and see you," she wrote.

That summer she went to the Riviera with Schlee; Salka continued to wait.

The most extraordinary event of 1962 was her invitation to dinner at the White House with President and Mrs. John F. Kennedy. Pinning down the exact date of this event is as elusive as Garbo herself—the private affair wasn't recorded on JFK's appointment calendar nor in the papers kept by social secretary Letitia Baldrige. An FBI background check, released under the Freedom of Information Act, shows that Garbo was approved for a White House visit on January 15, 1962. According to Nancy Tuckerman, Jacqueline Kennedy Onassis's trusted personal assistant, the former First Lady recalled that Garbo was the houseguest of Washington socialite Florence Mahoney. Both were invited to the informal dinner, along with Lee Radziwill, Mrs. Kennedy's younger sister, and K. LeMoyne Billings.

Lem Billings, JFK's longtime friend, had met Greta while cruising on Sam Spiegel's yacht the previous summer. Billings thought her wonderfully funny and hypnotically beautiful—doubtless touting her to Kennedy as *his* latest conquest. The evening was planned so that Garbo would arrive before Billings, "giving the President an opportunity to chat with the actress, and to make special arrangements with her for Lem's arrival." Greta and Mrs. Mahoney were escorted to the family residence on the second floor.

When the last of the guests had arrived, Greta walked into the dining room with the First Lady; Billings rushed to greet her. "There was a ghastly pause. Garbo looked at Lem blankly. She turned, puzzled, to the President. 'I have never seen this man before,' said Greta Garbo." Lem was in shock. Nothing seemed to refresh her memory about their meeting on the Riviera. "The President was full of earnest curiosity about how such a mix-up could have occurred. Perhaps Lem had become friends with someone who *looked* like Garbo. Lem testily declared that that was impossible. . . . In his befuddlement, the one possibility he did not consider was that Garbo's amnesia had been recently contrived by the President of the United States." The party managed to maintain their charade until the second course.

"It was a lovely, intimate dinner," Greta said. In honor of the occasion, she had worn one of her finest designer suits. "President Kennedy did not smoke and drank only water," she remembered. "I felt like one of the damned when I lit a cigarette." Her host inquired about her recent activities. Fumbling for a response, Garbo told him that she was a collector. " 'What do you collect?' Kennedy asked. 'Here's an example,' I said and opened my handbag to show him an article I had torn out of a magazine, which was about Kennedy. The president looked at me in surprise." JFK then asked her opinion on various issues—one of the rare times Garbo expressed herself in a political context.

"Greta was very attracted by the president. She boasted a little that instead of withdrawing to his study he had stayed with his guests after dinner 'longer than I have ever done since I became president,' " Kerstin Bernadotte reported. Mrs. Kennedy took the party on a private tour of the White House, including the popular Lincoln bedroom, where Garbo took off her socks and got on the bed. Thinking that she had too much to drink, she later told Sam Green that "one was unruly at the White House." She declined an invitation to stay overnight—a missed opportunity, she would suggest—but did receive an unusual souvenir from the president: a whale's tooth. "Mrs. *Jah-*kee" smiled. "He never gave *me* a whale's tooth," the First Lady said.

With the advent of television, the resurgence of international film festivals, and the European film market, Greta Garbo's cinematic immortality was confirmed while she herself remained intangible. Skeptics believed that Garbo's furtive flirtation with the public and press was actually a canny way of securing her legend, yet she did very little to support the myth of a glamorous, legendary movie star. Certainly a Ginger Rogers, Loretta Young, or Joan Crawford made a more conscious effort in this regard.

Gossip and the perpetuation of many Garbo myths were inevitable precisely because she failed to reveal herself to the public. Twenty years after she left motion pictures, interest in the Divine One continued unabated— and, in fact, was born anew during the 1960s. In February and March of 1963, Italy's lone television network, RAI-TV, screened a series of Garbo films on consecutive Sunday evenings, turning the star into "the greatest thing since *Perry Mason*" on Italian television with a record 10 million viewers tuning in each evening. The series was so successful, attendance at everything from movies to restaurants dropped dramatically during the hours the films aired.

A few months later, this success was repeated at the Empire Theatre in London. "The comeback of Greta Garbo to the West End of London is so successful that even MGM's expectations have been surpassed," a studio press release announced. By the end of the run, 90,000 people had attended the screenings, each week building on attendance from the last. Asked to comment on her latest triumph, Greta was dumbfounded. "I didn't think they'd remember me," she said.[7]

Perhaps her most profound effect would be on a new generation of moviemakers. Federico Fellini opined that Garbo was the only movie star to achieve the status of a religious icon. For him, she had the "austere looks of a cloistered empress. She was always an unreachable living myth whom I would describe as the founder of a religious order called the cinema. . . . She gave the cinema the sacredness of Mass."

As George Schlee's escalating health problems weighed upon her, Greta seemed to be reaching out for younger companions. She met Raymond Daum on a snowy New Year's Day at the Dakota apartment of Ruth Ford and Zachary Scott. Immaculately dressed in a pale violet turtleneck sweater and light gray slacks, Greta was seated on a hassock in the middle of the library. While Lauren Bacall, Jason Robards, Elia Kazan, Norman Mailer, Tammy Grimes, and others sipped Irish coffees and stood reverentially aside, Daum gathered the courage to approach her through Schlee. Greta perked up when she heard that Daum worked at the United Nations; she invited him to sit down, suggesting that "Schleesky" get her another vodka. During the course of their short but friendly conversation, she would learn that Daum was thirty-eight, single, and resided near the U.N. on Beekman Place; they were neighbors.

Five and a half months passed before he heard from her again. "She'd like to come today," Schlee announced, indicating that Greta was interested in Daum's offer to take her on a private tour of the U.N. Daum agreed to meet them at the main entrance. "George waited in the Delegates Lounge—Garbo explained that he was suffering from lumbago (a word she always used to describe her own back pain)—and she and I set off walking."

In time, Daum became a regular walking partner, often "trotting" with her down Second Avenue to Greenwich Village—a minimum of eighty

---

[7]Similar festivals would follow in France, Germany, and Holland. The success also inspired the 1964 release of an album from MGM Records entitled *Garbo!*, a compilation of clips from eight of her sound films.

blocks round-trip—three times a week. Greta walked quickly in long, easy strides, usually glancing neither left nor right until something in a shop window captured her attention. Then she would stop for a moment in front of the shop, returning to her walk when she became aware that she had "a customer." Though she was often recognized—and scrutinized— few admirers actually bothered her in New York; most would observe and then flee when they realized they had been detected.

Garbo and Daum spoke candidly about politics, art, religion, travel, literature, and even children—but rarely about her career in Hollywood, and then only in the most oblique terms. After her death, Daum termed any depiction of Garbo as "a lonely, pathetic woman . . . an empty vessel" to be a counterfeit portrait. "It is clear to me as a longtime close friend and neighbor of Miss G. that she was careful not to open up to many people. She would laugh with me at the continuing 'take' on her persona by so-called friends," he stated. "Garbo gave to friends only what she wanted them to know about her—and no more."

"Life is full of melancholy times," Greta quipped. "These things come, but luckily they go away . . . otherwise we'd jump in the East River, and it's so filthy."

When she visited Europe during the summer of 1963, merchants and admirers were delighted by the appearance of a rejuvenated Garbo. A few months later, she was seen in Barbados with Columbia Records president Goddard Lieberson and several other New York friends. Finally, at the island home of Claudette Colbert, Sweden's two greatest female stars came together socially. Remembering their cool encounter at Metro-Goldwyn-Mayer two decades earlier, Ingrid Bergman withdrew into the garden; Greta saw her and followed. "[She] sat down beside me. I didn't know what to say I was so nervous," Bergman recollected. "But she opened up the conversation, 'I understand you're in love with Barbados, and you're going to buy a piece of land here?' And I said, 'Yes, we just love the beach farther up from here, and we've plans for a little house.' "

Garbo became concerned that Bergman and her husband did not understand the risks. "Here they steal everything," she said. "They'll steal your clothes." Bergman wasn't worried; such things were easily replaced. If someone really needed her clothes badly enough to steal, they could have them, she replied. That effectively ended the conversation. Greta stood up and, without as much as a cordial good-bye, walked off. "Maybe that explains her attitude to life," Bergman remarked; "she's afraid *they're* going to steal it all away." It certainly explained the difference in philosophy between two Swedes born ten years and two worlds apart.

Greta's 1964 sojourn to Europe began with a meeting of friends in Switzerland. Brian and Eleanor Aherne had a home on Lake Geneva in a village of Vevey. The threesome joined forces with Noël Coward and on the fourteenth of July flew from Geneva to Rome. In Italy, the party rented a yacht for a short cruise. Before settling in Cap-d'Ail with Schlee, Greta squeezed in a side trip to Athens, where she toured the Acropolis. In the manner of the Greek tragedies, the newest drama in Greta Garbo's life was about to begin.

At the end of September, as per their schedule, Greta and George Schlee left Cap-d'Ail for Paris, checking into the Hôtel de Crillon on Place de la Concorde. Schlee had not been feeling well. On the afternoon of October 3, they met Betty Estevez for lunch. It was a day she would not soon forget. After lunch, the trio went for a walk down Rue Royale, looking in on the art galleries. Greta crossed the street. "All of a sudden, I don't know why, but George began across and was nearly hit by a bus. I thought Garbo was going to faint right there," says Estevez, "because we had both seen it happen. We went straight into a café near Maxim's to have a drink. They were both really shook up."

That evening, Garbo and Schlee had dinner with Cécile de Rothschild, whose eighteenth-century Parisian town palace on Rue du Fauborg Saint-Honoré is just around the corner from the back entrance of the Crillon. "Fate had ordained that [Cécile] should come to Paris on a certain day earlier than she intended—to find Greta & Schlee at the Crillon before leaving the next day for New York," Cecil Beaton wrote. Around 11:30 P.M., George escorted Greta back to the hotel and, according to Estevez, she went straight to bed. Restless and apparently unable to sleep, Schlee went for a walk a short time later. He was stricken with a heart attack on the street and staggered into a local bistro.

Before collapsing completely, he asked the proprietor to telephone his friend at the Crillon. Schlee was taken to Lariboisiere Hospital, where he was pronounced dead on arrival. In the meantime, Greta received a call from a man she did not know and could not understand because he only spoke French. She asked him to call Cécile de Rothschild, who now had the difficult task of informing Greta of her companion's death. The stories that filtered back to the United States differ in the details concerning Schlee's death as well as Garbo's response. *The Hollywood Reporter* stated that Schlee was stricken during a tour of the clubs; Jean Howard heard that he had been in a brothel; a stringer for *Time* magazine reported that he died in his hotel suite; another story implied that Garbo had abandoned

Schlee on the street after calling for help.[8] To this day, officials at the Crillon deny any knowledge of what really happened that evening. The original records kept by the Prefecture de Police have been destroyed.

Garbo left the hotel, seemingly disappearing into the crowd before the police could question her. Most people believed that, fearing a public spectacle, she placed herself in Cécile de Rothschild's hands, and the baroness secreted her out of harm's way before anyone knew that she was gone. "I'm afraid Garbo didn't cope very well," said one acquaintance. "She packed her bags and fled to a friend's place." The other side of the story, says Joe Lombardo, was that "Valentina came over and told her to get out. She said, 'He's my husband, what are you doing here?' And that really upset Garbo. It took her a long time to get over it—you know, to be treated like that."

A visibly distraught Garbo arrived at Kennedy Airport on October 7, the day of the funeral. The Russian Orthodox service was held at the Universal Funeral Chapel on Fifty-second and Lexington Avenue and was attended by an estimated eighty-five mourners, including Mr. and Mrs. William Paley, Mr. and Mrs. Sam Spiegel, Mr. and Mrs. Joshua Logan, Lillian Gish, and Anita Loos. Three of George's friends—John Gunther, attorney Eustace Seligman, and Dr. Alfred Frankfurter, editor of *Art News*—opened the half-hour service with their eulogies. "It's hard to talk about George, for he leaves no public record," Gunther told *The New York Times* prior to the service. "He was just a dear and delightful human being, a connoisseur of the art of living, a warm and sincere man." Dr. Frankfurter quoted from Pushkin's poem "Exegi Momentum": "I have erected a monument to myself, not built by hands; the track to it shall not be overgrown."

George Matthias Schlee was buried at Ferncliff Cemetery in Westchester County. According to one report, his widow ordered the groundskeeper to turn Garbo away if she ever showed up; as far as they knew, she never did. After her husband's death, Valentina obviously felt there was no need to "put on a show" any longer. When the estate (valued at more than $1 million) was settled, Valentina stripped Villa Le Roc of all photographs, mementos, and "relics of Garbo." (Her Academy Award, which had been brought out of the closet and put on display in George's private library, had been returned to Greta years earlier.) After having the grounds and building exorcised, she put it up for sale.[9] She also called in a Russian Orthodox priest to exorcise "that

---

[8]According to psychic Kenny Kingston, seeking forgiveness from George Schlee would be one of the primary focuses of his private séances with Greta Garbo.

[9]Ironically, according to a report in the *New York Post*, at the time of his death Garbo and Schlee were planning to sell the villa and purchase a yacht.

vampire" from her New York apartment. The ritualistic ceremony had included all of their belongings—even the refrigerator.

Certainly, Valentina Schlee's reaction was consistent with that of the wronged woman—but it also resembled that of a rejected lover. She never let go of the hate; in fact, she built a cool wall of alienation around it. She seemed to thrive on the drama. For the next twenty-five years, both she and Greta remained adversarial neighbors at the Campanile, making for many uncomfortable moments for residents, elevator operators, and doormen.

Once back in New York, Greta had to face the critical reaction of the press as well as Valentina's friends. Noticing that she was not on the plane bringing Schlee's body home nor at the funeral, critics remarked that, "If she loved him, she didn't realize it until afterwards." Perhaps, they suggested, she wasn't capable of love. Not so, says Betty Estevez. "I think she suffered terribly when George Schlee died because he had become a hero in her life, the man who took care of her." Her close friends saw another side of Garbo's grief. "She mourned deeply," Joe Lombardo confirms. "George Schlee was really a great love affair. Oh, yes. It took her years to get over that." Lombardo believes that Greta began going to a little church on Sixtieth Street around this time. "For a while, she went there every day."

When he saw Greta the following summer in Klosters, Jack Larson also observed a woman who was "absolutely grief-stricken" over Schlee's death. "She was terribly upset—definitely red-eyed. I never saw her cry, but you could tell she had been grieving," he says. According to Larson, she did not understand why she had been criticized for her behavior when she had simply stepped out of the way in order to allow Valentina to assume the public role of the grieving widow.[10]

Greta's friends rallied around her, sending her cards and notes offering a sympathetic ear if she wanted to talk. In response to a card sent by Sydney Guilaroff, Greta thanked a dear friend for thinking of her but apologized for her inability to speak with him personally. Eventually, she had to speak to *someone*. Raymond Daum received a call a few days after he had written a note of condolence. Greta wanted to come to his apartment for a visit. She arrived in less than an hour and was silent and disconsolate. Finally, after a long pause she spoke. There were tears in her eyes as she murmured softly, "Everyone I love dies."

Greta spent most of the next year avoiding places that reminded her too much of Schlee: She joined the Seligmans in Greenwich, Connecticut; visited the

---

[10]Three years later, Katharine Hepburn would also disappear into the shadows while Mrs. Spencer Tracy buried her husband; no one questioned Hepburn's feelings.

Gunthers at their home in Greensboro, Vermont; Nadea Loftus in Tucson (where she fought off an attack of sinusitis); and stopped in San Juan, Puerto Rico, on her way to the Virgin Islands. She had been battling sinusitis for more than two months, she wrote Cecil in April of 1965, and wondered why she never seemed to be able to shake it off. Could it be because she never had children or never married? Perhaps, she mused, she simply wasn't nice enough—though she hoped to find an answer so she would know what to curse!

When her mind had cleared, she accepted an invitation from Cécile de Rothschild to go on a cruise from Saint-Raphaël to the isle of La Maddalena (off the coast of Sardinia) and on to the Greek Isles on one of the family's smaller yachts, the *Sieta*. Other guests would include Austrian industrialist Friedrich Ledebur, Princess Jeanne-Marie de Broglie, and Cecil Beaton. All seemed to be forgiven between Greta and Cecil—though Beaton apparently thought Garbo's gray hair was the only significant sign of her maturity. "At first I was riled and irritated by the 'Is that so's' and 'never mind's,' 'Don't ask questions,' 'Not going to tell you,' etc. I couldn't imagine that there was not to be one moment of truth, but, no, she behaved like a mad child most of the time and that is all she wanted. So I soon learnt to talk gibberish like a monkey and she seemed perfectly content."

According to Beaton, Greta's relationship with Cécile was a kind of masochistic fantasy for the Baroness de Rothschild. Cécile assumed the mantle of protector and friend; in effect, filling the void left by Mercedes de Acosta's departure as well as Schlee's. A good-humored, kind woman, the baroness was one of the rare few who did not let her great wealth ruin her life; and she believed in doing interesting, creative, and unconventional things with her money. "Cécile was serious—heavily Rothschildian & slightly preoccupied," Beaton wrote of his hostess during the cruise. "She is very happy to have Greta on board—for she is besotted. She snickers at everything Greta does—even if it is a slap directed against herself. . . . With Greta she is a kid hynotised by a snake."

The fragile bond of trust that had existed between Greta and Cecil completely dissolved between them. For all intents and purposes, the summer of 1965 would mark the end of their friendship. If Greta suspected as much, she didn't seem to care; she had other things on her mind. She approached her sixtieth birthday with great sadness. *"Dans quelque jours, il sera l'anniversaire de la douleur que ne me quitte pas, que ne me quitte pas pour la reste de ma vie,"* she later shared with Raymond Daum, not quite sure why her feelings had been articulated in French: "In a few days, it will be the anniversary of the sorrow that never leaves me, that will never leave me for the rest of my life."

CHAPTER TWENTY-SIX

Survivor

Throughout 1966, Sven Gustafson fought a losing battle with heart disease. "Someone is very ill," Greta shared in a letter to Salka. "Since I am peculiar, I dont want to put facts into words, hoping if I dont for a miracle. But I am living in terror and utter sadness . . ." It was, unquestionably, a devastating time for her, coming so soon after George Schlee's passing. Greta stayed in New York awaiting word of some change in her brother's status, and finally in June there was a sigh of relief. "My patient is now home and I remain a rather confused, tired boy," she said.

She wondered what to do with herself for the summer, vacillating between an invitation from Cécile de Rothschild to go to Sardinia again and one from Princess Anja Chervachidze to spend time in Cap-Martin. But when August arrived, she had yet to leave New York. "I'm not sure of what to do," she admitted, "or rather how to do it."

Her trip to Europe during the late summer and early fall of 1966 reinforced a new bond—a circle of friends comprised of Cécile (and occasionally her sister-in-law, Liliane de Rothschild), Garbo, and the two Bettys: Betty Spiegel and Betty Estevez. Whether they met in Paris, Saint-Raphaël, St. Moritz, or New York, it was a circle completely independent of other attachments. For the next twenty years, here among these comrades, Greta would feel more protected than anywhere else. There were other friendships that meant as much to her—Salka Viertel, Jane Gunther—but none that made her feel so at ease.

"She loved to stay with Cécile because her life was comfortable and easy, and we would spoil her any time we could. All in our ways," Estevez says. "Cécile could spoil her a lot more than I could, of course, but we spoiled her." As with others who had embraced Garbo in friendship, what appealed to them was her vulnerability. "There was an endearing quality about her that you can't quite put your finger on," Estevez continues. At times, she could be selfish and self-absorbed, but "she made an effort to charm you if she liked you and if she wanted you to like her."

Then, too, these were women at leisure who—like Greta—had nothing but time on their hands. She first met Betty Spiegel, producer Sam Spiegel's young wife, at Betty Estevez's apartment in Paris. When Estevez told her that

Mrs. Spiegel was going to Monte Carlo to pick up the *Malahne*, Greta began to fantasize about a trip. "Her eyes got wide and she said, 'Oh, we could go to Corsica!' I'd never thought about that," Betty says. "She was very sweet."

Spiegel believes that the Garbo legend was just that—a legend, and a tremendous disservice to the woman behind it. "Everyone seems to want to imbue her with something that simply wasn't there," she says. "She wasn't a complicated person—that's what no one can get a fix on. There wasn't a helluva lot to share. . . . We didn't sit around and discuss Proust or Jung. They were very lighthearted, very light conversations: what we were going to have for lunch, what was the on the menu for dinner . . . sometimes a little bit of gossip, but nothing vicious. . . . G. just kind of sat back and listened . . . and enjoyed."

She did like to be entertained. "If she was in a small group . . . and we started acting silly or doing something or pretending to do a striptease in front of her, she'd laugh and think it was very funny," Betty Estevez offers. "She just wanted to be one of us, not be her." Estevez is convinced that from age sixty on, Greta "never had the sexual thing again—maybe even before. You could tell by her attitude about it." Once a maverick, she was now more of an observer.

Though some friends suspected that she might have had an affair with Cécile de Rothschild, they were never quite sure. Sam Green was. "Cécile and she were not lovers," he insisted. "I know what was happening. They had separate rooms. They went to bed at different times and got up at different times. And Garbo told me, long ago, 'All that sex business. I'm so glad to be over that.' She was past the point where her dignity would have allowed it."

She did like talking about sex, friends say. "I remember lying on the grass at my house in Oyster Bay, talking about which way one does it and which way is the best way," Horst, the renowned German photographer, recalled. "I was just back from Bangkok, and she wanted to know how you do it in Bangkok."

A long-standing joke had Greta picking up a sailor at Times Square on New Year's Eve. "You know, G., you keep joking about all these things. I think they're things you'd really like to do, but don't have the courage," Betty Spiegel once told her. Garbo smiled. Betty believed she knew what Greta's idea of a perfect date was: one evening, she announced to the two Bettys that a gentleman would be joining them for cocktails. "Betty and I looked at each other and I said, 'G., do you have a beau?' She said, 'He's my steady. I guess you could call him my steady.' I said, 'I didn't know you had a fellow' . . . and Betty said, 'Oh, come on, she's putting us on. It's a joke.' Well, she had a little doll dressed up like a boy and she had him sitting in a chair facing the other way. So she turned the chair around and that was the gentleman she had invited."

However good-natured one's intentions, one had to be careful when giving Greta a hard time. Amused by her tendency to use the royal "we" and "our" instead of I, me, or mine, Betty Spiegel once teased her, "Oh, were you a group?" Greta looked at her. "Sometimes when you teased her, she'd get a hurt look in her eyes. . . . I think that she sincerely didn't want to hurt anyone else. One sensed that. There was a fragility about her . . . I guess you felt that this poor lady's probably had so many people pulling and tugging and asking her for things all her life."

Garbo liked to feel safe with you, Betty Estevez emphasizes. "If you were ignoring her, in a way she felt happier—not by ignoring her but not asking questions, just talking about your own life. Sometimes I'd tell her things that happened to me in the nightclubs that would amuse her. But I think what she mainly wanted from people was a certain amount of loyalty." And a sense of belonging without feeling possessed.

Sven Gustafson died on January 27, 1967. He suffered an acute heart attack while under the care of doctors at the Desert Hospital in Palm Springs. Sven left his entire estate to his widow, Ethel Marguerite ("Peg") Gustafson—there was no mention of his sister in his will. The estate would deny the claim of his son out of wedlock by Elsa Hägerman, Sven Hägerman Gustafsson, although there was ample proof of his kinship, including letters, postcards, and photos.[1] When Sven Junior later filed suit to legally identify his father, Greta became concerned that he might come after her as well. She asked Joe Lombardo if he could recommend a good lawyer. "She said that her brother had an illegitimate child and she was worried that he might try and get some of her money," he recalls.

Protecting her money continued to be a major concern. When MGM began selling its films to television and revival theaters, Garbo, like most actors and actresses of that era, was unhappy that she wasn't allowed to participate in those residual earnings; she felt used. But unlike most of her peers, she made the money she did earn work for her long before she needed it. She didn't qualify for Social Security—thanks to her investments, she never needed it.[2] Neither would she tolerate losing a penny.

After George Schlee died, Greta turned to her niece, Gray Gustafson Reisfield, for help in maintaining her business affairs. But Gray had a young family to look after, and it was clear that her aunt needed someone who

---

[1] It appears that Sven Junior did not find out about his father's death for nearly five years.

[2] Although she did try to collect. She belatedly applied for a Social Security Number in 1962 but, according to Joe Lombardo, she didn't qualify because she had earned most of her money (as a resident alien) well before the period of eligibility.

could devote more time to her. Although others would claim they provided guidance, it was through Gayelord Hauser that Greta finally found someone who could help manage her investments. Anthony Palermo, who ran Hauser's natural foods company, Modern Products, was introduced to her when he first arrived in the United States. According to Palermo, Garbo and Hauser already owned a private hospital in Milwaukee. Together, the trio purchased commercial property along the 300 block of Rodeo Drive in Beverly Hills years before that area received its platinum rating. Greta's income from Rodeo Drive alone was around $10,000 a month.

By the mid-1970s, Palermo took on the responsibility of being Garbo's personal facilitator, dealing with her banks, investment brokers, property managers, and insurance agents. It was a full-time job that Palermo (who was married and the father of four children) managed to balance with his own business and home life. He would become a trusted advisor, confidant, and occasional escort on short trips abroad. Palermo remembered one trip in particular in which they flew to Switzerland just to look at a painting; Greta passed on the purchase and they got on the next flight to New York.

Throughout the late forties and fifties, her acquisitions had been sporadic; most of her art was secured from fellow collectors: Jean-Michel Atlan's *Composition* from Èlie de Rothschild, *Dame en Blanc, Assise* by Albert André from Charles Feldman, a pair of nineteenth-century paintings from Helena Rubinstein. Her primary interest had been the antique and secondhand shops in and around Manhattan, where she ferreted out antique furniture, rare books, and assorted decorative pieces for her apartment.[3] She continued to be drawn to color and balanced whimsical figures with historical ones; her collection kept friends guessing. (According to Joe Lombardo, she dabbled in painting herself and had her own painter's box, brushes, oils, and accessories.)

Her most daring acquisitions to date had been two paintings by Georges Rouault, *Pierrot Assis* and *Femme de Profil,* and an unidentified Wassily Kandinsky. Following Schlee's death, Greta took a major turn as an art collector, moving from the serenity of the French Impressionists to the "mad" brilliance of the Expressionists. Significantly, she purchased a major cache of paintings by Alexej von Jawlensky between 1966 and 1970. Although she was at a loss to explain why she bought them, it is clear that they were

---

[3]Her shelves were lined with volumes by Tolstoy, Goethe and Longfellow as well as Emerson, Hawthorne, Thackeray, Wells, Browning, and Dumas. Betty Spiegel was among those who were never quite sure that Greta read any of them. "I just don't know how people can read things and not discuss them."

more than mere investments. "I went to the gallery today and there was this painting; I mean a goofy painting. And I thought, 'What's the matter with me?' I can't stand horror and some of the pictures I buy are horror things—they stare at you," she said. "Oh well, maybe I'll get it. I don't know who the hell else would buy it. It's really very strange. I'll probably regret it. No. They're my colors. I do like it: They're my colors."[4]

Greta arrived in Switzerland during the first week of July 1967 and stayed through August. Salka arranged for a car to pick her up in Zurich and bring her to Klosters, enlisted the support of Peter's network of friends to secure a nearby apartment for her stay—at no charge—and filled her refrigerator. "For Garbo, Salka is like a nanny," an observer said. "She looks after her. In a way, it's like a daughter coming home." She spent September and October with Cécile and company.

When she returned to New York, there was bitter news from Cecil Beaton. After a cordial meeting on neutral territory, Beaton phoned Greta at her apartment and left word that he would like to have lunch with her to discuss the upcoming publication of *The Happy Years*.[5] Like Mercedes, he had too much ego (and pride) not to include his affair with Garbo—which he considered an important part of his life—in his published memoirs. But Greta did not want to hear his explanation and never returned the call.

Surprisingly, she *was* capable of being realistic when it came to the idea of people writing about her. Though she distrusted writers in general, Greta certainly had plenty of friends who made their living with words. She never attempted to stop Beaton from publishing his first volume (detailing their 1932 meeting)—nor did any recriminations follow. And she would not stand in the way of Salka Viertel. Eager to set the record straight and share some of her reminiscences of European theater before the war, Salka told Greta about her book before approaching publishers, and when she sold it in January of 1968, Greta was one of the first people to congratulate her. There would be very few personal revelations in *The Kindness of Strangers*; almost all of the Garbo references regarded her work with Salka—there were no betrayals of private moments.

* * *

[4]Conversely, she easily divested herself of the Picasso when she became unhappy with it. "It was a little, early Picasso which was not terribly attractive and she was quite right to sell it," David J. Nash, then an associate at Parke-Bernet, recalled. She conducted the entire transaction without speaking.

[5]The volume covered the years 1940–1948 and was published in the United States under the title *Memoirs of the 40's*.

The nature of Greta Garbo's celebrity dictated a life in which the fantastic constantly collided with the mundane. In March, a report that she had died prompted *Hollywood Reporter* columnist Radie Harris to call George Cukor—who was that moment entertaining Greta for tea. It was through Cukor that Greta would have one of her most curious Hollywood encounters. It began when she expressed a desire to meet Mae West, then enjoying a rebirth of sorts as college students began rediscovering her films along with those of W. C. Fields and the Marx Brothers.

"Garbo and Mae West met for the first time over the Easter weekend," Radie Harris reported. "Mae arrived first, in an off-white and pale green flowered long satin gown. Garbo, in her typical fashion style, wore a rose colored slack suit. She was accompanied by Gayelord Hauser, who reminded Mae that years ago, when she was at Paramount, he had tried to interest her in the same health foods he prescribed for Garbo." Greta sat in a low chair, virtually at Mae's feet, for most of the evening, appearing as fascinated by the famous "Carmen Miranda lifts," which the petite West wore in order to make herself look taller, as she was by her stories about her run-ins with censors and the law during the 1920s.

"Mae later complained that she had to do all of the talking that evening," Herbert Kenwith, a mutual friend, says. Kenwith denies that before she left, West complimented Garbo on her film work and encouraged her to get back in front of the camera—that she still had the looks and could always do character work. "Oh, no, no, no. Mae was more discreet than that." When prodded further about what they did talk about that evening, Kenwith says he was told, "She didn't say nuthin' worth rememberin'!"

On May 9, 1968, Mercedes de Acosta passed away at her home after a long illness. She died without ever reconciling with Garbo. Cecil Beaton wrote a somber tribute in his diary. "She became ill, she became poor, but she never became old. . . . She was one of the most rebellious & brazen of Lesbians." In her final years, he admitted, she had been a moody, demanding friend. "She became rather idiotic, petty & petulant. Looking for grievances, she found them," he recorded. "She managed to make it difficult for friends, impossible for her lovers." As the years passed, her friends got younger—and her patience shorter—but Beaton described her as a gallant soul when death approached. His only regret was not sending flowers in Greta's name (with no one the wiser).

With her collection safely tucked away at the Rosenbach, Mercedes sadly neglected one important detail: the topless photos of Greta at Silver Lake which she had used in her book. A collection of photographs was discovered in a trunk soon after she died. In time, they would find their way to sex magazines and tabloids. They would be Mercedes de Acosta's final legacy.

Inspired in part by another successful round of revivals (including a Venice Film Festival tribute), the Lincoln Center and Museum of Modern Art Film Festival presented twenty-six Garbo films to the public during the summer of 1968. The series was an immediate sellout and, according to Herbert Kenwith, even managed to attract a curious Garbo; she invited him to see *Queen Christina* with her.[6] They were ushered in through a side entrance and sat in two reserved seats in the back row. "We got to the seats, sat down, the picture began, and she said nothing to me at all," he remembers.

Sometime later, when Kenwith again saw the motion picture with director Rouben Mamoulian, he mentioned this later to "Miss Brown." "We were walking along Fifty-third Street going east toward the river," he says. As they crossed Third Avenue, Kenwith spoke of the tragedy of John Gilbert. "She had four or five small packages in her arms. Suddenly, she put her hands up to her ears and screamed at me—I don't remember what she said, she just yelled. A package of vegetables broke and rolled into traffic, and I was in the middle of the crosswalk trying to pick the other packages up before the light changed." Startled by her sudden display of emotion, Kenwith rescued the packages, "and we walked in silence until about Second Avenue. Then she started talking to me like nothing happened."

Garbo was still in flight from her cinematic shadow.

When she was on her own in New York, Greta was able to make part-time help stretch to meet her full-time needs. Claire Koger served as a housekeeper, seamstress, and cook during the week; on the weekends, there was an occasional secretary who "volunteered" to help with bills and correspondence; and an assortment of walkers accompanied her on various shopping trips, sometimes even running errands themselves.

In Europe, she took advantage of the Rothschild largesse: villas, yachts,

---

[6]Kenwith, a popular television director, frequently ran into Greta on the street. One day, unable to resist the temptation, he followed her and tried to strike up a conversation; she did not respond. After an afternoon of business meetings, he returned to the neighborhood—and again saw Garbo on the opposite corner. "Are you following me?" he teased. "And with that, she started to laugh and with a big gesture waved me over." As Kenwith walked her home, he told her about himself—his work for CBS and NBC, his friendship with George Cukor—always mindful that he must not call too much attention to "Miss Brown." Two days later, she found his number in the phone book, called him—and asked if he would help her pick out a new TV set. The invitation to accompany her to the *Queen Christina* screening followed.

private jets, chauffeurs, maids, cooks—as well as the means to secure her privacy. And Salka Viertel offered her the security of a lifelong friend who knew her before the myth was locked into place. Salka didn't have a lot of money, but she had a big heart and had generated enough goodwill to help make Greta's stays in Klosters eminently comfortable. Here, she could, as one pundit noted, wear privacy "like a warm, winter coat."

Klosters is located in the mountainous southeastern corner of Switzerland, a four-hour drive from Zurich (less than three hours by train). While the neighboring city of Davos exploded in population after World War II, choosing what locals call the "department store" approach to compete with resorts like St. Moritz, Klosters voted to severely restrict new construction in order to maintain its intimate look. The gamble paid off. In the 1950s, the town attracted a loyal group of semipermanent residents—Rex Harrison, Yul Brynner, John Kenneth Galbraith, William Buckley, Irwin Shaw, Robert Capa, Audrey Hepburn, et al.—who stayed on for four to five months, not weeks, extending their business well beyond the traditional high season.

Garbo preferred arriving in the late summer and often stayed well into the fall, depending on the weather and her accommodations. "Fate has chained me here," she claimed, yet Klosters seemed a perfect place to work on her eternal restlessness. "On the road from Klosters to Davos—uphill for seven kilometers—Garbo pointed out the paths and walkways she had wandered along over the years," one companion noted. "A couple of times she had walked through the forest, following a stream, all the way to Davos." She explored most of the paths in the area—sometimes with friends like Bodil Nielsen, ofttimes alone—and knew every inch of the walkway around Lake Davos.

When she wasn't "in motion" or socializing with Salka and friends, Greta spent the rest of her time in Klosters reading and waiting. "I don't know for what," she said. "I am restless everywhere and always have been . . ." But around Salka, her mood seemed to change. "Whenever I saw her, she was very compassionate to me, very warm," Jack Larson says, "and very mindful of Salka. I think Salka had a good effect on her."

Salka's project during the first part of 1969 was finding a new apartment for her; Gore Vidal, then enjoying some celebrity for his satirical novel *Myra Breckinridge*, had taken over the apartment Garbo had been using. The pair would come to know each other best between 1970 and 1975 when both frequented Klosters. Greta was especially fond of his "slightly lopsided" Australian terrier, which she had nicknamed Ratzski. "She was spectacular . . . very bright . . . very funny," Vidal said. "The spooky thing was when you watched her she had about six poses, and she did all six for you. And of course if you had been brought up on her movies you kept going out of time—finding yourself suddenly in the midst of *Conquest* or *Camille* . . . She knew she had this effect, too. She was rather mischievous."

As far as Vidal was concerned, there were never any rules with Garbo. "[They say] the main one was that she was not supposed to talk about her movies to you. But with me she did nothing but talk about MGM," he stated. "On our walks she remembered the names of everybody she worked with, the second cameraman, her problems with L. B. Mayer . . . She was meticulous about the making of every picture, and she [talked] about it." Ultimately, what her life was about, Vidal surmised, "was looking for that perfect pull-over, as she called it, sweater. She spent forty years looking for the perfect pull-over." She never found it.

Indeed, many friends would have stories to tell about her near-cataclysmic indecision in buying clothes or shoes. Greta was notorious among Klosters and Davos merchants for endless discussion and few actual purchases. Salka did so much for her and her needs seemed so spare that few store owners took real notice of her as a customer—but if Salka felt she had been cheated, the offending merchant soon heard an earful. Even as her own health problems began to multiply, Viertel remained protective of "Gruscha" and highly sensitive to her feelings and needs.

Most residents felt similarly protective toward their reclusive visitor. "When she was still alive, we never talked about her—ever," says Claude Botteron, the maître d' at the Chesa Grischuna, a charming, old-fashioned Swiss hotel in the center of town. Owner Dori Guler emphasizes that her late husband, Hans, did most of the fussing over Garbo. He became very fond of her, making sure that she was properly taken care of whenever she was in his restaurant and often accompanying her on walks about town.

If the routine seemed monotonous, it could also be tremendously reassuring. Bertolt Brecht once wrote about the "simple luck" of surviving loved ones: that "survival of the fittest" could be both an accusation and a curse. With more and more of her friends and former associates passing on, Greta looked on each change as the scripted ending to another chapter in her life. She filled her days with inconsequential things, as she always had, and somehow the "melancholy times" of her later years gradually slipped by.

John and Jane Gunther disappeared from the New York scene at the end of the 1960s, but Greta had remained a constant in their lives. When John died in 1970, she became even closer to Jane. "G.G. and I, alone then, never lost affection and concern each for the other. . . . In the last years we used to talk about nothing in particular several times a week. I suppose that is what friendship is about, and G.G. was that sort of friend."

Greta's mood brightened with a trip west. After George Schlee died, she relied more than ever on Gayelord Hauser and Frey Brown (until Brown's death in the early seventies). Hauser and Brown had lived in the same house since the late 1930s, a terraced estate on Angelo Drive in Coldwater Canyon. Though he had been hurt when Garbo ignored him in favor of Schlee, Hauser happily welcomed her back. Throughout the 1970s, the couple was often seen window shopping on Rodeo Drive in Beverly Hills. "It seemed to give her quite a kick, walking down our street," an employee of one of Rodeo's fashionable stores commented. Gradually, the fact that Garbo and Hauser owned a prize section of the commercial area, a few doors away from Gucci, became public knowledge.[7]

When Hauser and Brown weren't available, their neighbors Bill Frye and Jim Wharton often escorted Greta around town. During the day, they might go for coffee at the Farmer's Market; often in the evenings she would walk over to Frye's house because Hauser didn't drink and she liked her "Gutty Sark," as she referred to her favorite Scotch.

Her California friends learned that Greta was happiest working in the garden. "She used to go out in my garden very early in the morning," says Jean Howard, who also lived near Gayelord Hauser. "It wasn't very warm, but that girl loved to prune! My God, those roses never looked better. Gayelord used to say that, too." An amateur photographer, Howard resisted a very serious temptation to take a picture of Garbo in her element: in her straw hat and gloves with the early morning light hitting her face just perfectly. "I would have had a Renoir picture," she insists, "but I didn't want to have to lie about it."

Despite her various health complaints, Bill Frye remembers Garbo as being "so tough, even in her seventies." He would watch with amazement as she trimmed his oleanders, pulled out weeds, and removed dead vines. "Once she killed a rattlesnake with a hoe, and it quite thrilled her. When she told me about it over dinner, I was horrified and said I would've called the fire department. She said if it happened again just to call her instead. *She* would be the fire department."

During the fall of 1971, Greta returned from Europe with her arm in a sling; she had broken her wrist trying to ford a stream. But the press had pro-

---

[7]By 1979, with a booming economy propelling her investment to a record high, Garbo was reportedly considering divesting herself of her share of the property at 333, 335, and 337 Rodeo. She got out before the market again fell.

vided an even more brutal homecoming when she read "My Love Affair with Garbo," an excerpt from Cecil Beaton's journal which was picked up for syndication around the world.[8] Privately, Beaton claimed that it was partly due to Greta's "mistreatment" of Mercedes that he decided to go ahead and publish the next volume of memoirs. "I feel angry that she never made a gesture of forgiveness towards Mercedes . . . and I know she would not give any generous help to me if I were in need of it."

Yet most associates viewed Beaton's motives as purely self-serving. "His job was mythologizing himself, and that's what he did," says Sam Green. In so doing, he did "the one thing you can't do which was to betray her, exploit her, lie about a romance and do it for money and fame—which he did. The whole of Europe turned their back on Cecil Beaton; a lot of people never spoke to him again. . . . The royal family stopped having anything to do with him. He really did himself a great deal of damage [and] was punished very badly."

Not surprisingly, Beaton's name ceased to exist in Greta's vocabulary. Society closed ranks around the victim of his indiscretion. In May of 1972, Cécile de Rothschild confronted Beaton on her turf and accused him of deceiving a friend. "Let me ask you how much you made out of Garbo on the *McCall's*, *Times*, *Oggi* [pieces]," she queried. "I mean, how much with the *Vogue* photographs *et tout ça* during the past twenty years?" Beaton reluctantly estimated his profit to be around £4,000. "Not bad, eh? For someone who didn't need the publicity." Kerstin Bernadotte called the book "a pack of lies," adding that "Beaton has always been attracted to celebrities, but his strong side isn't exactly women."

Still, there were no legal repercussions for Beaton. Nor would there be for Polish author Antoni Gronowicz, whose *An Orange Full of Dreams* was published in late 1971.[9] The novel included a forward by "Greta Garbo"; Garbo never wrote it, but because she did not immediately contest its legitimacy, the writer succeeded in publicly establishing a relationship with the reclusive star that was fraudulent. Gronowicz would not give up on his obsession.

In New York that winter, Greta and Sam Green were reintroduced at Cécile de Rothschild's Regency Hotel residence. Green, then thirty-one,

---

[8]*The Happy Years* was published the following spring.

[9]The book is a fictionalized biography of a legendary actress named Greta Galingala. Her story combines elements of Garbo's life with that of Polish actress Helena Modjeska. (In 1956, the author announced to the world press that he had written a play about Modjeska at Garbo's request; it was never produced.)

had been carefully prepared for the meeting. "Sam embodied his family's social graces as well as its fondness for travel and good taste in art," said one observer. His father was a respected professor of art history and his mother a professor of social psychology—but Green was a college dropout who discovered the Andy Warhol crowd and thrived in their cutting-edge psychedelia. Before there were Lennons and Onos in his life, the freelance art dealer and curator became adept at introducing fashionable friends—from Diana Vreeland to Cecil Beaton—to the avant-garde.

In fact, when Beaton tried to tempt Green with an invitation to have dinner with Greta Garbo, the opportunity of meeting a Rothschild held equal allure for him. Garbo wasn't there (Beaton had made that up), but Cécile de Rothschild was suitably impressed and invited Sam on a cruise the following summer. "I realized that what she was doing was checking me out to see whether I was the kind of person she could introduce to Garbo," Green admits. "Because Garbo needed somebody to look after her in New York who wasn't going to be a sycophant."

After a three-year grooming process, Green finally met the elusive Miss G. at Cécile's house in Saint-Raphaël. "Previously, she had always asked me to leave the south of France the day before I knew Garbo was coming. The third year, after Cécile had determined that I was not going to embarrass her, she invited me specifically to come on the eighteenth." It was Greta's sixty-fifth birthday and Sam had rehearsed "a ridiculous speech about how cool I was, how I was impressed with her and it's nice to meet you. . . .

"I came downstairs at 8:00 and Cécile was reading the newspaper. Garbo wasn't in the room, so I made myself a drink. I was watching the staircase for her to come down . . . and suddenly there was somebody behind me. I turned around and there she was. I put out my hand and was just about to open my mouth when she said, 'Mr. Green, I have been waiting for such a long time to meet you. I know we're going to be good friends and that we're going to have a terrific time together.' She absolutely pulled the rug right out from under me so I couldn't make a fool of myself." After a friendly dinner, Garbo retired early, leaving Sam and Cécile to talk.

Greta's relationship with the young art dealer commenced with their meeting in New York more than a year later. Stricken with seasonal bronchitis, she eased into a schedule of walks with Green twice a week, augmented by daily phone calls. Every day that he was in town, Sam would call her around 11:00 A.M. and tell her everything about "what I had done the night before and who I was seeing and what I was doing, what this one said and what that one thought." He would soon be making reservations, writing checks for her basic needs, and covering all the minutia that was part of what he irreverently called "bedpan duty."[10] But another year would pass before she invited him up to her apartment.

As most New Yorkers learned, in their city Garbo walked . . . and walked . . . and walked. She averaged between two and four miles a day. She shopped at Bloomingdale's, and prowled the flea markets in SoHo, the stores on Second Avenue, and the art galleries around Fifty-seventh Street, with equal passion. Sometimes, she stopped by Jean Dalva's family-run store to watch the cabinetmakers at work, lingering long enough to wish them a good evening as they finished for the day.

It was on the aging concrete and asphalt streets of New York that the second Garbo legend, the legend of the hermit about town, was born. Truman Capote would compare Garbo to an abandoned temple, yet in a neighborhood where limousines and nannies were part of the accepted accoutrement, she was a magical presence. "I saw GG window shopping on Madison Avenue in the fifties a few days ago," Garson Kanin related in a letter to George Cukor. "She wore a helmety sort of head covering, an army jacket, ski pants and ski boots. A man touched my arm and said, 'Do you know who that is? That old lady over there?' 'Who?' I asked. 'Garbo,' he replied. 'Greta Garbo.' 'You're nuts,' I said. He was too, because she looked not at all like an old lady but like a radiant angel."

As she was a creature of habit, it was not difficult to find Greta in her neighborhood. Twice a week, she purchased groceries at the Nutrition Center, where her typical shopping list included eggs, honey, bran, dried apricots, English muffins, and whole milk. She bought her vegetables and fruit at a produce store on Fifty-third and Second. According to the proprietor, she loved zucchini and artichokes and was "crazy about persimmons." Meat was purchased at the Mid-City Food Market or Green Valley Foods on First Avenue. At the Dover Deli, she would buy lox, sturgeon, and Nova Scotia salmon. Her craving for more expensive fare was satisfied at a gourmet emporium on Madison Avenue or at Nyborg & Nelson, a Swedish deli on Fiftieth and Second.

She was a cash-paying customer who quickly ingratiated herself to local shop owners; even merchants who did not benefit from her patronage watched over her. "She's a very nice lady, but I worry about her," Silvio Faraci, co-owner of Salnet Produce, confided. "Last month she came in

---

[10]A bank balance was a difficult thing to keep when creditors failed to cash their checks—Garbo's signature was often worth more than the debit. To keep things straight, she asked Green to write checks on his own account and she reimbursed him.

looking pale and tired. I got a feeling she's very lonely . . ." One day, he recalled, Greta came in and they were joking around. "Maybe I'll come in here and work behind the counter for a few hours a day," she mused. "It would be good for me." Faraci's partner, Charlie Pasternack, thought they should take Garbo up on her offer. "In this neighborhood she could sell an apple for a hundred bucks and people would be lined up outside waiting for more just like it."

Showing discretion and sensitivity to her needs were the keys to maintaining Garbo as a customer. She reveled in the times when no one recognized her, and yet she expected that they would. Arguably, the subterfuge only took on significance when people did recognize her—which she occasionally acknowledged with a wink or by putting her index finger to her lips. Dan Squilanty, the owner of one of the health food stores she frequented, kept a photograph of her in his shop window even after Greta threatened to boycott his store if he didn't remove it. Squilanty felt she had been kidding—indeed, Garbo continued to patronize his store without bringing it up again.

As the years passed, "Garbo sightings" up and down the avenues and obscure corners from Forty-eight to Seventy-second Streets became commonplace. Garbo-watchers, it was noted, were divided into two categories: passive and active. Some chased; most watched from afar. Admirers were usually surprised to encounter, not a monotone figure in gray but a healthy-looking older woman who wore mascara, eye shadow, and lipstick; she was flesh and blood. She also knew how to fend for herself and often used her umbrella to excellent advantage. Pursued for blocks by a curious fan, Greta finally turned to face him. "If you follow me any more, I am going to call a cop," she said. The embarrassed Garbo-watcher blurted out an apology, professing his undying admiration. Greta's voice softened. "Then why do you follow me?" she asked as if speaking to a child. "Please don't at all."

The best relationship to cultivate with her on the street was an anonymous one. "I almost feel I know her—or I should say, my dog knows her," a resident of Sutton Place remarked. "Whenever I'm walking him and Garbo comes along, she'll bend down and pet him, tell him how nice he is, and walk off. She has never said a word to me; it's as if I didn't exist." But she did acknowledge the homeless who had become non-existent in the minds of many of her affluent neighbors. According to Raymond Daum, Greta "used to stop and give money to bums on the street. She always had empathy with the poor."

Throughout the 1970s, Garbo's face on the covers of publications such as *Life* and *Vogue* continued to sell her mystique as well as their magazines. Incredibly, there continued to be rumors of extraordinary movie offers. *Time* reported in March of 1971 that Luchino Visconti hoped to entice Garbo to play the Queen of Naples in his film adaptation of Proust's *Remembrance of Things Past*. "She has not said yes. On the other hand, she has not said no," the magazine divulged. "Actually, she has said nothing at all—only taken a plane to Nice and tried to dodge a waiting photographer." Her friend Sam Spiegel wanted her to play the dowager empress in *Nicholas and Alexandra*—coincidentally, the same role she had been asked to play fifteen years earlier in *Anastasia*. Bill Frye, who was producing *Airport 1975* at Universal, fantasized about adding Garbo to his passenger list, but she turned him down flat. "What could be worse than playing an old movie star?" she would say.

Work had long ago lost its appeal. If going to the theater was a hazard for her, watching friends like Katharine Hepburn and Deborah Kerr toil on stage was equally daunting.[11] "How can they do it, these women?" she asked Ray Daum. "The mere thought slays me." Jack Larson detected envy in her voice as she watched as Kerr prepare to go off and make a film. "Here was this beautiful woman with vitality rushing off to do a film, something she might have wanted to do—but couldn't."

Although she denied an earlier report that she had asked Jacqueline Susann to write her biography, Greta was confronted with yet another literary effort when *Publisher's Weekly* announced Antoni Gronowicz was shopping his "part biographical, part autobiographical" Garbo study at the 1972 Frankfurt Book Fair. Due to the Clifford Irving–Howard Hughes hoax the previous year (in which Irving had nearly succeeded in passing his book off as an official collaboration with Hughes), and the explicit sexual nature of Gronowicz's manuscript, publishers attempted to confirm the book's validity with Garbo's friends. All they got were denials. "They may do my biography after I'm dead, but now—never," she told Minna Wallis. "You know me well enough for that!"

In June of the following year, she again made the news when it was reported that she had cataract surgery at a hospital in Barcelona. It certainly was news to Greta, who had just returned to New York after spending the best days of spring with Gayelord Hauser in California. She did go to Europe that summer for a two-week cruise around Corsica with Cécile

---

[11]A casual theatergoer—she preferred matinees because they didn't intervene with her sleep schedule—she still managed to see most of the major shows. She went with Cécile de Rothschild to see Hepburn in the 1970 musical *Coco*; and Sam Green made the arrangements to see her in *A Matter of Gravity* (1976). Deborah Kerr was the star of *Seascape* (1975)—one of the rare times Garbo visited backstage as well. "Deborah warned everybody that if they said or did anything untoward, she would never forgive them," says Jack Larson. After the matinee, she went backstage with her escort, Joe Lombardo, and everyone behaved—it was Kerr who did the fussing.

de Rothschild, Sam Green, and two new friends, Joseph and Caral Gimpel Lebworth. Then, she promised, she was "going to baby-sit (I need a baby-sitter myself) with Mrs. Aherne for a few days."

For Garbo 1974 was a comparatively quiet year, highlighted by a trip to Tunisia with Carl Johan and Kerstin Bernadotte, and a reunion with Charles Boyer in the south of France. She made up for her low profile the following year; 1975 began quietly with a touching visit with Susan Hayward, who, unbeknownest to most of Hollywood, was dying from an inoperable brain tumor. Garbo had found out and paid her respects. But she was unable to keep her presence in Los Angeles secret for long.

"GeeGee's back in town," George Christy announced in *The Hollywood Reporter*. In honor of Gayelord Hauser's birthday, she hosted a Sunday brunch for two dozen friends at his home. Among the guests were George Frelinghuysen, Edith Head, Tony Duquette, Eleanor and Brian Aherne, Anthony Palermo, and Gayelord's nephew, Dieter Hauser. "Hair pulled back, Garbo wore her ubiquitous dark glasses, a pink cotton shirt, plaid madras slacks—and appeared affable, not aloof, even took a turn in the parking lot advising guests where to park their cars." Guests commented on "the great devotion and reliance" that Garbo and Hauser had for each other. "They've been friends forever," Christy noted.

After their reunion in 1962, Greta began writing Mimi Pollak again. Unlike with her previous correspondence, her brief, somewhat distracted letters from this period were written primarily in English. But like her letters of the past, they described similar routines: how she virtually lived on carrots, why she did not dare come home to Sweden (she feared she would be recognized). Early in 1975, she sent Mimi a poem she had written about not being able to touch the hand of her friend—someone, if times had been different, she might have been walking through life with. Curiously, in July of that year she managed to return to Sweden for the first time in more than a decade—but spent most of her time with Count and Countess Bernadotte at their country estate in Båstad.

The weather was ideal. On one notably spectacular midsummer day, they took a boat out to Hallands Väderö, a small island off the coast. "One should not go to places like this," Greta said; "nothing can be as perfect." At the end of July, they went to Copenhagen and attended a concert by Birgit Nilsson, the Swedish soprano, at the world-famous Tivoli Gardens. The Bernadottes later arranged for Garbo to have dinner with Nilsson and her husband.

The excursion tipped off the public as well as the international press. Crowds and cameras followed. Greta was a few months shy of her seventieth birthday and had been estranged from Hollywood for the better part of her life. That such scenes continued not only puzzled her but, as she got older, had become increasingly intimidating. Memories of a pleasant homecoming were further obscured a few months later when Kerstin Bernadotte, a former journalist, sold a relatively innocuous story about their twenty-five-year acquaintance, accompanied by photographs taken by the Count and Countess, to *Ladies' Home Journal.* It would be Garbo's final trip to Sweden.

During the first week of October, Sam Green brought Greta, Cécile de Rothschild, and Philadelphia Museum of Art curator Joseph Rishel to his cousin Henry McIlhenny's estate, Glenveagh Castle, in Ireland. From there they went to London, where Garbo's presence was kept secret until an invitation arrived from Buckingham Palace. Green wanted Greta to think that her discovery was purely accidental. Privately, he admitted suggesting to a well-connected friend that a royal invitation to tea might "amuse" Garbo. A few days later, an official-looking piece of correspondence was delivered to the Albany Apartments, where Garbo and Green were staying. Sam waited until after dinner and drinks to bring out the invitation. "Thursday, the 17th of October, you are requested for tea at Buckingham Palace at 4:30." Underneath this message, written in blue ballpoint pen, it read, "You will be alone. ER".

"What a thrilling invitation to have! Garbo did open a few doors, let's face it," Sam says. "She thought about it for a while and then said, 'Well, Mr. Green, of course I can't go. I have nothing to wear. But why don't you go?' She was very smart. Since the invitation was to me, she didn't have to go." Sam returned the invitation to the Albany doorman and let him deal with a rather awkward moment.

There was no point in arguing; Green had a more important mission. "When I got her to London . . . it was because I had a plan," he states. "She was going to do something for me—she was going to visit Cecil Beaton for the weekend." Beaton had suffered a severe stroke in July of 1974 and was now partially paralyzed and confined to a wheelchair. Green's friendship with the photographer predated his with Garbo; he didn't tell her his plan until they arrived in London. Greta stuck to her position. "No, I can't do it. I don't *want* to do it," she told Sam. Beaton had done "terrible things," she said. "I trusted somebody and he betrayed me."

Sam made an emotional appeal, characterizing the reunion as a dying wish. "He's so diminished. It's almost destroyed his life," he told her. " 'Please. Could you find it in your heart to be generous enough to do this?' I really worked on her. It took me three weeks! Finally, she didn't have any choice; I just wore her down." When they got to Waterloo Station, Greta had a change of heart. "I can't go," she pleaded. "I'm not going to go. What if he has reporters in the trees outside the train station?" She was really scared. To assuage her fears, Sam suggested they take an earlier train and walk around Salisbury for a while before going to Reddish House.

The meeting between Garbo and Beaton was "a real tearjerker," says Green. They arrived at the house around dusk. Greta was escorted to the drawing room by Beaton's secretary, Eileen Hose; Cecil was seated near the fireplace. "Beattie, I'm back," she said as she walked across the room and greeted him warmly with kisses on both cheeks. "She was generous for the first time, probably ever in her life—and he was undone. It was an amazing thing to see happen."

As Greta snuggled up to Cecil, Sam retired from the room with Beaton's secretary. According to Hugo Vickers, it was only after she saw him struggle to pull himself together for dinner that Greta realized how debilitating the stroke had been. Eileen Hose would never forget Garbo turning to her and saying, "Well, I couldn't have married him, could I? Him being like this!" Early the next afternoon, she bid him farewell. "Greta, the love of my life," Beaton sobbed as he attempted to hug her. Spotting the guest book on a table near the door, Greta broke free of his embrace to sign her name in the book. It was the only recorded time she ever rushed to *give* an autograph—and although she often got updates on his progress from Green, it was the last time she saw or spoke to Cecil Beaton.[12]

"It's so strange how life is," Greta later confessed. "You go along and you accept whatever is there as fact. You put on your face and your makeup and everything and you get going. All of a sudden, one day, there's a hand that comes—in my imagination, every seven or ten years or whatever—a hand that goes over the face and changes it a bit, puts more weakness in it. . . . And it's equally revolting each time."

In March of 1976, "Harriet Brown" turned up at a new location: the exclusive Galley Bay Surf Club on the Caribbean island of Antigua. Accompanying her was a heretofore "secret" companion: Greta's niece, Gray Reisfield. Few of Garbo's friends knew anything about her family in America, fewer still believed there to be a significant relationship between Greta and the Gustafsons: Sven's widow, Peg, and daughter, Gray. "All the years I've known Gay [Garbo], she never mentioned her niece or family," Nicholas Turner insists. The point is underscored by Sam Green. "She didn't express any great fondness for her family. She didn't even seem to know the family very well," he says. "I do know the niece came in once a month to pay her bills [and] that they took a winter vacation every year . . ."

[12]Beaton died on January 18, 1980.

Frustrated though she may have been by Sven's inability to make his own way in life, once they settled in Santa Fe, New Mexico, the Gustafsons successfully maintained a low profile. Many classmates of Gray's had no clue about her famous lineage until years later; neither did she parlay this association to gain advantage while at college. Her marriage announcement contained only information about her family in Santa Fe and background on the groom, Dr. Donald Reisfield.

More than likely, it was Greta's intention from the beginning that her friends keep out of "family business." The link was established when the Reisfields planted roots in New Jersey, scarcely an hour's drive from Manhattan. Joseph Lombardo was one of the few to bear witness to the family's existence, though Greta's behavior was reminiscent of an earlier era. "She used to go out to her niece's house once in a while," he says, "and I would drive her. The crazy thing was she would get out the block before—she wouldn't let me see the house. It was a beautiful home, but Garbo wanted to walk to the house without me looking or seeing."

As she had in Stockholm, Greta protected her privacy by concealing her family and their location from prying eyes. It was in her later years that friends became more aware of Gray. *People* magazine, reporting on the vacation in Antigua, made it official with pictures of Garbo and her niece. Voyeurs were far more interested in her daily ritual of morning and afternoon swims in the lagoon, capped by a few stolen, topless moments on the beach. "There, apparently unmindful of the hushed public attention, stood the woman who has personified shyness. 'My God,' breathed an attractive younger woman one day after Garbo had disrobed and then dramatically exited, 'I couldn't get away with that, and I'm thirty-three!' "

One reason why Greta Garbo's identity as the hermit about town seemed eternal was her sturdy appearance. The durability of this image was contradicted by Garbo's obsession with her health. She was continually looking for new physical remedies—be they new ways to cook or to exercise. Sam Green shared his interest in alternative medicine and spiritual enlightenment with her. "She was always interested in the odd, the abnormal. She didn't want to be Rolfed, but she did acupuncture, she did transcendental meditation, and she believed in reincarnation." Green arranged for her to have a private session with a certified TM instructor. Although the concept was surely not new to her, meditation would become part of her life for the next few years—until Sam and Greta discovered they had been given the same supposedly unique mantra to use.

Time made gradual dents in that robust veneer. During her 1976 visit to Klosters, Greta became so ill she thought she was going to die. It was also during this period that she discovered she had a cancerous lesion on her nose. Yet the one cancer she should have been threatened by—lung cancer—did not intimidate her nearly as much as stopping smoking. Despite warnings from doctors, her meager solutions in the past had been limited to switching brands, smoking filtered cigarettes with a holder, or cutting down on the number she smoked each day. But she was a chain smoker who couldn't quit. "I've inhaled since I'm seventeen years old, and now my dopey body waits for the next one," she told Ray Daum.

After her brother died, Greta went to a doctor in Zurich who claimed he could cure anyone of smoking by hypnosis. The treatment would take five days, he said, and on the final day, she would be completely free of the urge to smoke. "I went to him full of good intentions of giving it up," she said. After the fifth treatment, she went straight back to her hotel, looked at her watch, and told Anthony Palermo, "This is exactly five days," and lit up again. "Since then I have never been able to stop—Now I can't even be bothered to try."

Late in 1977, Simon & Schuster announced that they intended to publish Antoni Gronowicz's biography of Greta Garbo. Although friends had refused to confirm any part of his work, a cursory investigation of Gronowicz's credentials by the publishing house finally uncovered a "connection" between Garbo and the author. What the publisher did not suspect was that the press items used to "prove" Gronowicz's relationship with his subject were, most likely, plants by Gronowicz himself. Virtually every time a blurb mentioning Garbo and the author appeared in local papers or trade magazines, the subject in question was conveniently—and most notably—abroad.

Garbo advocates hastened to point out that, contrary to the author's intimation of a private understanding, the book was most definitely unauthorized. "In all the years Brian and I have known Garbo, we've never even once heard the name Antoni Gronowicz," Eleanor Aherne told Radie Harris. "Knowing her as well as we do, and her reticence about any intrusion into her private life, I cannot believe she would give a complete stranger permission to write about her. Or that she, herself, would agree to write the foreword."

Greta was furious about the book. So angry, in fact, that Sam Green took it upon himself to seek legal advice. A friend recommended an attorney named Lillian Poses. "I checked her out and found out she was definitely the right kind of person to handle Garbo's case. . . . I explained that there would probably be some difficulty about time. Garbo didn't like to sit and wait in an office . . . She said she understood the situation and would be happy to accommodate Garbo." But when Green presented his solution, Greta's temper again flared. "Don't you dare get involved with my business," she warned him. "I know you mean to help, Mr. Green, but you're not helping at all."

Ironically, Cécile de Rothschild came up with the same name. This time, a meeting was set. After a fair amount of time spent talking about everything except the case, Poses came to the point. What exactly did Greta hope to do about Gronowicz's book? "Stop them. Stop them."

On February 7, 1978, Garbo signed a sworn affidavit stating she had "never at any time entertained any type of human relationship" with the person known as Antoni Gronowicz. Furthermore, she offered in a second statement, "in connection with certain reports and news accounts of a purported biographical work on my life . . . I state unequivocally and categorically that I have never, at any time, collaborated with this person or anyone else, on my memoirs or any other biographical material. Nor have I ever authorized or given my approval of any such work." She denied "without reservation" writing an introduction to *An Orange Full of Dreams*.

The public declaration of Garbo's non-cooperation succeeded in consigning the biography to publishing limbo, for the time being.[13] But her book worries were far from over. During the summer of 1977, she had unwittingly become a participant in a new venture. British writer Frederick Sands used his acquaintance with Deborah Kerr to meet her mother-in-law, Salka Viertel, in Klosters. By his own account, Sands visited Salka often, but usually left early because she was ill and tired easily. On the second or third visit, she told him, "Come back for tea this afternoon and you will meet someone interesting." That surprise, of course, was Greta Garbo.

Having been validated by his association with Salka, the writer quickly ingratiated himself to her best friend. The next day, although it was gray and drizzling outside, Greta invited him to walk with her—and that was his cue to have a clandestine picture taken (photographer Eckhard Nitsche hid in the foliage as they walked around Lake Davos). After each outing, Sands returned to his hotel and hurriedly wrote down everything he could remember about their talks.

The Divine Garbo was published in late 1979. If Greta felt betrayed by Sands' sly pursuit, using an ailing Salka Viertel to get to her and documenting the meeting with secret photographs, that was nothing compared to her shock at the revelations contained in the text detailing her youth in

---

[13]Simon & Schuster decided not to publish "in her lifetime." In 1984, Gronowicz's latest work, an "autobiography" of Pope John Paul, was denounced as a fraud by the Vatican. With the unprecedented approval of the United States Supreme Court, the publisher recalled all unsold copies of the book and shredded them. Antoni Gronowicz died in 1985. His biography of Greta Garbo was published in 1990.

Stockholm—the first new research since a 1960 biography by Swedish author Fritiof Billquist. Garbo showed up at Irwin Shaw's flat with a copy of the book in hand. She was upset, says Jack Larson. "She felt completely betrayed. 'They're ruining Klosters for me. This is happening to me even here'. . . . She gave the book to Irwin and he looked at it. He tried to comfort her, saying, 'It's not so bad.' She burned it in his fireplace."

After having the ugliest, most powerful *bruja* (witch) in Cartagena place a ceremonial *protección* on his newly restored palace, Sam Green invited Garbo to Colombia. She arrived in February of 1978 for a three-week stay. Surprisingly, one thing Green did not consider when planning her visit was that it coincided with the Cartagena Film Festival. "The most astonishing thing is that Garbo walked all over that city—the biggest movie star ever to come to South America—and with every show-biz reporter in the Spanish-speaking world there, nobody recognized her," he recalled.

No sooner had she returned to New York than an item appeared in Suzy's gossip column about the trip. The leak occurred, Green explains, because his assistant erred in trying to correct a story about a May-December romance between Garbo and her young host. After the litany of recent betrayals, Greta was reticent about accepting Sam's explanation. "Do you really think, after all these years, I'd send a press release and use you to promote Cartagena?" he asked. She wasn't sure. "Well, there it is, you see, in the paper—everything we [did]. I cannot go anywhere where I have to deal with the people in your crowd because I get used for everything," she said. "I haven't been in motion pictures for a lifetime, and I'm *sick* of it. . . . I don't know if you're a scoundrel or an idiot."

In the past, Greta had disengaged from friends and associates because she was being exploited; death separated her from the others. Hörke Wachtmeister passed away in 1977; Salka Viertel's health was now so fragile that she required a nurse-companion. Jack Larson ran into Greta in New York and inquired about Salka. "We stopped to speak of her until I saw a disturbed look in Garbo's eyes. Suddenly she took my hand, said good-bye, and swiftly walked away." Her beloved friend died on October 30, 1978. Salka was buried in the small cemetery adjacent to Klosters' Protestant church.

"Take good care of Greta," Salka had instructed Lotte Friedländer, a semipermanent resident who lived in both New York and Klosters. When he wasn't in Marbella, Spain, Peter Viertel also looked after her. Lucienne Graessli, the proprietor of the Hotel Pardenn, delivered meals when she wasn't dining at the Chesa Grischuna; in time, Greta began staying at the Pardenn as well. Lotte's husband handled her fan mail, and Irwin Shaw and his pals pro-

vided the laughs. She spent her seventy-fifth birthday in Klosters. The celebration was modest. "Only a fool celebrates getting older," she said, quoting
George Bernard Shaw.

By the spring of 1981, Greta was back in Paris taking in her favorite
sights: Napoleon's tomb at Les Invalides and the Tuileries Gardens. The
year 1982 began with a visit to the Palm Springs home of Brian and
Eleanor Aherne, followed by a cruise to the Greek island of Poros as a guest
of Cécile de Rothschild and a wealthy French industrialist. She returned
home to New York only to discover that her apartment had been burglar-
ized. According to Joe Lombardo, the superintendent's son had let himself
into several apartments, leisurely helping himself to valuables throughout
the summer. "They didn't even leave her a spoon."

In the early 1980s Sweden recognized one of its own, first with a 1981
stamp (featuring a scene from *Gösta Berlings saga*) and next with a new
royal honor. Greta let it be known through "a mutual friend" that she
would love to have official Swedish recognition for service to her country,
said Wilhelm Wachtmeister, the Swedish ambassador to the United States.
Sweden's new king, Carl XVI Gustaf, agreed. Garbo's American citizenship made her eligible for the prestigious Commander of the Royal Order
of the North Star, First Class. The presentation was made on November 2,
1983, at Jane Gunther's apartment on East End Avenue.

"I had never met Garbo before, but it was not difficult immediately to
recognize her from the screen half a century ago. The profile, the smile, the
laugh, the voice, it was all there. Even though she looked her [78] years,
face drawn, she was still stunningly beautiful," Ambassador Wachtmeister
recounted. "She seemed happy to speak Swedish again, completely without an American accent. She liked to talk about her youth in Sweden,
where some relatives of mine happened to be her friends [Hörke and Nils
Wachtmeister]. However, an attempt to steer the conversation toward her
Hollywood years was abruptly rebuffed. I referred approvingly to somebody
who had resigned at the peak of his career 'like you.' 'That was not why I
resigned,' she retorted without inviting any elaboration."

Early in 1984, Greta was informed by her doctors that she had a rare
form of breast cancer, cancer of the nipple. Surgery was immediately recommended. On the advice of Cécile de Rothschild, she turned to Caral
Lebworth for moral support; Lebworth had also battled breast cancer. "I
spoke with her both before and after she had the mastectomy," Lebworth
stated. "It's absolutely terrifying when you're told that you have cancer.
You don't know how to deal with it, and she was nervous and worried
about the operation. . . . She asked me, 'Could I see your scar?' I said sure,
and I undressed for her and let her look at me . . ."

Greta was fortunate that a radical mastectomy had not been required. After the surgery, performed in New York under an assumed name, she made little effort to hide it. She did not wear a prosthesis because it required putting on a bra—and she refused to start now. Friends, in fact, were so accustomed to her sagging, braless look (even Garbo had to submit to the forces of nature) that it never occurred to them a change had taken place. "I didn't even know about it until one day when we walking along and some people were trying to take a photograph," Betty Estevez remembers. "She said, 'Do you think they notice anything?' And I said, 'Notice what?' Because she always wore these knit shirts and pullovers . . ." Then Betty saw the slightly concave look of her sweater and Greta told her about the surgery she'd had a few months earlier.

Her secret did not become public knowledge until after her death. When Garbo returned from her annual European retreat, she attributed her recent ill health to bronchitis. Neighbors who had been concerned about how she looked before she left were cheered by her near-complete recovery. "Now, she looks rested and apparently has bounced back from whatever was bothering her," Ted Leyson noted. "She is no longer limping and looks much more robust."

Ironically, it was Leyson, a persistent paparazzo, who was the most recent thorn in her side. A committed Garbo-watcher, he hung out on Fifty-second Street almost every day waiting for her to go out. Once on the trail, he would follow her throughout the city and take pictures. Greta didn't understand why someone who hadn't been in movies for decades was worth anything to anybody. "Why do they harass me?" she complained to Raymond Daum. "Pick on people who are *au courant*."

But Garbo would remain *au courant* as long as her legend continued to pervade the lexicon of popular culture. Literary references ranged from Ernest Hemingway's *For Whom the Bell Tolls* to Thomas Tryon's 1972 short story "Fedora." Recent musical references included the "Greta Garbo stand-off sighs" in Kim Carnes' hit song "Bette Davis Eyes," her name at the top of Madonna's list in "Vogue," and two songs by rock diva Stevie Nicks: "Greta" *and* "Garbo." In the art world, Andy Warhol presented her as one of the great modern myths.

Cinematically, the inspiration was more limited—perhaps because the legend was more intimidating. Garbo considered getting an injunction against "The Silent Lovers," the second episode in the 1980 TV miniseries, *Moviola*. The story was Garson Kanin's romantic retelling of the Garbo-Gilbert affair. During the fall of 1984, she avoided all public comment when Sidney Lumet's film *Garbo Talks* was released. A harmless fairy tale about an admirer's dying wish, it was considered an intrusion nonetheless.

Occasionally, Greta would indulge herself and watch one of her own films on television; mostly, she caught up with others. Her tastes varied from the sublime to burlesque. She loved watching soap operas and game shows: *General Hospital* in the afternoon; *Wheel of Fortune, Jeopardy,* or *The Hollywood Squares* (comedian Paul Lynde was a favorite) in the early evening. She analyzed Henry II's relationship with the archbishop of his church in *Becket;* mused about a missed opportunity in *The Picture of Dorian Gray;* and, according to Joe Lombardo, was a vocal admirer of Barbra Streisand's work as the producer, director, cowriter and star of *Yentl.* "My God, I've never seen such a picture!" she commented enthusiastically. "That's the most talented woman that I've ever known or ever heard about."

Another chapter in her life ended when Gayelord Hauser died on December 26, 1984. Greta attended the memorial service at All Saints Episcopal Church in Beverly Hills as well as the wake hosted by Anthony Palermo. "Garbo asked that no one be there but Gayelord's closest friends, not even the kitchen help," said photographer Ellen Graham. Graham usually thought of Greta as a sunny person. "She just came alive when she visited California, and with Gayelord especially, but she was so grim that day, not herself at all. I thought she wouldn't make it."

She knew she was slowing down. In one of her final letters to Mimi Pollak, written in 1984, Greta confided that she was sad, not very well, and afraid. Sweden remembered her on her eightieth birthday with celebrations in Stockholm and Högsby (where her mother was born),[14] and Swedish television broadcast a birthday tribute. Usually, Raymond Daum stated, her birthdays were uneventful. This year, there was an unplanned celebration. Greta and Cécile visited Château Lafite, one of the Rothschilds' famous French vineyards. After a tour of the caverns, Cécile's cousin Philippe invited them to "a little dinner" at Château Mouton to taste the new wines. Garbo was wary but felt obligated. She arrived at the château to discover a hundred people—including photographers and members of the press—milling about in the salon. Baron Phillipe de Rothschild swept in forty-five minutes late, presenting quite a picture as he stood at the top of the stairs in his golden caftan. "Greeeta, is that you? Greeeeta, my sweetness. We meet again!" he declared as he melodramatically played the moment for all it was worth in front of the crowd.

Greta, who had met the baron once before in 1938, gamely hid her embarrassment. "Under the circumstances, she behaved nobly," Sam Green remarked. The dinner menu featured most everything she could not

[14]Some Swedes believe, incorrectly, that Garbo was born there, as well.

or would not eat. "It was really awful," Green says. "But she did the whole thing. Toasts. 'What a wonderful wine.' She was performing." On the way back to Cécile's, there was absolute silence in the car. "Cécile was in the doghouse. Garbo had been set up [and] Cécile should have known better." The event was her final performance on the Rothschild stage. Her future relationship with Cécile was limited primarily to the telephone.

Sam Green also received his walking papers around this time. The culprit, he states, was another tabloid story broadcasting the news about an impending Garbo-Green hookup. "Mr. Green, you've done a terrible thing," she told him when he returned from Cartagena. When she hung up the phone, Sam immediately called back and tried to plead his case, to no avail. "Does this mean we're not speaking anymore?" he asked. "Right." Wasn't there anything he could do? "Yes, hang up."

Although Sam claimed to have been the victim of another overeager assistant, the problem, several Garbo intimates say, wasn't that simple. "She found out that he was taping her," Betty Estevez says. "I think he had made a tape or something for a party. . . . And some of the gay boys [who were there] told somebody who called her and told her about it." Green insists that Greta knew he was taping conversations to keep an audio journal much like his friend and mentor, Andy Warhol, did. Betty Spiegel never bought that argument. "She did say something to the effect that Mr. Green was not a nice man," she recalls.

Greta's private world continued to narrow.

In February of 1986, the Swedish government again recognized Greta Garbo for "her contributions to the art of film acting". The presentation of the new decoration, *Illis quorum meruere labores* (meaning "To those whose works deserve it"), took place on February 27, again in Jane Gunther's home on East End, with Ambassador Wilhelm Wachtmeister representing his country. The ambassador describes the recipient as "very happy" with the honor, although on this occasion, she "seemed considerably weaker physically. She had difficulty walking, but mentally she was just as alert and humorous as the first time."

The beginning of Garbo's decline went unnoticed by most of her friends. In March of 1987, she tripped over a vacuum cleaner in her living room and badly sprained her right ankle. Considering her age, the injury appeared serious enough to warrant a two-day stay at a local hospital. Fearful of being discovered, she checked out of the hospital early, her ankle now bound in a thick elastic bandage.

Claire Koger had been given a small room to facilitate overnight stays on special occasions and was asked to stay on to help Greta at home. Over the course of their thirty-one years together, Koger had earned her employer's trust; she was one of the rare few who never gossiped and never sold her story. Though she was scarcely a year younger than her employer and was herself ailing and arthritic, Koger diligently performed her job five days a week, battling rain, ice, and snow during the winter months to walk from her apartment on East Sixty-sixth Street to see to "the lady"; Greta always called her "my girl."

According to Koger, her employer was very generous privately and often gave away her clothes, shoes, miscellaneous household goods, and even jewelry. When they were alone, they were almost like sisters—Claire was one of the few people allowed to address Greta by her childhood name, Kata. It was a bond that stood the test of time.

Time, however, was no longer a luxury. Greta's fall prevented her from going on the long walks that had been such an important part of her life. "When she had to use a cane, she realized she was finished—which was a word she would have used. 'I'm a finished man. A miserable, wretched creature,'" a friend observed. "Always the most demonstrative, rarest words spoken slowly." By necessity, her neighborhood walks would become shorter—and slower—until shop owners no longer saw her in their stores or on the street. "Getting old is having to give up things one at a time," she had told Sam Green. Superficially, she was talking about vodka, caviar, cigarettes, and pâté de foie gras. In a larger sense, she meant her freedom.

Another Chapter Ended

The biggest controversy of Garbo's later years concerned whether or not she knowingly cooperated with the assortment of writers and journalists whose paths briefly intersected with hers. Close friends usually denied the association because it seemed unlikely to them that "Miss G" would talk to strangers about things she had never confided in them. Yet there are a number of verifiable instances where she did.

It would have been inhuman for Garbo not to have some pride in her cinematic legend. A perfect example of the subtle change in her attitude was her acquaintance with Swedish journalist Sven Broman. They met in Klosters during the summer of 1985. Broman was the editor of the popular Swedish magazine Året Runt (Year Round), a fact that he says he never hid from her. Gray Reisfield states that she warned her aunt that Broman was one of the writers involved in *The Divine Garbo*—but Garbo told her he had already admitted as much, saying that it was a "mistake of his youth" which he promised not to repeat.

Though reports of their encounter hit the press before she even returned to New York, Greta continued to socialize with Broman and his wife. Over the next five years, they would meet on and off in Klosters and New York. She enjoyed having someone to speak Swedish with; Broman also shared his Swedish magazines and newspapers with her. Garbo always spoke poignantly of home. "I don't know anything about the modern Sweden today," she said. "I only remember it the way it was."

In her final years, Sweden came to her. King Carl XVI Gustaf and Queen Silvia visited the United States in April of 1988 to help celebrate the 350th anniversary of New Sweden, the first official Swedish settlement in America. Before they left New York, the royal couple paid a courtesy call on the woman who remained Sweden's most celebrated international figure. The reception took place at the home of a prominent Swedish national. Garbo was deeply touched. "Sweden has the world's most beautiful and intelligent queen," she later told Broman.

Out of respect, the king and queen refused to release any details regarding their "private audience" or answer queries about Garbo's health. Interestingly, according to at least one source, they did carry a message: Jacqueline Kennedy Onassis, now an editor at Doubleday & Co., wanted to speak with her regarding an authorized biography. Several of Greta's friends had urged her to let someone write her autobiography "so it would be real correct and everything put forth accurately," Betty Estevez says. A brief meeting was arranged with Mrs. Onassis—but, after "serious consideration," the answer still was no.

When Greta arrived in Klosters in July of 1988, she was alone and confined to her bed for most of the time. Sadly, though she had often taken short walks in the village the previous summer, this year no one had seen her outside her hotel. A worried Lucienne Graessli confided to the Bromans that before they had arrived, Greta didn't seem to be eating. They sent her favorite Russian caviar up to her room, but nothing succeeded in drawing her out. Most of the time, the concerned proprietor reported, she appeared to be in a daze and was generally unresponsive to inquiries. "She just sits there," he said. Greta admitted that she had been "unenterprising"; because she was unable to walk any distance without assistance, the most exercise that she had gotten was a fifteen-minute walk around the hotel with Lotte Friedländer. "There have been so many days when I haven't gotten out of bed . . . I just couldn't."

By the end of the month, she perked up a bit and was seen in the bar of the Hotel Pardenn, complaining to the Bromans about the dollar's eroding market value against the Swiss franc. Traveling had become a burden for her, she said. "I regret coming to Switzerland. I should have stayed in New York, but I can't bear the heat in summer and I can't stand air-conditioning." She put the Bromans on notice they wouldn't be making any side-trips this year. "I can only walk a few steps," she said. "The life around me no longer seems real. It feels like I'm dying bit by bit."

In August, she suffered a mild heart attack. A local doctor attended her until Gray Reisfield arrived with her personal physician to bring her back to the States. "That was the first time she kissed me on both cheeks," Graessli remarked, "when she said good-bye. She had never done that before. It was like a last good-bye . . ." Other Klosters residents were upset about her sudden disappearance from the scene. She did manage to call Hans Guler at the Chesa Grischuna to explain that she probably would not be back. "Her doctor there is very close-mouthed," Peter Viertel told journalist Michael Gross. "But he said, 'She's not well at all.' "

Greta drew her immediate family closer to her. Gray moved into her aunt's apartment in order to help take care of her. Friday afternoon was family time: the Reisfields, their children (Scott, Craig, Derek, and Lian), and, in time, their mates. "I tried to explain to my husband that it took her a long time to warm up to the idea of new people," Gray Horan noted. "She did extend an invitation for him—after we had dated for seven years and been married for two. I had announced I was pregnant, and she wanted to meet 'the Papa.' Once he was admitted, he was completely embraced."

The Reisfields viewed their aunt's apartment on Fifty-second Street as her "sanctuary of peace and imagination." At sunset, she opened the French doors of the salon to let in reflected light from the river; golden highlights blended with her favorite colors of raspberry pink, rose, apricot, and moss green. "In her later years when the apartment became almost her entire world, she would jokingly say, 'How the mighty have fallen,' " Donald Reisfield said, "but she was quite content to be alone with her friends, the paintings she had so carefully chosen." There were make-believe friends, as well: a plastic inflatable snowman, dressed in a vest and top hat, was the only one allowed to sit on the eighteenth-century marquise; beneath one of her living room couches, a tribe of shock-haired troll dolls guarded her secret "underworld." "When she was in the mood to be happy, there was no one more fun or lighthearted," said Gray Horan.

On January 5, 1989, Greta was rushed by ambulance to New York Hospital. A spokesman for the Woman's Clinic refused to comment on whether or not she was a patient there or what she was being treated for. Though she was discharged a couple of days later, the cause of her infirmity had scarcely been treated; her kidneys had begun to fail and she refused to go on dialysis. By the end of spring, Garbo's doctors were making house calls in an effort to make her as comfortable as possible.

Anthony Palermo took credit for getting her to agree to the dialysis. "One day she didn't sound too well on the phone so I went out there. She looked terrible," he said. The Reisfield family had been unsuccessful in getting her to go in, but he had persisted—"We don't want you dead," he told her—and she relented. That June, he accompanied Greta and her niece back to the hospital. After an overnight stay, Gray Reisfield hired a limousine service and a nurse to begin taking her aunt to the Rogosin Institute at New York Hospital. Every Monday, Wednesday, and Friday, a blue Lincoln Mark V would park in front of the Campanile. Greta, dressed in loose-fitting slacks, knit cap, glasses, and bedroom slippers, would be helped to the car by the doorman or nurse. To ensure her privacy during the six-hour treatment, Garbo's doctors had arranged for her to use the in-patient dialysis unit at the Ralph Bunche Pavilion.

After her death, sensational stories would emerge charging that in her final days, Garbo had given into alcohol. Jeffrey Lawrence, the owner of the corner store where she bought most of her liquor, vehemently denied this. It had been months since she had ordered anything, he stated. "If I depended on clients like Greta Garbo, my shop would be locked and closed." Betty Spiegel, Betty Estevez, and Joe Lombardo all confirm that Garbo liked a cocktail in the evening, but that she never drank to excess. In fact, Estevez adds, when the problem with her kidneys became apparent, Greta drank only water with meals. "How does it feel not to drink?" Irwin Shaw had inquired when he ran into her in Klosters. "Like losing your mother and father," she responded.

According to Sven Broman, concerns about her liver had caused Garbo's physician to demand that she abstain—and she lasted only six months before seeking a second opinion. A detailed legal brief prepared by the attorneys for her estate contradicts this and specifically cites kidney problems. "It is not disputed that Miss Garbo had a kidney condition. However, except to the extent that Miss Garbo had to maintain a proper diet, drink fluids, and take bicarbonate of soda, Miss Garbo's renal condition did not require any treatment until 1988 . . ." Claire Koger would attest that "in the thirty years I worked for her, I never saw her drunk" and offered that any insinuation that her employer drank to excess was "false and mean"—a point that Jane Gunther, who regularly visited her and even took care of Greta at her own apartment, reiterated in her own affidavit.

Her intimate friends didn't deny that Greta sometimes became confused and didn't know what time it was—neighbors and employees at the Campanile occasionally helped her when she became disoriented late at night. However, her doctor, Stuart Saal, stated that he "never saw any evidence of 'chronic melancholia' or any other psychiatric disorder." What she was experiencing was "a very specific time-sense confusion," he said, an after-effect of her 1988 heart attack. Another physician who tended her certified that "[Garbo's] memory was unusually good for an elderly person with a chronic disease."

Greta made excellent progress during the first months of treatment. By July, she was back walking neighborhood streets, albeit with a sturdy cane. She began to retreat again in the fall.

Valentina Schlee died from complications due to Parkinson's disease on September 14, 1989. Garbo heard the news from the building's elevator operator—and burst into tears. Her nemesis was dead. No more rushing home before "Madame V" went out at 7:00 P.M.; no more anxiety when she rang for the elevator to see if it went up to the ninth floor first; no more chilling stares on the rare occasions when they did meet. Valentina and Greta had been close in age. Once they had had so much in common—and much to keep them apart; ultimately, the separation had suited them both.

The tears came more easily now that Greta was older, more frail, and simple tasks had become more difficult; but the absence of any real bitterness made her less of a pathetic figure. "People learn to accept death. If you die in good health," she told a confidant, "then you have not been trained nor made ready for death . . . I often think about death. I really wish I could believe, but I can't. For me it's over when it ends. Maybe I am too prosaic. And yet I do feel that life has been good in my old age."

She expressed similar, surprisingly warm feelings to her family. Her grand-niece described a memorable autumn day in 1989. She greeted them at the door wearing a paper party hat and led them into the drawing room. "She was wearing a gold medal on a sash around her neck, an honor from the King of Sweden. She had put her Oscar on a table next to a bottle of chilling champagne. With age, she had become a more fragile beauty. Her pale blue eyes remained incredible—bright, inquisitive, aware of everything. She said she had not had champagne in years but thought it would be good tonight. It was. She told the funniest jokes and stories. It was true Garbo. She was not performing. The evening, however, had all of her old screen magic."

Once she started to fade, everything seemed to shut down all at once. Sven Broman spoke with Garbo on the telephone the day before she went back into the hospital. She was coughing all throughout their short con-versation and appeared to have trouble breathing. "I think she gave up," he says. "She was just too sick."

No ambulance went screaming to the front door of 450 East Fifty-sec-ond Street. On Wednesday, the eleventh of April, Greta's driver picked her up as per their weekly schedule and took her to New York Hospital. The Reisfield family took turns sitting vigil at her bedside. She was resting com-fortably and seemed to be rallying. To the very end, her doctor stated, she was "gracious, alert, oriented, and independent."

Garbo took her leave quietly, peacefully at 11:30 A.M. on Easter Sunday, April 15, 1990.[1] A hospital spokesperson made a general announcement, honoring the family's request to withhold any details about her last days or what their burial plans might be. Mimi Pollak heard the news when she was awakened by a reporter at three in the morning. "Strange. The evening before the news of her death, I was sitting alone . . . and thinking intensely about her," Mimi told *Svenska Dagbladet*. She affirmed that it was her friend's wish to be buried in Sweden and that Greta had made her swear this would be done. When Mimi spoke with Gray Reisfield a short time later, it was clear to her that was her family's intention.

Greta Garbo's body was cremated at the Garden State Crematory in New Jersey. On the following day, April 17, a private memorial service was

---

[1]Although her kidneys and other vital organs were on the verge of failing, pneumonia was the actual cause of death. The official death certificate lists only "natural causes."

held for a small gathering of friends and family at Frank E. Campbell's Funeral Chapel on New York's East Side. The final disposition of her ashes was not made known. Her will was submitted for probate one week later. An uncomplicated nine-page document, Garbo's Last Will and Testament was written on March 2, 1984. Although she had been remembered as a minor beneficiary in the wills of several family members in the past, she did not respond in kind when her will was prepared. She bequeathed "all tangible personal property"—her name and likeness, all personal papers, records and copyrights—and her "residuary estate" to Gray Gustafson Reisfield, her "dearest living relative." She specifically denied the claims of any relations, including "any and all children and their descendants" of her deceased brother other than Gray and her children. Although Sven Gustafsson, Jr., had died in 1988, the codicil included a new name as "a possible non-marital child" of her brother: Åke Fredriksson.

"Everyone in Sweden doubted that [the document they heard about] was her will," states Åke Sven Fredriksson. Fredriksson, a simple, amiable man, isn't sure how his parents met, except that his mother was a worker at the Grand Hôtel during the twenties. Fredriksson was born in 1926, but says he did not learn the identity of his father until after the Gustafsons left Sweden. He met Sven Junior in the early 1980s and believes that Sven was the one to notify Garbo of his existence. Lawyers for the estate contacted him shortly after his aunt's death.

"It was for my children's sake," Fredriksson says, that he failed to identify himself earlier. He wanted his daughters to lead a normal life in Sweden. He is adamant that his motive for making a claim against Garbo's estimated $55 million estate was a simple desire for someone to acknowledge that he was, in fact, his father's son. "It wasn't for the money," he insists, although that would have been nice. By the time his aunt died, Fredriksson says, his children were old enough to deal with the notoriety involved in declaring their relationship. Unfortunately, whatever his intentions, the battle over Garbo's will included accusations of alcoholism and that Gray Reisfield had manipulated her aunt. The presiding judge ruled that there wasn't sufficient cause to invalidate the will; the claim was dismissed. But Fredriksson believes he made his point nonetheless.

He wasn't the only one seeking to prove his or her legitimacy. "I'm disappointed [at] not being in her will," Anthony Palermo told a Milwaukee reporter. "I took care of this wonderful person, and I didn't exist. I don't blame Miss G for that. It's not her fault. Just something that happened, that's all I'll say." Palermo was equally upset that Claire Koger wasn't mentioned. This did not surprise Claire. "I never considered myself, nor did Miss Garbo consider me, to be her companion in a personal sense," she stated for the record. "Miss Garbo never promised to leave anything to me by her Will. . . . Our relationship over the years was an employer/employee relationship."[2]

The residual value of Greta Garbo's estate became apparent in the weeks and months to come. Not in stocks and bonds—although they were considerable (the value of her investment in Fortune 500 companies such as Anheuser-Busch, Eastman Kodak, General Electric, General Motors, IBM, Ralston Purina, Time-Warner, and Texaco totaled nearly $10 million)—nor in real estate, most of which had been sold in the 1980s. The effect of her continuing mystique on the monetary value of her estate was felt most keenly when her art treasures, antique furniture, and assorted knickknacks went on the auction block at Sotheby's that November.

The three-day sale was highly touted in the print and broadcast media. A preview of the collection drew more than seven thousand people. The greatest surprise of the event wasn't that most of the "blue chip paintings" by Renoir, Jawlensky, Bonnard, and Rouault sold for well over their pre-auction estimates, but that Greta's Second Avenue tchotchkes brought such extraordinary prices. An ordinary canvas hardly worth more than $600 went for nearly $19,000; a pair of porcelain candlesticks with an appraisal between $800 and $1,200 sold for an incredible $31,000; a pair of Chinese figurines valued in the $1,000 to $1,500 range fetched over $25,000. The auction amassed over $19 million.

Garbo's name sold. To protect that name, the next step her estate would pursue would be to copyright it. She had spent a lifetime avoiding commercial endorsements, but had imposed no such restrictions on her heirs.[3]

For years, Greta intimated that one of the roles she had coveted was that of Dorian Gray. Oscar Wilde's story wasn't simply about youth or vanity, but also about a loss of innocence; Dorian Gray is tortured by twisted inner demons—a dark side few of his friends recognize because of his external beauty. The painting that Greta Garbo stashed away in real life was Renoir's portrait of his son, Edmond, an innocent young boy with long blond hair who bears an eerie resemblance to Greta as a naïve young schoolgirl. Perhaps *Enfant assis en robe bleue* impressed her because it represented something she could never recapture: her life in Sweden before she became an actress. Before she had become intoxicated by the sight of the actors

---

[2] The estate made a private arrangement to take care of Koger.

[3] In fact, in order to successfully maintain their copyright, the heirs must make use of it occasionally. These rights are now managed by Harriet Brown & Co., a Delaware corporation.

preparing for a performance at Södra Teatern—before Moje Stiller, Svensk Filmindustri, and Dramatiska Teatern ever touched her life.

Would Greta Garbo even recognize Stockholm today? The building at Blekingegatan 32 was demolished in 1973 and a new apartment structure was built in its place. Katarina Södra Folkskola has increased in size, expanding its playground and yard as well as its classrooms. The square adjacent to the school has been renamed Greta Garbos torg. Enskede, where Greta and her family tended their first garden, has been urbanized. PUB, the department store, fought off its competition for several decades before reorganizing under the name PUB-Interiör. Dramatiska Teatern is as popular as ever, but the acting school no longer exists—it is now incorporated as part of the University of Stockholm. Svensk Filmindustri built new offices and studios, and the fate of the historic studios at Råsunda now hangs in the balance.

The only thing that remains much the same as it was in Greta's youth is Södra Skogskyrkogården, the southside cemetery. Today, it is a ten-to fifteen-minute ride on the subway from the center of the city. Nowhere is the Swedish respect for land more evident than on the well-tended grounds of this *kyrkogården,* where pine, oak, maple, and elm exist in peaceful harmony with their man-made surroundings.

The modest plot that represents the Gustafson family grave, the burial place of Karl Alfred, Anna Lovisa, and Alva Maria, is in a secluded area of the cemetery. Hidden behind a perimeter of dog rosebushes, basking in the shade of tall Scotch pines, it must have seemed like a private place indeed when Anna Gustafsson first purchased the space in 1920. A humble place worthy of a working-class family. It may not be Greta Garbo's final resting place, but there can be no doubt it is where Greta Lovisa Gustafsson's heart is. "I want to go home to Sweden," she said a couple of years before her death. "I want to lie in Swedish soil."

Sadly, she did not make it home. Her niece inspected burial sites in Stockholm, Gnesta, and Högsby, but according to reports, found them "too accessible for plunder and for demonstrations of hysteria." Fearful of another incident akin to the ransacking of Charlie Chaplin's grave in Switzerland, Garbo's heirs have been unable to commit to a final resting place.

Even in death, Greta Garbo is apart from all that she loved and all that was part of her. She is still drifting.

SOURCE NOTES

ABBREVIATIONS:

AMPAS   Margaret Herrick Library/Academy of Motion Picture Arts & Sciences
BU   Special Collections/Boston University
CU   Oral History Project/Columbia University, New York
DL   David Lewis manuscript, original interviews 1976–1977
DOS   David O. Selznick collection/University of Texas at Austin
FBI   Case files, U.S. Department of Justice/Federal Bureau of Investigation
FN   Footnote
GC   Private collection of George Coupé, Sr.
INS   Case files, U.S. Immigration and Naturalization Service
KDT   Kungliga Dramatiska Teatern Archive, Stockholm
LC   Library for the Performing Arts at Lincoln Center, New York
MdA   Mercedes de Acosta collection/Rosenbach Museum, Philadelphia
MGSC   MGM Script Collection/University of Southern California, Los Angeles
MPPDA   Motion Picture Producers and Distributors Association collection/AMPAS
NA   National Archives and Records Administration
SF   Svenska Filminstitutet, Stockholm
Sjö   Victor Sjöström Archive/Svenska Filminstitutet
SMU   Oral History Collection/Southern Methodist University, Dallas
SRTV   Sveriges Radio-TV library, Stockholm
USDS   Case files, U.S. Department of State-passport and visa services
WWW   Walter Wanger collection/Wisconsin Center for Film and Television Research

CHAPTER ONE: A Scandinavian Profile

19   "Let's not talk . . .": "The Story of Greta Garbo" (pt. 1), *Photoplay*, 4/28.
20   Parish records concerning the Gustafsson and Karlsson families courtesy of the Vadstena/Jönköpings Län arkivet, Högsby Församling, and Landsarkivet in Visby.
22   Karl and Anna's betrothal announced: Katarina archivet, Stockholm.
23   "Where we lived . . .": "Greta Garbos ungdomsminnen," *Lektyr*, 1930 (SF).
23   "If God gives . . .": Sands and Broman, *The Divine Garbo*, p. 12.
23   Södra Maternity Hospital birth record, 9/18/05: Stadtsarkivet, Stockholm.
24   "My mother was . . .": Broman, *Conversations with Greta Garbo*, pp. 35–36.
24   "Born into a home . . .": "Garbo Finds Herself," *Photoplay*, 3/42.
24   "there [was] danger . . .": *Lektyr*, 1930 (SF).
24   "It was eternally . . .": ibid.
25   "If I see . . .": *Photoplay*, 4/28.
25   "That girl has . . .": "How Garbo's Fear of People Started," *Photoplay*, 3/32.
25   "We are on . . .": "The Garbo You've Never Read About," *Movie Mirror*, 8/35.
25   "I never enjoyed . . .": *Lektyr*, 1930 (SF).
25   "I used to think . . .": "An Unknown Chapter in Greta Garbo's Life" (pt. 1), *Liberty*, 8/18/34.

26 "Does uncle care . . .": Second draft, *Here Lies the Heart*, pp. 480–81 (MdA).

26 "I was awful . . .": Beaton, *Memoirs of the 40's*, p. 230.

26 "I had a certain . . .": *Lektyr*, 1930 (SF).

26 "Greta was stagestruck . . .": Payne, *The Great Garbo*, p. 30.

27 "I could never . . .": *Lektyr*, 1930 (SF).

27 "I didn't find . . .": Sands and Broman, *The Divine Garbo*, p. 37.

27 "She was a strangely . . .": Payne, *The Great Garbo*, p. 35.

27 "an occasional krona . . .": Sven Broman to author, 4/19/94.

28 "It worked . . .": Broman, *Conversations*, p. 25.

28 "a real cadger . . .": Sands and Broman, *The Divine Garbo*, p. 15.

28 "She wanted to . . .": "Greta Garbo Wanted to Be a Tight Rope Walker," *Photoplay*, 5/34.

28 Katarina school records: Stadtsarkivet, Stockholm.

29 "I think I used . . .": Broman, *Conversations*, p. 36.

29 "I used to go . . .": *Photoplay*, 4/28.

30 "even as a child . . .": "Greta Garbo, Onkel Drosschkenchauffeur und ihre Vorfahren," *Die junge dame*, no. 24, 1936.

30 "For a girl . . .": "My Little Admirer Named Greta," *London Sunday Express*, 6/1/30.

30 "She hesitated . . .": ibid.

31 "After that day . . .": "The Garbo You've Never Read About," *Movie Mirror*, 8/35.

31 "By this time . . .": ibid.

33 "The man told . . .": Walker, *Garbo: A Portrait*, p. 13.

33 "God, what a feeling . . .": *Photoplay*, 4/28.

33 "I often had . . .": *Lektyr*, 1930 (SF).

CHAPTER TWO: Dramatiska Teatern

34 "Lots of things . . .": Daum, *Walking with Garbo*, p. 32.

34 "we badly needed . . .": "Greta Garbos ungdomsminnen," *Lektyr*, 1930 (SF).

34 "One other thing . . .": GG to Eva Blomkvist, 7/7/20, quoted in Billquist, *Garbo: A Biography*, p. 23.

35 "The shop was . . .": "Greta Garbo—Home Town Girl," *Screenland*, 3/35.

35 "always kept her dignity . . .": "Greta the Barber Shop Girl," *Everybody's Magazine*, 12/33.

35 "Can you imagine . . .": GG to Eva Blomkvist, 8/7/20 (SF).

35 "I feel as though . . .": GG to Eva Blomkvist, 8/15/20, quoted in Billquist, *Garbo*, p. 24.

36 "very ambitious . . .": Sands and Broman, *The Divine Garbo*, p. 24.

36 "She had matured . . .": "My Little Admirer Named Greta," *London Sunday Express*, 6/1/30.

36 "Alva would come . . .": "An Unknown Chapter in Greta Garbo's Life" (pt. 2), *Liberty*, 8/25/34.

36 "one never feared . . .": "Garbo-biografien," unidentified publication provided by PUB-Interiör.

36 "Miss Gustafsson should . . .": Sands and Broman, *The Divine Garbo*, p. 25.

37 "a large, smiling man": *Lektyr*, 1930 (SF)

37 "I felt my heart . . .": *Lektyr*, 1930 (SF).

38 "When she put . . .": Taraba, *Den Gåtfulla Garbo*, p. 41.

38 "She is so beautiful . . .": "Garbo-biografien," PUB-Interior.

39 "because I was attracted . . .": Haining, *The Legend of Garbo*, p. 79.

39 "I remember we . . .": Gumpel, *Sagor och verklighet*, pp. 58–59 (Translation by Laila Nylund). Privately published by Gumpel for his children, *Sagor och verklighet* was written as a series of fables; there are very few real names used in the book. Garbo is alluded to but never specifically named. Her story, "Umwertung aller Werte," is a fairy tale about a shopgirl who becomes a great star.

39 GG's relationship with Gumpel: Broman, *Det handlar om kärlek*, p. 304.

39 "My father was . . .": Laila Nylund to author, 3/20/95.

40 "like the good friends . . .": Gumpel, *Sagor och verklighet*, p. 59.

40 "pretty indifferent . . .": GG to Eva Blomkvist, 8/27/21, quoted in Billquist, *Garbo*, p. 27.
40 "I was fascinated . . .": Sands and Broman, *The Divine Garbo*, p. 29.
41 "He stared at me . . .": *Lektyr*, 1930 (SF).
41 "Miss Gustafsson, in spite of her youth . . .": "Garbo-biografien," PUB-Interiör.
41 "Greta Gustafsson, the future film star . . .": Billquist, *Garbo*, p. 36.
42 "uncomprehending and startled . . .": ibid.
42 "a sudden rain squall . . .": ibid., p. 35
43 "I met an actor . . .": "The Story of Greta Garbo" (pt. 1), *Photoplay*, 4/28.
43 "She was so anxious . . .": Bainbridge, *Garbo*, p. 40.
44 Greta collected a letter from Ekengren: Sands and Broman, *The Divine Garbo*, p. 34.
44 "I remember it was . . .": *Photoplay*, 4/28.
44 "Then I just ran . . .": ibid.
44 "Oh God . . .": ibid.
45 Dramatic school curriculum: KDT.
45 "Greta was so excited . . .": Pollak, *Teaterlek*, p. 42.
46 "a little round . . .": "Jag minns här Greta drog en låt på Grand," *Svenska Dagbladet*, 4/22/90.
46 "until suddenly Greta . . .": Pollak, *Teaterlek*, p. 43.
46 "The school was . . .": *Photoplay*, 4/28.
46 Greta's student notebook: The book was left to the Svenska Filminstitutet when Sven Gustafsson, Jr., died in 1988. According to scriptologist Charles Sachs, who independently studied the work book in order to verify its authenticity, the first part of the book is not in Garbo's handwriting but clearly was written by someone in the Dramaten class. The last section features notes on a scene and can be positively identified as Garbo's writing.
47 "He came in . . .": "Då slipper jag namna om handdukarna! sa Greta," *Veckojournalen*, 9/6/77.
47 "Meeting the fellow . . .": "Hon fick avgiva ett heligt löfte att aldrig vidare ägna sig åt film," *Hänt i Veckan*, no. 2, 1970.
47 *La belle aventure* playbill: KDT.
48 *Swing* magazine review: Bainbridge, *Garbo*, pp. 37–38.
48 "The film surpassed . . .": Sjöberg, *Hänt i Veckan*, no. 2, 1970.
48 "We worked hard . . .": Pollak, *Teaterlek*, p. 48.
49 "The beauty that . . .": Sands and Broman, *The Divine Garbo*, p. 44.
49 "We had landed . . .": "Det Här Visste Ni Inte," *Röster i Radio TV*, 4/14/89.
49 "At that moment . . .": Pollak, *Teaterlek*, p. 63.
50 "The other pupils . . .": *Photoplay*, 4/28.
50 "for she never . . .": Billquist, *Garbo*, p. 48.
50 "You understand that . . .": ibid., p. 50.
50 "I remember that . . .": Bainbridge, *Garbo*, p. 42.
51 "Shortage of money . . .": Sands and Broman, *The Divine Garbo*, p. 42.
51 GG to Mimi Pollak: Undated letter, 1923.
52 "Happy is too big . . .": "The Story of Greta Garbo" (pt. 2), *Photoplay*, 5/28.

CHAPTER THREE: Flesh and the "Devil"

53 "I never get . . .": "The Story of Greta Garbo" (pt. 1), *Photoplay*, 4/28.
53 "Without so much . . .": "Greta Garbos ungdomsminnen," *Lektyr*, 1930 (SF).
54 "[Stiller] was really . . .": *Photoplay*, 4/28.
54 "Then he just . . .": ibid.
54 "The boys liked him . . .": "Kalla mig svägerska, sa gudomliga Greta," *Hufvudstabladet*, 3/10/71.
55 FN2: ibid., plus "Helsingforspojken Stiller," *Hufvudstabladet*, undated clipping (SRTV).
56 "one who was always . . .": Werner, *Mauritz Stiller: Ett Livsöde*, p. 9.
56 "He never shirked . . .": "As I Remember Him," *Film Comment*, Summer 1970.

56 Stiller's "darling favorite": Asther, *Narrens väg*, p. 31.

56 Esbensen under surveillance: Werner, *Mauritz Stiller*, p. 239.

57 "I was pleased . . .": "The Story of Greta Garbo" (pt. 2), *Photoplay*, 5/28.

57 "I was all shaky . . .": ibid.

58 "I venture the paradox . . .": ibid., p. 220.

58 "She has no technique . . .": Hood, *Sjöström och Stiller*, p. 223.

58 GG contract, 7/23/23: SF.

58 "She wanted to . . .": Sands and Broman, *The Divine Garbo*, p. 44.

58 "I'm not getting anywhere . . .": Broman, *Conversations*, p. 44.

59 "I think everyone . . .": *Film Comment*, Summer 1970.

59 "Frankly, we were inclined . . .": "Where Garbo Learned Her Trade," *New York Herald Tribune*, 12/20/36.

60 "Finally, everyone went . . .": *Photoplay*, 5/28.

60 "I have to break . . .": Payne, *The Great Garbo*, p. 62.

60 "Our desire to make . . .": *New York Herald Tribune*, 12/20/36.

61 "she cried . . .": Bainbridge, *Garbo*, p. 55.

61 "It was a love-hate . . .": Sands and Broman, *The Divine Garbo*, p. 53.

61 "As we cut . . .": "Hurr Stiller 'upptäckte' Greta Garbo," *Geffle Dagblad*, 1/27/33.

61 "It has been a . . .": *Filmjournalen* interview, 1923, quoted in Hood, *Sjöström och Stiller*, p. 223.

61 "She just sat . . .": Bainbridge, *Garbo*, p. 57.

61 "dull, uninteresting and . . .": Hood, *Sjöström och Stiller*, p. 223.

61 "I always had . . .": Broman, *Conversations*, p. 55.

62 "We loved Tora Teje . . .": "Då slipper jag namna om handdukarna! sa Greta," *Veckojournalen*, 9/6/77.

62 "She wanted a shorter . . .": Sands and Broman, *The Divine Garbo*, p. 49.

62 "modern and elegant . . .": "Kring Stiller, *Erotikon* och Greta Garbo", *Norrköpings Tidningars*, Christmas 1938.

62 "Greta thought it was . . .": Pollak, *Teaterlek*, p. 59.

62 Name change document: SF.

62 FN6: Gray Reisfield to author, 2/3/97.

63 "roaring like a lion . . .": Payne, *The Great Garbo*, p. 71.

63 "Don't be cautious . . .": Siwertz, *Lars Hanson*, p. 193.

63 "I have taught her . . .": Hood, *Sjöström och Stiller*, p. 224.

63 "Someone has to come . . .": Daum, *Walking with Garbo*, pp. 32 and 39.

64 "She adored Stiller . . .": Sands and Broman, *The Divine Garbo*, p. 45.

64 "probably ambivalent . . .": Werner, *Mauritz Stiller*, pp. 245–46.

64 "a promise for . . .": SF, *Svensk Filmografi: Volume 2 (1920–1929)*, p. 203.

64 "a semi-plump . . .": Werner, *Mauritz Stiller*, p. 169.

64 "too early to say . . .": Bainbridge, *Garbo*, p. 59.

65 David Schratter to Mauritz Stiller, 3/20/24: Stiller/Trianon correspondence (Sjö).

65 "We had to . . .": *Veckojournalen*, 9/6/77.

65 New Dramaten productions: KDT.

66 GG to Mimi Pollak: Undated letter, 1923.

66 Deal memo: Stiller/Trianon correspondence, 5/22/24 (Sjö).

66 "It is so wonderful . . .": *Photoplay*, 5/28.

66 Premiere invitation: Fritz Mischke to Mauritz Stiller, 7/12/24 (Sjö).

CHAPTER FOUR: Wilkommen

68 "This telegram has been . . .": David Schratter to Mauritz Stiller, 7/12/24 (Sjö).

68 "Get packed . . .": Mauritz Stiller to GG, 8/13/24 (GC).

69 "an old soul . . .": "The Story of Greta Garbo" (pt. 2), *Photoplay*, 5/28.
69 "a masterwork . . .": *Film-Kurier*, 8/20/24.
69 "The German people . . .": *Photoplay*, 5/28.
70 "It's a huge . . .": Broman, *Conversations*, p. 56.
70 "I didn't notice . . .": Asther, *Narrens väg*, p. 54.
70 FN1: Dramaten agreement, 4/8/25 (KDT).
71 "Several times I walked . . .": Asther, *Narrens väg*, p. 54..
71 "Dear little Greta . . .": Mauritz Stiller to GG, 10/19/24 (GC).
72 "HAVE HAD EXCELLENT . . .": A. Aronson telegram to Mauritz Stiller, 11/8/24 (Sjö).
72 "FEEL I HAVE INTERESTED . . .": A. Aronson telegram to Mauritz Stiller, 11/8/24 (Sjö).
73 "It was her eyes . . .": Selznick, *A Private View*, p. 60.
74 "a nice-looking . . .": ibid.
74 "I guess he looked . . .": *Photoplay*, 5/28.
74 "the same kind of . . .": L. B. Mayer to Mauritz Stiller, 11/27/24 (Sjö).
75 Departure from Berlin: GG 1925 datebook (GC).
75 *Odalisken från Smolna* story: "Stillers nya film," *Stockholms-Tidningen*, undated clipping circa 1924 (SF).
76 Trianon misusing government funds: "Six Talks on G. W. Pabst," *Cinemages*, no. 3, 5/55. (See Gösta Werner's *Mauritz Stiller: Ett livsöde* for more discussion of the film.)
76 "I do not know . . .": *Photoplay*, 5/28.
76 "from old, wilted men . . .": "Hur Stiller 'upptäckte' Greta Garbo," *Geffle Dagblad*, 10/27/33.
76 "One day . . .": de Acosta, *Here Lies the Heart*, p. 143.
76 Mercedes de Acosta passport records: MdA and USDS.
77 "HERE IT IS IMPOSSIBLE . . .": Mauritz Stiller telegram to GG, 1/20/25 (GC).
77 "It was a shock . . .": *Photoplay*, 5/28.
77 "Everything will take care . . .": Semitjov, *Garbo filmen vi aldrig fick se*, p. 78.
77 "In two days . . .": GG to mother, undated letter, quoted in Billquist, *Garbo*, p. 70.
77 "We know your people . . .": *Cinemages*, no. 3, 5/55.
78 "You can have her . . .": Walker, *Garbo*, p. 28.
78 "For this you will . . .": Sofar deal memo, 1/28/25 (GC).
78 " 'Gentleman,' it began . . .": Metro-Goldwyn Letter of Agreement, 1/30/25 (GC).
79 "I was a little . . .": "Garbo, the Sphinx, Speaks of Stiller and 'Dark Years,' " New York *Daily News*, 4/29/37.
79 "Whatever Mr. Stiller . . .": *Photoplay*, 5/28.
80 GG letter to Mimi Pollak: 3/25.
80 "Dearest Greta . . .": Mauritz Stiller to GG, 3/20/25 (GC).
81 "Haven't I told you . . .": Billquist, *Garbo*, p. 69.
81 "How is that darling . . .": Edgar Sirmont to Mauritz Stiller, 1/12/27 (Sjö).
81 Portrait of Berlin in 1925: Friedrich, *Before the Deluge*, pp. 124–30.
81 "To conquer Berlin . . .": ibid., p. 273.
82 "She moves through . . .": Payne, *The Great Garbo*, p. 82.
82 "the perfect sweep . . .": Eisner, *The Haunted Screen*, p. 260.
82 UFA contract: 4/20/25: SF.
82 "MY ABSOLUTE OPINION . . .": Mauritz Stiller telegram to L. B. Mayer, 5/18/25 (Sjö).
83 "WE HAVE CONTRACT . . .": L. B. Mayer telegram to Mauritz Stiller, 5/27/25 (Sjö).
83 "in no uncertain terms . . .": Söderhjelm, *Mina sju magra år*, p. 200.
83 "She was the same . . .": "The Garbo You've Never Read About," *Movie Mirror*, 8/35.
83 "to study different . . .": Metro-Goldwyn Letter of Intent, 6/20/25 (GC).
84 "It was strange . . .": *Photoplay*, 5/28.
84 GG letter to Mimi Pollak: 6/11/25.
84 "People here do not . . .": *Photoplay*, 5/28.

CHAPTER FIVE: Strange New Land

85   "I thought there . . .": "The Story of Greta Garbo" (pt. 2), *Photoplay*, 5/28.
85   "When we saw . . .": ibid.
85   Customs declarations: Manifest of Alien Passengers, SS *Drottningholm*, 7/6/25 (NA).
85   "Do what you can . . .": Marx, *Mayer and Thalberg: The Make-Believe Saints*, p. 65.
86   "I looked up . . .": "I Loved Garbo," *The New Movie Magazine*, 2/34.
86   "I remember . . .": ibid.
86   "the most exciting . . .": "An Unknown Chapter in Greta Garbo's Life" (pt. 2), *Liberty*, 8/25/34.
86   "She stayed on . . .": *The New Movie Magazine*, 2/34.
86   "We knocked on . . .": ibid.
87   "Miss Garbo says . . .": *Motion Picture*, 11/25.
87   "She simply crawled . . .": *The New Movie Magazine*, 2/34.
87   "Everyone treated it . . .": ibid.
87   Paying their own expenses: "What's the Matter with Greta Garbo?", *Photoplay*, 4/27.
88   "He had a great . . .": *The New Movie Magazine*, 2/34.
88   "Miss Garbo has . . .": "The Man Who Saved Garbo's Career," *Screen Book Magazine*, 7/34.
88   "Look at the dress . . .": ibid.
88   "They don't like me . . .": ibid.
89   GG signs MGM contract: GG 1925 datebook (GC).
89   "Are you satisfied . . .": *Liberty*, 8/25/34.
89   "I feel suicidal . . .": Sands and Broman, *The Divine Garbo*, p. 66.
89   GG to Lars Saxon, 8/30/25: Broman, *Conversations*, pp. 72–73.
89   FN3: Mauritz Stiller papers (Sjö).
90   "I know you . . .": Edgar Sirmont to Mauritz Stiller, 1/12/27 (SF).
90   Cross-country schedule: GG 1925 datebook (GC).
90   "Greta whispered to me . . .": Mauritz Stiller to Axel Nilson, 11/27/25, quoted in Hood, *Sjöström och Stiller*, p. 276.
90   Prohibition booze: "Heartbreaking Days in Hollywood," *Screen Play*, 8/33.
91   "I spent my first . . .": Beaton, *Memoirs*, p. 210.
91   GG re-signs her contract: Walker, *Garbo*, p. 35.
91   "Only one person . . .": Hood, *Sjöström och Stiller*, p. 273.
91   "They were a . . .": Bainbridge, *Garbo*, p. 83.
91   FN5: Hood, *Sjöström och Stiller*, p. 270.
92   Garbo's teeth: Charles Higham to author, 9/16/94.
92   "The studios are hideous . . .": GG to Lars Saxon, undated letter circa fall 1925, quoted in Sands and Broman, *The Divine Garbo*, p. 79.
93   "It could be . . .": ibid.
93   "The first year . . .": "Jag minns när Greta drog en låt på Grand," *Svenska Dagbladet*, 4/22/90.
93   "I'm dreaming of . . .": GG to Lars Saxon, undated letter circa fall 1925, quoted in Sands and Broman, *The Divine Garbo*, p. 72.
94   "to tell the story . . .": Dorothy Farnum scenario, 9/19/25 (MGSC).
94   "Meester Mayer . . .": "The Story of Greta Garbo" (pt. 3), *Photoplay*, 6/28.
94   "The salary was . . .": *Screen Play*, 8/33.
94   "Carpenters, electricians, painters . . .": ibid.
95   "Greta starts working . . .": Mauritz Stiller to Axel Nilson, 11/27/25, quoted in Hood, *Sjöström och Stiller*, p. 275.
95   "Can't we have . . .": "Garbo's Untold Story," *Screen Play*, 9/33.
95   "Without the guiding hand . . .": ibid.
95   "except those long . . .": ibid.
96   "Let him have them . . .": Billquist, *Garbo*, p. 110.
96   "I've been down . . .": "A Woman Alone," unidentified publication (LC).

96 "One evening late . . .": *Screen Play*, 9/33.
97 GG letter to Mimi Pollak: 12/6/25.
97 "I still can't describe . . .": ibid.
97 "Hemlängtan . . ." GG to Vera Schmiterlöw, undated letter circa 1926, Kungliga Biblioteket, Stockholm. (This is a handwritten copy of Greta's letter. As with another version of this correspondence, later sold at an auction in the U.S., it is *not* in Garbo's writing—but it is her voice.)
97 "We lit very much . . .": Higham, *Hollywood Cameramen: Sources of Light*, pp. 67–70.
98 "She's got it . . .": Marion, *Off with Their Heads!*, p. 134.
98 "We all thought . . .": Bainbridge, *Garbo*, p. 87.
98 "Greta Garbo, who showed . . .": Preview notes, 1/25/26 (MGSC).
99 "the find of the year . . .": *Variety*, 2/24/26.
99 "Young, slim . . .": *New York American*, 2/22/26.
99 "It almost makes . . .": Undated letter, quoted in Billquist, *Garbo*, p. 112.

CHAPTER SIX: Trial by Fire: Becoming Garbo

103 "The picture is not . . .": "Miss LaMarr's Strange Draw; Greta Garbo New Sensation," *Variety*, 3/3/26.
103 "Don had been . . .": "The Swedish Girl Was Scared," *Hollywood Studio Magazine*, 11/71.
104 "[Garbo] lost all faith . . .": David O. Selznick memo to Don King, 2/7/45 (DOS).
104 Background information on MGM and Louis B. Mayer: Carey, *All the Stars in Heaven: Louis B. Mayer's MGM*; Crowther, *Hollywood Rajah*; Gabler, *An Empire of Their Own*; Higham, *Merchant of Dreams: Louis B. Mayer, MGM and the Secret Hollywood*; Schatz, *Genius of the System*.
104 "Louis B. Mayer was . . .": DL (courtesy James Curtis).
105 "My unchanging policy . . .": Hay, *MGM: When the Lion Roars*, p. 19.
106 "In my country . . .": "Hollywood Surprises New Swedish Actress," *The New York Times*, 2/28/26.
106 "Ideally, I would like . . .": Mauritz Stiller to Axel Nilson, 11/27/25, quoted in Hood, *Sjöström och Stiller*, p. 275.
107 "He was remarkably . . .": Anita Loos manuscript notes (BU).
107 "the greatest mind . . .": *Variety*, 5/19/26.
107 "a conspicuous enchantress . . .": Dorothy Farnum synopsis, 11/27/25 (MGSC).
107 "Had a conversation . . .": GG to Lars Saxon, 2/14/26, quoted in Broman, *Greta Garbo berätter*, p. 86.
108 "I could never . . .": "The Story of Greta Garbo" (pt. 3), *Photoplay*, 6/28.
108 "If you call . . .": GG to Lars Saxon, 2/29/26, quoted in Sands and Broman, *The Divine Garbo*, p. 79.
108 "As soon as . . .": "Heartbreaking Days in Hollywood," *Screen Play*, 8/33.
108 Friendship with Edith Sjöström: J. J. Cohn interview with Linda Frank, 12/9/92.
109 "[She] was tortured . . .": Broman, *Conversations*, p. 62.
109 "Every Sunday . . .": ibid, p. 60.
109 "I honestly felt . . .": ibid, p. 62.
109 "I nearly drowned . . .": ibid, p. 64.
110 "We liked an audience . . .": Lillian Gish to Raymond Daum, 1978 (CU).
110 Marriage proposal from Saxon: GG to Mimi Pollak, 3/4/26.
110 "No. That wouldn't . . .": Broman, *Conversations*, p. 60.
110 "We understood each other . . .": "Greta Garbos ungdomsminnen," *Lektyr*, 1930 (SF).
111 Stiller's confusion: Walker, *Garbo*, p. 46.
111 "They brought me here . . .": Bainbridge, *Garbo*, p. 93.
111 Stiller's despair: Victor Sjöström manuscript notes (Sjö).
112 "He had his own . . .": Bainbridge, *Garbo*, p. 92.

112 "These two Metro . . .": "John Gilbert and Greta Garbo Will Play in *The Undying Past,*" *New York American,* 4/19/26.

112 "That is the hardest . . .": *Photoplay,* 5/28.

112 Stiller intercepted telegram: "Garbo's Untold Story," *Screen Play,* 9/33.

113 "and with a little . . .": ibid.

113 "In that case . . .": Marx, *Mayer and Thalberg,* p. 87.

113 "She would look . . .": Bainbridge, *Garbo,* p. 93.

113 "When this thing . . .": GG to Axel Nilson, 6/29/26, quoted in Hood, *Sjöström och Stiller,* p. 279.

114 "If I were . . .": GG to Lars Saxon, 7/6/26, quoted in Broman, *Greta Garbo berätter,* pp. 87–90.

114 "and phlegmatically accepted . . .": Marx, *Mayer and Thalberg,* p. 87.

114 "How I was . . .": *Photoplay,* 6/28.

114 "Given all that's happened . . .": GG to Lars Saxon, 7/6/26, quoted in Broman, *Greta Garbo berätter,* p. 90.

114 "I've never seen . . .": GG to Vera Schmiterlöw, undated letter circa 1926, Kungliga Biblioteket, Stockholm.

115 "I never saw anyone . . .": "The Most Intelligent Actress," *The Film Weekly,* 2/6/32.

115 Stiller's visa: Walker, *Garbo,* p. 95.

115 "bursting with energy . . .": Pensel, *Seastrom and Stiller in Hollywood,* p. 95.

115 "Oh, oh, oh . . .": GG letter circa summer 1926, quoted in Sjolander, *Garbo,* p. 61.

115 Borg as mediator: *Screen Play,* 9/33.

116 "Mister Mayer . . .": *Photoplay,* 6/28.

116 "I cannot see . . .": ibid.

116 L. B. Mayer to GG, 8/4/26: Higham, *Merchant of Dreams,* p. 111.

116 "They say, 'Greta Garbo . . .": *Photoplay,* 6/28.

116 "I don't understand . . .": GG to Lars Saxon, 7/6/26, quoted in Sands and Broman, *The Divine Garbo,* p. 81.

CHAPTER SEVEN: Conquest

119 Gilbert hailed Garbo: Marion, *Off with Their Heads!,* p. 132.

119 "Some instant spark . . .": "Garbo in Love," King Features, 1937 (LC).

119 "Every morning . . .": "The Story of Greta Garbo" (pt. 3), *Photoplay,* 6/28.

119 "I don't think . . .": "Up Speaks a Gallant Loser," *Photoplay,* 2/27.

120 "She did not love . . .": "John Gilbert," *Films in Review,* 3/56.

120 "God pity . . .": Quoted in the "Star Treatment" episode of *Hollywood,* Thames Television, 1980.

120 Jack's start in films: "Jack Gilbert Writes His Own Story" (pt. 1), *Photoplay,* 6/28.

120 The couple loved and quarreled: Fountain, *Dark Star,* p. 84.

121 "that all opportunities . . .": "Jack Gilbert Writes His Own Story" (pt. 4), *Photoplay,* 9/28.

121 "Acting, that very thing . . .": *Photoplay,* 9/28.

121 "is the most damaging . . .": "Vidor Ranks Heart First," *Los Angeles Times,* 9/22/26.

121 "He was an amazing . . .": King Vidor to Joan and Robert C. Franklin, 1958 (CU).

122 Garbo and Valentino: "Looks Like Pola Has Lost 'The Sheik'," *Variety,* 6/4/26.

122 "I do not recall . . .": Negri, *Memoirs of a Star,* p. 256.

122 "It was the damnedest . . .": Fountain, *Dark Star,* p. 125.

122 "They were in love . . .": Barbara Kent Monroe to Linda Frank, 9/14/93.

122 "They had been rehearsing . . .": Broman, *Conversations,* p. 62.

123 "There is something . . .": *Photoplay,* 2/27.

123 Details of wedding: "King Vidor Weds Miss Boardman," *Los Angeles Times,* 9/9/26; and "Vidor Wed to Eleanor Boardman," *Los Angeles Examiner,* 9/9/26.

124 "he was getting . . .": Brownlow and Kobal, *Hollywood: The Pioneers,* p. 193.

124 Gilbert and Mayer fight: Brownlow and Kobal, *Hollywood: The Pioneers,* p. 193; Fountain, *Dark Star,* pp. 130–31; and Marx, *Mayer and Thalberg,* p. 91.

124 Eleanor Boardman story included in the "Star Treatment" episode of *Hollywood*, Thames Television, 1980; and Fountain, *Dark Star*, pp. 130–32.

124 FN3: Vidor, *A Tree Is a Tree*, pp. 141–42.

125 "I asked Irene Selznick . . .": Leatrice Fountain to author, 10/26/92.

125 "Jack was on . . .": Harry Crocker unpublished memoir, *That's Hollywood* (AMPAS).

126 "he was always . . .": "Clarence Brown: Garbo and Beyond," *Velvet Light Trap*, Spring 1978.

126 "to convert a holy . . .": Walker, *Garbo*, p. 59.

126 "The results seared . . .": "Clarence Brown, Specialist in Film Romance, Picks 'Greatest Lovers'," Associated Press, 5/2/50.

127 "now being accepted . . .": "Gilbert-Garbo Engaged?" *Variety*, 9/21/26.

127 "If the stills . . .": Louella O. Parsons, *New York American*, 10/4/26.

127 "Garbo tried . . .": "Garbo's One Great Love—John Gilbert," *Screen Play*, 10/33.

127 "*Es ist ein Skandal* . . .": Thomas, *Thalberg: Life and Legend*, p. 108.

127 "That was rotten . . .": Billquist, *Garbo*, pp. 121–22.

128 "I was beneath contempt . . .": GG to Lars Saxon, 11/26, quoted in Broman, *Greta Garbo berättet*, p. 85.

128 "Slim as the proverbial . . .": "Greta and Moreno Score Artistic Triumphs in *The Temptress*," *Los Angeles Examiner*, 9/20/26.

128 "with intelligent restraint . . .": *The Film Daily*, 10/12/26.

128 "She may not be . . .": *Life*, vol. 88, no. 2296, 11/4/26.

128 "The consensus of opinion . . .": "Capitol's Record $74,342," *Variety*, 10/20/26.

128 FN6: E. J. Mannix/MGM box-office ledger (AMPAS).

129 "He loved people . . .": "Love, Laughter and Tears," *Los Angeles Examiner*, 1/21/51.

129 "she still contained . . .": "Stars Are Human After All," *Photoplay*, 9/36.

130 Anita Page recollection of party: Interview with Linda Frank, 9/18/94.

130 "Garbo would be there . . .": *Los Angeles Examiner*, 1/21/51.

130 Eleanor Boardman re San Simeon: "Garbo in Love," King Features, 1937 (LC).

130 "Yet, who could possibly . . .": Marion, *Off with Their Heads!*, p. 137.

131 "The most unexpected . . .": *A Private View*, pp. 82–83.

131 "There was a sudden . . .": Meryman, *Mank: The Wit, World and Life of Herman Mankiewicz*, pp. 206–207.

131 "Tell Miss Garbo . . .": Joseph Buhler to Mauritz Stiller, 11/1/26 (Sjö).

131 "GRETA GARBO OFF LOT . . .": *Variety*, 11/10/26.

132 Ultimatum: L. B. Mayer to GG, 11/5/26.

132 "marvelous . . . alluring . . .": Fountain, *Dark Star*, p. 138.

132 Stiller heartbroken: Negri, *Memoirs of a Star*, p. 292.

132 "GILBERT-GARBO ROMANCE OFF . . .": *Variety*, 11/17/26.

132 "a certain actor . . .": GG to Lars Saxon, 11/26, quoted in Bainbridge, *Garbo*, p. 111.

132 GG letter to Mimi Pollak: 11/26.

133 "We had a long . . .": Rowland V. Lee/AFI Written History, *Adventures of a Movie Director*, 1971.

133 "Love has no place . . .": "Garbo in Love," King Features, 1937 (LC).

133 "Away from the studio . . .": Marion, *Off with Their Heads!*, pp. 152–53.

CHAPTER EIGHT: MGM vs. Garbo: Contracts, *Love*, and Marriage

134 "I think I go . . .": "Up Speaks a Gallant Loser," *Photoplay*, 2/27.

134 "There isn't another . . .": ibid.

134 "Miss Garbo is a type . . .": "What's the Matter with Greta Garbo," *Photoplay*, 4/27.

135 "Four or five . . .": "The Story of Greta Garbo" (pt. 3), *Photoplay*, 6/28.

135 "is something nobody . . .": GG to Lars Saxon, 11/26, quoted in Bainbridge, *Garbo*, p. 111.

135 "Greta has no idea . . .": *Photoplay*, 2/27.

135 Gish caught in bicoastal feud: Lillian Gish to Dr. Ronald Davis, 1979 (SMU).

136 "They all point . . .": Lillian Gish to Louis Levy, 1/23/27, Manuscript Division, Library of Congress, Washington, D.C.

136 "From the moment . . .": Brooks, *Lulu in Hollywood*, p. 88.

136 "I couldn't speak . . .": Lillian Gish to Raymond Daum, 1978 (CU).

137 "sacrificed for money . . .": GG to Lars Saxon, 8/26, quoted in Sands and Broman, *The Divine Garbo*, p. 82.

137 "When you bring . . .": GG to Lars Saxon, 11/26, quoted in Bainbridge, *Garbo*, p. 111.

137 "That son of a . . .": Higham, *Merchant of Dreams*, p. 114.

138 "The way Greta . . .": Louella O. Parsons, *Los Angeles Examiner*, 12/11/26.

138 "a stout rope . . .": "Santa Claus! Here's What Picture Folk Want for Christmas," *Los Angeles Examiner*, 12/19/26.

138 "the luscious Swede . . .": "Speaking of Pictures," *Photoplay*, 12/26.

138 GG letter to Mimi Pollak: 11/26.

138 MGM using the INS against Stiller: Walker, *Garbo*, p. 54. (The studio may have been alerted to the rumors regarding Stiller early on in their relationship based upon the threat of a lawsuit from a former employee, Carlo Keil-Möller, as well as subsequent gossip about "Stiller's boys" in Berlin and rumored pick-ups in L.A.)

139 "People say that . . .": GG to Lars Saxon, 11/26, quoted in Bainbridge, *Garbo*, p. 111.

139 "Hers was to be . . .": Walker, *Garbo*, p. 65.

139 "Tell her that . . .": "Garbo's Untold Story," *Screen Play*, 9/33.

139 "The difficulties between . . .": Sven-Hugo Borg to Joseph Buhler, 12/1/26.

140 "My dear Sir . . .": Mauritz Stiller to L. B. Mayer, 12/18/26 (Sjö).

140 "Greta Garbo is a very . . .": "*Flesh and the Devil* Adds Woman to Old David, Jonathan Plot," *Los Angeles Times*, 11/14/26.

141 "Here is a picture . . .": *Variety*, 1/12/27.

141 Garbo drawing crowds: "Long Lines at Garbo Picture," *Los Angeles Times*, 1/16/27.

142 "Mildly exciting . . .": "Jack Gilbert Writes His Own Story," *Photoplay*, 9/28.

142 "In the end . . .": "A Swedish Siren," *The Picturegoer*, 5/27.

142 "My first impression . . .": Broman, *Conversations*, pp. 78–79.

142 "Always I hurry . . .": "They Learned About Women From Her," *Motion Picture Classic*, 8/27.

142 "Dove of Peace": "Greta Garbo Soon Returning to MGM for *Anna Karenina*," *Los Angeles Examiner*, 1/20/27.

142 "Perhaps Greta Garbo . . .": Louella O. Parsons, *Los Angeles Examiner*, 1/28/27.

142 Mayer talks to Lars Saxon: Broman, *Conversations*, p. 80.

143 "terribly restless . . .": *Photoplay*, 6/28.

143 Greta danced with Jack: Louella O. Parsons, *Los Angeles Examiner*, 1/11/55.

143 "Jack Gilbert and . . .": "Greta Garbo Almost Weds," Universal Service, 2/5/27 (AMPAS).

143 "GILBERT WEDS GARBO . . .": Louella O. Parsons, *Los Angeles Examiner*, 2/14/27.

144 "Well, if you must . . .": "John Gilbert, Greta Garbo Deny Betrothal, Marriage," *Los Angeles Mirror*, 2/24/27.

144 "We are not even engaged . . .": Louella O. Parsons, *Los Angeles Examiner*, 3/18/27.

144 "no trouble and . . .": *Photoplay*, 6/28.

145 "The popularity that . . .": "Under the Lights," *Los Angeles Times*, 1/30/27.

145 "Miss Garbo has surely . . .": "Swedish Actress Wins Fame by New Type; Leads Vamps," *New York American*, 2/13/27.

146 "When the new contract . . .": GG to J. Robert Rubin, 3/6/27.

146 "For the first time . . .": *Photoplay*, 6/28.

146 1927 contract: "Greta Garbo's Conditions," *Variety* 4/6/27; and Walker, *Garbo*, p. 69.

147 "We're going to be . . .": Moore, *Silent Star*, p. 204.

147 "Garbo said he drank . . .": Leatrice Fountain to author, 12/13/92.

147 "After a considerable . . .": Stewart, *By a Stroke of Luck*, p. 158.

148 Gilbert's behavior at the Miramar: Fountain, *Dark Star*, p. 136.

148 "You better run . . .": "John Gilbert is Jailed by Court," *Beverly Hills Citizen*, 4/21/27.

148 "I don't know . . .": "Hollywood's Police Record," *Motion Picture Classic*, 12/28.

148 "and they only told . . .": Moore, *Silent Star*, p. 204.

148 "GILBERT IN DUAL ROLE ON BLOTTER": *Los Angeles Times*, 4/16/27.

149 "He was madly . . .": Crawford and Ardmore, *A Portrait of Joan*, p. 31

149 "You go back . . .": "Garbo's One Great Love," *Screen Play*, 10/33.

149 "She never talked . . .": Bainbridge, *Garbo*, pp. 112–13.

150 "Of course, I have . . .": *Photoplay*, 6/28.

150 "Off again, on again . . .": *Photoplay*, 2/28.

150 "Garbo was at her best . . .": Fountain, *Dark Star*, p. 126.

150 "There are many things . . .": *Photoplay*, 6/28.

151 "The conventional thing . . .": *Photoplay*, 2/27.

151 "She never talks . . .": "They Learned About Women From Her," *Motion Picture Classic*, 8/27.

151 GG letter to Mimi Pollak: 5/27.

151 "The heavy-lidded droop . . .": *Motion Picture Classic*, 8/27.

152 "The condition of Greta Garbo . . .": "Greta Garbo Better, Physician Reports," unidentified publication, 4/30/27 (AMPAS).

152 "There is general concern . . .": Louella O. Parsons, *Los Angeles Examiner*, 5/7/27.

152 FN7: Abortion claims: Higham, *Merchant of Dreams*, p. 110.

152 "I happen to have . . .": Daum, *Walking with Garbo*, pp. 142–43.

152 Re pernicious anemia: Dr. Donald Reisfield to author, 2/7/97.

153 "M.-G.-M. officials found . . .": "*Karenina* is Suspended for Revision," *Variety*, 5/18/27.

153 "to let them see . . .": Louella O. Parsons, *New York American*, 5/23/27.

153 "I retired before . . .": "Tragedy Visits Screen Colony," *Los Angeles Times*, 6/4/27.

153 "It's an ill wind . . .": "Gilbert and Greta Will Be Co-Starred in *Anna Karenina*," *Los Angeles Examiner*, 6/6/27.

154 "Then, one day . . .": "When Greta Isn't Garbo," *Silver Screen*, 10/39.

154 "Is it that Americans . . .": "They Learned About Women From Her," *Motion Picture Classic*, 8/27.

154 "nervous, like a racehorse . . .": "That Languid Lure," *The Picturegoer*, 3/28.

155 "I know the person . . .": "Once Seen, Never Forgotten," by Malcolm H. Oettinger (SF).

CHAPTER NINE: Captive Beauty

156 "one of the bitterest . . .": Harry Crocker unpublished memoir, *That's Hollywood* (AMPAS).

156 "[Greta] tried to . . .": Bainbridge, *Garbo*, p. 114.

156 "Never, until two months . . .": "A Swedish Siren," *Picturegoer*, 5/27.

156 "She was, at this . . .": Fountain, *Dark Star*, p. 138.

157 "I don't recall . . .": Miller, *My Hollywood: When Both of Us Were Young*, p. 96.

157 The illicit nature of the affair: Marx, *Mayer and Thalberg*, p. 94.

157 "on evenings when lovers . . .": Dietz, *Dancing in the Dark*, p. 153.

158 Mona Mårtenson in Hollywood: "Mona Martensen in L.A.; M-G-M Going to Find Out," *Variety*, 8/7/27.

158 GG letter to Mimi Pollak: 9/15/27.

158 "This is the story . . .": Cutting Continuity Script, 1/11/28 (MGSC).

158 "I do not think . . .": "Film Imagery: Seastrom," *Close Up*, 1/29.

159 Synopsis of *The Divine Woman*: Cutting Continuity Script, 1/11/28 (MGSC).

159 "Good-bye to the Gish-type . . .": Victor Sjöström manuscript notes (Sjö).

159 "a softer, more easy-going . . .": Forslund, *Victor Sjöström*, p. 224.

160 "exceptional in every way . . .": Kevin Brownlow to author, 11/12/94. (The clip from *The Divine Woman* has been subtitled and is now a staple on Turner Classic Movies.)

160   "In Europe I enjoyed . . .": "American Film Industry," *Variety,* 8/3/27.

160   "got drunk, cursing Hollywood . . .": Asther, *Narrens väg,* pp. 96–97.

160   It was a painful farewell: Victor Sjöström manuscript notes (Sjö).

161   "My dear former Greta . . .": Mauritz Stiller to GG, 11/27 (GC).

161   GG letter to Mimi Pollak: 11/26/27.

162   "We shall continue . . .": Flamini, *Thalberg,* p. 110.

162   "The Embassy has finally . . .": *Variety,* 12/7/27.

163   "Her next picture . . .": Louella O. Parsons, *New York American,* 12/1/27.

163   "I have asked . . .": GG to Lars Saxon, 12/27, quoted in Sands and Broman, *The Divine Garbo,* p. 91.

163   "Whether I work . . .": ibid.

163   "Why are there . . .": Lawson, *Film: The Creative Process,* p. 104.

163   "The great difficulty . . .": Lorna Moon to Irving Thalberg, 11/17/27 (MGSC).

163   "Having made the most . . .": *Motion Picture Classic,* 3/28.

164   "Once she had been . . .": Walker, *Garbo,* p. 79.

165   "vivid, vital and dynamic . . .": Crawford and Ardmore, *A Portrait of Joan,* p. 31.

165   "You don't understand . . .": Meryman, *Mank,* p. 210.

165   "something wrong . . .": Hood, *Sjöström och Stiller,* p. 282.

165   "He was so glad . . .": ibid.

166   "Dear very missed Greta . . .": Mauritz Stiller to GG, 3/6/28 (GC).

167   "Greta Garbo, manless, heroless . . .": Louella O. Parsons, *Los Angeles Examiner,* 5/4/28.

167   Marion Davies snubbed: Davies, *The Times We Had: Life with William Randolph Hearst,* p. 85.

167   "the curious experience . . .": Louella O. Parsons, *Los Angeles Examiner,* 5/11/28.

168   *Mysterious Lady* Production Reports: MGM Special Collection, USC.

169   "a wonderful personality . . .": unidentified publication, 8/4/28 (LC).

169   "Girls ashamed of . . .": "Masculinity Menaces Movie Maidens," *Hollywood,* 7/15/28.

170   "I have some . . .": "The Story of Greta Garbo" (pt. 3), *Photoplay,* 6/28.

170   "one Sunday in the summer . . .": "Gish and Garbo: The Executive War on Stars," *Sight and Sound,* Winter 1958/1959.

170   "so intense and so eloquent . . .": Paris, *Louise Brooks,* p. 266.

170   Garbo "made a pass" at Brooks: Kobal, *People Will Talk,* p. 79.

170   "charming and tender . . .": Paris, *Louise Brooks,* p. 267.

170   Brooks was a "keen gossip": Kobal, *People Will Talk,* p. 74.

171   "Even eliminating what . . .": Reader's Report, 6/1/28 (MGSC).

171   "I'd rather you didn't . . .": Fountain, *Dark Star,* p. 160.

172   "together one day . . .": Douglas Fairbanks, Jr., to author, 10/14/92.

172   "Greta would write . . .": ibid.

172   "She is then . . .": "Greta Garbo," *Vanity Fair,* 10/30.

172   "I remember how . . .": Fairbanks, *The Salad Days,* p. 129. (Joan Crawford, who had recently completed *Our Dancing Daughters* at MGM, was still struggling to make a mark at the studio and frequently visited Fairbanks on the set.)

173   "I always found . . .": Douglas Fairbanks, Jr., to author, 10/14/92.

173   "The film presents . . .": *Los Angeles Times,* 7/28/28.

173   "Snapshots of Hollywood . . .": Louella O. Parsons, *Los Angeles Examiner,* 8/13/28.

173   "The director was . . .": Steichen, *A Life in Photography,* p. 8.

174   "She straddled it . . .": ibid.

174   "very easy-going . . .": Douglas Fairbanks, Jr., to author, 10/14/92.

175   It is a "majestic transformation . . .": Corliss, *Greta Garbo,* p. 66.

175   "Garbo is often called . . .": "Greta Garbo by Her Cameraman," *The Film Weekly,* 3/21/31.

175   "I am presently . . .": GG to Lars Saxon, 8/28, quoted in Sands and Broman, *The Divine Garbo,* p. 92.

176   "But even then . . .": "The Greta Garbo Legend Exposed," *Hollywood,* 10/30.

176   Scenario of *A Man's Man* (another lost film): Cutting Continuity Script, 3/27/29 (MGSC).
176   GG letter to Mimi Pollak: 9/29/28.
176   "The rumors of Miss Garbo's . . .": Louella O. Parsons, *New York American*, 8/29/28.
177   "YOUR MESSAGE MADE . . .": Edith and Victor Sjöström telegram to GG, 11/7/28 (GC).
177   Bengt Idestam-Almquist's deposition of Stiller's medical problems: Hood, *Sjöström och Stiller*, p. 283.
178   "When we were out . . .": Bainbridge, *Garbo*, p. 123.
178   "He was a fine patient . . .": Hood, *Sjöström och Stiller*, p. 283.
178   "When we passed London . . .": "As I Remember Him," *Film Comment*, Summer 1970.
179   "The nurse said . . .": Victor Sjöström manuscript notes (Sjö).
179   "I put my ear . . .": *Film Comment*, Summer 1970.
179   "MOJE PASSED AWAY . . .": Edith and Victor Sjöström telegram to GG, 11/8/28 (GC). (Stiller died at 1:15 A.M., Stockholm time, on November 8; Garbo received her telegram that same day in Los Angeles.)
179   "who did not arrive . . .": Daily Production Report, 11/8/28 (MGSC).
180   "She pressed her hands . . .": "When Greta Isn't Garbo," *Silver Screen*, 10/39.
180   "throughout all these years . . .": "Jag minns när Greta drog en låt på Grand," *Svenska Dagbladet*, 4/22/90.
180   "someone I have . . .": Beaton, *Memoirs*, p. 295.
180   FN10: E. Max Sarnoff to author, 1/13/93.

CHAPTER TEN: Femme Fatale

181   "ready very early . . .": Beaton, *Memoirs*, p. 296.
181   "You shall be saved . . .": Mauritz Stiller to GG, 11/27 (GC).
181   "You are free . . .": ibid.
181   "If I were to love . . .": Hood, *Sjöström och Stiller*, p. 283.
181   "You shall not think . . .": Mauritz Stiller to GG, 11/27 (GC).
181   "I have something . . .": Sands and Broman, *The Divine Garbo*, p. 95.
182   "After Moje died . . .": Bainbridge, *Garbo*, p. 126.
182   Garbo's warning: ibid.
182   "No one knew . . .": Broman, *Conversations*, p. 66.
183   "There were whispers . . .": Louella O. Parsons, *Los Angeles Examiner*, 11/25/28.
183   "THERE IS STILL TIME . . .": L. B. Mayer cable to GG, 12/3/28.
184   "Slightly better weather . . .": Billquist, *Garbo*, p. 152.
185   "Yes. I am glad . . .": "When Garbo Was Snubbed by a Prince," *London Sunday Express*, 10/7/34.
186   "A hearty reception . . .": ibid.
186   "Man, think of . . .": Bainbridge, *Garbo*, p. 129.
186   "When I saw . . .": *London Sunday Express*, 10/7/34.
187   Christmas at the Strand Hôtel: Broman, *Conversations*, p. 81.
188   "I don't want . . .": ibid.
188   Garbo's restlessness in Stockholm: *London Sunday Express*, 10/7/34.
188   Rumors about Stiller's estate: Sands and Broman, *The Divine Garbo*, p. 97. (Nils Asther also believed that GG was going to get everything. She got a small writing table.)
188   "I remember vividly . . .": Bainbridge, *Garbo*, p. 130.
189   "Finally it got to be . . .": ibid., p. 131.
189   "The next day . . .": Broman, *Conversations*, p. 64.
189   "I can only judge . . .": "Kalla mig svägerska, sa gudomliga Greta," *Hufvudstabladet*, 3/10/71.
189   "We rarely spoke . . .": "Helsingforspojken Stiller," *Hufvudstabladet*, undated clipping (SRTV).
190   "She enjoyed the reunion . . .": "Greta Garbo—Her Life Story," MGM bio, 1939 (AMPAS).
190   "She was stylishly . . .": "My Little Admirer Named Greta," *London Sunday Express*, 6/1/30.

190 Garbo, Prince Sigvard, and Wilhelm Sörensen: *London Sunday Express*, 10/7/34.

191 "Oh, how exciting . . .": ibid.

191 "Imagine our surprise . . .": Broman, *Conversations*, p. 107.

191 "how Greta used to . . .": ibid.

192 "The window, where we stood . . .": "Hon fick avgiva ett heligt löfte att aldrig vidare ägna sig åt film," *Hänt i Veckan*, no. 2, 1970.

192 "She had a sweet . . .": Broman, *Conversations*, p. 80.

192 "It feels so strange . . .": "En choklad kartong fylld av minnen, 55 års hågkomster av vânskap och behag," *MånadsJournalen*, no. 9, 9/85.

193 "If someone would . . .": Louella O. Parsons, *New York American*, 1/5/29.

193 "While Miss Garbo . . .": *The New York Times*, 1/21/29.

193 "the protective and . . .": "Individuality is Niblo's Word to Describe Garbo," *Houston Telegraph*, 7/28/28.

193 "No actress, before or since . . .": Walker, *Stardom: The Hollywood Phenomenon*, p. 144.

193 FN7: "What Garbo Thinks of Hollywood," *Photoplay*, 8/30.

195 "In my country . . .": "The Story of Greta Garbo" (pt. 1), *Photoplay*, 6/28.

195 "When I first . . .": "Hollywood's Cruelty to Greta Garbo," *Photoplay*, 1/32.

196 "Much has been written . . .": Crocker, *That's Hollywood*, unpublished memoir (AMPAS).

196 "She was charming . . .": "Critical Crisis as Garbo Learns to Talk," *Los Angeles Examiner*, 3/2/30.

196 "She would wander . . .": Dietz, *Dancing in the Dark*, p. 152.

198 "Every one of those . . .": "I Loved Garbo," *The New Movie Magazine*, 2/34.

198 "Let's not talk . . .": "The Hollywood Hermit," *The New York Times*, 3/24/29.

198 "At the Ritz . . .": Louella O. Parsons, *New York American*, 3/31/29.

199 "Prince or no Prince . . .": Louella O. Parsons, *New York American*, 3/21/29.

199 "THE SONG IS GONE . . .": Robert Reud to GG, 3/24/29.

199 FN10: Robert Reud to GG, 3/31/27.

200 "During the first . . .": "Mayer Advises Talkies to Keep Screen's Stars," *Los Angeles Examiner*, 2/3/29.

200 "The word 'contract' . . .": Louella O. Parsons, *Los Angeles Examiner*, 3/20/28.

200 "Sound was a great . . .": Walker, *The Shattered Silents*, p. 145.

201 "If they want me . . .": *The New York Times*, 3/24/29.

201 Garbo's purported sound test: *Film Dope*, no. 18, 9/79.

201 "You are a very . . .": "Love, Laughter and Tears: The Gilbert-Garbo Interlude," *American Weekly*, 1/21/51.

202 "I want always . . .": "Greta Lacks Temperament," *Los Angeles Times*, 1/8/28.

202 "Don't try and be . . .": Broman, *Conversations*, p. 65

202 John Mack Brown re working on *The Single Standard*: "The Garbo Legend Exposed," *Hollywood*, 10/30.

203 Garbo as Hamlet: LaVine, *In a Glamorous Fashion*, p. 53.

203 "She turned white . . .": "When Greta Isn't Garbo," *Silver Screen*, 10/39.

203 "Although I could hear . . .": Coffee, *Storyline: Recollections of a Hollywood Screenwriter*, pp. 187–88.

204 "Any love affair . . .": "Why Jack Gilbert Married," *Photoplay*, 8/29.

204 "and said she wished . . .": *Silver Screen*, 10/39.

204 "since Flicka and I . . .": *American Weekly*, 1/21/51.

CHAPTER ELEVEN: Okay for Sound: A Blonde with a Brunette Voice

205 "Since the marriage . . .": Louella O. Parsons, *Los Angeles Examiner*, 6/21/29.

205 "a Swedish log cabin . . .": Asther, *Narrens väg*, p. 136.

205 "To myself . . .": ibid., pp. 137–38.

206 "Greta, if you . . .": "No Man Is Safe from Her Witchery," *London Sunday Express*, 7/3/55.

206 "She can sense . . .": ibid.

206 "Every Sunday morning . . .": Loder, *Hollywood Hussar*, p. 96.

206 "Oddly, when I met . . .": Viertel, *The Kindness of Strangers*, pp. 142–43.

208 "alien, frightening and . . .": ibid., p. 128.

208 "Salka was a Rock . . .": Jack Larson to author, 10/3/92.

208 "When Greta told . . .": "The Private Life of Greta Garbo" (pt. 1), *Photoplay*, 9/30.

208 "If you really wish . . .": GG telegram to Wilhelm Sörensen, quoted in Sands and Broman, *The Divine Garbo*, p. 181.

209 "One morning . . .": *Photoplay*, 9/30.

210 "[Garbo] is one . . .": Louella O. Parsons, *New York American*, 7/16/29.

210 "I wonder if . . .": Lew Ayres to author, 9/23/92.

210 "To her I was . . .": Lew Ayres to Dr. Ronald Davis, 1981. (SMU).

210 "Miss Garbo has . . .": "Wait Till Greta She Speek! Then Hear One Artiste, Says Feyder," *Los Angeles Examiner*, 12/8/29.

211 "About the studio . . .": "The Garbo Legend Exposed," *Hollywood*, 10/30.

211 "best and most natural . . .": Billquist, *Garbo*, p. 146.

211 "I used to . . .": *Hollywood*, 10/30.

211 "She was far more . . .": Lew Ayres to author, 9/23/92.

211 "The great Garbo . . .": *Motion Picture Classic*, 10/29.

211 "The actress is . . .": *Variety*, 7/31/29.

211 "Garbo, the pash . . .": *Variety* 8/21/29.

212 "What's happened to Greta . . .": Louella O. Parsons, *Los Angeles Examiner*, 8/18/29.

212 "WILL COME IF . . .": *Photoplay*, 9/30.

212 "This is a very . . .": Sands and Broman, *The Divine Garbo*, p. 182.

212 "lived a life apart . . .": "The Man Who Tried to Elope with Garbo," *Photoplay*, 9/31.

213 "A thousand parrots . . .": "Hollywood Talks!", *Premiere*, Winter 1991.

214 "Jack went to Europe . . .": Moore, *Silent Star*, p. 206.

214 "a few more talker . . .": *Variety*, 10/9/29.

214 "It was very strange . . .", Fountain, *Dark Star*, p. 102.

215 "I have never . . .": Moore, *Silent Star*, p. 206.

215 "Now, it shouldn't have . . .": "Hollywood Talks!" *Premiere*, Winter 1991.

216 "all the dignity . . .": Lila Lee to Joan and Robert C. Franklin, 1959 (CU).

216 "I would like . . .": "The Hollywood Hermit," *The New York Times*, 3/24/29.

216 Sjöström discussions re *Anna Christie*: Forslund, *Victor Sjöström*, p. 228.

216 "What a superb . . .": Louella O. Parsons, *Los Angeles Examiner*, 3/27/29.

216 "It is a gorgeous . . .": *The New York Times*, 7/28/29.

217 "Garbo will fit . . .": Marion, *Off with Their Heads!*, p. 196.

217 "What do I need . . .": "The Day That Garbo Dreaded," *London Sunday Express*, 6/5/55

217 "a blonde with a . . .": "Crashing the Sound Gate," *Screenland*, 3/19/29.

217 "I was amazed . . .": Sands and Broman, *The Divine Garbo*, p. 183.

217 "I did not meet . . .": *London Sunday Express*, 6/5/55.

218 "Both of them . . .": ibid.

218 "I'll never forget . . .": "When Greta Isn't Garbo," *Silver Screen*, 10/39.

219 "I almost jumped . . .": *London Sunday Express*, 6/5/55.

219 "GARBO TALKS OK . . .", *Variety*, 10/23/29.

219 "It was always fascinating . . .": Marion, *Off with Their Heads!*, p. 197.

220 "She's a regular . . .": *Hollywood*, 10/30.

220 "Golden silence reigns . . .": *The New York Times*, 11/16/29; plus 11/24/29.

220 "No figure in . . .": *New York Telegraph*, 11/17/29.

221 "One day, I was . . .": Lew Ayres to author, 9/23/92.

221 "He missed nothing . . .": DL (courtesy James Curtis).

221 "the severest test . . .": "A Star Falls to Earth," *Los Angeles Times*, 1/26/30.

221 "Garbo is holding them . . .": Marion, *Off with Their Heads!*, p. 198.

222 "It's in the bag . . .": ibid, p. 199

222 "This is too good . . .": Hedda Hopper, *Los Angeles Times*, 4/21/40.

222 "alternately hatched and discarded . . .": Day, *This Was Hollywood*, p. 99.

222 "You have to . . .": Palmborg, *The Private Life of Greta Garbo*, p. 212.

222 "She had drawn . . .": Loder, *Hollywood Hussar*, p. 96.

223 "I thought the party . . .": Palmborg, *The Private Life of Greta Garbo*, p. 218.

223 "It may seem strange . . .": *Variety*, 1/8/30.

223 "People say Garbo . . .": *Los Angeles Examiner*, 12/8/29.

223 "depicts and sustains . . .": *Los Angeles Record*, 1/22/30.

223 "Even those who . . .": *Los Angeles Times*, 1/23/30.

223 "We entered the . . .": *London Sunday Express*, 6/5/55.

224 "Isn't it terrible . . .": Palmborg, *The Private Life of Greta Garbo*, p. 200.

224 "Other stars who . . .": "Critical Crisis Rises as Garbo Learns to Talk," *Los Angeles Examiner*, 3/2/30.

224 "an electric silence . . .": ibid.

CHAPTER TWELVE: The Peasant of Chevy Chase

225 "The talking screen . . .": *New York Telegraph*, 3/16/30.

225 "Now that the Great . . .": ibid.

225 "Great artistically and tremendous . . .": *Variety*, 3/19/30.

226 "Greta stays in her . . .": Louella O. Parsons, *Los Angeles Examiner*, 2/16/30.

226 "seems to have ended . . .": Louella O. Parsons, *Los Angeles Examiner*, 4/28/30.

226 "It wasn't long . . .": "The Man Who Tried to Elope with Garbo," by Rilla Page Palmborg, *Photoplay*, 9/31.

226 "the most amusing place . . .": "A Year in the Life of Garbo," *Film Weekly*, 3/25/32.

226 "When she is . . .": Heimann, *Out with the Stars*, p. 126.

227 "With photography misty . . .": "24 Hours with Greta Garbo," *Silver Screen*, 1/31.

227 "elegant and refined . . .": "I Go House-Hunting with Greta," *London Sunday Express*, 6/19/55.

227 "There was a . . .": "The Private Life of Greta Garbo" (pt. 1), *Photoplay*, 9/30.

227 "If any of . . .": Palmborg, *The Private Life of Greta Garbo*, p. 158.

228 "I never saw . . .": ibid., p. 151.

228 "We found we . . .": ibid., p. 115.

228 "Don't let anyone . . .": ibid., p. 116.

229 "All of a sudden . . .": ibid., p. 119.

229 "She generally kept . . .": ibid., p. 161.

229 "Then she would . . .": ibid., p. 133.

230 "In the year . . .": ibid., p. 180.

230 "Yet she has . . .": *Photoplay*, 9/30, and *Film Weekly*, 3/25/32.

230 Rilla Palmborg's two-part article: "The Private Life of Greta Garbo," *Photoplay*, 9/30 and 10/30.

231 "I don't like . . .": *London Sunday Express*, 6/19/55.

231 "I know how strange . . .": Beaton, *Memoirs*, p. 235.

231 "She did lie awake . . .": Palmborg, *The Private Life of Greta Garbo*, p. 137.

231 MGM doctors prescribed sleeping pills: GG told a number of friends about this, including Betty Estevez and Raymond Daum.

232 "Miss Garbo is reported . . .": "Greta's Second Talker," *Variety*, 10/9/29.

232 "They had a long . . .": Palmborg, *The Private Life of Greta Garbo*, p. 219.

233 "I will never forget . . .": "The Garbo Legend Exposed," *Hollywood*, 10/30.

234 "Some people insipidly . . .": *Hollywood*, 10/30.

234 GG letter to Mimi Pollak: 6/18/30.

235 "I never will . . .": Palmborg, *The Private Life of Greta Garbo*, p. 160.

235 "Garbo was all upset . . .": ibid., p. 161.

235 "In the days . . .": "Behind the Scenes in *Grand Hotel*," *Daily News*, 5/9/32.

236 "Playing *Anna Christie* . . .": Viertel, *The Kindness of Strangers*, p. 151.

237 "Her performance is . . .": Norbert Lusk, *Picture Play*, quoted in Conway, McGregor, and Ricci, *The Films of Greta Garbo*, p. 93.

237 "I can't go on . . .": *London Sunday Express*, 6/19/55.

238 "and was mildly snubbed . . .": ibid.

238 "to be simple . . .": Negulesco, *Things I Did . . . And Things I Think I Did*, p. 207.

239 "In this respect . . .": M. E. Greenwood to L. B. Mayer, 10/24/30.

239 Sörensen re Brown: "The Man Who Tried to Elope with Garbo," *Photoplay*, 9/31.

239 "I would not direct . . .": "Did Brown and Garbo Fight?", *Photoplay*, 3/31.

240 A tense on-the-set conference: "No Man Is Safe from Her Witchery," *London Sunday Express*, 7/3/55.

240 "She is incomparable . . .": *Film Weekly*, 6/32, quoted in Haining, *The Legend of Garbo*, pp. 169–70.

240 "Greta Garbo is not . . .": ibid.

240 "Temperamentally, Garbo is . . .": "Greta Garbo by Her Cameraman," *The Film Weekly*, 3/21/31.

241 "He admired her work . . .": Blanche Sweet to Raymond Daum, 1981 (CU).

241 "A sadly unconvincing . . .": *The New York Times*, 2/9/31.

241 "*Camille* without the cough . . .": *Motion Picture*, 3/31.

241 "Garbo is the strangest personality . . .": "Garbo Little Known in L.A.," *Variety*, 2/18/31.

CHAPTER THIRTEEN: Chiaroscuro (Shadows and Light)

242 "a glorious experiment . . .": Behlmer, *Memo from David O. Selznick*, pp. 26–27.

242 "often made them . . .": Gabler, *An Empire of Their Own*, p. 320.

243 "During the period . . .": Eisenstein, *Immoral Memories: An Autobiography*, p. 156.

243 "Let's get down . . .": "Exploding the Garbo Myth," *Photoplay*, 4/31.

243 "Garbo's a nice girl . . .": ibid.

243 FN1: Eisner, *Murnau*, pp. 221–24.

244 "If a magazine . . .": Introduction to *The Talkies* (Dover Publications, 1971).

244 "Greta can more thoroughly . . .": de Acosta, *Here Lies the Heart*, p. 318.

244 "Her uncounted thousands . . .": "Garbo vs. Dietrich," *Photoplay*, 2/31.

244 "indifference to all . . .": "The Great Garbo," *Vanity Fair*, 2/32.

244 "[Greta] seeks less . . .": *Film Weekly*, 6/32, quoted in Haining, *The Legend of Garbo*, p. 167.

244 "a loner in . . .": Douglas and Arthur, *See You at the Movies*, p. 89.

245 "roared with laughter . . .": Bull and Lee, *The Faces of Hollywood*, p. 31.

245 "a frightened schoolgirl . . .": ibid., p. 23.

245 "She comes in bounding . . .": "Photographing Garbo," *Movie Mirror*, circa 1931 (LC).

245 FN2: Bull and Lee, *The Faces of Hollywood*, p. 31.

246 "By the third year . . .": Rotha, *The Film Till Now*, p. 439.

246 "Soon after going . . .": "Leonard Tells Debut of Stars," *Variety*, 6/26/44.

247 "a new hero . . .": Carey, *All the Stars in Heaven*, p. 155.

247 "Naturally, I shall . . .": "Does Garbo Tank She Go Home Now?" *Motion Picture Classic*, 6/31.

248 "Plenty of turmoil . . .": "Garbo's Six Walkouts One *Lenox* Headache," *Variety*, 7/7/31.

248 "No one making films . . .": de Acosta, *Here Lies the Heart*, p. 217.

249 "an author and personality . . .": 1942 publicity bio (MdA).

249 "Although my father . . .": de Acosta, *Here Lies the Heart*, p. 11.

249 Mercedes raised as a boy: First draft, *Here Lies the Heart*, pp. 29–30 (MdA).

249 "with newspapers under . . .": de Acosta, *Here Lies the Heart*, p. 31.

249 "The feeling that . . .": ibid., p. 24.

250 "To the outward . . .": First draft, *Here Lies the Heart*, p. 33 (MdA).

250 "I suppose it was . . .": Second draft, *Here Lies the Heart*, p. 221 (MdA).

251 "She is very mannish . . .": Cecil Beaton diary entries, 12/15/28, 11/16/28, and 2/2/30, quoted in Vickers, *Loving Garbo*, pp. 39, 40, and 42.

251 Greta wasn't "so far a Lesbian . . .": Cecil Beaton diary, 2/2/30, quoted in Vickers, *Loving Garbo*, p. 42.

251 "as though straining . . .": First draft, *Here Lies the Heart*, p. 207 (MdA).

251 FN6: Schanke, *Shattered Applause: The Eva LeGallienne Story*, p. 64.

252 "I sat through . . .": de Acosta, *Here Lies the Heart*, p. 185.

252 "There is some element . . .": First draft, *Here Lies the Heart*, unnumbered page (MdA).

252 "I was too overwhelmed . . .": de Acosta, *Here Lies the Heart*, p. 214.

252 "Greta was already there . . .": ibid., p. 215.

253 "She looked tired . . .": ibid., p. 217.

253 "Garbo's gorgeous work . . .": "Garbo, Gable Sensations," *The Hollywood Reporter*, 7/13/31.

254 "My present prison . . .": de Acosta, *Here Lies the Heart*, p. 219.

254 "She told me . . .": First draft, *Here Lies the Heart*, unnumbered page (MdA).

254 "I must go away . . .": de Acosta, *Here Lies the Heart*, p. 222.

255 "I am on my way . . .": ibid., p. 223.

255 "If you turn up . . .": ibid., p. 224.

255 "How to describe . . .": ibid.

255 "with the dark mountains . . .": ibid., p. 226.

256 "No one can really . . .": ibid.

256 "There in Silver Lake . . .": Second draft, *Here Lies the Heart*, pp. 480–81.

256 "There was no sense . . .": de Acosta, *Here Lies the Heart*, pp. 224–25.

256 "extended retakes . . .": "*Susan Lenox* Sent Back for Retakes," *The Hollywood Reporter*, 8/11/31.

256 "I gave [Edington] . . .": "It's Funny About My Face," *American Magazine*, 6/34. (Beery was first quoted about the arrangement in *The Hollywood Reporter*, 12/22/31.)

257 "The *Susan Lenox* preview . . .": *The Hollywood Reporter*, 9/23/31.

257 "By far the most . . .": *The Nation*, 11/31.

258 Metro reconsiders *Mata Hari*: "Too Many Garbos, Says M-G, Irked by One Dietrich," *Variety*, 8/25/31.

258 "Anybody who knows . . .": *Film Weekly*, 6/32, quoted in Haining, *The Legend of Garbo*, p. 168.

258 "She'd feel a little . . .": Lamparski, *Whatever Became of . . .* (vol. 11), p. 88.

259 "The Garbo-Gable . . .": "Best Five for October," *The Hollywood Reporter*, 11/14/31.

259 Gossip re Garbo's lifestyle: "Rambling Reporter" columns, *The Hollywood Reporter*, August–November 1931.

260 "The most talked-about . . .": unidentified movie magazine, circa 1931 (LC).

260 "Everyone had to . . .": Sam Green to author, 2/9/93.

261 "It's nice to be held . . .": John Colton draft, *Mata Hari*, 7/1/31 (MGSC).

261 "No word of complaint . . .": "When Nordic Met Latin," *Photoplay*, 2/32.

262 Greta and Salka playing in the snow: "Rambling Reporter," *The Hollywood Reporter*, 12/3/31.

262 "a chance to play . . .": ibid., 12/11/31.

262 "Mercedes was the kind . . .": Jean Howard to author, 11/10/92.

262 Mercedes' clipping collection: MdA.

262 "New York is in a fit . . .": "Rambling Reporter," *The Hollywood Reporter*, 12/24/31.

262 "That I experienced . . .": Mary Anita Loos to author, 3/1/95.

262 "a very definite . . .": Luis Estevez to author, 7/1/94.

263 "at her worst . . .": Beaton, *Memoirs*, p. 223.

263 "To try and explain . . .": Riva, *Marlene Dietrich*, p. 168.

263 "When somebody like . . .": Paris, *Louise Brooks*, p. 267.

263 "She tried to be . . .": Fred Zinnemann to author, 6/13/94.
263 "looking more like . . .": "Greta, Incognito, Plays Tag with N.Y. Reporters," unidentified publication, 12/29/31 (AMPAS).
263 "No, I am not . . .": ibid.
264 "I can't say nothing . . .": "Garbo 'Can't Say Nothing', So She Runs," New York *Daily News*, 12/29/31.
264 "Reporters and admirers . . .": Viertel, *Schriften zum Theater*, pp. 343–44.
264 "The lobby, all exits . . .": ibid., p. 345.
264 "The story of my . . .": Daum, *Walking with Garbo*, p. 199.
265 "the hottest speakeasy . . .": "Rambling Reporter," *The Hollywood Reporter*, 1/6/32.
265 "Would Miss Co-o-ornell . . .": Cornell and Woodbury, *I Wanted to Be an Actress*, p. 106.
265 "I can't remember . . .": ibid., p. 107.
265 "No, I am not . . .": Bainbridge, *Garbo*, p. 172.
266 "Looks like a record . . .": "*Mata Hari* Panics Broadway at Capitol," *The Hollywood Reporter*, 1/6/32.
266 "Garbo, Novarro, Barrymore . . .": *Variety*, 1/5/32.
266 "GARBO ASKING FOR MORE . . .": *Variety*, 12/27/31.
266 FN14: E. J. Mannix/MGM box-office ledger (AMPAS).
267 "She's not a ballet . . .": Charles Brackett to Joan and Robert C. Franklin, 1959 (CU).
267 "in the core of . . .": Dressler and Harrington, *My Own Story*, p. 252.
267 FN15: ibid., p. 56.
268 "His sunny personality . . .": Marx, *Mayer and Thalberg*, p. 188.
268 "Losing the decision . . .": Marx, *A Gaudy Spree*, p. 57.
268 "Eddie was a . . .": DL (courtesy James Curtis).
268 "ADVISED PICTURE HE MADE . . .": L. B. Mayer cable to Irving Thalberg, 7/7/31.
268 "He had a way . . .": Marx, *A Gaudy Spree*, pp. 57–58.
269 Story conference, 12/26/31: Transcript, pp. 6, 10–13 (MGSC).
270 "Enthusiasm has replaced . . .": *The Hollywood Reporter*, 1/14/32.
270 "I didn't know . . .": Kobler, *Damned in Paradise*, p. 261.
271 "He was full of tales . . .": de Acosta, *Here Lies the Heart*, p. 234.
271 "She has less temperament . . .": "What Goulding Thinks of Garbo," *Picturegoer Weekly*, 6/18/32.
271 "When [Brisbane's] visit . . .": "One More Garbo Fan," *Photoplay*, 5/32.
271 "You have no idea . . .": Fowler, *Good Night, Sweet Prince*, p. 340.
271 "Her interest in her work . . .": "One More Garbo Fan," *Photoplay*, 5/32.
271 "The physical power . . .": ibid.
271 "She is a fine . . .": Kobler, *Damned in Paradise*, p. 263.
272 "No director has . . .": "What Goulding Thinks of Garbo," *Picturegoer Weekly*, 6/18/32.
272 "Finally I got up . . .": Daum, *Walking with Garbo*, p. 149.
272 "Retaliation against foreign . . .": "Foreign Stars on Pan," *The Hollywood Reporter*, 2/25/32; also "Will Garbo and Dietrich Be Deported?" *Motion Picture*, 7/32.

CHAPTER FOURTEEN: Dreaming of Snow

273 "This tree is . . .": de Acosta, *Here Lies the Heart*, p. 219.
274 "Instead of sinking . . .": ibid., p. 231.
274 Scenario for *Desperate*: Original screenplay, 1/21/32 (MdA).
275 "We have been building . . .": de Acosta, *Here Lies the Heart*, p. 233.
275 "You go and tell . . .": ibid.
276 "I took this up . . .": Harry Edington to M. E. Greenwood, 2/13/32.
276 "Our dressing rooms . . .": Kobal, *People Will Talk*, p. 281.
276 "We rarely saw Greta . . .": "The Old Days Were Fun," *The Chicago Tribune*, 11/10/46.

277 "I got down . . .": Kobal, *People Will Talk*, p. 281.
277 "Our contract with Garbo . . .": Memo, MGM Legal Department, 3/32.
277 "I reported to . . .": Douglas and Arthur, *See You at the Movies*, p. 88.
278 "in pictures we expect . . .": Melvyn Douglas to Joan and Robert C. Franklin, 1958 (CU).
278 "a very easy person . . .": Ross and Ross, *The Player: A Profile of an Art*, p. 33.
278 "in the poetic intensity . . .": Kenneth Tynan, *The Observer*, 7/11/65.
278 Re Von Stroheim's behavior: Noble, *Hollywood Scapegoat: The Biography of Erich Von Stroheim*, p. 101; also Curtiss, *Von Stroheim*, pp. 283–87.
278 "When Garbo sees . . .": "Second Thoughts on the Preview of *Grand Hotel*," *The Hollywood Reporter*, 3/14/32.
278 "GARBO NO SIGN . . .": *Variety*, 4/12/32.
279 "You could not . . .": *The National Board of Review* magazine, 5/32.
279 "Garbo dominates the picture . . .": *The New Yorker*, 4/16/32.
280 "Her face, this landscape . . .": "Hon fick avgiva ett heligt löfte att aldrig vidare ägna sig åt film," *Hänt i Veckan*, no. 2, 1970.
280 "The stories about . . .": de Acosta, *Here Lies the Heart*, p. 316.
280 Garbo lived "as others do . . .": "Garbo's Dread of Crowds Actual Mental Suffering," *Los Angeles Times*, 5/8/32.
281 "But you are . . .": Beaton, *The Wandering Years*, p. 257.
281 "he'd turn her upside down . . .": ibid., p. 259.
281 "Are you happy . . .": ibid.
281 "I'm for a law . . .": Sidney Skolsky, "Tintypes," News Syndicate column, 1931 (LC).
282 "I don't hate . . .": Beaton, *Memoirs*, p. 209.
282 A Viking child: de Acosta, *Here Lies the Heart*, p. 318.
282 "If she does go . . .": *Film Weekly*, 6/32, quoted in Haining, *The Legend of Garbo*, p. 168.
282 "If Greta Garbo's portrayal . . .": *The New York Times*, 6/3/32.
283 "A marked shrinkage . . .": "Beverly Bank Closes Doors," *Los Angeles Record*, 6/4/32.
283 "I had in the First National . . .": "Bank Failure Hits Screen Players," *Hollywood Citizen-News*, 6/6/32.
283 Greta transferred personal holdings to bank: "Strangest Holiday," *London Sunday Express*, 6/24/55.
283 Garbo bought risky bank shares: Broman, *Conversations*, p. 152.
284 "Unofficial but reliable . . .": "Film Bank Closing Laid to Depositor," *The New York Times*, 6/7/32.
284 "the bank officials were . . .": "Another Coast Bank Blows," *Variety*, 6/7/32.
284 Garbo identified by MGM as the mystery depositor: Mollie Merrick column, *Los Angeles Times*, 6/16/32.
284 "I'll wire President Hoover . . .": *Motion Picture*, 9/32.
284 "now that she is . . .": "Immigration Dept. Checks on Dietrich and Garbo," *Variety*, 6/14/32.
284 "It's slave labor . . .": Marx, *A Gaudy Spree*, p. 47.
284 "I have never been . . .": GG to Salka Viertel, circa 9/12/32.
285 "PLEASE FORGIVE ME . . .": Mercedes de Acosta telegram to President Hoover, 6/16/32 (NA).
285 Final status of First National Bank: *Beverly Hills Citizen*, 6/32–4/33.
285 Details of 1932 contract: Walker, *Garbo*, pp. 132–33.
285 FN8: Lawrence Quirk, *The Kennedys in Hollywood*. (Dallas: Taylor Publishing, 1996), pp. 69–71.
286 "Somebody joked that . . .": Beaton, *Memoirs*, p. 209.
286 "You will see . . .": *Screen Book*, 11/32.
286 "The Garbo-Mercedes business . . .": Anita Loos to Cecil Beaton, 9/29/32, quoted in Vickers, *Loving Garbo*, p. 4
286 "Not long after this . . .": de Acosta, *Here Lies the Heart*, p. 240.
287 "THANK YOU FOR EVERYTHING . . .": GG telegram to Salka Viertel, 7/28/32.
287 "I can't tell you . . .": " 'No Garbo,' Say Ship's Men; Star Sails," Associated Press, 7/30/32.
287 "Who is Garbo . . .": "How Does Garbo Get That Way?" *Motion Picture*, 10/32.

288   "I am not exactly . . .": "Thousands See Garbo Return," United Press, 8/8/32 (LC).
288   "People don't really . . .": "Garbo at Home Drops Cloak of Mystery," International News Service, 8/8/32 (AMPAS).
288   "I simply have . . .": ibid.
288   "By the way . . .": "Heja, Greta! Ropade Kålle," Dagens Nyheter, 8/9/32.
289   "My mother told me . . .": Riva, Marlene Dietrich, pp. 153–54.
290   "One day I received . . .": Gumpel, Sagor och verklighet, p. 59.
290   "Max arrived at . . .": Sands and Broman, The Divine Garbo, p. 186.
290   "Greta told me . . .": ibid.
290   "He was someone . . .": Laila Nylund to author, 12/8/94.
291   "To Garbo's credit . . .": "Garbo's Homecoming," Screen Book, 5/33.
291   Garbo at Tistad: Broman, Conversations, p. 109.
292   "frequented by hard-boiled women . . .": "Garbo Sees Lurid Paris Night Club," Los Angeles Times, 11/19/32.
292   Europe is dead . . .: GG to Salka Viertel, undated letter circa fall 1932.
292   "The world is absolutely mad . . .": GG to Salka Viertel, 12/31/32.
292   "If only I knew . . .": ibid.
292   Application for Immigration Visa, 1/16/33: USDS.
293   "It is yet undetermined . . .": "Garbo Contract at MG Renewed; May Film Abroad," Variety, 1/24/33.
293   "I don't know . . .": Daum, Walking with Garbo, p. 72.
293   "I liked being . . .": ibid.
294   "It is foolish . . .": Los Angeles Examiner, 3/14/33.
294   "I will take . . .": GG to Salka Viertel, 4/17/33.
295   "an excellent sailor . . .": "Admirers Greet Greta Garbo on Return to U.S.," New York Herald Tribune, 5/1/33.
295   "I am very happy . . .": "Greta Garbo Back, Talking!" Los Angeles Examiner, 5/1/33.

CHAPTER FIFTEEN: Drottning Kristina

299   The queen "was not like . . .": Ingvar Andersson, A History of Sweden (New York: Praeger Publishers, 1956), p. 185.
299   "Despite her sex . . .": "Queen Christina," Horizon, Summer 1967.
299   "Her lips, which were . . .": Stolpe, Christina of Sweden, pp. 41–42.
300   "I tell you . . .": Horizon, Summer 1967.
300   "The free-ranging philosophical . . .": ibid.
301   "Feelings of patriotism . . .": Andrew A. Stomberg, A History of Sweden (New York: Macmillan, 1931), p. 393.
301   "of feminine lure . . .": Reader's Report, 5/2/32 (MGSC).
301   FN4: Inga Gaate to Mauritz Stiller, 2/17/27 (Sjö).
302   "A fate and a life . . .": Inga Gaate to Mauritz Stiller, 2/17/27 (Sjö).
302   Thalberg re Mädchen im Uniform: Viertel, The Kindness of Strangers, p. 175.
303   "Always clever with . . .": "Greta Garbo—Her Life Story," MGM bio, 1939 (AMPAS).
303   "showed an enthusiasm . . .": ibid.
303   "Metro was the best . . .": Viertel, The Kindness of Strangers, p. 169.
303   "I know that I am . . .": GG to Salka Viertel, 9/12/32.
303   Sjöström asked to direct Christina: Variety, 1/20/33.
303   Garbo/MGM correspondence, 3/29/33–4/12/33: Walker, Garbo, p. 133.
304   Studio pressures Garbo re Mamoulian: Rouben Mamoulian to Dr. Ronald Davis, 1980 (SMU).
305   "because, from its box-office . . .": The Hollywood Reporter, 1/13/33.
305   "The crisis came . . .": Quoted in When the Lion Roars (pt. 1), Turner Television, 1992.

306 "If possible, one should . . .": H. M. Harwood to Walter Wanger, 4/24/33 (MGSC).

306 "Unconsciously, she resents . . .": H. M. Harwood to Walter Wanger, 3/23/33 (MGSC).

306 "A queen who shares . . .": H. M. Harwood draft of *Queen Christina*, 4/24/33 (MGSC).

307 "She is a most . . .": *Screenland*, 9/33.

307 "I read the manuscript . . .": John Barrymore to GG, 5/17/33, quoted in Kobler, *Damned in Paradise*, p. 263.

308 "Everyone in Hollywood . . .": "Male Leads Holds Up Garbo Picture," *The Hollywood Reporter*, 6/2/33.

308 "just about everyone . . .": "Olivier Set for Garbo Lead at MGM," *The Hollywood Reporter*, 6/29/33.

308 "If that is true . . .": Rouben Mamoulian to Dr. Ronald Davis, 1980 (SMU).

308 Most actors "don't know . . .": ibid.

309 "Across from them . . .": Jack Larson to author, 10/3/92.

309 "He would sit there . . .": Leatrice Fountain to author, 12/13/92.

309 "did everything he could . . .": Moore, *Silent Star*, p. 208.

310 "I went into . . .": "The Amazing Story Behind Garbo's Choice of Gilbert," *Photoplay*, 1/34.

310 "And then endless . . .": Kanin, *Hollywood*, p. 200.

310 "What they do . . .": Walker, *Garbo*, p. 134.

311 "so they raised . . .": Marion, *Off with Their Heads!*, p. 242.

311 "Three years ago . . .": Billquist, *Garbo*, pp. 203–204.

311 "for this last . . .": Moore, *Silent Star*, p. 208.

311 "both as to the benefits . . .": GG legal notice to MGM, 8/14/33.

311 "the screen personality . . .": *Variety*, 11/24/31.

312 "I don't think . . .": "When Greta Isn't Garbo," *Silver Screen*, 10/39.

312 "the utmost privacy . . .": "The Lowdown," *The Hollywood Reporter*, 9/8/33.

312 "I have been . . .": GG to Hörke Wachtmeister, late summer 1933, quoted in Broman, *Greta Garbo berättar*, p. 135.

312 "Jack Gilbert is back . . .": "Rambling Reporter," *The Hollywood Reporter*, 9/22/33.

312 FN10: Gil Perkins to Dr. Ronald Davis, 1986 (SMU).

313 "How could you . . .": Behrman, *People in a Diary*, p. 151.

313 "There's trouble afoot . . .": "Let Me Tell You About Greta Garbo," unidentified publication, circa 1934 (LC).

314 "Even with these changes . . .": James Wingate to E. J. Mannix, 8/7/33 (MPPDA).

314 "I'm half-done . . .": GG to Hörke Wachtmeister, fall 1933, quoted in Broman, *Greta Garbo berättar*, p. 135.

314 "Directing Miss Garbo . . .": "Rhythm on the Screen," *The New York Times*, 2/11/34.

314 Garbo listened to "None But the Lonely Heart": *Silver Screen*, 10/39.

314 "In California I learned . . .": Daum, *Walking with Garbo*, pp. 133 and 166.

315 "the best thing . . .": "Rambling Reporter," *The Hollywood Reporter*, 11/23/33.

315 "whose affairs were . . .": *Queen Christina* theatrical trailer, 1933.

315 "It seems to us . . .": James Wingate to E. J. Mannix, 8/7/33 (MPPDA).

315 "I think Miss Garbo . . .": Hays Office internal memo, 1/8/34 (MPPDA).

315 "*Queen Christina* is a skillful . . .": *The New York Times*, 12/27/33.

316 "How much of this . . .": Preview report, *The Hollywood Reporter*, 12/11/33.

316 "Hollywood jury" approves film: Memo to E. J. Mannix, 1/11/34 (MPPDA).

316 "Her appearance in *Queen Christina* . . .": Custen, *Bio/Pics: How Hollywood Constructed Public History*, p. 276.

317 "On top of all . . .": GG to Hörke Wachtmeister, January 1934, quoted in Broman, *Greta Garbo berättar*, pp. 136–37.

317 "Garbo is spending . . .": "Rambling Reporter," *The Hollywood Reporter*, 12/5/33.

317 "Greta Garbo and Mamoulian . . .": "Rambling Reporter," *The Hollywood Reporter*, 1/6/34.

317 "Finally, de Acosta went . . .": Riva, *Marlene Dietrich*, p. 158.

317 "She drove Garbo . . .": Mary Anita Loos to author, 3/1/95.
318 "To me, they were . . .": "Garbo Speeding for Hollywood with Mamoulian," unidentified publication, 1/17/34 (AMPAS).
318 "All this fuss . . .": "Garbo and Mamoulian Return," *Los Angeles Times*, 1/18/34.
318 "My son has . . .": *The Hollywood Reporter*, 2/7/34.
318 "It is a gross insult . . .": Col. Einhornung correspondence quoted in Walker, *Garbo*, p. 142.
319 "I am so ashamed . . .": GG to Hörke Wachtmeister, January 1934, quoted in Broman, *Greta Garbo berättar*, p. 136.
319 "It was a strange . . .": "Garbo," *American Scandinavian Review*, 3/38.
320 Gilbert's full-page ad: *The Hollywood Reporter*, 3/20/34.

CHAPTER SIXTEEN: Ars Gratia Artis (Art for MGM's Sake)

321 "Why should the picture . . .": "Tradeviews," *The Hollywood Reporter*, 2/2/34.
321 "It is a great . . .": "Tradeviews," *The Hollywood Reporter*, 2/13/34.
322 "a shack next to . . .": "Rambling Reporter," *The Hollywood Reporter*, 6/12/34.
323 "several friendly gestures . . .": Loy and Kotsilibas-Davis, *Myrna Loy: Being and Becoming*, p. 121.
323 "It seemed a little . . .": Jeanette MacDonald to Joan and Robert C. Franklin, 1959 (CU).
323 "Dear Miss Garbo . . .": "The Lowdown," *The Hollywood Reporter*, 6/20/34.
323 "some inexplicable tension . . .": "Garbo by Her Director," *Film Weekly*, 12/1/34.
323 "some pretty strong . . .": Joseph Breen to I. Thalberg, 4/2/34 (MPPDA).
324 "The latest scarer-awayer . . .": "Rambling Reporter," *The Hollywood Reporter*, 7/7/34.
324 "We've got to find . . .": GG to Hörke Wachtmeister, 7/28/34, quoted in Broman, *Greta Garbo berättar*, p. 170.
324 The celebrity name game: "The Lowdown," *The Hollywood Reporter*, 4/4/34 and 4/6/34.
325 "suave, if less than . . .": James Spada, *More Than a Woman*, (New York: Bantam Books, 1993) p. 90.
325 "a charming, caring . . .": ibid., p. 156.
325 "George Brent-Garbo rumors . . .": "Rambling Reporter," *The Hollywood Reporter*, 9/25/34.
325 "Everyone around one . . .": "Rambling Reporter," *The Hollywood Reporter*, 3/8/35.
325 "I found Greta . . .": "Garbo by Her Director," *Film Weekly*, 12/1/34; and "Garbo," *New York Evening Post*, 12/8/34.
326 "I have repressed . . .": Viertel, *The Kindness of Strangers*, p. 197.
326 Thalberg's opinion of Garbo: DL (courtesy James Curtis).
327 "It may be hard . . .": GG to Hörke Wachtmeister, undated letter, 1935, quoted in Broman, *Greta Garbo berättar*, pp. 171–74.
327 "I believe that Greta . . .": de Acosta, *Here Lies the Heart*, p. 258.
327 FN2: Kate Corbaley to David O. Selznick, 8/21/34 (DOS).
328 "I personally do not . . .": "Historic Facts on *The Life of Jehanne D'Arc*," compiled by Mercedes de Acosta, 8/4/34 (MdA).
328 "Greta complained during . . .": de Acosta, *Here Lies the Heart*, pp. 258–59.
328 Thalberg praised the script: ibid., p. 259.
328 "The following day . . .": ibid., pp. 259–60.
328 "If she has not . . .": M. S. Irani to Mercedes, 1/16/35 (MdA).
329 "Larry Beilenson, Garbo's attorney . . .": Selznick to L. B. Mayer, 10/31/34 (DOS).
329 Publicity re *The Painted Veil*: Script for theatrical trailer, 8/23/34 (MGSC).
329 "The chief fault . . .": *The New York Times*, 11/11/34.
329 "some good character portrayals . . .": MGM Reader's Report, 8/30/32 (MPPDA).
329 "Miss Garbo's new film . . .": *The New York Times*, 12/7/34.
329 "a bad picture . . .": *Variety*, 12/11/34.
330 "In a story . . .": Joseph Breen to L. B. Mayer, 9/25/34 (MPPDA).

330 "She wore long . . .": Viertel, *The Kindness of Strangers*, p. 198.

330 "We did not leave . . .": Dr. James Wingate to J. Breen, 10/23/34 (MPPDA).

330 "This decision was . . .": *Anna Karenina* Study Guide, p. 12 (AMPAS).

331 "with the skill . . .": Flamini, *Thalberg*, p. 262.

331 "How are you . . .": Hugh Walpole to George Cukor, 12/1/34. (Cukor, who was badly in need of money in later years, sold off much of his correspondence and deposited typewritten copies with AMPAS. This letter has been dated 1/21/35—but since it seems to be the impetus for Cukor's letter of 12/25/34, it is likely that the numbers for the date were transposed.)

331 "just couldn't face . . .": G. Cukor to Hugh Walpole, 12/25/34 (AMPAS).

331 FN5: GG to Hörke Wachtmeister, summer 1936, quoted in Broman, *Greta Garbo berätter*, p. 163.

332 David O. Selznick to GG, 1/7/35: DOS.

333 "LOOK LIKE DARK VICTORY . . .": Selznick draft of letter to J. Robert Rubin, 1/15/35 (DOS).

334 "For your information . . .": Selznick to Samuel Marx, 2/22/35 (DOS).

334 "As we see it . . .": Joseph Breen to L. B. Mayer, 3/5/35 (MPPDA).

335 "I was surprised . . .": Selznick to J. Breen, 3/7/35 (MPPDA).

335 "The moment she knew . . .": Reginald Owen to Charles Higham, 1971 (CU).

335 "I had to fight . . .": James Pendleton to author, 5/2/94.

336 "no reasonable objection . . .": Joseph Breen to L. B. Mayer, 3/20/35 (MPPDA).

336 "We had to eliminate . . .": *Anna Karenina* Study Guide, p. 12 (AMPAS).

336 "She was always . . .": Fredric March interview transcript, undated (WWW).

336 "Our reintroduction was . . .": Rathbone, *In and Out of Character*, p. 141.

337 "She has a zest . . .": "Debunking the Garbo Publicity," *The Hollywood Reporter*, 5/31/35.

337 "Formerly, it disturbed her . . .": "Garbo at Close Range," *New York Herald Tribune*, 6/30/35.

337 "She knew just . . .": Bainbridge, *Garbo*, p. 184.

337 "the most pliable . . .": "Greta Garbo—Her Life Story," MGM bio, 1939 (AMPAS).

337 "a very, very simple . . .": Reginald Owen to Charles Higham, 1971 (CU).

337 "I did not have . . .": *Focus on Film*, Summer 1974.

338 "the delicacy and distinction . . .": Behrman, *People in a Diary*, pp. 151–52.

339 1935 contract: Walker, *Garbo*, pp. 148–50.

339 "Betcha Garbo furnishes . . .": "Rambling Reporter," *The Hollywood Reporter*, 5/24/35.

339 "You know, my sister . . .": "Garbo Talks—for Publication," *Movie Classic*, 10/35.

340 "the extremes of agonies . . .": M. S. Irani to Mercedes, 12/31/34 (MdA).

340 "in spite of disappointments . . .": M. S. Irani to Mercedes, 7/10/35 (MdA).

340 "Mercedes d'Acosta is in Europe . . .": "Rambling Reporter," *The Hollywood Reporter*, 7/31/35. (Mercedes did divorce Abram Poole in 1935—although she says she went to Reno.)

340 Mercedes' travel itinerary: 1935 passport and visas (MdA).

341 "Can not believe . . .": GG to Salka Viertel, 7/10/35.

341 "A classic love story . . .": *The Hollywood Reporter*, 6/29/35.

341 "always superbly the apex . . .": *The New York Times*, 8/31/35.

341 "The problem confronting . . .": *Motion Picture Herald*, 7/6/35.

342 "She was content . . .": Broman, *Det Handlar om kärlek*, p. 307.

342 FN10: E. J. Mannix/MGM box-office ledger (AMPAS).

343 "This is my last . . .": GG to Salka Viertel, undated letter circa 1935.

343 "In her letter . . .": de Acosta, *Here Lies the Heart*, p. 268.

343 Mercedes arrives in Sweden: 1935 passport (MdA).

343 "In Hollywood Greta . . .": First draft, *Here Lies the Heart*, p. 578 (MdA).

344 "She made no comment . . .": de Acosta, *Here Lies the Heart*, p. 272.

344 "Yes, I accompanied . . .": Sorella Maria to Mercedes, 11/13/35 (MdA).

344 "So you have had . . .": GG to Salka Viertel, 11/22/35.

344 "Her terrified companion . . .": Beaton, *Memoirs*, p. 117.

CHAPTER SEVENTEEN: Tragic Muse

346 "but I have a friend . . .": Broman, *Det handlar om kärlek*, p. 309.

346 "I am in bed . . .": GG to Salka Viertel, 11/22/35.

346 "Sven is a nice . . .": L. L. Lawrence to L. B. Mayer, 12/3/35, quoted in Walker, *Garbo*, p. 148.

346 GG to L. B. Mayer, 12/8/35: Walker, *Garbo*, p. 148.

347 "On one of . . .": GG to Salka Viertel, undated letter circa 12/35.

347 "pure fabrication . . .": "Miss Garbo Makes Denial," *The New York Times*, 1/13/36.

347 "I do know . . .": Lesley, *Remembered Laughter: The Life of Nöel Coward*, pp. 176–77.

348 GG's last contact with Jack Gilbert: Leatrice Fountain to author, 10/26/92.

348 Details of Gilbert's death: L.A. County death certificate, 1/13/36.

348 "He was always . . .": Quoted in the "Star Treatment" episode of *Hollywood*, Thames Television, 1980.

349 "terribly distressed . . .": L. B. Mayer to GG, 1/10/36, quoted in Walker, *Garbo*, p. 148.

349 "AGREED. THANK YOU . . .": GG to L. B. Mayer, 1/15/36, ibid.

349 "Why must it be . . .": GG to Salka Viertel, undated letter.

349 "I'm worried about you . . .": Sorella Maria to Mercedes de Acosta, 2/6/36 (MdA).

349 "Only a few lines . . .": GG to Salka Viertel, undated letter circa 1936. (Original letter handwritten in capital letters.)

350 "I promised to . . .": "En choklad kartong fylld av minnen, 55 års hågkomster av vånskap och behag," *MånadsJournalen*, no. 9, 9/85.

350 Garbo's new visa: NA.

350 Shipboard press conference: "Garbo Talks; Frosty to Fifi," New York *Daily News*, 5/4/36; "Garbo Speaks; Amazes Press, Surprises Self," *New York Herald Tribune*, 5/4/36.

351 Robert Reud cable to GG: Rough draft, 5/4/37.

351 "The things which . . .": Daum, *Walking with Garbo*, p. 145.

352 "The great weakness . . .": James Hilton to I. Thalberg, 1/17/36 (MGSC).

352 "We have to live . . .": DL (courtesy James Curtis).

352 "Frances Marion was . . .": Lewis, *The Creative Producer*, p. 83.

353 "She had a tender . . .": DL (courtesy James Curtis).

353 "I expected someone . . .": DL (courtesy James Curtis).

353 "An hour sped by . . .": "Garbo and Me," *Picturegoer Supplement*, 9/4/37.

353 "She was polite . . .": Hedda Hopper notes for "Will Garbo Return to the Screen?" (AMPAS).

354 "hot impatience . . .": "Arsenic and Old Directors," *Esquire*, 4/72.

354 "It was apparent . . .": "When Greta Isn't Garbo," *Silver Screen*, 10/39.

354 "I suppose it is . . .": "Problems in Producing Classical Plays as a Screen Director Finds Them," *Kansas City Star*, 5/31/36.

354 "because they felt . . .": McGilligan, *George Cukor: A Double Life*, pp. 113–14.

355 Cukor with the ladies: Jean Howard to author, 11/10/92.

355 "always had been excessively . . .": McGilligan, *George Cukor*, p. 115.

355 "extraordinarily nice . . .": GG to Hörke Wachtmeister, undated letter circa fall 1936, Broman, *Greta Garbo berätter*, p. 176.

355 "Although she teemed . . .": McGilligan, *George Cukor*, pp. 108–109.

355 "government business . . .": G. Cukor to Dr. Ronald Davis, 1977 (SMU).

355 "so-called shenanigans . . .": Hedda Hopper notes for "Will Garbo Return to the Screen?" (AMPAS).

355 Garbo makes a request of Cukor: *New York Herald Tribune*, 7/11/51.

355 "She lives parts . . .": Hedda Hopper notes for "Will Garbo Return to the Screen?" (AMPAS).

356 "She believed in . . .": ibid.

356 "He told me . . .": DL (courtesy James Curtis).

356 "The public is interested . . .": Hedda Hopper notes for "Will Garbo Return to the Screen?" (AMPAS).

356   Garbo sitting in front of the mirror: DL (courtesy James Curtis).

356   "Her periods were . . .": ibid.

357   "but there was also . . .": de Acosta, *Here Lies The Heart*, p. 274.

357   "happy, glowing and inspired . . .": Viertel, *The Kindness of Strangers*, p. 210.

357   "a very sick woman . . .": Quoted in "Garbo," unidentified publication, circa 1937 (USC).

357   "I've got no time . . .": GG to Hörke Wachtmeister, undated letter circa summer 1936, Broman, *Greta Garbo berätter*, p. 183.

357   "It's a funny thing . . .": Quoted in "Garbo," misc. publication, circa 1937 (USC).

357   "an uncanny craftsman . . .": *Picturegoer Supplement*, 9/4/37.

358   Cukor arrested on morals charge: McGilligan, *George Cukor*, pp. 132–33.

358   "could be ruthless . . .": Viertel, *The Kindness of Strangers*, p. 200.

358   "absolutely devastated . . .": DL (courtesy James Curtis).

359   "[Garbo] must never create . . .": Thomas, *Thalberg: Life and Legend*, p. 308.

359   "Everyone in the studio . . .": DL (courtesy James Curtis).

359   "If you're going . . .": Broman, *Conversations*, p. 139.

359   "If I hadn't been . . .": GG to Hörke Wachtmeister, undated letter circa fall 1936, quoted in Broman, *Greta Garbo berätter*, p. 178.

359   "G's contract provided . . .": MGM Legal Dept. memo, 11/5/36.

360   "I was horrified . . .": DL (courtesy James Curtis).

360   "If you can get . . .": ibid.

360   "GRETA GARBO CATCHES FIRE . . .": *New York Herald Tribune*, 12/11/36.

360   "*Camille* never ends . . .": GG to Hörke Wachtmeister, December 1936, quoted in Broman, *Greta Garbo berätter*, p. 182.

361   "THANK YOU FOR YOUR TELEGRAM . . .": GG to Ambassador Bostrom, quoted in Broman, *Greta Garbo berätter*, p. 183.

361   Thalberg thought *Walewska* too complicated: Viertel, *The Kindness of Strangers*, p. 199.

361   "the advisability, or otherwise . . .": Charles R. Metzger conference notes, 5/25/35 (MPPDA).

361   FN9: GG to Hörke Wachtmeister, December 1936, quoted in Broman, *Greta Garbo berätter*, p. 182.

362   "The story deals with . . .": Charles R. Metzger to Joseph Breen, 12/5/35 (MPPDA).

362   Breen responds to screenplay: Joseph Breen to L. B. Mayer, 12/10/35 (MPPDA).

362   FN11: GG to Salka Viertel, 11/22/35.

363   "No more tragically . . .": *Daily Variety*, 12/12/36.

363   "It is because . . .": *The New York Times*, 1/23/37.

363   "This is a guiltily . . .": Mordden, *The Hollywood Studios*, p. 101.

364   1937 Academy Awards: *Inside Oscar*, pp. 78 and 82.

365   "This is prostitution . . .": Beaton, *Memoirs*, p. 248.

365   "the slightest idea . . .": Second draft, *Here Lies the Heart*, p. 495 (MdA).

365   "She seemed a lot . . .": "Garbo a Different Girl, Studio Copper Declares," *New York Post*, 10/30/37.

365   "She had never been . . .": DL (courtesy James Curtis).

365   Clarence Brown secrets Gilbert's daughter on set: Leatrice Fountain to author, 12/13/92.

365   "incredibly tired of being . . .": GG to Hörke Wachtmeister, April 1937, quoted in Broman, *Greta Garbo berätter*, p. 176.

366   Schratter files suit: Los Angeles County court records.

366   "She sat out there . . .": Gil Perkins to Dr. Ronald Davis, 1986 (SMU).

366   FN13: Geisler and Martin, *The Jerry Giesler Story*, p. 208.

367   "the difference between . . .": Schatz, *The Genius of the System*, p. 360.

367   "keep [Garbo] away . . .": Viertel, *The Kindness of Strangers*, p. 217.

367   Melchior Lengyel's story idea: "How Garbo Laughed," *The New York Times*, 1/4/48.

368   "If you can't make . . .": Irving Thalberg to David Lewis (DL).

368   "Madame Garbo's elegant . . .": *The New Yorker*, 11/6/37.

368 *Conquest* listed as a loss: E. J. Mannix/MGM box-office ledger (AMPAS).

368 "DIVORCE RUMOR LINKS . . .": *New York Post*, 10/20/37.

369 "Stoki didn't waste . . .": Bainbridge, *Garbo*, p. 190.

CHAPTER EIGHTEEN: Distant Thunder

370 "I want to thank . . .": GG to Hörke Wachtmeister, undated letter circa fall 1936, quoted in Broman, *Greta Garbo berätter*, p. 176.

370 "G.G., what do . . .": Zierold, *Garbo*, p. 83.

371 "Walter Wanger, who produced . . .": Raymond Daum letter to *The New York Times*, 5/7/95.

371 "Of course she's . . .": Vickers, *Loving Garbo*, p. 68.

371 "Ah, she is beautiful . . .": Daniel, *Stokowski: A Counterpoint of View*, p. 356.

371 "It didn't strike me . . .": ibid., p. 357.

371 "She was magnetic . . .": Lewis, *The Creative Producer*, p. 91.

371 "did not want . . .": Sands and Broman, *The Divine Woman*, p. 188.

371 FN2: Hepburn, *Me: Stories of My Life*, p. 287.

372 "He was a very . . .": Jack Larson to author, 10/3/92.

372 "great imagination and great humor . . .": Leopold Stokowski to Basil Moss, BBC-Radio, 9/2/69.

372 "where Garbo knelt . . .": Reinhardt, *The Genius: A Memoir of Max Reinhardt*, p. 303.

372 "No one close . . .": unidentified publication, 8/13/37, quoted in Daniel, *Stokowski*, p. 359.

373 "Now that Mrs. Stokowski . . .": Louella O. Parsons, *Philadelphia Inquirer*, 1/28/38.

373 "I will not deny . . .": "Friendly Garbo Giggles in First Real Interview; Wed Stokowski? Absurd," *New York Journal American*, 10/23/37.

373 "There is really . . .": "Garbo and Music," United Press story, 10/29/37 (USC).

373 "I guess I cant . . .": Quoted in original draft of "Garbo: Outtakes of a Life," by Jack Larson, 4/20/90.

373 "NO CABLE I MIGHT . . .": Robert Reud telegram to GG, 12/15/37.

374 "I don't look . . .": "Garbo Home for Christmas," *Sydney Morning Herald*, 1/25/38.

374 "We are only good . . .": "Garbo in Male Garb at Sea So She'll Be Alone," United Press story, 12/19/37.

374 "Will I be allowed . . .": "With Garbo at Home," *Screenland*, 4/38.

375 "I do not believe . . .": GG to Salka Viertel, undated letter circa 2/38.

376 Garbo "must be serious": Hedda Hopper, *Los Angeles Times*, 2/14/38.

376 "La Donna Misteriosa": Daniel, *Stokowski*, p. 364.

376 "He certainly must . . .": "Idyl," *Time*, 3/14/38.

377 "I live like . . .": Beaton, *Memoirs*, p. 207; plus p. 110.

377 Garbo's routine at Villa Cimbrone: "A Spanish Shawl for Miss Garbo," *The New Yorker*, 4/23/38.

378 GG re marriage: "Garbo and Stokowski Deny They Will Marry," *The New York Times*, 3/18/38.

378 "DEAR GODDESS . . .": Robert Reud to GG, 3/7/38.

378 "I am really . . .": GG to Hörke Wachtmeister, 3/16/38 (posted 3/17/38), quoted in Broman, *Greta Garbo berätter*, p. 184.

378 "so that Miss Garbo . . .": Daniel, *Stokowski*, p. 365.

378 "I only want . . .": "Not Married and Won't Be, Hounded Garbo Tells Press," *New York Post*, 3/19/38; plus *Philadelphia Evening Bulletin*, 3/17/38, and *New York Herald Tribune*, 3/18/38.

379 "The film star . . .": "Garbo Trip Revives Rumors of Nuptial," *New York Journal American*, 3/22/38.

379 "I was wondering . . .": GG to Hörke Wachtmeister, 4/25/38, quoted in Broman, *Greta Garbo berätter*, pp. 185–86.

379 "I'm a rather . . .": Daum, *Walking with Garbo*, p. 204.

380 "My first post . . .": Broman, *Det handlar om kärlek*, p. 309.

380 Mercedes' itinerary in Europe: 1937/1938 passport and visas (MdA).

380 Mercedes cable to George Cukor, 5/16/38: Cukor Collection (AMPAS).
380 "HE IS AN INSPIRATION . . .": George Cukor to GG, Paramount Pictures telegram form marked "Deferred 6/1/38" (AMPAS).
380 "WONDERFUL PLANS . . .": GG to G. Cukor, 6/7/38 (AMPAS).
380 "The maestro had suffered . . .": "Strangest Holiday," London Sunday Express, 6/24/55.
381 "DIDN'T WE ALWAYS . . .": G. Cukor and S. Viertel to GG, 6/29/38 (AMPAS).
381 "It may amuse . . .": Mercedes to G. Cukor, 7/10/38 (AMPAS).
381 "On days like . . .": Broman, Conversations with Greta Garbo, p. 170.
382 "but they also knew . . .": ibid., p. 171.
382 Sörensen arranges screening of Gösta Berlings saga: London Sunday Express, 6/24/55.
382 "When we set foot . . .": ibid.
382 GG applies for new re-entry visa: NA.
383 "a perfectly enormous . . .": Daniel, Stokowski, p. 370.
383 "exactly the opposite . . .": Richard Rodgers to Kenneth Leigh, 1968 (CU).
383 "You know how . . .": Daniel, Stokowski, p. 370.
383 "GARBO GOES CRUISIN' . . .": New York Daily News, 10/25/38.
383 "I am sending . . .": GG to Salka Viertel, 10/19/38.
384 "Poor Reggie Allen . . .": Daniel, Stokowski, pp. 370–71.
384 "My friend will . . .": GG to Hörke Wachtmeister, 5/39, quoted in Broman, Greta Garbo berätter, pp. 191–92.

CHAPTER NINETEEN: Box-office Poison: Garbo Laughs

385 "WAKE UP! HOLLYWOOD PRODUCERS": The Hollywood Reporter, 5/3/38.
385 Anita Loos re the failure of the studios to support their stars: Anita Loos papers (BU).
385 Salka Viertel re Marie Curie: Viertel, The Kindness of Strangers, p. 218.
386 "Now Aldous is . . .": Bedford, Aldous Huxley: A Biography (Volume One 1894–1939), pp. 359–60.
387 "a boy of the boulevards . . .": Ben Hecht–Charles MacArthur outline, 5/12/38 (MPPDA).
387 Joseph Breen to Bernie Hyman, 5/13/38: MPPDA.
387 "I was on . . .": Nelson, Evenings with Cary Grant, pp. 91–92.
387 FN3: Jacques Deval screenplay, 9/27/38 (MGSC).
388 Story conference notes re Ninotchka, fall 1938: MGSC.
388 "Garbo had a wonderful . . .": "I Go House-Hunting with Greta," London Sunday Express, 6/19/55.
389 "When Lubitsch entered . . .": de Acosta, Here Lies the Heart, pp. 239–40.
389 "I feel it is . . .": Charles Brackett to Joan and Robert C. Franklin, 1959 (CU).
389 "He wasn't just . . .": Eyman, Laughter in Paradise, p. 267.
389 "acceptable under the provisions . . .": Joseph Breen to L. B. Mayer, 5/16/39 (MPPDA).
390 "The class system . . .": Brackett/Wilder/Lubitsch/Reisch script, 4/8/39 (MGSC).
390 MGM employees attempt to sneak onto the Ninotchka set: Hedda Hopper, Los Angeles Times, 5/27/39.
390 "Dear Lady . . .": GG to Hörke Wachtmeister, 5/39, quoted in Broman, Greta Garbo berätter, pp. 191–92.
391 "AM HAPPY TO SAY . . .": Robert Reud to GG, 5/5/39.
391 "Now you go away . . .": "Garbo, As Seen by Her Director," The New York Times, 10/22/39.
391 "the actors all . . .": Joseph Newman to Dr. Ronald Davis, (SMU).
391 "I remember, one morning . . .": Beaton, Memoirs of the 40's, p. 239.
392 "I love to work . . .": "Hollywood's Old Settler," New York Post, 10/3/39.
392 "I wondered if . . .": Kanin, Hollywood, p. 105.
392 "In spite of . . .": Douglas and Arthur, See You at The Movies, p. 89.
392 "the most important . . .": ibid.
392 "In the scene . . .": ibid.

393 "I convinced her . . .": *New York Post*, 10/3/39.

393 "a vision of . . .": Hauser, *Treasury of Secrets*, pp. 310–311.

393 "I made it . . .": ibid.

394 "I could see . . .": Baldwin and Gardine, *Billy Baldwin: An Autobiography*, p. 299.

394 "That howl of discontent . . .": Hedda Hopper, *Los Angeles Times*, 8/25/39.

394 "as silent as . . .": Rathbone, *In and Out of Character*, p. 143.

394 GG talks to Jean Renoir re St. Francis: Jack Larson to author, 10/3/92.

395 "She was *so* excited . . .": *New York Post*, 10/3/39.

395 "He had this very serious . . .": Eyman, *Laughter in Paradise*, p. 271.

396 "a Garbo whose . . .": *The Hollywood Reporter*, 10/7/39.

396 "*Ninotchka* finds . . .": *The New York Times*, 11/10/39.

396 "We could easily . . .": W. G. Van Schmus to Joseph Breen, quoted in Breen letter to Bernie Hyman, 12/4/39 (MPPDA).

397 "for some reason . . .": Kanin, *Hollywood*, p. 105.

397 *Ninotchka* box-office: E. J. Mannix/MGM box-office ledger (AMPAS).

397 "I was just . . .": GG to Hörke Wachtmeister, 10/7/39, quoted in Broman, *Greta Garbo berättar*, p. 208.

397 The Gustafsons arrive in New York: Manifest of Alien Passengers, SS *Stavangerfjord*, 11/3/39 (NA).

398 "I still don't know . . .": GG to Hörke Wachtmeister, 11/14/39, quoted in Broman, *Greta Garbo berättar*, p. 211.

398 "Garbo was uncommunicative . . .": Maxwell, *R.S.V.P.*, p. 241.

399 "That skinny Swedish actress . . .": "The Great Garbo," *People*, 4/30/90.

399 "ardent admirer, 'protector' . . .": GG to "Darling Doc" Hauser, undated letter circa 1940.

399 "Life has been rather. . .": Gaylord Hauser to Mercedes, 11/9/39 (MdA).

399 "But as usual . . .": GG to Hörke Wachtmeister, 10/7/39, quoted in Broman, *Conversations*, p. 186. (Original comment written in English.)

399 "to travel to India . . .": ibid., p. 162.

399 A picnic in Tujunga Canyon: Jayakar, *Krishnamurti: A Biography*, p. 88; Anita Loos manuscript notes (BU); Hedda Hopper, *Los Angeles Times*, 12/9/39; and *Christopher Isherwood Diaries, Volume One: 1939–60* (New York: HarperCollins, 1996), pp. 49–51.

400 "As I became familiar . . .": Broman, *Conversations*, p. 174.

400 "She was naturally . . .": "When Life in Los Angeles Was a Cabaret," *Buzz*, 10/91.

400 "spent a great deal . . .": "Garbo Finds Herself," *Photoplay*, 3/42.

400 FN11: Anita Loos manuscript notes (BU).

401 "before her butterfly . . .": *Buzz*, 10/91.

CHAPTER TWENTY: A Celluloid Grave

402 Garbo's feelings about not doing her "bit" for Finland: GG to Hörke Wachtmeister, 3/15/40.

402 "People go like mad . . .": Daum, *Walking with Garbo*, pp. 58 and 164.

402 "There are always . . .": ibid., p. 164.

402 "Although an interesting . . .": Lewis, *The Creative Producer*, p. 164.

403 Wenner-Gren suspected of carrying munitions: FBI Report, 7/19/40, L.A. file #65-1824.

403 "They certainly feel . . .": GG to Hörke Wachtmeister, 3/15/40, quoted in Broman, *Greta Garbo berättar*, p. 212.

403 "The family is . . .": ibid.

404 "I read the papers . . .": GG to Hörke Wachtmeister, 4/22/40, quoted in Broman, *Greta Garbo berättar*, p. 213.

404 Garbo makes the first step toward citizenship: Preliminary Declaration of Intention, 6/10/40 (NA).

404 "Victor Saville, Sidney Franklin . . .": Higham, *Merchant of Dreams*, p. 301.

404 "On July 16 . . .": ibid., p. 302.

405 "wasn't intelligent enough . . .": Leif Leifland to author, 5/24/93.

405 "My life is . . .": GG to Hörke Wachtmeister, 8/29/40, quoted in Broman, *Greta Garbo berätter*, p. 214.

405 Alien Registration Form, 9/4/40: INS.

406 "a great act . . .": Hedda Hopper, *Los Angeles Times*, 10/20/40.

406 Declaration of Intention (#102407), 10/29/40: NA.

406 A change of tone in Reud's letters: Robert Reud to GG, 11/8/40.

406 Garbo and *A Woman's Face*: MGSC.

406 "I've had a cold . . .": GG to Hörke Wachtmeister, 12/40, quoted in Broman, *Greta Garbo berätter*, p. 215.

407 "quiet and pleasant . . .": Axel Wenner-Gren diary, 1/41 (courtesy Leif Leifland).

407 "My guess . . .": Leif Leifland to author, 5/24/93.

407 "Now that Garbo . . .": Hedda Hopper, *Los Angeles Times*, 1/15/41.

407 "Fur will fly . . .": Hedda Hopper, *Los Angeles Times*, 1/25/41.

408 "It is strange . . .": Gilbert, *Opposite Attraction*, pp. 240–41.

408 "and she would . . .": ibid.

408 "It never pleased me . . .": Beaton, *Memoirs*, p. 258.

408 "Anita [Loos] couldn't . . .": Carey, *Anita Loos: A Biography*, p. 192.

409 "The destruction of . . .": I. Thalberg to Nicholas Schenck, undated memo circa spring 1933 (courtesy James Curtis).

409 "I remember telling . . .": Bergman and Burgess, *Ingrid Bergman: My Story*, pp. 91–92.

409 "At one point . . .": "Saga of Greta Lovisa Gustafsson," *The New York Times*, 9/5/65.

409 "REGARDING BIRTH DATE . . .": Robert Reud telegram to GG, 5/10/41.

410 "It seems so odd . . .": GG to Hörke Wachtmeister, 5/31/41, quoted in Broman, *Greta Garbo berätter*, p. 213.

410 "As nothing divides . . .": Viertel, *The Kindness of Strangers*, p. 252.

410 "Due to the fact . . .": Joseph Breen to Bernie Hyman, 6/17/41 (MPPDA).

410 "In those days . . .": Reinhardt, *The Genius: A Memoir of Max Reinhardt*, p. 104.

410 FN3: Gray Reisfield to author, 2/3/97.

411 "I've started work . . .": GG letter to Hörke Wachtmeister, 6/23/41, quoted in Broman, *Greta Garbo berätter*, p. 217.

411 Melvyn Douglas's relationship with L. B. Mayer: Scobie, *Center Stage: Helen Gahagan Douglas*, p. 108.

411 "One gown, which . . .": Hedda Hopper, *Los Angeles Times*, 7/22/41.

412 "I don't know why . . .": Joseph Ruttenberg, AFI Oral History, 1972.

412 "Every time that . . .": ibid.

413 "I'm very sorry . . .": Paris, *Garbo*, p. 381.

413 "Garbo was exceptionally . . .": Robert Sterling to author, 10/14/92.

414 "If she starts . . .": "She Works with Garbo," *Lion's Roar*: vol. 1, no. 3, 1941.

414 "I'll soon be . . .": GG to Hörke Wachtmeister, 8/20/41, quoted in Broman, *Greta Garbo berätter*, p. 217.

414 "No one had remembered . . .": Kenneth Brown to Hedda Hopper, 10/30/55 (AMPAS).

414 "They went for . . .": Gilbert, *Opposite Attraction*, p. 241.

415 "She rolled up . . .": ibid.

415 "The most beautifully . . .": ibid., pp. 241–42.

415 "sang her entire . . .": Hedda Hopper, *Los Angeles Times*, 10/24/41.

415 "I tell her . . .": Gilbert, *Opposite Attraction*, p. 242.

416 "All laughed quite . . .": Ruth Gordon to George Cukor, 11/8/41; plus undated letter (AMPAS).

416 "a daring piece . . .": *Variety*, 10/22/41.

416 "I have finished . . .": GG to Hörke Wachtmeister, 10/24/41, quoted in Broman, *Greta Garbo berätter*, p. 220.

416 "rents are likely to . . .": ibid.

416 "You said I would . . .": GG to Robert Reud, 10/24/41.

416 "I learned that . . .": William A. Orr to Leigh L. Nettleton/INS Travel Control Division, 11/5/41.

417 "Her pictures are . . .": Hedda Hopper, *Los Angeles Times*, 12/14/41.

417 "[At] no time . . .": Production Code Administration interoffice memo, 11/26/41 (MPPDA).

417 Gottfried Reinhardt re Archbishop Spellman: Reinhardt, *The Genius*, p. 104.

418 "There is surprisingly . . .": "Film Ban Is Balm to Studio," *New York World-Telegram*, 12/10/41.

418 The campaign against *Two-Faced Woman*: *Time*, 12/22/41.

418 "Every last one . . .": Reinhardt, *The Genius*, p. 104.

419 "Having seen the original . . .": *New York Herald Tribune*, 1/11/42.

419 "For a woman . . .": Walker, *Garbo*, p. 161.

419 "The wickedness in . . .": Cecelia Ager, *P.M. Daily*, quoted in Conway, McGregor, and Ricci, *The Films of Greta Garbo*, p. 154.

420 "My father used to . . .": Douglas Fairbanks to author, 12/10/92.

420 "She shouldn't have . . .": Dick Shepherd. *Elizabeth: The Life and Career of Elizabeth Taylor* (Garden City, NY: Doubleday & Co., 1974), p. 30.

420 "People who've been . . .": Paris, *Garbo*, p. 434.

420 *Two-Faced Woman* box-office: E. J. Mannix/MGM box-office ledger (AMPAS).

420 "To adults she is . . .": *Dallas Morning News*, 9/9/41.

420 "Even while we . . .": Higham and Greenberg, *The Celluloid Muse*, p. 60.

421 Ruth Gordon re Valentina: "Ruthgar" to G. Cukor, 7/14/53 (AMPAS).

421 "a cosmopolitan of immense . . .": Niven, *Bring On The Empty Horses*, p. 187.

421 "Valentina was not . . .": Vickers, *Loving Garbo*, p. 83.

421 "as soon as George . . .": Joseph Lombardo to Milton Greene, 6/22/94.

422 "we ate our diamonds . . .": Vickers, *Loving Garbo*, p. 81.

423 "she has an inate . . .": "Garbo Stepping Out," *Newark Evening News*, 1/29/42.

424 Garbo unsure: Hedda Hopper, *Los Angeles Times*, 6/1/42.

424 "A series of . . .": Dragonette, *Faith Is a Song: The Odyssey of an American Artist*, pp. 252–54.

CHAPTER TWENTY-ONE: Transition: The War Years

425 "As long as . . .": Hedda Hopper, *Los Angeles Times*, 2/16/42.

425 "It was a most . . .": James Pendleton to author, 5/2/94.

425 Garbo and Elsie de Wolfe Mendl: Crocker, *That's Hollywood*, unpublished memoir plus essay on Lady Mendl (AMPAS).

426 "Axel [Wenner-]Gren wrote . . .": GG to Gayelord Hauser, undated letter circa early 1940s.

426 "Young lady, you won't . . .": "Garbo's Collection and a van Gogh Are to Be Sold," *The New York Times*, 7/19/90.

427 "Without turning around . . .": Sam Green to author, 2/9/93.

427 "Just before he painted . . .": "Garbo's Refuge," *The New York Times*, 9/2/90.

427 Garbo did not display her art: James Pendleton to author, 5/2/94.

427 FN4: David O. Selznick to Mel Dinelli, 4/5/46 (DOS).

428 "It was a moving . . .": Viertel, *The Kindness of Strangers*, p. 268.

428 "Perhaps Garbo's enthusiasm . . .": ibid.

428 Garbo refused the buy-out: Brownlow, *The Parade's Gone By*, p. 147.

428 "She simply existed . . .": DL.

428 Garbo loses her dressing room to Lana Turner: Guilaroff and Griffin, *Crowning Glory*, pp. 132–33.

429 "the ideal companion . . .": Niven, *Bring on the Empty Horses*, p. 187.

429 "I suppose everybody . . .": "When Life in Los Angeles was a Cabaret," *Buzz*, 10/91.

429 "a flawlessly cut . . .": "The Secret Life of Greta," by Jhan Robbins, *This Week*, 10/4/59.

429 "George Schlee overpowered . . .": Joseph Lombardo to Milton Greene, 6/22/94.

429 "one of the most . . .": Betty Spiegel to author, 6/2/93.

430 "Valentina never liked . . .": *W*, 7/26/74.

430 "I love her . . .": *Time*, 10/15/64.

430 "I think Valentina . . .": Betty Estevez to author, 5/3/94.

430 "We walked toward . . .": Gilbert Roland, unpublished memoir, quoted in "A Brief Affair," *Los Angeles Times*, 12/11/95.

430 "I desired her . . .": ibid.

430 "He answered the door . . .": Vickers, *Cecil Beaton*, p. 326.

431 "We were together . . .": Gilbert Roland unpublished memoir, quoted in the *Los Angeles Times*, 12/11/95.

431 Details of Garbo/Roland correspondence: Scott Harrison to author, 9/9/94 and 10/21/94.

431 "This is going . . .": GG to Gilbert Roland, 10/6/43.

431 Roland's family heirloom: Scott Harrison to author, 9/9/94.

432 Crocker hired a clipping service: Goodman, *The Fifty-Year Decline and Fall of Hollywood*, p. 264.

432 The price of Swedish neutrality: Wm. L. Shirer, *The Challenge of Scandinavia* (Boston: Little, Brown & Co., 1955), p. 114.

432 "were anxious to show . . .": Leif Leifland to author, 3/30/42.

433 "I wonder how . . .": "En choklad kartong fylld av minnen, 55 års hågkomster av vänskap och behag," *MånadsJournalen*, 9/85.

433 "For the rest . . .": Higham, *Merchant of Dreams*, p. 290.

433 "As a member . . .": Stevenson, *A Man Called Intrepid*, p. 58.

433 "I would have . . .": Broman, *Conversations*, p. 191.

434 Garbo and Dag Hammarskjöld: Daum, *Walking with Garbo*, p. 175.

434 "I thought this . . .": Hepburn, *Me: Stories of My Life*, p. 224.

434 FN8: Kanin, *Hollywood*, p. 164.

435 "He went on . . .": Viertel, *The Kindness of Strangers*, p. 271.

435 "Greta Garbo has . . .": Hedda Hopper, *Los Angeles Times*, 5/21/43.

435 "The California suggestion . . .": George Bernard Shaw to Gabriel Pascal, 9/1/38, quoted in *Bernard Shaw: Collected Letters 1926–1950*, p. 508.

435 "should be a . . .": Hedda Hopper, *Los Angeles Times*, 11/7/38.

435 "It was finally . . .": G. B. Shaw to Marjorie Deans, 3/22/43, quoted in *Bernard Shaw: Collected Letters 1926–1950*, p. 666.

435 "That was the first . . .": Beaton, *Memoirs*, p. 283.

436 "Garbo is simple . . .": "This is Garbo," *Collier's*, March 1952.

436 "After two-thirds of . . .": Viertel, *The Kindness of Strangers*, p. 277.

436 "I had been . . .": ibid.

436 "The Garbo-Lester Cowan situation . . .": Hedda Hopper, *Los Angeles Times*, 8/3/44.

437 "and also offered . . .": Pujol and West, *Operation Garbo*, p. 94.

437 Garbo surprised by a burglar: "Garbo in a Slide Down a Rain Pipe Foils House Thief," *Los Angeles Times*, 7/9/44.

438 "Greta looked up . . .": *MånadsJournalen*, 9/85.

438 "Spent my time . . .": GG to Hörke Wachtmeister, 6/5/45, quoted in Broman, *Greta Garbo berätter*, p. 221.

438 "Your friend, Miss . . .": G. Cukor to W. S. Maugham, 11/3/45 (AMPAS).

438 "In the meanwhile . . .": ibid.

439 "I think the fair . . .": W. S. Maugham to G. Cukor, 11/10/45 (AMPAS).

439 "Garbo was pretty . . .": G. Cukor to W. S. Maugham, 11/21/45 (AMPAS).

439 "I have been . . .": GG to Hörke Wachtmeister, 12/16/45, quoted in Broman, *Greta Garbo berätter*, p. 223.

CHAPTER TWENTY-TWO: Comeback

443 "I don't believe . . .": Louella O. Parsons, *Los Angeles Examiner*, undated column circa late 1945/early 1946 (AMPAS).

443 "Greta Garbo? . . .": Ruth Gordon, *Ruth Gordon: An Open Book*. (Garden City, NY: Doubleday and Co., 1980), p. 357.

443 Jimmie Fidler column circa 1945: contained in Garbo's INS file.

443 "had better offer . . .": INS correspondence, 12/45–5/46.

444 "She reminds me . . .": Bainbridge, *Garbo*, p. 229.

444 "Dearest, darling Hörke . . .": GG to Hörke Wachtmeister, 2/6/46, quoted in Broman, *Greta Garbo berätter*, p. 224.

444 "At the sight . . .": Cecil Beaton diary, 3/15/46, quoted in Beaton, *Memoirs*, p. 104.

445 "An historian should . . .": Vickers, *Cecil Beaton*, p. xvii.

445 "No advice or . . .": Beaton, *The Wandering Years*, p. 254.

445 "What about getting . . .": Cecil Beaton diary, 1/7/30, quoted in Vickers, *Cecil Beaton*, p. 131.

445 "always seemed to . . .": Beaton, *The Wandering Years*, p. 254.

445 "Garbo picked up . . .": ibid., p. 258.

445 "Suddenly the dream . . .": ibid., p. 259.

446 "She has a sense . . .": Cecil Beaton, *Cecil Beaton's Scrapbook* (London: Batsford, 1937), p. 55.

446 "Then she had been . . .": Beaton, *Memoirs*, pp. 104–105. (It is interesting to note that the original diary entry, dated 3/15/46, contained much less detail.)

446 "We 'steppe outte' . . .": ibid., p. 110.

446 "At first she . . .": ibid., p. 121.

447 1946 re-entry visa: USDS.

447 "Phew! I've been . . .": Beaton, *Memoirs*, p. 120.

447 "I think the . . .": Joseph Newman to Dr. Ronald Davis, 1984 (SMU).

448 "The high command . . .": Viertel, *Dangerous Friends: At Large with Huston and Hemingway in the Fifties*, p. 19.

448 FBI investigates the Viertels: Salka Viertel/FBI file, 1942–1955.

448 FBI report 4/22/43 on Salka: Viertel/FBI file.

449 "I have promised . . .": *StockholmsTidningen*, 7/18/46.

449 "She didn't stay long . . .": Laila Nylund to author, 3/2/95.

450 "She was always . . .": ibid.

450 "The Swedes have . . .": ibid., 3/20/95.

450 "I think she was . . .": ibid.

450 "You never saw . . .": ibid.

450 FN2: Jean Howard to author, 11/10/92.

451 "I always dreamt . . .": "Hon fick avgiva ett heligt löfte att aldrig vidare ägna sig åt film," *Hänt i Veckan*, no. 2, 1970.

451 "And then she . . .": *Hänt i Veckan*, no. 2, 1970.

451 "knowing no one . . .": Beaton, *Memoirs*, p. 192.

451 GG correspondence with Hörke Wachtmeister, 1941–1946, quoted in Broman, *Greta Garbo berätter*, pp. 220–24.

451 "I don't know . . .": Sven Broman to Marie Peterson, 11/3/95.

452 "Dockside roofs and windows . . .": "Greta Garbo Sails for U.S.," *The New York Times*, 8/25/46.

452 "at first tolerant . . .": "Greta Garbo Back—Not So Elusive Now," *The New York Times*, 9/4/46.

452 "could hardly believe . . .": Beaton, *Memoirs*, p. 122.

452 "I think he bought . . .": Paris, *Garbo*, p. 402.

453 "She said she . . .": Beaton, *Memoirs*, p. 145.

453 "As always, he was . . .": Viertel, *The Kindness of Strangers*, p. 299.

453 Garbo's real estate investments: Based on information from the Los Angeles County Assessor's Office and the archives of the *Milwaukee Journal*.

454 "[She] is the . . .": Hayman, *John Gielgud*, p. 156.

454 "I spoke to Hayward . . .": GG to Salka Viertel, undated letter, 1947.

454 "I SHOULD LIKE . . .": David O. Selznick to Daniel O'Shea, 4/19/47 (DOS).

455 "If there was . . .": Beaton, *Memoirs*, p. 272.

455 "It was like . . .": "Garbo: Outtakes of a Life," *The Washington Post*, 4/22/90.

455 "Why, when and where . . .": *London Daily Mail*, 8/18/47.

455 Details re the will of Edgar H. Donne: "Garbo Accepts Hermit Legacy to 'Dream Girl,' " *Los Angeles Times*, 7/5/47.

456 "She was just roaring . . .": Douglas Fairbanks to author, 12/10/92.

456 Garbo's problem with sleeping pills: Betty Estevez to author, 5/3/94.

456 "bared her soul . . .": Payn and Morley, *The Nöel Coward Diaries*, p. 91.

456 "It was no good . . .": Cecil Beaton to GG, 10/5/47, quoted in Vickers/Beaton bio, p. 316.

457 FBI efforts to link the Viertels to Communist activities: Viertel/FBI file.

457 "She wasn't a Communist . . .": Jack Larson to author, 10/3/92.

458 "[Schlee] wants to have . . .": Peter Cusick to G. Cukor, 10/17/47 (AMPAS).

458 "Her practical side . . .": Cecil Beaton diary, 11/3/47, quoted in Vickers, *Cecil Beaton*, p. 317.

458 "whose name would . . .": Hedda Hopper, *Los Angeles Times*, 7/25/46.

458 "as regal as . . .": Ram Gopal to Mercedes, 5/22/57 (MdA).

458 "My attitude to women . . .": Cecil Beaton diary, 10/9/23, quoted in Vickers, *Loving Garbo*, p. 45.

459 "they frighten and nauseate . . .": Cecil Beaton diary, 2/23/30, quoted in Vickers, *Loving Garbo*, p. 47.

459 "He can't do . . .": Nicholas Meredith Turner to author, 2/8/93.

459 "Why don't you . . .": Beaton, *Memoirs*, p. 274.

459 "Cecil definitely was . . .": Jack Larson to author, 10/3/92.

459 "With frozen face . . .": Vidal, *Palimpsest*, p. 299.

459 "I knew Cecil . . .": Sam Green to author, 2/9/93.

460 "Everyone in Hollywood . . .": Vickers, *Loving Garbo*, p. 49.

460 "She really liked . . .": Jean Howard to author, 11/10/92.

460 "Perhaps she is attracted . . .": "Garbo," *Sight and Sound*, 4/54.

460 "Don't be a dope . . .": Vickers, *Cecil Beaton*, p. 319.

461 "So you are . . .": ibid.

461 "I couldn't ever . . .": Beaton, *Memoirs*, p. 205.

461 "But just lately . . .": ibid., p. 108.

461 "It was such . . .": ibid., p. 216.

461 "To overcome her . . .": ibid., pp. 216–17.

461 "She goes under . . .": Tennessee Williams to Donald Windham, 7/15/47, quoted in *Tennessee Williams' Letters to Donald Windham 1940–1965*, p. 201.

462 "We sat in the . . .": Williams, *Tennessee Williams: Memoirs*, pp. 138–39.

462 "We talked about . . .": Beaton, *Memoirs*, p. 214.

462 "You must realize . . .": ibid., p. 209.

463 "Greta said there . . .": Cecil Beaton diary, 12/11/47, quoted in Vickers, *Cecil Beaton*, p. 321.

463 "Mercedes, unable to hide . . .": Beaton, *Memoirs*, pp. 222–23.

463 "Greta has a paralyzing . . .": ibid., p. 245.

463 "Typically, when on . . .": Vickers, *Loving Garbo*, p. 154.

463 "The little man . . .": Beaton, *Memoirs*, p. 232.

463 "Oh, I've said . . .": ibid., p. 234.

463 "He's been such . . .": ibid., p. 256.

464 Beaton encounters Schlee at the theater: Vickers, *Cecil Beaton*, p. 328.

464 *Ninotchka* in Italy: "Garbo Wins," *Motion Picture Herald*, 5/1/48.

464 "If she doesn't . . .": Beaton, *Memoirs*, p. 248.

464 "the most suspicious . . .": ibid.

465 "When we lived . . .": Vickers, *Loving Garbo*, p. 121.

465 "It's such a waste . . .": Beaton, *Memoirs*, p. 251.

465 "Each lives a life . . .": ibid., p. 259.

465 "I was on . . .": ibid., pp. 267–68.

466 Beaton tampered with journal entry: Vickers, *Cecil Beaton*, p. 329.

466 "Olympian while the lives . . .": Beaton, *Memoirs*, p. 212.

466 "A noise of . . .": ibid., p. 271.

466 "Well, well . . .": ibid., p. 288.

466 "It had never . . .": Beaton, *Memoirs*, pp. 299–300.

467 "I know if . . .": ibid., p. 292.

467 "looking better than . . .": Louella O. Parsons, *Los Angeles Examiner*, 4/48.

467 "I read the story . . .": GG to Salka Viertel, undated letter, 1948.

467 "What is back . . .": Peter Cusick to G. Cukor, 4/22/48 (AMPAS).

467 "*George Sand* could make . . .": Beaton, *Memoirs*, p. 212.

468 "just an unfurnished . . .": ibid.

CHAPTER TWENTY-THREE: Man Proposes . . . God Disposes

469 "If I disliked . . .": Beaton, *Memoirs*, p. 210.

469 "I appeared so old . . .": ibid., p. 284.

469 "Even if the public . . .": ibid., p. 211.

469 "It is impossible . . .": ibid., p. 291.

469 "I have been . . .": Salka Viertel to G. Cukor, 8/26/48 (AMPAS).

470 "There was a . . .": ibid.

470 "an utterly impossible . . .": ibid.

470 "You can have . . .": ibid.

471 "The one thing . . .": ibid.

471 *George Sand* deal memo, 8/4/48: WWW.

471 "Greta Garbo, the woman . . .": "Garbo Signs for Picture," *Los Angeles Times*, 8/19/48.

471 *George Sand* contract, 8/26/48: WWW.

471 "Greta is impatient . . .": Salka Viertel to G. Cukor, 9/28/48 (AMPAS).

471 "I thought it . . .": G. Cukor to W. Wanger, 9/13/48 (WWW).

472 Schlee convinced Wanger couldn't make a deal without him: G. Schlee telegram to W. Wanger, 9/15/48 (WWW).

472 "HAVE [JEAN] ANOUILH . . .": ibid.

473 "Don't you think . . .": G. Cukor to W. Wanger, 9/13/48 (WWW).

473 "My great concern . . .": W. Wanger to G. Cukor, 9/27/48 (WWW).

473 Garbo's new Declaration of Intention (#133227), 9/9/48: NA.

474 "There's not much point . . .": Cecil Beaton to GG, 8/24/48, quoted in Vickers, *Loving Garbo*, p. 145.

474 Beaton's covert love letters: Vickers, *Cecil Beaton*, p. 335.

474 "Do you swear . . .": Vickers, *Loving Garbo*, p. 148.

474 Letter of Agreement, 3/15/49: WWW.

474 "so that we can . . .": W. Wanger to G. Schlee, 2/21/49 (WWW).

476 " 'Irving,' he said . . .": Irving Rapper to Charles Higham, 1972 (CU).

477 "I remember she . . .": James Wong Howe to Charles Higham, 1971 (CU).

477 "The minute the cameras . . .": ibid.

477 "She seemed timid . . .": Hedda Hopper notes for "Will Garbo Return to the Screen?" (AMPAS).

478 "Greta admitted that . . .": Beaton, *The Strenuous Years*, p. 60.

478 "barely a script . . .": Bernstein, *Walter Wanger: Hollywood Independent*, p. 261.

478 Details of Wanger International financial setup: WWW.

479 Logan offered *La Duchesse*: Logan, *My Up And Down, In And Out Life*, p. 315.

479   "After a rather . . .": Henry Henigson to W. Wanger, 7/19/49 (WWW).

480   "Here she discovered . . .": Beaton, *The Strenuous Years*, p. 57.

480   "Signor Rizzoli . . .": "Garbo-Mason Film Meets Cash Hitch," *London Daily Express*, 9/2/49.

480   "The Greta Garbo–James Mason . . .": Hedda Hopper, *Los Angeles Times*, 9/8/49.

481   "WISH TO ADVISE . . .": Abe Lastfogel telegram to W. Wanger, 9/8/49 (WWW).

481   "BECAUSE IT IS . . .": Joseph Breen telegram to W. Wanger, 9/10/49 (WWW).

481   "Visibly indignant . . .": "Greta Garbo Annoyed," *London Daily Mail*, 9/10/49.

481   "no longer glamorous . . .": "Antagonism Seething Between Garbo, Italians," *Los Angeles Times*, 9/12/49.

482   "SCHLEE'S POSITION SINCE . . .": W. Wanger telegram to Roy Myers, undated communication on Western Union stationery (a handwritten note indicates that the wire was dictated but not sent); WWW.

482   New agreement between Garbo and Wanger, 9/22/49: WWW.

482   "She is now . . .": "Garbo in New Mystery: Come-Back is Put Off," unidentified publication (British Film Institute).

483   "her sufferings from . . .": Beaton, *The Strenuous Years*, pp. 56–57.

483   "As he tried . . .": Cecil Beaton diary, 10/2/49, quoted in Vickers, *Loving Garbo*, pp. 171–72.

483   "a person possessed . . .": Beaton, *The Strenuous Years*, pp. 61–62.

484   "I was very much surprised . . .": W. Wanger to Jules Stein, 1/3/50 (WWW).

485   "truthful understanding . . .": W. Wanger to GG, 2/17/50 (WWW).

485   "What happened . . .": Nicholas Meredith Turner to author, 2/8/93.

485   "People who have . . .": Niven, *Bring On the Empty Horses*, p. 187.

CHAPTER TWENTY-FOUR: Introducing Miss Brown

487   "The result of . . .": "That Gustafsson Girl," *Photoplay*, 4/30. (The 1928 date in the text is based on the fact that the source for this quote was Garbo's 1928 interview with Ruth Biery.)

487   "two faces, one for . . .": "Garbo Back; Refuses to Discuss Own Life," *The New York Times*, 10/8/38.

487   "She is decidedly . . .": "Adrian Answers 20 Questions on Garbo," *Photoplay*, 9/35.

487   "Greta Garbo the screen star . . .": Walker, *The Celluloid Sacrifice*, p. 112.

488   "We never travel . . .": Betty Spiegel to author, 6/2/93.

488   "It was just . . .": Sam Green to author, 2/9/93.

488   Sven Broman re "Harriet Brown": Broman, *Conversations*, p. 234.

488   Cecil Beaton re Harriet Löwenhjelm: Beaton, *Memoirs*, pp. 112–13.

489   "troubled by a dream . . .": de Acosta, *Here Lies the Heart*, p. 254.

489   "She didn't impress . . .": Patrice Hellberg to author, 9/22/93.

489   "Miss Brown . . .": Zierold, *Garbo*, p. 99.

490   "What she had . . .": "Reinhardt: The Son Also Rises," *Los Angeles Times*, 3/21/82.

490   "She was the best . . .": Sam Green to author, 2/9/93.

490   "I think she thought . . .": Betty Spiegel to author, 6/2/93.

490   "It was understood . . .": Sam Green to author, 2/9/93.

490   FN3: Betty Estevez to author, 5/3/94.

491   "She was charming . . .": James Pendleton to author, 5/2/94.

491   "To talk to . . .": Walker, *Garbo*, p. 170.

491   "Geler Lilla . . .": GG to Gayelord Hauser, undated letter.

491   "always waits mischievously . . .": "Let Me Tell You About Greta Garbo," *Modern Screen*, 3/34.

491   " 'Oh,' she said . . .": Dragonette, *Faith Is a Song*, p. 254.

491   "only the things . . .": Beaton, *Memoirs*, p. 112.

491   FN4: Daum, *Walking with Garbo*, p. 186.

492   "Any mortal being . . .": "No Man is Safe from Her Witchery," *London Sunday Express*, 7/3/55.

492   "Parents make it . . .": Beaton, *Memoirs*, pp. 227–28.

492   "in general . . .": Vickers, *Cecil Beaton*, p. 325; and *Loving Garbo*, p. 118.

492   "If the press . . .": Goodman, *The Fifty-Year Decline and Fall of Hollywood*, p. 293.

492   "Have you got . . .": Vickers, *Loving Garbo*, p. 182.

492   "I think of her . . .": James Pendleton to author, 5/2/94.

492   "People are trying . . .": Nicholas Meredith Turner to author, 2/9/93.

492   "I believe she . . .": Sam Green to author, 2/9/93.

493   "I just don't think . . .": Betty Spiegel to author, 6/2/93.

493   "technically bisexual . . .": Paris, *Garbo*, p. 279.

493   "I think not . . .": Raymond Daum letter to *The New York Times*, 5/7/95.

493   "I don't know . . .": Betty Estevez to author, 5/3/94.

493   "I will say . . .": Laila Nylund to author, 3/20/95.

494   "I still havent . . .": GG to Allen Porter, 9/6/50.

495   Preliminary Form for Petition of Naturalization, 9/18/50: NA.

495   "a member of the USA": GG to Allen Porter, L.A., 10/31/50.

495   "Miss Garbo has never . . .": Barney F. Potratz report, 11/21/50 (INS).

495   Salka Viertel's name included in the FBI Communist index: FBI memo, 12/10/51.

495   FN6: Jack Larson to author, 10/3/92.

496   "She seems more . . .": Cecil Beaton to Clarissa Churchill, 12/29/50, quoted in Vickers, *Cecil Beaton*, p. 334.

496   "We could see . . .": Laila Nylund to author, 3/2/95 and 3/20/95.

497   "It's rather frightening . . .": Beaton, *Memoirs*, p. 260.

497   Garbo writes re going through a "particularly sad" period: GG to Cecil Beaton, undated letter, 1951.

497   "It was as if . . .": Beaton, *The Strenuous Years*, p. 98.

497   "He knew enough . . .": Vickers, *Loving Garbo*, p. 95.

498   "She's got a lovely . . .": Hoare, *Serious Pleasure: The Life of Stephen Tennant*, p. 313.

498   "a long and emotional . . .": Vickers, *Cecil Beaton*, p. 355.

498   "a bit shy . . .": Alice B. Toklas to Carl Van Vechten, 11/27/51, quoted in Edward Burns, *Staying On Alone: The Letters of Alice B. Toklas* (New York: Random House, 1974), p. 247.

499   "I daresay I am . . .": Beaton, *The Strenuous Years*, pp. 108–109.

499   "You know, there's . . .": "A Glittery Party for Noël Coward," *Family Circle*, 5/52.

500   "Personally I would . . .": Nunnally Johnson to Alan C. Collins, 9/25/51 (BU).

500   "[Cukor] says he . . .": Nunnally Johnson to Darryl Zanuck, 3/11/52 (BU).

500   "that an interpretation . . .": Nunnally Johnson to Darryl Zanuck, 4/1/51 (BU).

500   "The passion was . . .": Stempel, *Screenwriter: The Life and Times of Nunnally Johnson*, p. 143.

500   "but as she went on . . .": Nunnally Johnson to Charles Higham, 1971 (CU).

500   "The goddess has . . .": Vickers, *Loving Garbo*, p. 211.

500   "He has infinite . . .": Cecil Beaton to Mercedes, 5/17/55 (MdA).

501   "The two women . . .": "Garbo and the Duke," *Esquire*, 9/75.

501   "Their rented yacht . . .": ibid.

501   "Greta still complains . . .": Cecil Beaton to Mercedes, 11/19/52 (MdA).

501   Capote re Garbo: Truman Capote to Cecil Beaton, 11/8/52.

501   "[Gayelord] Hauser had . . .": Cecil Beaton diary, 12/19/52, quoted in Vickers, *Cecil Beaton*, p. 359.

502   "When he didn't . . .": Bainbridge, *Garbo*, pp. 286–87.

502   "The night before . . .": Mercedes to Cecil Beaton, 10/5/53, quoted in Vickers, *Loving Garbo*, pp. 209–10.

502   "I had a hard . . .": Bainbridge, *Garbo*, p. 294.

503   "A large L-shaped . . .": Baldwin, *Billy Baldwin Remembers*, pp. 173–74.

503   "She knew just . . .": "Greta Garbo: The Legendary Star's Secret Garden in New York," *Architectural Digest*, 4/92.

503   "Better not get . . .": GG to Gayelord Hauser, undated letter, circa 1953/1954.

503   "compassionate, unchanged . . .": Viertel, *The Kindness of Strangers*, p. 331.

504   "what in God's name . . .": GG to Cecil Beaton, 12/53.

504   "Dear Darling Sir . . .": GG to Robert Reud, 3/9/54.

504   "It's sad that . . .": Cecil Beaton to Mercedes, 4/21/54 (MdA).

504   The Gustafsons in Santa Fe: based on conversations with residents, 2/4 and 2/6/94, plus research conducted at the New Mexico Historical Society.

505   GG writes Salka from "Desertland": undated letter circa summer 1954.

505   "She has plenty . . .": "Garbo's Romances—the Flames All Died," *Los Angeles Mirror*, 8/6/54.

505   "Greta returned three weeks . . .": Cecil Beaton to Mercedes, 12/3/54 (MdA).

505   "When she philosophises . . .": Cecil Beaton diary, 12/5/54, quoted in Vickers, *Loving Garbo*, p. 219.

505   "I was angry . . .": ibid., pp. 221–22.

506   "I knew that . . .": Negulesco, *Things I Did . . . And Things I Think I Did*, p. 210.

CHAPTER TWENTY-FIVE: Goddess Emeritus

508   "He didn't dare . . .": Broman, *Conversations*, p. 219.

508   "Madame, you are . . .": Evans, *Ari: The Life & Times of Aristotle Onassis*, p. 145.

508   "because she sings . . .": Negulesco, *Things I Did. . .* , p. 206.

508   "New Yorkers are . . .": Daum, *Walking with Garbo*, p. 218.

508   "Garbo works with . . .": Goodman, *The Fifty-Year Decline and Fall of Hollywood*, p. 294.

508   "Garbo was crazy . . .": Baldwin and Gardine, *Billy Baldwin: An Autobiography*, p. 166.

509   "a person of . . .": Cecil Beaton to Mercedes, 10/22/56 (MdA).

509   GG meets the Prime Minister: Vickers, *Loving Garbo*, pp. 235–36.

510   "to that dreary . . .": Cecil Beaton to Mercedes, 10/28/56 (MdA).

510   "Garbo began to complain . . .": *London Sunday Dispatch*, 10/6/57.

510   "She really has . . .": Cecil Beaton diary, winter 1957/1958, quoted in Vickers, *Loving Garbo*, p. 242.

510   Dr. Menford Sakel: Jean Howard to author, 11/10/92.

511   "a blessing in disguise . . .": Vickers, *Loving Garbo*, p. 243.

511   "a terrified creature . . .": Beaton, *The Restless Years*, p. 81.

511   "in the most cursory . . .": ibid., p. 79.

511   "for thirty years . . .": ibid., pp. 79–80.

511   "Soon a reassuring . . .": Vickers, *Loving Garbo*, p. 244.

512   "Well, we really . . .": Beaton, *The Restless Years*, p. 80.

512   Garbo visits Elizabeth Taylor: Geoff Blain (Ms. Taylor's personal assistant) to author, 5/7/93.

512   "a rather sad . . .": Goodman, *The Fifty-Year Decline and Fall of Hollywood*, p. 99.

512   Garbo looked after Harry Crocker: Joseph Lombardo to author, 6/27/94.

512   "She often asked me . . .": Jack Larson to author, 10/3/92.

512   "Churchill was very . . .": Broman, *Conversations*, p. 220.

513   "There was much . . .": Cecil Beaton to Mercedes, 11/16/58 (MdA).

513   "It crossed my mind . . .": Jean Howard to author, 11/10/92.

513   Garbo and Rothschild fight: Herbert Kenwith to author, 3/14/96.

513   "Well, well, well . . .": Vickers, *Loving Garbo*, pp. 249–50.

514   Garbo and Sam Spiegel: Luis Estevez to author, 7/1/94.

514   "Garbo has this effect . . .": ibid.

515   "I have always . . .": Cecil Beaton diary, winter 1961, quoted in Vickers, *Loving Garbo*, p. 259.

516   "I hope you . . .": Mercedes to William McCarthy, undated letter (MdA).

516   "deeply, deeply upset . . .": Beaton, *The Restless Years*, p. 125.

516   "It was hard . . .": Cecil Beaton to Mercedes, 10/61 (MdA).

517 "VALENTINA WILL NOT . . .": Broman, *Det handlar om kärlek*, p. 306.
517 "Greta repeated many . . .": Sands and Broman, *The Divine Garbo*, p. 45.
517 "The room was . . .": Bergman, *The Magic Lantern*, p. 250.
518 "He was so . . .": ibid., p. 241.
518 "I was shocked . . .": Vickers, *Loving Garbo*, pp. 250.
518 "When I dont . . .": GG to Sydney Guilaroff, undated letter.
518 "I am going to . . .": GG to Salka Viertel, undated letter.
519 "You would never . . .": GG to Salka Viertel, 7/10/62.
519 Garbo invited to a private White House dinner: David Powers and Letitia Baldrige to author, 11/92.
519 White House clearance: FBI background check request 1/8/62; approved 1/15/62.
519 Garbo stayed with Florence Mahoney: Nancy Tuckerman to author, 12/3/92.
519 "giving the President . . .": Michaelis, *The Best of Friends: Profiles of Extraordinary Friendships*, p. 177.
519 "There was a ghastly . . .": ibid., pp. 177–78.
520 "It was a . . .": Broman, *Conversations*, p. 219.
520 "Greta was very . . .": "Greta Garbo," *Ladies' Home Journal*, 4/76.
520 "one was unruly . . .": Sam Green to author, 2/9/93.
520 "the greatest thing since . . .": "La Dolce Greta," *Newsweek*, 3/11/63.
521 "The comeback of . . .": MGM press release, 8/14/63 (AMPAS).
521 "austere looks of . . .": *Today*, 4/17/90.
521 "She'd like to . . .": Daum, *Walking with Garbo*, p. 11.
522 "a lonely, pathetic . . .": Raymond Daum letter to *The New York Times*, 9/25/93.
522 "Life is full . . .": Daum, *Walking with Garbo*, pp. 51–52.
522 "[She] sat down . . .": Bergman and Burgess, *Ingrid Bergman: My Story*, pp. 92–93.
523 "All of a sudden . . .": Betty Estevez to author, 5/3/94.
523 "Fate had ordained . . .": Cecil Beaton diary, 9/65, quoted in Vickers, *Loving Garbo*, p. 266.
524 "I'm afraid Garbo . . .": Bainbridge, *Garbo* (Holt, Rinehart edition), p. 287.
524 "Valentina came over . . .": Joseph Lombardo to author, 6/27/94.
524 "It's hard to . . .": "Schlee Remains to be Flown Here," *The New York Times*, 10/8/64.
524 FN8: Kenny Kingston to author, 4/7/94.
525 "If she loved . . .": Bainbridge, *Garbo* (Holt, Rinehart edition), p. 287.
525 "I think she . . .": Betty Estevez to author, 5/3/94.
525 "She mourned deeply . . .": Joseph Lombardo to author, 6/27/94.
525 "She was terribly . . .": Jack Larson to author, 10/3/92.
525 Garbo responds to a note of sympathy: GG to Sydney Guilaroff, 10/28/64.
525 "Everyone I love . . .": "The Great Garbo," *People*, 4/30/90.
526 GG letter to Cecil Beaton: 4/2/65.
526 "At first I . . .": Cecil Beaton diary, 7/65, quoted in Beaton, *The Parting Years*, p. 33.
526 "Cécile was serious . . .": Cecil Beaton diary, 9/65, quoted in Vickers, *Loving Garbo*, pp. 270 and 272.
526 "In a few days . . .": "Garbo at 80," *Orange County Register*, 9/18/85.

CHAPTER TWENTY-SIX: Survivor

527 "Someone is very . . .": GG to Salka Viertel, undated letter, 1966.
527 "My patient is . . .": ibid., 6/18/66.
527 "I'm not sure . . .": ibid., undated letter.
527 "She loved to stay . . .": Betty Estevez to author, 5/3/94.
528 "Her eyes got . . .": Betty Spiegel to author, 6/2/93.
528 "Everyone seems to . . .": ibid.

528   "If she was . . .": Betty Estevez to author, 5/3/94.

528   "Cécile and she . . .": "Garbo's Last Days," *New York,* 5/21/90.

528   "I remember lying . . .": ibid.

528   "You know, G . . .": Betty Spiegel to author, 6/2/93.

529   "Oh, were you . . .": ibid.

529   "If you were . . .": Betty Estevez to author, 5/3/94.

529   Sven Gustafson will, 10/31/46 (submitted for probate 2/7/67): Santa Fe County records.

529   "She said that . . .": Joseph Lombardo to author, 6/27/94.

530   Re Anthony Palermo: "Garbo's Friend Keeper of Secrets," *Milwaukee Sentinel,* 7/23/90.

530   FN3: Betty Spiegel to author, 6/2/93.

531   "I went to . . .": Daum, *Walking with Garbo,* pp. 215–16.

531   "For Garbo, Salka is . . .": Bainbridge, *Garbo* (Holt, Rinehart edition), p. 289.

531   Garbo congratulated Salka on book sale: GG to Salka Viertel, 1/27/68.

531   FN4: *The Greta Garbo Collection,* American Movie Classics, 11/90.

532   "Garbo and Mae West . . .": "Broadway Ballyhoo," *The Hollywood Reporter,* 4/16/68.

532   "Mae later complained . . .": Herbert Kenwith to author, 3/14/96.

532   "She became ill . . .": Cecil Beaton diary, 5/68, quoted in Vickers, *Loving Garbo,* p. 281.

533   "We got to . . .": Herbert Kenwith to author, 2/3/93.

533   "We were walking . . .": ibid., 3/14/96.

533   FN6: ibid., 2/3/93.

534   "Fate has chained . . .": Sands and Broman, *The Divine Garbo,* p. 225.

534   "On the road . . .": Broman, *Conversations,* pp. 16–17.

534   "I don't know . . .": Sands and Broman, *The Divine Garbo,* p. 225.

534   "Whenever I saw her . . .": Jack Larson to author, 10/3/92.

534   "She was spectacular . . .": Dick Cavett interview, PBS, 1992.

535   "the main one was . . .": ibid.

535   "When she was . . .": Claude Botteron to author, 10/15/93.

535   Hans Guler and Garbo: Dori Guler to author, 10/14/93.

535   "G.G. and I . . .": "A Friendship," *The Greta Garbo Collection* Catalogue, 1990.

536   "She used to . . .": Jean Howard to author, 11/10/92.

536   "so tough, even in . . .": Daum, *Walking with Garbo,* p. 168.

537   "I feel angry . . .": Cecil Beaton diary, 9/68, quoted in Vickers, *Cecil Beaton,* p. 558.

537   "His job was . . .": Sam Green to author, 2/9/93.

537   "Let me ask . . .": Vickers, *Cecil Beaton,* p. 563.

537   "a pack of lies . . .": "Garbo Är Inte Sjuk," *Expressen,* 11/13/76.

538   "Sam embodied his . . .": Albert Goldman, *The Lives of John Lennon* (New York: William Morrow & Co., 1988), p. 576.

538   "I realized that . . .": Sam Green to author, 2/9/93.

539   "I saw GG . . .": Garson Kanin letter to Cukor, 1/13/70.

539   "She's a very nice . . .": "Garbo Walks," *New York,* 12/12/77.

540   GG's picture in a store window: "Garbo Lives," New York *Daily News* Sunday magazine, 10/14/84.

540   "If you follow . . .": "Garbo Walks!," *Show,* 6/63.

540   "I almost feel . . .": *New York,* 12/12/77.

540   "used to stop . . .": "Garbo at 80," *Orange County Register,* 9/18/85.

541   "She has not said . . .": *Time,* 7/19/71.

541   "How can they . . .": "The Great Garbo," *People,* 4/30/90.

541   "Here was this . . .": Jack Larson to author, 10/3/92.

541   "They may do . . .": *Los Angeles Times,* 1/12/72.

541   FN11: ibid.

542   "going to baby-sit . . .": GG to Salka Viertel, 6/22/73.

542   "GeeGee's back . . .": "The Good Life," *The Hollywood Reporter,* 5/15/75.

542 "One should not . . .": "Greta Garbo," *Ladies' Home Journal*, 4/76.

543 An invitation from Buckingham Palace: Sam Green to author, 2/9/93.

543 "What a thrilling . . .": ibid.

543 Green appeals to Garbo: ibid

544 "a real tearjerker . . .": ibid.

544 "Well, I couldn't . . .": Vickers, *Cecil Beaton*, p. 577.

544 "It's so strange . . .": "Garbo's Last Days," *Vanity Fair*, 2/94.

544 "All the years . . .": Nicholas Meredith Turner to author, 2/8/93.

544 "She didn't express . . .": Sam Green to author, 2/9/93.

545 "She used to go . . .": Joseph Lombardo, 6/22/94 and 6/27/94.

545 "There, apparently unmindful . . .": "Tourist 'Harriet Brown' Turns Out to be the Not-So-Reclu-
sive Garbo," *People*, 4/12/76.

545 "She was always . . .": Sam Green to author, 2/9/93.

546 "I've inhaled since . . .": *People*, 4/30/90.

546 "I went to him . . .": Sands and Broman, *The Divine Garbo*, p. 226.

546 "In all the . . .": "Broadway Ballyhoo," *The Hollywood Reporter*, 11/7/77.

546 "I checked her out . . .": Sam Green to author, 2/9/93.

547 "Stop them . . .": "Garbo's Last Days," *New York*, 5/21/90.

547 "never at any time . . .": GG's sworn affidavit, 2/7/78.

547 "in connection with . . .": Second affidavit, 5/2/78.

547 "Come back for tea . . .": "Garbo: Behind the Screen", *W*, 10/26–11/2/79.

548 "She felt completely . . .": Jack Larson to author, 10/3/92.

548 "The most astonishing . . .": "The Green House," *Vanity Fair*, 5/88.

548 "Do you really . . .": *Vanity Fair*, 2/94.

548 "We stopped to . . .": Jack Larson to author, 10/3/92.

549 "They didn't even leave . . .": Joseph Lombardo to Milton Greene, 6/22/94.

549 "I had never . . .": Wilhelm Wachtmeister letter to author, 4/18/94.

549 "I spoke with her . . .": Paris, *Garbo*, p. 536.

550 "I didn't even . . .": Betty Estevez to author, 5/3/94.

550 "Now, she looks . . .": "Garbo Strolls," New York *Daily News*, 10/15/84.

550 "Why do they . . .": Daum, *Walking with Garbo*, p. 138.

551 "My God, I've . . .": Joseph Lombardo to author, 6/27/94.

551 "Garbo asked that . . .": Daum, *Walking with Garbo*, p. 158.

551 GG letter to Mimi Pollak: Undated letter, 1984.

551 Garbo's 80th birthday: Sam Green to author, 2/9/93; plus *New York*, 5/21/90.

552 "Mr. Green, you've . . .": *Vanity Fair*, 2/94.

552 "She found out . . .": Betty Estevez to author, 5/3/94.

552 "She did say . . .": Betty Spiegel to author, 6/2/93.

552 "seemed considerably weaker . . .": Wilhelm Wachtmeister letter to author, 4/18/94.

552 Garbo's relationship with Claire Koger: Sam Green to author, 2/9/93.

553 "When she had . . .": *New York*, 5/21/90.

553 "Getting old is . . .": Sam Green to author, 2/9/93.

EPILOGUE: Another Chapter Ended

554 "mistake of his youth . . .": Gray Reisfield to author, 2/13/93.

554 "I don't know . . .": "Garbo Still Wants to Be Left Alone!" *New York Post*, 9/19/85.

554 "Sweden has the most . . .": "Garbo skålade för Feldt," *Expressen*, 7/28/88.

555 "so it would be . . .": Betty Estevez to author, 5/3/94.

555 "serious consideration . . .": *Los Angeles Times*, 5/10/88.

555 "She just sits . . .": Broman, *Conversations*, p. 183.

555   "I regret coming . . .": ibid., p. 179.

555   "That was the . . .": ibid., p. 205.

555   "Her doctor there . . .": "Garbo's Last Days," *New York*, 5/21/90.

555   "I tried to explain . . .": "Garbo's Refuge," *The New York Times*, 9/2/90.

556   "In her later . . .": "A Private Vision," *The Greta Garbo Collection* Catalogue, 1990.

556   "When she was . . .": *The New York Times*, 9/2/90.

556   "One day she . . .": "Garbo's Friend Keeper of Secrets," *Milwaukee Sentinel*, 7/23/90.

556   Garbo's drinking: "Elusive Star's Dark Ending: Illness, Booze and Confusion," *New York Post*, 4/17/90.

556   "If I depended . . .": *New York*, 5/21/90.

557   Garbo only drank water: Betty Estevez to author, 5/3/94.

557   "How does it . . .": "The Good Life," *The Hollywood Reporter*, 10/22/87.

557   Sven Broman re Garbo's health: Broman, *Conversations*, p. 182.

557   "It is not . . .": Kurz, Theodore A. "Memorandum in Opposition to Petitioner's Application to Vacate the Probate Decree," New York Surrogate's Court, 8/31/90.

557   Statement of Claire Koger: ibid.

557   Statement of Dr. Stuart D. Saal: ibid.

557   Statement of Dr. Sullivan: ibid.

558   "People learn to . . .": Broman, *Conversations*, pp. 179–80.

558   "She was wearing . . .": *The New York Times*, 9/2/90.

558   "I think she . . .": Sven Broman to author, 4/19/94.

558   "gracious, alert, oriented . . .": Theodore A. Kurz legal brief, 8/31/90.

558   "Strange. The evening . . .": "Jag minns när Greta drog en låt på Grand," *Svenska Dagbladet*, 4/22/90.

558   FN1: Certificate of Death (#156-90-022194), 4/15/90.

559   "all tangible personal property . . .": Greta Garbo, Last Will and Testament, 3/2/84.

559   "Everyone in Sweden . . .": Åke Fredriksson to author, 5/22/93.

559   "It was for . . .": ibid.

559   "I'm disappointed [at] not . . .": *Milwaukee Sentinel*, 7/23/90.

559   "I never considered . . .": Theodore A. Kurz legal brief, 8/31/90.

561   "I want to go . . .": Broman, *Conversations*, pp. 204 and 214.

561   "too accessible for . . .": "Garbo Still Awaiting Final Plot," *The Hollywood Reporter*, 4/27/93.

SELECTED BIBLIOGRAPHY

Acosta, Mercedes de. *Here Lies the Heart: A Tale of My Life*. New York: Reynal and Company, 1960.

Affron, Charles. *Star Acting: Gish, Garbo, Davis*. New York: Dutton, 1977.

Asther, Nils. *Narrens väg: Ingen gudasaga memoarer.* Stockholm: Carlssons, 1988.

Bainbridge, John. *Garbo.* Garden City, NY: Doubleday & Company, 1955; rev. ed., Holt, Rinehart and Winston, 1971.

Baldwin, Billy, with Michael Gardine. *Billy Baldwin: An Autobiography.* Boston: Little, Brown and Company, 1985.

———. *Billy Baldwin Remembers.* New York: Harcourt Brace Jovanovich, 1974.

Barthes, Roland. *Mythologies.* Paris: Editions du Seuil, 1957. (Translation by Jonathan Cape, Ltd., 1972.)

Baxter, John. *The Hollywood Exiles.* New York: Taplinger Publishing Company, 1976.

Beaton, Cecil. *Memoirs of the 40's.* McGraw-Hill: New York, 1972. [Published by Weidenfeld & Nicholson in London as *The Happy Years: Diaries, 1944–1948.*]

———. *The Parting Years: Diaries, 1963–1974.* London: Weidenfeld & Nicolson, 1978.

———. *The Restless Years: Diaries, 1955–1963.* London: Weidenfeld & Nicolson, 1976.

———. *The Strenuous Years: Diaries, 1948–1955.* London: Weidenfeld & Nicolson, 1973.

———. *The Wandering Years: Diaries, 1922–1939,* Boston: Little, Brown and Company, 1961.

Bedford, Sybille. *Aldous Huxley: A Biography (Volume One, 1894–1939).* London: Chatto & Windus, 1973.

Behlmer, Rudy, ed. *Memo from David O. Selznick.* New York: The Viking Press, 1972.

Behrman, S. N. *People in a Diary: A Memoir.* Boston: Little, Brown and Company, 1972.

Bell-Metereau, Rebecca. *Hollywood Androgyny.* New York: Columbia University Press, 1985.

Bennett, Joan, and Lois Kibbee. *The Bennett Playbill.* New York: Holt Rinehart and Winston, 1970.

Bergman, Ingmar. *The Magic Lantern.* Translated by Joan Tate. New York: Viking Penguin, 1988.

Bergman, Ingrid, with Alan Burgess. *Ingrid Bergman: My Story.* New York: Delacorte Press, 1980.

Bernstein, Matthew. *Walter Wanger: Hollywood Independent.* Berkeley and Los Angeles: University of California Press, 1994.

Bickford, Charles. *Bulls, Bats, Bicycles & Actors.* New York: Paul S. Erickson, 1976.

Billquist, Fritiof. *Garbo: A Biography.* Translated by Maurice Michael. New York: G. P. Putnam's Sons, 1960. [Swedish edition: *Garbo. Den ensamma stjärnan* (1959).]

Brion, Patrick. *Garbo.* Paris: Chêne, 1985.

Broman, Sven. *Det handlar om kärlek: Minnen från ett liv i tidningsvärlden.* Stockholm: Wahlström & Widstrand, 1993.

———. *Greta Garbo berätter.* Stockholm: Wahlström & Widstrand, 1990. [Published in U.S. as *Conversations with Greta Garbo,* New York: Viking Penguin, 1991.]

Brooks, Louise. *Lulu in Hollywood.* New York: Alfred A. Knopf, 1982.

Brownlow, Kevin. *The Parade's Gone By . . .* New York: Alfred A. Knopf, 1968.

Brownlow, Kevin, and John Kobal. *Hollywood: The Pioneers.* New York: Alfred A. Knopf, 1979.

Bull, Clarence Sinclair, and Raymond Lee. *The Faces of Hollywood.* South Brunswick and New York: A. S. Barnes and Co., 1968.

Carey, Gary. *All the Stars in Heaven: Louis B. Mayer's M-G-M.* New York: E. P. Dutton, 1981.

———. *Anita Loos: A Biography.* New York: Alfred A. Knopf, 1988.

Carr, Larry. *Four Fabulous Faces: The Evolution and Metamorphosis of Garbo, Swanson, Crawford and Dietrich.* New Rochelle, NY: Arlington House, 1970.

Castle, Terry. *The Apparitional Lesbian: Female Homosexuality and Modern Culture*. New York: Columbia University Press, 1993.

Ceplair, Larry, and Steven Englund. *The Inquisition in Hollywood: Politics in the Film Community 1930–1960*. Garden City, NY: Anchor Press/Doubleday, 1980.

Churchill, Winston S. *Memories and Adventures*. London: Weidenfeld & Nicolson, 1989.

Coffee, Lenore. *Storyline: Recollections of a Hollywood Screenwriter*. London: Castell & Co., Ltd., 1973.

Conway, Michael; Dio McGregor; and Mark Ricci. *The Films of Greta Garbo*. New York: Cadilac Publishing/The Citadel Press, 1968.

Cook, Bruce. *Brecht in Exile. New York: Holt, Rinehart & Winston, 1982*.

Corliss, Richard. *Greta Garbo*. New York: Pyramid Publications, 1974.

Cornell, Katharine, as told to Ruth Woodbury Sedgwick. *I Wanted to Be an Actress*. New York: Random House, 1938.

Cowie, Peter. *Scandinavian Cinema*. London: The Tantivy Press on behalf of Scandinavian Films, Nordic Cinema/Cinéma Nordique, 1992.

Crawford, Joan, with Jane Kesner Ardmore. *A Portrait of Joan*. Garden City, NY: Doubleday & Company, 1962.

Crocker, Harry. *I Read You Every Morning*. (Unpublished memoir on deposit at the Academy of Motion Picture Arts and Sciences.)

———. *That's Hollywood*. (Unpublished memoir on deposit at the Academy of Motion Picture Arts and Sciences.)

Crowther, Bosley. *Hollywood Rajah*. New York: Holt, Rinehart and Winston, 1960.

———. *The Lion's Share: The Story of an Entertainment Empire*. New York: E. P. Dutton & Company, 1957.

Curtiss, Thomas Quinn. *Von Stroheim*. New York: Farrar, Straus and Giroux, 1971.

Custen, George F. *Bio/Pics: How Hollywood Constructed Public History*. New Brunswick, NJ: Rutgers University Press, 1992.

Daniel, Oliver. *Stokowski: A Counterpoint of View*. New York: Dodd, Mead and Company, 1982.

Daum, Raymond. *Walking with Garbo*. Edited and annotated by Vance Muse. New York: HarperCollins Publishers, 1991.

Davies, Marion. *The Times We Had: Life with William Randolph Hearst*. Indianapolis: Bobbs-Merrill Company, 1975.

Day, Beth. *This Was Hollywood*. Garden City, NY: Doubleday & Company, 1960.

Dietz, Howard. *Dancing in the Dark*. New York: Quadrangle/The New York Times Book Company, 1974.

Douglas, Melvyn, and Tom Arthur. *See You at the Movies*. Lanham, Md., and New York: University Press of America, 1986.

Ducout, Françoise. *Greta Garbo: La somnambule*. Paris: Stock, 1991. [Updated edition.]

Dragonette, Jessica. *Faith Is a Song: The Odyssey of an American Artist*. New York: David McKay Company, 1951.

Dressler, Marie, as told to Mildred Harrington. *My Own Story*. Boston: Little, Brown and Company, 1934.

Durgnat, Raymond, and John Kobal. *Greta Garbo*. New York: Studio Vista/Dutton Books, 1965.

Eisenstein, Sergei M. *Immoral Memories: An Autobiography*. Translated by Herbert Marshall. Boston: Houghton Mifflin Company, 1983.

Eisner, Lotte H. *The Haunted Screen: Expressionism in the German Cinema and the Influence of Max Reinhardt*. Berkeley and Los Angeles: University of California Press, 1969. [Originally published in France as *L'ecran démonique*, 1952.]

———. *Murnau*. Berkeley and Los Angeles: University of California Press, 1973.

Evans, Peter. *Ari: The Life & Times of Aristotle Onassis*. New York: Summit Books, 1986.

Eyman, Scott. *Ernst Lubitsch: Laughter in Paradise*. New York: Simon & Schuster, 1994.

———. *Five American Cinematographers*. Metuchen, NJ: The Scarecrow Press, 1987.

Fairbanks, Douglas, Jr. *The Salad Days: An Autobiography*. Garden City, NY: Doubleday and Company, 1988.

Feyder, Jacques, and Françoise Rosay. *Le cinéma; Notre métier.* Vésenaz-près-Genéve: Pierre Cailler, 1946.

Flagg, James Montgomery. *Celebrities: A Half-Century of Caricature and Portraiture.* Watkins Glen, NY: Century House, 1951.

Flamini, Roland. *Thalberg: The Last Tycoon and the World of M-G-M.* New York: Crown Publishers, 1994.

Forslund, Bengt. *Victor Sjöström: His Life and His Work.* New York: New York Zoetrope, 1988.

Fountain, Leatrice Gilbert, with John R. Maxim. *Dark Star.* New York: St. Martin's Press, 1985.

Fowler, Gene. *Good Night, Sweet Prince.* New York: The Viking Press, 1944.

Friedrich, Otto. *Before the Deluge: A Portrait of Berlin in the 1920's.* New York: Harper & Row, 1972.

Gabler, Neal. *An Empire of Their Own: How the Jews Invented Hollywood.* New York: Crown Publishers, 1988.

Genthe, Arnold. *As I Remember.* New York: Reynal & Hitchcock, 1936.

Giesler, Jerry, as told to Pete Martin: *The Jerry Giesler Story.* New York: Simon and Schuster, 1960.

Gilbert, Julie. *Opposite Attraction: The Lives of Erich Maria Remarque and Paulette Goddard.* New York: Pantheon Books, 1995.

Gill, Brendan. *Tallulah.* New York: Harper & Row, 1972.

Gish, Lillian. *The Movies, Mr. Griffith and Me.* Englewood Cliffs, NJ: Prentice-Hall, 1969.

Gledhill, Christine, ed. *Stardom: Industry of Desire.* New York: Routledge, Chapman & Hall, 1991.

Goldsmith, Margaret. *Christina of Sweden.* Garden City, NY: Doubleday, Doran and Company, 1935.

Goodman, Ezra. *The Fifty-Year Decline and Fall of Hollywood.* New York: Simon & Schuster, 1961.

Guilaroff, Sydney. *Crowning Glory.* Santa Monica: General Publishing Group, 1996.

Gumpel, Max. *Sagor och verklighet.* Karlshamn: Ragnar Lagerblads Boktryckeri, 1948. [Privately published memoir; translation by Laila Nylund.]

Haining, Peter. *The Legend of Garbo.* London: W. H. Allen & Company, 1990.

Harrison, Rex. *Rex: An Autobiography.* New York: William Morrow & Company, 1975.

Hauser, Gayelord. *Gayelord Hauser's Treasury of Secrets.* New York: Farrar, Straus and Giroux, 1963.

Hay, Peter. *MGM: When the Lion Roars.* Atlanta: Turner Publishing, 1991.

Hayman, Ronald. *Brecht.* Oxford: Oxford University Press, 1983.

———. *John Gielgud.* New York: Random House, 1971.

Heimann, Jim. *Out with the Stars: Hollywood Nightlife in the Golden Era.* Abbeville Press, New York: 1985.

Hepburn, Katharine. *Me: Stories of My Life.* New York: Alfred A. Knopf, 1991.

Higham, Charles. *Hollywood Cameramen: Sources of Light.* Bloomington: Indianapolis University Press, 1970.

———. *Merchant of Dreams: Louis B. Mayer, MGM and the Secret Hollywood.* New York: Donald I. Fine, 1993.

Higham, Charles, and Joel Greenberg. *The Celluloid Muse: Hollywood Directors Speak.* Chicago: Henry Regnery Company, 1969.

Hoare, Philip. *Serious Pleasure: The Life of Stephen Tennant.* New York: Viking Penguin, 1991.

Hood, Robin. *Sjöström och Stiller.* Stockholm: Åhlén & Söner, 1939.

Isherwood, Christopher. *Christopher and His Kind.* New York: Farrar, Straus and Giroux, 1976.

Jacobs, Lea. *The Wages of Sin: Censorship and the Fallen Woman (1928–1942).* Madison: University of Wisconsin Press, 1991.

Jayakar, Pupul. *Krishnamurti: A Biography.* New York: Harper & Row, 1987

Kanin, Garson. *Hollywood.* New York: The Viking Press, 1967.

———. *Tracy and Hepburn.* New York: The Viking Press, 1971.

Kobal, John. *The Art of the Great Hollywood Portrait Photographers, 1925–1940.* New York: Alfred A. Knopf, 1980.

———. *People Will Talk.* New York: Alfred A. Knopf, 1985.

Kobler, John. *Damned in Paradise: The Life of John Barrymore.* New York: Atheneum, 1977.

Kracauer, Siegfried. *From Caligari to Hitler: A Psychological History of the German Film.* Princeton, NJ: Princeton University Press, 1947.

Kühn, Richard. *Greta Garbo: Der weg einer frau und künstlerin.* Dresden: Carl Reissner-Verlag, 1935.

Kwiatkowski, Aleksander. *Swedish Film Classics: A Pictorial Survey of 25 Films from 1913 to 1957.* New York: Dover Publications in association with Svenska Filminstitutet, 1983.

LaGuardia, Robert, and Gene Arceri. *Red: The Tempestuous Life of Susan Hayward.* New York: Macmillan Publishing Co., 1985.

Laing, E. E. *Greta Garbo: The Story of a Specialist.* London: John Gifford, Ltd., 1946.

Lambert, Gavin. *Norma Shearer.* New York: Alfred A. Knopf, 1990.

———. *On Cukor.* New York: G. P. Putnam's Sons, 1972.

Lamparski, Richard. *Whatever Became of . . . (Eleventh Series).* New York: Crown Publishers, 1989.

Laqueur, Walter. *Weimar: A Cultural History.* New York: G. P. Putnam's Sons, 1974.

LaVine, W. Robert. *In a Glamorous Fashion: The Fabulous Years of Hollywood Costume Design.* New York: Charles Scribner's Sons, 1980.

Lawson, John Howard. *Film: The Creative Process.* New York: Hill and Wang, 1964.

Leaming, Barbara. *Orson Welles.* New York: The Viking Press, 1985.

Lee, Rowland V. *Adventures of a Movie Director.* Los Angeles: AFI Written History, 1971 [unpublished].

Lesley, Cole. *Remembered Laughter: The Life of Noël Coward.* London: Jonathan Cape, 1976.

Lewis, David. *The Creative Producer.* Edited by James Curtis. Metuchen, NJ: The Scarecrow Press, 1993.

Loder, John. *Hollywood Hussar.* London: Howard Baker Ltd., 1977.

Logan, Joshua. *Josh: My Up and Down, In and Out Life.* New York: Delacorte Press, 1976.

Loy, Myrna, and James Kotsilibas-Davis. *Myrna Loy: Being and Becoming.* London: Bloomsbury Publishing, 1987.

McGilligan, Patrick. *George Cukor: A Double Life.* New York: St. Martin's Press, 1991.

Marion, Frances. *Off With Their Heads!* New York: Macmillan Publishing Co., 1975.

Marx, Samuel. *A Gaudy Spree: The Literary Life of Hollywood in the 1930's When the West Was Fun.* New York: Franklin Watts, 1987.

———. *Mayer and Thalberg: The Make-Believe Saints.* New York: Random House, 1975.

Maxwell, Elsa. *R.S.V.P.: Elsa Maxwell's Own Story.* Boston: Little, Brown and Company, 1964.

Meryman, Richard. *Mank: The Wit, World and Life of Herman Mankiewicz.* New York: William Morrow, 1978.

Michaelis, David. *The Best of Friends: Profiles of Extraordinary Friendships.* New York: William Morrow, 1983.

Miller, Patsy Ruth. *My Hollywood: When Both of Us Were Young.* New York: O'Raghailligh Ltd. Publishers, 1988.

Milne, Tom. *Mamoulian.* Bloomington: Indiana University Press, 1969.

Moore, Colleen. *Silent Star.* Garden City, NY: Doubleday and Company, 1968.

Mordden, Ethan. *The Hollywood Studios.* New York: Alfred A. Knopf, 1988.

Navasky, Victor S. *Naming Names.* New York: The Viking Press, 1980.

Negri, Pola. *Memoirs of a Star.* New York: Doubleday and Company, 1970.

Negulesco, Jean. *Things I Did . . . And Things I Think I Did.* New York: Linden Press/Simon & Schuster, 1984.

Nelson, Nancy. *Evenings with Cary Grant.* New York: William Morrow & Co., 1991.

Nerman, Einar. *Caught in the Act.* London: George Harrap, Ltd., 1976.

Niven, David. *Bring On the Empty Horses.* New York: Dell Publishing Company, 1976.

———. *The Moon's a Balloon.* New York: G. P. Putnam's Sons, 1972.

Noble, Peter. *Hollywood Scapegoat: The Biography of Erich von Stroheim.* London: The Fortune Press, 1950.

Palmborg, Rilla Page. *The Private Life of Greta Garbo.* London: John Long, Ltd., 1932.

Paris, Barry. *Garbo.* New York: Alfred Knopf, 1995.

———. *Louise Brooks.* New York, Alfred A. Knopf, 1989.

Payn, Graham, and Sheridan Morley, eds. *The Noël Coward Diaries.* London: Weidenfeld and Nicolson, 1982.

Payne, Robert. *The Great Garbo*. New York: Praeger Press, 1976.

Pensel, Hans. *Seastrom and Stiller in Hollywood*. New York: Vantage Press, 1969.

Pepper, Terence, and John Kobal. *The Man Who Shot Garbo: The Hollywood Photographs of Clarence Sinclair Bull*. New York: Simon and Schuster, 1989.

Petro, Patrice. *Joyless Streets: Women and Melodramatic Representation in Weimar Germany*. Princeton, NJ: Princeton University Press, 1989.

Pollak, Mimi. *Teaterlek*. Stockholm: Askild och Kärnekull, 1977.

Pujol, Juan, with Nigel West. *Operation Garbo*. New York: Random House, 1985.

Rathbone, Basil. *In and Out of Character*. Garden City, NY: Doubleday and Company, 1956.

Reinhardt, Gottfried. *The Genius: A Memoir of Max Reinhardt*. New York: Alfred A. Knopf, 1979.

Riva, Maria. *Marlene Dietrich*. New York: Alfred A. Knopf, 1993.

Robinson, David. *Chaplin: His Life and Art*. New York: McGraw-Hill Book Company, 1985.

Rosenberg, Bernard, and Harry Silverstein. *The Real Tinsel*. New York: Macmillan Publishing Co., 1970.

Ross, Lillian, and Helen Ross. *The Player: A Profile of an Art*. New York: Simon and Schuster, 1962.

Rotha, Paul. *The Film Till Now*. New York: Funk & Wagnalls, 1949. [Revised edition with additional material by Richard Griffith.]

Russo, Vito. *The Celluloid Closet: Homosexuality in the Movies*. New York: Harper & Row, 1981.

Sands, Frederick, and Sven Broman. *The Divine Garbo*. New York: Grosset & Dunlap, 1979. [Published in Sweden as *Garbo. Den gudomliga*. Stockholm, 1980.]

Sarlot, Raymond R., and Fred E. Basten. *Life at the Marmont*. Santa Monica: Roundtable Publishing, 1987.

Schanke, Robert A. *Shattered Applause: The Eva Le Gallienne Story*. New York: Barricade Books, 1992.

Schatz, Thomas. *Genius of the System: Hollywood Filmmaking in the Studio Era*. New York: Pantheon Books, 1988.

Schwartz, Nancy Lynn. *The Hollywood Writers Wars*. New York: Alfred A. Knopf, 1982.

Scobie, Ingrid Winther. *Center Stage: Helen Gahagan Douglas, A Life*. New York: Oxford University Press, 1992.

Selznick, Irene Mayer. *A Private View*. New York: Alfred A. Knopf, 1983.

Semitjov, Eugen. *Garbo Filmen vi aldrig fick se*. Stockholm: Bokförlaget Fabel, 1986.

Sennett, Ted. *Hollywood's Golden Year, 1939: A 50th Anniversary Celebration*. New York: St. Martin's Press, 1989.

Shaw, George Bernard. *Bernard Shaw: Collected Letters 1926–1950*. Edited by Dan H. Laurence. New York: The Viking Press, 1988.

Shipman, David. *Movie Talk*. New York: St. Martin's Press, 1988.

Shnayerson, Michael. *Irwin Shaw*. New York: G. P. Putnam's Sons, 1989.

Sinclair, Andrew. *Spiegel: The Man Behind the Pictures*. Boston: Little, Brown & Company, 1975.

Siwertz, Margit. *Lars Hanson*. Stockholm: P. A. Norstedt & Söners Förlag, 1947.

Sjölander, Ture. *Garbo*. New York: Harper and Row, 1971.

Söderhjelm, Alma. *Mina sju magra år*. Stockholm: Bonniers, 1932.

Steichen, Edward. *A Life in Photography*. London: W. H. Allen, 1963.

Stempel, Thomas. *Screenwriter: The Life and Times of Nunnally Johnson*. San Diego and New York: A. S. Barnes and Company, 1980.

Stevenson, William. *A Man Called Intrepid: The Secret War*. New York: Harcourt Brace Jovanovich, 1976.

Stewart, Donald Ogden. *By a Stroke of Luck! An Autobiography*. London: Paddington Press, Ltd., 1975.

Stolpe, Sven. *Christina of Sweden*. New York: The Macmillan Company, 1960.

Sundborg, Åke. *Greta Garbos saga*. Stockholm: Albert Bonniers Förlag, 1929.

Svenska Filminstitutet. *Svensk filmografi: Volume 2 (1920–1929)*. Uppsala: Almqvist & Wiksell, 1982.

Taraba, Anne. *Den gåtfulla Garbo*. Stockholm: Wahlströms, 1991.

Taylor, John Russell. *Strangers in Paradise: The Hollywood Émigrés 1933–1950*. New York: Holt Rinehart & Winston, 1983.

Thomas, Bob. *Thalberg: Life and Legend*. Garden City, NY: Doubleday and Company, 1969.

Thomson, David. *Showman*. New York: Alfred A. Knopf, 1993.

Torrence, Bruce. *Hollywood: The First 100 Years*. New York: New York Zoetrope, 1982.

Vickers, Hugo. *Cecil Beaton*. New York: Little, Brown and Company, 1985.

———. *Loving Garbo*. New York: Random House, 1994.

Vidal, Gore. *Palimpsest*. New York: Random House, 1995.

Vidor, King. *A Tree Is a Tree*. New York: Harcourt, Brace & Co., 1952.

Viertel, Berthold. *Schriften zum Theater*. Munich: Kösel-Verlag, 1948.

Viertel, Peter. *Dangerous Friends: At Large with Huston and Hemingway in the Fifties*. New York: Nan A. Talese/Doubleday, 1992.

Viertel, Salka. *The Kindness of Strangers*. New York: Holt, Rinehart & Winston, 1969.

Walker, Alexander. *The Celluloid Sacrifice*. New York: Hawthorn Books, 1966.

———. *Garbo: A Portrait*. New York: Macmillan Publishing Co., 1980.

———. *The Shattered Silents: How the Talkies Came to Stay*. New York: William Morrow, 1979.

———. *Stardom: The Hollywood Phenomenon*. New York: Stein and Day Publishers, 1970.

Weiss, Andrea. *Vampires & Violets: Lesbians in Film*. New York: Penguin Books, 1993.

Werner, Gösta. *Mauritz Stiller: Ett livsöde*. Stockholm: Prisma, 1991.

———. *Mauritz Stiller och hans filmer (1912–1916)*. Stockholm: Kungl. Boktryckeriet PA Norstedt & Söner, 1971.

Wifstrand, Naima. *Med och utan paljetter*. Stockholm: Bonniers, 1962.

Wiley, Mason, and Damien Bona. *Inside Oscar: The Unofficial History of the Academy Awards*. New York: Ballantine Books, 1986.

Williams, Tennessee. *Memoirs*. Garden City, NY: Doubleday and Company, 1975.

———. *Tennessee Williams' Letters to Donald Windham 1940–1965*. Edited by Donald Windham. New York: Holt, Rinehart & Winston, 1977.

Wollstein, Hans J. *Strangers in Hollywood: The History of Scandinavian Actors in American Films*. Metuchen, NJ: The Scarecrow Press, Inc., 1994.

Zierold, Norman. *Garbo*. New York: Stein and Day, 1969.

Zinnemann, Fred. *Fred Zinnemann: An Autobiography: A Life in the Movies*. New York: Charles Scribner's Sons, 1992.

Zolotow, Maurice. *Billy Wilder in Hollywood*. New York: G. P. Putnam's Sons, 1977.

———. *Stagestruck: The Romance of Alfred Lunt and Lynn Fontanne*. New York: Harcourt, Brace & World, Inc., 1965.

APPENDIX
THE FILMS OF GRETA GARBO

ADVERTISING FILM:

Herr och fru Stockholm or **Herrskapet Stockholm ute på inköp** (Mr. & Mrs. Stockholm, *formerly known as* From Top to Toe or How Not to Dress). *(23m.) Directed by Captain Ragnar Ring. Produced by Hasse W. Tullberg for Paul U. Bergström AB/Tullberg-Film.*
CAST: *Olga Andersson, Ragnar Widestedt, Greta Gustafsson, Erick Fröander.*
RELEASED: *December 12, 1920, in Stockholm.*

FEATURE FILM:

En lyckoriddare (*English title:* A Fortune Hunter *or* The Gay Cavalier). *Svensk Filmindustri/Skandias Filmbyrå (6 reels). Produced and Directed by John W. Brunius. Adapted by John W. Brunius and Sam Ask, from a story by Harald Molander. Photography by Hugo Edlund; Assistant Cameraman: Arthur Thorell. Art Direction by Vilhelm Bryde and Gustaf Hallén.*
CAST: *Gösta Ekman, Mary Johnson, Axel Ringvall, Hilda Forsslund, Nils Lundell, Vilhelm Bryde, Gösta Cederlund, Gull Natorp, Carlo Keil-Möller, Arthur Natorp, Semmy Friedmann, Alfred Lundberg, Anna-Lisa Baude. (Greta and Alva Gustafsson appear as extras in a tavern scene.)*
PREMIERED: *March 14, 1921, at the Sture Teatern in Stockholm.*

PROMOTIONAL FILM:

Konsum Stockholm Promo (*a clip from this film has been referred to as* Our Daily Bread). *(27m.) Directed by Captain Ragnar Ring. Produced by Hasse W. Tullberg for Tullberg-Film/AB Fribergs Filmbyrå in association with Konsumtionsföreningen Stockholm med omnejd (Stockholm Consumers' Co-operative Association).*
CAST: *Greta Gustafsson, Lars Hanson, and others.*
RELEASED: *October 7, 1921, in Stockholm, and featured as part of the Swedish exhibit at the Tokyo World's Fair.*

ALL OF THE FOLLOWING LISTINGS REPRESENT
FEATURE-LENGTH MOTION PICTURES:

Luffar-Petter (*English title:* Peter the Tramp). *Petschler-Film/Fribergs Filmbyrå (5 reels). Produced, Directed and Written by Erik A. Petschler. Photographed by Oscar Norberg. Assistant Director: Verner Nordlund.*
CAST: *Erik Petschler, Gucken Cederborg, Tyra Ryman, Greta Gustafsson, Iréne Zetterberg, Helmer Larsson, Carl F. Olsson, Mona Geijer-Falkner, Anna Brandt, Valdemar Dalquist, Carl-Gunnar Wingård, Mary Gräber, Lily Böös, Agnes Clementsson, Axel Westerlund, August Wiberg, Oscar Rudin, Teodor Ericson, Adolf Hultgren, Johan Widén, Ann-Margret Bergman, Elsa Nyholm.*
PREMIERED: *December 26, 1922, at the Odéon Teatern in Stockholm.*

Gösta Berlings saga (*variously known in English-speaking countries as* The Atonement / Legend / Story / Saga of Gösta Berling). *AB Svensk Filmindustri (12 reels). Directed by Mauritz Stiller. Adaptation by*

Mauritz Stiller and Ragnar Hyltén-Cavallius, from the novel by Selma Lagerlöf. Photography by J. Julius (Julius Jaenzon); Second Unit Cameraman: Carl Axel Söderström. Art Direction by Ragnar Brattén, Erik Jerken and Vilhelm Bryde. Costumes by Ingrid Günther. Special effects: Olof Ås and Nils Elffors. Original music score arranged by Rudolf Sahlberg and Gaston Borch. Historical consultant: Gustaf Upmark.

CAST: Lars Hanson, Gerda Lundeqvist, Hilda Forsslund, Otto Elg-Lundberg, Sixten Malmerfelt, Karin Swanström, Jenny Hasselqvist, Ellen Cederström, Torsten Hammarén, Greta Garbo, Mona Mårtenson, Sven Scholander, Svend Kornbeck, Hugo Rönnblad, Knut Lambert, Oscar Bergström, Jules Gaston-Portefaix, Albert Ståhl, Anton de Verdier, Axel Jacobsson, Jan de Meyere, Edmund Hohndorf, Theodor Buch, Signe Enwall, Birger Lyne, Tom Walter.

PREMIERED: March 10, 1924 (Part 1), and March 17, 1924 (Part 2), at the Röda Kvarn in Stockholm. (Synchronized, edited version [123m.] available from Video Yesteryear.)

Die freudlose Gasse (English title: The Joyless Street; U.S. title: The Street of Sorrows). A Hirschel-Sofar Filmproduktion (9 reels). Directed by G.W. Pabst. Adaptation by Willy Haas, from the novel by Hugo Bettauer. Photography by Guido Seeber, Curt Oertel and Robert Lach. Art Direction by Hans Sohnle and Otto Erdmann. Recording supervised by H. Landsmann. Assistant Director: Marc Sorkin.

CAST: Asta Nielsen, Greta Garbo, Werner Krauss, Einar Hansson, Valeska Gert, Jaro Fürth, Kl. Loni Nest, Robert Garrison, Henry Stuart, Tamara, Gregori Chmara, Gräfin Agnes Esterhazy, Karl Ettlinger, Hertha von Walther, Ilka Grüning, Max Kohlhase, Silvia Torf, Alexander Mursky, Mario Cusmich, Gräfin Tolstoi, Frau Markstein, Otto Reinwald, Raskatoff, Krafft-Raschig.

PREMIERED: May 18, 1925, at the Mozartsaal in Berlin. (Edited versions available from Kino Video [96m.] and Video Yesteryear [124m.].)

ALL OF THE FOLLOWING FILMS WERE PRODUCED BY METRO-GOLDWYN-MAYER AND DISTRIBUTED BY THEIR PARENT COMPANY, LOEW'S, INC.:

The Torrent (68m.). A Cosmopolitan Production. Directed by Monta Bell. Produced by Irving Thalberg (uncredited). Scenario by Dorothy Farnum, based on Entre Naranjos by Vicente Blasco-Ibáñez. Titles by Katherine Hilliker and H.H. Caldwell. Photographed by William Daniels. Edited by Frank Sullivan. Settings by Cedric Gibbons and Merrill Pye. Wardrobe by Kathleen Kay & Maude Marsh and Max Rée.

CAST: Ricardo Cortez, Greta Garbo, Gertrude Olmstead, Edward Connelly, Lucien Littlefield, Martha Maddox, Lucy Beaumont, Tully Marshall, Mack Swain, Arthur Edmund Carew, Lillian Leighton, Mario Carillo.

PREMIERED: February 21,1926, at the Capitol Theatre in New York and the Loew's State Theatre in Los Angeles. (Not available on home video.)

The Temptress (95m.). A Cosmopolitan Production. Directed by Fred Niblo. Produced by Irving Thalberg (uncredited). Scenario by Dorothy Farnum, based on La Tierra de Todos by Vicente Blasco-Ibáñez. Titles by Marion Ainslee. Photographed by Gaetano Gaudio and William Daniels. Edited by Lloyd Nosler. Settings by Cedric Gibbons and James Basevi. Wardrobe by André-ani. Assistant Director: H. Bruce Humberstone.

CAST: Greta Garbo, Antonio Moreno, Marc MacDermott, Lionel Barrymore, Armand Kaliz, Roy D'Arcy, Robert Anderson, Francis McDonald, Hector V. Sarno, Virginia Brown Faire, Alys Murrell, Steve Clemento, Roy Coulson, Inez Gomez.

PREMIERED: October 10, 1926, at the Capitol Theatre in New York. (Not available on home video.)

Flesh and the Devil (103m.). Directed by Clarence Brown. Produced by Irving Thalberg (uncredited). Screenplay by Benjamin F. Glazer, based on the novel The Undying Past (Es War) by Hermann Sudermann. Titles by Marion Ainslee. Photographed by William Daniels. Edited by Lloyd Nosler. Settings by Cedric Gibbons and Frederic Hope. Wardrobe by André-ani. Assistant Director: Charles Dorian.

CAST: John Gilbert, Greta Garbo, Lars Hanson, Barbara Kent, William Orlamond, George Fawcett, Eugenie Besserer, Marc MacDermott, Marcelle Corday, Polly Moran.

PREMIERED: January 9, 1927, at the Capitol Theatre in New York. (Note: The original roadshow version added a coda to Sudermann's story indicating the John Gilbert and Barbara Kent characters would eventually marry. Director Clarence Brown always objected to this ending, preferring to conclude the film with Garbo's demise in the icy water. This is the version that is shown at most film festivals, and is now the official video version from MGM/UA Home Video.)

Love (84m.). *Directed by Edmund Goulding. Produced by Irving Thalberg (uncredited). Scenario by Frances Marion, based on the novel* Anna Karenina *by Count Leo Tolstoy. Titles by Marion Ainslee and Ruth Cummings. Photographed by William Daniels. Edited by Hugh Wynn. Musical Score by Ernst Luz. Settings by Cedric Gibbons and Alexander Toluboff. Wardrobe by André-ani.*

CAST: *Greta Garbo, John Gilbert, George Fawcett, Emily Fitzroy, Brandon Hurst, Phillipe de Lacy, Edward Connelly. (Gilbert top-billed in advertising.)*

PREMIERED: *November 29, 1927, at the Embassy Theatre in New York.* (Not available on home video; Turner Classic Movies currently shows both endings with its broadcast version.)

The Divine Woman (80m.). *Directed by Victor Sjöström (Seastrom). Treatment by Gladys Unger, based on her play,* Starlight. *Scenario by Dorothy Farnum. Titles by John Colton. Photographed by Oliver Marsh. Edited by Conrad A. Nervig. Settings by Cedric Gibbons and Arnold Gillespie. Wardrobe by Gilbert Clark.*

CAST: *Greta Garbo, Lars Hanson, Lowell Sherman, Polly Moran, Dorothy Cumming, John Mack Brown, Cesare Gravina, Paulette Duval, Jean de Briac.*

PREMIERED: *January 14, 1928, at the Capitol Theatre in New York.* (Not available on home video; *The Divine Woman* has been listed by the American Film Institute as one of the ten most important lost films of the silent era.)

The Mysterious Lady (96m.). *Directed by Fred Niblo. Produced by Harry Rapf (uncredited). Treatment and continuity by Bess Meredyth, based on the novel* War in the Dark *by Ludwig Wolff. Titles by Marion Ainslee and Ruth Cummings. Photographed by William Daniels. Edited by Margaret Booth. Settings by Cedric Gibbons. Wardrobe by Gilbert Clark. Assistant Director: Harold S. Bucque.*

CAST: *Greta Garbo, Conrad Nagel, Gustav von Seyffertitz, Albert Pollet, Edward Connelly, Richard Alexander.*

PREMIERED: *July 27, 1928, at the Loew's State Theatre in Los Angeles.* (Available from MGM/UA Home Video.)

A Woman of Affairs (98m.). *Directed by Clarence Brown. Produced by Irving Thalberg (uncredited). Treatment and continuity by Bess Meredyth, based on the story* The Green Hat *by Michael Arlen. Titles by Marian Ainslee and Ruth Cummings. Photographed by William Daniels. Edited by Hugh Wynn. Art Direction by Cedric Gibbons. Gowns by Adrian. Assistant Director: Charles Dorian.*

CAST: *Greta Garbo, John Gilbert, Lewis Stone, John Mack Brown, Douglas Fairbanks, Jr., Hobart Bosworth, Dorothy Sebastian. (Gilbert top-billed in advertising.)*

RELEASED: *December 29, 1928, to select theaters nationwide.* (Available from MGM/UA Home Video.)

Wild Orchids (106m.). *Directed by Sidney Franklin. Produced by Irving Thalberg (uncredited). Adaptation by Willis Goldbeck, from the story* Heat *by John Colton. Continuity by Hans Kraly and Richard Schayer. Titles by Marion Ainslee and Ruth Cummings. Photographed by William Daniels. Edited by Conrad A. Nervig. Art Direction by Cedric Gibbons. Gowns by Adrian.*

CAST: *Greta Garbo, Lewis Stone, Nils Asther.*

RELEASED: *February 16, 1929, to select theaters nationwide.* (Available from MGM/UA Home Video.)

A Man's Man (76m.). *Directed by James Cruze. Produced by Harry Rapf (uncredited). Story adapted by Forrest Halsey, based on the play by Patrick Kearney. Titles by Joe Farnham. Photographed by Merritt B. Gerstad. Art Direction by Cedric Gibbons. Edited by George Hively. Wardrobe by David Cox.*

CAST: *William Haines, Josephine Dunn, Sam Hardy, Mae Busch, Gloria Davenport; with cameos by John Gilbert, Greta Garbo and Fred Niblo.*

PREMIERED: *May 25, 1929, at the Capitol Theatre in New York.* (A "lost" film; not available on home video.)

The Single Standard (72m.). *Directed by John S. Robertson. Produced by Hunt Stromberg (uncredited). Adaptation and scenario by Josephine Lovett, from the novel by Adela Rogers St. John. Titles by Marion*

Ainslee. Photographed by Oliver Marsh. Edited by Blanche Sewell. Musical Score by Dr. William Axt. Art Direction by Cedric Gibbons. Gowns by Adrian.

CAST: Greta Garbo, Nils Asther, John Mack Brown, Dorothy Sebastian, Lane Chandler, Mahlon Hamilton, Kathlyn Williams, Zeffie Tilbury, Robert Castle, Joel McCrea.

PREMIERED: July 27, 1929, at the Capitol Theatre in New York. (Available from MGM/UA Home Video.)

The Kiss (64m.). Directed by Jacques Feyder. Produced by Al Lewin (uncredited). Scenario by Hans Kraly, from the story by George M. Saville (a.k.a. Jacques Feyder). Titles by Marian Ainslee. Photographed by William Daniels. Edited by Ben Lewis. Musical Synchronization by Dr. William Axt. Art Direction by Cedric Gibbons. Gowns by Adrian.

CAST: Greta Garbo, Conrad Nagel, Anders Randolf, Holmes Herbert, Lew Ayres, George Davis.

PREMIERED: November 15, 1929, at the Capitol Theatre in New York. (Available from MGM/UA Home Video.)

Anna Christie (92m.). Directed by Clarence Brown. Produced by Irving Thalberg (uncredited). Adaptation by Frances Marion, from the play by Eugene O'Neill. Photographed by William Daniels. Edited by Hugh Wynn. Recording supervised by Douglas Shearer. Art Direction by Cedric Gibbons. Gowns by Adrian.

CAST: Greta Garbo, Charles Bickford, George F. Marion, Marie Dressler, James T. Mack, Lee Phelps.

PREMIERED: January 22, 1930, at the Criterion Theatre in Los Angeles. (Available from MGM/UA Home Video.)

Anna Christie (German language version, 82m.). Directed by Jacques Feyder. Produced by Irving Thalberg (uncredited). Adaptation by Frances Marion, from the play by Eugene O'Neill. German dialogue by Walter Hasenclever. German scenario by Frank Reicher. Photography by William Daniels. Edited by Finn Ulback. Recording supervised by Douglas Shearer. Art Direction by Cedric Gibbons. Gowns by Adrian. Music by Dr. William Axt.

CAST: Greta Garbo, Hans Junkermann, Theo Shall, Salka Steuermann, Herman Bing.

PREMIERED: December 22, 1930, in Cologne, Germany. (Not available on home video, but can be viewed occasionally on Turner Classic Movies.)

Romance (76m.). Directed by Clarence Brown. Produced by Paul Bern (uncredited). Dialogue continuity by Bess Meredyth and Edwin Justus Mayer, from the play by Edward Sheldon. Photographed by William Daniels. Edited by Hugh Wynn. Recording supervised by Douglas Shearer. Art Direction by Cedric Gibbons. Gowns by Adrian.

CAST: Greta Garbo, Lewis Stone, Gavin Gordon, Elliott Nugent, Florence Lake, Clara Blandick, Henry Armetta, Mathilde Comont, Countess De Liguoro.

PREMIERED: July 18, 1930, at the Loew's State Theatre in Los Angeles. (Available from MGM/UA Home Video.)

Inspiration (76m.). Directed by Clarence Brown. Produced by Irving Thalberg (uncredited). Dialogue by Gene Markey. Photographed by William Daniels. Edited by Conrad A. Nervig. Recording supervised by Douglas Shearer. Art Direction by Cedric Gibbons. Gowns by Adrian.

CAST: Greta Garbo, Robert Montgomery, Lewis Stone, Marjorie Rambeau, Judith Vosselli, Beryl Mercer, John Miljan, Edwin Maxwell, Oscar Apfel, Joan Marsh, Zelda Sears, Karen Morley, Gwen Lee, Paul McAllister, Arthur Hoyt, Richard Tucker.

RELEASED: January 30, 1931, to select theaters nationwide. (Available from MGM/UA Home Video.)

Susan Lenox: Her Fall and Rise (77m.). Directed by Robert Z. Leonard. Produced by Paul Bern (uncredited). Adaptation and continuity by Wanda Tuchock, from the book by David Graham Phillips. Dialogue by Zelda Sears and Leon Gordon. Photographed by William Daniels. Edited by Margaret Booth. Recording supervised by Douglas Shearer. Art Direction by Cedric Gibbons. Gowns by Adrian.

CAST: Greta Garbo, Clark Gable, Jean Hersholt, John Miljan, Alan Hale, Hale Hamilton, Hilda Vaughn, Russell Simpson, Cecil Cunningham, Ian Keith, Theodore von Eltz, Marjorie King, Helene Millard.

PREMIERED: October 15, 1931, at the Capitol Theatre in New York and the Loew's State Theatre in Los Angeles. (Available from MGM/UA Home Video.)

Mata Hari (90m.). Directed by George Fitzmaurice. Produced by Bernie Fineman (uncredited). Original story and screenplay by Benjamin Glazer and Leo Birinski. Additional dialogue by Doris Anderson and

Gilbert Emery. *Photographed by William Daniels. Edited by Frank Sullivan. Recording supervised by Douglas Shearer. Art Direction by Cedric Gibbons. Gowns by Adrian.*
CAST: *Greta Garbo, Ramon Novarro, Lionel Barrymore, Lewis Stone, C. Henry Gordon, Karen Morley, Alec B. Francis, Blanche Frederici, Edmund Breese, Helen Jerome Eddy, Frank Reicher, Mischa Auer.*
PREMIERED: December 31, 1931, at the Capitol Theatre in New York. (Available from MGM/UA Home Video.)

Grand Hotel (112m.). *Directed by Edmund Goulding. Produced by Paul Bern (uncredited). American play version by William A. Drake, adapted from the story by Vicki Baum. Photographed by William Daniels. Edited by Blanche Sewell. Recording supervised by Douglas Shearer. Art Direction by Cedric Gibbons. Gowns by Adrian. Assistant Director: Charles Dorian.*
CAST: *Greta Garbo, John Barrymore, Joan Crawford, Wallace Beery, Lionel Barrymore, Lewis Stone, Jean Hersholt, Robert McWade, Purnell B. Pratt, Ferdinand Gottschalk, Rafaela Ottiano, Morgan Wallace, Tully Marshall, Frank Conroy, Murray Kinnell, Edwin Maxwell.*
PREMIERED: April 12, 1932, at the Astor Theatre in New York. (Available from MGM/UA Home Video.)

As You Desire Me (71m.). *Directed by George Fitzmaurice. Produced by Paul Bern (uncredited). Adaptation and dialogue by Gene Markey, from the play by Luigi Pirandello. Photographed by William Daniels. Edited by George Hively. Recording supervised by Douglas Shearer. Art Direction by Cedric Gibbons. Gowns by Adrian.*
CAST: *Greta Garbo, Melvyn Douglas, Erich von Stroheim, Owen Moore, Hedda Hopper, Rafaela Ottiano, Warburton Gamble, Albert Conti, William Riccardi, Roland Varno.*
PREMIERED: June 3, 1932, at the Capitol Theatre in New York and the Loew's State Theatre in Los Angeles. (Available from MGM/UA Home Video.)

Queen Christina (100m.). *Directed by Rouben Mamoulian. Produced by Walter Wanger. Screenplay by H.M. Harwood and Salka Viertel, from the original story by Salka Viertel and Margaret P. Levino. Dialogue by S.N. Behrman. Photographed by William Daniels. Edited by Blanche Sewell. Musical score by Herbert Stothart. Recording supervised by Douglas Shearer. Art Direction by Alexander Toluboff. Interior decorations by Edwin B. Willis. Gowns by Adrian.*
CAST: *Greta Garbo, John Gilbert, Ian Keith, Lewis Stone, Elizabeth Young, C. Aubrey Smith, Reginald Owen, Georges Renavent, David Torrence, Gustav von Seyffertitz, Ferdinand Munier, Lawrence Grant, Akim Tamiroff, Cora Sue Collins, Muriel Evans, Sarah Padden, Paul Hurst, Eddie Gargan, Edward Norris, Barbara Barondess, Tiny Sanford, Fred Kohler.*
PREMIERED: December 26, 1933, at the Astor Theatre in New York. (Available from MGM/UA Home Video.)

The Painted Veil (86m.). *Directed by Richard Boleslawski. Produced by Hunt Stromberg. Screenplay by John Meehan, Salka Viertel and Edith Fitzgerald, from the novel by W. Somerset Maugham. Photographed by William Daniels. Edited by Hugh Wynn. Musical score by Herbert Stothart. Recording supervised by Douglas Shearer. Art Direction by Cedric Gibbons; Associates: Alexander Toluboff and Edwin B. Willis. Gowns by Adrian. Chinese Fantasy Conceived by Stowitts; Staged by Chester Hale.*
CAST: *Greta Garbo, Herbert Marshall, George Brent, Warner Oland, Jean Hersholt, Beulah Bondi, Bodil Rosing, Katherine Alexander, Cecilia Parker, Soo Yong, Forrester Harvey, Whitford Kane, Lawrence Grant.*
RELEASED: November 22, 1934, to select theaters nationwide. (Available from MGM/UA Home Video.)

Anna Karenina (96m.). *Directed by Clarence Brown. Produced by David O. Selznick. Screenplay by Clemence Dane, Salka Viertel, from the novel by Count Leo Tolstoy. Dialogue adaptation by S.N. Behrman. Photographed by William Daniels. Edited by Robert J. Kern. Musical score by Herbert Stothart. Recording supervised by Douglas Shearer. Art Direction by Cedric Gibbons; Associates: Fredric Hope and Edwin B. Willis. Gowns by Adrian. Ballet staged by Margarete Wallmann. Mazurka staged by Chester Hale. Vocal and choral effects by Russian Symphony Choir. Consultant: Count Andrey Tolstoy*
CAST: *Greta Garbo, Fredric March, Freddie Bartholomew, Maureen O'Sullivan, May Robson, Basil Rathbone, Reginald Owen, Reginald Denny, Phoebe Foster, Constance Collier, Gyles Isham, Buster Phelps,*

Ella Ethridge, Joan Marsh, Sidney Bracey, Cora Sue Collins, Olaf Hytten, Joe E. Tozer, Guy D. Ennery, Harry Allen, Mary Forbes.

RELEASED: August 20, 1935, to select theaters nationwide. (Available from MGM/UA Home Video.)

Camille (110m.). Directed by George Cukor. Produced by Irving Thalberg (uncredited). Screenplay by Zöe Akins, Frances Marion and James Hilton, from the play and novel La Dame aux Camellias by Alexandre Dumas fils. Photographed by William Daniels and Karl Freund. Edited by Margaret Booth. Associate Producer: David Lewis. Unit Manager: Ulric Busch. Musical score by Herbert Stothart. Recording supervised by Douglas Shearer. Art Direction by Cedric Gibbons; Associates: Fredric Hope and Edwin B. Willis. Gowns by Adrian. Dances staged by Val Raset.

CAST: Greta Garbo, Robert Taylor, Lionel Barrymore, Elizabeth Allan, Jessie Ralph, Henry Daniell, Lenore Ulric, Laura Hope Crews, Rex O'Malley, Russell Hardie, E.E. Clive, Douglas Walton, Marion Ballou, Joan Brodel, June Wilkins, Fritz Leiber, Elsie Esmonds.

PREMIERED: December 12, 1936, at the Plaza Theatre in Palm Springs; released December 25, to select theaters nationwide. (Available from MGM/UA Home Video.)

Conquest (113m.). Directed by Clarence Brown. Produced by Bernard H. Hyman. Screenplay by Samuel Hoffenstein, Salka Viertel and S.N. Behrman, from the novel Pani Walewska by Waclaw Gasiorowski, and a dramatization by Helen Jerome. Photographed by Karl Freund. Edited by Tom Held. Musical score by Herbert Stothart. Recording supervised by Douglas Shearer. Art Direction by Cedric Gibbons; Associates: William A. Horning and Edwin B. Willis. Gowns by Adrian.

CAST: Greta Garbo, Charles Boyer, Reginald Owen, Alan Marshall, Henry Stephenson, Leif Erickson, Dame May Whitty, Marie Ouspenskaya, C. Henry Gordon, Claude Gillingwater, Vladimir Sokoloff, George Houston, Scotty Beckett.

PREMIERED: November 5, 1937 at the Capitol Theatre in New York. (Available from MGM/UA Home Video.)

Ninotchka (110m.). Produced and Directed by Ernst Lubitsch. Screenplay by Charles Brackett, Billy Wilder and Walter Reisch, based on the original story by Melchior Lengyel. Photographed by William Daniels. Edited by Gene Ruggiero. Unit manager: Frank Messinger. Assistant Director: Horace Hough. Musical score by Werner R. Heymann. Recording supervised by Douglas Shearer. Art Direction by Cedric Gibbons; Associate: Randall Duell. Set Decorations by Edwin B. Willis. Gowns by Adrian. Make-up created by Jack Dawn.

CAST: Greta Garbo, Melvyn Douglas, Ina Claire, Bela Lugosi, Sig Rumann, Felix Bressart, Alexander Granach, Gregory Gaye, Rolfe Sedan, Edwin Maxwell, Richard Carle.

PREMIERED: November 10, 1939, at the Radio City Music Hall in New York. (Available from MGM/UA Home Video.)

Two-Faced Woman (91m.). Directed by George Cukor. Produced by Gottfried Reinhardt. Screenplay by S.N. Behrman, Salka Viertel and George Oppenheimer, from the play by Ludwig Fulda. Photography by Joseph Ruttenberg. Edited by George Boemler. Musical score by Bronislau Kaper. Recording supervised by Douglas Shearer. Art Direction by Cedric Gibbons; Associate: Daniel B. Cathcart. Set Decorations by Edwin B. Willis. Gowns by Adrian. Dance Direction by Bob Alton. Hairstyles created by Sydney Guilaroff. Jewels by Paul Flato.

CAST: Greta Garbo, Melvyn Douglas, Constance Bennett, Roland Young, Robert Sterling, Ruth Gordon, Francis Carson.

RELEASED: December 4, 1941, in select East Coast theaters; revised version released January 1, 1942. (Available from MGM/UA Home Video.)

INDEX